The Scarlett Letters

The Scarlett Letters

The Scarlett Letters

The Making of the Film
Gone With the Wind

Edited by John Wiley, Jr.

TAYLOR TRADE PUBLISHING
Lanham • Boulder • New York • London

Published by Taylor Trade Publishing
An imprint of Rowman & Littlefield
4501 Forbes Boulevard, Suite 200, Lanham, Maryland 20706
www.rowman.com

16 Carlisle Street, London W1D 3BT, United Kingdom

Distributed by NATIONAL BOOK NETWORK

Margaret Mitchell's letters © 2014 by GWTW Partners, LLC.
Notes and commentary © 2014 by John Wiley, Jr.

British Library Cataloguing in Publication Information Available

Library of Congress Cataloging-in-Publication Data

Mitchell, Margaret, 1900–1949.
  The scarlett letters : the making of the film Gone with the wind / [edited by] John Wiley, Jr.
     pages cm
  Includes bibliographical references and index.
  ISBN 978-1-58979-872-4 (cloth : alk. paper) — ISBN 978-1-58979-873-1 (electronic) 1. Mitchell, Margaret, 1900-1949—Correspondence. 2. Mitchell, Margaret, 1900-1949. Gone with the wind. 3. Georgia—History—Civil War, 1861-1865—Literature and the war. 4. Novelists, American—20th century—Correspondence. I. Wiley, John, 1938- II. Title.
  PS3525.I972Z48 2014
  813'.52—dc23

                              2014001554

∞™ The paper used in this publication meets the minimum requirements of American National Standard for Information Sciences—Permanence of Paper for Printed Library Materials, ANSI/NISO Z39.48-1992.

Printed in Canada

In memory of
Margaret Mitchell and David O. Selznick—
a "marriage" made in movie heaven,
and
Herb Bridges,
keeper of the *GWTW* flame, Georgia gentleman, and friend.

Contents

Foreword

Turney Allan Taylor

Most people immediately associate author Margaret Mitchell with her sweeping historical novel *Gone With the Wind*, which was published in 1936 and became a huge, worldwide bestseller. However, for me—and I count myself very fortunate—there is a far more personal connection to this illustrious southern writer.

* * *

My father, Allan Taylor, was born in Tennessee and always wanted to be a newspaperman. After graduating from Vanderbilt University, he worked on a paper in Chattanooga and then moved to Atlanta to join the *Atlanta Journal*. He met Margaret Mitchell for the first time in December 1922, when she was brought down to the newsroom. She had just been hired as a feature writer by the editor of the paper's *Sunday Magazine*, Angus Perkerson, and the only available seat was the desk she would share with my father. They soon became fast friends. (My father already knew John Marsh, who would become Mitchell's second husband, since they were roommates briefly after Marsh first moved to Atlanta.)

My mother, Lois Cole, met Margaret Mitchell for the first time at a luncheon in 1927. Mother had relocated recently from New York City to be the office manager of the southeastern branch of the publishing firm The Macmillan Company. To present her to Atlanta's female literary society, Medora Perkerson, the grand dame of Atlanta literati, gave a bridge luncheon at the Piedmont Driving Club. When my mother was introduced to her partner at one of the tables, she learned that her name was Margaret

Mitchell Marsh, affectionately known as Peggy. As the cards were dealt, my mother asked whether her partner followed any particular bridge conventions. Mitchell said somberly that she didn't know any and that she just led from fright. She then asked my mother what she led from, and my mother replied, "Necessity," at which Peggy grinned. They won the first hand, upon which they rose, solemnly, and shook hands across the table. With that, they became fast friends.

Months later, at one of the usual after-dinner coffee gatherings hosted by Peggy and John, Mitchell introduced Allan Taylor to Lois Cole with the words, to the effect, that she thought Allan had seen enough southern belles, and she wanted him to meet a really great northern gal. The two of them wed in 1930, and I was born several years later. Thus, I am present due completely to the good graces of "matchmaker" Margaret Mitchell, who was asked at my birth to be my godmother.

*   *   *

I met Margaret Mitchell for the first time in 1938, when I was just a few weeks old and she visited my parents on one of her infrequent trips to New York. Of course, I have no recollection of that event, nor really any other meetings when my godmother came north. I do remember that she regularly sent me birthday and Christmas gifts—a camera, a compass, and savings bonds that were put toward my college fund. She also gave me a wonderful set of stamps printed during the Nazi occupation of Slovakia and sent to her after the war by the foreign minister in gratitude for her book giving so many people encouragement to survive the German occupation. My earliest memory of Margaret Mitchell in person was when I was ten during the summer of 1948. Instead of going to our family's summer home in the Adirondacks, my parents took me and my sister, Linda, on a lengthy car trip to the South—to Virginia, Tennessee, and Georgia and back through North Carolina. Ostensibly, it was to inspect many of the battlefields of the Civil War, from Manassas to Fredericksburg to Richmond, and to visit the homes of several of our presidents, from Thomas Jefferson's Monticello to James Monroe's Ash Lawn. From Virginia we drove farther south to Knoxville and then down to Chattanooga, where we socialized with friends of my parents, as well as took in the sights, particularly the magnificent Lookout Mountain.

From there we motored on to Atlanta, where we connected with Margaret Mitchell and John Marsh. I remember "Aunt Peggy" as a short woman with tremendous vivacity, the most sparkling blue eyes I had ever seen, and a lively interest in all that we had done on our trip and all I was doing, from school to sports to my piano lessons. All of us had lunch at the Piedmont Driving Club, where Peggy escorted me and my five-year-old sister out to the pool. The three of us removed our shoes and socks (stockings in Peggy's case) and piddled our feet in the water. Our "excursion" turned into an all-out talkfest. The next day, Peggy took us to the Cyclorama, the huge amphitheater whose cylindrical walls are covered with a very realistic, detailed mural history of the Civil War battle for Atlanta. As she began to describe all the events depicted there, my sister kept tugging on my mother's dress until she got her attention. Linda said we should join the crowd of tourists being escorted by an attendant who was explaining the battle on the other side of the room. I'm sure my mother wanted to shush my sister and remind her that we had the world's greatest expert on what happened during those days in 1864, Peggy Mitchell, right with us. My mother was about to reprimand my sister when Peggy interrupted. She said that Linda was quite correct and that we should join the others in hearing the description from the official guide. So we all trooped over to the visitors, with my sister being very happy that she had made her point.

In retrospect, this incident at our visit to the Cyclorama illustrated how much Peggy Mitchell was concerned about what other people wanted, particularly if they were friends or family.

After our visit with the Marshes, we drove to Covington, Georgia, where we stayed with my father's elderly stepmother, and then drove through Asheville, North Carolina, and the Great Smoky Mountains on our way back to New Jersey. It was one of the most memorable trips that our family ever took together, especially our time spent with the spirited, thoughtful Peggy Mitchell and her kind husband.

*   *   *

What better way to understand what Margaret Mitchell underwent, with the popularity of her novel and the subsequent immense popular success of the 1939 blockbuster movie made from it, than to read in this volume her own letters to friends, family, colleagues, and professional people with whom she came into contact during those tumultuous years after 1936. The array of letters that makes up this book illustrate admirably all the characteristics of Margaret Mitchell that endeared her to so many people who knew her and made her a truly courageous, exceptional woman and novelist. Immersing ourselves in this correspondence provides us with great insight into the author and her world as she saw her long-in-the-works historical novel become one of the greatest American best-sellers and, in turn, a legendary motion picture.

For me, reading *The Scarlett Letters* reminded me anew how fortunate I was to have had Margaret Mitchell as a godmother, friend, and inspiration.

Introduction

On the evening of December 15, 1939, *Gone With the Wind* author Margaret Mitchell sat in a theater in Atlanta, waiting to see what Hollywood had done with her story. Producer David O. Selznick had invited her to the film's first preview that summer—even offering to move it from California to the Midwest to make it more convenient—but Mitchell declined; she feared that when word got out, she would have to "go through the mill of having the entire populace stopping me on the street and asking me which scenes were to be cut and is Mr. Gable too thrilling for words."[1] To allay her concerns, a Selznick associate suggested a private screening at the Long Island estate of John Hay "Jock" Whitney, the studio's chairman of the board, but again, the author said no.[2] She decided to see the movie for the first time at its world premiere.

Actor Clark Gable, who played Rhett Butler, sat to her left, with Mitchell's husband in between. (Rhett and his creator were supposed to be side by side, but the author and her husband switched places so the two men could talk.)[3] Whitney and Olivia de Havilland, who portrayed Melanie Hamilton, were on her right, and Vivien Leigh, the British actress making her American film debut as Scarlett O'Hara, sat in the row ahead. Throughout the auditorium were other cast members, including Laura Hope Crews, Evelyn Keyes, and Ann Rutherford; actress Claudette Colbert and Leigh's soon-to-be-fiancé, Laurence Olivier; nationally known figures such as World War I flying ace Captain Eddie Rickenbacker, Columbia Broadcasting System executive William S. Paley, and cosmetics queen Elizabeth Arden; and four honored guests—Confederate veterans of the Civil War, each in their nineties. But most of the 2,031 lucky ticket holders inside Loew's Grand Theatre were from the author's hometown, and it was they who were uppermost in Mitchell's thoughts. "I was thinking that I was the most fortunate woman in the world and my mind wasn't on 'G.W.T.W.' either," she wrote to a former newspaper colleague the next day. "I was thinking about the friends who had been so good to me."[4] It was a sentiment she would echo in her speech to the audience when the film ended.

Yet in those minutes before the lights dimmed and the curtains parted, memories of the past three and a half hectic years likely crossed her mind. As soon as she sold the film rights to Selznick in the summer of 1936, Mitchell was engulfed by a tidal wave of attention from a "movie-crazed" public, despite her repeated denials that she had nothing to do with the making of the motion picture.[5] Compelled by her southern manners, the author replied to almost every letter she received. She wrote to aspirant actresses desperate to play Scarlett, often providing words of encouragement and wishing them luck. She answered questions from the screenwriter and others about antebellum architecture, customs, and wallpaper, digging out early drafts of her manuscript for details she had cut from the book. She thanked people who offered their house, their grandmother's dress, or a song they had just written for use in the movie, encouraging them to contact the studio. She gossiped with a trio of Georgians who went to Hollywood as advisers on southern history and customs, delighting in their behind-the-scenes tidbits. And she declined hundreds of requests from "all the population of Atlanta . . . and the late Confederacy" who wanted to attend the premiere, noting that the distribution of tickets was out of her hands.[6]

This collection of more than 360 of her letters and telegrams, all related to the motion picture *Gone With the Wind*, provides readers a front-row seat as Mitchell learns the ins and outs of moviemaking and struggles to deal with a populace obsessed with the "Metropolis of Make Believe."[7] Along the way, she journeys from naive, first-time author to battle-hardened businesswoman, yet she never loses her sense of humor. Mitchell's ability to weave a story, so evident in her novel, is equally obvious in her exchanges with a who's who of the Golden Age of Hollywood—from Selznick, original director George Cukor, and screenwriter Sidney Howard to cast members Gable, Leigh, de Havilland, Leslie Howard, and Hattie McDaniel—as well as with journalists, fellow authors, entrepreneurs and star-struck fans. Most of her letters were warm and often witty. Yet she did not hesitate to scold the producer's over-the-top publicist who insisted on using her name to promote the movie, a former college mate who tried to feed off the author's fame with an "I-knew-her-when" magazine story, and her own publisher who demanded she take a cut in royalties to help him market two new editions of the book tied to the movie.

Mitchell was a "born storyteller" who "wrote as she talked," recalled longtime friend Lois Cole. The author "told her tales with such fun and skill that a whole roomful of people would stay quiet all evening to listen to her."[8] Yet, Cole admitted, "It is difficult to put Peggy on paper, to convey her gaiety, her interest in and profound knowledge of people, her range of interests and reading, her devotion to her friends, and the verve and enchantment of her talk."[9] Taking Cole's observation to heart, I have not tried to capture the story of Margaret Mitchell and the motion picture *Gone With the Wind* with *my* words. Rather, I am letting the author's own words—which reveal her humor, her kindness, her strength, and her sass—re-create the excitement that gripped the nation seventy-five years ago as millions of moviegoers awaited Scarlett's silver screen debut. It's like listening, enchanted, to Mitchell weave stories all evening.

John Wiley, Jr.
Midlothian, Virginia

A Note About the Letters

Margaret Mitchell's letters generally fall into two categories: those to friends and fans were usually light and conversational; sometimes they were short, other times they were quite lengthy and jumped from topic to topic. Those of a business nature were often verbose and always precise, written by a woman whose father and brother were lawyers. While my goal for this book was to let Mitchell "speak for herself," I also wanted to keep the focus on the motion picture *Gone With the Wind*. Therefore, while transcribing the letters, I left out sentences, sometimes paragraphs, about personal matters—from day-to-day occurrences and the health of family members to gossipy updates on mutual friends. I also removed sections that repeated information provided in earlier letters if these parts did not include new points. All such deletions are indicated by ellipses.

For style and grammar, I edited with an extremely light touch. I corrected a handful of what clearly were typos, especially with proper names, and standardized capitalization and the spelling of several words ("adviser"/"advisor" and "bedeviling"/"bedevilling," for example). Otherwise, I left intact the author's often-rambling sentence structure, her sparse use of commas, and alternate spellings from the time, such as "under weigh" and "et cetera."

As you read, you may wonder why certain key letters are not included, such as Mitchell's missives to Dolly Blount Lamar of the United Daughters of the Confederacy (UDC), whose statement on the casting of Vivien Leigh as Scarlett became national news, and those to Dorothy Bates Kelley, a friend living in California whose young daughter attempted to win a role in the film. Unfortunately, the carbons of these letters were among those destroyed by Mitchell's husband after her death, in keeping with the author's wishes. The Lamar and Bates/Kelley files (and several others) in the Margaret Mitchell Family Papers at the Hargrett Rare Book and Manuscript Library contain notes that detail the span of correspondence he discarded. In Lamar's case, I tried to track down relatives—she had no children—who might have inherited her original letters from Mitchell but was disappointed to learn that many of the UDC president's personal belongings were lost in a fire at her home in Macon, Georgia.

Prologue: The Making of a Masterpiece

Margaret Mitchell loved both books and motion pictures. As a small child, she enjoyed hearing the fairy tales of Mother Goose and the Brothers Grimm. "She had a strong memory and soon knew all of these by heart," Stephens Mitchell wrote in a memoir of his famous sister. "She would call on me to read them, but if I misplaced a word she was quick to spot it."[1] Once she learned to read, her tomboy tastes gravitated toward adventure series such as Tom Swift and The Rover Boys despite her brother's chiding. "I told her that the plots were all the same, and that the style was pretty terrible. She would answer, 'Well, if it is a good plot, it will stand being read over a good many times, and the style doesn't matter as long as you can understand what the characters are doing.'"[2] She then graduated to the classics, including Shakespeare and Dickens, and her parents rewarded her with dimes and quarters when she finished *Hamlet* or *David Copperfield*. "By the time she was twelve, she had read many grown-up books, and from then on her literary tastes were adult," her brother recalled.[3]

A new form of entertainment—the moving picture—also was an important part of her youth. Mitchell, born in 1900, came of age with the nickelodeon. The first so-called electric theater opened in Atlanta in 1904; three years later, there were more than a dozen such venues.[4] "When movies came in, about 1906 or 1907, we began going to see them," Stephens Mitchell remembered. "Father would take us downtown at night and, for a nickel each, we could all go to the movies." With each picture lasting about fifteen minutes, "you could see four or five in a night. Margaret always enjoyed them, particularly the comedies."[5] Like reading, moviegoing became a lifelong habit. As a freshman at Smith College, she and her fellow students sometimes cut class to catch the latest Norma Talmadge or Wallace Reid film.[6] She later was especially amused by the antics of the Marx Brothers, an affinity she shared with her second husband, John Marsh. "I don't know whether you are a Marxian," he wrote his mother. "If not, you may actually dislike them. Many people do, poor wretches. But I hope you are one of us superior folks who can appreciate what true geniuses the Marxes are."[7] Mitchell's friends joked that it was easy to find her in a darkened theater simply by following her yelps of laughter at Groucho, Harpo, and Chico.[8]

However, Mitchell was not content with simply absorbing stories told by others, whether on the printed page or on the silver screen. Like many voracious readers, she also had an irresistible urge to write. Probably the earliest surviving example of her fiction is a handmade storybook titled "Two Little Folk." In fewer than one hundred words, Mitchell wove a narrative in her childish printing about "two little people" who lived in her backyard: Tommy, "the boldest and the bravest," and "lazy" Sarah. She told of the couple eating breakfast and singing and saved the big reveal until the last sentence: Tommy and Sarah were a pair of ducks. When she was about eight, she began filling numerous copybooks with more complex tales: "The Knight and the Lady," "The Little Pioneers," "When We Were Shipwrecked," and "Dan Morrison, a Spy for the Confederacy."* The future novelist kept a journal and also created plays that the neighborhood children acted out; when she was fifteen, she staged an elaborate version of *The Traitor*, a 1907 novel by Thomas Dixon Jr. That same year, she completed a 107-page handwritten novella set in the South Seas titled *Lost Laysen*.† At Washington Seminary, the private girls' school she attended in Atlanta, two of her short stories were published in the school yearbook during her junior and senior years.

Mitchell also became a "distinguished letter writer," her brother recalled.[9] Like most young people of her generation and social class, she was taught early how to write a good letter. In 1918, when she went away to college in Massachusetts, her father found her missives home brimming with "more of life and liveliness than he had ever read before."[10] After her time

---

* Most of her surviving early stories were published in 2000 in the book *Before Scarlett: Girlhood Writings of Margaret Mitchell*, edited by Jane Eskridge. Some of the original copybooks, including "Two Little Folk," are in the Hargrett Rare Book and Manuscript Library at the University of Georgia and in the Kenan Research Center at the Atlanta History Center.

† The novella surfaced in 1994 among the papers of Henry Love Angel, a young man Mitchell knew in her youth. Scribner paid $1 million for the publishing rights, and the story was released in May 1996, making the *New York Times* best-seller list for two weeks.

at Smith was cut short by the death of her mother in 1919 and following an ill-advised marriage in 1922, she joined the staff of the *Atlanta Journal Sunday Magazine* as a feature writer. Over the next three and a half years, she produced more than two hundred feature stories, news articles, and book reviews, including an interview with Rudolph Valentino, the reigning sheik of the silents.[11] Again, her writing skills impressed the elder Mitchell. "It did not take Father long to see that she had a genius for words," Stephens Mitchell said.[12]

*   *   *

While working at the *Atlanta Journal*, Mitchell turned once more to writing fiction. She began a novel of the Jazz Age that featured a young woman named Pansy Hamilton, the daughter of a Georgia judge. The story opened with a nighttime car accident in which a friend of Pansy was injured, leading her to break into a drugstore for antiseptic and bandages.[13] But after about thirty pages, Mitchell gave up. She wrote a novella titled "'Ropa Carmagin." The title character, a woman named Europa who lived in the crumbling family home, was in love with a handsome mixed-race young man.[14] While the author finished this story, she apparently never tried to have it published.*

In 1924, Mitchell divorced her first husband; he apparently had a drinking problem and, on at least one occasion, had struck her. She married his best man, John Marsh, and the newlyweds moved into a cramped, ground-floor apartment that she christened "The Dump." When Mitchell reinjured a weak ankle, she quit her job at the newspaper but quickly became bored. Marsh encouraged his wife to work on a project, and in the fall of 1926, she turned to a period she knew well—the Civil War and Reconstruction era. As a child, she had spent Sunday afternoons on the "bony knees of veterans and the fat slippery laps of great aunts," listening to their firsthand tales of that era.[15] While most novels of the Civil War had focused on the battleground state of Virginia, Mitchell felt that the events in Georgia, especially Union General William T. Sherman's 1864 march on Atlanta, had "far more drama than anything else in the whole war."[16] She decided to tell a tale of her hometown, which was burned by Sherman, and the people who struggled through the war and the hard times afterward: "What quality is it that makes some people able to survive catastrophes

---

* Both the Jazz Age pages and the novella were destroyed, probably shortly after Mitchell's death.

and others—apparently just as brave and able and strong—go under?" she wondered. "I only know that the survivors of the Civil War used to call that quality 'gumption.'"[17]

Using a trick she learned as a reporter, Mitchell wrote the last chapter first. A strong ending was key to any piece, and she said it helped her write by knowing where the story was headed. She worked steadily on the new project and completed a first draft by 1929. Friends knew she was working on something, but she covered her typewriter and pages with a towel if visitors stopped by unexpectedly. Over the next couple of years, she "hit the book a few more licks," but as other tasks crowded her days, writing moved to the back burner.[18] Eventually, several piles of manila envelopes containing individual chapters, rewrites, and notes ended up throughout the apartment; after the couple moved in 1932, most of the manuscript was relegated to a closet. In April 1935, Harold Latham, an editor from The Macmillan Company, visited Atlanta on a book-scouting tour of the South. Tipped off by Lois Cole, an associate editor at the company and a friend of the author, Latham asked Mitchell several times about her project. At first, she told him she did not have a book. She later claimed the manuscript was not in good enough shape to share but promised he would be the first to see it if she ever finished. However, angered by catty remarks from an acquaintance and encouraged by her husband, Mitchell changed her mind and hurried to hand the pile of envelopes to Latham just as he was leaving his hotel to catch a train.

The editor forwarded the manuscript to New York, where Cole spent hours organizing the messy pile of papers. In her report, she praised her friend's "sure fire" plot and the "natural" dialogue.[19] A professor at Columbia University, a regular reader for Macmillan, weighed in as well. He called the story "magnificent" and urged, "By all means take the book."[20] On July 17, 1935, Latham wired Mitchell: "MY ENTHUSIASM YOUR NOVEL SHARED BY OUR ADVISERS WE WOULD LIKE MAKE IMMEDIATE CONTRACT FOR ITS PUBLICATION."[21] She signed the contract, which offered a $500 advance and 10 percent royalties, on August 6, 1935; the agreement also specified that the author retained both the dramatic and the motion picture rights.[22]

Mitchell spent the next six months rewriting, editing, checking her historical references, and ensuring consistency in dates and dialects. *Gone With the Wind* was published on June 30, 1936, and millions of readers soon discovered that same "genius for words" Mitchell's father had noted years earlier. The *New York Times* called the book "one of the most remarkable first novels produced by an American writer" and "the best Civil War novel that has yet been written."[23] The *Washington Post* agreed, declaring *Gone With the Wind* "the best novel that has ever come out of the South. In fact . . . it is unsurpassed in the whole of American writing."[24] And in the *Saturday Review of Literature*, Pulitzer Prize–winning poet Stephen Vincent Benet noted, "In spite of its length, the book moves swiftly and smoothly—a three-decker with all sails set . . . realistic in detail and told from an original point of view."[25] Several other reviewers called attention to the story's silver screen potential. "Here is material for twenty motion pictures—a broad canvas that throbs with color and life," wrote one. "Note to film editors: Stop at no figure, but bid lively," urged another.[26]

* * *

Hollywood got wind of Mitchell's novel early. The first inquiry from a studio came on February 12, 1936, when Samuel Goldwyn, Inc.'s East Coast office requested material on the "new Mary Mitchell book, *Gone With the Wind*, which you intend to publish shortly."[27] Macmillan informed the studio that galleys of the novel probably would be ready by mid-March.[28] At about the same time, a literary agent named Annie Laurie Williams approached Macmillan about the book's movie rights, "very anxious to take them on."[29] On March 9, at the agent's request, Lois Cole forwarded to Mitchell a letter of introduction in which Williams touted several properties she had sold, including 1929's *Magnificent Obsession*, by Lloyd C. Douglas, and *Tortilla Flat*, by John Steinbeck, published in 1935.* "From all I have heard from the Macmillan editors I feel that there is a fine picture in *Gone With the Wind*," she told Mitchell.[30] Cole also forwarded a letter from Monica McCall at the Ann Watkins agency, an established firm that Harold Latham favored. Whomever Mitchell chose, Cole reminded her, she should notify Macmillan so the publisher could send the agent galleys, the book's untrimmed typeset pages created for final proofing. "We intend, as you know, to make it a big book, and you ought to get a big price."[31]

Mitchell responded to both agents, politely putting them off by explaining that she was swamped with proofing pages.[32] To Cole, the author dismissed the entire idea of her story being translated to the screen, but Mitchell was among the few who harbored doubts. A month later, Cole

---

* *Magnificent Obsession*, starring Irene Dunn and Robert Taylor, was released in 1935 by Universal Pictures. *Tortilla Flat* was not produced until 1942; the Metro-Goldwyn-Mayer film starred Spencer Tracy, Hedy Lamarr, and John Garfield.

reported that "movie agents are pursuing me with their tongues hanging out," and studios were contacting Macmillan directly.[33] As a result of this rising tide of interest, the publisher began having second thoughts. Latham was headed to the West Coast on a scouting trip and decided he might be able to sell the rights himself.[34] If he were successful, the publisher would earn the 10 percent agent's fee. On a visit to Atlanta the following week, Latham discussed the situation with Mitchell and obtained her verbal assent for Macmillan to handle the sale. Mitchell's main concern was the screenplay. She promised not to be "tough-mouthed" about it but said she did not want Hollywood to have the Confederates win the Battle of Jonesboro or "Scarlett seduce General Sherman."[35] Latham, as naive as she about how movies were made, promised to push for the studio to grant her input on the movie script.

In mid-May, Macmillan began shipping copies of the 1,037-page tome to the New York story editors at all the major studios—Columbia, Metro-Goldwyn-Mayer, Paramount, RKO, Twentieth Century-Fox, Universal, and Warner Bros.—as well as two independent studios run by Goldwyn and David O. Selznick. Two days later, Katharine "Kay" Brown, the thirty-four-year-old East Coast story editor for Selznick International Pictures, sent a synopsis of the novel to her boss. In a teletype, she termed the story a "magnificent" possibility for either Miriam Hopkins or Margaret Sullavan, reported that one studio already had made an offer of $25,000, and urged Selznick to give the story his prompt attention.[36] The next day, Brown reiterated her enthusiasm and laid out a potential cast for the four leading roles: Hopkins or Bette Davis as Scarlett, Janet Gaynor as Melanie, Clark Gable as "Bret" (while bemoaning the fact that Ronald Colman, "perfect as to description," was so veddy British), and Franchot Tone as Ashley. Brown also predicted the book would bring $50,000, adding, "I am absolutely off my nut" about the story.[37]

After reading Brown's summary, Selznick admitted *Gone With the Wind* sounded like a "fine" story but said he felt the studio could not afford to take a gamble on the property without having under contract an actress suited for the role of Scarlett. "Most sorry to have to say no in face of your enthusiasm," he said, but gave Brown some hope by asking her to watch the book's sales. If *Gone With the Wind* showed signs of becoming another *Anthony Adverse*—a massive 1933 novel by Hervey Allen that sold 175,000 copies in the first six months—Selznick said he might reconsider.[38] About the same time, other studios that had expressed an early interest were dropping out: Twentieth Century-Fox said the initial asking price of $100,000 was too high, and the Goldwyn studio said it felt the part of Scarlett was too unsympathetic for Miriam Hopkins, the actress it had in mind.[39] Many producers steered clear, skittish about tackling another Civil War picture after the box office failure the previous year of Paramount's *So Red the Rose*, made from Stark Young's 1934 war novel.

Latham made some initial contacts about the movie rights but had no luck. He realized he needed Annie Laurie Williams's experience, so he agreed to join forces with the agent and split the 10 percent fee if she sold the rights.[40] Latham wrote to Mitchell seeking written authorization for Macmillan to market the film rights but made no mention of his arrangement with Williams.[41] In a follow-up letter to the agent, he stressed that their deal was confidential and that all negotiations with Mitchell were to be handled by his office.[42] When the author signed the letter of agreement and returned it to him, Latham again promised to try to give her "some measure of protection" on the film's screenplay.[43]

Williams was eager to close a deal and wanted Mitchell's preapproval on a price should she get a firm offer. As directed, she contacted Latham, who was on vacation; the editor wired Mitchell asking for her go-ahead if an offer came through of at least $50,000. He also told her that the company, as her agent, was "working through" Williams but did not mention their agreement.[44] Mitchell wired the next day that she accepted the amount "WITH UNDERSTANDING THAT CONTRACT WILL BE SUBMITTED TO ME FOR APPROVAL."[45]

One week after the book's release, on July 7, Selznick directed Brown to make an offer of $50,000. With Mitchell's acceptance in hand, Williams agreed, and that afternoon, Brown sent a jubilant teletype to the West Coast: "Hold your seat. I've closed for fifty thousand."[46] The next day, Cole wrote to Mitchell. She reported the studio was considering filming the movie in Technicolor and was going to take its time with casting. She also noted that Williams said the final price was the highest she could get "when it came right down to writing a check." The agent asked that all questions about the selling price be answered by saying, "Something over $50,000." Cole thought that was stretching the truth but added, "She says she got paid an extra cent so she could say that."[47]

*   *   *

Like Mitchell, David Selznick also developed an early love of books and movies. Born in 1902 in Pittsburgh, his fascination with the new world of film was in his genes: his father, Lewis J. Selznick, was an early pioneer of the fledgling East Coast motion picture industry. In 1918, when he formed

Selznick Pictures Corporation, Lewis Selznick named sixteen-year-old David company treasurer.[48] The father, who came to America from Eastern Europe as a boy, was drawn to literature while learning to speak and read English, and he passed on this appreciation for the classics to his youngest son. David Selznick, whose room was full of books as a boy, claimed to have read *Anna Karenina* and *David Copperfield* at an early age.[49] Years later, he made film versions of both novels—as well as of *A Tale of Two Cities* and *The Adventures of Tom Sawyer*—and his reverence for authors and literature was evident in his on-screen work. In 1935, when Margaret Mitchell saw *David Copperfield*, she realized that "here was a producer of both genius and integrity who was breaking all Hollywood rules by producing the book the author wrote."[50]

Selznick also showed an aptitude for writing. He dabbled in poetry and usually worked closely with his screenwriters, sometimes crafting sections of scripts himself. But the producer is best known for showering employees and bosses alike with voluminous memos addressing a variety of topics in minute detail. The habit began early. As a young executive in his father's companies, he found it easier to express himself in writing as opposed to face-to-face sessions with employees often much older than he. Later, working at Metro-Goldwyn-Mayer and RKO studios, he found his memos made him stand out in a telephone-centric workplace. Dictation also helped him "think a thing through to its conclusion more clearly," and his memos created a written record of what was actually said.[51] A feature story in the *Saturday Evening Post* dubbed him "The Great Dictater," noting that Selznick's obsession with the smallest details of moviemaking possessed him "to dictate or die."[52] In Margaret Mitchell, the producer met a kindred soul who shared his loquacious attention to detail.

*   *   *

Mitchell received the movie contract on July 15. After reviewing its sixteen pages with her husband, who was her business manager, and her brother, an attorney, she decided the document was "the stupidest contract" she had ever seen and one "no rational person could sign, regardless of the amount involved."[53] The three of them had many questions; John Marsh wrote an eleven-page, single-spaced letter laying out their concerns, noting he hoped "getting the contract revised and signed won't be as laborious as the job of getting this very long letter written."[54] He was to be disappointed. Marsh and Stephens Mitchell tried to get answers over the telephone, but to no avail. By month's end, the author and her brother decided to go to New York to meet face-to-face with representatives of Selznick International. "I will lose my mind certainly if this thing isn't settled soon," she told a friend.[55]

Gone With the Wind had touched a chord in a Depression-weary nation, and readers poured out their hearts to Scarlett's creator. Seemingly overnight, Mitchell became one of the most famous women in the country. Fans swamped her with mail; some days, hundreds of letters, along with dozens of copies of her novel to be autographed, arrived at her Atlanta apartment. Mitchell was grateful for the public's appreciation of her work and felt duty-bound to respond and thank them for their kind words and answer their questions. But her replies, warm and friendly, encouraged many readers to write a second time, often leading to a series of correspondence. For advice on what to do "when one has been so unfortunate as to become a best seller," she turned to Stark Young, the Mississippi author of *So Red the Rose*:

> For instance, when I am expecting a hellishly busy day and five close friends telephone, announcing that their Aunt Minnies from Keokuk are visiting them and will have a stroke if they do not see what I look like—what am I to do? Northerners have said bluntly, "Tell your friends you'll be jolly well pleased if their Aunt Minnies have two strokes as long as they don't bother you." But you are a Southerner and you know the intricate and courteous relationships between friend and friend and kin and kin in this section. They are not to be dealt with cavalierly.[56]

"You hit the nail on the head," Young replied, agreeing that "it's the Southern in us that complicates" matters. He advised her to take a trip to Mexico or New Orleans under her married name—"there nobody would bother you"—or to take advantage of the "big city's privacy" of New York.[57] But he admitted there was no long-term solution.[58]

Fans already had begun writing her about the movie, and Mitchell believed selling the film rights would shift that burden onto Selznick. She and Stephens Mitchell took the train to New York. At Selznick's Park Avenue office, Macmillan was represented by company treasurer Richard Brett. (Latham was still on vacation.) From the studio were John Wharton, Selznick's attorney and treasurer of Selznick International Pictures, and Kay Brown. Mitchell and her brother took an immediate liking to the story editor. "Margaret and I had not been in New York fifteen minutes . . . before we both whispered to each other that you were the smartest person around," Stephens Mitchell told Brown years later.[59]Also present was Annie Laurie Williams; Mitchell was still under the impression the agent was simply helping Macmillan.

The author and her brother were "as ignorant as a babe unborn"[60] about the issues they faced, and Stephens Mitchell admitted he was intimidated by Wharton, one of the country's leading theatrical rights attorneys.[61] The first day of talks did not go well. Using Marsh's lengthy letter as a guide, Mitchell's brother raised several points that were dismissed as mere technicalities. And any hope they held of the studio allowing the author a say in how the book was translated to the screen was quickly dashed. The contract specifically gave Selznick the right to make "any and all changes and substitutions in the property," including plot, action, and dialogue.[62] By the end of the day, the Mitchells considered simply walking away, but the author wanted to put the matter behind her, so they decided to stay. That evening, the pair had dinner with Lois Cole and her husband, who encouraged the author to try to retain the television rights. The following day, Mitchell won a partial concession in that area. She also had a section removed from the contract that obligated her to offer the movie rights to her next novel to Selznick before anyone else and insisted on inserting a line in the section about commercial tie-ups—items such as dolls, games, and figurines manufactured to promote the film—that directed her name not be used in promoting such products. That afternoon, July 30, Mitchell signed the contract, selling the movie rights to *Gone With the Wind* to David O. Selznick for $50,000. She received $45,000, and Macmillan and Williams split the remaining $5,000 as their commission.

In Mitchell's mind, her dealings with Hollywood were over. Selznick was free to make the motion picture he wanted from her book, and she would bear none of the blame should it fail. Contractually, the studio could not use her name to endorse "Wade Hampton Hamilton Bran Flakes" or "Scarlett O'Hara-Hamilton-Kennedy-Butler Toilet Water."[63] Mitchell would not bother the people making the movie, and they would not bother her. However, the author's innate curiosity and a maternal interest in what Selznick was doing with her literary "baby"—along with the public's unshakable belief that Mitchell was their ticket to Hollywood— meant she could not stay aloof for long. And, as she soon learned, not everyone took contracts and promises as seriously as she did.

CHAPTER One

Hollywood Comes Calling
1936

I can't imagine the movies buying it any way. I don't see how
it could possibly be made into a movie unless the entire book
was scrapped and Shirley Temple cast as "Bonnie," Mae West
as "Belle" and Stepin Fetchit as "Uncle Peter."

—Margaret Mitchell to Lois Cole
March 14, 1936

Miss Annie Laurie Williams   *Atlanta, Georgia*
New York, New York   *March 10, 1936*

My dear Miss Williams:

Thank you for your nice letter. Lois has written me most glowingly of
you and your firm—will you think me very unappreciative if I ask you to let
me defer business matters till such a time as I am able to attend to them?
I am on the last go-round of the galley proofs and am very late in getting
them finished, due to illness and an injury to my right arm and hand which
makes any writing a torment. And, due to my efforts to make my dead line,
I am as nearly insane as a person can get and still remain at liberty.

I will write you just as soon as I can.

Miss Lois Cole   *Atlanta, Georgia*
The Macmillan Company   *March 14, 1936*
New York, New York

Lois, dearie—

Both checks arrived and thanks.* Will you notify proper departments of their arrival? I do not know who to write.

The proofs will all be off on tomorrow's 5 a.m. air mail. . . .

About Miss Williams and Miss Watkins.† I dropped short notes to each saying that you had mentioned them most favorably but that I was in too frenzied a state, trying to read proof to talk business and I would write them just as soon as I got from under. Lois—I know nothing of agents, as you know. If taking Miss Williams will ease you out of any embarrassment, great or small, I'll take her. Please don't mind saying so. If she didn't sell it, I wouldn't hold you responsible. I can't imagine the movies buying it any way. I don't see how it could possibly be made into a movie unless the entire book was scrapped and Shirley Temple cast as "Bonnie," Mae West as "Belle" and Stepin Fetchit as "Uncle Peter."‡ I do thank you and Mr. Latham for your interest and thought in this matter. I never dreamed publishers could be so nice.

My god, I wish I had more time to write you for I am in a lather about your and Allan's new book and want to know all about it and know damned well you haven't the time to write me.§ I wish I could get as enthused about my own opus as I can about the opi (or is it oppuses?) of my friends. . . .

In haste

Miss Lois Cole   *Atlanta, Georgia*
The Macmillan Company   *April 27, 1936*
New York, New York

Dear Lois,

I am glad you warned me that your playmate Annie Laurie was in the neighborhood. She called me from Pinehurst or Aiken or some where night

---

* On March 11, Macmillan mailed Mitchell a check for $250—the remaining half of her $500 advance, due on delivery of her manuscript. The publisher also sent a check for $10 as reimbursement for a new photograph the author had had taken in Atlanta.

† Ann Watkins was the head of A. Watkins, Inc., a New York literary agency.

‡ Stepin Fetchit was the stage name of vaudeville comedian Lincoln Perry, who became the first millionaire black film actor.

§ *Drums in the Forest*, by Lois Dwight Cole and her husband, Allan Taylor, was published in 1936 by Macmillan under the pseudonym Allan Dwight.

before last. I'm going to tell you about our conversation so she can't cross me up. She picked a bad day to call me but she couldn't know that. I had intended staying in bed all day so I would be fit to go to opera that night (we had three nights of semi-Metropolitan for our Dogwood Festival)—but before breakfast a perfectly strange woman crashed in. She had read my book and reviewed it for something or other and wanted to see what I looked like. Needless to say, having had no coffee, I looked like Hell. Really she was very nice but I missed my breakfast. And while she was still camped here there came a call from Dot Bates that her mother had broken her hip and her child was into something or other.* Would I look after Mamma? That meant x-rays and the hospital and threatening to castrate several nurses so I didn't have lunch either. Bessie, now private secretary as well as cook, collared me at the hospital and told me the mournful news that an indigent old lady friend, slowly dying of heart failure, was being evicted from her house.†

Well that took till after supper. I had twenty minutes to eat and dress and get to the opery when who should phone but Annie Laurie. Hunger and weariness had taken toll of my good manners but I tried to be sweet and girlish and told her I'd been ill. Yes, she knew about that and was so sorry but she had understood that I wanted her to proceed as my agent in the matter of the movies and so—Well, I blew up then. It was just the last straw of a day full of straws. And I said coldly that she was in error. That I had given her no such authority. My letter to her had merely been an acknowledgment of her letter. I had written her that I was sick and was in no condition to attend to business.

Well, she backed water quite hastily and said she wanted to come down to Atlanta to see me and talk the matter over. By this time John was doing a fandango to get me away from the phone and Bessie was changing my stockings for me and I saw all chances of a meal disappearing. So I told her that I'd love to meet her, you having written so many nice things about her and her work but that if she was coming down here to talk business she was out of luck because I wasn't going to talk business. I said that I was still feeble and that, at present I had no intention of deciding anything because I thought that when sick people made decisions they were always wrong.

---

* Dorothy "Dot" Bates Kelley was a childhood friend of Mitchell's and a bridesmaid at her first wedding in 1922.
† Bessie Berry (later Jordan) was Mitchell's longtime housekeeper and cook.

Moreover I told her that the book wasn't good movie material and invited her to read it. If she wanted to come here socially I'd love to see her but in a business way, no. At this point Bessie dragged my evening dress over my head, no mean feat, I must say. So Annie talked at great length about her firm and how good it was and said she'd write to me from N.Y. I was in a state by the time I got to the opera and had to go out and eat a hamburger between the acts. It wasn't till after midnight that I began to get good and mad about her saying that she understood I wanted her as agent. . . .

Excuse this mad letter but I am all in. Just wanted to let you know about Annie Laurie and to tell you that I haven't signed up with her. . . .

Miss Annie Laurie Williams   *Atlanta, Georgia*
New York, New York   *May 5, 1936*

Dear Miss Williams:

Just a note to tell you that I wrote to The Macmillan Company and asked them to give you a set of galley proofs of "Gone With the Wind." I hope you have them by this time.

I was very glad I had the opportunity to talk to you—even if the operator did keep shouting "Three minutes is up!" every three seconds. I was not only glad to hear from you personally, for Lois Cole has written me so many things about you and your work, but I was glad to have the occasion to correct any misunderstanding that may have arisen about the matter of the moving picture rights of "Gone With the Wind." You indicated that you had gotten the impression somehow that I had authorized you to act as my agent in this matter and as I have not, this misunderstanding naturally might have led to embarrassment for both of us. I can't quite understand just how your misunderstanding might have arisen as I thought I made my position quite clear in my previous letter to you. As I stated to you in our telephone conversation I have not authorized anyone to act as my agent, either tentatively or temporarily, in handling the movie rights of "Gone With the Wind." I am not ready to even think about such problems as movie rights now as I am too engaged with other pressing matters at this time, my own health, family affairs, business matters neglected during the months when I was preparing the book for publication. If at some future date I wish to ask you to act as my agent I will communicate with you.

Thank you for your card.

Mr. Harold Latham   *Atlanta, Georgia*
The Macmillan Company   *May 25, 1936*
New York, New York

Dear Mr. Latham:

I have signed the contract giving Macmillan the right to try to sell the book to the movies and I'm enclosing it. I feel very relieved about having it in your hands instead of an agent's. That's not disparaging agents but then, I don't know agents and I do know you. Further more I am so impressed with what you did about the English publication that I know you can do far more about movie people than any agent would.*

If possible I should like to have something in any contract you may make with a movie producer that I can have some say so about the final scenario. I won't be tough-mouthed about the changes—that is, some changes. I know that the book will be a difficult one to make into a movie, if, indeed, it can be made into a movie. And I know too that many things are easy in a novel and difficult, even impossible, to reproduce on the screen. I know that some changes are necessary in transferring any book to the screen, characters have to be completely eliminated, incidents collapsed into each other, etc. But there are a few changes I wouldn't put up with. I wouldn't put it beyond Hollywood to have General Hood win the Battle of Jonesboro, Scarlett seduce General Sherman and a set of negroes with Harlem accents play the back woods darkies. By the way, is your new "agency department" going to handle dramatic rights, too?

Your note about Mr. Leigh came this morning and I thank you for it and for your trouble in writing me.† I have already written him so don't you bother with writing him. I told him I couldn't lecture, that it just wasn't in me. For, as I told you, what would I lecture about? He suggested the "Urge to Write," at which I fell on the sofa and bellowed because I have no urge to write and never had, loathing writing above all things, except perhaps, Wagnerian opera and tap dancing. . . .

---

* In late April, Mitchell's publisher brokered a deal with Macmillan & Co. Ltd., its former parent company in London, for a British edition of *Gone With the Wind*. The novel was released in England in September.

† W. Colston Leigh of the Leigh Bureau of Lectures and Entertainments wanted to arrange a paid speaking tour for Mitchell to promote her book.

Lois Cole   *Atlanta, Georgia*
The Macmillan Company   *June 15, 1936*
New York, New York

JUST RECEIVED TELEGRAM MISTER LATHAM SENT YESTERDAY RECOMMENDING THAT I ACCEPT FIFTY THOUSAND DOLLARS CASH FOR MOTION PICTURE RIGHTS IF OFFER IS MADE STOP WILL ACCEPT THIS AMOUNT WITH UNDERSTANDING THAT CONTRACT WILL BE SUBMITTED TO ME FOR APPROVAL AS STATED IN HIS WIRE.

Miss Lois Cole   *Atlanta, Georgia*
The Macmillan Company   *July 3, 1936*
New York, New York

Dear Lois,

Feebly I take my typewriter in hand to ask just what the Hell Annie Laurie means by jumping on me about rumors that Fox Films had bought the book. At present I am hunting for some one to jump on about all the damn movie rumors which are driving me nuts. In fact, for four days after Mr. Latham's wire about the definite price I didn't even tell Father and then told him only in the capacity of a lawyer, in connection with expected income tax affairs. I said nothing nor did John or Father yet during those four days rumors that I had sold for fifty thousand up to five million boiled all over town, in fact, all over the state.

People are driving me crazy, folks on the relief rolls asking for a hundred because I won't miss it out of my many millions, etc. Friends wondering why in Hell I persist in driving a 1929 model car and wearing four year old cotton dresses and fifty cent stockings and calling me an old Hetty Green to my face. None of these rumors started from me. Finally they got so bad I had the newspapers here deny the rumors in large print. Perhaps you saw Dudley Glass's story, denying that I had sold, denying that Clark Gable had personally phoned from Hollywood saying he'd cut his throat if I didn't let him play Rhett, etc.

It isn't confined to this section. My ex roommate at Smith (now in N.Y. with United Artists films) wrote me that her book seller had told her that a Macmillan salesman had told him that I had refused forty thousand smackers and, dearie-lamb, that's a hellavu lot of smackers to refuse. A friend in Chicago wrote about the same thing, saying that in a round about way they had heard from some one in the Macmillan organization that I had sold for seventy five thousand, to an unnamed film company. In-laws on the Pacific coast write to me that they heard through librarians who had heard through Macmillan people that I had sold for a million and our congratulations to you, dear Peggy.

Recently, I have run into a number of book men from other publishers (from N.Y.) and one and all refuse to believe me when I say I haven't sold. They say they all had it straight from the horse's mouth in the N.Y. Macmillan office that I had sold and what am I trying to do—dodge the income tax collectors? Why jump on me? I've never said a word except in denial but it looks like the Macm. salesmen have spread it. I wish there was some way of calling them off as the whole situation is running me crazy.* . . . Please tell Bonnie Annie that I do appreciate what she is doing and I have done my best to cooperate but what the hell?

Lois I will write you at length about this dreadful week when I get the energy. I just came to the end of everything yesterday and blew up with loud explosions and went to bed and have the tired shakes so bad this a.m. that I can hardly hit the keys. I'm trying to get away on Monday. John can't go with me, alas. I think I'll just get in the car and ride. Probably to the mountains. I'll be less likely to run into people I know up there. Should you wish to locate me, wire John at the Georgia Power during the day and here at home at night. I will phone him each night where I am.

Dear God, Lois. NOT Janet Gaynor! Spare me this last ignomy or else tell Bonnie Annie to hold her up for a million. May I ask which part she intends to play—Belle Watling? Miriam Hopkins has been my choice from the beginning but I knew what I had to say wouldn't matter so said nothing. She has the voice, the looks, the personality and the sharp look. And I wish that lovely creature (I think her name is Elizabeth Allan) who played David Copperfield's mother could do Melanie.† And I wish Charles Boyer didn't have a French accent for he's my choice for Rhett. Next to him, Jack Holt is the only person I can think of.‡

I'll write you soon. Everyone has been wonderful, so wonderful that I'm nearly dead. I think the sales went over all right. I believe Luise Sims has already worked off three hundred and seventy copies in three days

---

* On July 7, Macmillan sales manager Alec Blanton promised his employees they would be notified when the movie rights were sold. Until then, he cautioned, "you should, if asked, say that they have not as yet been disposed of."

† Allan played Clara Copperfield in the 1935 film version of *David Copperfield*, produced by David O. Selznick at Metro-Goldwyn-Mayer.

‡ Holt, best known for his work in westerns, was a leading man who got his start in silent pictures.

which is a record in Atlanta.* I go on the air tonight with Medora and then everything will be over. Tonight's my last appearance as Margaret Mitchell unless they come after me with a rope.†

My love to you and thanks for everything you've done and are doing.

P.S. Tomorrow is our eleventh wedding anniversary! Good Heavens!

Mr. Duncan Burnet   *Atlanta, Georgia*
Athens, Georgia   *July 3, 1936*

Dear Mr. Burnet:

You said in your nice letter that "this requires no reply." But I must reply to thank you for it and to tell you that I *haven't* sold the movie rights for three to ten million dollars, as rumor has it. In fact, I haven't even had an offer from the movies. I don't know where this rumor started but it's about to run me crazy. Of course, I'd *like* to sell it but don't see how the book could be made into a movie. You can help me a lot by denying the story. As you can imagine, every one in Georgia on the Relief Rolls is after me to give them a thousand dollars and they get mad when I say I've never had the thousand, much less three million!

Miss Ginnie Morris   *Atlanta, Georgia*
United Artists Corporation   *July 11, 1936*
New York, New York

Dear Ginnie,

The hell you say, I used to borrow your tooth brush! Everybody at Smith College was under the impression that you never owned a tooth brush.

I don't know where the rumor started that I turned down 40,000 smackers from the movies. It seems a very wide spread rumor, but there is no truth in it. Now I ask you, can you imagine poor folks like me turning down $40—much less $40,000?‡

---

* Sims was the head of the book department at Atlanta's Davison-Paxon department store, which hosted Mitchell's first book signing on publication day, June 30.

† On the evening of July 3, Mitchell was featured on WSB Radio's "Editorial Hour." The carefully scripted "interview" was conducted by Medora Perkerson, the author's former colleague on the *Atlanta Journal Sunday Magazine*.

‡ On July 23, 1936—one week before the contract was signed—Selznick issued a press release announcing, "David O. Selznick Outbids All Producers for 'Gone With the Wind.'" While neither Selznick International nor Macmillan announced the selling price, the rumor mill

Weren't the New York reviewers wonderful to me? I am still so breathless that my tongue is dry—and I thank you so much for saying that you like my book.

I will write you more later when life settles down—if it ever does. For two weeks I have been running like a rabbit.

Mr. Herschel Brickell   Atlanta, Georgia
New York Post   July 28, 1936
New York, New York

My dear Herschel,

I intended to write you immediately. And as you see, I didn't. I found Bessie and John beleaguered by salesmen of every type and people who wanted me to receive at teas, Father and Steve going round and round on the contract and one thousand letters, some of a most urgent nature that required instant handling.

I hadn't been home a hour before it seemed as though I'd never been away at all.* No, I won't say that. God knows that trip was a life saver and I came home mean and full of beans and determined to tell people where to head in. How very kind you and Edwin were! Now that I look back on it I am even more impressed than I was at the time. If I had been kin you two could not have been sweeter or more sympathetic or more understanding. It's due to you two that I *did* come home full of beans and mean as a two year old colt.

But this letter isn't the one I intended to write. The main purpose of this letter is to ask you just what your home address is and how I could lay hands on you should I come to N.Y. any time in the very near future. I know you live in N.J. but have forgotten where and I recall you saying that you didn't have a phone. (Oh, wise man! Or should I say Oh, wise woman?) I may be in N.Y. some time this week and will probably not stay more than a day. Rather I will stay no longer than is necessary for me and brother Steve to clear up this damned contract. We've been trying to handle it by letter

---

quickly filled in the blank. United Press reported Mitchell was paid $52,000. "Sally Forth," the *Atlanta Constitution*'s society columnist, pegged the amount at $54,000, adding that the author would "receive royalties from the picture that, with the cash payment, will exceed $100,000 in two years." Hollywood gossip columnist Louella Parsons claimed Mitchell was paid "no less" than $65,000.

* Mitchell had attended a writers conference at Blowing Rock, North Carolina, where she met Brickell, who reviewed *Gone With the Wind* in the *New York Post*, and Edwin Granberry, who reviewed the book in the *New York Sun*. The author began corresponding regularly with both men and their wives, Norma Brickell and Mabel Granberry.

and long distance and not getting very far. It seems sensible for us to go up and polish the matter off, one way or another.

I do not want to go. I have no clothes and no time to buy any. I have been sick in bed for the last three days and do not feel like tackling a hot trip. But I will lose my mind certainly if this thing isn't settled soon. Just now I don't care which way it is settled.

So—Steve and I won't be in N.Y. long and we will see few people. The fewer the better. I am asking the Macm. to not let anyone know I am coming. Otherwise there's half a hundred visits I'd have to make. I'd rather wait and make them when I come North later in the year—if I come. But I would like to see you and I would very much like to meet Norma. In every detail she sounded like everything I like. But Herschel, if when I land in town either Norma or you are busy, do, for Heaven's sake tell me so frankly. God knows, I know how inconvenient it is for people to drop in from Oshkosh and expect me to drop everything I've planned and see them. I feel sure that you will be perfectly frank about this. I am sure you know me well enough. Certainly any man who has publicly held a woman's head during altitude nausea should have no qualms about saying he and his wife are busy!

Will you either wire me your address or air mail it? I don't know when we'll get off. I am in the hands of my men folks and the minute they take a notion to load me on a train, then that very minute I'll know I'm on my way. . . .

Mr. Harold Latham   *Atlanta, Georgia*
Onteora Club   *August 13, 1936*
Tannersville, New York

Dear Harold:

(Have I called you Harold since you invited me to do so?)

I have been on such a dead run since publication date that I cannot recall whether or not I have written you during the past month. At any rate, I call you Harold even though I feel exactly as though I had referred to God Almighty familiarly as "G.A."

I wish I could use the typewriter myself now, for there are so many thousands of things I want to write you, so many thousands of things I want to thank you for, but unfortunately, the strain of answering hundreds of letters has finished what reading proof did to my eyes. For ten days I have been in a dark room with a black bandage over my eyes, forbidden by the doctor to even think of any kind of work or writing, so this letter will be brief as I have not yet caught the trick of dictating. . . .

Yes, the moving picture deal was closed up about two weeks ago. However, I was ill at the time, and as my eyes were going bad on me I made a quick two day trip to New York with my brother, who is a lawyer. I went off in a lather of rage about the contract, all ready to throw it in the movie company's face. It was the stupidest contract I ever saw, a contract that no rational person could sign, regardless of the amount of money involved. The contract held me liable for so many things, such as damage suits, that I could not sign it. Also, the contract was worded idiotically. In many items it referred to me as the holder of the copyright.

The Selznick lawyers were mighty nice. So were the pretty young ladies in the Selznick office. They smoothed me down. They made concessions and I made concessions and the contract was rearranged so that it was possible for me to sign it. I know, too, whom I have to thank for making this contract possible, and I am thanking you again. . . .

Miss Annie Laurie Williams   *Atlanta, Georgia*
New York, New York   *August 13, 1936*

Dear Miss Williams:

I have delayed a long time in thanking you for all you did in the matter of the movie contract. My delay has not been due to my lack of appreciation but to the fact that I have been ill in bed almost since I last saw you. I am suffering from very severe eye strain and have been unable to read or write. I am dictating this letter just to say "thank you for everything."

Could you send me Miss Kay Brown's address? She and Miss Modisett were so very nice that I want to write them and thank them, too.*

Miss Katharine Brown   *Atlanta, Georgia*
Selznick International Pictures, Inc.   *September 3, 1936*
New York, New York

Dear Miss Brown:

You and Miss Modisett must have thought me several kinds of a varmint for not writing you sooner to thank you for what you did in the matter of the sale of "Gone With the Wind" and also for your many courtesies to me. I have delayed writing you in the hope that I could write you

---

* Dorothy Modisett was Kay Brown's assistant in New York.

personally but can delay no longer and so must struggle through a dictated letter. Dictation is new and strange and fearsome to me.

My eyes were so bad when I was in New York that I could barely see. That was the reason for my unmannerly desire to get the contract closed up immediately. I had overstrained my eyes badly on the proof reading of the book and had about finished them on the heavy correspondence that followed the publication of the book. At the time I went to New York I was supposed to be in bed in a dark room, giving them a complete rest. Since I saw you last that's what I have been doing and it has been a wearisome and boring period of time.

Thank you both so much for your enthusiasm about the book, your cordiality to me—and the cocktails! Being a "Provincial Lady" and coming from a state that has been bone dry for about fifty years, the cocktail was about the first legal cocktail I ever drank!

My best to Miss Modisett and to you.

Miss Katharine Brown   *Atlanta, Georgia*
Selznick International Pictures, Inc.   *September 23, 1936*
New York, New York

Dear Miss Brown:

Some days ago I received a letter from Miss Annie Laurie Williams in which she said that Mr. Selznick wanted me to come to Hollywood about the script of "Gone With the Wind." I regret very much my delay in answering this letter but I have been ill. I was also having so much trouble with my eyes that I could neither read nor write. The truth of the matter is, I did not even see the letter until a day or so ago.

It will be impossible for me to go to Hollywood, for many reasons. The main ones are the two stated above, my health and my eyes. If I go anywhere at all during the coming six months, it will be a brief trip of two or three days, to New York. The Macmillan Company wish to give me a tea. Until my eyes are better and I can gain ten or more pounds, I won't even get to New York. Another reason for not going to Hollywood is that I simply hate traveling and hate to leave Atlanta even for a day or two.

You said, at the time of the signing of the contract, that someone from your organization might come to Atlanta. If they do, please don't forget that I'd be glad to do all in my power to assist them in any way. Should you wish to communicate with me about this or any other matter, will you please write me directly, instead of through Miss Williams? She is not my agent. The Macmillan Company was my agent for the sale of the motion picture rights in my novel, and I understand that they employed Miss Williams to assist them in the transaction.

Mr. Harold Latham   *Atlanta, Georgia*
The Macmillan Company   *September 23, 1936*
New York, New York

Dear Harold:

Here I come bothering you again and after I had promised myself that I would not worry you while you were vacationing. But this matter was so serious that I wanted you to know about it.

The enclosed letter to Mr. George Brett contains information I thought you should know. I had been proceeding confidently in the belief that The Macmillan Company had been my agent in the sale of the motion picture rights and that when I went to New York some two months ago The Macmillan Company, represented by Mr. Richard Brett and Mr. Swords, appeared at the conference with the Selznick people in my behalf and to look after my interests. A recent letter from Mr. George Brett, Jr. stated that The Macmillan Company was not my agent and that Mr. Richard Brett and Mr. Swords had appeared at the conference at the Selznick office, not in my behalf, but solely to protect the interests of The Macmillan Company.

I found this most upsetting and distressing. It was especially so, coming as it did when my eyes were in such condition that I could neither read nor write and was laid up in bed with my eyes bandaged. My brother, also my lawyer, set forth the information in the enclosed letter for me and it was mailed to Mr. Brett Monday.* I have also sent a carbon to Lois for she, of course, knew about my refusing to have Miss Williams as my agent. I had sent a copy of my letter to Miss Williams to Lois.

I find myself in a most embarrassing position about Miss Williams. I gather from correspondence from her that she may still think herself my agent. Evidently the Selznick Company thinks this too, for they have requested me to come to Hollywood, *through* Miss Williams. A recent article in the Wall Street Journal gives the impression that Miss Williams is my

---

* On September 21, the author's brother wrote a lengthy and sharply worded letter to George Brett Jr., president of The Macmillan Company, asking him to notify Williams that she "is not now and never has been Mrs. Marsh's agent but participated in the sale of the motion picture rights only as an employee of The Macmillan Company."

agent. She is not my agent and has never been. I have nothing against her and think she did a good job, for The Macmillan Company, in selling the motion picture rights. But, just the same, she isn't my agent. It is embarrassing to me to have to write to her again and tell her that she isn't my agent but then, I don't want any unauthorized person seeming to be my agent. As you know, I was besieged with requests from people wanting to be my agent, Miss Williams among others. I refused them all and would never have had any agent had you not offered the services of Macmillan.

I am so very upset and distressed about it all. I'm sorry to bother you but thought you should know.

Miss Annie Laurie Williams   *Atlanta, Georgia*
New York, New York   *October 1, 1936*

Dear Miss Williams:

I am so terribly sorry to have delayed so long in answering your letter and also in thanking you for the wire you sent me about the broadcast. I have not been very well and have put off writing from day to day in the hope that I would be able to use the typewriter myself. But that day seems far distant and I will delay no longer.

As I told you in New York, I do not want to go to California. I haven't changed my mind about that and I believe that even the thought of such a trip would be foolish, when I am unable to do any close work. If I should change my mind about the trip, I will take up the matter with Mr. Selznick or Miss Brown.

I so appreciated your wire and listened to the broadcast with great interest, as you can imagine. I had never listened to a radio until the last two months. But it has certainly been a Godsend to me since I have been unable to read. I was very pleased, of course, that the radio people used my dialogue practically word for word.*

---

* On September 17, *Then & Now*, a new radio program sponsored by Sears, Roebuck and Co., featured Robert Montgomery and Constance Bennett performing the scene in *Gone With the Wind* in which Rhett proposes to Scarlett. In its review, *Variety* said Bennett's voice "lacks rounded cadence" and that Montgomery "romps through his lines in a way suggesting he was in Chicago between trains." Mitchell's husband agreed. In a letter to his mother, he wrote, "We were told, however, on fairly good authority," that the pair "had *not* been selected for the movie. If you happened to hear the program, I think you will agree that the message was hardly necessary, as both of them are so completely unsuited for the part."

Thank you so much for your many courtesies and please forgive my long delay in acknowledging them.

Miss Katharine Brown   *Atlanta, Georgia*
Selznick International Pictures, Inc.   *October 1, 1936*
New York, New York

Dear Miss Brown:

I had not forgotten about the copy of "Gone With the Wind" for Mr. Selznick. But I delayed sending it for two reasons, first because I haven't been well enough to stir about much and, second, because I wanted to find a first edition for him. The only first editions I can locate are in the hands of my family and close friends. They became incensed and show their teeth when I suggest that they give them up. I haven't even one first edition of my own. I never thought the book would sell one-half of one edition, so I didn't lay in a supply. I am mailing an autographed copy to Mr. Selznick today in your care.*

Will you please thank Mr. Selznick for me for his renewed invitation for me to go to California. I just do not think that it will be possible. But I am appreciative of the invitation just the same. . . .

I do not know when I will be in New York, as my trip depends on my eyes. They are very sensitive to lights at present, so I will not be doing any traveling until this condition clears up. But I do want to see you when I get to New York.

P.S. It will be a pleasure to me to meet Mr. Cukor and your scenarist and I will be so glad to do anything I can to make their visit to Atlanta pleasant and interesting and to help them meet anyone they would like to talk to, but I don't believe that I personally could be very helpful in the business of turning a novel into a movie.† I hope things will work out so that you can come to Atlanta with them. As you may have gathered from "Gone With the Wind" I think a lot of this town and I would enjoy showing it to you.

---

* Mitchell inscribed the book, "To David Selznick with admiration for your many artistic achievements—Margaret Mitchell, Atlanta, Ga., October 1, 1936." The volume was sold at a June 2, 1971, auction at Christie's in London for £260, or $624.

† Selznick announced in a press release on September 11 that George Cukor would direct *Gone With the Wind*. Selznick and Cukor had worked together on several films, including *David Copperfield*, *What Price Hollywood?* (1932), and *Dinner at Eight* (1933).

Mr. Louis Sobol   *Atlanta, Georgia*
The New York Evening Journal   *October 1, 1936*
New York, New York

Dear Mr. Sobol:

I have just received a clipping of your column of Thursday, September 24th, in which you made mention of my book, "Gone With the Wind." I wanted to write you and correct an error in it. I am confident that the error was no fault of yours but it does an injustice to a charming young lady and I feel that it should be corrected.

You state that "Scarlett O'Hara" in the book is modeled after Miss Betty Timmons, of Atlanta. Certainly that is no compliment to any girl, for "Scarlett" was not a very nice person. I am not personally acquainted with Miss Timmons (she is not my niece nor is she a relative of mine) but I know many of her friends and know she is a girl of charm and beauty and character. "Scarlett" was not the same type of person as Miss Timmons and I am distressed that so fine a girl as Miss Timmons should be compared with her. I did not take the character of "Scarlett" from anyone, living or dead.

Miss Katharine Brown   *Atlanta, Georgia*
Selznick International Pictures, Inc.   *October 6, 1936*
New York, New York

Dear Miss Brown:

I hope you will let me know as far ahead as possible when and if Mr. Cukor is coming to Atlanta. As I told you, I am very anxious to be here then. However, I have ahead of me a trip to New York for the Macmillan's tea, just as soon as my eyes are in good condition again. When this will be, I do not know, so my plans are somewhat uncertain.

I want to render any aid possible to Mr. Cukor. For that reason, I am writing you this information. Mr. Wilbur Kurtz of Atlanta is a well known architect and painter. More than that, he is our greatest authority on the Civil War in this section. He has studied every campaign, been over every battlefield, mapped out the positions of troops. He has also a fine collection of early Atlanta pictures. He would be the proper man to show Mr. Cukor around. Of course, I would go too but Mr. Kurtz is the real authority. I am sending to you the Red Barrel, which has a story about me in it.* Most of the facts of the story are errors but I am sending it to you so you can

---

* The September 1936 issue of *Red Barrel*, the in-house publication of the Coca-Cola Company, featured a seven-page article titled "Gone With the Wind," by Ralph McGill.

see some of the drawings of Mr. Kurtz. I want to call your attention especially to the picture on Page 18. It shows a typical house in before-the-war
Atlanta. Atlanta was not a city of white columned houses and it would be
pretty terrible if it was pictured that way. The picture on Page 16, showing
Five Points, is probably a scene in the 1840s. I believe that the Cyclorama,
a portion of which is shown on Page 14, would be a great help to anyone
staging battle scenes. This Cyclorama is enormous and the only thing of
this kind in the world. It shows the complete Battle of Atlanta.

Life has been awful since I sold the movie rights! I am deluged with
letters demanding that I do not put Clark Gable in as Rhett. Strangers
telephone me or grab me on the street, insisting that Katharine Hepburn
will never do. It does me no good to point out sarcastically that it is Mr.
Selznick and not I who is producing this picture.

P.S. I have not talked to Mr. Kurtz and so do not know if he will be
available as he is pretty busy. If you like I will get in touch with him.

I forgot to say that not only do strangers assault me about not having
Gable and Hepburn and Bankhead in the picture but they assault me with
demands that Lamar Trotti do the scenario.* When I wearily reiterate that
after all Mr. Selznick is producing the picture, they say, "But there's no one
but Mr. Trotti who can do it. I shall never speak to you again if he doesn't
do the scenario."

Lamar Trotti is an Atlantan, you see, knows the section and has made
a deep study of this period. Everyone feels that he wouldn't let a character
say "you all" while addressing one person. (This one thing, I may add, so
incenses Southerners that they want to secede from the Union again every
time they hear it in a movie.) Is there any chance that Mr. Trotti will do
the scenario?

You mentioned that someone would come down with Mr. Cukor to see
me about "changes in the continuity." Of course, I would love to help out
in any way I can but I have no ideas at all about any changes and could be of
no help whatsoever in such a matter. Besides, if the news got out that I was
in even the slightest way responsible for any deviations from the book, then
my life wouldn't be worth living. You see, this section has taken the book
to its heart and that is something which makes me prouder than anything
else. But each and every reader feels that he has part ownership of it and
they are determined that nothing shall be changed. I am dogged by people

---

* Actress Tallulah Bankhead, born in Alabama, was the daughter of U.S. Speaker of the
House William B. Bankhead. Trotti, a former reporter with the *Atlanta Georgian*, was a producer and screenwriter at Twentieth Century-Fox.

who say they'll never speak to me again if "I let the movie people change one line." So I would not be of any assistance in the continuity.

I suppose you know that casting this picture is the favorite drawing room game these days and every newspaper has been after me to say just who I want to play the parts. It has been difficult but so far I have kept my mouth shut. I wish to goodness you all would announce the cast and relieve me of this burden!

Mr. Louis Sobol   *Atlanta, Georgia*
The New York Evening Journal   *October 8, 1936*
New York, New York

Dear Mr. Sobol:

You were very kind to reply so promptly to my letter and I appreciate it very much. No, I wouldn't want you to print anything further in your column about Miss Timmons and the mix-up. I thoroughly agree with your ideas on the matter and your reasons for not wishing to say any more about it. I wouldn't want anything printed that would embarrass her in any way.*

Miss Betty Timmons   *Atlanta, Georgia*
New York, New York   *October 13, 1936*

Dear Miss Timmons:

It was a mix-up, wasn't it? I hope it hasn't bothered you. I know it wasn't your fault and I have long since become hardened to newspaper errors. I am enclosing some Atlanta clippings, which may interest you. Even after I explained that we were no blood kin, the reporter insisted on quoting me as saying that we were kin!

I hope you have all the luck in the world in the movies. I'd be mighty proud if you were my niece!†

---

* Sobol wrote Mitchell on October 6 that the information came from Timmons herself and added that he "wouldn't be a nice man" if he made a liar out of the young woman in his column. Yet, in his "The Voice of Broadway" that same day, Sobol quoted from Mitchell's letter and defended himself by repeating that the "charming Miss Timmons, who insists she is a niece of Miss Mitchell," was his source.

† Timmons's paternal uncle was married to Aline Mitchell, a sister of the author's father. When Timmons continued her public campaign to wrangle a screen test for the role of Scarlett, Mitchell's opinion of the "fine" young woman changed. Eventually, the author and others at the studio began referring to Timmons as "Honey Chile."

Miss Katharine Brown   *Atlanta, Georgia*
Selznick International Pictures, Inc.   *October 19, 1936*
New York, New York

Dear Miss Brown:

I wish that I had known my brother was going to call on you.* I would have sent you a thousand messages. My husband and I were so interested in the details of his conversation with you. We are glad to know something of the mystery of Miss Timmons. As he probably told you, she is not related to us and we have never even met her. Life has been a merry hell since that story broke for everyone has been wiring and writing me that if I can get my niece in the movies, then I can get them in too, and also their tap-dancing daughters, their grandmothers and their colored cooks and chauffeurs. Things got so bad that three days ago I gave a statement to the papers, disclaiming any part in the producing, casting or costuming of "Gone With the Wind." I stated that I felt that Mr. Selznick, having been in the business for some time, was probably far more capable than I at deciding such matters. Aren't people movie-mad? I am beginning to realize that I am probably the only woman in the world who never wanted to be in the movies!

My brother told me of your ideas for Scarlett, and they seem so absolutely sound to me. I hope things work out that way. I am keeping that under my hat as I am being deviled daily by news services demanding who I want to play the part. I never realized what one got into in selling a book to the movies.

I am pleased—very pleased—about Mr. Howard, and it will be such a pleasure to meet him if he comes South for I have always admired his work.†

I had the nicest letter from Mr. David Selznick yesterday, saying that he might come to Atlanta with Mr. Cukor and Mr. Howard. I can think of nothing nicer. I only hope that by the time he gets here the painters will have cleared out of the apartment, the Armenians will have returned the rugs and the upholsterers will have given me something to sit on. At present, the house looks like General Sherman had made a successful raid. I should hate to seat Mr. Selznick on a bridge chair but I am so anxious to meet him that I would shamelessly seat him on the floor, if necessary.

---

* Stephens Mitchell went to New York to meet with Macmillan officials, who were conveying the foreign publication rights of *Gone With the Wind* to the author. He also met with Marion Saunders, who would become the author's agent for her overseas publishing contracts.

† Selznick announced in a press release on October 29 that Pulitzer Prize–winning playwright Sidney Howard would write the screenplay for *Gone With the Wind* and pledged that the studio would give the novel the "most complete treatment ever accorded a literary work."

You were so very kind to give my brother an interview for I know how busy you are. He appreciated it so much and so do I.

Mr. David O. Selznick   *Atlanta, Georgia*
Selznick International Pictures, Inc.   *October 19, 1936*
Culver City, California

Dear Mr. Selznick:

I was so happy to have your letter and delighted to know that there is a possibility that you may come to Atlanta with Mr. Cukor and Mr. Howard. I hope you will not think me very selfish if I ask you to please let us—my husband and I—have you out to our apartment for supper on at least one night. I know very well that everyone in Georgia will descend upon you as soon as you arrive, but we do want to see you and hope you will save us at least one evening.

Yes, Miss Brown wrote me that Mr. Howard was to do the adaptation and I was very pleased. I have long admired Mr. Howard's work in the theatre and of course I know of his screen adaptations. I saw "Dodsworth" just this week and thought it a real and moving affair.*

I would like to take this opportunity to tell you how very happy I am that my book has fallen into your hands. I have seen the care and the patience which you have lavished on your other productions and so I know that my book will enjoy the same happy fate.

Hoping to see you.

Mr. DuBose Heyward   *Atlanta, Georgia*
Charleston, South Carolina   *October 21, 1936*

My dear Mr. Heyward:

I hasten to write you to tell you that of course I will be glad to do anything I can in the movie matter—but I doubt if there is much, if anything, that I can do.† I know that calls for an explanation and this is the explanation.

I have nothing to do with the production of "Gone With the Wind," nothing to do with the dialogue, casting, directing, costuming, nothing

---

* *Dodsworth*, produced by Samuel Goldwyn Productions in 1936, was adapted by Howard from his 1934 stage version of the novel by Sinclair Lewis.

† Heyward, author of the 1925 novel *Porgy*, on which the musical *Porgy and Bess* was based, wrote to Mitchell seeking her help in securing a job writing dialogue for the *Gone With the Wind* screenplay.

even in an advisory capacity. That was settled when I signed the movie contract in New York in July. Due to an erroneous news story, many people think that I do have something to do with it. I am just finding out what you probably discovered many years ago—how many errors can get into newspapers and how impossible it is to combat them. The newspapers have had all kinds of stories—that I am going to Hollywood (and I am not going), that I am to write the dialogue (and I am not going to write it), that I have chosen my niece, Betty Timmons, to play Scarlett (and she is not my niece and I have never even laid eyes on her and I have not chosen her for anything). The Selznick people have not consulted me in any way or upon any subject since the contract was signed.

But here's a way in which I might possibly do some good. (I hope and pray that you will keep this very dark for it will cause me untold grief if it gets out.) There is a possibility that Mr. Selznick will be in Atlanta some time in the very near future. He is talking of coming here to look over the scenery on the chance that some of the background shots might be made here. I will probably meet him and if I do I will be only too glad to bring the matter up. I am proud that you think well enough of my book to want to protect it from being butchered.

By the way, Sidney Howard and not Jane Murfin will do the adaptation. . . .*

Mrs. Louella Parsons   Atlanta, Georgia
Hollywood, California   October 29, 1936

My dear Mrs. Parsons:

Everybody in the world reads your column and that is why I am appealing to you for assistance. I am appealing as an harassed and weary author, sadly in need of a rest and unable to get it because of the mail and telegrams that flood in on me due to rumors which seem to be circulating all over the country.

I am the author of "Gone With the Wind." When I sold the motion picture rights to Mr. Selznick it was on the understanding that I was to have nothing to do with the movie production. I was utterly weary from the hard labor of getting my large book to press, I had lost a lot of weight, and I had been told to take a six months rest and try to regain all the weight I had lost. Therefore, it was understood that I would do no work on the adapting

---

* Murfin was a playwright and screenwriter. She and Adela Rogers St. Johns wrote the screenplay for Selznick's *What Price Hollywood?*

of the book for the screen, would have no voice in the casting and would not go to Hollywood. However, rumors are abroad that are very different from this. The story has even been printed that I am to select the entire cast! Mr. Selznick knows how to make movies and I most certainly do not and I have nothing to do with picking the actors, but these stories and rumors have brought down on me a deluge of requests that I get people into the movies. That foolish story about my "niece," Miss Betty Timmons, of Atlanta, being chosen by me for the part of "Scarlett," caused me endless trouble. It made people refuse to believe me when I told them that I had no part in the casting of the characters. They said if I could get my niece in the movies, I could certainly get them in too. The truth is, Miss Timmons is not my niece and is not related to me in any way. I have never even seen her and I have certainly never chosen her for anything, but the flood of letters, telegrams and personal calls have so distracted me and made my work so heavy, that I have been unable to get any rest for weeks.

On top of this, the persistent rumor which has appeared in many papers, and appeared in your column too, on October 22nd, that I am going blind has caused me much work and worry. You see, I'm not going blind and have no intention of going blind. I strained my eyes pretty badly in the final work on my book and they are still tired and so am I. My eyes will be all right again just as soon as I can get some rest. But whenever such an item appears in a paper, my friends and relatives scattered all over the United States, write and wire me in panic. I have so many wonderful friends and naturally such items alarm them. When these letters come, I must get out of bed and write letters from morning till night, telling them that my eyes are all right, so you can see I do not get much rest!

I am begging you if ever again the rumor comes to your desk that I have something to do with the movie production of "Gone With the Wind" or that I am going blind, that you will deny them. I know I am taking a lot upon myself in asking this of you. My only excuse is that I have always read your column with the greatest interest and enjoyed it so very much and so I feel freer in writing to you than I would ordinarily to a stranger, which perhaps is presumptuous of me. My other excuse is that I am very tired and really do need a rest and I haven't been able to get it for months because I have been kept so busy answering letters and telegrams and telephone calls and personal calls.

I know you would laugh at some of the amusing things that have occurred. Several ladies have wired me that their little daughters tap dance beautifully and do the "splits" most elegantly and can't I get them into "Gone With the Wind"? (No, they haven't read the book, they admit.)

People turn up with their colored cooks and butlers and demand that I send them to Hollywood to portray "Mammy" and "Uncle Peter." If I can ever get a rest, I can probably laugh at such things, too, but just now—

Mr. Otis Brumby   *Atlanta, Georgia*
Cobb County Times   *November 3, 1936*
Marietta, Georgia

Dear Otis:

I came home from a trip this morning and found the clipping from the October 22nd Times.*

In the matter of choosing actors for the movie production, I have not suggested anyone. So many fantastic suggestions have been made for some of the parts in the movie, and one night recently when John and I and Sam Tupper, Jr., the novelist, were having supper, we started joking about an imaginary cast of our own.† Sam said he thought Mae West was the only logical candidate for the role of Grandma Fontaine. I replied that I thought the four Marx Brothers would be wonderful as the four Tarleton boys, and John said that Kay Francis was the only person to portray Mammy. Some people at the next table heard us and by the next morning friends were calling me to ask if this cast had really been selected and to protest about it. One lady was quite emphatic in her protests that Mae West was not the right person to play Grandma Fontaine.‡

Thank you again for your kind mention of the book.

Miss Louella Parsons   *Atlanta, Georgia*
Hollywood, California   *November 9, 1936*

Dear Miss Parsons:

How can I thank you enough for your mention of me in your column on Sunday! Not a person has called me, either yesterday or today, and

---

* Brumby devoted his entire "Jambalaya" column to *Gone With the Wind*, noting that "very sensibly Miss Mitchell refused to take any part in the game of naming the movie stars." He also warned readers of the novel that they should "be prepared to drop everything else—it is that interesting and once you get into the story, you just simply can't put it down to go to sleep, to work, or anything else."

† Tupper, a reporter on the *Atlanta Journal*, was a friend of Mitchell and her husband and had reviewed *Gone With the Wind* for the newspaper. A line from his critique—"a book to own and re-read and remember forever"—was used as a blurb on the back of the novel's later dust jackets.

‡ The character of Grandma Fontaine was not included in the motion picture.

asked me to get them in the movies! And there was not a single letter in today's mail, asking the same thing. If you only knew what a load you have taken off of me. I certainly appreciate it more than I can ever tell you.

I thank you for your letter. I appreciated it so much and all the nice things you wrote me about "Gone With the Wind." If I ever do get to California (and I may come some day, for I have a sister-in-law living in Los Angeles), I so sincerely hope that I can meet you. I have always read and admired and enjoyed your column so very much.

Thank you again for your courtesy and your help.

Miss Ruth Waterbury   *Atlanta, Georgia*
Photoplay Magazine   *November 11, 1936*
New York, New York

Dear Miss Waterbury:

I thank you so much for your letter and the many fine things you wrote me about "Gone With the Wind." Coming from an editor, I naturally appreciated them all the more.

I am very sorry to have to refuse your kind request for an article for Photoplay. This is my situation. When I sold the motion picture rights, I said that I would have no connection with the production and also that I would give no interviews about who I thought should play the characters in "Gone With the Wind." Since that time I have had many requests for my opinion but I have never voiced this opinion. The truth of the matter is that I know nothing about the making of movies and feel that it would be presumptuous of me to state flatfootedly that I thought any particular actor or actors would be more suitable than others. Mr. Selznick has done such marvelous things with his past productions that I feel my book is in good hands and he will cast it well.

But I thank you so much for your request.

Miss Katharine Brown   *Atlanta, Georgia*
Selznick International Pictures, Inc.   *November 17, 1936*
New York, New York

Dear Miss Brown:

I am sorry I have delayed so long in answering your letter but the apartment has been so crowded with out-of-town company for a week and this is the first chance I have had to write.

I was so happy to hear that you were coming to Atlanta, as well as Mr. Cukor and Mr. Howard. Will you wire me just when to expect you? Also, when Mr. Howard and Mr. Cukor are coming and, if possible, how long they will be here? The reason why I ask is that I want to arrange my own plans before you and they arrive.

I am anxious to line up any people you may want to see. We have a little theatre here but I have seen none of their work for two years. Also, the colleges in this section all have dramatic groups. Could you include in your wire whether or not you wanted me to line them up for you and the time when you would like to see them? By this I mean would you like for me to call the Georgia Tech Dramatic Club and ask them to call on you at your hotel at a certain time? Would you like for me to round up the interested members of the Atlanta Historical Society and make a definite date for them to meet you? I think it would be necessary to have definite dates.

Macon, Georgia has probably the best little theatre group in the State. Fortunately, one of my best friends is in it and I will hand you to her with an easy heart, knowing that she will be capable of giving you the utmost help.*

I am really so thrilled about your visit. I do want you to meet my husband. I wish to heaven that all the patriotic societies and interviewers and time stealers would let me alone for a week so I could really entertain you. As it is I am promising myself a vacation from work when you get here.

I hope you told Mr. Howard that I am not doing anything about the adaptation for I don't want him to come down here with a false impression. I will be so happy to meet him, but the truth of the matter is I am so harassed with many things that I scarcely am able to know my own name, much less be of any assistance on anything that takes brain work.

I do hope I get the chance to go to some of the smaller Georgia towns with you. They are so lovely and I am sure when they know who you are they will give you the town!

Miss Mabel Search   *Atlanta, Georgia*
Pictorial Review   *November 17, 1936*
New York, New York

Dear Miss Search:

I was so happy to have your letter and of course I was thrilled and flattered at the very mention of Faith Baldwin coming down to interview me. Miss Baldwin wrote me the loveliest letter when my book was brand new

---

* Susan Myrick, a reporter and columnist on the *Macon Telegraph*, was a charter member of the Macon Little Theatre.

and no-one knew that it would run the way it has run. I appreciated her letter and would so like to meet her.

You asked whether an engagement during the first week of December would suit me. I will have to tell you frankly what my situation is. The Selznick International Pictures, Inc., to whom I sold "Gone With the Wind," is sending representatives down here at the end of this month. While I have nothing to do with the adapting of my novel for the movies, I have promised to put myself at their disposal during their visit. My job is to introduce them to any and all who might prove helpful to them. I will have to be out of the city a good deal as it will be necessary to take them about the State, showing them historic spots, good backgrounds, etc. They have been very indefinite as to the exact day of their arrival and equally indefinite as to the length of their stay. As I have promised to do all I can for them, I cannot say definitely that I would even be in Atlanta during the first week in December. However, I have just written an air mail-special delivery to them asking them to please be definite as to the time of their arrival and departure. As soon as I hear from them I will write you.*

I hate very much to be so indefinite in this letter but you see my situation. Thank you very much for your interest.

Miss Katharine Brown
Selznick International Pictures, Inc.
New York, New York

Atlanta, Georgia
November 18, 1936

Dear Miss Brown:

Your letter has just arrived and I'm trying to get you off a quick answer. If this letter sounds choppy, please over look it. This is one of those days when the phone is going like mad, autograph seekers arriving, and strangers calling "just to see what I look like." . . .

I think the whole idea of scouting through the South is a swell one for if you don't find anyone who will do it will still be worth a million dollars in publicity. And there's just a chance you will turn up a nugget. Count on me for any help you need.

Now, I come to the publicity business. I don't think you know anything of my back ground so I must explain. I worked here on the Atlanta Journal, an evening paper. My husband has worked on the Journal and the Georgian (it's Hearst and also an evening paper). I have many good friends

---

* Baldwin came to Atlanta in early December, and her article "The Woman Who Wrote *Gone With the Wind*, An Exclusive and Authentic Interview" appeared in the March 1937 issue of *Pictorial Review*.

on the Constitution which is the only morning paper. In fact most of my friends are on these papers and they have been kinder than anyone can imagine to me since the book came out. I have found myself in the queer and not too pleasant position of being the best little bit of copy in town, for the last five months and I've had to play ball honestly and faithfully with each paper which isn't as easy it sounds, especially when one of the papers is my old paper. They all look to me for newsbreaks on everything connected with my business or the book or the movie. They don't want to be scooped by the opposition papers, nor if possible by the out of town papers on stories which they feel belong to me—and to them.

So I'd like, if possible to give them a break on your trip south. Your trip may not be a big story up north but it *is* a big story in this section. The very idea that a movie company thinks enough of a story to send a talent scout and a director and an adaptor down here will go over big. And moreover, it makes people who've always refused to go to any movie about the south think very kindly of Mr. Selznick and makes them feel that he honest to God wants to do a real southern picture with real southern color. Oh, yes, it will be a big story. I know your outfit isn't averse to publicity and publicity will be a great help to you in your search for new faces (and also a great burden, too, I do not doubt!).

So this is what I want to know—

When will you arrive in Atlanta and where will you stay?

Will Atlanta be your first stop in the South or perhaps Richmond or Charleston? (You see if you go there first the news break would come from those towns.)

What is your full title with the Selznick company?

And most important, do you mind this story being broken before you come South? Probably there will be some story out of N.Y. about your trip. If you do not want the first publicity in the Atlanta papers but want it to come out of N.Y. can you fix it so the Atlanta papers will get an even break by getting the news as soon as the N.Y. papers do?

Does all this sound very muddled? I am sure it does. I doubt if you make heads or tales of it! The reason I want to know when you will arrive and where you will stay (I advise the Biltmore, by the way) is that, if the story does break before you come here, I want to have an "out" for myself. I'm afraid the storm will break about my head and the countless scores who want me to get them in the movies will be back on my neck. And if this starts I'll just have to leave town for I couldn't go through it again and keep my sanity. So if it were known when you were coming and where you were staying, I could disclaim all connection and merely route people over to you. Yes, that's grief for you but I am becoming the most selfish of swine and derned keerful about my own hide!

So—could you wire me when you are coming, where you are staying, whether you are willing for me to break the story of your trip immediately and if Atlanta is your first stop on the way South? If it will hamper or embarrass you in any way to have the story broken before you get here, don't hesitate to tell me. But if you've already written some of the Southern colleges I imagine the story is already floating around.

I hope you'll let me give you a brawl of sorts—probably a cocktail party to meet the press. You see, I've been dying to give a party for them to thank them but had no excuse. And I wanted to have an excuse for holding it to the press because otherwise I'd have to give a huge reception and I don't want to do that. So please be my excuse!

Also, you might wire me if you want me to round up the Junior League. I don't want to mention them in any news story without having first sounded them out. They can get pretty horsey sometimes.

Mr. Sidney Howard   Atlanta, Georgia
Tyringham, Massachusetts   November 21, 1936

My dear Mr. Howard:

I was so pleased to have your letter and am happy to know that you are coming South. You were very kind to write me so many nice things about "Gone With the Wind" and I especially appreciated your remarks about the negro dialect which was just about the toughest job in the book.*

But my pleasure at your coming is somewhat dimmed by the fear that there has been a misunderstanding about my part in the production of "Gone With the Wind." I hasten to write to you for I would not have you come South under a misapprehension.

When I sold the book to the Selznick Company, I made it very plain that I would have nothing whatsoever to do with the picture, nothing about additional dialogue, nothing about advising on backgrounds, costumes, continuity. They offered me money to go to Hollywood to write additional dialogue, etc. and I refused. I sold the book on that understanding. Not more than a week ago, I wrote Miss Katharine Brown of the Selznick Company and asked her if you were familiar with my attitude and she wired me that you were.

---

* In his letter to Mitchell on November 18, Howard called the black characters in *Gone With the Wind* "the best written darkies, I do believe, in all literature. They are the only ones I have ever read which seem to come through uncolored by white patronizing."

But now your letter arrives and I realize that they have not told you and I am very distressed about it. I still have no intentions of doing anything about additional dialogue or even looking at the script. There are many reasons for this and I will try to list them as briefly as possible.

In the first place it would do no good for me to look over the script—any more than looking over a Sanscrit grammar. I know just as much about Sanscrit as I do about writing for the movies. A script would mean nothing to me and it would take me weeks or months to figure it all out.

In the second place, I haven't the time. I never dreamed writing a book meant losing all privacy, leisure and chance to rest. Since July 1, I've averaged an engagement every forty minutes from nine in the morning till long after midnight. And, between these engagements, I've had to handle an enormous mail and try to see my family.

The third reason is this. I know it sounds like a silly one but it is an important one to me. If I even so much as looked over the script, without even passing judgment on it, and there was some small item in the finished production that incensed or annoyed the people of this section, then I'd get the blame for it. Southerners have been wonderful to my book and I am grateful indeed that they like it and are interested in the forthcoming picture. Not for worlds or for money would I put myself in the position where, if there was something they didn't like in the picture, they could say, "Well, you worked on the script. Why did you let this, that and the other get by?" I would never live it down and I could never explain that I really had nothing to do with the script. It won't matter to them if there is something in the movie they don't like that you may be responsible for. You didn't write the book and you do not live here in Atlanta and if they do not like something then you will be excused.

From the minute the news of the movie sale broke, I have been deviled by the press and the public for statements about who I wanted in the picture, who I wanted to do the adaptation, where I wanted it filmed. I have never opened my mouth on any of these subjects for it occurred to me that such statements would be the greatest presumption on my part as Mr. Selznick and you are most competent people and know how to produce good pictures. Moreover, having said I'd have nothing to do in any way with the production, I've published it in Ascalon and told it in Gath that I have no connection with the film of "Gone With the Wind."* To be frank, I do not care who they put in it or where they film it. To be

---

* "Tell it not in Gath, publish it not in the streets of Askelon; lest the daughters of the Philistines rejoice, lest the daughters of the uncircumcised triumph." 2 Samuel 1:20.

quite frank, I have all confidence in you and Mr. Cukor and Mr. Selznick so why should I rush about issuing statements to the press on matters that are none of my business?

I did tell Miss Brown that I would be only too happy to do this for her—that if she, or Mr. Cukor or you, came South I would do all I could in making contacts for you for finding new talent, for rounding up research workers and local historians who know what really went on down here in those days. I said I'd take her from Dalton to Milledgeville, showing her old entrenchments, old houses and introducing her to people in each town along the way to help her. That's going to be a tough assignment in itself. But I can't do anything about the script or about additional negro dialogue. I just can't. I'm too nearly crazy now with the load I'm carrying to even consider it, even should I want to do it.

I know this foregoing doesn't sound hospitable nor obliging! But I had to write it for I realized that the Selznick Company had not explained the situation to you and I was very upset at the thought of you coming all the way down here in the belief that I was going to be of any assistance on the picture beyond making contacts.

May I tell you now, how sincerely happy I was when I heard that you were going to do the adaptation? I did so want the book to fall into good hands and was so pleased when it did!

Speaking of Civil War monuments—you should see our Southern ones. I believe they were put out by the same company that put out the Northern ones. They are twice as ugly and three times as duck-legged!*

Katharine Brown
Selznick International Pictures, Inc.
New York, New York

Atlanta, Georgia
November 23, 1936

MY TELEPHONE HEMLOCK SIX TWO FIVE ONE STOP NEWS LEAKING THROUGH PEOPLE YOU WROTE AND NEWSPAPERS PICKING UP RUMORS STOP AM HOLDING THEM OFF BEST I CAN FROM BREAKING STORY IN GARBLED FORM BUT URGE PROMPT ANNOUNCEMENT STOP CAN BIRDWELL RUSH NEWS RELEASE TO ME

---

* In the same letter, Howard related that he had purchased a farm in New England "in a village with ninety Yankee inhabitants and a Civil War Monument," adding, "Some day I am going to ascertain how the soil of rural New England which won't produce anything now was ever able to pay for so many Civil War monuments."

PERSONALLY STOP* PLEASE GIVE ME AS MUCH ADVANCE NOTICE
AS POSSIBLE ON DATE FOR PRESS TEA.

Russell Birdwell   *Atlanta, Georgia*
Selznick International Pictures, Inc.   *November 23, 1936*
Culver City, California

UNDERSTAND FROM KATHARINE BROWN THAT YOU WILL WRITE
ME TODAY ABOUT NEWS RELEASE ON TALENT SEARCH STOP NEWS
IS LEAKING AND URGE IMMEDIATE ANNOUNCEMENT TO AVOID
PREMATURE BREAK STOP WIRE COPY OF NEWS RELEASE TO ME
PERSONALLY AND PLEASE DO IT AS EARLY TODAY AS POSSIBLE.

Russell Birdwell   *Atlanta, Georgia*
Selznick International Pictures, Inc.   *November 24, 1936*
Culver City, California

THANKS FOR PROMPTNESS IN SENDING STORY BUT MUST SET
YOU STRAIGHT ON MY CONNECTION WITH FILM JOB STOP MY
CONTRACT SPECIFICALLY PROVIDES THAT I HAVE NOTHING TO
DO WITH THE MOVIE AND I HAVE STATED PERSONALLY AND
BY LETTER TO VARIOUS SELZNICK PEOPLE THAT I WILL HAVE
NOTHNG TO DO WITH TALENT SEARCH CASTING ADAPTATION
OF STORY OR FILMING BUT APPARENTLY I MUST REPEAT THIS
TO EACH NEW MEMBER OF ORGANIZATION I COME IN CONTACT
WITH STOP WHEN MISS BROWN AND OTHERS COME TO AT-
LANTA I WILL FEED THEM FRIED CHICKEN, SHOW THEM STONE
MOUNTAIN AND INTRODUCE THEM TO ANYBODY THEY WANT
TO MEET BUT ALL PARTS OF FILM JOB ARE ON THEIR HANDS
AND NOT ON MINE STOP AM RELEASING STORY TO ATLANTA
AFTERNOON PAPERS TODAY AFTER DELETING REFERENCES TO
ME AND MR BIRDWELL PLEASE MAKE THE SAME CORRECTIONS
IN ANY RELEASES YOU GIVE OUT STOP ON THIS AND ANY FU-
TURE STORIES I WANT NO REFERENCES MADE TO ME EXCEPT AS
AUTHOR OF THE BOOK.†

---

* Russell Birdwell was director of advertising and publicity at Selznick International.

† Birdwell's press release began by saying that Mitchell "may get her wish for a Southern actress" to play the part of Scarlett. He also claimed that Brown and Howard would "confer" with the author about casting and the screenplay.

Katharine Brown   *Atlanta, Georgia*
Selznick International Pictures, Inc.   *November 24, 1936*
New York, New York

STORY RECEIVED FROM BIRDWELL BUT IT STILL LINKS ME WITH
ENTIRE JOB OF TALENT SEARCH AND CASTING MOVIE STOP HAVE
RELEASED STORY TO ATLANTA PAPERS TODAY AFTER DELET-
ING REFERENCES TO ME AND HAVE WIRED BIRDWELL TO MAKE
THESE SAME CORRECTIONS IN HIS RELEASES ON THIS AND ANY
FUTURE STORIES STOP WONT YOU PLEASE INFORM ALL SELZNICK
OFFICIALS WHAT YOU KNOW ALREADY THAT I HAVE NOTHING
TO DO WITH CASTING OR ANY OTHER PART OF FILM JOB STOP I
WROTE THE BOOK AND THAT'S ALL STOP UNLESS MY POSITION
CAN BE MADE CLEAR TO YOUR PEOPLE AND CORRECTLY STATED
IN YOUR PUBLICITY I AM LEAVING ATLANTA IMMEDIATELY AND
WILL STAY AWAY UNTIL TALENT SEARCH EXCITEMENT IS OVER.

Mr. Stuart Rose   *Atlanta, Georgia*
The Saturday Evening Post   *November 29, 1936*
Philadelphia, Pennsylvania

Dear Mr. Rose:

Thank you for the trouble you took with Sam Tupper's stories. I'm
sorry they wouldn't do. While I hadn't read them, I hoped for the best. . . .

The tempest had begun to subside and then the Selznick people, who
bought "GWTW" for the movies decided to come South and try to dig
up "new faces" for the film. Naturally, everyone who thinks they can play
Scarlett—and that means every female under seventy—is in a state and the
town in an uproar. The Selznick people arrive on Wednesday and I pale
at the thought of what the next ten days will bring forth. I firmly believe
I am the only woman in the world who never wanted to be in the movies.
But—well, even I would like to play opposite Donald Duck!

Why aren't all editors as nice as you? We so enjoyed your visit. And
we hope to see you again when life has resumed its leisurely way and the
"wind" has stopped blowing.

Mrs. Mary Marsh   *Atlanta, Georgia*
Wilmington, Delaware   *November 29, 1936*

Dear Mother:

I have been a long time in thanking you for the birthday present—so
long a time that the slip and the panties have already been worn and sent

to the wash three times! At first, I did not write because I wasn't sure where you were but thought you were visiting somewhere in Ohio. Then, I delayed in the hope that John and I could come up and spend Thanksgiving with you and Frank and Gordon.* I thought I could thank you, in person, then, with a squeeze which, alas, cannot be sent through the mail. As you see, we didn't get there. It seems that we never get anywhere these days, but like Alice and the Red Queen, we only manage to stay in the same place by dint of running till our tongues hang out.

The material of the slip and pants was lovely and they fitted perfectly, after, of course, whacking off a little of the slip's bottom, which I must do with all garments. Now I do not feel that I will be embarrassed if caught in fitting rooms of department stores by autograph hunters. For weeks and months I've been too busy to buy any dresses or underclothes and my underwear was in sad shape, with lace unwhipped and straps hitched by small gold safety pins. Several times when I was trying to buy dresses and was standing in these worn and faded garments, waiting for the saleswomen, strangers pushed into the fitting room and were interested and outspoken on the condition of my petticoat. Now, I feel that I can face them with calm, even with pride, in my new slip. . . .

I think life will settle down soon. I hope so, at any rate. People here in Atlanta are beginning to take me for granted and let me alone. My friends, with a few exceptions, have been grand and haven't come to see me since July. And acquaintances are beginning to realize that even if their bosses do want to meet me, I don't want to meet the bosses and so there is no use telephoning me. . . . And when we finally get over the hump of the movie people's invasion, which will end around December 15, we ought to be able to breath.

I do not know whether or not you read the story of the movie folks' visit in the papers. The Selznick Company is trying to get "new faces" for "Gone With the Wind," Southern faces, Southern voices. So they are giving "auditions" (whatever that may mean) throughout the South to Junior Leaguers, debutantes, Little Theatre groups, college dramatic clubs, etc. I have stated until I am hoarse that I have nothing to do with the movies or with the casting, filming, auditions etc. The papers here, realizing how harassed we had been by scores of people bedeviling us to get them into the movies, were very kind in issuing pleas to the public not to bother me but to bother the Selznick people when they arrived. So, mercifully, we've had a little peace from the movie-crazed.

---

* Francesca "Frank" Marsh was the wife of John Marsh's youngest brother, Ben Gordon Marsh.

But, in a weak moment, I promised to help out on introductions to Junior Leaguers, local historians, etc. That means some grief, of course, and keeps me from bolting out of town as I would love to do. Then, too, I have to give a cocktail party for the Selznick folks and Sidney Howard, the dramatist who is adapting the book to the screen. I say "have to" but I do not mean it as it sounds. It's one party I shall take pleasure in giving for I want to invite the press, both of Atlanta and neighboring cities, the reference librarians, the book sellers, the book reviewers—all the people who have been so kind to me and done so much for me. I'm using the movie folks as an excuse to give the party so I can thank everyone at one time. For people certainly have been good to me....

My love to you all. I wish we could have been with you.

Mr. Sidney Howard   *Atlanta, Georgia*
Tyringham, Massachusetts   *December 1, 1936*

Dear Mr. Howard:

I was just as mortified as Jimmy Durante when I learned that the Selznick company had said nothing to you about my attitude on the film.* They had assured me that you knew all about it. I know you must have thought my abrupt letter the height of discourtesy, but it was written in the belief that you already knew the situation. I hope you will forgive any seeming rudeness.

I am perfectly well satisfied to have my book in your hands and those of Mr. Cukor and Mr. Selznick. You all have taste and talent and intelligence. The truth of the matter is, as I wrote you before, that I haven't the time to work on the picture; I haven't the inclination; I haven't the experience—and moreover, I do not want to let myself in for a lot of grief. That is why I have been so obstinately "hands off" in this matter.

Reading your latest letter gave me the correct understanding of your previous letter, and I thank you most sincerely for the thoughtfulness and consideration of your offer to let me look over the script. Now that the misunderstandings have been cleared away by your letters, I am even more confident than before that the book is in good hands.

I hope that you do decide to come to Atlanta, for I would be most happy to meet you. The date of Mr. Cukor's arrival is still uncertain but is supposed to be around the 10th of the month. I have been planning to leave on a vacation trip on December 15, but I am holding my plans in abeyance until I hear definitely whether you or he are coming.

---

* "I'm mortified!" was one of the comedian and actor's signature lines.

Mr. Russell Birdwell   *Atlanta, Georgia*
Selznick International Pictures, Inc.   *December 5, 1936*
Culver City, California

Dear Mr. Birdwell:

Your letter with the carbon of the story arrived today but as I have been away from the house since early morning, I have just read it.

I thought you understood my position in the matter of the filming of "Gone With the Wind." I've written it time and again to the Selznick Company, I've told it to its representatives and I've published it in many newspaper statements. I have nothing to do with the filming of "Gone With the Wind." I have nothing to do with the casting of it and have never once even hinted that I would like for anyone to play any role. I have never even said (as you quoted me in your story) that I would like to see a Southern girl in the leading role. I have no suggestions to make about the casting. I have no suggestions to make to Mr. Cukor and will make none. Of course, I will be charmed to meet him when he comes here and pleased to introduce him to anyone who may be of assistance to him. But that is as far as my connection with the film goes. I have said time and again that I will have nothing to do with the adaptation, with writing or even suggesting additional dialogue. I have written Mr. Howard and told Miss Brown and others of the Selznick organization that I will not even look at the script. I'll be very glad to meet Mr. Howard, for whom I have a vast admiration, but I will not read a line of the script.

If I had wanted to be tied up with the filming of my book I would have signed a contract and gone to Hollywood. But I didn't want to have anything to do with it, I said as much, I signed no contract. I do not wish to be tied up with the publicity of the film or talent search in any way except when it is unavoidable—such as that I happen to be the author of the book.

If your story goes out, making it appear that I am giving the tea for the Selznick representatives, I will have to recall my invitations and hold no tea. I am giving this party for my friends in the press who have been so kind to me and to my book. It is the only way in which I can show my gratitude to them. And it's *their* party and in *their* honor. I thought it would be very nice if Mr. Cukor and Mr. Howard and Miss Brown were here to attend it so that they could meet people who might be of some assistance to them.

But my invitation to them to attend the tea is purely a *social* courtesy, whereas your story makes it appear to be an important part of a business promotion and puts me in the position of taking a prominent part in the talent search. I am taking *no* part in the talent search and I must insist that my position shall not be misrepresented in publicity.

I have a very cordial feeling toward the Selznick company and all of its officials I have had the pleasure of meeting. Naturally when Mr. Cukor and Mr. Howard visit my home city, I wish to be hospitable to them. I would like to introduce them to my friends and do whatever I can to make their visit to Atlanta pleasant. This is exactly the same as I would do for any other visitor in whom I was interested.

Please do not misconstrue these simple courtesies. They have nothing whatever to do with your talent search and if they are going to be used in your publicity so as to link me with the talent search, then you will simply compel me to refuse to even meet Mr. Cukor and Mr. Howard when they come to Atlanta.

Elizabeth Sweet   *Atlanta, Georgia*
Jacksonville, Florida   *December 6, 1936*

NEWSPAPER STORIES WRONG STOP I HAVE NOTHING TO DO WITH PICKING GIRLS FOR CAST OF FILM STOP NO CONNECTION AT ALL WITH FILM STOP KATHARINE BROWN ATLANTA BILTMORE HOTEL GIVING AUDITIONS STOP HAVE YOUR FRIEND COMMUNI-CATE WITH HER BEST WISHES.

Mrs. Wilbur Kurtz   *Atlanta, Georgia*
Atlanta, Georgia   *December 8, 1936*

Dear Mrs. Kurtz:

I've been out of town for a few days and when I came back I found your "Old Field School."* I haven't read it yet but am saving it for a quiet moment tonight after I've gone to bed. I know I'll like it and I thank you so much for it.

The movie people have come and gone—thank Heaven—They were only looking for faces, not research workers. However, I have implanted a seed about Mr. Kurtz being the only authority in the section on historical matters and I hope it will bear fruit when the research department of The Selznick Co. comes here in the early part of the year. I told one of the Selznick people that they couldn't possibly produce the picture unless they had him in California.

---

* "Old Field School" was a story Annie Laurie Kurtz wrote about a small country school-house in Clayton County, Georgia, that her father attended as a boy.

When "this cruel war is over" and John and I have some peace and quiet we would love to come sit in your studio. I have been longing to talk of your book and see how far you have gotten and whether or not Mr. Kurtz is doing any new pictures for it.

Miss Ginnie Morris   *Atlanta, Georgia*
United Artists Corporation   *December 9, 1936*
New York, New York

Dear Ginnie,

Yes, I'd love to inscribe the books. However, I am leaving town at the end of the week and will be gone until perhaps February. I am having no mail forwarded. If you want the books in a hurry, I am afraid there isn't anything I can do about it at present. If you don't mind waiting, I'll autograph them as soon as I get back and take great pleasure in doing them.

Thank you for the pub stuff you sent.* But could you do something for me? I have never expressed the wish to see a Southern girl in the role of Scarlett O'Hara. I have never expressed any wish of any type about the cast of the picture. I will never express any wish, so help me God. I wish whenever you see me quoted, you will strike it out—also, I am not going to confer with either Mr. Cukor or Mr. Howard about the filming of the adaptation. I do not intend to even look at Mr. Howard's script. I have nothing whatsoever to do with the film and I do not want to be tied up in any way with the publicity. Of course, if Mr. Cukor comes to town I intend to have him out for dinner, but I do not want the social end of this affair confused with the business end. "Gone With the Wind" is the Selznick's baby and they can hold it without any help whatsoever from me, and I know they'll do a good job of it.

Forgive my haste. My love to you.

Mrs. W.H. McAloney   *Atlanta, Georgia*
Atlanta, Georgia   *December 9, 1936*

Dear Mrs. McAloney:

Thank you so much for the grand compliment you paid me when you wrote that you would like for me to appear in the film of "Gone With the Wind." I must admit that the idea had never occurred to me and honesty forces me to admit that my age and my type would not appeal very much to the movie directors, but I think you were more than kind to write and tell

---

* United Artists had a contract to distribute the films of Selznick International Pictures, so the studio's press releases were issued through United Artists.

me about this. Thank you, too, for your congratulations about the book. I think I will write Miss Katharine Brown, of the Selznick Company who was giving auditions here, and tell her to hurry back that the one and only Scarlett has been right under her nose! She is a well-bred young woman but I am afraid she will blast me if I do this.

Miss Katharine Brown   *Atlanta, Georgia*
Selznick International Pictures, Inc.   *December 11, 1936*
New York, New York

[Dear Katharine]:

Thanks for your wire. I'd love to know if the N.O. [New Orleans] prospects were *really* good. *Thousands* have assailed me since y'all left.

I rooted in "the county" yesterday for a house. Didn't find any. Suddenly remembered one in Jonesboro, not a plantation but a town house. Vaguely like Cyclorama one. Columns but not very impressive. It may appear in Xmas issue of "Life" with caption about it being used as Federal Hospital after battle of Jonesboro.*

Had a swell time with y'all. Loved it all. Missed you and wished I'd gone to N.O.

Mr. W.T. Anderson   *Atlanta, Georgia*
Macon Telegraph Publishing Co.   *December 12, 1936*
Macon, Georgia

Dear Mr. W.T.:

I was plum outdone to find you away from Macon. The movie people were outdone, too, and said frankly that I had lied about promising them the treat of seeing you as a Gentleman of the Old School. They were disappointed and so was I.

I hadn't thought about Sue for the purpose you mentioned because, to tell the truth, my only thought on this movie business was to get from under it all without being killed. However, now that I do think about it, it sounds like a swell idea, and I promise you if these people come back (as I fear they will!), I will certainly beat the drum for her.†

---

* Mitchell apparently was referring to the Warren House, which was used as a hospital for Union soldiers injured in the 1864 Battle of Jonesboro. The December 28, 1936, issue of *Life* featured a four-page spread on Mitchell and her novel, but it did not include a photograph of the house.

† In a letter to Mitchell on December 9, Anderson recommended that the author's friend Susan Myrick be "deputized" to "fight to keep the picture off the rocks." He also jokingly suggested that he and Mitchell go to Hollywood to ensure "your book is properly filmed."

I can just see the gorgeous headlines, if you and I went to California, leaving John and Mrs. "A" to console each other! I believe we'd put Eddie and Wallie in the shade!*

Miss Katharine Brown   *Hotel Alabama*
Selznick International Pictures, Inc.   *Winter Park, Florida*
New York, New York   *December 22, 1936*

We are here at this hotel, under the names of Mr. and Mrs. John Munnerlyn, the same being my middle name. And we intend staying here until December 30, if no one finds out who I am. The first person who asks me for an autograph, or wants to know if it's hard to write a book, or the first reporter who turns up—away we go to some other town, or home to Atlanta. We've been on the move constantly since leaving town or else I would have written you before this.

About Mr. Cukor's visit South to see me. Does he still want to come? Is he still willing to come to Florida to see me? If so, barring accidents such as the discovery of my identity, we will be here until December 30 and then we start back to Atlanta, making a leisurely trip and stopping over for brief visits at Quitman, Ga. and probably Macon, too. Would Mr. Cukor be able to come down here to Winter Park before December 30? Or would he like to arrive on December 30 and ride back to Atlanta with us? Or ride back part of the way, if his time was limited? We would be happy to see him here or to ride him home with us. Can you please wire me here at this hotel or long distance me, if you prefer, and tell me if we are to expect him or not? And could you please ask him if he could come without publicity? You see, if the story got out that he was coming here to see me, then we'd have to leave quickly. The reason is that we not only want to dodge the autograph seekers, etc., but because we know so many people throughout this section, many old friends, many newspaper people and we haven't been to see a single one. We were both so very tired that we just didn't have the energy to look people up. And if it got out that we were here and hadn't looked up our friends, it would be just too bad. Fact is, I don't want you to let anyone but Mr. Cukor know where we are or what name we are registered under—or that we are even travelling under an alias. It would make us both look pretty silly and as though we thought we were pretty damned important to hide out this way. And it isn't that we feel important. It's only that we are both so bone tired that we can't stand up under any more publicity or bother.

---

* King Edward VIII had recently abdicated the throne of England so that he could marry American divorcee Wallis Warfield Simpson.

If it should so happen that we were forced to leave Winter Park in a hurry, I will, of course, wire you immediately telling you where we were going and how you and Mr. Cukor could reach us. The wire won't be signed Mitchell, Marsh or even Munnerlyn but "John and Peggy Munroe." That's our next alias.

I cannot tell you how much I enjoyed being with you and Tony and Harriett.* It was not only lots of fun but a most welcome break in the long, long run of horrors which began last July. I enjoyed the trip to Macon so much, too and hope you all did. The Macon folks were simply agog about you and not because you were movie folks but because they liked you personally so very much. Of course, hundreds of people in Macon and Atlanta were simply furious because they didn't get to meet you three. I hope you are getting nice long letters from all the hundreds of people I have referred to you. The mail came down like the waters came down at Ladore, after you left—or perhaps I should say, thick as Autumn leaves at Valombrossa, all demanding that I get so-and-so in the movies and all stating their qualifications in twelve or fourteen handwritten pages.† I referred them all to you, telling them what a nice sweet interested person you were and how you were simply yearning to hear from all the Melanies and Scarletts in the South.

If I had my way, I'd stay out of Atlanta until my money runs out but as John's vacation is up soon and it wouldn't be any fun away from him, I'll have to go home and take up the weary load again. This has certainly taught me a lesson and it'll be a cold day in August before I write another book and get myself in such a fix. I keep thinking and praying that this mess can't go on much longer but it seems to get worse. I don't believe it will settle down till after the film comes out so please hurry up and get the film over with! I hope you saw Lois Cole after you got back and told her all about your trip. I've been aiming to write to her ever since you were down here for she was most interested in the matter but I never got around to it. In fact, this is the first letter I've written since I've been away.

Give my Christmas greetings to Harriett and Tony and Miss Modisett and the lawyer gentlemen who were so nice. And John and I hope you and yours have a bang up Christmas.

All the best to you and hoping to hear soon about Mr. Cukor's visit.

---

* Director Anton "Tony" Bundsmann helped Brown with the auditions in Atlanta. Harriett Flagg was Brown's secretary. Neither Cukor nor Howard made the trip.

† Lodore, a waterfall in England, is the subject of an 1820 poem, "The Cataract of Lodore," by Robert Southey: "All at once and all o'er, with a mighty uproar, And this way the water comes down at Lodore." Vallombrosa is a Benedictine abbey referenced in *Paradise Lost*, John Milton's 1667 epic poem: "Thick as autumnal leaves that strow the brooks in Vallombrosa."

CHAPTER Two

A National Pastime
1937

> In an effort to divert ourselves we fell to talking about
> the coming production of G.W.T.W. (as you probably know
> where ever two or more of ye are gathered together these days,
> the two or more talk about the movie).
>
> —*Margaret Mitchell to Katharine Brown*
> *February 14, 1937*

Mr. Russell Birdwell   *Atlanta, Georgia*
Selznick International Pictures, Inc.   *January 2, 1937*
Culver City, California

Dear Mr. Birdwell:

Please forgive my seeming rudeness in not answering your letter of December 15 sooner. The truth is, I've only read it just this minute. My husband and I went to Florida on December 15 and have just returned. We had no mail forwarded to us. I hope my delay has not inconvenienced you too much.

As to the pronunciation of "Melanie"—the accent is on the "MEL"—both "e's" are short. "MEL-anie." "MELon-y" comes nearest. I have never in my life heard it pronounced "Me-LANE-y" until after my book was published and I heard it thus pronounced over the radio several times. And it gave me a grue as it sounded so "Cracker" and tacky.

Wish you could have been here when Katharine Brown and her crew were auditioning Atlanta. They wished for you, too—when they had the time to do anything beside audition.

In haste,

Mr. Sidney Howard   *Atlanta, Georgia*
New York, New York   *January 4, 1937*

Dear Mr. Howard:

I returned to Atlanta, yesterday, after spending three weeks in Florida, and found your telegram waiting for me. I'm sure you must think me the rudest of mortals for not acknowledging it sooner and thanking you for your holiday greetings. But my husband and I had no mail forwarded to us, or telegrams either, and the telegram was shoved under the door.

You were nice to think of me and I appreciated it. I *did* have a nice Christmas, even if I was forced to spend it away from home. It was a quiet Christmas, spent driving through Florida orange groves, discussing with my husband abstract things like the gold standard (of which I know absolutely nothing), discussing many things which had, thank God, nothing to do with the writing of books or the producing of movies.

You see, in the early part of December, the Selznick company sent down a crew to Atlanta to "audition" people with the possible hope of picking up a new face for the cast of "GWTW." As I wrote you before, I have nothing to do with anything connected with the filming of the book. I didn't want to have anything to do with it as I know that every one in the U.S. except me is movie crazed and yearns to act. And I knew if I had any connection with the film, life would be more of a burden than it has already been for six months. But, of course, when the audition crew arrived, the populace of six states descended on me, demanding that I endorse each and every one of them for the role of Scarlett, etc. The phone went every minute and wires and special deliveries deviled me and shoals of people camped on the door step and clutched me if I went out. No one seems to believe that I have nothing to do with the movie and it seems to be beyond human comprehension that any mortal does not yearn to be connected with movies. Even after the crew left things were terrible—so terrible that we had to leave town and spend Christmas away from home. Alas where has my quiet peaceful life gone? I will be so glad when the picture actually goes into production, then perhaps some of my problems will be over. Do you know when this will be? I probably know less about the whole affair than any one in the United States.

I hear vague rumors that Mr. Cukor, who did not come south with the audition crew, as he intended, may yet pay Atlanta a visit at some undetermined date. Is there any chance that you will come, too? I should so love to meet you. And I've been afraid, ever since that hasty letter I wrote you, that you would think me the rudest creature, for refusing point blank to have any thing to do with additional dialogue. I wish you would come. Then I could tell you to your face, much better than I can in writing, just how happy I am that "GWTW" fell into your hands and not into the hands of several others I could mention.

Katharine Brown   *Atlanta, Georgia*
Selznick International Pictures, Inc.   *January 5, 1937*
New York, New York

IMPOSSIBLE TO SEE MR. CUKOR UNTIL AFTER THE 16TH OF JAN STOP MADE DATES FOR JANUARY BEFORE I LEFT TOWN STOP ALL NEW YORK ON MY NECK ALSO SEVERAL WEDDINGS IN THE FAMILY STOP ENGAGEMENTS OVERLAPPING NOW I AM SORRY.

Miss Katharine Brown   *Atlanta, Georgia*
Selznick International Pictures, Inc.   *January 8, 1937*
New York, New York

Dear Katharine:

Thought the enclosed might interest you as it pretty well sums up the reaction to the announcements about Clark Gable and Tallulah Bankhead.* On the way back from Florida we sounded out every one we saw along the road. What they said is pretty well expressed in this clipping. Just between younme *have* they decided who will have the roles? I'll keep it quiet if you want to tell me but if it ain't any of my business, just don't tell me.

Has Mr. Cukor any further plans? Sorry about having to put him off. I expected him to come to Florida and so made many many dates for January with folks from out of town, mostly New York. And with two weddings in the family on top of it, I am in a state.

---

* The undated newspaper clipping reads, in part, "If Clark Gable is cast for Rhett we don't think we shall even go to see the picture. If Tallulah Bankhead gets the part of Scarlett we know we shall not see it." The unidentified writer called Gable "the dominant male" and Bankhead "the faintly talented, palely purple attenuated wraith of what women once were." Bankhead was given a screen test for the role of Scarlett on December 22, 1936, in New York.

Mr. Russell Birdwell   *Atlanta, Georgia*
Selznick International Pictures, Inc.   *January 11, 1937*
Culver City, California

Dear Mr. Birdwell:

Couldn't you just say that I pronounced Melanie with the accent on "Mel" and let it go at that? For all I know there may be thousands of people who pronounce it "ma-LANEY." And I wouldn't for worlds hurt their feelings or embarrass them. I just don't want to be quoted directly on anything connected with the publicity for the picture. I know by now you must think I am very uncooperative and tough and hardboiled about this matter, but, really, this is not true. It is a matter of self-protection, for people have nearly driven me distracted about the forthcoming picture. Katharine Brown, when she was here, said she had no idea of the grief which had descended on me due to the public interest in the picture. My name has only to be mentioned in a movie column and hundreds of people descend on me wanting me to get them parts in the film or jobs in the technical end or chances to write dialogue. And there are scores who want me to get their houses used as background or their colored servants used as atmosphere. So I have discovered that I cannot afford to have my name connected in any way with the publicity.

So, if you could just say that you had inquired of the author as to the correct pronunciation and that she had given it to you. I would certainly appreciate it.

P.S. The clipping you sent me has just arrived and I thank you so much for it. Good heavens! Who would ever have thought I'd land among the "Ten Women of the Year"!*

Miss Jean Self   *Atlanta, Georgia*
Asheville, North Carolina   *January 11, 1937*

Dear Miss Self:

Thank you so much for your long and interesting letter. Of course, it makes me very happy to have people care about the moving picture production of my novel. I am very interested in who will play in it too, but I must tell you the truth about the situation.

I have nothing whatever to do with the production of the film. I am not adapting it to the screen, or writing additional dialogue, nor have I any voice whatsoever in the choice of the cast. So I can only wait until the film is produced to see how it turns out. I do know, however, that the Selznick

---

* On January 8, Durward Howes, editor of *American Women*, named Mitchell one of the country's 10 Women of the Year. The list also included actress Norma Shearer and photographer Margaret Bourke-White.

International Pictures, Inc., 230 Park Avenue, New York, are very interested in getting new talent, and Southern talent for this picture. May I suggest that you write Miss Katharine Brown at the above address and send her your picture, profile and full face, and state your qualifications. Miss Brown went through the South recently giving auditions to girls who had had no previous theatrical experience. Of course, it's probably one chance in a million that an untried girl will land a part, but nothing risked nothing gained!

Wishing you success,

Mr. Sidney Howard	*Atlanta, Georgia*
New York, New York	*January 12, 1937*

Dear Mr. Howard:

This is just a hasty note to acknowledge your note, and you need not reply for I know how busy you must be. I just wanted to tell you how happy my husband and I would be if you and your wife should come through Atlanta and see us. If it is possible that you are to be in our section at any time I wish you would give me some advance warning, for it would be just my luck to have you come when I was either out of town or loaded up with engagements, and I cannot bear the thought of that.

I talked by long distance with the Selznick New York office yesterday and they were so enthusiastic about your script that I had goose bumps up and down my back. How glad I am that you wrote it!

Miss Katharine Brown	*Atlanta, Georgia*
Selznick International Pictures, Inc.	*January 19, 1937*
New York, New York	

Dear Katharine:

...Mr. Plunkett arrived and is swell.* Saw him briefly at lunch and then had to leave him for two ministers from N.Y. The ministers didn't show up, stood me up, the so-and-sos. I sicced all the papers on Mr. Plunkett. If I can work my way through the mail, a family funeral and a delegation from a patriotic society before noon tomorrow, I'm taking Mr. Plunkett jaunting. God knows I've earned a day off so maybe we'll go to Jonesboro.†

No sign yet on the pub. release from Hollywood about Susan and Louisa.‡

---

* Costume designer Walter Plunkett visited Atlanta and other cities in the South to study antebellum and Civil War-era clothing.
† Jonesboro is the county seat of Clayton County, where Mitchell located Tara.
‡ The studio was arranging auditions and possible screen tests for two young women from Georgia—Susan Falligant, a student at the University of Georgia, and Louisa Robert,

Mr. Telamon Cuyler   *Atlanta, Georgia*
Wayside, Jones County, Georgia   *January 23, 1937*

My dear Mr. Cuyler:

The registered package containing your pictures has just arrived and I hasten to inform you of their safe arrival and of my appreciation.* This will only be a brief note as I have out of town guests on my hands.

Mr. Plunkett has left Atlanta and I do not know his forwarding address on the West Coast. However, may I keep these pictures for a few weeks? Some of the other people from the Selznick Company may be here and I should like to show them the pictures. Please be frank with me if you prefer that I return them to you immediately, registered mail. I know their value to you and they are so charming! I mentioned you and your collection to Mr. Plunkett. He was very interested but his visit to Atlanta was such a brief one that there was no time for him to do any travelling in this section.

Miss Katharine Brown   *Atlanta, Georgia*
Selznick International Pictures, Inc.   *January 23, 1937*
New York, New York

Dear Katharine:

Here are some more clippings.

Mr. Plunkett and I took a day off and jaunted to Jonesboro. The poor man had the worst cold you ever saw and his mouth had the loveliest collection of fever blisters ever exhibited in these parts. I urged him to stay in bed at the Biltmore for a day before going to Savannah and Charleston. He attempted to do this but was forced to leave town due to the scores of people who called on him bringing costumes of the Sixties. Half of them believed he wished to buy them. What finally drove him from his bed of pain was a woman who produced the actual dress Scarlett had worn at the barbecue. This made Mr. Plunkett wonder if he had become delirious.

Since his departure all of the hundreds of people who either wished to sell costumes of this period or wished to show pictures of such costumes have descended on me. They have telegraphed, written and called in per-

---

a member of the 1932 U.S. Olympic women's swim team and daughter of L. W. "Chip" Robert Jr., Atlanta businessman and secretary of the Democratic National Committee. Neither woman was hired.

* Cuyler was a Georgia lawyer, writer, and collector of Confederate memorabilia. He often sent Mitchell original documents and images from his collection.

son. It has been pretty terrible. So terrible that I actually dread the thought of Mr. Cukor's proposed visit. I really want to meet him very much and so does John, but I know from past experience that [in] the weeks after his visit life will be unendurable. The entire Confederate States of America will be on my neck. Do you think Mr. Cukor would mind coming down here under an alias? I do hate to make that request of him and I hope he will understand. If, for instance, any publicity on his visit was broken from Hollywood or in the Atlanta papers I would have to go to Siam for the next four weeks, leaving John and my unfortunate secretary to interview movie aspirants and answer letters. I just can't put this off on them. If it is possible in any way for Mr. Cukor to come quietly or for me to meet him in some other Southern town, I would certainly like to work it out.

Mr. Plunkett was a grand person, and my day with him was like a picnic. Thank you so much for sending him to me.

In haste,

Miss Katharine Brown   *Atlanta, Georgia*
Selznick International Pictures, Inc.   *February 5, 1937*
New York, New York

Dear Katharine:

I just couldn't come to New York to see Mr. Cukor. I would as soon cut my throat as go to New York. I would have to stay at least six weeks in order to see everyone I would have to see and I do not want to be away from Atlanta for six minutes.

It isn't that I do not want to see Mr. Cukor, for I know John and I would have a marvelous time. It is the weeks of aftermath that I dread. However, I do not see any help for it and I suppose will have to live through it somehow. A great part of this aftermath comes in the form of letters and calls. I am enclosing a couple of letters which I thought might be of interest to you. They are rather typical of scores of letters, and of course they must be answered and this takes forever. I thought you might be interested in the fact that people are even worked up about the knots on head rags. There is no detail too small, it seems, to bring forth a letter or a call. Please send these letters back when you have read them.

Let me know in advance, if you can, when Mr. Cukor will be down here, and John and I will handle things as best we can. I am afraid the press tea is off for when I tentatively put out a half-dozen invitations I was stormed by at least a thousand non-press people who said they would never speak to me again if I didn't invite them. At present the city auditorium is undergoing repairs and it is the only hall large enough to include the number who want to come. . . .

Is there any further news on the casting? Rumors are afloat in this section that Clark Gable is out due to the fact that his owners want too much rent for him.*

Miss Katharine Brown   Atlanta, Georgia
Selznick International Pictures, Inc.   February 14, 1937
New York, New York

Dear Katharine:

Yesterday I had to go to Macon on the saddest trip I'll ever make to that town. Aaron Bernd, who was your and my host at Teeter-on-the-Jitters during your trip to Macon, had died of pneumonia and I went over for the funeral.† As he was as good a friend as John and I had, it was a pretty desolate day. He had so very many friends, both Jewish and Gentile, and we all hung together after the funeral and went out to Teeter that night for the last time. In an effort to divert ourselves we fell to talking about the coming production of G.W.T.W. (as you probably know where ever two or more of ye are gathered together these days, the two or more talk about the movie). As I listened to Susan Myrick talking an idea dawned on me that made me wonder why I hadn't thought about it before. I spent the night with her and encouraged her far into the night to talk about the picture. She had such good ideas (at least I thought them good) that I came home determined to write you.

You know what my attitude has been all along in the matter of not making any suggestions to any of you Selznick folks about the film. You know the fight I have put up against the general public who wanted to get in the picture as actors, script assistants, costumers, advisers etc. Half of my fight has been, frankly, because I didn't want any more grief than I already had. The other half was because I sincerely believe that you people know your business far better than I'll ever know it and I did not want to hamper or embarrass you with suggestions that were useless or impractical. I've even refused as much as five hundred dollars to name the cast I'd like because I thought it might embarrass y'all in some small way. So this is

---

* Gable was under exclusive contract to Metro-Goldwyn-Mayer, but studios sometimes loaned actors and other personnel, for a fee, to work on films being made by other studios. † Bernd, the literary editor of the *Macon Telegraph*, was a good friend of Myrick's. "Teeter on the Jitters" was his weekend country house, which got its name after a guest who had drunk too much declared that he was "wobbling on the threshold of the D.T.s."

my first suggestion and for Heaven's sake, if it sounds foolish to you, don't mind telling me because it won't hurt my feelings and no one else except John will ever know about it.

My suggestion is—why not take Susan Myrick out to the Coast in some capacity while the picture is being made? (I say "in some capacity" for I do not know just what sort of title such a job would carry.) You said that you'd like to have me there to pass on the authenticity and rightness of this and that, the accents of the white actors, the dialect of the colored ones, the minor matters of dress and deportment, the small touches of local color etc. Well, I can't go and you know why. But I thought if you really wanted a Georgian for the job there wouldn't be any one better than Sue. In fact, she'd be a better person for the job than I would because she knows more about such matters than I do. I hope you will not gag when I explain why. I know you are sick and tired of people who want to get into the picture "because of their lovely Southern back ground." I know I am. But I have to drag in Sue's back ground for explanation.

Her Grandpa, old General Myrick had the biggest and whitest colyumned house in Georgia, at Milledgeville. It's still there, a lovely place but no longer in Myrick hands. The family lost it due to hard times. Sue is the youngest child of a Confederate soldier and God knows she's heard enough about the old days. Being poor as Job's turkey, she was raised up in the country and she knows good times and bad, quality folks and poor whites, Crackers and town folks. And good grief, what she doesn't know about negroes! She was raised up with them. And she loves and understands them. Since going on the paper, she has been the paper's official representative at most of the negro affairs of her section. Mr. W.T. Anderson, owner of her paper (I wish you could have met him) is strong for the colored folks and tries to get a square deal for them and the saying among the colored folks in the district is that "De Race is got two friends in dis County, sweet Jesus and de Macon Telegraph." So when ever there's a colored graduation if Mr. W.T. can't be there to make a speech, Sue goes and if the colored P.T.A. wants to be addressed by Mr. Anderson and he can't make it, Sue does the addressing—The same holds for funerals and awarding of prizes.

Moreover Sue is as competent a newspaper woman as we have in this section. She can—and does—do everything from advice to the lovelorn and the cooking page to book reviews and politics and hangings. But the main thing that recommends her to me is her common sense and her utter lack of sentimentality about what is tearfully known as "The Old South." She knows its good points and she doesn't slur over its bad points. She knows her section and its people and she loves them both but she is not unaware of either the faults or the charm of both people and section. In other words she's a common sense, hard headed person with an awful lot of knowledge about Georgia people and Georgia ways, not only of this time but of times past. So I'm handing the idea on to you of using her on the picture.

Now, Katharine, please don't think you've got to consider her seriously just because I suggested her or just because she's a friend of mine. If the idea doesn't seem good to you, just tell me now. It won't bother me and Sue will never know that I've ever written you so there'll be no skin off anyone's nose.*

Life is somewhat more endurable these days because I now have an office and I rush to it at dawn and stay there till all hours.† I have no phone. No one but John and Bessie know where the office is so no one can get me. I even have a sofa here so that I have been able to catch up on sleep. Poor Bessie has to wrestle with phoners and callers which is tough on her but fine for me. I think thank God, that things are quieting a little for a friend of mine tried to sell a N.Y. paper a story about me and the editor wrote her back that they were not using anything more on Mitchell unless Mitchell shoots a Yankee. My friend, in need of cash, had already picked out the Yankee for me to shoot and was grieved at my refusal. I think this is a straw in the wind which shows that the excitement is almost over. Given another few months and I can emerge and walk the streets lak a nacherl 'oman.

Hope you had a good time on the Coast. John sends you his best. If you see Tony tell him I saw his kin folks in Macon at the funeral and they sent their best to him. And the Macon people you met wish to be remembered to you. They all likes you all so much.

Mr. George Collier MacKinnon   *March 1, 1937*
Daily Record   *Atlanta, Georgia*
Boston, Massachusetts

Dear Mr. MacKinnon:

I won't have you saying you have been "pestiferous" in writing to me because I have appreciated your letters and your interest so very much. I would have answered your last letter, but at the time it arrived so many of my friends and relatives were ill with influenza that I had to let my mail slide for the time being.

---

* Myrick was hired by Selznick International as a technical adviser in the area of southern manners and customs. She spent the first six months of 1939 at the studio while *Gone With the Wind* was being filmed.

† Mitchell rented a nearby efficiency apartment to serve as her office.

I couldn't help smiling at the clipping from "Variety" which you forwarded to me.* I do not know the source of "Variety's" statement that I was going to Hollywood to assist in the filming of "Gone With the Wind," but the source of this statement was certainly not me. I have not changed my decision not to go to Hollywood. I have never had any intention of going. And, as for assisting with the script of "Gone With the Wind"—Mr. Sidney Howard is doing the script and I am sure my novel is in excellent hands and not in need of assistance from me. I have no connection with the film in any way at all, not even in the most minor advisory capacity. I do not intend to go to Hollywood.

Thank you for sending me the clipping. I am at a loss to understand how such a rumor got about, but I was glad to know about it.

Miss Katharine Brown
Selznick International Pictures, Inc.
New York, New York

Atlanta, Georgia
March 8, 1937

Dear Katharine:

It will be marvelous if you and Harriett can come to Atlanta with Mr. Cukor. I hope nothing happens to upset your plans to come. John and I will be so happy to see you again.

I have thought over the matter of Mr. Cukor and his visit and the inevitable aftermath and, as I believe I wrote you before, I have decided that the best thing is for him to come with all the loud trumpets possible. You are absolutely right about the press and the public being offended if he attempted an incognito visit. It would be bad on the Selznick Company and the picture, and, as you know, I am most anxious for people down here to like the film. There is nothing I can do to stave off the public and I realize it and am resigned to it. There is only one thing I can do. That is when I know the date of Mr. Cukor's arrival and the hotel at which he will stay, I can throw myself on the mercies of the Atlanta newspapers and ask them to run appeals to the public not to devil me but to devil Mr. Cukor. This will help a little but, of course, there will be no defense against the various organizations in the small towns of Georgia which will bring pressure to bear on me to make Mr. Cukor come to their towns and give screen tests to their hopefuls. But I am feeling fine now and have gained weight, and so this will not bother me so much. If things do get tough I can always leave

---

* The February 24 issue of *Daily Variety* carried a small notice that Mitchell was "changing her attitude" and "will likely sit in on the scripting at Selznick-International."

town after seeing Mr. Cukor, and let Bessie handle the movie aspirants. I wish to God you could have seen the white woman who turned up last week with a can of blacking in her pocketbook and the determination of playing Mammy. I sat on the blacking so she couldn't put it on her face, and for forty minutes watched her play Mammy up and down the rug.*

So tell Mr. Cukor to come on at any time convenient to him and let me know as far in advance as possible. Let me know too, if you can, just what he would like to see in this neighborhood. For instance, if he wants to see the line of old fortifications between Atlanta and Dalton or those at Jonesboro, I want to get hold of Wilbur Kurtz who, as I told you, is about the only living authority on these campaigns. He knows every foot of ground in two hundred miles, the old houses, who lived in them, what generals died in them, et cetera. As a matter of fact, if you wanted an honest to God expert on the War part of the picture, you couldn't do better than kidnap Mr. Kurtz and take him to Hollywood.†

Of course, we'd love to see Mr. and Mrs. Howard, and I would not tip the newspapers off to his presence here or even breathe it to anyone. Please tell him to let me know as far ahead as possible when he would be here so that I would not be entertaining the senior class of some high school on that day. Tell him we would want them to spend the afternoon with us and see Atlanta's few sights and have dinner with us.

Here is something for your own ear, which came to me third hand. Probably you have already heard about it. I heard that the families of the two Atlanta girls were raising some objections about their daughters posing for advertising stills. I didn't get much information on this matter, but simply pass this bit on to you.

Whoever told you that I was in Florida was wrong. I haven't been there since my last trip at Christmas time. But then, recently I have heard that I was in all points of the United States, including Reno where I was divorcing John. By the way, did you know I had a wooden leg? I just heard that Saturday and, as you can imagine, was a little surprised. . . .

---

* Mitchell was contacted by several white women intent on playing Mammy in blackface. In October 1936, a "Southern Woman" in California wrote, declaring, "I want to play your Mammy in the picture; I want to crawl into the skin of her and make her a *real* throbbing *living, living being.*" The author replied, politely telling the woman that she had nothing to do with casting, but did not refer her to the studio.

† Kurtz was hired by Selznick International as the film's historian. He went to Hollywood for several weeks of preliminary work in early 1938 and returned full-time that November, remaining for more than a year.

Miss Day Redmayne   *Atlanta, Georgia*
Santa Monica, California   *March 15, 1937*

Dear Miss Redmayne:

Thank you so much for your letter and your many good wishes. I appreciated them all.

In the matter of suggesting Gloria Swanson and Charles Laughton for the parts of Scarlett and Rhett, I have nothing to do with the film production of "Gone With the Wind" and I have no influence with the producers. So I can only sit back like any other movie fan and await the picture with interest.

Miss Katharine Brown   *Atlanta, Georgia*
Selznick International Pictures, Inc.   *March 16, 1937*
New York, New York

Dear Katharine:

As I cannot remember the exact ages of your little girls, the dolls I am sending them may be too old for the baby and too young for the young lady, but I am sending them just the same. They are made in Macon, and called Scarlett's Mammy. I do not know who the baby Mammy holds is. Some folks say it's Bonnie and others that it's Wade.*

The publicity about the Southern girls has been uniformly good. Of course, I'm anxious to know how the tests will come out. Please give the young ladies my best wishes.

I'm looking forward to seeing the Howards.

Miss Vivian Latady   *Atlanta, Georgia*
Birmingham, Alabama   *March 18, 1937*

Dear Vivian:

It was so grand hearing from you again. . . .

As to how my life is going—it is going much better, thank Heaven. I was forced to rent an office two months ago as the movie-crazed populace was doing its level best to kill me. I really believe that nine-tenths of the people in the world do not read newspapers. Otherwise, they would realize that I do not have anything to do with the moving picture of "Gone With

---

* In the novel, Bonnie is the daughter of Scarlett and Rhett. Wade is Scarlett's son from her first marriage to Charles Hamilton.

the Wind." They made it so tough for me that I took an office without a telephone, and I go there early in the morning and remain there till quite late. In this manner I manage to get some peace and rest, and the result has been that I have gained ten pounds and feel marvelous. I will be so happy when the picture finally goes into production and the cast is announced, for then I will not be at the mercy of movie aspirants. . . .

Miss Mahala Star   *Atlanta, Georgia*
Decatur, Georgia   *March 18, 1937*

My dear Miss Star:

I understand from the papers that Mr. George Cukor who is to direct "Gone With the Wind," will be in Atlanta at some time in the near future. I do not know exactly when, for in the matter of the filming of my book I am like Will Rogers, "all I know is what I read in the papers." I have no connection whatever with this film and do not even hold correspondence with the Selznick company about the casting. When I sold my book it was like a grocer selling a pound of butter, the sale is final and the grocer does not tell the customer just how to use the butter. It is all in the hands of the Selznick company and my advice to you is to see Mr. Cukor when and if he does come to Atlanta. A further suggestion is that you immediately write Miss Katharine Brown of Selznick International Pictures, Inc., 230 Park Avenue, New York (she, as you will recall, was the person who gave auditions here). Send her your picture, and write her your qualifications. She might take up this matter with Mr. Cukor before he came South, and so, make it easier for you to secure an audition with him if he comes here.

I hope you will understand me when I tell you that it would not do any good for me to give you my opinion about your capacities for the part of Scarlett. You see, I cannot give any opinion, having told the Selznick company that I would not ever, publicly or privately, express any opinion of this type. As I am not in their employ, it would not be my place to do this, and it might prove hampering or embarrassing to them. Another reason why I believe an interview between us would be of no help is that I know nothing whatsoever about movies or acting and I am no judge of anyone's fitness for the screen. I do not have any ideas about who should or should not play the part of Scarlett. I am in the position of any other movie fan and can only sit back and await the picture with interest.

With all good wishes for your success,

Miss Katharine Brown   *Atlanta, Georgia*
Selznick International Pictures, Inc.   *March 20, 1937*
New York, New York

Dear Katharine:

I was so happy to know that you were coming South again and I know I will enjoy your visit in spite of the fiends in human form who wish to get into your movie.

We are again being swamped with hundreds of movie aspirants. The Associated Press carried a story which said that, as Mr. Cukor could find no Scarlett in New York or Hollywood, he was coming to Atlanta "to confer with me about the matter." This information has seemingly unhinged the minds of a number of people who feel that they are the one and only Scarlett, and we are again leading hunted lives. When the papers queried me about Mr. Cukor's visit and his reasons for coming I told them that, as far as I personally was concerned, his visit with me was purely of a social nature. His visit to the South, of course, was because he sincerely felt that he should see the background of the book and Southern people before he undertook the production. I reiterated (and this did not get into print, worse luck!) that people were asses of no uncertain variety if they thought moving picture companies paid a lot of money for books and spent millions on the production and then permitted an author who knew nothing of moving pictures and actors to choose the cast. But the gullible public is firmly convinced that I and I alone am going to do the casting. If Mr. Cukor should make another statement to the press, couldn't he, please, say that his desire to see me is prompted either by courtesy or plain morbid curiosity, or something innocuous like that and also state that, of course, I have nothing to do with the casting of the picture? I am just being swamped all over again.

I'll send you the list of the newspaper people on Monday. I will make a very full list, as I do not know how many you wish to invite. I will indicate on the list the important ones, such as editors, publishers and movie critics, and you can decide how many you want to invite. In view of the Mayor's letter (see clipping) I am wondering whether or not you should invite him.* However, a delicate situation arises. He is the Mayor, this is a dry State, and you will serve cocktails. I do not know the Mayor's personal stand in the matter of alcohol, but his official position may be agin it. If only newspaper people

---

* On March 20, the *Constitution* carried an article about a letter that Mayor William B. Harts-field had written to Selznick urging the producer to hold the film's premiere in Atlanta.

are present it would be all right. If, however, members of the Woman's Club and of the Better Films Committee et cetera are attending, they might be incensed at the Mayor's tolerating cocktails. I think I will call personally on the Mayor and sound him out on this matter. He is a very fine person and I would not want to get him in an embarrassing situation.

Mrs. Myrtle B. Hodgkins   *Atlanta, Georgia*
Pooler, Georgia   *March 20, 1937*

My dear Mrs. Hodgkins:

I have been so swamped with letters from people who believe that I can get them into the cast of "Gone With the Wind" that I have despairingly given up trying to answer them. But your letter impressed me so much that I'm answering it because I do not want you to think I do not appreciate your situation or your interest.

The newspaper stories about Mr. Cukor coming here to "confer with me about the cast" are all wrong. I have nothing whatever to do with the movie production of "Gone With the Wind." I have nothing to do with the casting. I have not even had any correspondence with the Selznick Company on any matter concerning the picture. If Mr. Cukor comes here and does see me, it will be purely a social call and the picture will not even be discussed. That is the arrangement I have with the Selznick Company— that I have no connection whatever with the film. So I cannot help you in the matter of getting into the cast. It would do no good for us to have a personal interview with me because I could not recommend you to Mr. Selznick. That is not my place for an author never has any voice in the casting of a picture. Moreover, I know less than nothing about moving pictures or actors so my opinion would be of no value. If you wish to write to Mr. George Cukor direct, his address is care the Selznick International Pictures, Inc., 230 Park Avenue, New York City.

You see—I liked your face and I liked your determination! I wish I could help you but I can't.

Mrs. W.F. Melton   *Atlanta, Georgia*
Atlanta Woman's Club   *March 20, 1937*
Atlanta, Georgia

Dear Mrs. Melton:

I wish that I could help you and the Woman's Club, but I cannot be of any assistance in the matter of attending the Woman's Club dinner with Mr. Cukor. I advise you to write him direct about the dinner. . . .

I will have to state my position fully on this matter, and I hope you will understand. I have no connection at all with the forthcoming picture, yet, despite my efforts, people continue to believe that I have the entire production on my back. The truth of the matter is I do not even hold correspondence with the Selznick company on the subject of the film, and I have never had any personal communication with or from Mr. Cukor. If he meets me while he is here in Atlanta, it will be a purely social matter. I will, of course, have him out to dinner, as that is the only polite thing possible, but I will not even discuss the picture with him. That is the understanding the Selznick people and I have had from the beginning. Swamped, as I am, by people who think I can get them into the cast or use their ante bellum homes for background or get Mr. Cukor to speak—I cannot afford even to be seen publicly with him, and I do not intend to lay myself open to more grief than I now have by appearing publicly with him and giving an untrue impression that I have some connection with the picture. Moreover, I have refused so many invitations to make "public appearances" here in Atlanta that, if I attended the proposed Woman's Club banquet, I would offend a number of my relatives who have been kind enough to invite me to their own organizations.

I think that if you write to Mr. Cukor direct, or to Miss Katharine Brown of the same address (she was the charming young woman who gave auditions here before Christmas), they might accept your invitation, if they intend to be in Atlanta more than one night. I do not imagine their stay will be long, as I think they are making only a few hours' stopover on the way to Hollywood. . . .

Katharine Brown
Selznick International Pictures, Inc.
New York, New York

Atlanta, Georgia
March 23, 1937

CAN YOU WIRE ME WHEN HOWARD WILL BE HERE HAVE ALREADY KEPT THREE DAYS OPEN FOR HIM AND MY FUTURE PLANS DISARRANGED BY THE UNCERTAINTY.

Miss Katharine Brown
Selznick International Pictures, Inc.
New York, New York

Atlanta, Georgia
March 23, 1937

Here is the list. As I wrote you, I do not know how many you wish to invite, nor do I know whether you want to invite the wives of newspapermen as well. So, I have indicated those who are married with an "m." The ones I have put check marks by are the most important ones.

I called on Mayor William B. Hartsfield, Atlanta City Hall, yesterday and discussed the matter of cocktails mentioned in my last letter. He said it wouldn't bother him, and so I took it upon myself to invite him. I hope you do not mind my forwardness in this affair, but the Mayor is passionately interested in getting the world premiere of "Gone With the Wind" here. Besides, he is well aware of the valuable publicity to Atlanta that will come from this film and is very anxious to cooperate with you people in any way that will give Atlanta more publicity.

I hated to wire you a few minutes ago about Mr. Howard, but I am rapidly getting into a jam on my future engagements because I have put off people for the last three days, thinking Mr. Howard might be here. I have to see these people sometime between now and the time you arrive, and I would have a fit if Mr. Howard came and I was so dated up that I could not see him.

Mr. Edwin Granberry   *Atlanta, Georgia*
Winter Haven, Florida   *March 24, 1937*

Dear Edwin:

Here is a copy of the photograph used in Collier's.* The Macmillan Company just sent it to me. God only knows what happened to it in the reproduction, but I appear to have met up with a tomcat who scratched my face vigorously.

"Pester" us with fruit, comfort us with apples, or rather, comfort us with whatever fruit is in your neighborhood. We would love to have it.

We are momentarily expecting the dam to burst. Mr. Cukor, who is to direct "Gone With the Wind," will be here in the next few days with entourage and loud tooting trumpets. The only reason he is coming is sheer curiosity to see what kind of woman I am who refuses a good salary in Hollywood. However, the natives think he has come here on his knees to beg me to tell just who I think he should pick as Scarlett. As nine-tenths of the natives have already picked themselves for Scarlett, this complicates our lives a little. Of course I want to meet Mr. Cukor, but I will be very glad when his visit is over. I wish he would hurry up and cast the picture, then most of my trouble would be over.

---

* Granberry began working on an article about Mitchell in the fall of 1936, and the author and her husband saw the piece as an opportunity to stem the tide of public interest in her personal life. The article, heavily edited by Marsh and titled "The Private Life of Margaret Mitchell," appeared in the March 13, 1937, issue of *Collier's*.

We had a nice note from Mr. Littauer, saying that he might be in Atlanta sometime soon.* I hope so, because we liked him so very much. Edwin, your article has helped a great deal. No one asks me to autograph their copy, and many letters show a very comforting appreciation of my position and a "good for you" attitude. How lucky I was to meet a "gentleman with a Mississippi accent"!

Mrs. Elsie Adams Seeger   *Atlanta, Georgia*
Patterson, New York   *April 1, 1937*

My dear Mrs. Seeger:

. . . I thank you for your letter and I shall treasure the things you wrote me about "Gone With the Wind." I am so glad you liked that first conversation between the thoughtless twins and Scarlett. I wrote that first chapter seventy times in an effort to make it simple and casual and to make those three grownup children (and Jeems) normal frolicsome young people.

In the matter of the moving picture—I sold my book outright and I have nothing more to do with it, so I do not know what will happen to it. During the last week Mr. Cukor, who is to direct "Gone With the Wind," was here in Atlanta with a large staff, looking at old houses, old earthworks and riding the rutted roads of our rural counties. He seemed very anxious to convey the book to the screen with authenticity, and he told me that the first draft of the scenario preserved my ending of the book. What will happen to this ending in Hollywood neither he nor I know.

With renewed thanks for your kindness,

Mr. Peter Porohovshikov   *Atlanta, Georgia*
Oglethorpe University   *April 1, 1937*
Atlanta, Georgia

My dear Uncle Peter:

Please forgive my delay in answering your letter. This is the first moment I have had to write in a week. The moving picture people have been here investigating backgrounds and I have been working until past midnight every night. Having an ardent desire for the backgrounds of "Gone With the Wind" to be authentic, I have done and am doing my best. Just to show you what this involves, I am drawing up the plans of the four houses mentioned in my book, with every staircase, room, window, door and fanlight complete, and every outbuilding, woodpile and shrub in its place. I

---

* Kenneth Littauer was the fiction editor of *Collier's*. He attempted several times to woo Mitchell to submit a short story for the magazine, but to no avail.

am no architect, and, so, this will keep me busy for some weeks and make me travel the country districts of this section for some time to come. . . .

Mrs. George H. Keeler	Atlanta, Georgia
"Tranquilla"	April 2, 1937
Marietta, Georgia	

Dear Mrs. Keeler:

I can never thank you enough for your kindness to me and the moving picture people. You did me such a great favor when you permitted us all to see your lovely house. I was so very anxious for Mr. Cukor and Mr. Erwin to see a home that had beauty and grace and tradition.* Of course, "Tranquilla" has all those things and more, and I was so happy that the Selznick people had the opportunity to see the very best of the old South and the best of the new South at one time. The whole party sang your praises and "Miss Hattie's" all the way home from Marietta. Thank you so much for your courtesy.

Mrs. Lloyd Harris	Atlanta, Georgia
The Marietta Journal	April 2, 1937
Marietta, Georgia	

Dear Fannie Lou:

All of you were marvelous to us the other day and you certainly saved my life. I was so anxious for the movie people to see Marietta and Marietta people for, as I have often told you, Marietta, to me is really so beautifully old South. They saw the things they wanted to see and were so enthusiastic.

The newspaper articles were grand, both yours and the man reporter's (I can't remember his name). I showed the latter to Mr. Cukor and, of course, he carried it off with him. Could I have another copy for my scrapbook?

Tell Frances Mr. Cukor will return here on Tuesday and I will get his autograph for her.

Many thanks and love to you all,

Mr. Peter Porohovshikov	Atlanta, Georgia
Oglethorpe University	April 4, 1937
Atlanta, Georgia	

Dear Uncle Peter:

. . . I am sorry if I gave you the impression that I am connected with the filming of GWTW for nothing could be farther from the truth. I am not

---

* Hobart "Hobe" Erwin, a New York interior decorator, was doing preliminary design work on the film.

connected with it in any way. The members of the technical staff of the film were my guests and I was—and am—tendering them the courtesies and assistance always due guests. My visitors from the North always want to see the countryside, old houses, old furniture, cemeteries, etc. The movie people are even more anxious to see them. They are anxious too to know the floor plans of all the houses I wrote about and as I am the only one who knows the floor plans, I am the only one who can assist them. So I show them dozens of old houses so that they can see where stairs ran and how windows looked and how wide floor boards were. But, thank God, I have nothing to do with the filming nor do I intend to have anything to do with it.

Mr. George B. Ward   *Atlanta, Georgia*
Ward, Sterne & Co.   *April 5, 1937*
Birmingham, Alabama

Dear Mr. Ward:

   . . . I want to tell you that your mother's "testimony" has gone to Hollywood, where I hope it will do much good.* Mr. Cukor, the director of "Gone With the Wind," was in Atlanta last week and we spoke together at great length concerning the relations between slave and mistress in the old days. I knew your mother's words would make that life more vivid than anything I could say, and he was delighted with it. I did, of course, recommend many volumes written by Southern ladies after the War, but I thought your mother's would be more valuable. He was especially interested in how mistresses brought sick Negro children into their own rooms and nursed them. . . .

Miss Katharine Brown   *Atlanta, Georgia*
Selznick International Pictures, Inc.   *April 7, 1937*
New York, New York

Dear Katharine:

   The enclosed clipping about the latest adventure of that charming madcap, Honey Chile, does not tell all, and I thought you might be interested in the rest of it. My long-suffering aunt called me on Sunday and told me that Honey Chile, who had heretofore never honored her with a visit, had flown from New York and was staying with her. "She says if they put anyone else in as Scarlett the picture will be ruined. Lots of people have

---

* Ward's mother, Margaret Ketchum Ward, testified in 1883 before the U.S. Senate Committee on Relations between Labor and Capital about wartime conditions in Georgia. Mitchell used Ward's testimony while researching and fact-checking *Gone With the Wind*.

the gall to think she is my daughter. Good Heavens! She intends to see Mr. Cukor and that is why she has come. She intends to see you too."

Well, she didn't see Mr. Cukor or me. But, while I was at lunch with him and Erwin and Darrow yesterday at the Biltmore, she had sixteen bellboys paging him.* Mr. Cukor told each bellboy to tell her that he was not in the hotel. Finally, Erwin and Darrow went out to lure her upstairs for an audition while Mr. C. and I made our escape.

Last night Yolande called me, practically incoherent.† Honey Chile had phoned her at a quarter to six at the Constitution, a short while before the paper went to press. This merry romp screamed over the phone that she had discovered the train on which the badgered George was to leave and she had bought a ticket and was going to New Orleans.

"If I talk to him he will realize I am the only Scarlett. I must see him. I *will* see him. I will go all the way to Hollywood with him if necessary. I am now at the Terminal Station." Yolande said that she was overcome with horror and pity for the Selznickers. All of you had been so wonderful to her that she could not bear to think of the weary trio being captured by this determined belle. She rushed to the city editor and asked for fifteen minutes off so that she could go to the Station and warn the unsuspecting George. The city editor roared like a bull, snatched a photographer out of a trash basket, called a taxi and threw Yolande and the photographer in.

"Warn Mr. Cukor! You cover that story if you have to go all the way to New Orleans."

In the taxi Yolande wrote a note on a bank deposit slip to give Mr. Cukor if time was short. When she arrived at the Station Honey Chile was racing up and down beside the train, and she yelled to Yolande, "Either they aren't on the train or they are in hiding, but I will find them." She leaped on the train and the photographer banged away. Thereafter for ten minutes Yolande said Honey Chile tore through the train jerking open stateroom doors, disconcerting honeymoon couples, arousing sleeping children, and catching several gentlemen who had taken off their pants. The train was in an uproar, and the whole crew was pursuing her. Convinced that they were not on the train, she leaped off and ran down the tracks, telling her troubles to all and sundry, announcing that she would make a perfect Scarlett. Yolande said that, personally, she was mortified as the Station was packed and everyone showed an appreciative interest. One old lady sat down on her suitcase and said, with enthusiasm, "This is every bit as good as a movie!"

---

* Talent scout John Darrow, a former actor, was helping Cukor with auditions.

† Yolande Gwin was a society writer for the *Atlanta Constitution*.

Then Yolande had an idea. The train was very long and she suggested that Honey Chile wait at the end of the Pullmans while she, Yolande, watched the stair. Honey Chile took off like a rabbit at the suggestion. In a few minutes down the stairs came the trio, all unsuspecting and very weary after seeing hundreds of applicants. Yolande jumped at them crying, "Something dreadful has happened!" All three, bless them, questioned, "Is Mrs. Marsh hurt?" "No, something far worse. Miss T. is going to New Orleans with you."

Yolande said they evidently agreed with her that this news was far more dreadful than hearing that I had been mangled by a truck. And George positively paled. He told John Darrow to hold Honey Chile off the train at any cost, and the weary John sprinted for the end of the train, with Yolande and the photographer close behind. Yolande peeped over her shoulder and she took oath that George and Hobe Erwin dived into the coal car. Miss T. leaped upon Darrow, crying, "I don't want to see you. I have already seen you. My God, anybody can see you. I must see Mr. Cukor. This is the turning point of my life!" John soothingly took her hand and addressed her as sweetheart and told her Mr. Cukor had gone to New Orleans by motor. "Then, I will go to New Orleans," cried the determined Honey Chile. "What would you advise me to do?" "I would advise you not to chase him. Men don't like to be chased. The more you pursue him the less chance you have. Go home and forget about it, and perhaps when we come back to New York we'll see you." He held her hand till the whistle blew and then leaped aboard.

Yolande said the young lady had given no one any intimation that your company had already seen her in New York.

When Yolande got back to the paper the city editor almost threw a slug at her. "If you had been worth your salt you'd have pushed her on that train and we'd have had a fine story." "But Mr. Cukor had been so nice to me." "Bah," said the city editor.

All this is to let you know that this charming Dixie belle hasn't given up and will probably be on your neck ere long.*

I so enjoyed seeing you, but I wish our visits together could take place in quieter times. I hardly felt that I had seen you, and I didn't tell you 1/100 of the things I wanted to tell you. Judging by the Southern clippings, your outfit went over like a breeze and everyone fell in love with all of you. I do not know if your trip had any value in a material way, but in good will and advertising it must have been worth a million. You are all charming people.

John sends his best and so do I.

---

* On April 8, Kay Brown wired Mitchell, asking if the movie rights were available for the "Life Story of the Adventures of Honey Chile," a narrative "comparable in scope" to *Gone With the Wind*.

Mr. Herschel Brickell   Atlanta, Georgia
New York Post   April 8, 1937
New York, New York

Dear Herschel:

If you have had the same mild winter and early spring we have had you and Norma are probably back in the country now enjoying the fruits of your bulb planting. I wish I could see your place now for I remember from many years ago how beautiful Connecticut is in the spring.

Everything is marvelous here in the country now. Mr. Cukor, who is to direct "Gone With the Wind," has been here with his technical staff, and I took them over all the red rutted roads of Clayton County. The dogwood was just coming out and the flowering crabs blooming like mad. The movie people wanted to see old houses that had been built before Sherman got here and I obligingly showed them. While they were polite, I am sure they were dreadfully disappointed, for they had been expecting architecture such as appeared in the screen version of "So Red the Rose." I had tried to prepare them by reiterating that this section of North Georgia was new and crude compared with other sections of the South, and white columns were the exception rather than the rule. I besought them to please leave Tara ugly, sprawling, columnless, and they agreed. I imagine, however, that when it comes to Twelve Oaks they will put columns all around the house and make it as large as our new city auditorium.

The "Hollywood girl" you mentioned meeting, whose name is Katharine Brown, was down here with them. She is a charming person and I like her very much. I am always amazed that anyone so young and pretty can hold such a responsible position. By the way, she isn't in the Hollywood end but the New York end of the Selznick company. . . .

I feel perfectly wonderful these days, and have for the last couple of months. As a matter of fact, I am looking for a wildcat so that I can offer the wildcat the first bite before we mix up. I have almost regained all my lost weight and my mirror tells me that I am looking like a human being again. The main reason for this wonderful state is my office, which I think I wrote you about. I took it in January. It is a small room and jammed with file case, desk and sofa. Clippings and letters are knee high. I go there early in the morning and stay most of the day. There is no telephone and no one, except the family, knows my address. The admirable Miss Baugh keeps house for me in the office and has contributed at least seven of my ten missing pounds by her good work. . . .*

---

* Margaret Baugh, who had worked in The Macmillan Company's southeastern office in Atlanta, became Mitchell's full-time secretary in January 1937.

P.S. . . . The clipping you sent me from the negro magazine has just arrived and I want to thank you for it and tell how interesting I found it. I have followed the course of GWTW in the "Daily Worker" (that *is* the name, isn't it?) with much enthusiasm.* They do not like it at all, to put it mildly, any more than any radical periodical likes it. On the negro angle they disliked it so much they called on negro readers to write to Mr. Selznick, owner of the movie rights, and forbid him to produce the picture, threatening to boycott the picture if he did—and do worse things. They referred to the book as an "incendiary and negro baiting" book. Personally, I do not know where they get such an idea for, as far as I can see most of the negro characters were people of worth, dignity and rectitude—certainly Mammy and Peter and even the ignorant Sam knew more of decorous behavior and honor than Scarlett did.

The negroes in this section have read it in large herds and while I have not heard as many comments as I would like to hear, my friends are continually telling me what colored elevator operators, garage attendants etc. tell them and these colored people seem well pleased. Our wash woman, a middle aged woman and a worthy citizen if ever there was one, the owner of three houses, a tax payer and a pillar of rectitude remarked about the book, "It just goes to show that white folks in the old days had more sense than they have now. In those days white folks raised fine colored folks and they had sense enough to let the fine colored folks raise the white children. And the colored folks knew what was what and they didn't ever let the white children forget it. Now days, the white folks don't let the colored folks have any say-so in the raising of the children and look at them—sassing their elders, saying bad words, disobeying. Let me tell you, no old fashioned mammy would have let a child 'express itself' like children do now. 'Express itself'! . . .

Mr. George Cukor   Atlanta, Georgia
Selznick International Pictures, Inc.   April 14, 1937
Culver City, California

Dear George:

On Monday I smelled like honeysuckles, on Tuesday I smelled of heliotrope, today I am lilaced to the ears and am as happy as a tomcat in a fresh bed of catnip, tomorrow I will smell of rose geranium, and I can scarcely wait until next Sunday when the fragrance of sweet olive will envelope me. Thank you so much for the perfumes. My preliminary sniffings tell me that the rose geranium is more suitable for me, but I love them all. They all lack

---

* The *Daily Worker* was the newspaper of the Communist Party USA.

the heavy musky sweetness of many perfumes and also the sharp chemical odor of most flower scents. Thank you a thousand times.

I hope you are getting something from some of the books I lent you. As you remarked, many of the memoirs of that era are dreary affairs. It is maddening to have to read seven books about faith in God and the sacredness of states' rights in order to discover just how many petticoats a belle of the sixties wore. As I could not find some of the books I wanted you to have, I have had my book dealer advertise for them and we should have them shortly.

Yolande Gwin called me and told me of your dramatic exit from Atlanta. I think it should go down in history side by side with General Hood's retreat from Atlanta. And I only wish discretion did not seal my lips for the whole thing would make a wonderful anecdote.

Through clippings I have received and telephone calls I learn what I already knew—that is, that you charmed all the regions you visited and everyone liked you so very much and felt that "Gone With the Wind" was in perfect hands.

If I can be of help to you let me know.

John sends you his best. And please remember us both to John Darrow.

P.S. I am enclosing two letters, the first of which is self-explanatory. The second I am sending you with the request that you please route it to the correct department of your organization. I do not know whether or not Selznick International has a "permissions department." Anyway, this woman wants her "recording" returned to her. Naturally, I wrote her that I could not give her a letter of introduction to Mr. Selznick as I had not yet had the pleasure of meeting him.

I am mailing you today "The Story of the Great March" which is written from the Yankee soldier's viewpoint. The pictures, especially the ones of "The Bummer" and of a Yankee squad hunting for buried silver, may interest you.

Mr. Hobart Erwin   *Atlanta, Georgia*
Jones & Erwin, Inc.   *April 14, 1937*
New York, New York

Dear Hobe:

How do you like this one? It's an old house near Nashville. Take off the triangle above the columns, lengthen the first floor windows in the midsection to the porch level, square in the fanlight and perhaps turn one of the wings into a porte-cochere. And the chimneys should be taller.

If the pressure of work lets up next week I am going out on a hunt for other old houses for you. There is one between here and Dalton (about forty miles from Atlanta) that I want to see. I am borrowing a camera and, if I find anything interesting, I'll send you pictures.

Mrs. Clara G. Seay   *Atlanta, Georgia*
Selma Times-Journal   *April 14, 1937*
Selma, Alabama

Dear Mrs. Seay:

Thank you so much for sending me the clipping. Of course, I enjoyed it immensely.

Mr. George Cukor, the director of "Gone With the Wind," was here recently with a part of his technical staff. They stayed in Atlanta several days and then, at my suggestion, toured about the South. They wanted to listen to Southern voices and see old houses and furniture and to gather atmosphere. When he returned from his tour he told me that everyone he had met had been so wonderfully cordial and helpful. "But," he said with a laugh, "they all told me that if I let a single character say 'you all' to one person the late Confederate States would again secede from the Union! So, you can be very certain I will not make this error." He also said that he intended to follow the book completely and not "dress it up" in order to conform with the peculiar notions people out of the South have of Southerners. As I have nothing to do with the production of my novel, I can only sit back like any other movie fan and hope that the real South will come to life in his hands.

Miss Virginia Morris   *Atlanta, Georgia*
United Artists Corporation   *April 21, 1937*
New York, New York

Dear Ginnie:

I am sorry about the delay. I thought I had better write you this air mail special, rather than wire you, because I knew I could not put everything I wanted to say in a wire.

Ginnie, I just can't give you the story and I regret it more than I can say. I'm sorry because it's you I'm refusing and I'm sorry on account of Photoplay. I haven't got a thing against the magazine. I like it and I have read it for years and I know what a high type of publication it is. My reasons run far deeper than anything of that sort, and I hope that I can explain them so that you and the magazine will not think that I am merely being stubborn or unreasonable.

To begin with, it would be practically impossible for me to see you any time within the next six weeks. The dates you asked for are already promised to my publisher, Mr. Latham, who is coming to Atlanta on his annual visit. The exact time of his arrival isn't certain, but I have business as well as personal reasons for wishing to see him, so I am holding that week open. Right after that, we have an engagement with a New York magazine editor who is a good friend of ours. Following that is a tangle of engagements with several good friends who are coming home for visits and with other folks who will have to be seen for business or social reasons, so that I wonder how I will find time to breathe.

The crowded calendar just ahead isn't, of course, a vital reason in itself for refusing the interview; you and the magazine might be willing to wait until a later date. But it may throw some light on my real reasons, if you understand that crowded calendars like that have been my normal life ever since last June, plus an interminable flood of letters that must be answered, plus business matters of all kinds that must be attended to, plus a telephone that never stops ringing. And before last June, I put in several months of day-and-night work, seven days a week, getting my manuscript ready for the printers, checking historical facts, checking typescript, reading proofs, etc.

Ginnie, I'm tired out. I want to get out of the spotlight more earnestly than you or anyone else could possibly believe. And this is the first reason why I don't want any more interviews published if I can possibly get out of it. Every time one of them appears in a magazine, it stirs up a fresh storm of letters, telephone calls, invitations, requests for other interviews. And those are the very things I don't want stirred up these days. Poor John hasn't played golf in nearly a year, because he puts in all his Saturdays and Sundays—and his nights, too—helping me handle the business end of this job, but even with both of us working harder than we ever worked before, we never get caught up. We want to get away from this sort of thing, back to the quiet life we had before, and an interview in a national magazine with a circulation like Photoplay's wouldn't help a bit along that line.

I haven't given anybody an interview since last December when Edwin Granberry interviewed me for Collier's, although I have had numerous "opportunities" to give others. I keep hoping that public interest in me will wane and I have done everything in my power to assist its waning. I am happy to say that things have quieted down somewhat from their worst since the Collier's and Pictorial Review articles were published, but an interview in Photoplay would merely just stir them up again.

In fact, an interview in Photoplay would stir them up worse, I believe, than almost anything that could happen to me. And this is my second important reason for not wishing to be interviewed.

Ginnie, the movie angle of my situation has been responsible for at least 75 per cent of my troubles during the past year, which has been like a madhouse when it should have been the happiest time of my life. In spite of the fact that my contract with Selznick states, just as emphatically as I could make it, that I have nothing to do with the movie production in any way, shape or form, the public continues to act as if I were running the whole show. I refused to look at the script, I refused to go to Hollywood, I have steadily refused to consult or advise about the movie—in fact, I haven't done *anything* with reference to the movie except be polite to the Selznick people when they came to Atlanta.

But, in spite of all that and in spite of the fact that the Georgia newspapers and radio stations broadcast the truth and asked people to leave me alone, the public continues to flock to my door, demanding that I get them or their tap-dancing daughters into the cast, demanding that I make Mr. Selznick do this and not do that, demanding that I announce my selection for Scarlett and Rhett, and on and on and on.

The movie-mad public—and apparently one needs only to mention the word "movie" and half the public goes mad—are the folks who have made my life a hell this past year. I am not using "hell" in any light manner. I really mean it. And, Ginnie, you know as well as I do that your interview in Photoplay would link my name up with the movie more tightly than it ever has been before. It wouldn't matter whether your article was about me and the movies or about me and Einstein's theory. The effect would be the same. It would arouse interest in me personally on the part of thousands of people—Photoplay's habitual readers—who hadn't given much thought to me before, and it would bring down on me a fresh avalanche of letters. Of course, you could say in your article that I have nothing to do with the casting, etc., but the Georgia papers have done that time and again and it doesn't do any good. People just don't read carefully, it seems. They would see my name and my picture there in connection with the movie, and that is all they would need to give them the notion that *I* am the very person to get them in the cast, or jobs as property men, or passes into some movie lot, and they would be down on me like a duck on a June bug.

You may think I am exaggerating, but here is an example of what has happened. A while back, Photoplay carried an article about some of the leading candidates for the various parts.* You wouldn't think such an innocuous article could have troubled me, but it did. Inside of a week after that issue of Photoplay hit the stands, I received several hundred letters of the kind mentioned above, and some of the writers got quite nasty and argumentative when I tried to explain to them that I had no connection with the movie. They had seen my name in Photoplay, so they reckoned they knew more about it than I did.

My final reason is this—if I did give you an interview, I would most certainly not say anything about the movie of "Gone With the Wind," who should play the various parts, how I wanted it produced, etc. And if your article was not about me and the movies, then I don't know what it could be about. Faith Baldwin in Pictorial, Edwin Granberry in Collier's, and several nationally syndicated articles and series of articles in newspapers have already covered the story of "Margaret Mitchell and her record-breaking novel" from beginning to end. Moreover, there have been countless articles in smaller magazines and newspapers. There isn't anything new to be written out of Margaret Mitchell. She wrote a book and it sold a million and a half copies, and that's an old story now.

You may say that there is plenty to be written about my childhood, my girlhood and my married life. Perhaps there is, although I personally, as an ex-newspaperwoman, do not see anything that would make good copy. But the fact remains that I am not going to give any interviews about my childhood, etc. After all, my private life is my own, and I am not an actress who must, because of the very nature of the relationship between her and the public, reveal her private life and intimate thoughts.

I have gone into the situation in such detail because I want you to understand. I haven't been with you during this past year to tell you about this situation and, as I have been working sometimes twenty hours a day, I haven't had the time to write you about it. So, I don't know if I have succeeded in explaining why I cannot give you the interview. I hope especially that I haven't given you the impression that I am unappreciative of my book's success and ungrateful for the public's interest. I am both appreciative and grateful, more than I can say. It's only that the job of being a celebrity—which is the last thing in the world I ever expected

---

* The article, "Gone With the Wind Indeed!" by Kirtley Baskette, appeared in the March 1937 issue of *Photoplay*.

or wanted to be—has brought with it problems and burdens heavier than I am able to carry. So I have been forced to do anything I could to lighten the burden. An article about me in Photoplay would only increase the burden—hence no interview.

My friends who understand my predicament have been trying to help me and they have turned down a large number of offers to write "I knew her when" articles—and that is another factor that would have to be reckoned with if I gave you the interview. Some of them would be certain to be offended if you got an interview and they didn't. So many complications to be thought about!

Ginnie, I would like to see you but when you come to visit us, I want it to be when there is plenty of time and leisure to do you proud and give you some parties and have the time to sit and talk interminably. Anything like that would be impossible now, with life so feverish. But this situation can't last forever, and when things have quieted down, I hope you will come, for pleasure and not for business, and then we will both enjoy it.

Love to you from both of us,

Miss Olla Blaucet Black   *Atlanta, Georgia*
Memphis, Tennessee   *April 22, 1937*

My dear Miss Black:

Thank you so much for your letter and all the nice things you wrote me about "Gone With the Wind." I appreciated them very much. Your letter, with its descriptions of your old home place, was most interesting.

It is with regret that I am returning your two songs to you. I only wish there were some way in which I could assist you in marketing these songs, but I cannot help you.*

I know the rumor is widespread that I am assisting in the production of the film of my novel, but nothing could be further from the truth. I am not connected in any way with the film, for I sold the book outright to the Selznick company. I do not have any more influence with them than any other movie fan. I do not even know whether they are using any songs in the picture. The only suggestion I can make is for you to send the songs to Mr. George Cukor who is to direct "Gone With the Wind." . . .

With many thanks for your good wishes.

---

* Black sent Mitchell two songs she had written. "Blue Dusk" was a "sweet, simple waltz . . . very good to use in some of your ball or entertainment scenes," while "Those Unseen Hands" was a spiritual for "negro choir or plantation singers."

Miss Katharine Brown   *Atlanta, Georgia*
Selznick International Pictures, Inc.   *April 22, 1937*
New York, New York

Dear Katharine:

Thanks so much for your long letter and the details about Mr. Sinclair and the set-up for the actual tests.* Of course, I was very interested. I do hope Alicia Rhett turns out well.† I liked her pictures very much and she has a lovely air about her.

Thank you for offering to send the preliminary tests to Atlanta for us to see. Of course, you can imagine how much we would like to see them, but I do not think you had better ship them. The reason is that, despite all of our efforts to keep it quiet, it would get around because the theatre people and the newspaper people live in each other's pockets. When the news did get around we would have both press and public on our necks asking exactly what we thought about the girls and their possibilities. But thank you for offering to send them.

I thought Mr. Cukor had gone to the Coast and so I wrote him there. I gather from your letter that he is now in New York, so I am shipping in your care two more reference books he requested me to buy, and I would appreciate it if you would forward them to him.

The day before Honey Chile left town she called upon John. He had never had the pleasure of her acquaintance before and was naturally intrigued when she wafted into his office.

I had heard nothing about an article about me for the Ladies' Home Journal. I wonder if this is another one of those rumors that are continually rising up about me? I keep hearing that I have sold manuscripts for several million dollars to various magazines, and I wonder if this is an allied rumor. No one has interviewed me for the Journal, nor has Mr. Stuart Rose, of that publication, intimated anything about it in a letter to me. Next time you write me, please tell me where you heard this news.

I know how busy you are and I appreciate your letters. If you get a chance to let me know how things progress I would love to hear from you, but if I do not hear I will understand.

John sends his best, and so do I.

---

* Robert Sinclair was a stage director hired by Selznick to coordinate casting tests in New York.
† Rhett, discovered by Cukor in Charleston, South Carolina, briefly was considered for the role of Melanie or Carreen but eventually was cast as Ashley's sister, India Wilkes.

Mrs. H.R. McKinnon   *Atlanta, Georgia*
Adel, Georgia   *April 23, 1937*

My dear Mrs. McKinnon:

I wish there were something I could do to assist you in getting your little girl into the cast of "Gone With the Wind." But I have no more to do with this film than any other movie fan. So it would do no good for me to see little Patti-Sue, for I have no influence with the movie people at all and no voice in the matter.

The only suggestion I can offer is that you send a picture of Patti-Sue, preferably a full length one which will show her size, to Mr. George Cukor, of Selznick International Pictures. . . . He is directing "Gone With the Wind" and he is the only one who chooses the actors. . . .

Mr. Telamon Cuyler   *Atlanta, Georgia*
Wayside, Jones County, Georgia   *April 27, 1937*

Dear Mr. Cuyler:

I received the envelope made from Confederate stamps and I appreciate it so very much. I have never seen anything like it before. . . .

I saw the picture of you and Mr. Cukor in the Atlanta Georgian, and I am forwarding it to Mr. Cukor. Your face and carriage fit the Confederate coat so well, and I only wish that you were going to play in the picture! Why don't you write and tell Mr. Cukor you'd like to play the part of Ashley Wilkes's father? No one could possibly do it in so distinguished a manner.

You never did write me about where Rhett went that night. So, hurry up and do it because, naturally, I am eaten with a very unladylike curiosity.*

With best regards and many thanks for your courtesies,

---

* In a letter on April 13, Cuyler wrote to Mitchell, "How merrily you will laugh over my tale of where 'Rhett' went that last night." A nearly sixty-page handwritten story titled "Rhett's Journey," dated December 5, 1938, is in the Telamon Cuyler Papers at the Hargrett Rare Book and Manuscript Library. Whether Mitchell read the piece and returned the pages to him is unclear from their correspondence. As late as April 1946, Cuyler told the author, "I so want to finish that 'Rhett's Journey' wherein I found in the book, the material to show where he went that last night."

Mrs. Duncan McDonald   *Atlanta, Georgia*
Miami, Florida   *April 29, 1937*

Dearest Irene:

I was so glad to have your letter and think you were awfully sweet to write such a long one when you are so busy. . . .

Irene, there isn't a thing I can do about Clark Gable taking the part of Rhett. It isn't stubbornness on my part entirely which keeps me from mixing up in the movie. The truth is that authors never have anything to do with the casting of their books. I have no voice in the matter and no influence whatever. However, my information is that Clark Gable will not be in the picture because the company that owns him will not turn him loose. Mr. Cukor and his staff were here a couple of weeks ago giving auditions and you can imagine the excitement in Atlanta. I was practically homeless during their stay because every movie-struck individual in the Southeast was determined that I could get them into the movie and they nearly deviled the life out of me and refused to believe that I had no influence at all. . . .

Mr. John Darrow   *Atlanta, Georgia*
Selznick International Pictures, Inc.   *April 30, 1937*
New York, New York

Dear John:

Think nothing of the clippings from the Columbia, South Carolina, paper. I know how those things happen. I ought to as they have been happening to me for nearly a year. Even when the reporter has the best intentions in the world, he will sometimes make things sound very differently from the way they were intended.*

I have followed your progress through the South (by clippings) with great interest, and I do hope you found some wonderful prospects.

Personally, I think a man who looks like you should not be permitted to go about our Southland for you are a positive menace. Scores of young ladies have called upon me to ask whether or not you were married and several young girls told me that when they went to you for auditions they swooned when you looked at them. I know you didn't realize you were cutting such a swathe, but the young ladies said they didn't mind being turned down for parts when it was you who did the turning down.

---

* While interviewing students at the University of South Carolina for possible roles in *Gone With the Wind*, Darrow was quoted in the local newspaper as calling Mitchell "an intelligent woman who will always get what is coming to her . . . and very charming!"

For your interest I am enclosing a couple of pictures of Colonel Cuyler and Mr. Cukor. Colonel Cuyler is a most striking looking old gentleman, isn't he? You needn't return the pictures.

John and I were sorry too that we did not get to see more of you while you were in Atlanta, but you were busier than a bird dog. I do hope you get back this way someday and have a little leisure, for I know we would enjoy you so very much. I appreciated your letter because I know how busy you must be. As you know, I am as interested as any other movie fan in how the picture progresses and anytime you have the opportunity to drop me a line I would appreciate it. Please remember if there is anything I can do in any way to assist you I want you to call on me.

Mr. George Cukor   *Atlanta, Georgia*
Selznick International Pictures, Inc.   *May 5, 1937*
New York, New York

Dear George:

Thank you so much for your telegram of congratulations.* I know what a busy person you are these days, so I appreciate your thoughts all the more.

I had intended writing to you last week but, of course, the tempo of life has quickened incredibly and I did not have the time. You have probably noticed news items about the suit of plagiarism brought against "Gone With the Wind."† It is all foolishness, but still, as you can realize, it will be troublesome, annoying and expensive. While I do not know yet upon what the old lady is basing her claim, I feel that I will probably have to produce all my references from "Gone With the Wind" to defend my book against her claims. That is why I am asking you to return the four books I lent you. I am not referring to the books I ordered for you and have sent you from time to time, but the following four which were my own:

---

* After Mitchell won the Pulitzer Prize for fiction, Cukor wired, "I ALWAYS KNEW YOU HAD IT IN YOU."

† Susan Lawrence Davis, author of a 1924 book, *Authentic History of the Ku Klux Klan, 1865–1877*, sued Mitchell in April 1937 for plagiarism. The elderly Alabama woman claimed that *Gone With the Wind* copied from her book such historical figures and organizations as General John B. Gordon and the Freedman's Bureau and that both volumes were bound in Confederate gray. The suit was dismissed in July. Davis died in April 1939, but her family refused to give up. When the movie *Gone With the Wind* opened in Birmingham, Alabama, in early 1940, Davis's sister and executor of her estate unsuccessfully sought an injunction to halt the screenings and damages of $5,000, claiming the producer had used her sister's copyrighted material in his film without authorization.

"Social Life in New Orleans" by Eliza Ripley
"Hospital Life" by Kate Cummings
"Four Years in Rebel Capitals" by DeLeon
"Memories" by Fannie Beers

I hope that you have already skimmed what little cream there may be in these books and that returning them will not inconvenience you. By the way, my bookseller phoned today that they had located another book for you and I am having it mailed on.

I follow your progress with great interest through my clipping bureau, and of course I am waiting with as much eagerness as any other movie fan the results of your auditions. While the volume of requests to me personally have declined enormously since you made your radio address here, I still get a few letters and refer the people on to you. Several pictures sent to me seemed to have possibilities as the young ladies not only were pretty but appeared to have intelligence.

Thanks again for your wire. John sends his best and so do I.

Mrs. B.L. Moore
Columbia, South Carolina

Atlanta, Georgia
May 5, 1937

My dear Mrs. Moore:

First, let me tell you my position in the matter of the film of my novel, "Gone With the Wind." I have no connection with this film in any way as I am not employed by the Selznick company even in an advisory capacity. It is true that when the moving picture people were here in Atlanta I saw them, but it was purely a social affair. I have nothing to do with the writing, costuming or casting of the picture, and have no influence with the producers. So I cannot help you in getting into the cast.

But let me make this suggestion: I know that Mr. George Cukor, who is directing the picture, is moving heaven and earth to get new talent. He came through the South several weeks ago giving screen tests. Last night I read in a New York paper that he was still giving auditions. Write him directly and set forth your qualifications for playing the part of Melanie—that is, if you have had any experience whatsoever in amateur dramatics, little theatre groups et cetera. I do not think such experience will weigh particularly with him, but if you have had any experience you might as well tell him about it. Send him these snapshots which you have sent me. I think it might help if you sent him two closeup pictures of the studio type, one profile, one full face, and without a hat. If you do not mind a personal remark, I liked your face so very much because it was not only a good-looking face but one with sweetness and strength of character. I hope Mr. Cukor agrees with me. . . .

Thank you for the nice things you wrote me about "Gone With the Wind." I am so glad that Melanie appealed to you because I liked her too. I am returning your poems to you and I thank you for letting me see them. I should confess here and now that I cannot write poetry myself. I am one of those bromidic people who "know nothing about poetry but do know what I like," and I do like your poems. I hope you have luck in selling them in the future.

Your little boy is the handsomest child I have ever seen. How proud you must be of him.

With all good wishes,

Mr. John Embrey Horan   *Atlanta, Georgia*
Dalton, Georgia   *May 7, 1937*

My dear Mr. Horan:

I have delayed unpardonably long in answering your letters and I hope you will forgive me. My generally quiet life has speeded up enormously in the last two weeks and I have not been able to read my mail, much less answer it.

I think the little dolls are as attractive as can be.

What I am going to write you about the commercial manufacture and sale of these dolls will be disappointing and perhaps confusing to you. But I myself am still a little confused about my right to give permission for the manufacture of any dolls named for the characters of "Gone With the Wind." For several weeks past I have been endeavoring, through my lawyer, to establish just what my rights in matters such as this are. At present this clause in my contract with the Selznick International Pictures, Inc., who own the film rights of "Gone With the Wind," is being clarified. Just as soon as I know how far my rights run I will communicate with you. I am very sorry to delay you in the manufacture and sale of your attractive dolls, but I can do no more than tell you the truth about the matter. . . .

Mr. George Cukor   *Atlanta, Georgia*
Selznick International Pictures, Inc.   *May 12, 1937*
New York, New York

Dear George:

The Mary Chess perfumes arrived and I must again congratulate you on your knowledge of scents, and I must thank you for sending it. While

I like all of these, I think the mimosa is the most delightful. I had tried someone's brand of mimosa many years ago, but it was heavy enough to be used as an anesthetic for a major operation. This brand is so sweet and faint and the loveliest part about it is that it reminds me of old mimosa groves far back in the country on a still, hot day with the bees demented in the blossoms. You were grand to think about me and I appreciate it.

As luck would have it, I did not get to see Miss Bankhead's performance.* Of course, I was eager to go, but the show opened the night after the Pulitzer Award arrived. The Vice President of The Macmillan Company was in town and he gave me a party that night. I hoped to see her the following night, but the house was so filled with friends and excitement that I could not go to the theatre. I was very disappointed for everyone was charmed with her. So few people here have liked her in her films, and I am afraid many of them went to see her play determined not to like it. But everyone was most enthusiastic about her and the phone rang all day long as people told me how charming she was.

Mr. David O. Selznick   Atlanta, Georgia
Selznick International Pictures, Inc.   May 13, 1937
New York, New York

My dear Mr. Selznick:

Thank you so much for your letter of congratulations about the Pulitzer prize.† I appreciate your thoughtfulness very much.

Mr. Lester Martin   Atlanta, Georgia
The Loom-Tex Corporation   May 13, 1937
New York, New York

Dear Mr. Martin:

I have received your letter requesting my permission for The Loom-Tex Corporation to use the name "Scarlett O'Hara" in connection with one of the garments you manufacture. I am very sorry that at present I can neither give nor withhold my permission in this matter. At this time my attorney is in correspondence with the attorneys of the Selznick International Pictures corporation who own the moving picture rights to "Gone With the

---

* Bankhead was touring the country in *Reflected Glory*, a comedy by George Kelly. Atlanta was the play's final stop.

† On May 10, Selznick wrote, "Please permit me to extend my heartiest congratulations on your winning the Pulitzer Prize."

Wind." They are clarifying the clause in my contract which has to do with just such matters as you wrote me about. I will communicate with you as soon as this is settled.

Thank you for your letter and the interest expressed therein.

Mrs. Myrtle B. Hodgkins   *Atlanta, Georgia*
Pooler, Georgia   *May 26, 1937*

My dear Mrs. Hodgkins:

I am very sorry that I must refuse to send a letter of yours to Mr. Cukor. As I think I wrote you before, my agreement with the moving picture people was that I would have nothing to do with the film, and would not hold any correspondence with them on the subject. I have had to refuse to forward so many letters from people who wished to get into the cast that I do not feel it would be right to make an exception. Moreover, it will be of little value because I have no influence with the producers. I am very sorry.

Mr. Sidney Howard   *Atlanta, Georgia*
Tyringham, Massachusetts   *June 9, 1937*

Dear Mr. Howard:

When Mr. Cukor talked to me over long distance from New York about your proposed trip to Atlanta I was sorely tempted to tell him that I would do anything he wanted if only you and your wife would come to see us! Because, seriously, my husband and I look forward to meeting you. I hope you will understand me—what stiffened my spine was a hunch that you personally were not very anxious to make a wild, flying one-day trip to Atlanta for no particular reason. I thought that when you decided to come to Atlanta you would like to come in peace and at leisure. I hope I read your mind correctly. I kept trying to discover exactly why they wanted you to come, but I did not learn the reason and I was somewhat puzzled. Your letter clears up that puzzle.*

I know so little about the movies that I thought the script was already finished. If it wasn't finished what was that thick pile of manuscript that lay on George Cukor's desk during his visit to Atlanta? By heroic self-control I did not look at it. I knew if I did I could not honestly tell newspaper reporters and friends that I had no idea what the script was like. I wanted to be in the position of complete ignorance when asked whether

---

* Howard told Mitchell that "none of those connected with the picture has yet got down to brass tacks," so they wanted him to visit the author "to give themselves the illusion of action."

my ending had been retained and what characters and episodes had been omitted. I am not an extraordinarily good liar, and I knew if I looked at the script I could never say with any plausibility that I didn't know anything about it. Of course, I was terribly interested, and I hope to have the opportunity in the not too far distant future of discussing it with you.

I gather from your letter that you have no more idea than I when the production will start.

I hope you will understand when I say that I felt very comforted when I heard that you had had two plagiarism suits.* Being new to this writing profession, I had an uncomfortable feeling as though I contracted the itch—innocently enough, but still embarrassing—and that no really nice person had the itch, no matter how innocently acquired. I was glad to learn other writers were similarly afflicted. I do not anticipate any difficulty in the winning of this suit and I doubt if it will ever come to trial, for I imagine any judge would throw it out of court. The suit is based, among other things, on the fact that my book was bound in Confederate gray and so was Miss Davis's book. And it seems that the lady has a copyright on every Southern general from Lee on down, for, among her other accusations, are some stating that I mentioned General Gordon and General Wade Hampton and she did too. However, the suit will be a bother to me and an expense too. It seems a pity that people cannot be forced to post bond for court costs and attorneys' fees before they file a plagiarism suit.

I was glad to learn that you do intend to come to Atlanta sometime, but do not think you can buy us a dinner. It is going to be our dinner or nobody's. So get ready for it.

Mr. John Embrey Horan   Atlanta, Georgia
Dalton, Georgia   June 10, 1937

Dear Mr. Horan:

Yes, I know about the Chattanooga woman who is making dolls.† She is not the only one. Since a month after my book was published people have been doing this. They are doing it at their own risk, and are in danger of being sued not only by the Selznick company but by the novelty manufacturers to whom the Selznick company has given the exclusive rights of manufacturing such articles.

---

* The playwright was accused of plagiarism on two of his best-known works—*They Knew What They Wanted* (1924) and *The Silver Cord* (1926)—but was cleared in both cases.

† The June 7 issue of the *Chattanooga News* featured an article about Mrs. Lee Battle, who was making "Mammy Lou" dolls based on the character of Mammy.

I know that you are impatient about my delay in answering you, but the delay rises from the fact that legal matters proceed with maddening slowness, especially when they are conducted by mail. We are waiting for a reply from New York now.

Mr. John Darrow   *Atlanta, Georgia*
Selznick International Pictures, Inc.   *June 17, 1937*
New York, New York

Dear John:

Your letter was a pleasure and I was so glad to hear news of the picture. I had wondered what effect the Actors' Guild strike would have and I thought it was one of the reasons for the delay.* I am looking forward to the fate of the Southern belles you wrote about and I sincerely hope some of them will justify your trouble. . . .

Thank you so much for your offer to do things for me in New York. It was sweet of you to think of this but there is nothing I need now. Just drop me a line whenever anything interesting turns up about the picture, for I would love to hear it.

John sends you his best and so do I.

P.S. I saw in the paper that Betty Timmons had married a New Yorker last week, so, I suppose your troubles from that source are over.†

Mr. Harold Latham   *Atlanta, Georgia*
The Macmillan Company   *June 18, 1937*
New York, New York

Dear Harold:

This is just a note to acknowledge your letter of June 15th about the sale of the serial rights. Thank you for this letter and the information in it.‡

You wrote that the sale would depend in part upon the date of the motion picture release. Confidentially and for your information, I have heard that the picture will not go into production until February 1938. This delay is due to the recent Actors' Guild strike, to casting difficulties and

---

* Darrow told the author that because the studios had to rewrite their standard contracts in a settlement with the new Actors' Guild, testing for more than a dozen young women from the South for possible roles in the film had been delayed.

† Timmons married Harold Wilkinson Hixon Jr. on June 7. The announcement made no mention of Mitchell or the new bride's previous ambitions to play Scarlett.

‡ Serial rights involve the reprinting of books and plays in serialized, or chapter, form in newspapers and magazines.

to the indecision of the Selznick outfit about technicolor. Of course, they may change their minds and start production tomorrow, but the foregoing is my latest information.

Lois and Allan were here for a too brief visit and we enjoyed their stay very much.

Miss Virginia Morris   *Atlanta, Georgia*
United Artists Corporation   *June 21, 1937*
New York, New York

Dear Ginnie:

Thank you very much for the suggestions in your letter of June 2nd. I would have written you sooner except that the matter of exploitations of the title and characters of the book is in somewhat of a tangle, and I thought that by waiting a while I might be able to have some more definite information about the situation. That hasn't happened yet, but I didn't want to delay any further in answering your letter.

Briefly, the situation is that when I sold the movie rights to Selznick I also sold them the right to make commercial tie-ups. So, they will get whatever profits are to be made out of commercial articles that tie up with their movie. They are also claiming the right to use the title and names of the characters for exploitations that do not tie up directly with the movie. My understanding of the contract was that I did not grant them this latter right. But there is some vague and confusing language in this section of the contract, and we are now in correspondence with the Selznick lawyers, trying to get the situation clarified. . . .

Miss Katharine Brown   *Atlanta, Georgia*
Selznick International Pictures, Inc.   *July 3, 1937*
New York, New York

Perhaps you can settle this question for me. However, if it takes any trouble, don't bother about it because I'm only asking for sheer curiosity.

I have had a number of clippings about a Mrs. Elizabeth Hearst, of Hollywood, "the only Southern technical advisor in motion picture work." She is evidently visiting about the South while on her vacation and she speaks in these interviews about having an appointment with me and, also, about acting as technical adviser for "Gone With the Wind." I am beginning to get inquiries about her connection with the film. These inquiries I always answer truthfully, that I know nothing at all about the production and all such questions should be referred to Mr. Russell Birdwell. However, I'd like to know personally if she is technical adviser, for she intends to visit here in Atlanta where she has relatives and, for all I know, the newspapers may come after me for some sort of statement about her.

The reason why I'm asking questions on this not-so-important matter is that back in May I had a brisk workout from a young woman who represented herself as being from the script department of Selznick's in Hollywood. She alleged to be doing research work here. She nearly ran us all crazy and deviled John, me, my secretary, my friends on The Journal, and friends at the radio station to death. I never did give her an interview, although she pushed her way into our apartment, telephoned a thousand times and ambushed me at the radio station.* We had our suspicions about her connection with your outfit, and a letter from Mr. O'Shea in Culver City told us our suspicions were correct.† I have decided that hereafter I would not see anyone purporting to be from your organization, unless they were heralded by introduction from you or the West Coast office.

The foregoing would lead you to think that I believe this Mrs. Hearst an equally illbred imposter, and I hasten to tell you that I do not think this at all. Some time ago she wrote me an exceptionally nice letter, asking to call while she was here in Atlanta. I could not give her the engagement, as July is always my busiest month as everyone in the world comes to visit me. She did not state in her letter that she was technical adviser for "Gone With the Wind" or else I would have tried to work in an engagement at 4 a.m. or some other time when my guests are gone to bed. So, can you please let me know if she is acting in this capacity? You know I want to be of all possible help to any of your people who are here in Atlanta in the interest of the film.

The choice of Walter Connolly met with universal approval throughout this section. He has always been very popular down here.‡

---

* The young woman was a would-be actress from Columbus, Georgia, named Thelma Wunder. According to an article in the *Atlanta Constitution* on October 1, 1937, Wunder went to Hollywood to test for the role of Honey Wilkes in *Gone With the Wind*. (The character of Honey, Ashley's youngest sister, was not included in the motion picture.)

† Daniel T. O'Shea was secretary of Selznick International Pictures.

‡ An article in the July 4, 1937, issue of the *Atlanta Journal* announced that Connolly was the first actor "definitely selected" to play a role in *Gone With the Wind*—that of Scarlett's father, Gerald O'Hara. Connolly, who also portrayed a plantation owner in the 1935 motion picture *So Red the Rose*, was the readers' choice for Gerald in an April casting poll conducted by the *Journal*.

My brother Stephens will be in New York sometime in the next week and hopes to see you.

Mrs. W.F. Bryan   *Atlanta, Georgia*
Allendale, South Carolina   *July 26, 1937*

Dear Mrs. Bryan:

Thank you for your letter and the picture of your lovely house. I appreciated the interest which prompted you to write to me.

The name of the company which will produce "Gone With the Wind" is Selznick International Pictures, Inc. . . . As I have no connection with the filming of my novel, I suggest you write to them about your house. I should tell you, however, that I have learned through newspaper reports that they intend to produce the picture entirely in Hollywood and will film no scenes in the South.

Lizzie McDuffie   *Atlanta, Georgia*
Atlanta, Georgia   *July 30, 1937*

My dear Lizzie McDuffie:

I was very glad to learn your address from the story about you in this morning's paper for I have been wanting to get in touch with you since you phoned me several days ago.* Of course, I want to see you and hear about your moving picture experiences. Would it be possible for you to come to see me this afternoon between four and five o'clock? I expect to go to the country for a little vacation tomorrow and may not return before you leave Atlanta.

Will you call my home when you receive this letter and tell my maid, Bessie Berry, whether or not you will be able to come this afternoon? I will be at my office but she will bring me your message. My new phone number is Hemlock 2733. I live in a cream colored brick apartment house on the corner of Seventeenth Street and West Peachtree Street and the apartment number is 9. The address is The Russell Apartments, 4 East 17th St. N.E.

My good friend Elinor Hillyer wrote me that you had been her nurse so perhaps you and I met when I was a little girl.

---

* McDuffie, born in Covington, Georgia, and raised in Atlanta, was a personal maid to First Lady Eleanor Roosevelt. In April 1937, Roosevelt wrote to Kay Brown and encouraged the studio to audition McDuffie for the role of Mammy, noting that she "was brought up where the scene is laid" and "has a great deal of histrionic ability."

Miss Katharine Brown   *Atlanta, Georgia*
Selznick International Pictures, Inc.   *August 13, 1937*
New York, New York

Dear Katharine:

Thanks for the letter with its budget of news. I'm sorry if the letter about Mrs. Hearst put you all to any trouble. I did not mean to imply in my letter about her that she had personally claimed to me that she was "technical advisor," but the clippings my bureau sent me which arrived prior to her Atlanta visit claimed this position for her. As I wrote at that time, I was rather busy, and I did not see her. That was about the time the plagiarism suit was waxing hot and we were a bit rushed.

While I was never worried about the final outcome of that suit, it did take a lot of time, for I knew if it went to trial (instead of a hearing before a judge) I would be called upon to prove that my historical references came from documents which antedated the publication of Miss Davis's book in 1924. As you know, I had at least seven million historical references. Wanting to be prepared if we did go to trial, I had routed out a number of references and had them copied and indexed. I suppose this isn't lost labor, for Miss Davis still has time to appeal the case.

Things are ever so much nicer now and life is practically normal. Only occasionally am I ambushed by someone wanting to be Scarlett, although a few letters on the subject still dribble in and I refer them to John Darrow. I am devoting this quiet interlude trying to make the hair at my neckline grow an inch and a half. It has reached the nasty stage and refuses to grow any more. It gives me a ratty appearance and leads strangers to say that I am one of those eccentric authors who have no pride in personal appearance.

Your item about the possible Prissy whetted my interest. I have been especially interested in who would play this little varmint, possibly because this is the only part I myself would like to play. For this reason whoever plays Prissy will be up against a dreadful handicap as far as I am concerned, for I will watch their actions with a jealous eye.*

Lizzie McDuffie, Mrs. Roosevelt's maid, who tried for the part of Mammy was the nurse of one of my good friends, Elinor Hillyer, formerly on the staff of the Delineator and now with Altman's. Elinor told Lizzie to phone me when she came to Atlanta recently, and Lizzie did and I had a most pleasant and interesting visit with her. She is a woman of great

---

* The part of the twelve-year-old slave girl Prissy was played by twenty-eight-year-old Butterfly McQueen.

dignity and intelligence and it was a relief to sit and talk with someone who didn't ask me if it was hard to write a book. She was very reticent about her experience in your studio, but said with great enthusiasm how nice you had all been to her.

Your information about the Richmond girl who did not want a long contract was most interesting.* I can't help but wondering what her reasons are, probably she is engaged and intends to get married soon. It seems a pity if she really is a good prospect.

I enjoyed the article about you in the August 1st New York Mirror but, being an ex-feature writer, I wanted to add to this story. To tell the truth, ever since I laid eyes on you my old newspaper blood has been surging again through my veins. You are, as you probably know, the world's best copy. The trouble about writing a story about you would be that there is of a necessity a great deal of material that would have to be omitted. That sounds as though I were accusing you of having a lurid past, but I hasten to correct that impression. As I have sized you up, you are the best "public relations" woman I have ever seen and about the smartest. But three-quarters of the value of a public relations expert lies in the fact that no one knows they are a public relations expert. So, in any story written about you that would have to be omitted. The nice part is that you do "look like a debutante" and not like someone who keeps this, that and the other warring element and temperamental personality smoothed down. . . .

Steve was sorry he missed you. He had brought his wife and oldest little boy to New York for a vacation after his work was finished and the child saw everything except the Aquarium. He even went to some literary cocktail parties and was gorged on so many hors d'oeuvres that he gained four pounds. Carrie Lou was outdone because he insisted on saying "ain't" on every possible occasion at these literary teas.†

Of course, we want to hear all the news you care to send us about the picture. And be assured if any of it is confidential no one else will ever hear about it.

---

* Brown had mentioned a "charming girl" from Richmond, Virginia, who hoped to play the role of Scarlett. The woman, Em Bowles Locker, was given a screen test on February 15, 1938, in New York.

† Carrie Lou Reynolds was Stephens Mitchell's wife. Their oldest son, Eugene Mitchell, was named after his grandfather.

Mr. Hobart Erwin   *Atlanta, Georgia*
Jones & Erwin, Inc.   *August 18, 1937*
New York, New York

Dear Hobe:

A friend of mine in Charlotte, North Carolina, sent me the enclosed cards. I thought the sketches most interesting, especially the one labeled "An Old Camden Mansion," and I am sending them on to you in hopes that you will find them interesting too. These scenes are typical of South Carolina and not of Georgia, although the one labeled "A South Carolina Cabin" is typical of all rural Southern Negro cabins.

Kay Brown wrote me that your article would be in the September Harper's Bazaar and, of course, we are looking forward to it with great interest.

We had all hoped that you would be back in Atlanta long ere this for a quieter visit than your last one was. But after hearing in roundabout ways that the picture had been postponed until next spring we decided that your trip would be postponed too. Or do you intend to come back to Atlanta? John and I and Wilbur Kurtz and Sue Myrick would love to see you should you come. We really mean that, so do not get any foolish idea that you would be taking up our time or imposing on us. We all like you and it would be a pleasure to drive you around the countryside.

Mr. Joe Beamish   *Atlanta, Georgia*
The Post-Standard   *August 27, 1937*
Syracuse, New York

Dear Mr. Beamish:

Thank you for sending me your column from the Post-Standard.* As you guessed it would, it certainly gave me a laugh. I know that you wrote this article about casting "Gone With the Wind" as an amusing article. But I do not believe you know how true it is. I have heard hotter arguments about who shall play Scarlett than I ever heard about the Supreme Court, and some of the most remarkable people are advanced as candidates. During

---

* In his "Matches and Jo" column of April 18, Beamish imagined a discussion between friends about who should play various characters in *Gone With the Wind*, and Mae West as Belle Watling was the only clear winner. "We decided Mae had won the game—in every way, shape and manner. (Especially shape)," he wrote.

these arguments I sit timid and silent because I seem to be the only person in the United States without a violent opinion on this matter. I have nothing to do with the production of the film in any way and I do not intend to go to Hollywood, and I am content to let the movie people make their own decisions. But this does not keep my friends, when in the heat of argument, from calling upon me to back up their particular actress.

Mr. Hobart Erwin   *Atlanta, Georgia*
Jones & Erwin, Inc.   *September 17, 1937*
New York, New York

Dear Hobe:

As I have just returned from a vacation which did not include mail, I just received your letter of September 2nd. I was so glad to have the latest news from you and I thank you for it.

The wallpaper business sounds elegant and you certainly have all of my good wishes for its success. In the matter of the wallpaper in the houses in "Gone With the Wind," I probably cannot be very helpful. You doubtless gathered when you were in Atlanta that I was appallingly ignorant about periods of decoration and the terminology of your trade, but I will do my best and try to make clear to you how I saw the walls of these houses. There was no wallpaper at all in Tara. I have seldom seen wallpaper in old Georgia houses of this section. The walls generally are plastered over the laths and then a smooth coat of white plaster goes on. I think this is called "sizing" but I am not sure. When these walls became soiled they were smoothly white-washed. There were seldom any pictures upon them, and I believe it was these long stretches of bare white walls which gave the lovely coolness in summer and the hellish cold in winter. I believe this was also the reason why the rooms in these old houses always seemed enormous and bare in spite of the massive furniture in them. If you saw the bedrooms at "Westover" at Milledgeville you may recall that, in spite of two towering wardrobes, two enormous four-poster beds, a chest and an assortment of chairs, the rooms still seemed scantily furnished. So, Tara, as I saw it, had no wallpaper but white walls. I cannot tell you clearly about the wallpaper at Twelve Oaks, except that there was none of that type of pictorial paper (by that I mean the lower half of the wall a solid paper and the upper half a scene of hunting or some historical scene). I only know the paper was formal, correct, in good taste, a little faded and utterly colorless.

I can tell you of three wallpapers in Scarlett's Victorian house which she built in Atlanta. All of the downstairs (with the exception of the dining room), including the hall by the stairs, was done in a tasty, solid, dried blood, red color. The paper was not a slick type of paper, nor was it rough like the modern kind which, I believe, is called "oatmeal." It was soft and porous, something like blotting paper. The dining room was of a teeth-on-edge purple in which blue predominated and the figure was a gold fleur de lis about the size of a cabbage. These fleur de lis were scattered with a prodigal hand. The fleur de lis were done in solid gold and outlined all around their border with tiny gold dots, as I shall indicate below.

Scarlett's bedroom walls were a riot of roses of various sizes with watermelon pink predominating. All of the roses were opulent and slightly overblown. I know about these papers because since receiving your letter I have gone through some of the earlier drafts of the book and found the above descriptions, which I eliminated in the last draft when I realized how long the book was.

About Aunt Pitty's house, I can tell you nothing of the wallpaper in Scarlett's bedroom. That in Melanie's room was a little faded, sweet, austere. I suppose that means that there were small, formal bunches of flowers not too close together. Aunt Pitty's hall and stairway were dark and ill lighted and had some dull tannish brown paper. The living room walls were fussy and cluttered and yet not in bad taste as were those in Scarlett's house. There was an accent of black in the wallpaper but I can't tell you exactly where—perhaps in the swag wreaths near the ceiling, perhaps narrow twisting lines of black going in and out of the main small floral design. I am not very helpful, am I? I can see the things and know the feeling they gave the beholder, but I cannot get down to actual designs very well.

You were so nice to offer John and me your extra bedroom and we do thank you. It sounds like a sanctuary and we would both love it, but I am afraid we will not be able to take you up on it on the occasion of our first visit North. This visit will not be a pleasant one, as I will be forced to see about four million people at all hours of the day and night. I intend to get these interviews over with for good and all on my first visit and then return to New York later in the hopes of having some fun. So we have decided when—and if—we go to New York to stay at a hotel. However, for your own information, I believe it will be a very long time before either of us goes North. As I told you when you were here, I do not want to stir out of Atlanta till I am off the best seller list.

I, too, had heard that the shooting had been postponed till February, though I never learned why. I will look forward to your visit to Atlanta, and your remarks about the numbers of underscorings on which you will consult me make me pale! I have not read my own book since the last galleys left my hands in the spring of 1936 and I have mercifully forgotten most of it. Give me warning before you come so that I can re-read it!

I hope to see Sue soon and will convey your regards to her personally.

John and I send our best, and want you to call on us in any way if we can be of assistance to you.

P.S. I neglected to send this off to you, so will add a postscript. In re-reading your letter I notice you asked me to send you any old wallpaper I might come across for documents, and that you would "do the regular" by me in the matter. I would not know where to turn in the matter of old wallpaper. Due to hard work in the last three years, I have lost touch completely with people who are interested in such things. I wish I could be helpful about this but I can't. You were nice to offer us paper for a room, but I do not feel I deserve it as I have not been of any assistance. Please disregard what I have said about the walls when you make your designs. I know you want the sets to be lovely and to picture well, and I am sure whatever you decide to put on the various walls of "Gone With the Wind" will be all right with me.

If the following request will be troublesome to you in any way, please disregard it. Do you remember when you were in Atlanta that you had some sketches of costumes and scenes of "Gone With the Wind" done by a young New York woman? One of them showed Scarlett sitting on Aunt Pittypat's front porch, leaning against the pillar. I liked it very much and I have remembered it in every vivid detail since then, and I should like to have it to frame for my living room. If the young lady has not disposed of it and does not want a couple of million dollars for it, I would like to buy it. Could you ask her, please, to write me and tell me if she is willing to let me have it and what the price would be?

Mr. Sidney Howard   *Atlanta, Georgia*
New York, New York   *October 8, 1937*

My dear Mr. Howard:

As you and I are inextricably entwined like Siamese twins in the newspapers, I am able to keep up with you through my clipping service. Recently my heartfelt sympathy went out to you when I learned that the entire Selznick organization had descended on you at the same time you were rehearsing your new play.

Offhand I cannot answer your questions for this reason. The decorators are running mad in my apartment and I cannot get my hands on any notes or books, as everything is piled helter-skelter under tarpaulins. However, this afternoon I will go to our reference library and see what I can dig up for you. I have a vague memory of a half-page newspaper advertisement in an 1864 paper about the arrival of new blockade goods. If I can find it I will get a photostat for you.

Some of the things I am going to say now may upset your plans. For instance, you wrote of "cast iron balconies." If ever there was a cast iron balcony in pre-War Atlanta I never heard of it or saw a picture of one. That type of architectural decoration was not peculiar to this up-state section. It is found two hundred miles away in the coast section around Savannah and, of course, reached the height of its beauty in New Orleans. Moreover, most of the iron in Atlanta had been donated for munition purposes long before Gettysburg because the pinch of the blockade was felt before the summer of 1863.

About the depots for feeding and clothing refugees from Tennessee— if there were such depots I never heard of them. But this afternoon I will query not only the library but my elderly friends who would recall them if they existed. This was the way the refugee problem was generally handled. Practically everybody in the South was vaguely kin to everybody else and if they weren't kin they had friends in other states. The idea of anything like organized charity would have been abhorrent to refugees. Generally the refugees arrived in a strange town and were taken into the houses of relatives, friends or kind-hearted strangers. I recall that one of my relatives, when refugeeing to Macon, was taken into the house of a stranger and this stranger already had under her roof twenty other refugees who slept on pallets in the halls and in the linen closets. The various churches had circles for the relief of refugees. It is my impression that the ladies took the garments they had made and the food they had collected and went about in little groups calling on the refugees and giving where gifts were needed. However, I may be wrong and I will check this point, and also look in the newspapers for names of ladies' auxiliaries and church organizations, as you requested.

And about Doctor Meade blowing up the blockade runners—would it be possible for him not to blow up the whole tribe of blockaders? If he damns them all there will be a wild howl of rage from the South, for many of the blockaders were honest patriots who obeyed the government rules and came out of the War poor as church mice.

I'll write you more as soon as I can dig it up.

Mrs. Erma Fisk Austin   *Atlanta, Georgia*
Hollywood, California   *October 9, 1937*

My dear Mrs. Austin:

Thank you so much for your letter and the interest in "Gone With the Wind" which prompted you to write it. I appreciate the many fine compliments you paid my book and I am happy that the characters seem so real to you.

I am very sorry that I cannot send you an autographed copy of "Gone With the Wind." I have not autographed a copy in nearly a year, not even for relatives and close friends. Last year the volume of requests for autographs exceeded the number of copies sold and the situation in regard to autographs became an impossible one. So, I was forced to establish this rule.

While I appreciate very much the compliment you have paid me in wanting to make a model of me from a photograph for exhibition purposes, I will have to refuse. I do not see how it would be possible to make a lifelike model from a photograph, especially as none of my photographs resemble me in the slightest. And I would rather not have a model that did not look like me. The photographs you mentioned have not yet arrived, but I shall look forward to them with great interest.*

I hope you will understand when I say that I cannot at present give permission for the dolls you made to be named after characters in "Gone With the Wind." There are legal complications in my contracts which make it uncertain as to how far my rights extend in such matters. My attorneys are now investigating this situation and I hope it will be clarified in the near future. As soon as these matters are arranged I will communicate with you.

Mr. Sidney Howard   *Atlanta, Georgia*
New York, New York   *October 11, 1937*

Dear Mr. Howard:

As the paper hangers still obstinately refuse to remove furniture from in front of the door to the closet in which my reference books and notes are stored, I still cannot cite you "page and line." However, I will add some more information (from memory) to that which I sent you Saturday.

I telephoned all the old people of my acquaintance yesterday and not a one of them recalled a single iron balcony in Atlanta during the War period. Nor did any of them recall any signs on churches calling for iron

---

* Austin sent Mitchell photographs of the dolls—"ten of your children"—she had created of various characters from *Gone With the Wind*.

or, for that matter, calling for anything. The churches did not ever have such signs upon them. Any appeals of this type would have appeared in the Atlanta papers. I doubt if there would have been handbills bearing such appeals, as the paper shortage was always acute. There may have been placards bearing appeals on the office of the provost marshal but I cannot establish this definitely.

As far as I know, the last appeal for old iron was in 1862, a year before Gettysburg. General Beauregard issued this appeal throughout the Confederacy and he was asking for church bells. I cannot tell you the exact date of Beauregard's appeal, but I am having it looked up in the old newspapers at our library. It may also appear in the Records of the War of the Rebellion.* I do not know about the general response to this appeal: I only know that the Methodist Protestant Church in Atlanta, of which my great-grandfather was minister, gave their bell in 1862.

The memories of old timers agree with what I had heard about there being no charitable centers for refugees. The best help I can give you on this matter is as follows. Adjoining the railroad tracks and the depot was the city park. It would be in this park that refugees who came by train would pause. Here they would wait with their baggage until friends and relatives came in their carriages to get them. The refugees who had neither friends nor relatives would probably sit here for a while until some kind-hearted citizen offered them shelter, or they would sit in the park for a while until they started the weary tramp around the town to find what already overcrowded boarding houses could take them in.

About the blockaders' stores—blockade goods were sold in several ways. Many storekeepers (retail merchants) went to Wilmington and bought goods on the docks at auction and shipped them back to Atlanta to their stores. Others had large warehouses in Atlanta. They had their agents in Wilmington ship the goods to the warehouses and they held auctions in these warehouses for the benefit of retail merchants and any citizens who wished to bid. Men engaged in blockading cotton to England had offices here in Atlanta for the purpose of purchasing cotton from the rural districts around the city. These establishments—wholesale, retail and cotton offices—would probably have borne no other signs than the names of the proprietors. As I wrote you Saturday, the stores usually announced the arrival of new blockade goods by advertisement in the newspapers, although I have seen a handbill which ran vaguely like this, "Blank & Blank beg to

---

* The War of the Rebellion: Official Records of the Union and Confederate Armies, a 128-volume set, was published beginning in 1880.

announce that they have just received a consignment of goods through the blockade, toothbrushes, ladies' merinos, fine tarlatans, etc." I am still hunting for one of these ads so I can send you a photostat.

The only names of ladies' charitable societies that I know of are: The Soldiers' Friend, The Soldiers' Aid, The Volunteer Aid Society, The Thimble Brigade, The Ladies' Defense Association, The Wayside Homes, The Ladies' Clothing Association, The Ladies' Industrial Association, The Ladies' Christian Association. I never heard that these organizations had anything to do with refugees. They correspond somewhat to the ladies' canteen workers of the last war in that they met all troop trains with baskets of food, socks et cetera. They also cooperated with the doctors in getting the wounded off the trains, nursing in the hospitals and taking convalescents into their homes.

I hope this is some help but a very large bird tells me in a loud, squawking voice that it probably isn't helpful but is very upsetting to things you already decided to do!

Tuesday, October 12th

General Beauregard's appeal appeared sometime shortly before March 27, 1862. The original is in the Beauregard Collection of the Confederate Memorial Museum, Richmond, Virginia. The Confederacy was placarded with it and it appeared in newspapers too. I am quoting a part of it below:

"More than once a people fighting with an enemy less ruthless than yours . . . have not hesitated to melt and mold into cannon the precious bells surmounting their houses of God, which had called generations to prayer.

"We want cannon as greatly as any people who ever, as history tells you, melted their church bells to supply them; and I, your General, entrusted with the command of your army embodied of your sons, your kinsmen and your neighbors, do now call upon you to send your plantation bells to the nearest depot, subject to my orders, to be melted into cannon for the defense of your plantations.

"Who will not cheerfully and promptly send me his bells under such circumstances? Be of good cheer; but time is precious."

Today I had every historical organization in the city, as well as the WPA research workers, looking for the refugee center references. As we have found nothing at all, I would imagine my first report to you on this subject was correct. I would also say definitely that no church ever bore a placard of a secular nature. No appeal for iron was made in Atlanta in midsummer of '63.

The photostats of blockade ads will go to you tomorrow, as well as a picture of The Calico House (so called because it was painted to resemble that material. And very dreadful looking it was, too, as it looked like a modern camouflaged battleship.) The Calico House was the closest approach to a relief center the town had. All garments, packages, bandages and food for soldiers and the needy were assembled there.

My husband and I look forward to seeing you in Atlanta some day when this cruel war is over.

Mr. Hobart Erwin   *Atlanta, Georgia*
Jones & Erwin, Inc.   *October 13, 1937*
New York, New York

Dear Hobe:

The picture in its beautiful frame arrived yesterday and, in spite of the fact that painters and paper hangers are running amuck in our apartment, I hung it in the bedroom where I could examine it and re-examine it. The picture itself is every bit as charming as I recalled, and as for the frame—if that is some of your "handiwork" then I am even more in favor of your handiwork than I was before. You were so sweet to do the picture up so beautifully for me, and it was just the thing I needed to pep me up at the end of a ghastly week of redecorating and chaos in the apartment.*

I must admit I feel embarrassed about you and Miss King giving it to me because I honest-to-God wanted to buy it and now here I am in that pleasant but embarrassing position of having seemed to hint and having gotten far more than I hinted for. Anyway, thank you both so very much. I am enclosing a letter to Miss King, which I hope you will forward as I do not have her address.

The prospect of your possible trip South pleases us both very much and I hope you can work Atlanta in on the Aiken trip. By the way, Sue Myrick visited me last week-end and asked for news of you and wanted to be remembered. Mr. Kurtz sends his regards too.

---

* The framed drawing of Scarlett, by fashion designer Muriel King, is in the Margaret Mitchell Collection in Special Collections at the Atlanta-Fulton Public Library System.

Miss Muriel King   *Atlanta, Georgia*
c/o Hobart Erwin   *October 15, 1937*
New York, New York

My dear Miss King:

Your lovely sketch of Scarlett on Miss Pittypat's front porch arrived, beautifully and suitably framed by Hobe Erwin. I look at it with pleasure, elation and embarrassment. The pleasure and elation spring from my joy in possessing so charming a picture and the embarrassment because I know I seem to have hinted for it at the top of my lungs. Honesty forces me to admit the elation far outweighs embarrassment, and I thank you so very much for your kindness and your generosity.

I must tell you a little about my feelings for your sketch. When Hobe was here with the Selznick people I went to the Biltmore to have lunch with them. You cannot imagine what a stew they were all in, for since General Sherman captured Atlanta the town had not had so much excitement. Every female between diaper age and wheelchair was crowding the hotel for an audition for the part of Scarlett, phones were ringing, and would-be Scarletts were popping out of cracks in the floor. Hobe drew me aside and showed me your sketches. In the last year and a half I have seen many sketches of Scarlett and of war scenes, and none have appealed to me as much as yours. I had only the briefest moment to look at them for Mr. Cukor dragged me away. But the memory of them persisted and I have thought of them so often. The soft, dim blue background of the night appealed to me as much as the weary frown on Scarlett's face and the lovely dress.

I wanted to get another look at the sketches before Hobe left but their visit was anything but a quiet one and the opportunity never arrived. I thought of the picture so much that I finally decided to ask Hobe to buy it for me. Really, Miss King, I did want to *buy* it! You were so very kind about the matter and I hope, someday when I am in New York, that Hobe will bring me to see you and I can thank you in person.

Mr. David O. Selznick   *Atlanta, Georgia*
Selznick International Pictures, Inc.   *November 3, 1937*
New York, New York

Dear Mr. Selznick:

I have just been talking to Katharine Brown and she told me that she thought you would like to see the illustrations which appeared in the Danish edition of "Gone With the Wind." Mr. Hasselbalchs, the publisher, sent me a set of them and I was delighted with them. They aroused a great deal of interest here in Atlanta and the three newspapers reproduced them. I think they are all most remarkable, considering that the illustrator had never been in the United States.

If I may judge by what Mr. Hasselbalchs writes me, and by the clippings of reviews from Denmark, Sweden and Norway, the book is having a very excellent sale. The reviews have been so overwhelmingly kind that I will never again think of Scandinavians as being a cold and reticent race. I am telling you about the career of "Gone With the Wind" abroad because I know you will be interested in it from the viewpoint of its advance publicity for the picture.

The German edition has been out about a month but I have received no reviews as yet. However, a friend in Germany wrote me last summer that the English edition was having a good sale all over Germany. The Polish edition should be published quite soon and sometime in the early future the Hungarian, Czech and Finnish will appear in print. At present I am negotiating with France and Italy and trying to arrange for a Slovine edition too. But, of course, these last are not signed up yet. Last May I heard that the English edition had sold 80,000 and the reviews from the British Isles, Australia, South Africa and India have been good enough to take my breath away. I certainly never expected all of this!

I keep up with you and other members of the Selznick organization through my clipping service, for it seems that the Selznick people and "Gone With the Wind" are tied like Siamese twins in the public prints. Of course, I am just as interested as any other movie fan in who will play what part. I never go anywhere that I do not run into heated discussions as to the suitability of various movie stars for different parts. Everyone feels so violently that it frightens me into silence or else I mumble apologetically that I think Donald Duck would be wonderful as Rhett.

Mr. Herschel Brickell   *Atlanta, Georgia*
Ridgefield, Connecticut   *November 4, 1937*

Dear Herschel:

I may have let you in for a job that will be troublesome to you, so, if you do not wish to undertake it, have no hesitancy in refusing. Here is the how-come of it.

I had a long telephone conversation with Katharine Brown, of the Selznick International Pictures in New York. She wrote me some time ago that you had met her at a tea. She said they were testing a well known actress for the part of Belle Watling. The actress was born in Wisconsin and, naturally, did not have a Southern accent.* In the midst of the test it suddenly occurred to the studio that Belle Watling not only had a Southern accent but probably a different accent from the more educated characters. So, Miss Brown got me on the phone and asked if Belle's accent would have been different from Scarlett's and Melanie's and in what way. I did the best I could over the phone. I told her that the accent would have varied as it always does between the educated and the illiterate. I told her too that most of the prostitutes of the day were recruited from freshly landed immigrants or (here in the South) the daughters of small farmers who had been led astray, cracker families and poor white mountaineers. I said that in pronunciation they generally changed e's and i's—calling a pen "a pin," men "min" and accenting such words as settlement and government on the last syllable, "settle*mint*" and "gover'*mint*." In many cases they changed i's to e's, such as "sengle" for single. I told her the voices would be flat and slightly nasal.

I realized as I was speaking that all I said was confusing. Katharine then asked if I could suggest any Southerner in New York who would be able to sit in on an audition for Belle and correct the accent. I know very well that an ear for accents is born in one like an ear for music. And the only people I could think of were you and Norma and Elinor Hillyer, and Katharine crowed with delight at the mention of the Brickells and said she would get in touch with you. Knowing the movie people and their ways, I would not be at all surprised if they had dispatched Rolls-Royces with couriers and outriders to Ridgefield last night to kidnap you and Norma.

So, the purpose of this letter is to tell you and Norma that it won't hurt my feelings if you refuse to have anything to do with the matter.

Mr. Herschel Brickell   *Atlanta, Georgia*
Ridgefield, Connecticut   *November 12, 1937*
Dear Herschel:

As it appears that today is going to be "one of those days" when all hell busts loose, I do not know how long this letter will be. But I wanted to tell you that I am violently interested in the literary row about Hemingway. Of course I want the Saturday Review of Literature for I missed it.† And I

---

* The actress being tested for the role of Belle was Lenore Ulric. She was born in Minnesota but began her stage career in Wisconsin. The part eventually was played by Ona Munson.
† The November 6 issue of *Saturday Review of Literature* featured a review of Ernest Hemingway's *To Have and Have Not* titled "Hemingway and the Critics." Elliot Paul judged the book

want your reply and anything else you might write on the subject. If convenient, I'd like anything interesting other columnists may have written, for I have not seen a New York newspaper in weeks. I suppose it was only natural that the argument should resolve itself into a Tory-Left Wing alignment and the real question—whether it was a good book or a bad one—should be forgotten.*

I have heard no more from Katharine Brown, and so, I do not know what they decided to do about Belle's accent. My modest and old fashioned family have become accustomed to anything in the last year and a half and, like the Queen in "Alice in Wonderland," get up every morning ready to believe six impossible things before breakfast. Even Father was convulsed at the idea of someone telephoning from New York to discover how the madam of a Confederate bordello talked.

Mrs. Lillian K. Deighton   *Atlanta, Georgia*
Selznick International Pictures, Inc.   *December 6, 1937*
Culver City, California

Dear Mrs. Deighton:

I was very interested to hear that work on "Gone With the Wind" was getting under weigh and I am glad to do what I can to be of assistance to you.

As to a list of reference books, which you requested, I am enclosing this on a separate sheet of paper. Practically all of them are out of print and many are very difficult to get. . . . I do not have a complete bibliography of books I used. They ran into the thousands and I have never had the time since "Gone With the Wind" was published to collect and arrange them. So, I am including on the enclosed list only a few. I do not know whether you want purely military books or just "human interest" ones, but I will throw in a few military memoirs for good measure.

You will notice perhaps that a great number of the memoir type of books do not deal with Georgia and are mainly about Virginia. For the most part, however, the experiences of Confederate women in all parts of the South which were overrun by Federal troops were practically the same.

As to the "reproduction of scenes in Atlanta" prior to and during the Civil War, which you requested, I will refer you, first, to Miss Ruth

---

the author's best and scored critics, including Brickell, who were "surly, flippant, in some case insulting" to the novelist.

* One critic said *To Have and Have Not* spoke favorably of "social consciousness," while another termed it "vaguely Socialist."

Blair, Secretary, The Atlanta Historical Society, Biltmore Hotel, Atlanta. A short while ago she had an interesting display of old photographs, approximately forty of them, showing Atlanta streets during this period. She also has some lithographs and military sketches of the period. Mr. Cukor and Mr. Hobe Erwin conferred with her while in Atlanta. If you will write directly to her, telling her in detail exactly what you want and stating that the Selznick Studios will bear the cost of photostats, messenger service et cetera (if it is photostats which you require), I am sure she will be happy to cooperate. Ask her to write on back of pictures dates & locations.

Miss Alma Jamison, the Reference Department, Carnegie Library of Atlanta, may possibly be helpful too. I do not know about the photograph collection of the Reference Department at the Library. I do know, however, that Miss Jamison has in her files old newspapers and old magazines with pictures of Atlanta. Frequently, however, photostats of old magazine pictures are very unsatisfactory.

Mr. Telamon Cuyler, of Wychehil, Wayside, Jones County, Georgia, has a remarkable collection of Confederate material. It is a very valuable collection. Just how much deals with Atlanta I cannot tell you. Mr. Cukor met Mr. Cuyler, too, and it might be well for you to consult with Mr. Cukor before communicating with Mr. Cuyler. The reason for this is that Mr. Cuyler wished to assist on this film in some capacity, preferably as a technical adviser. I know he has written Mr. Cukor about this, but I do not know the outcome.

Mr. Wilbur Kurtz, 907 Penn Avenue, N.E., Atlanta, is our leading Southern authority on this period. He is an artist, an architect and an historian, and he has done many paintings and sketches of Atlanta during that period. He is soon to publish a History of the Atlanta Campaign with his own illustrations. I believe he has a large collection of photographs. I would suggest, as I did about Mr. Cuyler, that you confer with Mr. Cukor before writing to Mr. Kurtz. My reasons for this suggestion are confidential, and these are the reasons. When Mr. Cukor, Mr. Darrow, Mr. Erwin and the others were in Atlanta I rallied all the authorities on old Atlanta to meet them. Mr. Kurtz was, of course, among them and all the organizations—patriotic and otherwise—in the State were clamoring for him to be sent to Hollywood as a technical adviser. While Mr. Cukor was here he had conferences with Mr. Kurtz and the upshot of it all was that an announcement was made in the newspapers that Mr. Kurtz would go to Hollywood in this capacity. While I have not seen Mr. Kurtz in a long time, I do not believe anything further came out of it. It is, as you can see, a somewhat embarrassing situation for him, as the publicity about his going to Hollywood was very widespread. For all I know, Selznick International may have engaged him in some capacity. However, I thought I would tip you off to the situation so that you would not enter into communication with him without knowing about this.

If I can be of any further assistance to you in matters of research, I hope you will call upon me. While, as you know, I have no connection with the film, my interest in it is naturally very great, and the authenticity of the background is of greater moment to me than who will play what character.

For your information, I sent Mr. Cukor some eight or ten books I used. If it is not possible for you to obtain some of the books I am listing, perhaps you can get the ones I sent him.

Atlanta during the period of which I wrote was a new, raw town. It lacked the beautiful homes that could be seen in Charleston, Savannah, Richmond, New Orleans and other old towns. By that I mean it was not filled with gorgeous, enormous columned, white houses such as were seen in "So Red the Rose." It possessed no houses with wrought iron balconies and stair rails; it had none of the half-basement houses of the deep South, such as were seen around Mobile and New Orleans. Atlanta did have a few beautiful places and I hope the Historical Society has pictures of them. For your information, the Leyden house was about the loveliest mansion in town and one of the few possessing white columns. It stood on Peachtree Street between Miss Pittypat's house and Five Points. If you use the scene where Scarlett goes for the doctor and passes down Peachtree Street, the Leyden house will be on the right-hand side of the street. The nicest group of houses faced upon the Court House Square. Scarlett went to the Court House Square the day she went to see Rhett when he was in prison in the old fire house. The Court House was not destroyed and I think you can get a photograph of it. I know Mr. Kurtz has one, and he also has a beautiful sketch he has done of it. A number of the large houses were destroyed but some remained and were used as headquarters for Federal officers. In writing to Miss Blair it might be well for you to ask especially for pictures of these houses. I know you can get a photograph of the old Solomon house, as it is still standing.

If you will write Miss Ella May Thornton, State Librarian, at the Capitol, Atlanta, and request a picture of her mother's girlhood home which was occupied by General Sherman in 1864, I believe she will oblige you. I cannot tell you whether or not this house stood on the Court House Square, but I think it did. And I do not know whether or not it was burned when General Sherman left Atlanta, but Miss Thornton can give you this information.

Mrs. G.M. Bacon   *Atlanta, Georgia*
St. Nicholas Hotel   *December 6, 1937*
Albany, Georgia

My dear Mrs. Bacon:

I have just received a letter from Mrs. Abbott about the black lace mantilla which you own. I am sorry that I cannot give you much information as to whether or not it could be used by the actress who plays Scarlett in the film of "Gone With the Wind." I have no connection at all with the moving picture production of my book, and know no more about it than other moving picture fans. However, I do not believe that the actress has been chosen yet to portray Scarlett.

The only suggestion I can make is for you to write direct to Mr. Walter Plunkett, in care of Selznick International Pictures, Inc., Culver City, California. Mr. Plunkett is the man who is designing all the costumes for the picture and he could tell you whether or not he could use your mantilla.

Miss Katharine Brown   *Atlanta, Georgia*
Selznick International Pictures, Inc.   *December 10, 1937*
New York, New York

Dear Katharine:

I appreciated the very long letter for I know that you are a very busy person these days.

Of course I am interested in the fate of Lizzie McDuffie. I have not had a great number of pleasant occasions during the last year, but the time I spent talking to Lizzie was most enjoyable. Of course business at the White House will be at a standstill until Lizzie's fate is known! If our Bessie was up for a screen test I know John and I would be so a-twit that the Power Company, Dutch publishers and the raids of autograph hunters would be as nothing.

I haven't mentioned the young lady you told me about over the phone and will not, of course. I immediately forgot her name, which is a help. Of course I'd love to know what happens to her or to any of the Scarletts and think it would be grand if you did telephone me about it.

Mr. Harold Latham is in Atlanta now on his annual visit and one of the first things he told me was about meeting you. He enjoyed it so much and liked you and I believe from the length of his conversation you charmed him completely.

About the manuscript of "Gone With the Wind" which Mr. Whitney wants to buy—here is the situation.* I do not even know if it is in existence,

---

* John Hay "Jock" Whitney was chairman of the board of Selznick International Pictures.

for I intended to destroy it and probably did nearly two years ago. Time has telescoped during these two years and so many things have happened that many past events are a blur. It may be that all or part of the manuscript is in the basement, inextricably mixed with thousands of sheets of re-writes. Some day I pray I will have the time to get into the basement and burn all papers connected with "Gone With the Wind." At present I do not have the time to wash my ears more than once a week.

Even if the manuscript is in existence it isn't for sale. But I wish you would thank Mr. Whitney for his interest in it. I think it's a wonderful compliment. Even if it is in existence I am afraid I could not sell it to him as almost every university, historical organization and library here in the South have been after it too, as well as my family, and I should be outlawed if I let it cross the Mason-Dixon Line. The whole truth of the matter is that I do not care where my book, as a book, goes, but I do not want even one sheet of manuscript or one line of notes to survive.

Just for your own ear, there is a slight rise in feeling against Clark Gable for Rhett. However, I gather he is the one slated for the job. Is it definite that Dorothy Jordan will be Melanie?* I have heard nothing but enthusiasm for the choice.

I had hoped that long ere now normal life would have returned and that John and I would be taking a winter vacation in New York, and we looked forward to seeing you. But, if it ain't one thing it's another, and this unauthorized publication of "Gone With the Wind" in Holland has kept us busy recently and will continue to do so until I win out.† As you may have seen from the newspapers, I went to Washington to the Department of State to get aid in stopping the publication. I do not yet know what will become of it.

Give my best to Harriett and to Tony if he is in New York. Our regards to you and our good wishes for a wonderful Christmas.

Miss Lillian K. Deighton   *Atlanta, Georgia*
Selznick International Pictures, Inc.   *December 21, 1937*
Culver City, California

Dear Miss Deighton:

As to your question about the costumes Scarlett and Melanie wore when they nursed the wounded in the hospital—do I understand this to

---

* Louella Parsons reported on December 8 that Dorothy Jordan, an actress and the wife of *King Kong* (1933) producer-director Merian C. Cooper, would play Melanie.

† Mitchell was seeking an injunction against Dutch publisher Zuid-Hollandsche Uitgevers Maatschappij for publishing *Gone With the Wind* in Holland without her permission. The matter was not settled until after World War II.

mean "did they wear any type of nurse's uniform?" The answer to this question is, no, I never heard of women here in the South wearing any type of nurse's uniform. Prior to the War the profession of trained nursing was practically unknown, and the social status of the few women who did what is now called "practical nursing" was very low. I except, of course, the orders of the Catholic nuns who were devoted to nursing. During the War there were a few Confederate women who might be called professional matrons of hospitals. Kate Cummings was one of these, but you will perhaps note that she was a Scotchwoman. During the War a number of ladies, who had heretofore led secluded lives, stepped into hospitals and proved themselves masterly executives. They made excellent matrons and superintendents of hospitals and they harried and bullied army surgeons, inexperienced orderlies and patriotic young ladies with all their might. But they wore no nurses' uniforms, nor did they consider themselves professional nurses. Mrs. Merriwether, for instance, was one of this type.

As far as I have been able to discover from my reading and my conversation with old ladies who lent willing if inexperienced hands to nursing, there was no uniform. They wore whatever dresses they pleased, preferably their oldest dresses and their plainest ones. They pinned towels or cloths about their heads, so they told me, to keep the gangrene smell and the smell of tobacco out of their hair. And they wore the largest aprons possible and the aprons had the largest possible pockets. In these pockets they carried scissors, pins—if they were fortunate enough to have them—pieces of candy or sweetmeats for the wounded, and, most of all, writing paper. So many of the wounded were unable to read or write, and one of the heaviest jobs the worthy lady volunteer nurses had was writing letters to the families of wounded men.

On page 158 I have mentioned Scarlett with her "hair tied up in a towel"; on page 302 I mentioned her "oldest calico frock"; on page 303 I spoke of the dress as "the mended lavender calico." By this time, 1864, Scarlett was in "second mourning." If she is shown nursing when she first came to Atlanta, in 1862, she would be dressed in mourning—solid black with no trimming, not even a white collar. The basque would be plain and the collar a small round one, a narrower collar than the style we call "Peter Pan." It might have been worn with an onyx mourning brooch.

For your information, I am enclosing a picture of the depot. I do not doubt you will get a better one from some Atlanta source. This shows the depot after Sherman captured the city and before he burned it. It also shows the household goods of the people Sherman sent to Rough and

Ready. This scene took place after Scarlett and Melanie had fled Atlanta. For your information I am giving this item, taken from an 1860 newspaper:

> "The depot is 300 feet long and 150 feet wide; the roof, spreading in a graceful curve from wall to wall, is without a column to support it; four tracks pass through it, two on either side of the platform down the middle on which inner buildings of wood have been erected for ticket offices, waiting rooms etc. . . . Atlanta does not present the look of Western towns of mushroom growth built mostly of white painted wood. Atlanta is built almost wholly of brick. There are, however, a few very substantial edifices of stone."

Should you see Mr. Cukor I wish you would ask him a question for me. Is it true that the girl who is to play Scarlett is to be a redhead? So much of the newspaper publicity I have recently read spoke of the picture being filmed in technicolor and the attendant difficulties of getting a redhaired girl for Scarlett. Of course, Scarlett did not have red hair. Her hair was black. The first mention made of the color of her hair appears in the first paragraph of page 55.

In my first letter to you where I wrote (on the last page) of the houses on "City Hall Square," I inadvertently called this section of Atlanta "Court House Square." This was an error and I meant to say "City Hall Square." The two places are one and the same, and I feared my error might confuse you.

With best wishes of the Christmas season,

Mr. Walter Plunkett   *Atlanta, Georgia*
Selznick International Pictures, Inc.   *December 28, 1937*
Culver City, California

Dear Walter:

The lovely plaque arrived and I thank you so much for it and for remembering me at what must be a very busy time in your life.

I have thought of you so often recently as I had heard that "Gone With the Wind" was to start production on February 1st. Of course, I wondered whether or not it would be in technicolor and if you had to re-design the costumes with an eye toward color.

I cannot help recalling with amusement your exit from Atlanta, pursued by ladies with Scarlett's own, actual dresses which they wished you to use. I hope the next time you are in Atlanta such ladies will let you alone, and the sun will shine, and you will not have a bad cold.

With best wishes for the New Year,

Mr. George Cukor   Atlanta, Georgia
Selznick International Pictures, Inc.   December 28, 1937
Culver City, California

Dear George:

Hell is paved with good intentions and there is a new paving stone in hell this month, labeled "the Christmas telegram I was going to send George Cukor." A lot of work descended on me just before Christmas, so, telegrams and cards could not be gotten out. We appreciated your telegram so very much, especially as we know how very busy you are now.

I gather from rumors and newspaper items that production starts around February 1st. Of course, I am terribly interested and just as curious as anybody else to know what actors will be cast in the picture. As always my best good wishes go to you for the forthcoming film. I've always been so happy to know that you were to direct it.

John sends his best and so do I.

Mr. David O. Selznick   Atlanta, Georgia
Selznick International Pictures, Inc.   December 29, 1937
New York, New York

My dear Mr. Selznick:

I know that you are just as interested in the foreign sales of "Gone With the Wind" as you are in the sales here in the United States, for I realize how important the foreign sales of a film are. So, I am writing to tell you of the career of "Gone With the Wind" abroad.

I have been breathless with excitement over the news I have heard from Europe. Since I wrote you last, in early November, I have heard from my German publishers, Goverts. They have sold 40,000 and have printed 60,000. They expect to sell this 60,000 by the first of January. With very few exceptions, the German reviews have been excellent. I did not expect German people to be interested, so I was glad to learn the reason behind their interest. The reviewers all draw comparisons between the defeat of the Confederacy and the defeat of Germany, and the bitterness of Reconstruction in the South with the bitterness of post-War Germany.

Little Denmark had sold 21,000 on the first of December and expected to push the number up considerably in Christmas sales. The Norwegian first edition was 8,000, and I do not know how many they printed in their second edition. The Hungarian translation is just out and I have no news of its sale. The first volume of the Polish edition appears in January. I will keep you informed of the foreign sales.

If it is possible to judge from newspaper items, I understand that "Gone With the Wind" will go into production sometime in February. My good wishes to you, as always, for the success of the picture. All of your pictures are so excellent that I am looking forward with great enthusiasm to your handling of my own novel.

CHAPTER Three

When This Cruel War Is Over

1938

At this date I would not care if the picture was produced with an all
Abyssinian cast, provided it was produced immediately.

—Margaret Mitchell to Mabel and Edwin Granberry
July 22, 1938

Lizzie McDuffie   *Atlanta, Georgia*
The White House   *January 4, 1938*
Washington, D.C.

My dear Lizzie:

Thank you so much for letting me know the result of your screen tests.
I was very disappointed at the outcome for I, too, had hoped that your
many trips to New York meant that they would choose you. It would have
been wonderful, of course, if a born Georgian had been chosen to play this
Georgia part, and I am sure that many other Atlanta people who have been
keeping up with your screen tests through the newspapers will feel disappointed too. Two days ago Walter Winchell announced over the radio that
you had definitely been chosen for the part of Mammy and this morning
the Atlanta Constitution ran a story. I am sending you a clipping.

I do not know whether Mr. Marsh and I will be here in April when the
President and his party come South, as we are making plans for a long

vacation in the early spring. I think it most kind of Mr. Roosevelt to show interest and he was most understanding in the matter of no publicity.*

Thank you again for your letter. I appreciated it, even if it did bring bad news.

Miss Katharine Brown   *Atlanta, Georgia*
Selznick International Pictures, Inc.   *January 24, 1938*
New York, New York

Dear Katharine:

Thanks so much for the letter and the copy of the letter to me from Miss Louise McKeehan. Her letter reads exactly like the ten thousand other would-be-Scarlett letters I have received. I generally answer them with a letter stating that I have nothing to do with the casting of "Gone With the Wind," and so I can be of no assistance to them. And then, dearie, I refer them to you. So, if you are kind enough to want to answer her, you can tell her the same thing and state that you don't want her.

I was glad to hear about the May 15th starting date. All the gossip columns put it at February 1st. . . .

It may interest you to know that there is the same sort of interest and curiosity in the movie cast abroad as there is here in America. "Gone With the Wind" has been going like a breeze in Germany and the publishers want me to send them every possible detail about the forthcoming movie. The foreign fan mail that has begun to trickle in all wants to know who will play Scarlett, just as much as folks in Opp, Alabama, and Portland, Maine, want to know.

I certainly appreciate the way you keep me posted about things.

In haste, and best from us both,

Miss Lillian K. Deighton   *Atlanta, Georgia*
Selznick International Pictures, Inc.   *February 8, 1938*
Culver City, California

My dear Miss Deighton:

Several days ago I learned, with interest and pleasure, that Mr. Wilbur Kurtz, of Atlanta, had gone to Hollywood for a two weeks' conference about "Gone With the Wind." My pleasure at this news was twofold—first, because

---

* On January 1, McDuffie wrote to Mitchell that when President Roosevelt came to the Little White House at Warm Springs, Georgia, in April, he "would like to meet you." She added that the president promised "there would be no publicity" about the visit.

I am happy to know that the picture will soon go into production, and, second, because I know how truly valuable Mr. Kurtz's knowledge of old Atlanta can be. Had I known when I wrote you before that Mr. Kurtz was really going to Hollywood, I would have told you more about his background. At the risk of inflicting a long letter on you, and perhaps information in which you are not interested, I want to tell you further details about him.

We have many people here in Atlanta who consider themselves "authorities" on our local history, but I found, to my sorrow, that when you tried to pin such people down on details they generally became quite vague. For instance, they could not tell whether the stairs of the newspaper office I mentioned were inside the building or outside; they did not know whether this or that house was of brick or wood; they were apt to place certain hotels two or three blocks away from where they should be. All of this may seem very unimportant, but it really was not in my case. I knew that if I made one small error of location all the people over sixty years old in this section would rise up and denounce me as an ignoramus (Georgians are fearfully vocal about historical errors!).

Mr. Kurtz has spent his life running down not only great historical matters, such as army campaigns, but also small matters such as I have listed above. As an artist and architect he was interested in houses, and for a great many years he has been photographing and sketching old houses and scenes around Atlanta. It is fortunate that he did this, for in the last twenty years most of our landmarks have vanished. Had it not been for Mr. Kurtz's interest and diligence in collecting pictures taken years before, taking his own pictures and making sketches, our collection of Atlantiana would be poor indeed. Mr. Kurtz really knows his stuff, and the purpose of this letter is to tell you that you can rely on what he says. He is very well known throughout this section, and when the newspaper reports appeared last year stating that he was going to Hollywood, hundreds of people expressed gratification. As one old lady said, "Mr. Kurtz may keep them from having General Sherman fall in love with Scarlett and decide not to march to the sea."

Lest you think that statement a deliberately rude one, I hasten to say that the South and Southern history have not always fared so happily in Hollywood. Unfortunately, most of the people in the South know our history very well and it makes them indignant when backgrounds, accents and historical matters are improperly portrayed. Errors which would not annoy other sections of the country call forth great indignation here—"The Buccaneer," for instance. In this film, which was most excellent entertainment, it appeared that Lafitte's pirates won the Battle of New Orleans. While no one denies the great aid they were to General Jackson, great indignation was expressed because no emphasis was placed on Old Hickory's Kentucky, Tennessee and Georgia backwoodsmen with their long rifles. Practically everybody's great-grandfather was in that battle (including mine) and people in this section know the fight play by play. They snorted loudly because little credit was given to these hunters and all credit bestowed on a bunch of smugglers.*

My reasons for wanting to see the background of "Gone With the Wind" done accurately are far from selfish! Despite hundreds of denials in newspapers, thousands of people believe I have something to do with the production of the film. I am constantly stopped on the street and told that if I do not get thus and so right dreadful things will happen to me. I do not want dreadful things to happen to me simply because mammy's head rag is knotted in the back instead of the front.

I hope by now you have met Mr. Kurtz and found him of assistance. Please remember if there is any other way in which I can assist you at long distance I am only too happy to do so.

Miss Katharine Brown   Atlanta, Georgia
Selznick International Pictures, Inc.   March 8, 1938
New York, New York

Dear Katharine:

John and I have been out of town for three weeks, with no mail forwarded, so that explains why I haven't answered your letter of February 11th about the alleged sequel to "Gone With the Wind" that I was supposed to be writing.

Tell Mr. Selznick that I am not writing anything of any type at all these days. This rumor about the sequel rises and falls like a tide, and the tide is high about every two months. I wish you'd tell him for me how much I appreciate his interest in the sequel, and thank him for wanting to know about it. I note with some interest that in today's paper Walter Winchell says I am writing a series of articles for The Nation. This ain't so neither and will probably cause me no end of grief, as every editor I've turned down during the last year will probably be on my neck shortly.

This isn't the letter I intended to write, but things are jammed up today, so I'll write you at length later. I just wanted to let you know I wasn't writing a sequel.

P.S. Discovered the woman writing for The Nation was Margaret Marshall and my name was a typo error!

---

* *The Buccaneer* (1938), produced and directed by Cecil B. DeMille, starred Fredric March as Jean Lafitte.

Miss Katharine Brown   *Atlanta, Georgia*
Selznick International Pictures, Inc.   *March 16, 1938*
New York, New York

Dear Katharine:

I haven't seen Wilbur Kurtz since his return from the West Coast, for John and I have been busy and Mrs. Kurtz has been laid up with a cold and we have been unable to get together. I hope to see him in the next day or so, for, as you can imagine, I am simply hopping with excitement to hear all. Wilbur is a close-mouthed individual and would not even tell me anything interesting over the telephone. When he left Atlanta he told no one where he was going and why, except John and me. The news leaked out from Hollywood, and when he returned he gave a very good interview to The Journal. But I am anxious to hear about the script and the background and the plans, and the cautious Wilbur does not even trust the telephone operators.

I did hear one amusing story from Hollywood, that spawning-place of rumors. Another friend of mine has recently been there visiting a relative who is a director. At a party given him he asked the everlasting question, "But who is going to play Scarlett?" and the assemblage set upon him with derision. They told him that he, being from Atlanta, should know better than anyone: the author, Margaret Mitchell, was to play the part, and she had been in Hollywood for four months being groomed and tutored. They all thought Mr. Selznick had been clever as hell to keep her so quiet. My friend's jaw dropped on his chest, for he'd been seeing me at least once a week for the last six months. He told them so and remarked that I had no histrionic ambitions. I gather, too, that in his indignation he ungallantly stated that I was something like fifty years too old for the part. But the movie people merely patted him kindly and told him that he did not know what he was talking about. This rumor caused John and me to roll on the floor with delight. I just hope my relatives in Los Angeles and my friends there don't believe it, for they will think I am mighty high-hat not to have called them up. . . .

I hear by the grapevine route that some Northern organization whose title is, I believe, The Society for the Dissemination of Correct Information About the Civil War, has been flooding the California office with their mimeographed stuff about what a horrible and unladylike person I am and how utterly false is the picture I presented in my book.* This outfit never had the courage to send me any copies, but they have been circulating them sub rosa. I got a copy from a gentleman whose sister-in-law is a

---

* The actual name of the group, based in Evanston, Illinois, was The Society for Correct Civil War Information. Several of its bulletins included articles attacking the historical accuracy of *Gone With the Wind*.

well known slick writer. This gentleman, a Northerner by birth, was furious because I had out-sold her, and he annotated this mimeographed stuff for me. The annotations showed obvious indication of violent indignation at my sales records. Most of the material consisted of "letters from subscribers" which appeared a year ago in the columns of a Boston newspaper. A majority of them were pitched on a personal angle—that is, personal about me, referring to me as "the Atlanta midget." Many of them were along this general line: "A Northern lady (they were very careful not to give her name), recently returning from a trip South, says that Southern people are indignant at "Gone With the Wind" and say that the author is not a person of good family" et cetera, et cetera. Most of the stuff was pure mouthing, and there never was a direct accusation of inaccuracy which I could answer with about sixteen references from Northern and Southern authorities. . . .

By another grapevine I learn that there are chain letters circulating here in the South (and in the North, too, for all I know), asking that correct Southern accents be used in the picture. I haven't seen one of these letters yet, but I will try to secure one and send it to you. Frank Daniel, on the Atlanta Journal, is using these letters as a springboard for a story entitled "Just What is a Southern Accent?" He is pointing out, and very truly, that there is no definite Southern accent. Here in Georgia alone there are at least five different accents, and a native Georgian can spot someone from the mountains or coast or wire grass section by the time they say, "How do you do?" I will send you a copy of the story. . . .

If you have any news about the casting of even minor characters, such as Miss Pittypat or Mrs. Merriwether, of course, I'd love to know about them, and I would not spread the news. I have been credited for months with knowing who was to play Scarlett and being plain dog mean and close-mouthed for not telling anyone. Did you ever dream when you bought the movie rights from me that there'd be this public interest? Heaven knows I didn't.

Mr. David O. Selznick   *Atlanta, Georgia*
Selznick International Pictures, Inc.   *April 13, 1938*
Culver City, California

Dear Mr. Selznick:

I am sorry to take up a busy man's time on a matter which you will probably deem of little importance, but my relations with the Selznick organization have been so pleasant that I do not wish any misunderstandings, however slight, to mar them. So, I am writing you in some detail about a matter which may come to your ears.

Since "Gone With the Wind" was published I have had many thousands of letters, and a great number of them have come from Northern people whose grandfathers fought in the Union Army. With the exception of two or three, all the letters have been most kind and generous and I have been made very happy by the repeated statements in these letters that "Gone With the Wind" had given the North a better understanding of the old South and the new. About six months ago I received a very intemperate and critical letter which enclosed a bulletin put out by the "Society for Correct Civil War Information." I had never heard of this organization and, in spite of diligent research, could find no one in this section who had heard of it. This pamphlet deliberately misquoted me many times and deliberately misrepresented historical facts.

This appealing little brochure gave me and my friends great pleasure and amusement, and we quoted lines from it frequently for our entertainment. I thought no more of it until recently rumors began to drift east from Hollywood that this organization had been sending its bulletins to the Selznick International Pictures in an effort to make it appear that I had written a completely inaccurate book and that Sherman's March to the Sea was simply a good will tour sponsored by the Federal government. I still was somewhat amused by this information. However, many people here in the South were not amused and were violently indignant. Recently, I was in Macon, Georgia, and called on Mrs. Walter D. Lamar, one of our most prominent Southern women. She is the President-General of the United Daughters of the Confederacy, a very large organization here in the South and one devoted to charitable work and to fighting inaccuracies concerning Southern history. I discussed with her the pamphlets and their contents. She asked me what would be the probable reaction of you and your organization to this propaganda. I replied that all I had heard of you made me believe you were a fair man and a just man and that you were determined to produce a picture that was historically accurate. Then she asked me, changing the subject, when the movie would go into production, and I said I did not know.

All the foregoing is leading up to a letter I have received this morning from Mrs. Lamar. She said she has written to several people about this pamphlet and she was under the impression that one of the reasons "Gone With the Wind" had been delayed in reaching the screen was that you had lent a very attentive ear to the propaganda of the Society for Correct Civil War Information! Apparently something I had said gave Mrs. Lamar this impression but what it may have been I do not know, as such an idea had never entered my head.

Lest you think I am putting too much weight on this matter, I will tell you that I have been appalled since "Gone With the Wind" was published at the way totally erroneous rumors have arisen about me personally, my activities and my statements. I have read with stupefaction remarks attributed to me that I would die rather than make, and have had casual, joking statements come back to me so garbled that I could scarcely recognize them. So, fearing lest, by the time the rumor gets to you, it will have grown enormously and I will be credited with saying that the reason why "Gone With the Wind" has not gone into production is that you are afraid you will arouse the ire of Northern patriotic societies, I am hastening to write you the truth of the matter. I am writing Mrs. Lamar today to give her the correct information on this point. She is a very fine person and a fair one, and I know she will do her part toward correcting this error. I hope nothing comes of it, but I have had so many remarkable things happen along this line that I did not want to take a chance.

My husband and I have been away on a two months' vacation, with no mail forwarded and no clippings, and I have not yet caught up on the progress of the film. I am looking forward to spending a pleasant visit with Mr. Wilbur Kurtz who was in Hollywood a couple of months ago, for I am so interested in his experiences and want to hear all about them.

Mr. Herschel Brickell   *Atlanta, Georgia*
Ridgefield, Connecticut   *April 14, 1938*

Dear Herschel:

I might as well break the news to you brutally. I weigh 120 pounds and have to unzip all my dresses to breathe. I am breaking ground for my third chin and I never felt better in my life. I recall your remarks that you never could hand fat people a thing. I do not wish to go under false colors for I am as hefty as a hog at killing time.

We had a wonderful vacation, drifting about small Florida towns. No one knew who I was and no one asked for autographs. We went to see Mabel and Edwin, of course, and had a most enjoyable two days with them....

You harrow me when you tell me the ladies at White Plains were still interested in me. While we were away the Herald-Tribune's best seller list included me out except for two stores and last Sunday I was included completely out.* I thought this a definite indication of waning interest and I am going to continue to believe this as it makes me feel more comfortable.

---

* The *New York Herald Tribune*'s best-seller list in its weekly "Books" supplement reported the top-selling titles at more than fifty bookstores across the country.

You asked about news of the movie. Here is the latest I know, and it is six weeks old. I have a friend who is perhaps the world's leading authority on the Atlanta campaign and all historic events centering around Atlanta. His knowledge is not just book knowledge. As a young man he went over battlefields when veterans were still spry enough to take him. He knows where every battery stood and where every mule got its ears shot off; he is an architect and an artist; he has also written a military book on the Atlanta campaign. When the movie folks were here a year ago I persuaded him to take them about the countryside. They were impressed by him and in February sent for him to come to Hollywood for "a preliminary conference" on the background of "Gone With the Wind." I saw him last night and he told me most interesting stories. Evidently, the ground has been broken for the production, even if the four main characters have not been cast. His job was picking flaws in the old Atlanta sets, fighting to keep too many tall, white columns off of houses, et cetera. He said the research department was working overtime as were the art department and the set-building department. But no one had any idea when the actual shooting would begin. It can't begin until all this preliminary work is done and the costs of production estimated. He said that if there had been anyone definitely chosen for Scarlett or Rhett he believed the news would have leaked out on the lot. He said that Sidney Howard had adhered very closely to the book. Naturally, he had had to drop out many characters and situations to shorten the script and he had been forced to condense. I gathered that it was a good script and that the ending was as I had written it. Of course, the script may be re-written twenty times more before it is shot. . . .

Colonel Telamon Cuyler   *Atlanta, Georgia*
Wayside, Jones County, Georgia   *April 22, 1938*

My dear Colonel Cuyler:

As Miss Baugh wrote you, John and I went to Florida for a long vacation. We returned through Macon, arriving there on a Saturday night. It was our intention to pay you the long-deferred call. However, we learned that during our absence our apartment had been burglarized and many articles, including my fur coat, John's suits et cetera, had been stolen. We hastened home to confer with the police and insurance people and to make a complete check on our losses. I must admit that one of the first thoughts that leaped to my mind was of your copy of The Illustrated London News, which I have put away in a closet. I feared lest our burglars had been of the intellectual type and had taken it. I was greatly relieved to find it. I want to return it to you on your next visit here. I do not wish to mail it as, pack it as carefully as I might, the back might be loosened or damaged in shipping. . . .*

You asked about the progress of the movie and I am wondering if you have talked at any length with Wilbur Kurtz since his return from Hollywood or merely had a letter from him. His news is the latest I have had. I understand that the building of sets and the choosing of backgrounds goes on apace and that the interior designs have been finished. But, except for the three or four minor characters already announced, no actors have been chosen. Wilbur said there was not even a whisper of gossip as to who would play the central characters. Nor was there a whisper as to when the actual shooting would begin, although he thought it might be around June.

For your information, I pass on to you the first sensible reason I have heard of for the delay on the film. I believe the movie people are waiting until details of "Gone With the Wind" have faded from the minds of readers and only the highlights remain. It will be necessary, of course, to cut the story considerably in order to condense it into the usual film length. Many incidents and many characters will be completely eliminated. I realize the necessity for this and do not feel annoyed by it in the slightest. However, some readers may feel differently. For instance, people who liked Will Benteen, and who were especially interested in his oration at Gerald's funeral, might be indignant if Will were omitted from the picture entirely. If the producers wait long enough readers will only remember war and reconstruction and a violent four-cornered love affair, and will not criticize the producers for their necessary omissions. Does that seem logical? . . .†

Mrs. Myrtle B. Hodgkins   *Atlanta, Georgia*
Pooler, Georgia   *April 25, 1938*

Dear Mrs. Hodgkins:

In your recent letter you asked for advice on getting into the cast of "Gone With the Wind." Unfortunately, I am in the same position I was in when you wrote me several months ago—I know less than nothing about the picture or the progress toward filming. The only news I have comes from newspapers, and the newspaper stories are bewildering and conflicting. I do not know whether they have chosen any actors to play my characters beyond the two or three minor parts which have been announced. And

---

* *The Illustrated London News*, a weekly British newspaper begun in 1842, featured extensive coverage of the American Civil War.

† The character of Will Benteen was not included in the motion picture.

I do not know the reason for the delay in the production of the film. So, you see, I am a poor person to advise you! I don't suppose it would do any harm to keep on trying to get into the film. If you have any additional pictures of yourself you might try sending one to Miss Katharine Brown. . . .

I wish I could be more helpful, but no one knows less about the moving picture of "Gone With the Wind" than I do.

Mr. David O. Selznick   *Atlanta, Georgia*
Selznick International Pictures, Inc.   *May 11, 1938*
Culver City, California

Dear Mr. Selznick:

Thank you for your long letter and your understanding of the situation I put before you. Mrs. Lamar of Macon is, as I wrote you, a very fair-minded person and, on learning of her error, she wired and wrote letters to those whom she had misinformed. She regretted very much her misunderstanding and she did all she could to straighten matters out. As a result of her prompt action, the story appears to have been stopped before it had spread beyond those to whom she had communicated it. I was sure that you were one person who would understand my anxiety about the spread of false rumors because you, in the moving picture business, must be plagued by them a million times more than I am.

I appreciated very much your explanation about the eliminating of the Ku Klux from your film. I agree with you most heartily in this matter and I am very happy that you are not calling this organization by name. The original Klan grew from a bitter necessity and Southern people respected it for they owed much to it. The present day Klan was a despicable organization and one abhorrent to all decent Southerners. In the early 1920s we suffered much from Klan activities here in Georgia. Nowadays we hear little of it, for it is practically dead, thank Heaven. I personally would feel very sorry if the moving picture version of "Gone With the Wind" helped even in a small way to bring it back to life. I would feel this way even if you had not received protests from Negro organizations and anti-Fascists. . . .

I was so happy to learn that you were pleased with Mr. Kurtz's work. We think so highly of him here, for he is probably the best informed man in all the world on the military and social history of this section. Both of us are so busy these days that we have little opportunity for seeing each other. However, on Sunday we took a day off and drove up the road over which Sherman and Johnston fought their campaign. Both of us love old battlefields; my husband and my secretary wanted to go over the old earthworks at Resaca, Adairsville, Cass Station et cetera; so, we spent a happy day climbing hills and tramping through underbrush. Mr. Kurtz and I burst out laughing when we said simultaneously while standing on an overgrown gun pit, "I wish Mr. Selznick could see all this."

Mr. Kurtz told me of many interesting experiences in your studios and, of course, I hung on his words. I think we were a comfort to each other, as we could speak freely. Neither of us dares discuss anything about the picture with casual friends for fear of finding ourselves misquoted in a garbled manner. For the same reason I find it pleasant to write to you, as I can indulge myself in the luxury of expressing opinions without fearing that my remarks will find their way into print.

I hope your casting problems will soon be over and I am sure that the actors you choose will be the very best possible.

Mr. Nelson M. Shipp   *Atlanta, Georgia*
Columbus Ledger-Enquirer   *June 15, 1938*
Columbus, Georgia

Dear Mr. Shipp:

You must be a mind reader, for I had intended writing to you. John and I have been out of the city on the Georgia editors' convention and when we returned I found a clipping of your story of June 11th. Of course I was immediately interested in your "little nation-wide campaign."* And now your letter and additional clippings arrive. Thank you so much for them.

While I have nothing to do with the moving picture production of "Gone With the Wind," I am naturally tremendously interested in it. I, like every other Southerner, have been torn between amusement and indignation at the way Southerners, their accents and their habits, have appeared in moving pictures and on the radio. So, of course, I hope "Gone With the Wind" will portray Southerners as they really are.

Last year Mr. Cukor, who will direct the picture, was here in Atlanta giving screen tests. It seemed to me that he was just as interested in Southern voices as he was in applicants for the part of Scarlett. He is a

---

* In a Memorial Day speech, Shipp, editor of the *Columbus Enquirer*, charged that Hollywood traditionally showed southerners as "no more than a lot of lazy, slow-drawling, sun-basking, good-for-nothing, mint-julep-drinking people who bestow the title of 'colonel' upon the one who can say 'you-all' the loudest." In a follow-up article in the newspaper, Shipp touted his remarks as the beginning of a campaign to "save 'Gone With the Wind' out of Hollywood from the kind of 'Southern talk' and manners that have detracted so from a number of otherwise more or less creditable cinema productions."

brilliant man and his ear for accents made us all marvel. He had not been in Atlanta twenty-four hours before he could tell the differences between North Georgia voices, Coast voices and Mississippi voices. He said that he was going to do everything in his power to make the picture one that would please Southerners. Nothing was too small to interest him. For instance, he wanted to know whether the "head rags" of colored mammies were tied in the back or the front, and whether the little black boys who trotted from kitchens to dining rooms with hot bread wore shoes or went barefooted.

Of course, there is no way of knowing what the final result will be when the movie eventually finds its way to the screen. I am merely saying that we were impressed by Mr. Cukor's desire to make the picture truly Southern.

Thank you again for your interest. Many wonderful things have happened to me and my book in the last two years, but the thing that has gratified me the most and made me happiest has been the kindness and enthusiasm of the people in my own section.

Miss Katharine Brown   *Atlanta, Georgia*
Selznick International Pictures, Inc.   *July 7, 1938*
New York, New York

My dear Katharine:

As you may have gathered from the New York newspapers last week, I was in the modern Babylon.* It was my intention to have you for lunch or dinner if you could work me in, for there were—and are—so many things I wanted to talk over with you. Unfortunately for my plans, I had to come home almost immediately after the newspaper stories broke, for once I get into the papers in a town I find it high time to retreat home. I thought, as I packed madly for the Southern retreat, that I would at least talk to you over the telephone, but then I ran up against the long weekend and the Fourth of July holiday with everybody in New York out of town.

John and I hope to get North in the fall for a little while and we want to see you.

I got out of Atlanta with every newspaper and press association on my neck about the Gable-Shearer announcement, and I ran head on into

---

* On June 30, the second anniversary of the publication of *Gone With the Wind*, Mitchell visited the Macmillan offices on Fifth Avenue, where she personally greeted employees "from the telephone operators who handled my frenzied long distance calls to the boys on the bottom floor who sent the books on their way."

the same situation with the New York press.* It has been my policy since I put the movie rights into Selznick International's hands not to issue any statement of any kind on the subject. Personally, I have always felt it was not my place to state preferences or dislikes or opinions as to how the film was being handled. The result was I did some pretty fancy footwork last week and said nothing at all. Some New York newspapers said as much, but others quoted me as bridling and blushing and saying that Mr. Gable should be a landslide. The truth is I made no such statement.

Do, please, tell me if it is true that George Cukor is out of the picture. I have very little interest in who will act in the picture, but I am sorry if George will not direct. I thought him a grand person and a brilliant one. Of course, if the answer to that question is a confidential matter, just skip it. However, I can keep my mouth shut on such matters if you care to tell me about it.†

I was so tremendously glad that the two leading characters were announced, even if the press did give me a fine badgering about it. And I will be gladder still when the whole cast is announced and the picture goes into production. Selznick International may think GWTW is a headache to them, but dearie, the film has been a Grade A headache to me! And, alas, I have nothing to do with the matter. As you doubtless know, I am lots more interested in who will play Ashley and Melanie than in any other characters. I always felt that any competent actor and actress could do Rhett and Scarlett, but it is difficult indeed to portray complex people who think instead of act. If you have any advance dope on who will play these parts I would love to hear about it.

While in New York the press hammered one question at me above all others. They wanted to know how I would feel if the character of Scarlett was completely changed and tailored to fit Norma Shearer, thereby making Scarlett a poor put-upon creature instead of a hellion. As such an idea had never occurred to me I simply hung my mouth open and said that I had had no information that such a change had been made in the script. Since coming home this rumor has risen up and roared in my ears from every side. I thought I would pass this along to you for what it's worth, for in your job you have to know about ten thousand rumors. . . .

---

* Newspapers across the country, including the *New York Times*, announced on June 24 that Gable and Norma Shearer would play the roles of Rhett Butler and Scarlett O'Hara.
† In her reply on July 8, Brown noted that other directors had been mentioned for *Gone With the Wind* but that Selznick "very much" wanted Cukor.

Mr. Steen Hasselbalch   *Atlanta, Georgia*
Steen Hasselbalchs Forlag   *July 7, 1938*
Copenhagen, Denmark

My dear Mr. Hasselbalch:*

Your letter of June 7th, containing the "Hausorden," arrived, causing great excitement and pleasure in our household. I thought the medal a beautiful one in itself, and your kind thought which came with it makes it even more valued. My husband and I were entertaining guests at dinner the night it arrived, and so, I wore it and was very impressive.

The day after I received it I went to New York for a brief visit. It was the first trip I had made to New York since "Gone With the Wind" made its success two years ago. I went to call on my publisher, Mr. George Brett, of The Macmillan Company, for I wanted to meet all of his staff and thank them for their helpful cooperation. I told Mr. Brett that I was not meeting him on an author-publisher basis any more and that he could no longer terrify me with editorial thunderings. I was now his equal, as I was an honorary member of the publishing firm of Steen Hasselbalch, and I expected the dignity and respect due my new and elevated position. Of course, he enjoyed it as much as I did. . . .

I was so very charmed by your invitation to come to Denmark for a visit at the time the film of "Gone With the Wind" is first shown there. Your thoughtfulness as to my comfort while in your country touched me and I appreciate it very much. But when you spoke of my actually meeting their Majesties the King and Queen—well, I was made timid! Should such a wonderful happening ever take place, you and your whole staff would have to be with me for support.

Just before I went to New York the newspapers announced that Norma Shearer would play Scarlett and Clark Gable would play Rhett. There was a good deal of excitement about this and the newspapers here and in New York did their best to make me say what I thought of these two actors. I have always felt that it was not my place to make any statements about the cast for, after all, I am not connected with the making of the moving picture. If I still retained a part interest in it or had anything to do with the scenario, then, perhaps it would not be out of place for me to venture comments good or bad. So, I reluctantly kept quiet on the subject, but it

---

* Hasselbalch was Mitchell's publisher in Denmark.

was not easy. Clark Gable has been the popular choice for Rhett ever since the movie rights were sold.*

I notice from newspaper stories that George Cukor, who was to direct the picture and who had been doing research on it for sixteen months, is not to direct it after all. I am sorry about this, as I had met him personally and found him an interesting, charming and highly intelligent person. I had liked his "David Copperfield" so very much. I do not mean from the foregoing that Mr. Van Dyke, of the Metro-Goldwyn-Mayer company, who will direct "Gone With the Wind" in Mr. Cukor's place, is not a wonderful director. He has many fine and artistic films to his credit. It is only that I knew and liked Mr. Cukor.†

Melanie and Ashley and Miss Pittypat and other minor characters have not been chosen. Walter Connolly will play Gerald O'Hara; Margaret Tallichet, a beautiful "unknown," will play Carreen; and Charles Murphy, a young man with a small amount of stage experience, will play Charles Hamilton. . . .‡

Again, my sincere thanks for the "Order of Merit" and the honor it implies. I am sure you never bestowed it on anyone one-half so appreciative.

Mr. Nelson M. Shipp   *Atlanta, Georgia*
Columbus Ledger-Enquirer   *July 11, 1938*
Columbus, Georgia

Dear Mr. Shipp:

I have just returned from New York and found your kind letter and the many clippings about the proposed memorial to me and "Gone With

---

* Privately, Mitchell and her husband were not fans of Gable for the role. In a letter to his sister, Frances Marsh Zane, the day after the movie rights contract was signed, John Marsh wrote, "A great many people have picked him for Rhett, but he is persona non grata to the Marsh-Mitchell family. In our opinion, his he-man stuff is synthetic. He just doesn't ring the bell. . . . He was good as a tough but he has never gotten over with us parts where the force and violence are more subtle." But, Marsh, added, "I suppose it would be difficult for any movie actors to please us in any part, because the people in the book are so much like real people to us."

† Louella Parsons reported on June 24 that as part of Selznick's deal with MGM to get Gable, Cukor would be replaced by an MGM contract director—either Woody "One-Take" Van Dyke, who had directed Gable in *San Francisco* (1936), or Jack Conway, who had directed Selznick's *Viva Villa* (1934) and *A Tale of Two Cities* (1935).

‡ None of these actors were in the film. Thomas Mitchell portrayed Gerald O'Hara, Ann Rutherford played Carreen O'Hara, and Rand Brooks played Charles Hamilton.

the Wind."* I regret very much my delay in writing and thanking you for your interest and the honor you wish to bestow on me, but the business and social engagements I was trying to fill in New York kept me moving so fast that John did not forward any mail to me.

What I am going to write you now is for your eyes alone, and not for publication. I feel so very proud and grateful to you for your thought of me and my book that I would like to write you frankly what is on my mind. If I thought there was any chance of this letter being published, or even spoken about, I am afraid my words would dry up and I would sound very self-conscious and stilted. So, I am writing you this letter in confidence, hoping that you will understand my appreciation, even if I must refuse the honors you wish to confer on me and my book. If I could see and talk with you I believe I could make myself clearer. But I shall do my best on paper.

It is not mock modesty or a desire to be urged which makes me say that I do not want a memorial such as you so kindly suggested. It is that the spirit which animated your desire to do this for me is memorial enough. I have had many unbelievable and wonderful things happen to me in the past two years but, as I wrote you before, the most wonderful thing of all has been the kindness and encouragement of the people of Georgia. The world has been good to me and there has come money and what passes as fame, and these are indeed fine things. But to me the finest thing of all has been the letters which say, "You have set our much maligned South before the world in its true light, showing our courage, our endurance and our brave spirit in the face of overwhelming odds." I know it sounds sentimental when I say that I want no other memorial than words like these and no greater honor than the feeling that I have done a little toward presenting the true story of our South to the world.

One reason behind my objection to the erection of an "ante bellum Southern home with its white columns" (July 6) is this: the Tara of "Gone With the Wind" wasn't the traditional white-columned Southern mansion beloved in song and story. Here in North Georgia during the period of which I wrote there were few such stately mansions, for the land was new. If you will re-read the third chapter of my book, you will see how strongly I emphasized the fact that North Georgia's civilization was young and raw and crude—at the time Gerald built Tara—by contrast with the refined and cultured life of Savannah and the older sections of Georgia.

---

* In an effort to promote tourism in his part of the state, Shipp proposed converting a state park building to "Magnolia Hall" by adding a columned façade and a Margaret Mitchell "shrine" inside.

The Tara I wrote about was not a beautiful place and it had no white columns at all. On page 48 I speak of it as "a clumsy, sprawling building built by slave labor." On page 57 I wrote, "the house had been built according to no architectural plan whatever, with extra rooms added where and when it seemed convenient." Again on the same page, I referred to "the awkward lines of the house." I am sure you must have seen a number of these ugly old North Georgia houses, large and cool and comfortable, beautiful only because they meant home to those who lived in them. I have spent two years fighting the idea that Tara looked like the thick-columned, beautiful Natchez houses portrayed in the film "So Red the Rose." When the moving picture people were here I fought them to a standstill because they, too, thought Tara an elegant mansion, while I had described it as a comfortable and large but unlovely up-country plantation home. I did not feel that a man, such as I pictured Gerald O'Hara to be, would build a home of charm and grace. Such charm and grace as Tara had were an emanation from its mistress, Ellen. So, if your plans to build a white-pillared and symmetrical Tara worked out, it would be an erroneous conception and would give people the wrong idea of the house.

Your story of July 6th also said that the proposed building would be constructed of native stone. That also would make it untrue to Tara as I portrayed it. Tara was built of whitewashed brick and some of the additions were of wood.

Now, I will tell you another reason which probably will seem foolish to you. But it is a serious matter to me. I did not write about actual people or actual places, and I went to incredible pains to make sure no such houses as I described ever existed. Yet, despite all my efforts in this direction, thousands of tourists have insisted on believing that this or that home or ruin in Clayton County was Tara. When the letters from tourists who wrote that they had seen Tara rose to unbelievable proportions I went to Clayton County myself and, unrecognized, was shown four Taras in one afternoon. I could not help being incensed about this, for I have no respect for authors who write about real people and houses and thereby cause embarrassment to living people. So, I have vigorously fought any and every rumor about the reality of Tara. I fear that if a beautiful house, such as you suggest, should be erected, it would cinch matters in the minds of tourists and make it doubly erroneous because your Tara would be located in a terrain vastly different from that of the actual locale of the story.

The possibility that Southern voices and Southern speech may not be faithfully presented in the motion picture of "Gone With the Wind" is very offensive to you and you have been crusading against it. To me, it is just as important that the appearance of the houses shall be faithfully presented, because if the houses don't look right it will convey a wrong impression of the people who lived in the houses. But if you build a Tara that looks like my Tara, I am afraid it won't be very attractive to tourists. And, if you don't, it will be a cause of endless trouble to me in trying to explain what Tara really looked like. . . .

I do hope that nothing I have said will cause you to believe that I am unappreciative of the great honor you have paid me by your proposal. It is an exciting and also an humbling feeling to know that you and the people of my state wish to do so wonderful a thing for me. But I must refuse. Apart from the problem you would have in trying to build Tara as it really was, I seriously don't want to be memorialized at all. I cannot help feeling that memorials are for the great and the dead. I have achieved a temporary notoriety but I am not great—no one knows it better than I do—and I am very much alive!

You will accept this letter, won't you, as for your eyes only? And, accept, too, thanks that come from the heart.

Miss Katharine Brown   *Atlanta, Georgia*
Selznick International Pictures, Inc.   *July 13, 1938*
New York, New York

Dear Katharine:

Thanks for the grand, long letter. I appreciate your details all the more when I know how busy you are. I will keep the information you sent me confidential.*

It wasn't Louella Parsons or Jimmie Fidler who started the rumor about the change in script in Norma Shearer's behalf. The New York reporters had that item several days before those two commentators signed off, and they nearly ran me ragged about it. They also had the dope that the actual contracts with Shearer and Gable had not been signed, and they tried to get it out of me whether I thought the announcement was a trial balloon. As if I should know!

Here is what has come to my ears about these two. I get reactions from letters, phone calls and people who catch me in department stores and

---

* In her letter, Brown discussed Shearer in the role of Scarlett, noting that she thought the actress would have been "brilliant casting" a year and a half earlier but that she was now "old hat" after *Marie Antoinette* (1938). Brown also continued to tout Ronald Colman as "better in the part" of Rhett than Gable and reported that Martha Scott was being considered for Melanie.

beauty parlors. I haven't heard a word against Norma Shearer as an actress or a woman. She is, of course, enormously popular and everyone prefaces their statements with the remark that they think she is a wonderful actress. However, everyone thinks she is sadly miscast in the part of Scarlett. They think she has too much dignity and not enough fire for the part. As to Clark Gable—I believe I told you once that he was not as popular here in the South as in other sections of the country—in tough and hardboiled roles, yes; but in other roles, no. He has never been the choice for Rhett down here. People think he is a very fine actor, too, but they think he does not look Southern or act Southern and in no way conforms to their notion of a Low-Country Carolinian. In looks and in conduct Basil Rathbone has been the first choice in this section, with Fredric March and Ronald Colman running second and third. All of the foregoing is confidential, of course. I thought you might want to know the reaction of this section.

Lois Cole did not know that I was coming to New York till I was practically there. She was so busy producing a new son shortly before my trip that I did not know whether I'd be able to see her. She was doing fine and I did see her and the baby too. He is a fine child and I am to be his godmother, which, naturally, makes me quite setup about myself.

Between eleven and twelve at night we get phone calls from people who have been arguing about the cast (and probably drinking about it too) since dinner-time. They call us up in a fury to find out whether or not we like Gable and Shearer. John is patience itself and soothes indignant ladies who just can't bear Mr. Gable's dimples. He tells them that Mr. Selznick would dearly love to have a letter from them on the subject. I know Mr. Selznick must appreciate our urging people to write to him.

Mrs. Herbert May Sternburgh   *Atlanta, Georgia*
Reading, Pennsylvania   *July 13, 1938*

Dear Mrs. Sternburgh:

Thank you for letting me see the letter which the Selznick International Pictures sent you in reply to your letter about the cast of "Gone With the Wind."* I was interested in it. I am returning it to you.

The first thing I knew about Clark Gable being cast as Rhett was when the newspapers descended on me, both here and in New York (where I

---

* The mimeographed form letter from casting director Charles Richards thanked Sternburgh for her comments but noted that most movie stars are under exclusive contract to various studios and that Selznick International "cannot hope to make everyone happy" with its casting choices.

spent a few days recently). They all wanted to know what I thought about Norma Shearer and Clark Gable. It has been my rule not to express any preferences for the cast, as I have felt that it was not my place to do so. I kept saying to the reporters that both Miss Shearer and Mr. Gable were fine actors but that I had never seen anyone who looked like my characters. Of course, such a noncommittal statement did not please the press and some of them quoted me as "blushing and bridling" at the mention of Mr. Gable's name. Others implied that I was very pleased with the choice. The truth is that I did not say anything one way or the other.

I do thank you so much for your interest in my book and in the picture.

Mr. Nelson M. Shipp   *Atlanta, Georgia*
Columbus Ledger-Enquirer   *July 20, 1938*
Columbus, Georgia

My dear Mr. Shipp:

Many, many thanks for your understanding answer to my letter. I feared after I mailed it that I had overburdened you with too many explanations. Now, I am glad I went into details. I could not help smiling at your statement that you were engaged in "a slow retreat." It was an amusing phrase and an accurate one and I found much pleasure in it. . . .

In your postscript you asked confidentially what I thought of the reported plan of changing Scarlett for Norma Shearer's benefit. I will have to admit that I, like Will Rogers, know only those things which I read in the papers. The day I left for New York the announcement of Clark Gable and Norma Shearer came to me through the Atlanta newspapers. As I have no communication with Hollywood, it was my first intimation that they had been chosen. Arriving in New York, I ran into an alarming number of New York reporters who had heard the rumor of the possible change in Scarlett's character. There was nothing I could tell them in answer to their questions, because my last news from Hollywood had been that Mr. Sidney Howard's script adhered closely to my book (with, of course, omissions and condensations necessary to cram so long a story into a feature length picture). Since talking to New York reporters I have listened to radio broadcasts and read statements purporting to come from Norma Shearer which led me to believe that Scarlet's character will not be "sweetened up." I also heard that neither Miss Shearer nor Mr. Gable had actually signed a contract to play Scarlett and Rhett and that the report had been a news leak and not an official announcement. I have heard the cry of "wolf, wolf" (or should it be "Rhett, Rhett"?) so often in the last two years that I have decided not to believe anything until I am seated in a movie watching the actual film unroll. I do not believe the moving picture people realized when they bought my story that they were going to have a bear by the tail. I do not think they realized—and certainly I never did—that the South was going to rise up and speak its mind about Southern accents, Southern conduct and Southern background. I can't help being amused by the predicament of the movie people, and I would be just as amused and pleased at the fighting spirit of the South if it was another Southerner's book and not my own.

With renewed thanks for your kindness,

Mr. and Mrs. Edwin Granberry   *Atlanta, Georgia*
Winter Park, Florida   *July 22, 1938*

Dear Mabel and Edwin:

I have been wondering whether you two went to New York, as you planned. I wondered, too, if you came through Atlanta while I was away and John in Macon. We hate to think we missed you if you did come. I haven't a notion where you all are now—at Winter Park or Little Switzerland or New York or the Beach. . . .

During the last week of June I went to New York and ran into more than I expected. I had hoped to pay a quiet visit to The Macmillan Company; inspect my new godson, lately born to Lois Cole and Allan Taylor; spend a night with the Clifford Dowdeys and see Norma and Herschel. I managed to do those things, but not with the leisure I hoped. The movie announcement about Clark Gable and Norma Shearer had just come out and I was descended upon by the New York press who demanded statements as to my feelings on the subject. At this date I would not care if the picture was produced with an all Abyssinian cast, provided it was produced immediately. I felt it would scarcely be tactful to make such a statement, and so, was very non-committal. However, I found myself quoted variously as being non-committal and endorsing Clark Gable. My private belief is that this announcement was a leak instead of an official announcement. And my still more private belief is that it was a trial balloon to see how the public would react. The sensitive and nervous public has reacted at the top of its voice, to judge by the clamor of newspapers and the still louder clamor of our telephone. No one seems to want Norma Shearer in that part and very few (in this section, at least) can endure the thought of Clark Gable attempting a Charlestonian. If the Selznick company would only start shooting the damned picture, perhaps we'd get some rest. . . .

Miss Katharine Brown   *Atlanta, Georgia*
Selznick International Pictures, Inc.   *August 6, 1938*
New York, New York

Dear Katharine:

I called Western Union to find out why you hadn't received my wire and discovered that they sent it day letter!

I'm enclosing clippings from the Atlanta papers showing approximately what I said when Miss Shearer declined.* I also said that I, "like all other movie fans" was anxious to see the picture go into production but until I sat down in a theatre seat and saw the film unroll I wasn't going to get worked up about it. I also said (and I've said this same thing every time I've been queried during the past two years), that the picture was not my problem, that I knew nothing about the making of pictures and that Mr. Selznick knew all about it. I had all confidence in his ability to make this picture just as grand a picture as others he had turned out. Grander, I hoped. But you see, the papers won't quote me as saying that any more. I've said it too often; it's old stuff; they want something new and I don't blame them. All I can do is reiterate it whether they see fit to print it or not. As I told you over the phone, I told the N.Y. press that S.I.P. had been most thoughtful of me, most careful of technical details of the picture (costumes, scripts, sets etc.) and that our relations were most happy. But who printed that? Only the Greenwich Village paper. When I was asked if I "was mad" at the Selznick company for the delay, I laughed and said no, why should I be? I wasn't producing the picture, wasn't going to Hollywood, wasn't working on the script and didn't see that it was my place to be mad or glad whatever S.I.P. did or didn't do. Besides you had casting problems with which I was very sympathetic. Well, who quoted that? Nobody. But I was quoted as saying "You may think I'm mad but I'm not going to Hollywood." I also remarked how nice I thought the S.I.P. crew were who came to Atlanta. But it didn't draw a line. Of course if I had said that K. Brown was a so and so and George C. was a so and so and of all the so and sos D.S. was the biggest so and so I'd ever run across, it would have drawn eight column streamers.

I can't endorse anybody for reasons you may know and which would take too long to tell—mainly because I really don't care so much. I know

---

* On July 31, Shearer issued a statement that she was withdrawing from consideration for the role: "I have decided that I should not play Scarlett. I am convinced that the majority of fans who think I should not play this kind of character on the screen are right. I appreciate tremendously the interest they have shown."

you'll get a good cast and they'll turn out a whale of a show and three fourths of the public will be satisfied, me amongst them. I can and will reiterate my complete confidence in Mr. Selznick's ability, his honest desire to do a wonderful picture, his artistic integrity and his wish to please the southern movie fans. I've said it before and I'll say it again but whether it will be printed, I don't know.

Sue Myrick was here last Sunday and we gave a newspaper party for her. The staffs of three papers and four news services were well represented. "A magnificent collation was served and a good time had by all," as the country newspapers would put it. We had just ushered the last city editor out the door and taken off our shoes and said, "Oof!" when the U.P. had me on the phone announcing that Miss Shearer regrets and what did I think? I was caught short as I wondered if it were really true and I muttered something about it being a graceful and big thing for her to do if that was the way the fans felt. I hung up the phone and the cold sweat dripped off me. If the call had come a half hour earlier with seventy five newspaper people in the house, I'd have been sunk. Sue's train was not to leave for an hour but we packed her and rushed out of the house and stayed at the station for hours and then went to a movie, getting home after midnight.

I AM sorry about your vacation. What a bad break for you. But it might have been worse. You might have had to come to Atlanta! Seriously, you know we'd love to see you anytime in the world but we'd hate for you to have to make a mad and hurried trip, when your life is probably very mad and hurried just now any way. If the papers call me about the Gable announcement, I'll tell them what I've written on the previous page and if Mr. S. will send me a telegram, I'll read it to them and tell them how nice he was to wire me personally and how glad I am to hear officially that production will begin on such and such a date with such and such actors, etc.

Come to see us some time when you don't hafter come!

Miss Katharine Brown   Atlanta, Georgia
Selznick International Pictures, Inc.   August 11, 1938
New York, New York

Dear Katharine:

I seem to be having many afterthoughts these days, but over long distance I can seldom think of many of the things I want to say. I know you must think that a very fortunate state of affairs, for Heaven knows what your phone bills would be if I did think of everything.

It occurred to me after talking to you that you and I were really talking about the same thing and both of us were in agreement about any statement I should make. The only difference of opinion, as far as I could see, was the "official statement."

To amplify—as I understand it, you wanted me to make an official announcement re-affirming my confidence in Mr. Selznick's ability to make a wonderful picture. In my letter and over the phone I told you that I had been saying just this thing for nearly two years until the papers were loath to carry it any more, as there was no news value in it. On this particular occasion you wished me to make such a statement, using the official announcement of Clark Gable as the peg on which to hang it. There are two reasons behind my inability to oblige you. In the first place, in this section at least, the *official* announcement of Clark Gable will have very little news value, because the public has been convinced that he had the part ever since the unofficial Shearer-Gable announcement. An official announcement from Mr. Selznick will be a nice confirmation, but not news, and I do not think it will get much space except in moving picture trade journals et cetera. The public made up their minds many months ago that Mr. Gable was going to be Rhett, and that was that. So, any official statement from me coupled with the official announcement of Gable would hardly draw a line of space, at least not here in the South where both these items are old news.

The second reason behind my lack of enthusiasm for an official announcement is this: I'm just not the type to make formal and official statements. I never have and probably never will. Most of the newspaper people here in this section have known me since I could chin myself on a space bar and, should I take it into my head to make a pronunciamento of a formal and official kind, they would give me the bird—and rightly too, for they would think I had grown far too large for my nether garments. They'd think that I was a stuffed shirt (to mix my metaphors), or why else would I be issuing typewritten statements to old friends—especially when the statements I issued were of little news value. Of course, they might overlook such an action on my part if I were announcing that Alice Longworth was going to play Scarlett and Eleanor R., Melanie.* But, outside of so exciting a contingency as this, they wouldn't care much for an official statement. I do not know if I've made myself clear, but I hope I have. Most of my friends are newspaper people and they are in the habit of getting me on the telephone whenever they want to know anything. They expect me to play fair

---

* Alice Roosevelt Longworth was the eldest child of President Theodore Roosevelt and a cousin of both Franklin and Eleanor Roosevelt.

with them and tell them something that will make a good story, and I try to do my best because they have, for the most part, been very good to me.

I've gone into these details because I hated to seem so mule-headed over the telephone and I hated not to be obliging in what must have seemed a very unimportant matter to you. But, as I've told you, I've been on the ground with this situation for over two years and I know what will work and what won't work.

Let me amplify that rumor I mentioned to you over the phone. I thought you had heard it or else I would have written you about it some time ago. You are so close to the movie industry and you know so much about it that perhaps you do not realize the vast ignorance of the public on such subjects. Just how "releasing" is done they do not know and do not care. No sooner had the unofficial news of Gable and Shearer broken than this rumor started, namely, that all Mr. Selznick retained in "Gone With the Wind" was the actual ownership of the rights. Metro-Goldwyn-Mayer was to do the producing and releasing; Metro-Goldwyn-Mayer stars were to act in it; the MGM director was to direct it; and it was to be filmed on the MGM lot. I myself have seen some of these items in various newspaper stories. The public gets the notion that in order to get Clark Gable Mr. Selznick had had to surrender practically all of his rights in the picture. I know this sounds strange to you, but in the last month I have met with this story in a thousand variations and have had many questions asked me. I have laughed and said, "What a stupid idea. Of course that isn't true." But people continue to believe it and they are vastly indignant at MGM for putting the pressure on Mr. Selznick so that he had to give up "Gone With the Wind."*

I wanted so to meet you in Virginia! After your day's work was over you and I could have talked for hours (if you still had the strength) in some hotel bedroom, and I should have enjoyed it so much. But I know too many people in Virginia and, careful though I might be, the news would get out that I was there and the next news would be that I was personally selecting Scarlett. Then the next news would be that I was in a padded cell.

If the papers give me a ring I am going to make a statement which I think and hope will please Mr. S. and will cover all the ground, but I just can't make an "official" statement. I hope the papers see fit to carry it.

---

* MGM agreed to loan Gable to Selznick International for the role of Rhett and put up half—$1.25 million—of the then-estimated $2.5 million cost of making the film. (The movie's final production cost was $3.96 million.) In exchange, MGM received 50 percent of the film's profits after its parent company, Loew's, Inc., took 20 percent of the box office receipts for distributing the film.

Mr. Herschel Brickell   Atlanta, Georgia
Ridgefield, Connecticut   August 12, 1938

Dear Herschel:

The political races are on and the air thick with campaign speeches. Yesterday Mr. Roosevelt invaded Georgia to try to swing the senatorial election from the Conservative Democrats. I listened to the speaking and I hope sincerely that the Selznick company was not listening. The reason is this—many Southern newspapers have been running campaigns urging Mr. Selznick to use real Southern accents in GWTW. They've raved about the beauty of the Southern voices, the accuracy of pronunciation and enunciation; they've threatened to boycott the movie if the Southern accent isn't right. Yesterday, after listening to a vast number of Southern accents, I thought how bewildered Mr. Selznick would be. I don't believe Southerners realize how they sound. Those on the air yesterday were not illiterate country folk—they were college graduates and the flower and chivalry of our dear Southland—and they said: "Sarroldy" for Saturday, "yestiddy" for yesterday, "neye-eece" for nice, "guh-munt" for government, "intehdooce" for introduce, "instuh-munt" for instrument, and "puhzuhve" for preserve.

If the bewildered Mr. Selznick made his puppets speak like this the South, suh, would secede and declare that we had all been insulted. . . .

Things are almost normal now. The mail is off. It is true John works four nights a week on odds and ends left over from those chaotic months, but another two months should see the end of them. We felt so cheered about the return of peace and quiet that last Sunday we hauled Sue Myrick, of the Macon Telegraph, up here and used her as an excuse for a debut party. We had between fifty and sixty newspaper folks and it must have been a good party because one editor held on to the kitchen table and refused to be dragged home by his wife, declaring that this was the first good time he had had since the bank holiday in the first Roosevelt term. Sue is a grand person and a good storyteller. Unfortunately, she is full of dialect stories about Negroes and Crackers. She inspires John and me to similar stories. After an hour of this we are unable to talk grammatically in normal social intercourse and for days after Sue had been here we sound like a group of Erskine Caldwell's characters having a reunion with the characters of Joel Chandler Harris. . . .*

---

* Caldwell's books, such as *Tobacco Road* (1932) and *God's Little Acre* (1933), featured poverty-stricken characters in the rural South. Harris's series of "Uncle Remus" books in the late 1800s used the characters of Br'er Rabbit and Br'er Fox to relate African folktales adapted to the South.

Miss Katharine Brown   *Atlanta, Georgia*
Selznick International Pictures, Inc.   *September 12, 1938*
New York, New York

Dear Katharine:

Your letter of September 6th, with its request for the loan or purchase of all or part of the manuscript of "Gone With the Wind" for exploitation and advertisement of the picture, has arrived. Far from being "cross" at you or Mr. Selznick or Mr. Whitney, I am naturally flattered to death by their interest. But I can't let you have all or even a part of it.

The truth is that I set out to destroy the original manuscript right after the book was published two years ago and I think all of it went into the furnace. If any part of it survived, it was only because it got buried under the avalanche of things that descended on me in those days, and if any stray sheets turn up in the future, I intend to destroy them too. I never wanted any part of it to pass out of my hands for addition to literary collections or for display purposes, so the sensible thing seemed to be to burn it up. I felt and still feel so strongly about the matter that when I was making some revisions in my will last month I included a stipulation that should any pages of manuscript or notes et cetera turn up after my death they should be destroyed immediately and should neither be sold nor given away nor exhibited. I do not care who gets "Gone With the Wind," as a book, but I do not want manuscript sheets floating about.

Someone misinformed you about the manuscript of "Gone With the Wind" being shown at the Book Fair, but it is easy to see how such an error got about. The Macmillan Company wanted the manuscript and when I could not produce it they asked for any part of it for the exhibition. I had not completed my work of destruction then and I let them have one or two pages which they returned to me after the Book Fair. About that same time, Collier's Magazine was running a story about me, and they asked me for a page from one of the several chapters I had eliminated from the book before it was published. After considerable searching, I managed to find one and they used it in their lay-out.*

These three pages are the only part of my manuscript that have ever been exhibited and I have always regretted that I let those sheets go out of

---

* When Macmillan inquired in October 1936 about exhibiting some of the manuscript at the *New York Times* Book Fair, Mitchell realized the publisher had never returned the pages. The manuscript was located in Macmillan's vault and shipped to Atlanta. The author then selected three pages that were shown at the fair; another page was used to illustrate Granberry's article.

my hands, even temporarily, for they caused me an enormous amount of labor and inconvenience. Libraries and private collectors bombarded me with offers for the manuscript; editors of many magazines descended on me and are still descending, trying to buy the chapters I had eliminated from the published version of "Gone With the Wind." For a long time it seemed as if no airplane landed here without an editor determined to wrest one of these chapters from me. Bessie was kept so busy frying chickens and I so busy saying "I'm sorry but I can't" that we were practically exhausted. The public arrived by mail and in person, wanting to view the original manuscript, demanding to know in detail what had been in those unpublished chapters; newspapers wanted to print them; the rumor arose that I had written a final chapter (after the published one) which I or The Macmillan Company would sell for a dollar. You cannot imagine the uproar in which we lived, and we were already having uproar enough to keep us busy. There were editors to see and newspaper stories to deny and hundreds of letters to be written and tourists to be gotten rid of as gracefully as possible. I wouldn't go through all that again for a million dollars.

Even if some remnants of the manuscript or the discarded chapters were to show up some day, I don't see how I could let Mr. Selznick have them after I have refused them to universities and historical societies and like organizations here in the South. By this time, he has had enough experience with the South and Southern people to know that that would never do.

As you can gather, I have been in a strange and difficult situation about this matter and it has been made more difficult by the fact that many people do not understand that I really have violent objections to letting even a page of corrected galley proof get out of my hands. I object for the same reason that caused me to resist the many efforts to publish "intimate" stories and pictures of my private life. I want to keep my private life private if there is any way possible to do so, and I always regarded my manuscript as an intimate and personal thing.* Please tell Mr. Selznick and Mr. Whitney how sincerely I appreciate their interest and their

---

* The bulk of the original manuscript of *Gone With the Wind*, along with most of Mitchell's notes and the majority of the corrected typescript, were destroyed after her death. The author's husband saved two envelopes containing selected pages from the manuscript, some of her research notes, several of the original manila envelopes in which chapters were organized, and pages from the typescript sent to Macmillan, and these envelopes remain in a safe deposit box in an Atlanta bank. As directed in a codicil to Marsh's will, the envelopes are to be opened only if needed to prove that Mitchell wrote the novel.

requests. I do think it is grand of them both to want the manuscript even if I can't let them have it.

By inference I gather that plans for the beginning of production must be under weigh and, of course, I was interested. And of course, too, I will be interested in knowing how Alicia Rhett's tests turn out if you decide to bring her up from Charleston. I was sorry the young lassies of the Barter Theatre did not work out very well. I hope you had a good time in Virginia even if you didn't pan any paydirt.

I did my best after your (Mr. Selznick's) telegram came but the sumtotal of the newspaper publicity was the enclosed clippings.* If I can find another clipping I will send it too. It was by an Atlanta columnist who briefly stated that he had seen a telegram from Mr. Selznick to me officially confirming Clark Gable. The truth is the Atlanta papers (and probably many others) are waiting for the first official break on the casting of Scarlett and the first official news on the beginning of production before they turn loose any publicity. I do not believe that they would run another line unless I eloped with Mr. Selznick to Tahiti, and as he is very busy at present, and I am too, I don't know how we could manage it just now. . . .

Mr. Chester P. Smoak   Atlanta, Georgia
Charleston, South Carolina   September 21, 1938

My dear Mr. Smoak:

I thank you so very much for your letter. It gave me great pleasure to know that people of high school age liked "Gone With the Wind" and I appreciated the nice things you wrote me about it.

You asked me to state what actress I would like to see portray Scarlett O'Hara in the film version of my novel. I am sorry that I can be of no assistance to you in this matter. To tell the truth, I have no preference at all. I suppose the reason is that I am the only person in the world who knows just what Scarlett looks like and, naturally, no actress looks like her. She was an entirely fictitious character whom I created in every detail. So, I am willing to leave the casting to Mr. David Selznick. I have no connection with the film at all, and so I shall wait like any other movie fan until I see it unroll upon the screen.

---

* As Mitchell predicted, the announcement of the casting of Gable as Rhett received scant attention in the Atlanta newspapers. The *Constitution* ran a one-paragraph wire story on page 10 headlined "Gable Set for Role in 'Gone With Wind.'" The *Journal* ran a stand-alone publicity photo in the lower right corner of page 1 of Gable, Selznick and Louis B. Mayer of MGM signing the loan-out agreement.

Mr. M.D. Mermin   *Atlanta, Georgia*
Cohen, Cole, Weiss & Wharton   *September 30, 1938*
New York, New York

My dear Mr. Mermin:

When I decided to write you this letter, my thoughts naturally went back to the time I first met you, when I came to New York in 1936 to sell the motion picture rights in "Gone With the Wind" to Mr. Selznick. I can hardly believe it was only a little more than two years ago. It seems like a lifetime, for so many strange, fantastic experiences have been crowded into these two years. I am especially amused when I remember that I was thinking, as we sat in the Selznick offices that day, that when the movie contract was signed my work would be finished and I could get some rest after the strenuous experiences I had been having since publication of my book, a month before. I haven't yet gotten that rest and I sometimes wonder if I ever will.

However, a lull has finally come and I am using this opportunity to attend to various matters, including the writing of this letter, which had to be neglected while the "Wind" was blowing a gale. When your movie is ready to go on the screen, it will stir up another burst of popular excitement, and I am desperately anxious to get my affairs reorganized and in good shape before this or some other cyclone sweeps into my life.

One of the matters which I hope to get cleared up during this period of comparative quiet is a point in my Selznick contract which I have never understood very well, and that is why I am writing to you. Being uncertain of its meaning leaves me in doubt as to what you expect of me. The doubtful point is Article 3 which requires me to "prevent the Property . . . from vesting in the public domain." Just what that language may mean has always been a mystery to me, and I hope you can give me your idea of its meaning, so I can work in harmony with you, if I have not already done so.*

I realize that this is a matter that could be handled better by personal conversation than by letter, and that is one reason why I have delayed so long in taking it up with you. I hoped long ago that I might have an opportunity to talk it over with you, but "Scarlett O'Haras," who were good tap dancers if nothing else, camped on my doorstep and refused to believe I could not make Mr. Selznick put them in the movie, Billy Rose's efforts

---

* Basically, the 152-word sentence, which Mitchell and Brett referred to as the "God Almighty clause" because of its convoluted language, obligated the author to protect the book's copyright around the world to prevent anyone else from making a motion picture version of her novel.

to take possession of my dramatic rights had to be stopped and other law-suits fought through the courts, endless visitors had to be entertained or evaded and endless invitations to make speeches refused, foreign contracts had to be negotiated, fan mail had to be answered and a thousand other things kept me busy morning, noon and night, with the result that trips to New York were impossible.* I finally did get to New York for a few days this summer and I planned to call on you then, but the newspapers found out I was there, and I beat a hasty retreat back to Atlanta. Now, with my father in poor health, I am very uncertain as to when I can come back to New York, so I must attempt to explain my problem by letter or leave the matter unsettled for another indefinitely long period.

I am afraid the letter will be very long and I apologize in advance for imposing it on you, but I hope you will have the patience to read it through.

When this problem first came to my attention many long months ago, I knew, even without getting an expression of your ideas about Article 3, that there were certain steps I ought to take. I knew that copyright protection for my book ought to be obtained if possible in any country in which I authorized publication, and this has been done. What I did not know was to what extent the Article was intended to obligate me to take steps in countries in which I was not authorizing publication. Not being clear on this point, at the same time I was determined if possible not to fail in any possible obligation to Selznick. I accordingly decided to obtain protection in all of the important countries where protection was possible, and this also has been done. But there were many small and unimportant countries in which I considered that copyright registration was of no importance, either to Selznick or to me. I wanted to get your ideas as to which countries fell into the latter classification, instead of attempting to decide this myself without consulting you. But with other things demanding every minute of my time, there was no opportunity to consult you, so I gave my attorneys blanket instructions to obtain copyright protection as widely as possible. Even if this should cost me a lot of money and even though it resulted in my going far beyond what you would have asked me to do, I figured it couldn't do any harm. Pending the time when I could talk the situation over with you, I preferred to err on the side of doing too much rather than

---

* In June 1937, Broadway showman Billy Rose mounted a revue in Fort Worth, Texas, that featured a musical segment based on *Gone With the Wind*, with ballerina Harriett Hoctor as Scarlett, a white-columned mansion burned by Yankees, and a song titled "Gone With the Dawn." Mitchell sued over the unauthorized use of her dramatic rights and won a $3,000 settlement and a public apology.

too little. As matters now stand, I have obtained copyright protection for the book in all of the important countries (except those like Russia where it is impossible to obtain protection), and in a great many of the small and unimportant countries, including a number of the latter which I am confident you would have not asked me to bother with if I had taken the matter up with you in the beginning. . . .

You know without my saying it that obtaining the registrations in a large number of countries, especially the smaller ones, has been very expensive, as well as a complicated and troublesome job. And I am convinced that a great deal I have done has been needless from the standpoint of any practical benefit to Selznick. Naturally, I don't want to go on endlessly, obtaining registrations in more and more countries, if that will benefit nobody and will mean nothing but waste of effort and waste of money. So, I am laying the problem before you in the hope that we can reach a mutually satisfactory understanding, as we have done on other matters that have arisen from time to time in the past. Frankly, I am hoping you can tell me that I have done enough. But if you can't do that, it would be a great help if you would designate the additional countries in which you would like to have the book protected. . . .

I don't like to waste money any more than the next person, and you may be surprised to know that this copyright protection job has already cost me a very considerable part of the total amount Selznick paid me for the motion picture rights. Unless I call a halt pretty soon, I may end up spending *more* than Selznick paid me.* That is my business, of course, especially as I might have saved a lot of this money if I had written you this letter two years ago. And even if I should end up by losing money on my trade with Selznick, I am not complaining. I do think, however, that this is worth mentioning as an evidence that I have not held back in looking out for Selznick's interests, and as a reason why I feel justified in asking your help in preventing a bigger waste of money on something that does nobody any good.

I think I am also entitled to mention another matter that has made me carry a heavier burden than anybody anticipated at the time we signed the contract. That is the long delay in producing the motion picture version of "Gone With the Wind." I am not blaming Mr. Selznick for this. I know he can't help what has happened, and he has my very sincere sympathy because I know that his problem is one of the most difficult a man ever had to

---

* By 1940, Mitchell had spent an estimated $80,000 protecting her copyright around the world.

tackle. But I think you will recognize that the delay has given me a problem which nobody figured on when the contract was drawn up. If the movie had been produced in the normal length of time, you would have gotten copyright protection on your finished product a year or more ago, and the danger of a pirated movie would have been off our minds. But your movie wasn't produced in the normal length of time, and may not be ready for another year, and all of this time I am standing in front of you and protecting you. I have been doing this, to the best of my ability, and it has cost me a lot of money. So, it would seem only fair for you to assist me in avoiding *needless* expense, if you can. And you can, by giving me the expression of your ideas about Article 3 which I am asking for. . . . Of course, if you wish to discuss these matters with me personally, I will be glad to come to New York. I doubt that there is much I could add to what I have written in this letter and my personal preference is to make no unnecessary trips to New York at this time, but I can and will come if you want me to.*

Mr. George Brett, Jr.   *Atlanta, Georgia*
The Macmillan Company   *October 31, 1938*
New York, New York

Dear George:

I hope what I am going to write you will not offend you and I hope that you will not think I am angry with you in any way, but I must tell you this and hope that you will understand. I cannot in the future accept from you any letter of introduction of strangers, nor wires of introduction, nor introductions by telephone. During the last year I have been forced to refuse letters of introduction from all my friends in New York, except you, and now I am very sorry that I must refuse yours too. The reason for this is the recent conduct of Mrs. Ogden Reid who has caused me a great deal of worry, trouble and embarrassment by her statement to the New York papers that I had endorsed Katharine Hepburn for the part of Scarlett. I did not do this, as I have never endorsed anyone and never intend to do so and I told Mrs. Reid this. I do not know why she should deliberately cause me so much trouble. I explained to her over the phone at some length the difficulties that would arise should I endorse anyone. The most I said about Miss Hepburn was a polite remark which anyone would have made under

---

* On December 7, after reviewing a report on Mitchell's actions over the past two years regarding foreign copyrights, Mermin informed the author that she had met her obligations to Selznick International under her contract.

the circumstances, that she was a charming young actress and looked pretty in "Little Women."*

Lest you think I am putting too much importance upon so small an error getting into the public prints, I will explain. For over two years the newspapers and the magazines of the country have been trying to get me to make a statement as to my preferences for actors for "Gone With the Wind." I have been offered a great deal of money for a very few words on this subject, and I have refused them all. Of course, as soon as Mrs. Reid's statement reached the New York papers, I began to hear about it from all over the country. Naturally, the Atlanta papers called me in some justifiable indignation and bewilderment.

They wanted to know why I had chosen to break this piece of news in New York after refusing for two years to give it to them. They also wanted to know when Mrs. Ogden Reid had visited me here in Atlanta, for one of the New York papers stated that she had been my guest. (I am sure Mrs. Reid never made this last statement and that it was a reportorial error.) I was forced to make a flat denial that I had endorsed Miss Hepburn and another denial that Mrs. Reid had visited me. I tried to make it as tactful as possible by saying that the phone connection was bad and perhaps she had misunderstood me. Thereafter all day newspapers in other parts of the country were on my neck, wanting to know why I had issued this statement in New York after refusing it to them for many months past. My father was very ill that day and my presence was needed at the hospital. I was unable to be with him as I had to sit at the telephone making denials. I could not help resenting Mrs. Reid's action for I had given her no cause for making such a statement. I made notes of my conversation with her and, moreover, there were two witnesses to my talk.

A year or more ago you wired, asking that I cooperate with the representatives of Life Magazine because your friend, Mr. Luce, wished to get pictures.† We were leaving on vacation that very day, but we postponed it and I put in the whole day with the photographers, going to great trouble

---

* Helen Rogers Reid was vice president of the *New York Herald Tribune*. On October 25, when introducing Hepburn to a forum in New York, Reid proclaimed the actress her choice for the role of Scarlett and added that Hepburn was the author's choice as well, "first, last and always." Mitchell told reporters that when Reid called to invite her to the forum, "I told her I thought Miss Hepburn looked pretty in the hoopskirts worn in *Little Women* [a 1933 film directed by Cukor] and I liked that picture very much. I have never expressed a preference and I never will. If Mrs. Reid understood me to say I felt a strong preference for Miss Hepburn in the role, I owe her and Miss Hepburn an apology."

† Henry Luce launched *Life* magazine in the fall of 1936.

to make sure that the captions were historically accurate. It turned out that they wished to obtain photographs of me in negligee and in the kitchen in an apron whipping up a dainty little custard for John. They were very annoyed when I refused. For this reason or some other, they printed completely erroneous and cleverly misleading and utterly ambiguous captions under their pictures. I am still having trouble from these captions. As the captions stated that *I* had given the information, I had most of the historical societies of the section on me about the errors. Worst of all, they printed a deliberate lie under John's picture, stating that he hated to hear the name of my book mentioned and giving the impression that he was resentful of my success. This last was probably one of the causes of the unfortunate rumors of our divorce, which have plagued us for months.

These unfortunate occurrences were no fault of yours and I hope I can make it plain to you that I understand that they were no fault of yours. But I cannot any longer expose myself to such infinite trouble and worry. Nor do I want to expose you to the embarrassment of having people you introduce to me act so strangely.

I wrote earlier in this letter that I had been forced to refuse letters of introduction from other people in New York. The reason has been the same in all cases, a series of annoying, embarrassing and very troublesome experiences that resulted from meeting strangers who were introduced to me in this way. So, it has seemed safer for all concerned for me to accept no introductions. I am very sorry to have to write you this letter but, after thinking it over, it seemed more sensible to set the matter forth in detail now than to wait until some future date when you might telephone me and ask me to receive some friend of yours. Then we would both have the unfortunate experience of my having to refuse to meet your friend or talk with him. I could not expect you to understand such a point-blank refusal, seeming to come out of the clear sky and from no apparent reason. . . .

Miss Adelaide du Bose   *Atlanta, Georgia*
Durham, North Carolina   *November 4, 1938*

My dear Miss du Bose:

Your letter arrived yesterday afternoon but the picture you mentioned has not arrived. However, I am answering you immediately, as I have engagements during the coming week-end which will keep me so busy I will be unable to write to you for several days.

I did not know that a Selznick talent scout was in this section—but then, I probably know less about the production of "Gone With the Wind" than any movie fan.* I am not connected with the picture in any way. . . . So, you see, I can be of no assistance to you in getting you the part of Scarlett. I have read in the papers that it is the intention of the producers to do the picture in technicolor and it is probably for that reason that they decided against you, on account of your dark eyes.

I hope you will not think me cold or curt when I tell you that a personal interview with me would do you no good at all. You see, I could not recommend you because, as I stated above, I have nothing to do with the picture and when I sold the movie rights to my book I sold them completely. So, it would be impossible for me to make any recommendation.

Here is the only suggestion I can make, and I do not know if it will be of any value. Last year when the Selznick talent scouts were in Atlanta Miss Katharine Brown, of that organization, was with them. Her title is, I believe, Story Editor, but it appeared that she was in charge of the search for Scarlett. New York newspapers state that she is now on her vacation and, of course, I do not know how long that vacation will last. Why not write to her and send her several of your pictures? Set out your qualifications and description and tell her what Mr. Arnow has said. . . .

I am so very sorry that I cannot help you.

Mr. George Brett, Jr.   *Atlanta, Georgia*
The Macmillan Company   *November 8, 1938*
New York, New York

Dear George:

I hasten to thank you for your very understanding letter for I appreciate your attitude. It was for your sake as much as for mine that I set out the facts, for I wanted to spare you some possible future embarrassment. A number of my friends in other cities have suffered likewise and have been nonplussed and irritated at the actions of people they introduced, so it has seemed better all the way round to stop the letters of introduction. By the way, I was glad to see that Life Magazine for November 7th published my denial along with Mrs. Reid's remarks about my recommendation of Miss Hepburn.†

---

* That fall, Maxwell Arnow conducted a last-ditch talent search throughout the South. Over eighteen days, he met with members of community theater groups and college and university dramatics programs in nine states from Virginia to Louisiana. One young woman from Shreveport, Louisiana, Marcella Martin, eventually played the role of Scarlett's friend, Cathleen Calvert.

† The magazine noted that when Reid "intimated" that Hepburn was the author's choice for the role of Scarlett, Mitchell "politely" denied it and "said she had no preference."

My grapevine information is that the movie will start on January 7th with whatever Scarlett happens to be nearest to hand. I was startled to learn this week that a Selznick talent scout had gone quietly through Atlanta, Charleston and other cities giving auditions to Southern girls. There was no fanfare of publicity and the scout, Max Arnow, seemed to be trying to avoid newspaper people. I learned of his presence in the South by a desperate letter from a South Carolina girl who had been tried and found wanting and who hoped that an endorsement from me would get her the part. Other sources state that Mr. Arnow admitted they were still desperately hoping for a miracle to turn up and the right girl to walk into their hands.

When you told me over the phone about the cheap edition and your expectation of a large sale, I must admit that I thought you unduly optimistic. I apologize for my thought and I have decided never again to argue with anyone in The Macmillan Company when they make a statement, for it is very obvious to me by this time that all of you know about what will sell, and I know nothing. Today I went by Norman Berg's office and he broke the news to me that he had just sold five thousand copies to *one* Atlanta book store and that the rest of the territory was clamoring.* He told me that reports from the rest of the country indicated a sale of such proportions that it sounded like light years to me instead of books. I think he said something about over a half million, but my mind became too enfeebled by the shock to take in the figures. I wish I could figure out who is buying the book because every one of the three dollar copies you sold has been read by at least ten people. It is my own notion that the small towns and villages are now buying it—places where there are no book stores or even lending libraries. When the Sales Department is able to issue figures on this sale I would certainly appreciate having them. . . .

Colonel Telamon Cuyler   Atlanta, Georgia
Wayside, Jones County, Georgia   November 9, 1938

My dear Colonel Cuyler:

I was sorry that I had to leave the costume party but our New York guest had to return to her hotel. I had hoped to see you on Sunday but it appeared that Father needed me on that day. I have given him your good wishes and he thanks you. He has been home from the hospital for several days and is recovering nicely. He is, however, still weak enough to need the

---

* Berg was the trade manager of Macmillan's southeastern office in Atlanta. In November, Macmillan issued a so-called cheap edition of *Gone With the Wind* that retailed for $1.49. The book sold 338,000 copies in two weeks.

services of a nurse. He is still unable to do any reading, as he is easily tired, and this is an annoyance to him for, as you know, he has spent the greater part of his life reading. . . .

I am glad your photographs came back from Mr. Cukor, for I had become alarmed though I did not wish to mention it to you. I do not mean that Mr. Cukor would have been careless with them, but studios are large places and pictures are easily lost. Your photographs are too valuable to be lost.

Friends who came through here last week-end had seen "Kiss the Boys Goodbye." They said it was a burlesque on Selznick's search for Scarlett. They said that it was amusing in spots but that the author evidently hated every one of her characters so much that it was impossible to feel sympathy for them. It was a malicious comedy all the way around. In the end, however, the apparently dimwitted little Southern girl who had been chosen to play "Velvet O'Toole" turned on her Northern tormenters and routed them, butting one anti-Southern columnist in his fat stomach, shooting an amorous movie producer, telling the literati what bad manners they had, winning the heart of a millionaire polo player, et cetera. They said, though the girl who played the part was an Alabama girl, the Southern accent was laid on with a trowel.*

Now, do you not think that you have known me long enough to call me Margaret? I would be very pleased if you would.

Mr. Robert Sykes ·
Durham, North Carolina

Atlanta, Georgia
November 10, 1938

My dear Mr. Sykes:

I appreciate your courteous letter so very much. I thank you for the understanding of my position which you displayed. So often in the last two years when I have been forced to refuse to help Southern girls get into the cast of "Gone With the Wind," I have had a very uncomfortable feeling that the young ladies and their families were thinking me most uncooperative and ungenerous. My helplessness in this matter has been a source of considerable worry to me and, frankly, I will be the most relieved person in the world when the picture finally goes into production. As I wrote your ward, Miss du Bose, I have no connection with the picture, though I am widely credited with producing it single-handed. Moreover, I am not so old

---

* *Kiss the Boys Goodbye*, by Clare Booth Luce, premiered on Broadway in September 1938. The play told the story of Hollywood director Lloyd Lloyd and his discovery of southern belle Cindy Lou Bethany for the role of Velvet O'Toole for his screen version of a best-selling Civil War novel.

that I do not remember how terrible the disappointments of the late 'teens are, and I hate to write letters that bring disappointment. That is why I appreciate your letter and its spirit so very much.

I am so glad Miss du Bose got the trip to Bermuda and I hope that makes up in part for Mr. Arnow's verdict. Her picture arrived shortly after I had mailed my letter to her, and I have returned it. She is indeed a beautiful girl and has personality written all over her face.

Mrs. Ruth A Leone   *Atlanta, Georgia*
Selznick International Pictures, Inc.   *November 29, 1938*
Culver City, California

Dear Mrs. Leone:

Your letter of November 21st, with the list of research questions, has just arrived. I will be very glad to assist you on these questions whenever the opportunity arises. Unfortunately, at present my father is recovering from a serious illness and I spend a great part of my time with him, my husband's mother is visiting us and the rest of my time goes to her. I have not read "Gone With the Wind" since the last galley proofs went out of my hands and all of my notes are packed in the basement. When Mrs. Marsh's visit is over I will re-read the book, exhume my notes and tell you all I can.

Mr. Wilbur Kurtz, of Atlanta, who was in Hollywood last spring as technical adviser on "Gone With the Wind," is now in Hollywood and will be there for two or three days before returning to Atlanta. It is my information that he went to California from New York with Mr. Selznick. If he has not left Hollywood perhaps you can secure the answers to some of these questions from him.

I will answer one question—No. 6, "Hospitals in Atlanta in Wartime"—now. The question ran "Could it be located in a church which had been turned into a makeshift hospital?" If any Atlanta hospitals were located in churches I never heard it. But perhaps they might have been pressed into temporary service to take care of the enormous overflow of wounded after the Battle of Chickamauga.* Atlanta had been a base hospital town from early in the War and the hospitals were rather well organized and not makeshift affairs. I do not recall whether I stated at exactly what hospital Melanie, Mrs. Merriwether and the others nursed, but in my mind I thought of the Female Institute Hospital. The Atlanta

---

* In the motion picture, Scarlett is shown nursing wounded soldiers in a makeshift hospital inside a church during the siege of Atlanta.

Female Institute was a girls' academy before the War. Being a larger build-ing, it was adapted for hospital purposes. I tried to locate a picture of it for Mr. Cukor a year ago but was unable to do so. It is possible that Mr. Kurtz, who has an enormous number of pictures of old Atlanta, has had better luck than I.

I hope to write to you very soon.

Miss J.G. Shain   *Atlanta, Georgia*
The Smart Library   *December 8, 1938*
Melbourne, Australia

My dear Miss Shain:

I thank you for your letter and for your continued interest in "Gone With the Wind" and in me. You asked if I was writing another book and, if so, what was the book about. I am not writing anything at all and I do not know when I will have the opportunity to write again. I have heard many rumors that I was writing a sequel to "Gone With the Wind" and other rumors that I was writing a novel about present day Atlanta, but there is no truth in either of these rumors.

I know when I tell you that I have not had the leisure in over two years even to think about writing you will wonder why and wonder what I do with my time. To answer that fully I would have to write a book as long as "Gone With the Wind"! So, I will try briefly to give you a few reasons why I am doing no writing. My mail is especially heavy. I would not have you think that I am complaining or that this is a burden, because letters from readers all over the world have made me very happy and I feel that they are the very best payment any writer can have for her work. I am deeply appre-ciative of the interest readers have taken in my characters and I do my best to answer letters. This takes a great deal of time, as you can imagine. Then, there are the business problems that have arisen in the train of "Gone With the Wind." My book has been published in thirteen countries, and doing business of any nature in so many countries takes a great deal of time. Now, I will tell you something which you may find amusing, but to me it has been far from amusing, and frequently very pathetic.

I sold the motion picture rights to "Gone With the Wind" in 1936 and, as you know, the production of the film has not yet started. I sold the book outright and have nothing to do with the filming; I have not worked on the scenario and I have no voice in the casting; I do not even intend to go to Hollywood to watch the picture being made. However, thousands of people believe that I am the one who is selecting the cast for the movie.

Thousands of people wish to portray my characters on the screen, and so, they write to me or come to see me in the belief that I can secure the part of Rhett or Scarlett for them. I cannot help them in any way, but I find it hard to convince pretty little eighteen-year-old girls who believe they could play Scarlett if they had the chance. These movie aspirants have come to me in hundreds during the last two years, each one certain that if I saw her I would certainly realize that she could do the part to perfection. My helplessness in the face of their hopefulness has been saddening. I will be very happy when work on the filming begins on January 5th, for then this problem will be lifted from me and I will have more leisure. Clark Gable will play Rhett, according to latest reports, and the actress who will portray Scarlett will be announced at Christmas time.

Thank you for telling me that "Gone With the Wind" is still being read in Australia.

Mr. Harold Latham   *Atlanta, Georgia*
The Macmillan Company   *December 10, 1938*
New York, New York

Dear Harold:

Thank you for writing me so promptly about the dinner of the Southern Society. And thank you, too, for covering the story in such detail. I think the world lost a Grade A reporter when you went into publishing, for after reading your letter John and I felt as if we had actually been at the dinner.*

Of course, we read every word with great interest, and our only regret was that your modesty kept you from being very detailed about what Mr. Palmer said about you.

I thought your speech of acceptance was absolutely perfect and could not have been improved. You said what was in my own heart and what I would have tried to say had I been there. (Only I could never have gotten the words out and it would probably have taken all the Georgia delegation to have held me up, as my knees act very peculiarly in such instances.) I am so very happy that you were willing to accept the medal for me and I thank you all over again. I think if I couldn't be there you were the logical person, and everyone else who has talked to me about the matter agreed with me completely. People you never met and probably never will meet went out of their way to tell me how appropriate they thought it was for you to rep-

---

* On December 7, Latham accepted on Mitchell's behalf a medal from the New York Southern Society in recognition of her novel's success. The award was presented by society president Thomas W. Palmer at a dinner at the Waldorf-Astoria Hotel.

resent me. As you doubtless gather from that remark, almost everything that happens to me and to "Gone With the Wind" is public property down here, and strangers have no hesitancy about stopping me on the street and giving me their opinions on this and that. . . .

It really looks as if the filming of GWTW has started. On Thanksgiving Day Wilbur Kurtz, the artist who did that picture I gave you, went to Hollywood as technical adviser. He wrote that the studio was humming and they were working on nothing else but this film. He was working all hours on the sets which are now being built, and checking such props as Scarlett's wagon, the color of red Georgia mud, the railroad cars, et cetera. He said that Gable would be on the lot on January 5th. Mr. Selznick gave a statement in Chicago on his way West with Wilbur and in this statement he said Scarlett's name would be announced between Christmas and the first of the year. If they are putting out money for a technical adviser and for the building of sets, I suppose the picture is definitely under weigh, and no one can be happier than I am. While the aspirants for the part of Scarlett have stopped arriving at our door in droves, there still are enough of them to constitute a problem. The same applies to people who want me to get them jobs as technical advisers, dialect experts, costume designers and authorities on social customs of the old South. I can't help any of these people and it takes a great deal of time convincing them of this.

Another reason why I feel certain the filming is ready to start is that I heard, in a roundabout way, that the movie people were interested in a cheap edition of "Gone With the Wind" illustrated with stills from the picture. This is confidential news. Probably they have already approached you and Mr. Brett on this matter, but, if they haven't, please keep it quiet.

I'll let you know as soon as the medal arrives. And, again, all my thanks for the trouble you took in this matter and the wonderful words of acceptance you spoke.

Mrs. Ruth A. Leone   *Atlanta, Georgia*
Selznick International Pictures, Inc.   *December 14, 1938*
Culver City, California

Dear Mrs. Leone:

With Christmas closing upon me I cannot be as helpful to you in research matters as I would like. I do not know when I will have the opportunity to give the proper time and thought and reading necessary to answer the questions you asked me. I never like to give offhand answers to such questions without consulting all my authorities and listing them. As I lay no claim to being an historian, I do not try to carry such things in my mind, but always check back to authorities when I need the information. However, here are a few items.

I'd like to say something about the barbecue I described in "Gone With the Wind." I mentioned the smoke from the pits which could be seen as guests approached Twelve Oaks, and also, on page 100, I spoke of "puffs of smoke from the long barbecue pits floating over the crowd." To people familiar with barbecues these mentions of smoke will be understood, but to those unfamiliar it may appear that clouds of smoke choked the guests. At a correctly managed barbecue there is practically no smoke because the fires in the pits are down to coals. From a distance, however, a thin, colorless smoke can be seen, and this arises from the cooking meats. The "puffs of smoke" will come from the drippings of the bastings poured upon the meats. If too much basting is used the liquid falls suddenly on the coals, making a sizzling noise and giving off a sudden puff. If the wind is in the direction of the guests, they get this smoke.

I notice Mr. Kurtz has sketched for you some peacock fans and has mentioned the palmetto fans and folding fans. I would like to add for what it is worth, that fans of guinea feathers, almost circular in shape and attached to handles slightly longer than a hand's grip, were very popular. Many elderly ladies liked turkey feather fans.

About the Red Cross insignia—I do not believe it was in use at this time, certainly not in the South. I have never seen a picture of the insignia or heard a mention of it. It is my impression that the medical corps was known as the "Sanitary Corps" or the "Sanitary Service." Mr. Kurtz can tell you about this. By 1864 the Confederates were not worrying very much about insignias on ambulances. With the shortage of heavy material covering ambulances, many kinds of materials were used. I recall hearing of an ambulance which was covered by a canvas tarpaulin pieced out with blankets and a crazy quilt.

The Negro labor battalion would not be in uniform. They were hired from their owners and they would be dressed in the same clothing they wore at home. The labor corps of which Big Sam was a member would number about a hundred.

There would be no sheep on the lawns of the big houses. It is hard to grow grass, except Bermuda grass, and people were very proud of their lawns. They did not even want chickens to scratch there. The sheep would have been in the sheep pasture, perhaps next to the cow pasture, but not a part of the cow pasture as sheep cut the grass so much shorter than cows.

On some plantations the sheep were rotated through several pastures in order to give the grass time to grow again.

Aunt Pitty had only two servants, Uncle Peter and Cookie. Prissy was added to them.

Yes, colored children and white children played together. It was the custom then for each white child to be given a colored child as a "play child" and the children were inseparable. (As the "play children" of the little girls grew up they became maids to their mistresses. Many of the "play children" of the boys, when they grew up, went off to the War with their masters.) White children frequently went into tantrums if their "play children" could not accompany them to fetes such as the barbecue.

I am very glad that Mr. Wilbur Kurtz is in Hollywood, for he is a walking encyclopedia of knowledge about the South in war times. I gather from Mrs. Kurtz that he has met you and I know that he will be of great value to you. I want to thank you for the obvious painstaking accuracy of your Department, for, as I wrote Mrs. Deighton last year, accuracy of background means so much to Southerners. We have seen so many moving pictures about the old South which made us roar with laughter.

Please give my regards to Mr. Kurtz when you see him.

Mr. Wilbur Kurtz   *Atlanta, Georgia*
Selznick International Pictures, Inc.   *December 16, 1938*
Culver City, California

Dear Wilbur:

I have just received the letter of December 10th from you and Marian Dabney.* I am addressing the reply to you instead of her because I have been wanting to tell you how much I have enjoyed your journals.† John has found them so interesting too, and we are grateful to you for writing in such detail, and for permitting us to read them.

I'm glad you didn't bet a dime with Mr. Selznick on the color of the convicts. They were white. If they had been black Scarlett would not have permitted them to be mistreated because she liked colored people and, in common with most of her generation, she would have felt that Negroes had a market value, even after freedom. (Old ideas will hang on.) If they

---

* Marian Dabney worked in Women's Wardrobe at Selznick International.

† Kurtz kept a journal about his experiences on the set of *Gone With the Wind* and shared it in sections with his family and the Marshes. Some of the diary was published in 1978 in a special edition of the *Atlanta Historical Journal* under the title "Technical Adviser: The Making of 'Gone With the Wind,' The Hollywood Journals of Wilbur G. Kurtz."

had been Negroes Archie would not have cared what happened to them because he hated Negroes.

I am enclosing a clipping from the Macon Telegraph about Sue Myrick. I do not know and she does not know exactly when she will go to Hollywood, but it is probable she will not leave as soon as Annie Laurie does.*

I'm returning the sketches of the head rag, and you will note that I have not ok-ed them. My reasons for not ok-ing them are two in number. The first is that I am not connected with the film and I do not think it my place to pass upon anything of this nature. During the past year or more I have received several letters from the Selznick offices asking for information of one kind or another. I have answered some of the questions and have been glad to do it if the information was readily available. I was also glad to assist the Selznick people in getting a list of books and people they might consult in their research work. However, I am not a technical adviser on this job. I have given some pretty broad hints of my attitude in several of my previous letters, but now I think I had better state my position more directly. I haven't minded discussing certain matters informally, as I have done in some of the previous letters, but I don't intend to give official ok's on any part of the film. That would put on me a responsibility I don't wish to have.

It would also be directly in conflict with the position I have taken for the past two and a half years. From the minute I sold the film rights, I said that the picture was Mr. Selznick's and I did not wish to have anything to do with it. You know how the public has hammered on me, trying to get me to take a hand in the selection of the cast, trying to get me to make Mr. Selznick do this or do that, trying to get me to mix myself into something that is none of my business. You also know how stubbornly I have resisted all of this pressure on me. Having withstood it all of this time, I certainly don't intend to reverse myself at this late date and actually take a hand in the production as an adviser, officially or unofficially. That just isn't my job.

My second reason is that, even if I were inclined to act as an adviser, I haven't the time to do it. As you know, I am no authority on the period covered by my book, and I do not try to carry a lot of details in my head. Whenever I want to know something I sit down and check all my references, no matter how minor the point may be—and no matter whether I have looked it up just the week before. I do not like to give offhand judgments, even on head rags. When I was writing my book I remember having seen several pictures of head rags that were tied the way they ought to be tied, and there was one in particular that I thought would be helpful to

---

* Annie Laurie Kurtz joined her husband in California in late December and served as his assistant.

you. This morning I went through the twenty or more memoirs of ladies of the Sixties I have here at home and did not find the photograph I wanted. I do not know in exactly what book it appears, but I know the picture I want, and several others, are either at the Carnegie Library or the Historical Society because I looked them up once before. Miss Blair is away on vacation and I haven't the time to put in a day or two at the Carnegie Library running down this piece of information. John and I are, as usual, up to our necks in work and the recent sale of 380,000 of the cheap edition of "Gone With the Wind" has doubled our work; Father is convalescing but takes a great deal of my time; Atlanta is full of old friends home for Christmas and each one is firmly convinced that I should spend a day with her. On top of all this, I have an auditor here who is trying to close up my books for the year. The news that the picture is actually going into production has stirred a number of people to fresh frenzies—would-be Scarletts are arriving at my door again and people who want to be technical advisers, dialect experts, or who want me to get them on the Selznick lot "just for a look around" are bedeviling me. So, you can see I wouldn't have the time for any research work, even if my life depended on it.

In other words, I don't mind being obliging and I am hopeful that the picture will be accurate as to the background, costumes, etc., but I can't and won't take on the responsibilities of serving as an adviser and we might as well understand each other on that point before we go any further. I have a letter today from Mrs. Leone which indicates that she has some understanding of my position. She says she would not have sent me her last list of questions—only a few of which I commented on—if she had known you were coming to California as early as you did. When Sue Myrick and Annie Laurie get there, you three ought to be able to handle the situation without needing any help from me and much better than I could.

I read with interest the news that Tara would have columns and I was sorry to hear it, although I suppose it was only to be expected. When the picture is shown I am afraid the reporters may ask me, "did Tara have columns?" and I will have to reply truthfully that it had no columns at all. A week does not pass without this question coming up, and I imagine it will come up again when the picture is presented.

Keep on with the journal. I cannot tell you how interesting it is. I think you would have made a wonderful war correspondent.

Tuesday, December 20

I am sorry this letter did not get off sooner. Sue Myrick came up for the week-end to do some shopping for her trip and to tell us goodbye in case she was called West suddenly. We went to see Annie Laurie Sunday morning and had a big time. Annie Laurie has been having quite a siege with the dentist and her jaw on one side was a little swollen. However, she was full of enthusiasm and excited about her trip. Everyone who knows you and her is enjoying a vicarious excitement and we are all so happy that both of you will have the trip and the interesting experience. Of course, Sue wanted to travel with Annie Laurie but she has not yet been notified when to leave. I suppose Annie Laurie will go tonight.

Thank you so much for the carbon of the letter to Mr. Palmer.* We thought it a fascinating description and I took it up and read it to Father who was vastly interested. You are so nice to keep me posted and I appreciate it more than I can tell you.

By the way, (not that it matters) Scarlett did not leave town by the McDonough Road: page 383—"Rhett turned the horse's slow feet westward from Peachtree"; page 384—"Circling round the center of town, . . . get through to the southwest part of town without any danger." With the main body of the explosion to the east of Atlanta near Oakland Cemetery, and the frightened and drunken crowds in the center of town, the wagon avoided them by a wide westward curve back to eastward and into the Macon Road. I put in a week in the car with old maps figuring out what streets and roads and lanes the wagon could have taken. I know this hasn't anything to do with the picture, but I thought you might be interested personally.

With best wishes from John and me,

Mr. Harold Latham   Atlanta, Georgia
The Macmillan Company   December 21, 1938
New York, New York

Dear Harold:

The copy of "Tom Watson" which you sent to Father in my care arrived yesterday and I took it to him.† He was so very pleased, not only with the book (which he has not read) but at your thought of him. He has just reached the point in his convalescence where he is beginning to take an interest again. He has been suffering from acute neuritis in one arm,

---

* On December 14, Kurtz wrote a lengthy letter to C. F. Palmer, president of the Atlanta Chamber of Commerce, describing the filming of the Atlanta fire sequence on the Selznick studio back lot the night of December 10. He called the event, during which old sets from *King Kong* and *The Garden of Allah* were burned, "a notable chapter in movie history."

† *Tom Watson: Agrarian Rebel*, by C. Vann Woodward, was published by The Macmillan Company in 1938. Watson was a Populist Party politician from Georgia.

which has prevented him from holding books in any comfort. I am giving him a bed table with a book rack for Christmas, and "Tom Watson" will be the first book to occupy the rack. Your gift was so well chosen, for, as you know, Father's life overlaps the span of Watson's life, and Father knows first hand many of the things Mr. Woodward wrote. I told Father I would thank you for him because as yet his arm permits little writing. He asked me to assure you of his pleasure and to wish you a fine holiday season. I am sure our family will have a happy, if quiet, Christmas Day because Father will be at the dinner table with us.

I do not know whether the enclosed picture was printed in New York newspapers, so I am sending it to you.* By this token, I am convinced that the picture has begun. Wilbur Kurtz, of Atlanta, the technical adviser mentioned in the story, wrote us such an interesting letter about the making of these box cars in the Selznick workshop and the care lavished upon such details as to whether the planks on the cars ran up and down or sidewise. He said that when the fire was started the director had three wagons and horses and three sets of doubles, in case of emergency. As one of the wheels on the first wagon came off smack in the middle of the railroad track between two burning box cars, it was necessary to rush the second wagon through.

Merry Christmas to you,

---

* Mitchell included a newspaper clipping from the *Los Angeles Times* featuring a photograph of the Atlanta fire scene under the headline "Flames Look Real And Are Real, But It's Only Make-Believe."

CHAPTER Four

Scarlett at Last
1939 (January–June)

> While I have nothing to do with the production of the film of my book, I cannot help feeling a thoroughly normal pleasure that the role of Scarlett has fallen into the hands of a girl whose photographs show her to be so charming.
>
> —*Margaret Mitchell to Vivien Leigh*
> *January 30, 1939*

Mr. and Mrs. Clifford Dowdey
Fort Worth, Texas

Atlanta, Georgia
January 2, 1939

Dear Helen and Clifford:

I think you may be interested in the latest Marsh mangled metaphor. Someone asked John recently if I intended to write another book and he replied, "A wet hen avoids the fire." . . .

There's no particular news from us. The end of the year always means a lot of hard work but it's about over now. We had a fine Christmas and after a family dinner we went calling and eggnogging. It has been four years since we did that and it was so much fun. A great part of the fun lay in the heartening fact that people no longer treated me as a curiosity but took me for granted just as if I had been a successful lady embalmer or life insurance salesman. I expect there will be one more upsurge of public interest and then I think it will all be over. The upsurge will come during the next two weeks when Mr. Selznick will announce to the popeyed world just which little lady will play Scarlett. . . .

Mr. and Mrs. Wilbur Kurtz   *Atlanta, Georgia*
Washington Hotel   *January 2, 1939*
Culver City, California

Dear Annie Laurie and Wilbur:

I have been trying not to have the flu recently, so this letter must be excused. Certainly, I cannot hope to write as marvelous ones as you two have given me. Annie Laurie, your letter of December 26th was greatly appreciated both for its length and its details. . . .

We had a quiet and happy Christmas, which was made even happier by Father's continued recovery. He stayed downstairs all Christmas Day and enjoyed the children so much. We expected to have a giddy New Year and call on all the friends we had not seen in four years (and to do some eggnogging) but I felt poorly, so we stayed at home.

I am enclosing a clipping about the Governor's Mansion for your interest, also one from the Macon Telegraph. Colonel Cuyler was in town three days ago and phoned me. He said Susan had been going over his entire collection. I think Colonel Cuyler is very disappointed that he was not invited to be an adviser of some sort and even more disappointed not to play Ashley Wilkes's father in his daddy's Confederate coat. However, he was a good sport and has turned over his collection to Sue. As you know, she has been working on her job for two years and she is now making a final roundup of information from old people in her section. She still does not know when she will leave.

I know the announcement about Scarlett will have to be made in the next week or so and, naturally, we are waiting with great interest. I wish it would hurry up. It's like a delayed Christmas Day. . . .*

Of course, I was so interested in your impressions of Mr. Selznick. He must be so very nice. Everybody likes him.†

---

* In late December, Brown and Marsh discussed a possible joint announcement in Georgia and California, with Jock Whitney and Brown flying to Atlanta to give Mitchell a private screening of the tests for the three actors chosen for Scarlett, Ashley, and Melanie just before their names were revealed in Los Angeles.

† In her first letter to Mitchell from Hollywood, Annie Laurie Kurtz told of meeting Selznick at the studio's Christmas party, which was held Christmas Eve on one of the soundstages: "He is so genial, so cordial and not at all hard to like. He seems very popular with his employees. He asked about you. Said this was his biggest undertaking and added that if 'twas

We are waiting for the next installment of the journal, and waiting with far more interest than ever felt for an installment of a Mary Roberts Rinehart mystery in the Saturday Evening Post.

John sends his best to both of you and so do I. Please give our regards to George Cukor and our best wishes to Mr. Selznick.

Mr. and Mrs. Wilbur Kurtz   *Atlanta, Georgia*
Washington Hotel   *January 4, 1939*
Culver City, California

Dear Annie Laurie and Wilbur:

I hope you both will forgive me when I confess that I have been screaming with pleasure ever since I read your letter about the pitfalls and ambushes set for your feet by Mrs. Hearst and the other people who have axes to grind. I feel for you, of course. Who in the world could understand your situation better? But misery loves company and I have been fighting that sort of thing since July 1936. I have gotten very tired of people saying "but what do you do with your time?" If I wanted to speak frankly, which I seldom do these days, I'd answer that I spent my time fighting off people who wanted to use me for their own purposes—and trying to do it in the manner of a Southern lady of the old school.

Now, about Mrs. Hearst: around June of 1937 my clipping service began sending me items about her. She was on her way South to visit Atlanta, her home town. The items said she was the "only woman technical advisor and the only Southern technical advisor in Hollywood." The newspaper stories said she wanted to see me or intended to see me. She talked at some length about her ideas for the cast of "Gone With the Wind." While *she* did not say it, the newspaper accounts gave the impression that she was to be the GWTW technical adviser. I was loath to believe this as I had confidence that Katharine Brown or someone in Culver City would have notified me. I was a trifle nervous, however, for I realized Atlanta papers would begin querying me about her and I did not wish to appear rude by saying that I never heard of her and did not think she was on the Selznick payroll.

She wrote me a very pleasant letter asking to see me when she was in Atlanta. She told me of her work on Southern pictures. She did not ask for endorsement or recommendation. I wrote her that I could not give her an engagement because June was my busiest month and everyone I had ever

---

not the success the public wished, it would not be because he had not put forth the best that was in him to make it so."

known was visiting here at that time. I wrote Katharine Brown about her, as I feared I might have been very abrupt with a bona fide member of the Selznick organization. David Selznick sent a memo, "Please have Katharine advise Margaret Mitchell that we do not know anybody named Mrs. Elizabeth Hearst and also that no one should be connected with us or with the picture unless properly accredited by Katharine or yourself, or Mr. Cukor or myself."* I never heard from Mrs. Hearst again. I'm telling you all this for fear she may claim to be a friend of mine or claim that I did endorse her or recommend her to Mr. Cukor. You, Annie Laurie, and Wilbur are new at this strange business but you have already learned a lot. I realized long ago how very careful I would have to be. The strangest people claim to know me and try to use my name to get things for themselves. So I take no chances and wherever possible I air the truth, as I am doing to you now.

By the way, if a dreadful little mess named Thelma Wunder, who has violently blondined hair and who wears perfume you can smell a block off, should turn up claiming to know me, please push her down the nearest elevator shaft. She is the kind of person who will claim anything, if I may judge by my experience with her. A year or so ago she wired me saying she was from the Selznick script department and wanted an interview with me. Neither Katharine nor Mr. Selznick or any of the movie people had sent a letter of introduction, so I had no intention of seeing her. Moreover, she arrived in town at about the same time I received the Pulitzer Prize, and I will never be busier than I was then. I told her over the telephone that I could not see her, but she was of the same breed as your Mrs. Hearst. I believe she wanted to get an interview with me to sell to a movie fan magazine. I had already turned down scores of friends who wished to write me up for the movie magazines. To try to brief this story, she called dozens of times; she tried to make the three newspapers make me receive her; she tried to dig up from the newspapers information about me. Finally, she pushed her way past Bessie and Margaret and rushed through the apartment like a wild animal. Fortunately, I had some warning and locked myself in the bathroom. Then she went to John's office and deviled him. That night I was at WSB on a hookup program with all the Pulitzer Prize winners. It was just about my first and last radio appearance and I was weak with terror. When I went off the air Miss Wunder, who had been lurking outside, leaped upon me like a hunting leopard, firmly seized me in her grasp, kissed me and crushed my orchids. It took John and Lambdin Kay to part us.† The WSB outfit held her bodily while John and I escaped. To hear her talk she was something remarkable in Hollywood and she will probably come to see

---

* Selznick sent the memo to O'Shea.
† Lambdin Kay was public service director for WSB Radio in Atlanta.

you. John wrote Mr. O'Shea about her and Mr. O'Shea said she had been employed for two weeks as a stenographer on the lot.

I could tell you scores of like experiences. I seldom tell them to people because no one will believe such things. I know you and Wilbur will.... I'm telling you these things so that you two will not be nice to brazen strangers because you think they are friends of mine.

I'm going to show this letter of yours to your family, for I don't think you would mind. I was so glad to hear that Wilbur had a new installment of the journal almost ready and I can hardly wait to see it.

Yes, I know what you mean by the studio being particular about no conversation from people working on the lot. For two years John and I have been keeping our mouths tightly closed about a number of movie doings, and we will continue to do so about anything either of you write....

John and I are so happy to know that you both are enjoying yourselves. We are so proud of Wilbur. Of course we've always known his worth and his knowledge and had the greatest appreciation for his ability. It makes us feel good to know that he is appreciated in far places.

Katharine Brown   *Atlanta, Georgia*
Selznick International Pictures, Inc.   *January 10, 1939*
Culver City, California

IMPOSSIBLE TO ANSWER QUESTIONS WITH OUT SEEING ENTIRE PLAN OF PLANTATION, INCLUDING BIG HOUSE, PASTURES, OUT HOUSES, SLAVE QUARTERS, BURYING GROUND ET CETERA. I DISCUSSED THIS POINT AT LENGTH WITH KURTZ & HOBE ERWIN WHEN ERWIN WAS HERE. KURTZ AND MYRICK THOROUGHLY CAPABLE OF ADVISING ON THIS....*

Miss Blythe McKay   *Atlanta, Georgia*
The Macon Telegraph   *January 12, 1939*
Macon, Georgia

Dear Blythe:

You were the one who sent me the copies of The Telegraph and News, weren't you? Thank you so much for them. If it was George Burt or someone else on the paper instead of you, please thank them for me.

Blythe, I ate up every word of your story about Sue's departure and the excitement preceding it. I feel certain that if I had never heard of Sue or you or the others I would have enjoyed it almost as much. It was a grand story

* On January 10, Brown sent Mitchell a telegram about the landscaping of the Tara set on the Selznick back lot, asking how close the plowed fields should come to the house.

and written at the tempo and pace of the events it described. I read it and then laid it on the table by the bed for John to read the next morning. I thought he was so tired from a hard day that he would not feel like reading. I thought he was asleep and tiptoed back to the bedroom and found him sitting up with the paper, grinning like a possum, all his weariness forgotten. He said, "Please tell Blythe for me how fine her story is. Somehow it brought a lump to my tough old throat for, while I was happy to know that Sue was going to have this exciting experience, I felt sad about her going."

After I had finished your story I thought of a number of people in New York who have no idea that there is a world outside of New York, a world full of people completely different from New Yorkers. I wanted to send them your story and say, proudly, "This is really the South, this represents the Southern towns where people have friends they love and appreciate, where everyone (including the telegraph operators) may know everyone else's business but their interest is so genuine and affectionate that no one minds. This is where people have pride and unselfish pleasure in the good fortune of their friends."

Can you imagine people in the large Northern cities driving ninety-six miles to see a friend get on a plane? And wanting to bawl because the friend would be gone a few months? I don't think it would be possible.

I haven't heard from Sue, but today I had a letter from Mrs. Wilbur Kurtz. While the information I am going to quote is certainly innocuous, please don't let it get into the paper because perhaps Mrs. Kurtz would not wish it. "I met Sue at the airport Saturday morning at 9:45, the plane being an hour late. As Wilbur was busy . . . , I went alone in a big Studio car which called for me at the hotel. Wilbur will tell you all about Sue's arrival in his next letter, so I will not repeat. After getting Sue established in her room at the hotel, I took her over to the Studio and I did not see her again till night—and *was* she tired! They had shown her everything and introduced her to everyone at once. She is now established in a lovely office in the main building, one adjoining Mr. Cukor's. . . . Lamar Trotti phoned yesterday. Sue, Wilbur and I are to have dinner with them next week."

Love to you and all the other nice Macon people.

David O. Selznick   *Atlanta, Georgia*
Selznick International Pictures, Inc.   *January 13, 1939*
Culver City, California

SO HAPPY OVER YOUR ANNOUNCEMENTS. THANKS FOR SENDING ME THE FULL DETAILS. COULD NOT WIRE SOONER AS I HAVE BEEN

After her book was published, Margaret Mitchell received thousands of fan letters and felt compelled to answer almost every one. Courtesy of Hargrett Rare Book and Manuscript Library/University of Georgia Libraries.

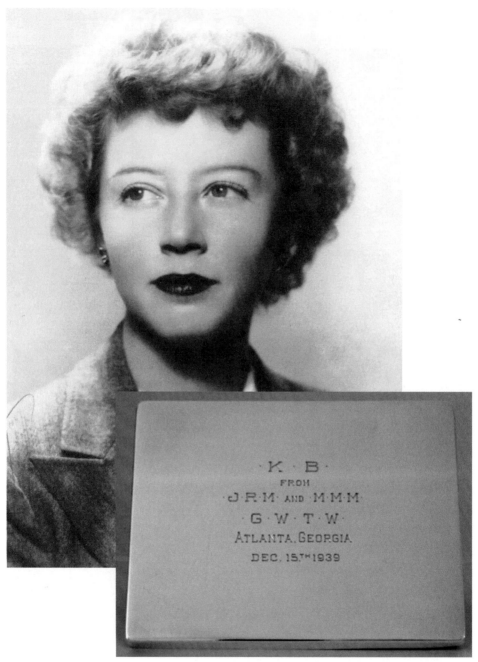

Katharine "Kay" Brown, producer David O. Selznick's East Coast story editor, saw the "magnificent" movie possibilities of *Gone With the Wind* and pressed her boss to buy the rights. Inset: In 1939, to commemorate the film's world premiere, Mitchell and her husband, John Marsh, presented Brown an engraved silver cigarette case. Courtesy of Kate R. Barrett.

Selznick "put forth the best that was in him" to bring *Gone With the Wind* to the silver screen in a way that would please the author. Academy of Motion Picture Arts and Sciences.

In one of the few times she expressed an opinion about casting, Mitchell said Georgia-born actress Miriam Hopkins had the voice, the personality, and the "sharp look" for the role of Scarlett O'Hara. John Wiley, Jr., Collection.

Were it not for his French accent, actor Charles Boyer was the author's choice for Rhett Butler. John Wiley, Jr., Collection.

The only other person who came to Mitchell's mind for Rhett was cowboy star Jack Holt. John Wiley, Jr., Collection.

For Melanie, the author mentioned the "lovely creature," Elizabeth Allan, who played David Copperfield's mother in Selznick's 1935 film version of the Dickens novel. John Wiley, Jr., Collection.

A reader from California begged Mitchell to suggest "small, dainty" Gloria Swanson, 39, who "looked and acted like a child of seventeen," for the role of Scarlett . . . John Wiley, Jr., Collection.

. . . and "tender, terrible, remorseful" Charles Laughton, who once described himself as having "the face of a departing pachyderm," for Rhett. John Wiley, Jr., Collection.

Dramatist Sidney Howard corresponded frequently with Mitchell while writing the movie's screenplay, but the two authors never met. Tom Heyes Collection.

Mitchell teased former actor John Darrow, who worked as a talent scout for Selznick, that he was a "positive menace" to the young women of the South and that his good looks caused many of them to swoon. John Wiley, Jr., Collection.

Colonel Telamon Cuyler, a Georgia lawyer, writer, and collector of Confederate memorabilia, wore his great-uncle's Confederate uniform to pose with George Cukor when the director visited Atlanta in April 1937. Courtesy of Hargrett Rare Book and Manuscript Library/University of Georgia Libraries.

Mitchell often told people that the Danielsville, Georgia, birthplace of Crawford Long—who in 1842 first used ether for surgical anesthesia—was similar to what she had in mind for the O'Hara home. Crawford Long Museum.

Another house the author cited as looking like Tara was Liberty Hall, the Crawfordville, Georgia, home of Confederate Vice President Alexander Stephens. Georgia Department of Natural Resources.

The façade of Tara built on the studio back lot was not the rambling farmhouse that Mitchell described in her book but was closer to her description than the grand house that Selznick created for Twelve Oaks. Courtesy of Hargrett Rare Book and Manuscript Library/University of Georgia Libraries.

Wilbur G. Kurtz served as historian on the motion picture *Gone With the Wind* and used his artistic talents to create several props, including the bank draft Scarlett used to pay the taxes on Tara. Courtesy of Hargrett Rare Book and Manuscript Library/University of Georgia Libraries.

Annie Laurie Fuller Kurtz joined her husband in California, where she served as his assistant and wrote chatty letters to the author. She is shown with actor Harry Davenport, right, who played Dr. Meade. Courtesy of Hargrett Rare Book and Manuscript Library/ University of Georgia Libraries.

Susan Myrick, a newspaperwoman from Macon and friend of Mitchell who served as a technical adviser on the film, shares a laugh with actors Fred Crane, left, and George Reeves, who played the Tarleton boys. Courtesy of Hargrett Rare Book and Manuscript Library/University of Georgia Libraries.

From the beginning, Clark Gable was the leading choice for the role of Rhett Butler—at least outside the South. Herb Bridges Collection.

After a two-year "search for Scarlett," Selznick chose little-known British actress Vivien Leigh to play the role of the century. Herb Bridges Collection.

Forty-five-year-old Leslie Howard, also British, reluctantly portrayed twenty-six-year-old Ashley Wilkes. Herb Bridges Collection.

Best known for her roles opposite Errol Flynn, Olivia de Havilland played Melanie, the true heroine of the book, according to Mitchell. Herb Bridges Collection.

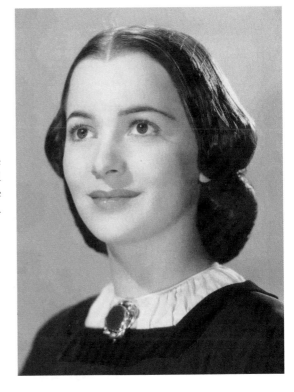

While filming the opening scene of Scarlett on the front porch of Tara, the set was crowded with crew members and equipment. Courtesy of Hargrett Rare Book and Manuscript Library/University of Georgia Libraries.

Many people begged the author to get them into the studio. Here, an unidentified visitor of the Kurtzes strolls down the Atlanta street set built on the back lot. Courtesy of Hargrett Rare Book and Manuscript Library/University of Georgia Libraries.

Director Victor Fleming, who took Cukor's place, poses with Howard and Leigh while holding a copy of Mitchell's novel, an ever-present guide on the set. Herb Bridges Collection.

In the fall of 1939, Mitchell pointed out to MGM two errors on the studio's *Gone With the Wind* letterhead—"Melanee" instead of "Melanie" and "Wilks" instead of "Wilkes." However, she apparently missed one herself: the misspelling of "Carreen." John Wiley, Jr., Collection.

Director Victor Fleming, who took Cukor's place, poses with Howard and Leigh while holding a copy of Mitchell's novel, an ever-present guide on the set. Herb Bridges Collection.

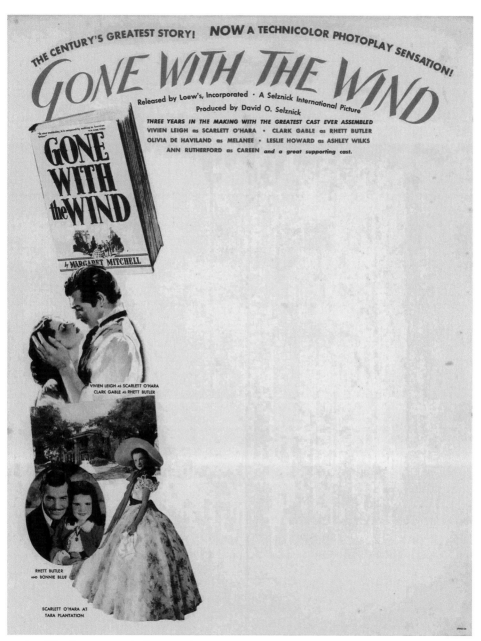

In the fall of 1939, Mitchell pointed out to MGM two errors on the studio's *Gone With the Wind* letterhead—"Melanee" instead of "Melanie" and "Wilks" instead of "Wilkes." However, she apparently missed one herself: the misspelling of "Carreen." John Wiley, Jr., Collection.

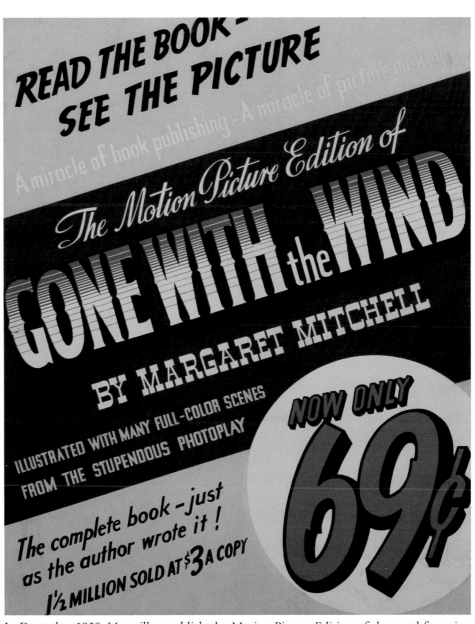

In December 1939, Macmillan published a Motion Picture Edition of the novel featuring color stills from the film, and the book sold 700,000 copies in a few months. John Wiley, Jr., Collection.

Gone With The Wind

A deluxe movie program was created that sold for twenty-five cents in theater lobbies. Mitchell wrote several lengthy letters to MGM about the program and the use of her photo inside. John Wiley, Jr., Collection.

ENGAGED WITH THE PRESS. THEY SHOWED GREAT INTEREST AND
ENTHUSIASM. PLEASE GIVE MY THANKS TO MISS LEIGH, MISS DE
HAVILLAND AND MR HOWARD FOR THEIR TELEGRAMS. MY BEST
WISHES TO THEM AND TO YOU. WILL WRITE TOMORROW.*

Mrs. James Barrett [Katharine Brown]   *Atlanta, Georgia*
New York, New York   *January 14, 1939*
RELAX AND REJOICE. LANDSLIDE FOR LEIGH. CLIPPINGS IN MAIL.

David O. Selznick   *Atlanta, Georgia*
Selznick International Pictures, Inc.   *January 14, 1939*
Culver City, California

My dear Mr. Selznick:

I would have telephoned you last night to tell you of my pleasure in
your announcements but, after spending three hours between the Western Union office and the offices of the Associated Press and our morning
newspaper, The Constitution, I was rather tired. I am sure the excitement
of the evening contributed to this tiredness! But I didn't mind being weary
in so good a cause.

Yesterday afternoon (Friday) The Journal, one of our afternoon papers,
carried a copyrighted UP story about Miss Leigh, which I am enclosing.
It bore the earmarks of being an "official release" but, on second reading,
appeared to be a news leak. None of our three papers queried me about
it. Around nine o'clock your first wire came and the Western Union girl
told me that a long wire was on the way and segments of it would arrive
at fifteen minute intervals. It seemed sensible to avoid delay in delivery by
going to the Western Union office, so John and I did this. Three sheets telling about Miss Leigh had arrived by the time we reached the office; I knew
our morning paper was going to press and of course I wanted the home
town papers to have the break on this story, so I left John at the Western
Union office to wait for the remainder and I went to The Constitution office. By good luck, they had a photograph of Miss Leigh and they tore out
part of the front page, put her picture in, and began setting your wire.† At

---

* Selznick wired Mitchell the evening of January 13 that he was ready to announce the casting for the remaining three principals but was holding the story for one hour to enable the
author to give the news first to the Atlanta newspapers. The producer said he hoped Mitchell
would be "completely satisfied" with his film version of her novel.

† The *Constitution*'s page 1 article trumpeted, "Scarlett Officially Named! English Actress
Wins Role."

intervals the rest of the wire came in. It was all very exciting and reminded John and me of our own newspaper days.

As you will notice from the enclosed clippings, Scarlett's home town is very interested in her progress and equally interested in Mr. Howard and Miss de Havilland. I am very grateful to you for sending me so long and detailed a wire, for I am grateful to the Atlanta papers and Atlanta people for their interest and I was glad to have so much information to give them.

If I can judge from the reactions of the newspaper men last night and that of the men on the afternoon papers who have called me this morning, they are well pleased with the choice of Miss Leigh. Everyone thought it was a fine thing to have a girl who was comparatively unknown in this country because her rendition of Scarlett would not be mixed up by past performances of roles of a different type. Mr. Howard has always been the almost unanimous choice of Southerners for the role of Ashley. And the announcement of Miss de Havilland was hailed with pleasure. (For a bad five minutes it looked as if a picture of Miss de Havilland in a scanty bathing suit was going to appear in the morning paper, bearing the caption "Here is Melanie, a True Daughter of the Old South." That picture was the only view of her the file clerk could find at first. I made loud lamentations at this, especially when the editor said, "We can explain that Sherman's men had gotten away with the rest of her clothes." Finally, we found the sweet picture with the old fashioned bangs.)

I know that you must feel a great sense of relief this morning—a relief far greater than mine. It is fine to have the announcement over and the picture ready to go into production. As always, you have my heartiest good wishes for the success of the film.

Forgive this jerky letter, but I am writing in haste as I want to get this to you on the next air mail.

P.S. No one with whom I have talked made any objection about Miss L. being English & not American. This letter is personal and confidential, please!

Miss Katharine Brown   *Atlanta, Georgia*
Selznick International Pictures, Inc.   *January 14, 1939*
New York, New York

Dear Katharine:

I hope the enclosed will please you and Mr. Whitney.

We spent a wild evening, John in the Western Union office taking the telegram by half-pages, I in the City Room of The Constitution, office boys trotting between the paper and the telegraph office, and the front page of the paper being torn up to make room for the announcement. One old timer on the staff said that the way the story kept coming in in short chunks reminded him of the sinking of either the Titanic or the Lusitania. At the moment he could not recall which. This morning the afternoon papers and the news services have been on the phone. I don't think you need to worry about the reaction down here.

I'll write you a longer letter next week. Since the first of the year I haven't drawn a breath, as there were three weddings and a party every forty minutes for each of the brides. It looks to me as if people are getting married today who have never gotten married before and, after so much party food and a wrecked complexion, I am ag'in' it.

P.S. I've sent Mr. S. copies of these clippings. Dearie, it looks to me like we've gone to town!*

Miss Susan Myrick   *Atlanta, Georgia*
Washington Hotel   *January 16, 1939*
Culver City, California

Dear Sue:

Thanks for your letter of January 11th, which I will answer when the dear public gets out of my hair. Bedlam has broken loose since the announcement Friday night and things are every bit as bad as they were a year or so ago. Thus far the reaction to Miss Leigh has been excellent. I believe Henry Kurtz sent his parents the Atlanta papers, so borrow them and read The Constitution. We would have made the top headline except for the fact that Congress had rebelled against the President and the harassed city editor, torn between Franklin D. and Scarlett, felt he'd better leave the top banner as was. However, they gave the paper over to Miss Leigh. Someday I will tell you about the wild three hours we spent between the Western Union office, where Mr. Selznick's wire was coming in in paragraphs, and The Constitution office, where the front page was being torn out and everyone screaming and running and grabbling in files like a movie of a newspaper office.

---

* Mitchell was careful in her statements to the Atlanta newspapers about the casting. She complimented Leigh's "grand smile" and said she thought "one with an English accent can easily be trained to speak with a genuine southern accent." Leslie Howard is a "marvelous actor," the author said, "and I've never seen him turn in a poor performance." She mentioned de Havilland's appearance in the 1935 movie *Captain Blood*, noting the actress "looked simply lovely in the costumes of that film. . . . I think she will make an excellent Melanie."

Here are two clippings for your scrapbook. More power to you, dearie. And please tell Miss Leigh I will answer her lovely wire, and those of Miss de Havilland and Mr. Howard, whenever things settle down enough for me to have good sense. Of course, The Constitution printed their wires with yelps of joy, and the public seemed to like them too.

Miss Katharine Brown   *Atlanta, Georgia*
Selznick International Pictures, Inc.   *January 16, 1939*
New York, New York

Dear Katharine:

Here are some more clippings. Things are holding up very well, as you can see, but don't feel bad if there is a reaction. Such a reaction is almost inevitable after such an outburst of good stuff, but it will not matter and the pendulum will swing back to a favorable position. Please send these clippings on to Mr. Selznick. I'd send him some direct except that I would have to go to town to get them, and personally I do not want to get out on the streets. I get stopped every four feet and it takes hours to buy a spool of thread.

Will you please ask Mr. Selznick and Mr. Birdwell, if they use any of this Atlanta stuff in publicity, that they will not use such nauseous and personal things as I have marked in ink. Such items are the reason why I loathe making any announcement, no matter how impersonal. It opens the gate for well-meaning people to write things that neither John nor I like and which cause us a great deal of trouble and profitless correspondence.

The morning paper had John up early asking whether there had been a bad reaction because of Miss Leigh's nationality. He told them no. I do not know whether this means that the paper has had any reaction. I'll send you the clippings. For your own information, yesterday we had to go to three parties. Had we not accepted them long ago we would have stayed at home. The first was a "breakfast" to Atlanta authors—reaction to all three actors announced, most excellent. The next party—ditto. This was a gathering of serious minded folks who are trying to do something about economic conditions in the South. The third was a large tea given by the Atlanta women of the press with husbands and guests there—everybody seemed pleased enough. I had to pour coffee at this last and, after three hours of people screaming in my ear and asking questions about Miss Leigh, I poured coffee everywhere except in cups.

In haste,

Miss Rosa Hutchinson   *Atlanta, Georgia*
The Macmillan Company   *January 17, 1939*
New York, New York

Dear Miss Hutchinson:

Again I want to tell you about how far and wide your items go. The notes about the medals and the amount of paper used in "Gone With the Wind" have made every large newspaper in the United States and are now coming in from the country weeklies—and also from European papers! My old newspaper, the Atlanta Journal, bears on its masthead, "The Journal Covers Dixie Like the Dew"—I think you should adopt a somewhat similar slogan but not confine your activities to Dixie. . . .

The story about Vivien Leigh, Leslie Howard and Olivia de Havilland broke Friday night and here in this section it pushed Doctor Frankfurter and a number of other prominent political figures off the front page.* To tell the truth, I was very surprised at this as I thought after two years of rumors about Scarlett there would be little interest in the announcement. There has been a great deal of interest and my husband and I have led as wild lives since Friday as ever we did when "Gone With the Wind" was hovering around the million mark. We are thankful that the cast has finally been announced and hopeful that this is the last flareup of public interest in us. Hereafter we hope Mr. Selznick or Miss Vivien Leigh will be the object of public curiosity and not I.

Mrs. Wilbur Kurtz   *Atlanta, Georgia*
Selznick International Pictures, Inc.   *January 17, 1939*
Culver City, California

Dear Annie Laurie:

I am deeply distressed about the clipping I am sending you about Wilbur, Senior's request for red mud. I am writing you hastily so that you will not think any of your family was to blame for this getting into the paper. It is all my fault and, if there can be any excuse for my breach of confidence, here it is.

The papers and the public have been hammering on us since Friday night when the Vivien Leigh story broke. I don't mean "hammering" in any bad way. It is just that public interest has been so great that everyone wants

---

* Felix Frankfurter was nominated to the U.S. Supreme Court by President Roosevelt in early January.

to know every thing and we have been swamped. The newspaper stories (which Henry Harrison said he would send you) have been exceptionally good and have practically pushed Doctor Frankfurter's appointment and the crisis in Europe off the front pages.* Everything was very favorable to Miss Leigh in spite of the fact that she is not an American or a Southerner. Naturally, for Mr. Selznick's sake (and to a lesser degree for your and Wilbur's and Sue's sakes), we hoped this favorable publicity would keep up. Our experience in such matters has been that there is usually a very natural reaction from favorable publicity. We hoped it would not occur in this case.

When the newspapers began calling to know if I had received any protests about Miss Leigh's nationality, I said "no," but I felt that perhaps the expected reaction was on the way and that something unfavorable might be written. I was asked if the picture was to be in technicolor and when I replied that it was the question came, "Then, what will they do about the red Georgia dirt? There isn't a teaspoonful of red mud in California. They simply couldn't manage that at all." I could see a story going out about what a flop the background would be in technicolor and I said, hastily, "That will be arranged perfectly. Why do you suppose Mr. Kurtz is in Hollywood? He is taking care of such matters. There is at least a teaspoonful of red dirt in Hollywood now for Mr. Kurtz wrote home for some." Of course, I asked them not to say anything about it, but either in the excitement of the Vivien Leigh story they forgot or else they thought it too good to keep, for here it is, and I feel very sick about it.† I think perhaps you'd better not write me anything else that is confidential, for occasions will doubtless arise in the future where I will have to exercise my judgment quickly as to what is the correct thing to say, and my judgment will doubtless run contrary to yours and Wilbur's. I want you to know that everyone who has mentioned this item to me has been amused and interested and has taken it as an excellent sign of Mr. Selznick's desire to do right by Georgia. If anything should be said about this leak at your end, please throw all the blame on me where it belongs.

The journal and your letter arrived yesterday afternoon. . . . John and I thought this section of the journal the most fascinating one of all, especially the part about buying the furniture and other props for the

* Henry Harrison Kurtz was one of the Kurtzes' five children.
† On January 16, the *Constitution* ran an article headlined "Hollywood Orders Red Georgia Mud: 'Gone With the Wind' Characters Will Be Spattered With the Right Hue." The container of red dirt sent to Kurtz in Hollywood is now in the collection of the Atlanta History Center.

various houses. Annie Laurie, I have stopped thinking that your situation in regard to people wanting to get jobs is amusing. I think it is terrible. Having gone through a great deal of this myself, I know how wearying and embarrassing it is and how finally one almost shrinks from one's fellow man for fear that fellow man has an axe to grind. When John laid down your letter he said, "She's so sweet and I hope she comes home with some faith left in human nature." I had thought that the studios were protected from people like that.

You are one up on me! No one has yet offered me money (or tried to) for a movie job.

Of course we were very excited about the news that little Adele Kelley might have a bit part.* Of course I have not seen her since she went West but she was a lovely child then with the most endearing good manners, and I never saw a more graceful dancer. Moreover, she was always so sweet about the lack of money in the family and never whined about how much other little girls had in comparison to her own possessions. I think it was fine of you to make all this possible, and I am sure Adele is remembering you in her prayers every night. For you to take so much trouble when you are so busy is a sure sign that you have not lost your faith in human nature! . . .

I am so glad the cast has been announced but I will be far gladder when the present ravenous interest has been satisfied. Things have been pretty bad since Friday. When people can't get me over the phone they worry John, making it difficult to get any work done. Everyone who meets me on the street tries to sell me some of their grandma's furniture to be used in the picture.

P.S. Give Sue my love & tell her I'm writing her soon.

Miss Susan Myrick   *Atlanta, Georgia*
Georgian Hotel Apartments   *January 19, 1939*
Santa Monica, California

Dear Sue:

. . . Sunday John and I had a brief but entertaining visit at the Biltmore Hotel with Mark and a perfect swarm of New Dealers who are doing something or other for the white trash in this section.† Just what I cannot tell you, as they were all as mysterious as a group of small boys playing

---

* Adele Kelley was the teenage daughter of Mitchell's friend Dorothy Bates Kelley.
† Mark Ethridge was editor of the Louisville *Courier-Journal*.

Dick Tracy or Operator 13. The suite was bedlam personified, with groups calling each other into the bath room for conferences, long distance phones ringing in bedrooms, and newspapermen popping in and out. . . . I think this is a pretty fine country after all, when two Tory Conservatives can be welcomed with enthusiasm and smacking kisses by a group varying from palest pink to Red. . . .

Jimmy Pope, who was present, saw Vivien Leigh on the stage in London and had many fine things to say about her, but we did not get the opportunity to talk at length with him.* He made this rather interesting statement about the difference between English voices and Southern voices. He said English people generally spoke with a challenging note and the voice rising at the end of each sentence as if they confidently expected to be interrupted by their listeners and were determined that this should not happen. Southerners talked as if they believed everyone was interested in their words and would wait patiently all day for their own turn—and the Southern voice had a tendency to drop at the end of each sentence even when it was a questioning sentence. Sue, I can hardly wait for you to come home and tell us all that you cannot write or that you have not time to write. I certainly feel for you.

About writing, I know how busy you are, so don't bother to do it unless you have plenty of time. I would not want you to force yourself when you were tired. Just remember, however, we will devour anything you write, with relish and appreciation.

I gather that Hobe Erwin is out, as he feared he would be. Is this true? Who is doing his job and why did Hobe lose out?† When I think of all the time all of us put in with Hobe it seems a pity because of the waste. But he was so nice it was worth it.

Things are beginning to quiet down again after the hoorah of the announcement. It does not take me more than five hours to buy a paper of pins now, whereas last Monday I could not move one step on the streets without being swarmed about and questioned. If we could only get away for two or three weeks till this has blown over it would certainly be wonderful, but I see no chance. There is so much to do that we can't get away, and the announcement of the cast has trebled our work. I never dreamed there would be so much interest after two years. Gladstone Williams's bland an-

---

* Jimmy Pope was the editor of the *Atlanta Journal*.
† Erwin reportedly resigned because the continued delay in the film's production affected business at his design firm. Edward G. Boyle and Joseph B. Platt, a consultant for *House & Garden* magazine, handled the interior decoration of the sets.

nouncement that the premiere would be held here has given me as much trouble as anything else.* I have reached the point of saying, savagely, that that story was not an official release and I know nothing about it and care less, and why don't people write Mr. Selznick who, I have heard, is producing the picture. . . .

Give our best to everyone who knows us and, as for you, lots of love and may the Lord strengthen your arm and your voice and stiffen your neck.

P.S. I am enclosing a letter from Miss Dorothy Blackmar. We spoke of her the Sunday you were here. Please return the letter when you have read it. I believe she is an authority on this subject. Just to refresh your memory, her grandfather was a music publisher in Augusta and New Orleans during the War. The "hobby" she refers to is the collecting of all her grandfather's imprints. If the movie folks need her stuff, please see if you can get them to offer her a decent amount of money. I am sure she is one of these courteous and well bred Southerners who would never think of the money angle. But, like most of us Southerners, she can probably use it.

Your letter, the first written from Santa Monica, has just come. Your characterization of R.B. was wonderful.† John will love it. . . . I liked what you said about Leslie Howard. I have always thought him most intelligent looking.‡

Hooray for you for keeping cotton out of the front yard at Tara. In God's name, what will they think of next? Probably cotton on the front porch of Tara like porch-cotton Crackers. And three cheers for taking the English riding britches off Gerald. You know no Irishman would wear English-cut pants. I hope you win your battle against the pink bows on the pickaninnies' hair. Any self-respecting head woman of a plantation would have worn such bedizened pickaninnies out with a cotton stalk. I don't see why plain "wropped and jucked" hair isn't pictorial as well as accurate. I grieve to hear that Tara has columns. Of course it didn't and looked nice and ugly like Alex Stephens's Liberty Hall and the birthplace of Doctor

---

* On December 26, 1938, the *Constitution* featured an article by Gladstone Williams announcing the premiere would be held in Atlanta in September 1939.

† In her letter of January 15, Myrick complained about Russell Birdwell's heavy editing of the columns she was writing for newspapers in Georgia and called him "the revolving bastard if ever there was one (The Revolving Bastard, in case you don't know, is a bastard any way you turn him)."

‡ Myrick also expressed reservations about the casting of "three Britishers" in the leading roles (both Leigh and Howard were British, as were de Havilland's parents) but said she thought Howard "will get it all right. He has more sense than anybody I've seen around here—except Cukor, who is a grand person."

Crawford Long at Danielsville (both pictures are in Emily Woodward's "Empire").* Of course, I shall have to state in answer to questions (when the picture is released) that Tara is all wrong and never had any columns at all. I know I will be asked this question seven million times and by seven thousand papers because it is the favorite question I am asked, next to "did she get him back?"

Your news about Laura Hope Crews *was* news, and good news too. Please let us know right away if William Farnum is chosen. As Florence Atwater so aptly put it, he was once my very ideel. I can't place Hattie Mc-Daniel, so please tell me what pictures she has played in. I'm glad Eddie Anderson looks good to you. I remember Noah in "Green Pastures" here in Atlanta but do not know if he played it. (Do you mean he and Oscar Polk were in the movie or the stage play of "Green Pastures"?)†

What you say about George bears out our impression of him. Although we met him under most trying circumstances, he seemed not only a fine person but one of the few geniuses we had ever met. I'm so glad you have got a grand person to work with.

Now, my pretty, this will have to be all. Thanks for writing at such length.

Miss Katharine Brown   *Atlanta, Georgia*
Selznick International Pictures, Inc.   *January 21, 1939*
New York, New York

Dear Katharine:

Enclosed is your reaction, which arrived on schedule time and from the expected sources.‡ Whether the contagion will spread I cannot predict, but I will keep you informed. As you will gather from this story, Mr. Daniel is, to use a vivid but vulgar phrase, "kidding the pants off the ladies." I should state here and now that I did not say a word attributed to

---

* *Empire: Georgia Today in Pictures and Paragraphs* was published in 1936 by Ruralist Press of Atlanta. Released in September, the book is the only one for which Mitchell wrote a dust jacket "blurb."

† Crews played the role of Aunt Pittypat. Farnum, a major star from the silent era, was being tested for the role of Gerald O'Hara, and McDaniel was being discussed as Mammy. Anderson, who played Uncle Peter, portrayed Noah in Warner Bros.' 1936 film version of *The Green Pastures*; Polk, who played Pork, was Gabriel in the same film.

‡ The Ocala, Florida, chapter of the United Daughters of the Confederacy issued a resolution on January 19—the birthday of Confederate General Robert E. Lee—protesting "any other than a native-born southern woman playing the part" of Scarlett and vowing to boycott the film.

me in this story, although it sums up my sentiments fairly well. John was handling the early morning telephone calls yesterday while I tried to get a cup of coffee, and he told Frank Daniel a few things. Frank attributed them to me and, using them as a springboard, he dived headlong into the Florida ladies.*

The Associated Press had me on the phone for nearly an hour last night about this story. In fact, everyone in creation has had me on the phone for hours during the last two days. Things were never this bad, even when GWTW was selling around a million. Newspapers make up part of the calls; others come from people who wish to sell me old fashioned beds and bowl and pitcher sets (and matching chambers, for all I know) to be used in Mr. Selznick's film; numbers of the calls are from people who are being "just neighborly," as charming Miss Janet Gaynor so accurately expressed it in one of her recent films. (I have had to handle the phone calls recently because Bessie, our cook, has been chief witness for the defense in a murder trial. Both the defendant and the deceased were dear friends of hers and the killing took place in her front yard, and the lawyers are reserving her testimony as the last testimony before the jury goes out. Bessie has been having a perfectly wonderful time in court and I have been one-half a jump ahead of a fit here at home.)

If there was any possible way for us to get out of town at this time, of course we would leave. But it takes weeks of preparation for John to leave the office, so we are caught between the lines with the shooting going on from both sides. It is most unpleasant.

The people who talk to me on the phone and who corner me on the streets seem pleased enough about Miss Leigh—not violently enthusiastic but pleasantly interested and curious about how she will do. I've had a few letters of protest, probably not over six.

Katharine, I do not want to tell you all how to run your business, but here is a suggestion. It came to me last night when I was talking to the AP man. He was reading me a dispatch from Memphis about the woman who feared Mr. Selznick would not "accurately reproduce Dixie's sacred drawl." I told the AP man that Mr. Selznick had hired three Georgians and was paying them good money just to take care of this matter. He said, "Yes, but

---

* On January 20, Frank Daniel, in an article in the *Atlanta Journal* headlined, "First 'Secession' Comes Over Vivien Leigh as Scarlett of the Screen," pointed out that there is a wide variety of Southern accents, dependent on geography, education and class. He noted that Scarlett's accent was probably a combination of her father, "a shanty Irish," and her mother, who was of French descent.

millions of people do not know that." What he said is true. If there has been any publicity about Mr. and Mrs. Kurtz and Susan Myrick, except in this vicinity, I have not seen it. Oh yes, there were two small items about them which appeared when they arrived at the Coast. My suggestion is why not give them and their work a great deal of publicity? As John and I have said over and over in answering telephone calls recently, the very fact that Mr. Selznick went to the trouble to get them proves his good intentions and his honest desire for accuracy. The general public knows nothing of their presence there nor of their work. I do not know if the three will become bullheaded about personal publicity, but, for your own information, here is something about the Kurtz-Myrick backgrounds.

No one could possibly be more Middle Georgian than Sue, in family, traditions and upbringing. Her grandfather was General Myrick of Milledgeville (which was then the capital of the state)—an exceptionally prominent man in his day and the possessor of one of the most beautiful Southern colonial homes in the State. It is really a dream. However, it is no longer in the Myrick family. Sue's own father was a Confederate soldier, one of those pitifully young boys who went out in the last days. Sue was the youngest child and was brought up in the deep country on a plantation twelve miles from Milledgeville. The atmosphere in which she was reared was unchanged from ante bellum days; her playmates were the little colored children on the place. She is in the odd situation of straddling three generations, having been brought up in one tradition which had passed fifty years before her birth and living in this present time.

As for the Kurtzes—Mrs. Kurtz's people, the Fullers, lived on a plantation in Clayton County, approximately twenty miles from where Tara was supposed to have been. Her father, Captain Fuller, was the hero in one of the most exciting exploits in all Confederate history, for he was the man responsible for the capture of the Andrews Raiders. Their capture postponed the fall of the Confederacy by at least a year. Andrews and a party of Union spies made a gallant effort to burn the railroad bridges between Atlanta and Chattanooga, having stolen a Confederate engine for this purpose. Captain Fuller, pursuing in another engine, overtook them before they could do this. The engines were the Texas and the General. The Kurtzes can give you all the details.

Mr. Kurtz was born in Indiana, but he has devoted his life to the study of the history of this section. He really is the best authority possible. Our local Historical Society endorsed him, you may recall.

Your publicity department has done nothing with them in the way of dramatizing them and showing just what good assistants Mr. Selznick has. I believe there is a man named Price at the Studios. Isn't he an Atlanta man too?* There has also come to my ears fifth-hand the news that an Atlanta girl, Patricia Stewart, daughter of Mrs. John P. Stewart, is acting as social secretary to Vivien Leigh. I remember last year that there were newspaper stories about her little sister Peggy being considered for a part in GWTW. If Patricia Stewart is acting as secretary, there is another Atlanta angle for you.

What I have written above is not publicity—it is the truth, and it is news. Moreover, I think it an excellent argument for your defense.

The Hearst papers have just had John on the phone on the same blanked story. We will certainly be glad when this subsides. I will hold up this letter to get the afternoon papers for you. I will send copies of these clippings directly to Mr. Selznick and, if I can get them, copies to Mr. Birdwell.

Your letter of January 19th has just arrived. Thanks for offering to hold the tests in case we might come to New York. Katharine, we appreciate this very much, but I see no chance of getting to New York and we feel it the [better] part of both valor and discretion not to see the tests. If we see them the news would be sure to leak out, and then every paper in the United States would be on me. Of course, I'd like to see them, and so would John, but, unfortunately, there are many things in this world I'd like to do but find it better not to do.

This will be all until the next shrapnel explodes.

P.S. I realize that the reiteration of what I am now going to write has doubtless become wearying to you but I must write it again—please don't let anything I write you get into the papers or even into other hands. My letters are for you alone and are confidential and if they got any publicity, I couldn't write any more and I would get into a lot more trouble. And I have troubles enough as it is. (By this I do not mean that you can't tell Mr. Selznick and Mr. Whitney any thing I've written—if you think it will be of interest to them. But no one else and please ask them not to quote me. You see, during the last two years, casual innocuous letters of mine have had a way of turning up in news stories and gossip columns until now I never write anything except very dull and formal letters.)

And please, should your organization see fit to do anything with my suggestion about the Kurtzes and Susan, keep me out of it. Please don't

---

* William H. "Will" Price served as a dialect coach on the film. He also worked as dialogue director on *The Hunchback of Notre Dame* (1939), starring Charles Laughton and Maureen O'Hara. Two years later, Price and the actress were married.

say that "this publicity was broken at the suggestion of Miss Mitchell" and please don't say or intimate that I endorsed them or suggested them for their jobs. Even the items out of Hollywood when Sue arrived which read "she is a good friend of Miss Mitchell" has brought down on me all the bothersome and tedious people who for two years have been trying to get me to get them on the lot "just to watch the filming" or jobs as speech experts or technical advisers, etc. "If you got Miss Myrick on you could get me on etc. etc." Dear me, what a strange world we live in, to be sure!

Miss Susan Myrick   *Atlanta, Georgia*
Georgian Hotel Apartments   *January 22, 1939*
Santa Monica, California

Dear Sue:

Here are some more clippings. The Georgian story refers to the Ocala U.D.C. ladies' objections to Miss Leigh. Frank Daniel took the Ocala ladies for a ride in Friday's Journal. I haven't an extra copy to send you but have sent one to Mr. S. this morning. See if you can wangle it from him. Frank landed on the ladies like a d. on a j.b.* . . . Some one from Macon may send you a clipping of this same Georgian (today's) which I am sending you, an early edition, which is full of errors I got corrected in this edition. Cliff Fligg, who wrote it, stated that you lived on a gorgeous old plantation and, Miss Fanny, how you managed to get your copy into the paper from the old plantation, God only knows.† Cliff also picked up some of Frank Daniel's kidding story and attributed it to me. Frank had remarked that a great number of Georgia's early settlers had been from English debtor prisons and that probably gave them an English accent. I nearly tore my hair when the Georgian picked up this remark and put it into my mouth. It is not only inaccurate (as this up-country was settled so long after Oglethorpe's debtors) but I didn't say it and all the patriotic societies will probably come down on me.

As you can gather life has been a Hell since this Leigh story broke—remarkably enough, however, I've personally heard few protests about her. Every one seems pleased in a mild way. But the phone hasn't let up one minute and the papers have been on my neck constantly. I don't see why the west coast publicity department doesn't do something. It isn't my business to fight their battles or to do their publicity. They should have antici-

---

* "Duck on a June bug" is one of Scarlett's favorite expressions in the novel.
† Myrick wrote an advice column for the *Macon Telegraph* under the name of "Fanny Squeers."

pated what was coming and been prepared. Anyone could have predicted exactly what would happen—and John and I, for two, did predict it. From now on, I'm giving out no statements because everything gets twisted and I get into trouble.

Dearie, get together with the Kurtzes on the matter of writing a story for a national magazine. By that I mean, ask Annie L. to let you see a letter I wrote her last week about it. She (like you) talked to me about whether I should drop a line to some editors I knew about a story on technical advising. You three get together and decide when you want me to do this and what sort of story each of you will write so there will not be any conflict. By the way, I sent K. Brown one of your Macon stories and she thought it swell and interesting.*

Mrs. J.R. Barton ·   *Atlanta, Georgia*
Jacksonville, Florida   *January 23, 1939*

Dear Mrs. Barton:

I appreciate the interest in "Gone With the Wind" which prompted you to write to me about the selection of Miss Vivien Leigh to play the part of Scarlett. As always, I am grateful to Southern people for their kind reception of "Gone With the Wind." But your protest against Miss Leigh was mailed to the wrong person! You see, I have nothing whatever to do with the film production and I have no part in the selection of the cast. That difficult task belongs to Mr. David O. Selznick, who owns the film rights. I can see you feel very deeply about this matter. Why do you not write him at his Culver City, California, studios?

Miss Katharine Brown   *Atlanta, Georgia*
Selznick International Pictures, Inc.   *January 23, 1939*
New York, New York

Dear Katharine:

The enclosed clipping probably means that this particular worry is at an end in this section. Mrs. Lamar, of Macon, is not only President-General of the United Daughters but a person of great prominence and authority

---

* During the filming of *Gone With the Wind*, Myrick wrote a column called "Straight from Hollywood" about her experiences on the set. The articles appeared several times a week in the *Macon Telegraph* and the *Atlanta Georgian* from January through July. In 1982, a compilation of most of her columns, edited by Richard Harwell, was published as *White Columns in Hollywood: Reports from the GWTW Sets*.

in Georgia. In fact, many people refer to Miss Dolly as "the Duchess of Georgia," and they do not mean it in a joking way.*

I continue to get amusement from hearing my own words come back to me from every conceivable source—my words about the accents of old time Southerners being more English than American.

Have you any news about who will play Pittypat and Ellen? Having digested Miss Leigh, people are now asking me about the minor roles.

P.S. I intended to send you this story from the Macon Telegraph long ago. I thought it might amuse you, as it gives a perfect picture of Macon, Georgia, and how everyone knows the business of everyone else—and also how genuinely people love Sue. John and I went out to the airport to tell her goodbye, thinking she might be a little lonely. Good Heavens, half of Macon was there and the staffs of the two Macon papers. The airport restaurant was so jammed with them that other travelers could get nothing to eat. I asked who was getting out the Macon Telegraph that night and they replied that it was in the hands of the office boy, the antique colored porter, and Mr. W.T. Anderson, owner and publisher. Practically everyone burst into tears when the plane took off, because Sue was going to be away from Macon for a few weeks. Believe it or not, the Mayor of Macon issued a public statement to the press, proclaiming a "period of mourning" during her absence.

Miss Katharine Brown   *Atlanta, Georgia*
Selznick International Pictures, Inc.   *January 24, 1939*
New York, New York

Dear Katharine:

I thought you might be interested in Mrs. Lamar's full statement, especially her remark about Scarlett being "thoroughly objectionable." The first time Miss Dolly called on me, two years ago, she told me this to my face, and we have been good friends ever since!

I have no duplicate of this clipping, so, if you think Mr. Selznick or Mr. Birdwell would be interested, please send it to them. My secretary informs me that Miss Dolly's remark about Scarlett was on the radio yesterday.

---

* Lamar issued a statement that called Leigh's selection "an excellent solution of the problem, in which all the country has been keenly interested." She added, "I have known many delightful English people, and have often been told by them that they consider the intonations and English of cultured southern people more like that of the mother country than any found in any other section of the United States."

Miss Susan Myrick   *Atlanta, Georgia*
Georgian Hotel Apartments   *January 26, 1939*
Santa Monica, California

Dear Sue:

I have been sending you the clippings, not John, and I will continue to send you any which I think will interest you. Don't bother about acknowledging them for I know how busy you are. We appreciated your last letter about the ending of the "final script." We suspected that hell would be moved and Heaven disturbed in an effort to get a happy ending. I arise to ask, feebly, what Mammy was doing with Scarlett in the last scene, as I had thought I sent her back to Tara permanently several chapters before. Maybe that was just a hallucination.*

You probably have this Macon clipping about Miss Dolly stating that Scarlett was "thoroughly objectionable," but I am sending it just the same. I agree with Miss Dolly heartily, but we seem to be in a minority.

Henry Harrison Kurtz told me that Annie Laurie had written about your remark that you had had seven Belle Watlings in your office one morning. This convulsed John and me and called forth remarks that cannot be put on paper. How much I wish I could be with you for some conversation!

The press and public are beginning to let up a little on me about Miss Leigh, but unabatedly the phone rings and people plead with me to get them and their relatives into the cast in bit parts and as extras, scores want letters of introduction to Mr. Cukor and Mr. Selznick and other scores want me to use my influence "just to get them on the lot so they can watch." So, I can feel for you. . . .

Mr. David O. Selznick   *Atlanta, Georgia*
Selznick International Pictures, Inc.   *January 30, 1939*
Culver City, California

My dear Mr. Selznick:

I am sorry I have delayed so long in answering your three letters—the one written shortly after the announcement of the cast, the letter of January 24th about the difficult scene at the barbecue, and your last letter concerning the Associated Press dispatch about the Ocala ladies. I realize

---

* Myrick reported that the final scene in the latest version of the screenplay had Mammy comforting Scarlett after Rhett's departure: "He'll come back. Did'n I say de las' time? He'll do it agin. Ah knows. Ah always knows." In the novel, Mammy returned to Tara shortly after Bonnie's death.

that you wanted an immediate reply to the one about the barbecue scene, but this is the first time in more than two weeks that I have had the opportunity or the leisure to think coherently. Since the announcement was in the papers my life has been a bedlam. Of course, my life during the past two years has been lived in practically the same circumstances, very largely because of the thousands of people who thought I was producing "Gone With the Wind" single-handed in my back yard and who believed that I, and I alone, could give them parts in it. But the last two weeks have broken all records. I have been living in the pockets of the newspapers for days and they telephone at all hours about all subjects; requests for minor parts in the picture come in every minute; people who wish to sell me their grandparents' furnishings to be used in the picture have swamped me; anxious folks who want to know if you are going to do right by the South must be soothed; and, on top of it all, an incredible number of people want personal letters of introduction to you so they can get on the lot and watch the entire proceedings. As you can imagine, the handling of such people calls for endless time, patient explantation and greater understanding and tact than I possess. So, please forgive my delay in answering your letters.

About the scene at the barbecue where Melanie is first introduced—yes, I see your problem perfectly, for you set forth the difficulties so clearly.* I understand, too, the reason why you must make Melanie's first entrance a telling one—an entrance which will establish her for exactly what she is. To tell the truth, difficulties of this nature had not occurred to me until I read your letter, for I know so little about script writing. The technique of novel writing is, I now observe, a very different one. As Melanie was one of the characters I wished to build continually throughout the book, I intentionally did very little with her in her opening scenes—merely introduced her and thereafter let her grow. But I can see your problem very clearly.

I am so very sorry that I cannot help you with this problem. No matter how much I might wish to help you, by writing the dialogue or sketching the scene, it would be impossible. I am a slow writer and writing takes time, uninterrupted time. For nearly three years, I have had not time for writing of any kind. With hundreds of letters coming in, with the telephone constantly ringing, with people clamoring for "introductions to Mr. Selznick"

---

* Selznick asked Mitchell to write a version of the scene in which Ashley and Melanie are first introduced to viewers. (In the novel, the couple's meeting with Scarlett is recounted in retrospect.) The producer, who claimed 90 to 95 percent of the dialogue in the film would be in Mitchell's words from the book, said several attempts at creating the scene did not capture the "flavor" of the author's writing.

and newspapers bedeviling me for statements on subjects which do not concern me, I have had no time even to think about creative writing, must less attempt it.

Some time ago I abandoned any thought of writing, at least until after the "Gone With the Wind" storm subsided, and it shows no signs of subsiding, for the remarkable public interest in your film is constantly stirring it up again.

So I must ask to be excused but not without regret that I am in no position to help. I am proud that you wish to keep the whole film true to the book and I would help if I could.

I want to take this occasion to correct a wrong impression of my attitude which you may have gained from the newspaper stories published at the time of your announcement of the cast. I was quoted as saying that I thought Miss Leigh could easily learn to talk like a Southerner because she is English. I have forgotten the exact words, but that was the general meaning of the statement credited to me.

I did not say this. I said that Miss Leigh's nationality was not in itself a disqualification, because Southern voices and English voices are frequently similar, and often more similar than the voices of Southerners and those of people in other sections of the United States.

I did not attempt to get the misquotation corrected because I know how futile it is to try to get statements like that changed after they have been published, but I do not wish you to be left under the misapprehension that I think Miss Leigh or any of the others should try to "talk Southern." I have scrupulously avoided interfering in your business by offering suggestions about your film but the misquotation forces me to state what my real attitude is.

Good quality stage voices are not distinctively Northern or Southern or Eastern or Western, and natural voices of that kind will be far more acceptable to the South than any artificial, imitation "Southern" talk. Of course, a voice with distinctively un-Southern qualities, a New England twang or a Mid-Western rolling "r," would be out of place in a Southern film, but I don't believe even that would be as offensive as pseudo-Southern talk in the mouth of a person who did not come by it naturally. If Miss Leigh says "bean" for "been" and uses a broad "a," naturally it would be desirable to attempt to eliminate such Britishisms, but I doubt the wisdom of attempting to go much further. Eliminating distinctively un-Southern accents or pronunciations of words will be fine, but attempting to teach her to "talk like a Southerner," as I was misquoted as saying, will probably do more harm than good.

This is partly because Southerners have been made sensitive by the bogus Southern talk they have heard on the stage and screen so often. But it is also due to the fact that there is no one "Southern accent." There are at least five different Southern accents in different sections of Georgia alone, and Georgians talk differently from other Southerners. Virginia people have a very distinctive accent and Charlestonians speak differently from everybody else. Louisiana and Mississippi lie side by side but the people in the two states do not talk alike. And so it goes.

So many Southern people have expressed the wish that your actors will talk in good quality natural stage voices, instead of imitation "Southern," leaving the atmosphere to be built up by the Negroes and other actual Southerners who may be in the cast. I believe this is the dominant public sentiment and it conforms so directly with my own ideas, I would be embarrassed if you were given a wrong impression of my attitude by reasons of a misquotation in the newspapers.

You were kind enough to offer to send me stills of the cast in costume. Of course I will be very happy to have them and thank you so much for offering to send them.

As to your letter about the AP statement attributed to me in the matter of the Ocala U.D.C. Chapter—I'll have to confess I have not seen it, as it did not appear in the local papers. I do not know what kind of story it was, as I told the Associated Press that I had no statement to make in the matter beyond what I had said the day before—that Miss Leigh was very charming looking and I was very happy the picture was going into production.

Miss Olivia de Havilland   *Atlanta, Georgia*
Selznick International Pictures, Inc.   *January 30, 1939*
Culver City, California

My dear Miss de Havilland:

Certainly, it was not my intention to wait two weeks to thank you for your charming wire.* I was so pleased with it that I intended to acknowledge it immediately. However, the sudden upsurge of public interest in "Gone With the Wind," as a result of the announcement of the cast, has kept me busy night and day. I realize that interest in the forthcoming film is national, but here in Georgia where the scenes are laid, practically every-

---

* De Havilland wrote, "THIS NEWS THAT I AM TO PLAY MELANIE MEANS A LONG CHERISHED DREAM REALIZED. NOW I HOPE FOR ONE THING MORE IMPORTANT. THAT IS TO PLAY THE ROLE TO YOUR SATISFACTION."

one takes a personal interest in each new development, and such a flood of letters and telephone calls came in, I have not had a moment of my own.

Your wire to me, which was printed in our morning paper the day after the announcement, delighted everyone—as it did me. The letters I have received and personal comments I have heard indicate that your selection for the part of Melanie has met with general approval. It will interest you to know that the neighborhood theatres in Atlanta are now re-running your picture "Captain Blood" to full houses.*

I am sending my sincere good wishes to you. I know better than anyone else how difficult a part Melanie's will be. She is one of my favorite characters in the book and I am looking forward to the day when I will see you portray her on the screen.

Mr. Leslie Howard   *Atlanta, Georgia*
Selznick International Pictures, Inc.   *January 30, 1939*
Culver City, California

My dear Mr. Howard:

Thank you so very much for the wire you sent me on January 13th when Mr. Selznick announced your selection for the part of Ashley Wilkes.† Your telegram pleased not only me but thousands of others (if I may judge by the comments I have heard), for it appeared in our morning paper the day after the announcement.

I have little privacy these days and, whether I like it or not, almost everything that happens to me becomes public property—as your telegram did. I feebly told the newspaper editor that yours was a personal wire, but little good that did! Now I am not sorry that it was published for everyone thought it amusing and charming. I suppose you know that from the beginning you have been the choice of the people of this section for the part of Ashley. Here in the South a sigh of relief went up when the announcement about you was made.

I have your enjoyed your work in many other roles and I look forward with intense interest to the time when I can see you as Ashley Wilkes. My very best wishes to you.

---

* *Captain Blood*, a 1935 film from Warner Bros., marked the first of eight on-screen pairings of de Havilland and Errol Flynn.

† Howard wrote, "I AM NOT AT ALL ENVIOUS OF RHETT BECAUSE THANKS TO YOU, IT WAS MELANIE, MA'AM, THAT I WANTED. BUT SERIOUSLY, I FEEL IT A GREAT HONOR TO HAVE BEEN SELECTED TO ENACT ONE OF THE ROLES OF YOUR BOOK, THE TITLE OF WHICH ESCAPES ME AT THE MOMENT."

Miss Vivien Leigh   *Atlanta, Georgia*
Selznick International Pictures, Inc.   *January 30, 1939*
Culver City, California

My dear Miss Leigh:

I realize that my long delay in acknowledging your telegram must seem discourteous to you.* But you yourself are the cause of the delay! Ever since January 13th, when the announcement came that you are to play Scarlett, you have been such an active subject of discussion I have had no time to write. Here in Atlanta, where Scarlett was supposed to have lived, interest in her and in you is very high. The newspapers have been full of stories about you and they telephoned me every five minutes, it seemed. Friends, relatives and strangers also telephoned to ask me questions, most of which I could not answer, and every time I went to town to shop I could never do any shopping because people stopped me on every corner to talk about you and to say how pleased they are that the film is at last getting under way.

I have read that some people have protested your selection because they believe that an American girl, and not an English girl, should portray Scarlett. You will be pleased to know that I have encountered none of this sentiment in Atlanta and very few letters of protest have come to me from other places. Most of the letters I receive are favorable, and the people who stop me on the streets to talk about you seem very pleased with your selection and charmed by your appearance in your photographs.

Your telegram to me, which was printed in one of the Atlanta newspapers, pleased everyone so much. I hope you do not mind the fact that it *was* printed. I will tell you how that came about. I am a former newspaper reporter and when Mr. Selznick sent me an enormously long telegram announcing that you had been selected, I knew my friends on the paper would want to see it and I carried it to them myself. While this story was being set up in type my husband arrived with your wire. He called across the city room to me that he had a wire from you, and the editor who was putting the story into the paper simply snatched it from him and rushed to the composing room with it. *I* did not get to see it till two hours later.

Thank you again for your wire and for the sentiments you expressed in it. Please know that my sincere good wishes go to you. While I have noth-

---

* Leigh wrote, "IF I CAN BUT FEEL THAT YOU ARE WITH ME ON THIS, THE MOST IMPORTANT AND TRYING TASK OF MY LIFE, I PLEDGE WITH ALL MY HEART I SHALL TRY TO MAKE SCARLETT O'HARA LIVE AS YOU DESCRIBED HER IN YOUR BRILLIANT BOOK."

ing to do with the production of the film of my book, I cannot help feeling a thoroughly normal pleasure that the role of Scarlett has fallen into the hands of a girl whose photographs show her to be so charming.

Miss Katharine Brown .   *Atlanta, Georgia*
Selznick International Pictures, Inc.   *January 31, 1939*
New York, New York

Dear Katharine:

Thank you for your letters of January 24 (about the minor characters) and of January 26 (with your question about the advisability of writing to Mrs. Lamar). Answering your last letter first—if I were you I do not believe I would write her or have Mr. S. do it either, unless he should happen to receive some direct communication from her. You probably do not know it, but during the past two years she has written him once or twice, and it may be that she will write to him again at some time. If so, it would be appropriate for him to mention the matter in his reply.

Otherwise, I believe such a letter would be unadvisable. Here are my reasons for thinking so. Mrs. Lamar was speaking her mind truthfully and sincerely; a letter of thanks from your organization might make it appear that you thought her statement was made just to please you, to win your thanks, and that she didn't really mean it. All the fiends in hell could not force Mrs. Lamar into saying something she did not believe and she might resent being thanked for doing something that she considered only the proper thing to do. Here is another reason. You recall that the Ocala ladies said their say one day and Mrs. Lamar said hers the next evening, giving the appearance that she disagreed with the Ocala Chapter and was putting them in their place. I gather that this is not the case. At a recent reception for one of the innumerable brides of the season I talked with a Macon visitor. I must admit that conversation was difficult as the noise and screaming of the close-packed crowds equaled the noise of the fall of Atlanta. The Macon visitor told me that Mrs. Lamar did not know of the action of the Ocala Chapter when she issued her statement. Her remarks were made in answer to an editorial in a Boston newspaper. Unfortunately, the newspapers construed her remarks about Vivien Leigh as a reprimand to the Florida Chapter. I imagine this may have been a source of embarrassment to both the Chapter and Mrs. Lamar.

The third reason is that Mrs. Lamar's statement could hardly be classed as an endorsement of Vivien Leigh. Her remark that it was well that an English woman and not an American was to play "so thoroughly objectionable" a character as Scarlett is scarcely complimentary. I am sure, however, Mrs. Lamar meant no personal slap at Miss Leigh.

I am not sure that the above makes sense. I am coming down with a cold and my mind feels very dull and sluggish.

The excitement about Vivien Leigh is subsiding, which is a blessing. I do not believe the Selznick company need worry about the picture being boycotted. At least, not here in the South. I believe even those who protested about Miss Leigh will attend so that they will not feel left out when the matter is discussed. After all, if they do not see the picture how will they be in a position to criticize it?

I am enclosing some more of Sue's stuff which, as I told you, is appearing here as well as in Macon. I am grateful that it is running in Atlanta as it answers the questions people asked me. Mrs. Kurtz wrote me, very confidentially and not to be repeated outside, that she was spending some time with Laura Hope Crews so that Mrs. Crews could listen to her accent. Mrs. Kurtz is a darling person and she has a sweet, soft, breathless way of talking, so Mrs. Crews couldn't do better. John and I whooped at the thought that Aunt Pittypat might appear with the face of Mrs. Crews and the voice of Mrs. Kurtz.

Not that it matters, but I want to keep the record straight. In a previous letter to you I told you that Wilbur Kurtz had been "endorsed" by the Atlanta Historical Society. I am in error there, for when I went to the secretary to check up the matter I discovered that no formal action of endorsement had been taken by the Society. Practically everyone informally put in a word for him when Mr. Cukor was here. Mr. Cukor attended a reception my family gave to the Historical Society and all the members told him how valuable they thought Wilbur would be. But no action was taken formally by the Society. I am correcting this error I made because I do not want to get either the Selznick company or myself in trouble because of my mistake.

I am enclosing a clipping from this morning's paper about Mr. Whitney. You will note that he was questioned about the possibility of the world premiere of GWTW being held here in Atlanta. In the past two months, Atlanta has been in quite a stew about this. It all started, as far as I can tell, from a newspaper story out of Washington which stated flatfootedly, but without quoting any authority, that the premiere would be here.

I mention this because you may receive a letter from the Atlanta Junior League about a costume party they wish to stage as a part of the premiere festivities. One of the League members had me on the phone for an hour yesterday telling me of their plans and insisting that I get

Mr. Selznick to send the whole cast to their party—it would help them to make so much money, it seems. Shamelessly, I referred her to that "charming, attractive and understanding Miss Brown who auditioned the Junior League last year."

Other organizations and individuals may write you about premiere matters, because I intend to push them all off on you, just as I have done with the would-be Scarletts. But don't believe it if any of them tell you that I have endorsed or recommended their plans. And don't let any of them give you the impression that I am urging, promoting or sponsoring the idea of having the premiere staged here.

I have told everybody simply that "I know nothing about it and I have nothing to do with it," but often people think I am not telling the truth about matters like this (they just can't believe I know as little about the movie as I do), and probably I will be credited with having said a lot of things that never entered my mind.

I really dread the months ahead until the picture has actually been produced, for literally hundreds of people have already come down on John and me for seats at the premiere. Some of them want passes but the great majority want our promise that they will get seats, that they won't be crowded out. With interest already so high, this coming year may be even harder on us than 1936 was. I think you know that attending any premiere would be an ordeal for me, so don't believe any stories you may hear that I am the one who is promoting the idea of holding the premiere in Atlanta.

The Editor	*February 2, 1939*
The Hollywood Reporter	*Atlanta, Georgia*
Hollywood, California	NOT SENT

Dear Sir:

I have received a clipping from your publication, dated January 18, 1939, in which this mention is made of me:

"Although the dailies and the press services batted the Vivien Leigh-Scarlett story around, none kicked the gong by asking Margaret Mitchell what SHE thought about it, and now it's too late, for Selznick has whipped her into line for an accolade on the choice."

I think you have been very unjust to the "dailies and the press services," to Mr. Selznick and to me. At no time has Mr. Selznick attempted to "whip me into line" and at no time have I bestowed "an accolade on the choice."

The statement I made at the time when the choice of Vivien Leigh for Scarlett was announced was simple and it was truthful. Having never seen Miss Leigh on the screen and having seen only one photograph of her, I could only say that I thought her very pretty and that she had a charming pair of Irish eyes. As to her capabilities, I said nothing for I did not then—and still do not—know her capabilities. Ever since "Gone With the Wind" was sold to Mr. Selznick, some time after its publication, I have deliberately refused to express myself on any and all of the Scarletts who were advanced by the press and by movie gossip columnists. Having nothing to do with the production of the film, I did not think it my part to express any opinion. I still think an expression of an opinion by me would be decidedly out of order.

When I wrote above that you had done an injustice to the dailies and the press services I meant that the lack of a statement from me was not their fault. Since September 1936 scarcely a day has passed that some paper or news service has not queried me on who I would like to play Scarlett or what I thought of the leading contender. At the time the announcement was made about Miss Leigh the papers and the press services naturally asked me these questions. I replied as I stated above.

Mr. Selznick and his organization have been courtesy itself to me. They understand my hands-off attitude and my reiterated statement that the picture and all pertaining to it was their affair and not mine.

The Right Rev. Gerald O'Hara   *Atlanta, Georgia*
Bishop's House   *February 6, 1939*
Savannah, Georgia   *CONFIDENTIAL*

My dear Bishop O'Hara:

Stephens has told me of your letter and I have obtained his approval for writing you, instead of attempting to reply indirectly through him. Please do not feel that Stephens violated your confidence by showing your letter to me. He thought I should see the letter, not only because it so directly concerns me but also because he has confidence in my ability to keep such matters confidential, which I most certainly will.

I thoroughly understand and deeply sympathize with your attitude. I have had so many experiences comparable to yours and I know how wearing they can become. I know what it means, just as you do, not to be able to go anywhere without having my connection with "Gone With the Wind" brought into the conversation. I have shared your feeling of relief when the public interest began to subside and I have the same dread that you have of the period ahead when the motion picture will produce a fresh upsurge of public interest.

So I am not being heartless and indifferent when I say that I do not think anything can be done along the lines you suggest. I would gladly do it if I could but I believe the time has passed when it is possible.

Actual "shooting" of the movie began about three weeks ago and the producers have already completed several different scenes in which Gerald appears. Making the change you suggest would require re-making these scenes entirely and I doubt that the producers would be willing to stand the expense which this would involve.

But expense is not the most important consideration. You are familiar with the long delay in making the movie, because of the producers' inability to find a satisfactory cast. Now that the cast has finally been selected and the filming has begun, time is important to the producers and I doubt that they would look favorably on any changes that would involve loss of time in re-making several scenes and otherwise revising the script, advertising material, et cetera.

I have mentioned these factors in the producers' situation, because they, the Selznick company, are the ones who would have to decide the question you have raised. I might suggest a change in Gerald's name, but they would be under no obligation to adopt my suggestion. When I sold the motion picture rights, I made an outright sale. I have no control of any kind over the movie, I am not employed in any advisory capacity and I rarely have any information about what is being done except that which I read in newspapers. A great many people seem to believe that I have the deciding voice in everything the producers do, but this is the exact reverse of the truth. I am merely the person from whom they bought a piece of property back in 1936. It is their property now and if I attempted to tell them how to manage it, they would probably pay mighty little attention to me, especially if the adoption of my suggestions involved them in a substantial loss of time and money.

I regret the embarrassment you have suffered and I can say with all sincerity that I would have been happy to save you from all of it, and I have tried my best to save you from it. If you had come to Savannah a few months, or even a few weeks, earlier than you did, there would have been no Gerald O'Hara in my book. I would have changed his name without any request from you and without you even knowing about it.

I went to endless pains to avoid using names that would cause embarrassment to anyone. Before I adopted the name of Gerald O'Hara, I made lengthy investigations to make certain that no person by that name had lived in Savannah, Atlanta or Clayton County during the period of my book. The same was true of all of my other characters. Of course, I also avoided using the names of prominent living people. It required months of tedious research but I have been rewarded by the fact that none of the names of my many characters has caused embarrassment to anyone, excepting Gerald O'Hara alone. And that one name would have been changed if I could have foreseen that a strange quirk of fate would send a Bishop to Savannah with the exact name of Gerald O'Hara after it was too late for the change to be made.

When I first read in the newspapers of your coming to Georgia, I was stunned. I had worked so hard to avoid using the wrong names, and here was an almost malicious turn of affairs to upset my well laid plans. My book had already been finished, it had been delivered to the publishers and it was far advanced in production. I wired my publishers explaining the situation and begging for time to change the name, but they said it was too late to attempt to make the change. Gerald's name appears so often in the book, it would have required a wholesale re-setting of the type and there was not time in which to do that. And so Gerald O'Hara kept the name he had had for nearly ten years before you came to Georgia, to your embarrassment and mine.

I have often wished to give you this explanation and I am glad that your letter has given me the opportunity. Before ending this long letter, I want to add one thing more. It is merely an opinion of mine and I offer it for whatever it may be worth.

Even if you or I had the power to change Gerald's name in the motion picture, it would be far better from *your* standpoint to leave it as it is. Changing it to some other name would, I firmly believe, cause you a thousand times more embarrassment than you have experienced so far. The interest in and knowledge of "Gone With the Wind" is worldwide and changing the name would only serve to give worldwide advertising to the fact that the Bishop of Savannah-Atlanta has the same name as my Gerald O'Hara.

If I should attempt to persuade the producers to change Gerald's name—and persuasion is all that I could use; I have no power to command—it would be necessary for me to give my reasons in full and that would force me to tell them of your situation. I would not, of course, violate your confidence and tell them you had asked me to make the request but, according to my view, it does not matter who makes the request. The mere making of it would multiply your embarrassments, for it would quickly become known to the newspaper gossip columnists. Hollywood is a whispering gallery. No matter how confidentially I might attempt to handle the matter with the producers, the story would be in the newspapers within a week, for apparently nothing can be kept confidential in Hollywood longer than a few days.

Your predicament has had some publicity locally, but it has never been publicized on a big scale. My clipping service brings me the newspaper items about my book from all parts of the world and your name has been mentioned in them only a few times. But the attempt to change Gerald's name probably would put stories about you in newspapers throughout the nation, perhaps throughout the world.

However, suppose that I was able to accomplish the impossible. Suppose the producers did agree to change Gerald's name and also succeeded in keeping my request confidential. Even this would not avoid unpleasant publicity, for the circumstances would become known sooner or later. An unbelievably large number of people know Gerald O'Hara by name and love him, and the first time it became known that his name had been changed to John O'Hara, for example, protests would begin to roll in, along with many inquiries as to *why* such a change had been made. The newspaper writers would promptly put two and two together and you would get the credit for the change, even if you had never suggested it. Newspaper stories would go round the world about it and you, and I am afraid that many of the stories would treat it as a joke. As a result you would be subjected to the very kind of publicity you wish to avoid but on a magnified scale, far surpassing anything that might happen if Gerald's name is left as it is.

I base this opinion on some of my own experiences with "Gone With the Wind." The book is my own creation but it has long since gotten out of my hands. It belongs apparently, not to me, but to its readers, and the number of them is greater than I have ever been able to comprehend. Just today the mail has brought me letters from Belgium, Poland, Sweden, South Africa, Brazil, Ireland and Czecho-Slovakia, as well as those from people in this country. The lady who wrote me from Poland said, "It would surprise you to know how much interest we have in your characters and how much we talk about them here in this little village in the Carpathian hills." The same thought runs through many of the other letters.

Personal experience has shown me that the public interest centered around "Gone With the Wind" is a force of such magnitude that it is not to be trifled with. I do not trifle with it myself and I would not advise anyone else to trifle with it. If Gerald's name were changed, I seriously believe that it would cause widespread resentment and a considerable part of that resentment would be directed at you, no matter how innocent you might be. Of course, I may be wrong about all this but it is my opinion.

You asked that your letter be kept confidential and I will do this. I also ask you to keep my letter confidential. My notoriety has taken away a considerable part of my freedom of speech and I have expressed myself much more freely in this letter than I ordinarily do.*

Mrs. John Huske Anderson   *Atlanta, Georgia*
Raleigh, North Carolina   *February 9, 1939*

My dear Mrs. Anderson:

Thank you so much for your note and for the column by Nell Battle Lewis.† I always enjoy Miss Lewis's column.

Of course I was relieved when Mr. Selznick announced the cast for "Gone With the Wind." After more than two years of having people believe that I was producing the picture single-handed in my living room, I was naturally relieved. So many thousands of people thought that I could get them into the movies, and of course I couldn't, as I have no connection with the film and no influence with the producers. I know nothing about Miss Leigh beyond the fact that her photographs show a very pretty young woman. I believe that if the producers are willing to trust her with an investment of several million dollars, they must have faith in her ability. However, it is not up to me to either endorse the pretty lady or criticize her. And so, I have done neither.

Miss Susan Myrick   *Atlanta, Georgia*
Georgian Hotel Apartments   *February 10, 1939*
Santa Monica, California

Dear Sue:

Laughs have been few and far between recently, as I have been laid up with a cold and a persistent fever. (I'm much better now.) But your letter had a laugh in every line. I must admit some of my laughter was on the wry side—especially when you described Twelve Oaks. I had feared, of course, that it would end up looking like the Grand Central Station and your

---

* The bishop replied on February 17, thanking Mitchell for her explanation and noting, "The coincidence of names was unfortunate, but of course I do not attach blame to anyone for it."

† In her January 22 "Incidentally" column, Lewis noted the selection of a British actress was a better choice than "a Scarlett from Kansas." Mitchell had created a character "with so much personality in her own right, that a suitable interpreter was hard to find."

description confirms my worst apprehensions. I did not know whether to laugh or throw up at the *two* staircases. Probably the Twelve Oaks hall will be worse than the one in "So Red the Rose." People here in Atlanta got up and left the theatre in herds when that hall was shown. And I will never forget the pungent remarks about the level of Hollywood brains. God help me when the reporters get me after I've seen the picture. I will have to tell the truth, and if Tara has columns and Twelve Oaks is such an elegant affair I will have to say that nothing like that was ever seen in Clayton County, or, for that matter, on land or sea. This would be somewhat embarrassing to me and perhaps to the Selznick company, but I am not going on record as telling a lie just to be polite. When I think of the healthy, hardy, country and somewhat crude civilization I depicted and then of the elegance that is to be presented, I cannot help yelping with laughter.

I wish you'd write something about Scott Fitzgerald when you get the time. If anyone had told me ten or more years ago that he would be working on a book of mine I would have been stricken speechless with pellagra or hardening of the arteries or something. I dearly loved his books and still do and re-read them ever so often. "This Side of Paradise" is the most perfect crystallization of an era in all American fiction. It makes me feel sad when I think how utterly past that era is now. I'm sure Mother and I picked him up in our car one day when he was at Camp Gordon during the war. The streetcar tracks had not been laid that far at that time and we usually hauled twelve soldiers to town every time we went out to see Stephens. After he got famous and I saw his picture I remembered him.*

Sue, it does sound incredible that the script is not yet finished. I have an idea (and correct me if I'm wrong) that they are using Sidney Howard's script for the first part of the movie—and it followed (so I was told by Mr. Howard) the book closely. I imagine they are following the book up to the end of the War with few changes, but telescoping the Reconstruction period as much as possible.

God forbid that Scarlett's Reconstruction house should be a poem of good taste. That would throw out of balance the whole characterization of the woman. Hurrah for George and Mr. Platt for standing up for a bad-taste house. Hobe Erwin had some swell ideas on that house and we had a hot correspondence on wallpaper and many other details, including a perfectly ghastly gas lamp fixture which stood at the bottom of the

---

* Novelist F. Scott Fitzgerald, on loan from MGM, spent about two weeks in January working on the screenplay of *Gone With the Wind*. In the spring of 1918, he was stationed at Camp Gordon, near Atlanta.

stairs (my own idea), a large brass nymph, discreetly draped and bearing aloft the gas fixture. . . .

Dearie, your Georgian articles are fine. Not long ago my barber, who does not know I know you, talked about them during an entire hair-setting. Everybody enjoys them so much.

Later

Wilbur Kurtz, Junior just phoned and told Margaret Baugh that his father had wired him that SIP was keeping him on for another ten weeks. For a number of reasons besides my personal liking for the Kurtzes, this news cheered me. On the chance you are interested, I will give you the reasons.

You are clear across the continent and living a very sequestered life, so I know it is hard for you to understand what turmoil and excitement has been going on in the South (and in the North, too) since the Vivien Leigh announcement. I should add that the Selznick company is not out of the woods yet on the matter of giving two leading parts to foreigners after all their talk about getting Southerners. My clipping service keeps me in touch with public reactions and I imagine I know more about them than even Selznick's publicity department. A number of people from out of this section smiled in a superior manner at some statements I made in "Gone With the Wind" to the effect that Southerners were violent people, still untamed, though very polite. They have changed very little, and there has been plenty of violence recently. There I was caught between the lines. I had nothing to do with the picture and little interest either, except that I be let alone, but I caught the barrages from both sides. The final statement I gave out to the papers seemed to have a very quieting effect; the Associated Press carried it all over the country. I said that Miss Susan Myrick, well known newspaper woman of Macon et cetera, and Mr. and Mrs. W.G. Kurtz of Atlanta, well known et cetera, have been taken to Hollywood for the express purpose of passing on the accuracy and authenticity of Southern backgrounds; I said that your presence in Hollywood, at Mr. Selznick's invitation, was the surest guarantee of his good faith and his desire to do right by our much maligned Southland. People have been chewing that over and it tastes very well. With no disrespect meant to Mr. Selznick or Mr. Cukor, the fact remains that all that stands between them and a violent Southern revolt is you and the Kurtzes in Hollywood and, I may add, my own noncommittal but pleasant attitude. If two weeks after such a statement appeared in every small town paper in the South the Kurtzes came home, I know exactly what would happen. Every paper would rise up editorially and denounce Mr. Selznick, saying that all he wanted was the use of your name and the Kurtzes' name for publicity and when he had gotten that publicity he let you out. They would point out that this was perfect evidence that Mr. Selznick had no desire to do a true Southern epic but intended to produce another Hollywood Southern horror full of boners, bulls, inaccuracies and material offensive to the South. Next people would begin writing letters to the newspapers, then boycott would raise its head months before the picture was half shot. I'd be between the lines again, pulled hither and thither by papers and public who would want to know just what I thought about the whole affair. There would be no other thing for me to say except that I had no idea why you three were let out when the picture had hardly begun. The headlines above such an innocuous state-ment would read "Author Denounces Selznick for Double Dealing." (This may sound fantastic but it fits in with my past experience. I made the most non-committal statement about Vivien Leigh but hundreds of papers head lined it "Author Okays Leigh" and "Author Satisfied With Leigh." Some were even stronger.)

You know me well enough to know that I am not an alarmist nor do I borrow trouble. But I have always been one to take "the long view." More-over, for nearly three years I've had a box seat with an excellent view of the reactions of the public mind, especially the Southern mind. It sometimes seems to me that "Gone With the Wind" is not my book any longer; it is something about which the citizens of Economic-Problem-Number-One rally. These citizens are sensitive and sore at real and fancied slights and discriminations and are ready to fight at the drop of a hairpin. With pub-lic emotions barely cooled about Vivien Leigh, I think it would have been complete folly if Mr. Selznick had let Wilbur and Annie Laurie come home. Mr. S. is not a Southerner, of course, and knows practically nothing of our psychology and he would have, unwittingly, let himself in for more trouble and wrangling than he or his publicity department could ever handle.

I feel certain that if he had let the Kurtzes out and a storm broke over him, he or Katharine would have been on the phone in no time asking me to help them or give them advice. And, of course, there would have been no help to give and no advice either.

After more than two years of having my life upset by this movie, I shud-der to think what I would have gone through with if the embattled South had gotten sore about the Kurtzes being let out. I am so desperately tired of standing in the middle ground between the movie folks and the public and I do not know if I could have gone through with another barrage so close to the Vivien Leigh barrage.

Annie Laurie wrote that you had met Katharine Marsh Bowden.* I hope you get to see the family as they are swell people. Annie Laurie also included casually a bit of information that turned my few remaining hairs white. She spoke of the bazaar scene with Scarlett and Rhett dancing together, and mentioned that Scarlett had on a bonnet and veil. In the name of God, what was she doing with a hat on at an evening party where everybody else was bareheaded and wearing low-cut gowns? My temperature jumped seven points at the news. I cannot image even Scarlett showing such poor taste. I foresee that I will get at least one good belly laugh out of this picture, and it will be during this scene.

Mrs. Wilbur Kurtz
Selznick International Pictures, Inc.
Culver City, California

Atlanta, Georgia
February 13, 1939

Dear Annie Laurie:

Several days ago, Wilbur, Junior telephoned and told Margaret Baugh of receiving a wire about the extended contract. Margaret and I whooped with pleasure and from that minute my cold began to get better! John, Margaret and I had felt very depressed ever since you wrote us that your contract was up and the good news made us all happy. Then came your letter of February 8th with details and the wire from you yesterday. Thanks for them both.

I know you and Wilbur have been so happy in Culver City, knew you were enjoying every minute of it—and I hated to think your fun was over. Now—hurrah for another ten weeks in Make-Believe!

I think the sewing room girl who offered to send the scraps from the costumes must be a very sweet person indeed. If she sends them (and if I ever again have time I can call my own) I will make old fashioned patchwork pillows of them, briar stitching the scraps together. I have always liked sewing and embroidering and have missed them so much during the last few years.

Miss Crews sounds like such a *real* person. No wonder you like her so much. I haven't seen her since "The Silver Cord." She was marvelous in it.

And now I must talk about something that is not so pleasant. It is the letter you wrote Mr. Cukor about Adele Kelley. If you had consulted me in advance I never would have authorized such a letter, and the use of my name without my permission was directly contrary to my wishes. The

---

* Katharine Bowden was Marsh's oldest sister and lived in southern California.

whole thing has made me feel very discouraged, for I have had such a desperate struggle over improper uses of my name, and it has thrown a cloud over my natural pleasure in hearing that Adele has gotten a part.

Except for the fact that I was sick, I would have written you just as soon as I received your letter about Adele. I did not want to write such a letter when I was already feeling bad, and perhaps the delay was for the best, as it has resulted in an alteration of my plans. I originally intended to write also to Mr. Cukor or Mr. Selznick, telling them that your letter about Adele was unauthorized. On further thought, I realized that this might be an unduly harsh way of handling the situation. Knowing you as I do, I was confident you would *want* to correct the error yourself when you understood my position, and I am leaving the job in your hands.

I have still another reason for wishing to handle the matter in the way that will cause you the least possible embarrassment. It is that I do not hold you entirely responsible for what happened. I know Dorothy Bates and her beguiling ways and I know, just as well as if I had been there and seen it happen, how she played on your sympathies one minute and sweet-talked you the next, until she got you convinced that you ought to do something which your own judgment probably told you was against my wishes.

But that is neither here nor there. For your own sake, and Wilbur's I do not want to embarrass you unnecessarily, and my thought is that it will be less embarrassing for you to handle the job yourself than it would be if I handled it direct with Mr. Selznick or Mr. Cukor. However, if you prefer for me to write to them, please let me know.

Here is a re-statement of my position—I have not in the past endorsed anybody for a part in the movie, I am not endorsing anybody now, and I will never endorse anybody in the future. I have never permitted anyone to use my name for an endorsement, and on the innumerable occasions when people have used my name without permission to promote their candidates I have not hesitated to expose them.

I had a deep and sincere conviction from the very beginning that it would be improper for me to attempt to pick Mr. Selznick's cast for him, when I know less than nothing at all about the making of movies. Everybody agrees that my rule is the right one but everybody apparently wants me to break it in so far as their own particular candidates are concerned.

You certainly must know what an unending battle I have had in holding to what I believe is right. Every imaginable kind of pressure has been put on me. Governors and other high officials have tried to force me into backing their candidates, utterly false stories have been published saying that I endorsed some particular pet candidate, with the deliberate purpose of putting me into such an embarrassing position I would hesitate to deny the fake "endorsement" (I have not hesitated to deny every one of them), one of the richest and most influential women in the United States called me over the long distance telephone to talk about other matters and then used that conversation as the basis of announcing that I was backing a certain actress for Scarlett, and on and on. Friendship, kinship, imaginary kinship and every other possible emotional appeal has been used over and over.

This pulling and hauling on me from all sides, the innumerable difficult situations from which I have had to extricate myself, the thousands of letters I have had to write because of this one problem, have accounted for such a big part of *all* my problems and worries since GWTW was published, I could have led a reasonably happy life these past two and a half years except for this one problem alone.

It is unnecessary for me to tell you that if I were to make a change of front now (or *seem* to make a change), I would plunge myself into the worst possible situation I have ever experienced. I would not make such a change because it would be a betrayal of one of my most serious convictions, but I would not do it also for the simple reason that it would get me into endless trouble. It would bring down on me, like a swarm of hornets, the thousands of people to whom I had previously refused endorsements and it would advertise me to the world as a hypocrite and a liar.

Almost these same effects would be produced if somebody else used my name in endorsing candidates. My only protection would be to deny that I had given any endorsement and to say that my name had been misused. That is why it is important to get this matter straightened out with Mr. Cukor and do it *quickly*. Every minute that passes increases the danger that a story will get into the newspapers saying that Adele was given a part at my request or because of my friendship for her, and if that happens I will have no choice but to deny it and tell the whole story of what happened. I would have to say that I had not seen the child in three years, didn't know what she looked like, had no idea of her dramatic ability, and that you and Dorothy had used my name without permission and against my wishes. Of course, this would be the end of any friendship between me and the Bateses.

This is what I want you to do—

1st—Tell Mr. Cukor or Mr. Selznick right away that your letter was written without my knowledge or approval, that I did not endorse Adele and that my position about not endorsing people has not changed in the slightest.

2nd—Ask them to tell their publicity department not to put out any stories about Adele in which my name is mentioned in any way. *This is very important.* Even if the stories did not say I had endorsed her, I would get the credit for having done so and that would make me out a liar to all the people I have told I was giving no endorsements to anybody.

3rd—Tell Sue about this and ask her not to include me in any mention of Adele she makes in her column. She can say Adele is "formerly of Atlanta" or something of the sort without bringing me into it.

4th—Caution Dorothy and Adele of the dangers in this situation and ask them to say just as little about me as possible. If they go around saying things of the kind you wrote in your letter about my sponsorship of Adele, it will certainly get into the newspapers. I am sure you must know how the gossip columnists are constantly picking up items on the movie lots. Anybody you meet may be one of their spies, and if Dorothy and Adele go around saying I helped Adele get a part, it will get into the newspapers sooner or later. If anything should be published intimating that Adele is my protégé, I will be forced to expose the whole story. I would be very sorry about that, not only on your account, but especially on Adele's account. I am fond of her and I am hopeful that she makes a big success in her career, on her own merits. But you and Dorothy have created a situation that may force me to say something that might make Adele unhappy. So please tell Adele, Dorothy, all of the Bateses, Sue, Wilbur and anybody else who knows about the situation that the less said about me in connection with Adele the better it will be, not only for my protection against untrue stories getting into the newspapers but also to save Adele from what might be an embarrassing situation. Other people are to blame for all this, not Adele, but it might work out that she would be the chief sufferer.

Don't let Dorothy put all of the blame on you. She had warning long ago of how I feel about all these things, for she has tried time and again to get me to endorse Adele and to use my influence to get her in the film, and I have told her in detail why I could not do it. So, if worse trouble develops out of this, it will not be because Dorothy did not know in advance what she was heading into. Considering all of the things that have happened in my relations with her and her family over a period of years, it makes me very depressed to think that she would go out of her way to cause me worry and trouble, as she has done in this instance.

One thing more, John was not at all pleased about your using his name to get Katharine and Anne into the Selznick lot.* We do not want our

---

* Anne Bowden was Marsh's niece.

names used at all by other people. We have followed a strict policy of not asking any favors of the Selznicks, and we do not wish to be put into the position of having asked favors by reason of other people using our names without our permission.

I know all of this probably sounds very harsh. It isn't and you would agree that it isn't if you could understand all of the reasons back of my position. You would agree that it is just plain common sense if you had been through the same hell as I have these past few years. I have never succeeded in getting an outsider to understand it, so I will not try to explain it. I simply ask you to take my word that there is a good reason behind everything I have asked you to do or not do. I ask you also, most sincerely, to believe that not one word of this letter has been written for the purpose of wounding you and that I would have been most happy if I could have escaped writing any of it.

You see, Annie Laurie, I know you and I understand you. I know how utterly scrupulous and conscientious you are. I know you'd die before you'd use my name or that of any of your friends to help *yourself*. But I know how sympathetic and kind hearted you are about helping *others*. That is why I hate to write this letter, penalizing you for your kind heartedness. But if it were John or Father or Steve who had gotten me into such a position, I'd have to ask them to get me out of it, just as I am asking you.

I hope you can get the situation in hand before something worse happens. Let me know what Mr. Cukor says and any other developments. . . .

Miss Marcella Rabwin   *Atlanta, Georgia*
Selznick International Pictures, Inc.   *February 15, 1939*
Culver City, California

My dear Miss Rabwin:

The seven pictures arrived yesterday afternoon. I thank you for sending them and I thank Mr. Selznick for his courtesy in wanting me to see them. A number of the cast have been merely names to me and, of course, I was curious to see what they looked like. I had never seen Barbara O'Neil, Ann Rutherford, Fred Crane, George Besselo or any of the Negro characters except Hattie McDaniel.* Of course the pictures interested me very much. There is one thing I find especially touching—perhaps that's because I am the author—Carreen looks so much like her mother's child, in expression

---

* O'Neil played Scarlett's mother, Ellen; Rutherford played her youngest sister, Carreen; Crane and Besselo (who shortly afterward changed his name to George Reeves) played the Tarleton boys; and McDaniel played Mammy.

and gesture and dependence. I do not know how such things are managed in the moving pictures, but this seems beautifully subtle to me.

You wrote that these pictures were for my private use and not for publication and you requested that I keep them from "the prying eyes of the news hawks." Of course I will do this, and any other pictures or communications which may come to me from you or Mr. Selznick will be held equally confidential. I write you this so that you will not think I betrayed your confidence and gave to the newspapers the pictures which appeared yesterday and which I am enclosing. They are from our morning paper. One of our afternoon papers carried an entire page of stills. They were different from the morning paper, with the exception of the one of the O'Hara family. I would send you these but I do not have an extra copy of the afternoon paper. I do not know where the papers got the pictures, but they did not come from me.

I will be happy to have any other photographs you wish to send me in the future. With thanks and best wishes to you and Mr. Selznick,

Miss Susan Myrick   *Atlanta, Georgia*
Selznick International Pictures, Inc.   *February 15, 1939*
Culver City, California

Dear Sue:

Here are some more clippings. The Constitution carried a full page spread of stills too, different ones from the ones in the Georgian. Yesterday, the day they appeared, Mr. Selznick's secretary kindly sent me some very lovely stills which were for my own private interests and I was requested to keep them out of the hands of the newspapers. Just about the time I was looking at them the newspapers came out with a half a dozen apiece. Is this a case of the right hand not knowing what the left hand is doing, or did the Atlanta papers get someone to swipe the stills for them?

I'm also sending you the clippings about George's walkout.* Did you write the story in the Constitution? We can't help feeling bad about George quitting the picture. You know how much we liked him personally and how impressed we were with his mind and his ability and his lovely simplicity. And we don't like many people. How will this affect you, Sue? Will you get along with George's successor? I've been so glad that you were

---

* On February 14, Selznick and Cukor issued a joint statement that the producer and director were parting company over a "series of disagreements between us over many of the individual scenes" in the film. It was announced that director Victor Fleming would be pulled off MGM's *The Wizard of Oz* to take Cukor's place.

having a good time, even if they were working the socks off you, glad that you liked George and geed with him. I hope you'll find the next director as pleasant to deal with.

If you have time and care to do it, write us any inside dope you have on the George-Selznick split. If you don't care to put it on paper, tuck it away in your head and tell us about it when you see us.*

The more I look at the picture of the bonnet and the veil that Scarlett was wearing at the bazaar the worse it gets. Queen Marie of Roumania never had quite such a getup after Ferdinand's death, and even she didn't wear it to evening parties. I suppose this must be one of the things that come under the head of "pictorial." And nary a wounded man at the bazaar and nary a uniform that had been through the mud of Virginia.

Mr. Harry Haggas   *Atlanta, Georgia*
Pudsey, North Leeds   *February 16, 1939*
England

Dear Mr. Haggas:

Thank you so much for your letter and the many nice things you wrote me about my book. Naturally, it pleases me very much to know that an English reader is interested in Scarlett and her friends. No, I do not intend to write a sequel to "Gone With the Wind," for, to tell the truth, I do not know what happened to my characters after the last page.

Since your letter was written you have doubtless read in English newspapers that the part of Scarlett in the film has been assigned to Miss Vivien Leigh, an English actress. I have never seen Miss Leigh on the screen, as her only American film was "A Yank at Oxford" and I missed it.† Her photo-

---

* In a letter to Mitchell on February 14, Myrick related that the dispute centered around the screenplay, which was still being rewritten: "So George just told David he would not work any longer if the script was not better and he wanted the Howard script back. David told George he was a director—not an author and he (David) was the producer and the judge of what is a good script (or words to that effect) and George said he was a director and a damn good one and he would not let his name go out over a lousy picture and if they did not go back to the Howard script (he was willing to have them cut it down shorter) he, George was through. And bull-headed David said, "'Okay, get out!'"

† *A Yank at Oxford* starred Robert Taylor and Maureen O'Sullivan, with Leigh in a supporting role. The 1938 film, produced by MGM's British subsidiary, has an early scene in which Taylor's American character is asked by his British tutor what he is "reading"—meaning his field of study—but Taylor misunderstands and replies, "Well, I'm still reading *Gone With the Wind*, but I'm only halfway through."

graphs show her to be a very charming young woman. I understand from reading our newspapers that production on the film began on January 13th and is being pushed rapidly. Clark Gable has the part of Rhett; Leslie Howard, Ashley; and Olivia de Havilland, Melanie.

Colonel Telamon Cuyler   *Atlanta, Georgia*
Wayside, Jones County, Georgia   *February 17, 1939*

My dear Colonel Cuyler:

This is just for your confidential ear. I was greatly distressed by the story the Constitution ran at the time the pictures of the film were published. The headline was completely at variance with the story, for the headline read "Margaret Mitchell Puts Okay on First Screen Stills of Novel." A careful reading of the story will show that I put no okay on anything. But who reads carefully? Doubtless you know of my long struggle to keep from either endorsing or criticizing anything about this film. I have felt that either course would be presumptuous on my part, as I had nothing to do with the picture. Yet, I am continually misquoted, and in the future I intend to say "no comment."

Far from "okaying" the pictures, I cried "Godlmighty" in horror before I caught myself. My eye had lighted on Scarlett's widow's bonnet and long veil in the midst of the décolleté gowns of the Atlanta belles. I cannot imagine even Scarlett having such bad taste as to wear a hat at an evening party, and my heart sank at the sight of it. Probably the reporter mistook my exclamation for one of pleasure. A quick view of the uniforms show not a one that looked as if it had seen active service. Nor was there a wounded man to be found even with a microscope. The Armory looked vaguely like Versailles and not like the rough room in which drills were held. However, it was not my place to remark on these things, as the Constitution had only requested that I identify the chapters from which the scenes were taken. Should I be asked at some later date if these scenes were correct in detail, I will be in an embarrassing position for I will have to tell the truth. I have an idea that Mr. Kurtz and Susan were overridden on these points. After all, they can only suggest and can do nothing if their suggestions are not followed.

The news about George Cukor's retirement came as a shock and I know no more than what has appeared in the newspapers. I am anxious to read Sue's next article to see if she will cast any light on the matter. The more I read about Hollywood the gladder I am that I decided long ago I would have nothing to do with it! . . .

Mrs. Wilbur Kurtz   *Atlanta, Georgia*
Selznick International Pictures, Inc.   *February 18, 1939*
Culver City, California

Dear Annie Laurie:

I feel so very rich this morning (and guilty too) because I received one letter from you yesterday afternoon, a special last night for supper, and on this morning's mail there arrived your third letter, written Wednesday, February 15th, with the clipping from the Hollywood Reporter. I know what an enormous amount of time these letters took and I do thank you most sincerely for your trouble. With everything on the lot so upset about Mr. Cukor's resignation, I appreciate the letters all the more. . . .

Now, Annie Laurie, let me tell you how much I appreciate your understanding of my letter and my situation. I have been so worried lest I might have hurt you or upset you, and I did not wish to do either. So, thank you, and now let us put the matter behind us.

The news about Mr. Cukor was terrible, of course, and I can imagine that everyone, from Mr. Selznick on down, has a sense of uncertainty. I gather from newspaper stories that the cause of Mr. Cukor's withdrawal was that he did not like the script he was given. Maybe some day we will all know the whole story. I do feel sorry for Sue because she worked in close contact with Mr. Cukor and seemed to get along with him so well. I hope all three of you like Mr. Fleming and find him easy to work with. . . .

Miss Susan Myrick   *Atlanta, Georgia*
Selznick International Pictures, Inc.   *February 23, 1939*
Culver City, California

Dear Sue:

This letter is just a bouquet for Miss Myrick.

Of course John and I have thought your articles for the Georgian the best things that ever came out of Hollywood. Generally Hollywood stuff is the dreariest drivel in the world and only fit to be read while sitting under a drier in the beauty parlor. It is so press agentish that I do not understand how even the ten year old mind can tolerate it. Your stuff is so fresh and interesting and, in other words, dearie, we think it's swell.

Tuesday I heaved my flu-ridden carcass from the bed to attend a party given by Medora Perkerson for the Atlanta Women's Press Club. Medora has just been elected president. There are about forty-five members and I believe every last one rushed up to me and, completely unprovoked, cried, "Susan Myrick's stuff is simply marvelous!" When you get such enthusiasm from your fellow-professionals you are indeed good. Furthermore,

I heard no note of envy nor of criticism; everybody seemed pleased and proud that "one of our girls" was in the game pitching and being a credit to her State. Lib Whitman, society editress of the Georgian, said proudly, "You've been so sick I guess you haven't seen the Georgian trucks recently. For the last two weeks all Georgian trucks have had enormous banners on them screaming, 'Read Susan Myrick's Hollywood Stories—Exclusive in the Georgian.'" The Journal and the Constitution girls looked as though their vitals were being gnawed. Of course, I swole up as if you were my daughter or something and I had everything to do with each word you put down. Next time you come to Atlanta I want to give a Press Club party for you. The truth is the Press Club is pressing such a party upon me.

I think you would be touched by Colonel Cuyler's solicitude for you since Mr. Cukor's departure. In letters he refers to you as "dear Susan." He thinks your stories are grand, too.

I wish you could get your stuff syndicated in the North. Ellen Wolff, formerly of the Journal staff, is just back from New York and she found herself the center of attention because she quoted from your stories. She told everyone she saw that she could not understand why the New York papers were not running them.

The picture of Melanie in labor, with "Gone With the Wind" clutched to her and Scarlett anxiously cooling her brow, was wonderful. John says the expression on Miss de Havilland's face is precisely the expression I wore during the time I was writing the book. One still sent me by Mr. Selznick showed Mrs. Merriwether at the bazaar and, I give you my word, I practically cringed before her. She looked like a combination of all the dowagers who harrassed me in my young days driving me to wait on tables at Georgia Products dinners and to sell tickets on Tag Days. . . .

If you see George C. these days give him our best and tell him that we understand (as well as people can understand at so long a distance) the reasons why he walked out.*

Miss Susan Myrick   *Atlanta, Georgia*
Selznick International Pictures, Inc.   *February 28, 1939*
Culver City, California

Dear Sue:

I did not get to the Press Institute, as I still felt wabbly in the knees. I knew I could never stand up for countless hours on the tiles, nor could

---

* Cukor stopped by the studio on February 20 and asked Myrick to tell Mitchell that "he is sorry not to finish this production because he liked you and the book so much but he just couldn't go on with the thing when he felt it wasn't as good as it should be."

I stay up till all hours listening to New Dealers. However, John went over for Friday and Saturday. I hope you'll be glad to know that he said it was the quietest Convention he had ever attended, nice but not much fun. You weren't there, nor were any of the Telegraph. . . .

Your last letter, having to do with Mae West, practically ruined me.* What a pity you are not writing such tidbits as this for the local press. I am sure there are thousands of readers who would be interested. We appreciated this long letter, as we have appreciated your others.

Sue, if you have not already read a book published last year, "I Lost My Girlish Laughter," I entreat you to get it.† I had read it when it first came out and thought it amusing. Last week, after reading some of your letters, I bought me a copy and re-read the book. I got a great deal more out of it. The information in your last letter, about Ben Hecht and John Van Druten being called in on the script, sent me into gales of laughter, for the situation was identical with one in the book.‡ I suppose there's nothing left of Sidney Howard's script by now.

I hate to say "I told you so" but there is no one but you to whom I can say it. When movie agents were hounding me in 1936 to let them unload GWTW on the movies, I refused, saying it wasn't possible to make a movie out of it. This remark drove them to hysteria. Finally, I let The Macmillan Company sell it. Before I signed the contract I told Katharine Brown and the other Selznickers assembled in the room they were making a great mistake, for a picture could not be made from that book. They all laughed pityingly and patted me, saying "there, there." They said it was a natural and just look at all that dialogue! Why they would not have to write another line. I said yes indeed and thank you, but I knew how that book was written. It had taken me ten years to weave it as tight as a silk pocket handkerchief. If one thread were broken or pulled an ugly ravel would show clear through to the other side of the material. Yet, they would have to cut for a script, and when they began cutting they would discover that they had technical problems they never dreamed about. They all said I

---

* On February 23, Myrick wrote about makeup artist Monte Westmore's visit to actress Mae West's apartment: "Mae's bed, he told us, is wide enough for six men to sleep in— then without a change of countenance he added 'no doubt six men had slept in it' and cont[inue]d the tale."

† *I Lost My Girlish Laughter*, written by Silvia Schulman, a former Selznick secretary, was published by Random House in 1938 under the pseudonym Jane Allen. The book tells the story of movie producer Sidney Brand, a character clearly based on Selznick.

‡ Playwrights Hecht and Van Druten had been brought in to rework the script before Fleming took over.

was overwrought and were very sympathetic and sent Miss Flagg and Miss Brown out with me to buy me a cup of tea.

Now they have run into exactly the problem I foresaw. And may God have mercy on their souls.

Heaven only knows what Mr. Fleming will shoot if he comes to this section of Georgia. If he intends to go on location in Clayton County around the scene of the crime, he is going to waste a lot of money. I remember the section before it was lumbered out and it was beautiful; I remember it before the boll weevil. Now it almost hurts to ride those back roads. When times got hard the folks sold everything they had, and that meant most of the trees. Where there were formerly miles of wooded hills on the Clayton County side of the River there are now miles of stumps, and the Flint River is a sad and unprepossessing little yellow creek lying open to the sky instead of being shady and being banked with willows.

I took George Cukor and Hobe Erwin through that section. George tried to be polite but his disappointment was terrible. Of course the few remaining old houses were a shock to him. He tried to be polite about them and murmured feebly that they did have "charm." But they didn't look like the State Capitol at Montgomery nor the old Capitol at Milledgeville nor those ghastly sets from "So Red the Rose." There was no reason why they should have looked that way, as this section was never very handsome, architecturally speaking. When we finished the trip he and Hobe were in agreement that they had not seen anything that would serve as a location.

For Heaven's sake, make them finish the picture by September. The Press Convention will be held then at Calhoun, which is just up the road a piece above Marietta. . . .

Do let us know more about Mr. Hecht and Mr. Van Druten. I somehow picture them and Mr. Selznick in a pose not unlike that of the Laocoon group.*

March 1, 1939

P.S. . . . The news about Ben Hecht and Van Druten will be kept confidential. Rumors are rife around here that not only will all the footage George shot be thrown away but Miss Leigh and Mr. Gable as well. I had a truly dreadful time yesterday down town. I wanted to buy chintz for a slip cover and I went to three stores to get away from people. I got no chintz but I

---

* "Laocoön and His Sons," also called the "Laocoön Group," is a marble sculpture that depicts the Trojan priest and his offspring being strangled by sea serpents. The piece, circa 25 BC, is in the Vatican Museums.

did get fallen arches as I stood up for hours, mainly listening to Charleston people howling about Clark Gable and demanding that Basil Rathbone be given the part. I finally said, "So South Carolina is still fighting lost causes," and lit a shuck.

If they do re-shoot the bazaar, I hope you get the bonnet off Miss Leigh. I have had to endure so much conversation about that bonnet that I do not want to get out of the house. I am enclosing, for your interest, Colonel Cuyler upon the subject.* Please let me have it back. . . .

Mr. and Mrs. Wilbur Kurtz   Atlanta, Georgia
Selznick International Pictures, Inc.   March 11, 1939
Culver City, California

Dear Annie Laurie and Wilbur:

. . . No, I have not seen your last family letter (the one you said was to "Brother and Margaret"). I am hoping to go over to your house tomorrow, so I will ask for it. You said that in this letter you had told about the business of opening the picture with the firing on Fort Sumter. I must confess that at this news John and I yelled with laughter. I have yet to see a War picture which did not open with Fort Sumter, and it was too much to hope that "Gone With the Wind" would be different. Movie producers are just like vaudeville actors. I once asked a vaudeville actor why he and others of his profession persisted in cracking jokes that came from Joe Miller's joke book.† I felt than an occasional new joke would be relished by the public. He said, seriously, that I was all wrong. Far from relishing a new joke, the public resented one bitterly. They were confused by the newness and did not know whether to laugh or not. They knew what to expect when an actor said, "Who was that lady I seen you with last night?" and they laughed dutifully. Probably Mr. Selznick feels that audiences are accustomed to Fort Sumter and will know when they see it that a picture about the War will inevitably follow. Please tell me whether this Fort Sumter business means that your cotton press will not appear. You remember how we dis-

---

* Cuyler wrote to Mitchell on February 23, predicting that "if the dancing scene is a sample, I foresee trouble." Not even Scarlett "would have been so utterly lacking in taste as to wear a bonnet at a party." He also noted the bazaar scene missed "the sheer drama of the ragged uniforms and the wounded. . . . I am sure Susan and Wilbur would never have allowed all these errors. They must have made valuable suggestions only to see them put aside."

† Joe Miller was an eighteenth-century British actor whose seriousness led his friends to ascribe all new jokes they heard to him. After his death, a book titled *Joe Miller's Jests* was published, followed by a companion piece, *Joe Miller's Joke Book*.

cussed the picture opening with the cotton press in operation? I sincerely hope the press sequences will not be eliminated.

Annie Laurie, I have enjoyed your articles in the Constitution so much and have clipped them for my files.* Everybody who reads them stops me on the street to tell me how interesting they are. How you find time to write them I do not know, but I hope you keep up the good work. Wilbur's pictures reproduce beautifully, as usual, and add so much charm to the page. Do keep up the good work for all of us who like to read about what is going on. . . .

Have they got a script yet? I read in some theatrical paper that the last people who were hired to do the script refused to do a day-to-day job and said that they had to be at least ten days ahead. That sounded as if the script were not completed yet. In accordance with your request, I have not breathed a word about Ben Hecht working on the script. Night before last I met a Hollywood producer who is visiting a friend of mine and he told me that Robert Benchley had been approached with an offer to work on the script too. I regret to state that I was overtaken by unseemly merriment and laughed until I cried. I could not tell the man why I laughed, but I was thinking that Groucho Marx, William Faulkner and Erskine Caldwell would probably be on the script before this business was over. As you can gather, I do get a great deal of fun out of this affair, and my greatest enjoyment comes from a sense of thanksgiving that I have nothing to do with it and am not in Hollywood.

Mr. David O. Selznick   *Atlanta, Georgia*
Selznick International Pictures, Inc.   *March 13, 1939*
Culver City, California

My dear Mr. Selznick:

I have just received a clipping of a UP story, published in the New York Telegraph on February 28th, about a letter Selznick International wrote to Congressman Hugh Peterson, who had objected to the choice of Vivien Leigh for Scarlett.† Here follows a portion of the story:

---

* Annie Laurie Kurtz wrote a series of weekly articles about the filming of *Gone With the Wind* that ran in the *Constitution* from mid-February until mid-June. From November 28 to December 12, the newspaper also featured daily excerpts from a diary she kept while in Hollywood.

† When Leigh's selection was announced, U.S. Representative Hugh Peterson of Ailey, Georgia, told the press, "I don't like it. Not at all. Many of the scenes are laid in my district and there are some grand actresses of the South who are steeped in traditions of the Civil War period and could have played the part to perfection." In response, the congressman

"The film company, in a three-page, single-spaced letter, attempted to set him right on the matter. It said Margaret Mitchell, author of "Gone With the Wind," had approved Miss Leigh in the following elegant manner:

"'She looks like she has plenty of spirit and fire, not at all like a languid Hollywood girl.'"

When the selection of Miss Leigh was announced, I neither "approved" nor disapproved her, and I have not done either since then. On the night of your announcement, when the newspaper reporters asked me my opinion of Miss Leigh, I told them that I knew nothing about her. They then showed me a photograph of her, the first one I had ever seen, and I remarked, in effect, that she appeared to be a young woman of spirit and fire, with a very decided Irish look in her eyes.

That politely noncommittal comment is the only statement I have ever made about Miss Leigh. Certainly no one could construe it as an "approval." However, hundreds of newspaper items were published the following several days stating that I had "put my ok" on Miss Leigh or otherwise approved her. It was very embarrassing to me to find myself in this false position, but I did not write you about it, as I was reluctant to believe your Publicity Department was responsible for this distortion of my meaning. I was willing to believe that it was a product of the carelessness in language that sometimes gets into newspaper stories.

The item of February 28th, however, seems definitely to place responsibility on someone in your organization for circulating the false statement that I have "approved Miss Leigh." Again, the newspaper writer, rather than your organization, may have been responsible for this language, but the same item (as published in some other papers) stated that Mrs. Lamar, president general of the United Daughters of the Confederacy, had also "approved Miss Leigh's selection." With these two misstatements in the same article, I am forced to believe that the Selznick organization must have been at least partly at fault. I know what Mrs. Lamar said and it could not be construed as an "approval," any more than my comment was. Neither of us is the kind of person who would approve any actress for the difficult role of Scarlett without knowing much more about her than we

---

said, he received a letter from Selznick International that reported Mitchell had approved of Leigh's casting and invited Peterson to Hollywood to meet the actress. He declined, noting his constituents would not appreciate him "trotting out to the West Coast to look over the film girls."

know about Miss Leigh. Both of us might make polite comments about an actress whom *you* had selected but we would naturally feel resentful if our politeness was abused and our comments twisted into something we did not say.

I am writing to ask you to caution your Publicity Department and the rest of your organization (including MGM) against the misuse of my name in connection with Miss Leigh or any other matter involved in the filming of "Gone With the Wind."

I am confident you understand what my position is, and I know Katharine Brown does, but if the rest of your organization (and MGM) does not cooperate, I will be forced to do something that will be embarrassing to all of us. If publicity is put out or statements circulated saying or even hinting that I am responsible for your cast, your script or any part of the film (other than my book), I will be forced to go into the newspapers or on the radio and tell what the true situation is. I would regret to do that very much. It would lead the public to believe that you and I are on bad terms and perhaps create the impression that I disapprove of everything you have done. But unless you can control your publicity and prevent it from misrepresenting my position, I will have no choice but to tell the public myself what my position really is.

In issuing instructions to your organization, it ought not to be difficult to make clear what my position is. It is simply that I wrote the book, *and that is all*. I am responsible for my book but I am not responsible for the motion picture. My connection with the motion picture ended on July 30, 1936, when I signed the contract selling you the film rights. I sold them to you lock, stock and barrel and from that day forward they have been yours, to do with as you please.

You have done with them as you pleased, according to your own judgment and without interference from me. That is entirely proper, for you are the owner and producer. I am not. You are risking your money and reputation on the film. I am not. I am the author and that is all and I have stubbornly stayed in my position as author and stayed out of your business as producer.

What I am asking is that your publicity leave me in my position as author and not attempt to drag me into the position of co-producer. I do not intend to have my name used to back up your decisions, when I have had nothing to do with the making of the decisions. I have carefully remained on the sidelines, I have repeatedly insisted that you should have a free hand in making the film, without interference from me or anybody else, and I believe this has been an asset to you. At least, I have not added to your troubles by permitting my name to be used by various groups who were trying to force you to make decisions that might have been embarrassing. For all of these reasons, I am entitled to ask that your Publicity Department show me the consideration of not misrepresenting my connection with the film.

Perhaps I may seem to be writing a long and very serious-minded letter about a small thing, the newspaper item of February 28th. It is not a small thing to me, for it involves a question of publicity policy that is a large and important one. During the coming months, as work on the picture progresses, you and MGM will be putting out more and more publicity and it will be to your advantage as well as mine if we have a clear understanding now as to how the publicity will be handled.

Nothing in this letter means that I feel any ill will toward Miss Leigh or you. My purpose is simply to set things straight about a matter of considerable seriousness to me. Ever since the summer of 1936, your film has been a subject of public controversy and, for no good reason at all, I have been caught in the storm center of the controversy. A large part of the public apparently believes that I have complete control over you and everything you do in making the film. This has created a problem for me many times greater than any of my other problems as the author of "Gone With the Wind." If I did have control over the film and you, I would take the situation philosophically and make the best of it. But having no control over any detail of the film and no connection with it of any kind, I cannot permit my life to be made more burdensome by publicity items linking me up with the film more closely than the facts justify.

It may be that your Publicity Department has been encouraged to do this by the friendly attitude I have taken all along toward you and the film. In fighting my own fight against the popular misconception of my connection with the film, I have also fought for you. I have assured thousands of people of my confidence in you, and I have also made friendly comments, when I could sincerely do so, such as I made about Miss Leigh. But if my friendly attitude is taken advantage of and my polite comments are twisted into something very different from what I said, I will be forced to abandon both friendliness and politeness. If I am to be rewarded for my courtesy by being placed in a false position and having my name misused, I will be forced to take steps of my own to make my position perfectly clear to the public.

With best regards to you and best wishes for the success of "Gone With the Wind" in the films. . . .

Miss Katharine Brown   *Atlanta, Georgia*
Selznick International Pictures, Inc.   ·   *March 13, 1939*
New York, New York

Dear Katharine:

This is just a hasty note to acknowledge your letter to John about Mr. Whitbeck. It has just arrived and he has not seen it yet. I know he will thank you, even as I do, for your trouble in the matter and for Mr. Selznick's attitude.*

I am enclosing a copy of a letter I sent Mr. Selznick today. I wrote it with a great deal of regret and embarrassment but it was a letter that had to be written. I feel that Metro-Goldwyn-Mayer does not understand what my attitude has been in this matter. Mr. Whitbeck's plan of getting me to pose for a trailer shows this very plainly. Things have been intolerable enough for two years and if M.G.M., not understanding my attitude, tries to use me in their publicity I will have to do something drastic.

I keep hoping that things will settle down enough for me to write you a long letter some day, but work seems to get heavier all the time. We've been trying to get away on a vacation since Christmas and hope to manage it sometime during the next week.

Miss Virginia Morris   *Atlanta, Georgia*
United Artists Corporation   *March 16, 1939*
New York, New York

My dear Ginnie:

Your letter of March 13th, telling me you had written an article for Photoplay Magazine about our days at Smith, has just arrived. To be quite frank, the news came as a bombshell.

I have just been looking over the letters we exchanged back in 1937 about a similar matter. At that time you were interested in doing an interview for Photoplay. I wrote you at length telling of the many incredible happenings in my life since "Gone With the Wind" was published and

---

* Brown alerted Marsh that Frank Whitbeck, who produced MGM's movie trailers, wanted to come to Atlanta and shoot footage of Mitchell for a *Gone With the Wind* promotional film but that Selznick told him "not to pursue Peggy." In late 1939, MGM released a short titled *The Old South*, which was narrated by Whitbeck and for which Wilbur Kurtz served as historian. While not directly tied to *Gone With the Wind*, the 11-minute film told the story of the South's reliance on "King Cotton" and ended with Whitbeck noting that the people of the region were working "to reclaim their heritage . . . and to reconstruct with their cotton a glorious nation which hath gone, gone with the wind."

explaining why any magazine article about me—whether an interview or not—would add to my burdens. You answered that you "understood," that you would never have asked me if you had known of my desire to avoid publicity and that you would not for anything bring more troubles upon me.

In case you do not have copies of the correspondence in your files, I am enclosing a few excerpts from the two letters. The quotations show clearly that I was not talking about an *interview only* but about magazine articles in general. On that basis, I understood that you made statements amounting to a promise not to use me for copy. I thought you were one friend I could rely upon not to parade before the public what few remnants of my private life I have left. Whether you did make such a promise I will let you decide for yourself.

You also wrote in that same letter, "Ruth Waterbury wanted me to do any kind of story but I told her we hadn't seen each other in some time and I wouldn't put a word to paper without talking to you personally." That confirms that you did understand we were talking about "any kind of story," not just an interview, and it also makes it almost impossible for me to believe that you have actually delivered the article for publication without even consulting me or letting me look over what you wrote.

Does it mean, Ginnie, that you have been living with the movies and their publicity for so long you have forgotten that some people, many people, like to keep their private lives private? Did you think I was lying when I told you of my honest desire to get out of the limelight? When I thought you were giving me the promises of a trusted friend, were you just giving me soft soap? You wrote that you thought I was "distrait" and taking a hysterical view of the situation. I didn't like that a bit. If there was ever a less hysterical person than I am, I haven't met her, but I didn't write you of my resentment then. I forgave you because I thought your comments were the sincere, if misguided, remarks of a friend. Now, am I to believe that you didn't mean any of your promises, that you were merely saying "soothing" things because you thought you were dealing with someone suffering from hysteria?

I don't know that I can get you to understand but I will make one more effort. My book belongs to the public. Anybody who wants a copy can buy it and can do anything with it he pleases. Whether people like it or dislike it, and whether they say good things about it or bad, is their business, not mine. But my own life is my own. I have got a right to some privacy and I intend to hold on to it if I possibly can. I haven't paraded myself around before the public and I don't want other people to parade me around. I don't get my pictures published in newspapers with my thighs exposed to attract attention to myself and boost the sale of my book, and I don't like it when other people expose my intimate affairs. I have tried to do what I think an author *ought* to do—to stand or fall on my book and not on my personality. I know that is the right stand. Why should my supposed friends try to drag me off it?

I would like to keep my childhood and my girlhood and the rest of my life to myself. They mean a lot of me, and I am happy that not much of my private life has yet gotten into public print. I hope it never will but if it should ever *need* to be done, because of circumstances which have not yet developed and probably never will, I think I am the one who should have the right to say who shall do the writing. At least, I should have the right to know that what is written about me is accurate.

Ginnie, isn't there something you can do to get Photoplay not to publish this article? If you wrote it because you need the money, I will be glad to pay you whatever the magazine offered. No, I will have to take that back. If I did pay you, it would probably leak out somehow and then the gossips would be spreading the story that you had blackmailed me or there was something scandalous in your article which I had to get suppressed, and that would be very bad for both of us. (That's the hell of the situation I'm in, Ginnie. Every little thing I do and every "harmless little piece" that's published about me has got dynamite in it. I wish you could understand.) So I can't pay the money but I would like for you to know that I would be willing to keep you from losing money on me if it wasn't too dangerous for me to try it.

I am writing Photoplay today that I was not consulted about the article, that its publication is contrary to my wishes and that the magazine is publishing it at its own risk. Whether the article is "innocuous" or not, its publication will mean the end of any friendship between you and me. I hope you can withdraw it.*

Excerpts from my letter of April 21, 1937 to you, and your reply of April 29, 1937.

---

* The article was not published, but Mitchell and Morris never spoke again. On October 20, 1942, Morris returned this letter, which she termed a "ghoulish document," to the author, joking that she was "thwarting the day when my money-hungry heirs would surely sell it to The Georgia Historical Society!" She recalled that "there had never been a more exciting or more treasured friend than the pre-success Peggy" and added that the real reason she was returning the letter was in hopes "it may be read by that lost Peggy who will join me in a spontaneous and vociferous 'Opera!'" Mitchell did not acknowledge the contact.

(My letter)—"Ginnie, I'm tired out. I want to get out of the spotlight more earnestly than you or anybody else could possibly believe."

(Your letter)—"Indeed, I understand perfectly and I wouldn't add an ounce to your burden for anything."

(My letter)—"Ginnie, the movie angle of my situation has been responsible for at least 75 per cent of my troubles during the past year, which has been like a madhouse when it should have been the happiest time of my life."

(Your letter)—"It's indeed a shame, Peggy, that you can't enjoy the terrific success of your book."

(My letter)—"It wouldn't matter whether your article (in Photoplay) was about me and the movies or about me and Einstein's theory. The effect would be the same. It would arouse interest in me personally on the part of thousands of people—Photoplay's habitual readers—who hadn't given much thought to me before and it would bring down on me a fresh avalanche of letters."

(Your letter)—"I have no real conception of what besets an author."

(My letter)—"My private life is my own."

(Your letter)—"There's not the slightest reason why anyone should inquire into your private life."

(My letter)—"The job of being a celebrity—which is the last thing in the world I ever expected or wanted to be—has brought with it problems and burdens heavier than I am able to carry. An article about me in Photoplay would only increase the burden."

(Your letter)—"I wouldn't add an ounce to your burden for anything."

(My letter)—"My friends who understand my predicament have been trying to help me and they have turned down a large number of offers to write 'I knew her when' articles."

(Your letter)—"Indeed, I understand perfectly."

Miss Ruth Waterbury   *Atlanta, Georgia*
Photoplay Magazine   *March 16, 1939*
New York, New York

Dear Miss Waterbury:

Virginia Morris, of United Artists, New York City, has just notified me that she has written an article about me, based on her recollections of my days at Smith College, which Photoplay may publish in the near future. Virginia did not consult me about this article, I did not give my permission for it and I was not shown the manuscript. Publication of the article would be objectionable to me and I am notifying you that its publication will be at your risk.

You have been very considerate of me in the past when you requested articles or interviews and I asked to be excused. I hope you can show me the consideration now of not publishing this article. This is not because I have an ill will toward you or Photoplay. I am an admirer of the magazine and I read it frequently. It is simply that I am making a sincere effort to withdraw from the spotlight and return to a normal life. Naturally, an article about me in a magazine with your wide circulation would stir up interest in me again, at a time when I am happy to say it appears to be waning. Beyond that, I have an especial reason for objecting to this article. An article of the personal reminiscence or "I knew her when" variety is particularly distasteful to me, for it takes away what few shreds I have left of my personal privacy. I would like to keep my private life and I will be grateful if you can help me to keep it so.

Mr. David O. Selznick   *Atlanta, Georgia*
Selznick International Pictures, Inc.   *March 24, 1939*
Culver City, California

My dear Mr. Selznick:

Your letter of March 16th made me very happy, and I would have answered it immediately except that I have been ill with a mild but very persistent case of influenza. When I wrote my letter of March 13th, I did not *want* to believe you were responsible for the unpleasant things I mentioned, and your explanation that no one in the Selznick organization was to blame for them was more than welcome.* You and the members of your staff whom I have met have been so uniformly courteous it would have depressed me greatly if others in the organization had actually done the things about which I was complaining—without justification, as I now understand. Please accept my very sincere regrets.

Probably my letter would not have been written if it had not been preceded by a series of incidents which had gotten my nerves on edge. Even though I know you were not responsible for them, they got me into the right state of mind to send you the kind of letter I wrote when the Peterson incident occurred. They began with the hundreds of newspaper items saying that I had "okayed," "endorsed" or "approved" the selection of Miss

---

* Selznick insisted that the letter to Peterson quoted only what Mitchell had approved and that the congressman, "not content with the publicity he received," had misrepresented the studio's response.

Leigh. As I hope you noticed in my previous letter, I recognized that these misstatements—and the Peterson item, too—could easily have resulted from reportorial carelessness, rather than from any other cause, but they were irritating nevertheless. Then there was a very nasty item in the Hollywood Reporter saying you had whipped me into line about endorsing Miss Leigh, or some such remark. Also I received a number of letters from theatres over the country asking me to make personal appearances when "Gone With the Wind" was shown or to do other things in connection with their commercial promotion of the film. To top everything off, there was the MGM advertising man who wanted to make a movie of me for use in the advance publicity for the picture.

These and several similar things occurred in the past two or three months and they seemed to point to a change in publicity policy on the part of someone from what it had been before then, when your people had always shown me great consideration. I thought that MGM might be responsible but I did not write direct to them, as all of my dealings have been and will continue to be with you. What was happening had the appearance that someone was trying to use me personally in the film promotion, which would be very distasteful to me, so I cannot tell you how pleased I was to receive your assurance that your own policy is unchanged and that you have again cautioned MGM not to misuse me or my name.

As to the particular matter of the Peterson letter and similar matters, the policy you have outlined is all that I could ask. Using exact quotations of my comments on Miss Leigh, in the form I sent them to you, is just the way they should be handled. I stand back of what I actually said and I would not have made my comments in the first place if I had not intended to keep on standing back of them. You have my permission to use these quotations in any proper way, and as long as you follow this policy, I will not hold you to blame if other people misquote them or misrepresent them. I suppose some of that is unavoidable as long as human beings are human.

I am, of course, glad to tell you again of my friendly attitude toward you and the motion picture of "Gone With the Wind." I am sorry that my letter put doubts in your mind on that score and I am especially sorry that my misunderstanding of things added to your worries, for I realize, probably better than anyone else, how many worries and problems you have had. I know what difficulties and problems have surrounded you from the beginning, and I have admired the way you have overcome one obstacle after another.

If anything was said to Miss Leigh about my previous letter, please tell her that I have never blamed her for getting entangled in my public problems. Far from feeling any resentment toward her personally, because the controversy about her has caused me some annoyances, I have the highest admiration for the way she had conducted herself. Her dignity and sweetness in her very difficult situation have won friends for her everywhere.

For your private ear and not for repetition, I am impressed by the remarkable number of different faces she has. In the stills you have been good enough to send me, she looks like a different person every time she is shown in a different mood. In the last batch of stills sent me by Miss Rabwin, the one of Ashley and Melanie on the stairs was beautiful, and I was amused by one of the bazaar scenes showing Maybelle and her little Zouave. He looked exactly like the "out-of-town" boy who would have caused Southern matrons to flutter if he had paid his attentions to a girl as sweet and innocent as your Maybelle.

Miss Susan Myrick   *Atlanta, Georgia*
Selznick International Pictures, Inc.   *April 17, 1939*
Culver City, California

Dear Sue:

I know you'll have a crown in Heaven for the great joy your letters have given us. Your last one, which announced that Sidney Howard was back on the script, kept us laughing all day. Every time we thought of the history of the script and the full circle which has been made we laughed again. It is all too incredible. I suppose Mr. Howard discovered that there was practically nothing left of his original script. I would not be at all surprised to learn that the script of the sixteen other writers had been junked and Mr. Howard's original script put into production.

For months I have had to restrain myself from writing Mr. Howard and telling him about the goings-on over the script. Something told me he'd be the type who would appreciate the information. But, as usual, I kept quiet, for I never discuss anything about the picture with anyone. I have never met Mr. Howard but his letters have led me to believe that he is a grand person and one who has a sardonic appreciation of the strange ways of Hollywood.

My congratulations for your success in the matter of the dresses which were to defy the laws of gravity and stand up by themselves.* I consider

---

* At one point, the script for the afternoon nap scene at the Twelve Oaks barbecue called for the camera to pan over six gowns standing in a row, supported by their crinolines. Plunkett, with Myrick's help, eventually persuaded Selznick that dresses rigid enough to stand on their own would be impossible to wear.

this victory in the same category as the Miracle of the Marne. I wish Mr. Selznick could be put into a corset and laced down to sixteen inches and be laid upon a bed with the request that he get some beauty sleep. I think he might then understand the reason for loosened stays.*

The picture of you and Miss Crews was so good and she looks too cute to be true. She sounds as if she'd be so much fun. Confidentially, we have been expecting to see upon the screen Miss Pittypat with the face and form of Miss Crews and the voice of Annie Laurie. I knew Annie Laurie was so fond of Miss Crews and had been with her so much and I did not see how Miss Crews could resist annexing for her own use a Clayton County voice.

John begs me to ask you not to lose the memorandum about not coaching the Yankee officer for Southern accent.† He says that he and I will believe such a thing but no one else will without documentary proof. We laughed about that all day too.

Of course, I was very interested in what you wrote about Hall Johnson and the musical background.‡ I also got a laugh out of Mr. S.'s memorandum that he understood I objected very strenuously to having Negroes singing as a background. He is utterly wrong about this and I am so glad that you set him right by stating that I did not want the field hands to suddenly burst into song on the front lawn of Tara. John, not I, was the one who made this objection, but he spoke my ideas. He told George Cukor that everyone here was sick to nausea at seeing the combined Tuskegee and Fisk Jubilee Choirs bounce out at the most inopportune times and in the most inopportune places and sing loud enough to split the eardrums. And even more wearying than the choral effects are the inevitable wavings in the air of several hundred pairs of hands with Rouben Mamoulian shadows leaping on walls.§ This was fine and fitting in "Porgy" but pretty awful in other shows where it had no place. I feared greatly that three hundred massed Negro singers might be standing on Miss Pittypat's lawn waving their arms and singing

---

* In the same scene, when Myrick insisted that a young woman would loosen the stays in her corset before lying down, the producer worried this would "let the bust sag."

† While the crew was preparing to shoot the scene of Rhett in jail after the war, Selznick sent Myrick a memo noting it was "probably superfluous" to remind her that the actor playing the Yankee officer did not need to be coached in a southern accent.

‡ Hall Johnson was a Georgia-born choral director and composer dedicated to preserving Negro spirituals, which his Hall Johnson Choir performed for more than thirty years.

§ Mamoulian directed the 1927 play *Porgy* on Broadway as well as George Gershwin's "folk opera" version, *Porgy and Bess*, in 1935.

"Swing low, sweet chariot,
Comin' for to carry me home"
when Rhett drives up with the wagon. By the way, speaking of musical scores—I hope they keep the music soft. Sam Tupper went with us to see "Wuthering Heights" last night.* Every time the action became tense and the voices dropped to a low key the music blared out loud as a symphony orchestra and drowned out every word. We followed the picture by the pantomime, which, fortunately, was excellent. But we hardly heard a word of dialogue.

Going back to Hall Johnson—thank you for telling me that he thought "GWTW" was good and that it made him "unhappy that some of his race failed so miserably to understand it and criticized the black and white angle" of it. Coming from a person like him and a person of his background, I appreciated it very much, for I have been in a rather odd spot. I do not need to tell you how I and all my folks feel about Negroes. We've always fought for colored education and, even when John and I were at our worst financially, we were helping keep colored children in schools, furnishing clothes and carfare and, oh, the terrible hours when I had to help with home work which dealt in fractions. I have paid for medical care and done the nursing myself on many occasions; all of us have fought in the law courts and paid fines. Well, you know what I mean, you and your people have done the same thing. The colored people I know here in Atlanta had nothing but nice things to say, especially the older ones. Shortly after the book came out the Radical and Communistic publications, both black and white, began to hammer, but all they could say was that the book was "an insult to the Race." For two years they could not think up any reason why. I asked a number of Negroes and they replied that they did not know either but guessed it was some Yankee notion. The Radical press tried to use "Gone With the Wind" as a whip to drive the Southern Negroes into the Communist Party somewhat in the same manner that "Uncle Tom's Cabin" was used to recruit Abolitionists. Of course you know how happy it made me to have the Radical publications dislike "Gone With the Wind." I couldn't have held up my head if they had liked it, but the Negro angle bothered me, for Heaven knows I had and have no intention of "insulting the Race." . . . I have had enough twisted and erroneous and insulting things written about me and

---

* *Wuthering Heights*, a 1939 film by Samuel Goldwyn Productions, featured Laurence Olivier, Vivien Leigh's lover, in his American film debut. He was nominated for Best Actor for his role as Heathcliff.

"Gone With the Wind" to make me sore on the whole Negro race if I were sensitive or a fool. But I do not intend to let any number of trouble-making Professional Negroes change my feelings toward the race with whom my relations have always been those of affection and mutual respect. There are Professional Negroes just as there are Professional Southerners and, from what I can learn from Negroes I have talked to, they are no more loved by their race than Professional Southerners are by us. If you see Hall Johnson again please give him my very sincere thanks for his words.

As soon as I could get up from the flu we went on a trip to the Gulf Coast, hoping for warmer weather. We got rain and bitter cold and came home after a week, but it was a nice rest and I am getting fat again.

I can't help feeling curious about an item which has been appearing in various movie magazines. This item states that Vivien Leigh's Southern accent is growing by leaps and bounds because she has living in her home "a family friend of Margaret Mitchell." Well, dearie, neither you nor the Kurtzes are living with her. I have heard that an Atlanta girl named Patricia Stewart is her secretary, but I do not know her and never heard of her until I read these articles.

The latest stills which Miss Rabwin sent me showed the exteriors of Tara and, so help me God! there were white-painted, barred fences. Not a split-rail fence was to be seen. Everyone who saw the pictures spotted that immediately and yelled bloody murder. Couldn't Mr. Selznick have rented the elegant split-rail fences from the "Jesse James" company?*

John sends his love and so do I.

P.S. Give our best to George Cukor when you see him.

Mrs. Wilbur G. Kurtz   *Atlanta, Georgia*
Selznick International Pictures, Inc.   *May 8, 1939*
Culver City, California

Dear Annie Laurie:

. . . I've been intending to tell you how fine and solid and real the Atlanta backgrounds look. They appear to have been there always. I know the credit for this goes to Wilbur and my hat is off to him. They are wonderful. Thanks for the snapshots.

The Ladies Memorial Society invited me to review the parade with them and I sat next to Wilbur, Junior and enjoyed it. We wished for both

---

* *Jesse James*, starring Tyrone Power, Henry Fonda, and Randolph Scott, was released by Twentieth Century-Fox in 1939.

of you. I didn't get to the cemetery but heard Mr. Selznick sent a lovely wreath—the biggest one on the monument, Miss Nina said.* Looks like he's a plumb unreconstructed Rebel!†

We read about Mr. Fleming's illness and were so very sorry.‡ It does seem as if there is a jinx upon this picture. I know all of you must be working day and night if you are trying to finish it by the middle of June. I have no idea how far along the production is but from what I have read in the papers it would seem that there is at least a quarter of the book to be filmed. However, I know nothing about the script and the last quarter of the book may be telescoped and condensed. Have you any news—rumor or otherwise—about when it will be released? If it's finished in mid-June perhaps it will be released in September. I read a newspaper statement recently that it would not appear until Christmas.

I know you must miss Ruth Leone. Why did she go? Please give my regards to Mrs. Deighton. In the past I had some very fine letters from her.

Annie Laurie, John and I have had more pleasure over your "socializing" than anything else. It has delighted us that you not only have interesting work in the office but a good time outside the office. Naturally, the studio likes for you to go to luncheons and make speeches. What better person could they get to represent them? Your Southern voice, your lovely manners and your genuine interest in people make you a grade A representative. And to think of you blossoming into a speaker! I admire that more than anything else. No, I won't tell anybody about it, although I would like to brag about you. I will let you come home and do your own bragging. And if you do not brag I will tell on you.

Mr. Selznick has sent me, from time to time, stills of the picture and of course they have been very interesting. I give you my word that when John and I saw the interiors of Twelve Oaks we laughed till we cried. Such gorgeous elegance was never seen in Clayton County and I wonder if it was

---

* Nina K. Fuller was a sister of Annie Laurie Kurtz.

† Georgia and other southern states celebrate Confederate Memorial Day on April 26. Selznick sent a wreath of laurel leaves and calla lilies. In California, Annie Laurie Kurtz had suggested that Selznick International fly the Confederate flag that day "as a friendly gesture to the country of G.W.T.W." (To mark the official start of filming on January 26, Mary "Bebe" Anderson of Birmingham, Alabama, who portrayed Maybelle Merriwether, had raised the Confederate flag in front of the studio's administration building.)

‡ On April 29, Fleming withdrew from the film, citing exhaustion. He was replaced by Sam Wood, who had directed two of the Marx Brothers' best-known films, *A Night at the Opera* (1935) and *A Day at the Races* (1937). Fleming returned to Selznick International in mid-May, and Wood remained to shoot scenes concurrently to make up for lost time.

seen anywhere at that time. When I think of the bare, comfortable rooms of Clayton and Fayette County houses in which I visited as a child I laugh till I am sore. Twelve Oaks must be at least six hundred feet long and the hand of the interior decorator is evident everywhere. Tara is almost, but not quite as bad, but the oil paintings, prism crystals, the gorgeous upholstery with fringe, the expensive rugs give me great glee. I suppose I should feel bad about the way the simple houses I wrote about are gorgeoused up, but I do not because I knew from the start that this was what would happen. After all, I had seen "So Red the Rose" and other Southern pictures and I knew the movies were afraid to present a true South because that would run counter to the moving picture public's conception of the way we lived. So, I get a lot of hilarity out of the matter and an increasing sense of thanksgiving that I am not connected with the picture. I am going to be in an embarrassing spot when the picture comes out if any curious reporters ask me if Twelve Oaks and Tara are the way I imagined them. I can't lie and I will probably have to say "I can make no comment." . . .

Mr. George Brett, Jr.   *Atlanta, Georgia*
The Macmillan Company   *May 12, 1939*
New York, New York

My dear George:

I am so very sorry that I have delayed this long in answering your letter of April 27th, about the party which you wish to give me when—and if—the GWTW premiere is held in Atlanta. I wanted to write you immediately but it seems as if the letters I am most anxious to write are always delayed. The annual summer deluge of visitors began earlier this year and until today I've hardly had time to draw a comfortable breath.

First of all, I want to tell you how genuinely pleased and grateful I was when Lucien Harris and Norman Berg told me of your desire to give me a grand party.* It was very thoughtful of you and kind too, and I do appreciate the invitation, even if I am not able to accept it. I do not know whether Lucien went into any details about my "previous commitment" to the ladies' Press Club. On the chance that he did not, I will give you the details, for there is a great deal of background to this whole premiere situation.

The ink was hardly dry on my movie contract before various Atlanta organizations, civil and social, began angling with Hollywood for an At-

---

* Lucien Harris Jr., a grandson of "Uncle Remus" author Joel Chandler Harris, was the manager of Macmillan's southeastern office in Atlanta.

lanta premiere. All of them wanted me to "use my influence" with Mr. Selznick to get the premiere here. In line with my policy of standing clear of all things pertaining to the film, I refused to do anything about it. Mr. Selznick has never yet said that the premiere will be in Atlanta, but many people have gone ahead with plans for premiere parties and I have received invitations to a great number of them. They came from civic organizations, social organizations and individuals, some were for benefits for very worthy charities, and still others were of a thinly veiled commercial nature. These invitations came in by the dozens and I have refused them all. That was also in line with my "policy" since "Gone With the Wind" was published. With the exception of the banquet when the Bohnenberger medal was given me, I have made no "public appearances" in the past two and a half years, nor have I been guest of honor at any function, social, civic or otherwise.* I realized in 1936 that if I accepted one invitation I would have to accept all, and the invitations were—and still are—too numerous for one human being to handle. Atlanta people have been very good to me and I have always regretted having to decline their invitations but I do not know what else to do.

After the filming of "Gone With the Wind" got under way in January, Atlanta's interest in the premiere increased to the point where the event, as far as I was concerned, assumed the proportions of a major problem. In addition to the invitations to parties, literally hundreds of people begged me for introductions to the movie stars (if any should come) or asked me to get them passes to the premiere. Even more were willing to pay for their seats, but demanded that John, Stephens, Father and I guarantee that they would be able to get seats. If only the people who have spoken to us personally were to attend, there isn't an auditorium in Atlanta big enough to hold them all. And of course the demand for seats will get heavier as the event approaches.

Altogether, it looked like an intolerable situation for me, and still does. My impulse was to get as far away from Atlanta as possible, if the premiere should be held here. But I couldn't do that. So I decided on the next best thing—to leave Atlanta two weeks before the premiere, return just in time to dress for the performance, and leave immediately after the last reel. I have made only one alteration in that plan, and that brings me to my "previous engagement."

* On October 29, 1938, at a banquet in Atlanta, Mitchell accepted the Southeastern Library Association's Carl Bohnenberger Memorial Medal for "the most outstanding contribution to southern literature in the past two years."

The only organization I have joined in the last three years is the Atlanta Women's Press Club. The members are all active newspaper women. I am the only non-working member, and I am very proud of my membership, for most of the girls are old friends of mine and I am happy that they are still willing to accept me as one of them—as Peggy Mitchell, newspaper woman, rather than Margaret Mitchell, author. In addition, I am under great obligations to them, for they have played an important part in making life endurable for me these past three years. Their consideration for me in their newspaper work has eased my burden in a way that would be hard to describe. Instead of making my life more difficult, as some newspaper people might have done, they have done everything possible to shield me from unpleasantness, and I am under obligations to them that I can never repay.

Some time ago at a meeting the president arose and, after warning me to keep quiet and not interrupt, announced that the ladies of the press were going to give me a buffet supper and cocktail party directly before the premiere. They said that I had not ever permitted anyone in Atlanta to entertain for me and that, whether I liked it or not, they were going to give me a party. The fact that they were my close friends of many years' standing not only gave them a prior right over other people to entertain me, but, she said, my acceptance of their invitation, from a group of old friends, would give me a reason for declining other invitations. Moreover, their party would be small, informal and friendly—not a gawdy Hollywood affair with spotlights, champagne and ballyhoo (as some of the others to which I was invited are to be). She said that Club members knew I wouldn't go to a party of that kind—and she was right.

She said further that their plans were already complete: each member could invite her husband or beau; I could invite my family; the managing editor of the three papers, the Mayor and the Governor were to be invited; an invitation had been sent to Mr. Selznick, Katharine Brown and any members of the cast who might be here. They told Mr. Selznick that this would be the only affair I would attend, and Miss Brown has accepted for the Selznick organization—tentatively, of course, for there is no certainty that the premiere will be held here.

Although taken aback by the unexpectedness of the invitation, I accepted it. I did it partly because of old friendships, partly because of my obligations to the members of the club, but chiefly because of the *nature* of the party they were planning—one that would be simple, unpretentious and in good taste, not only because the ladies know my preferences for parties of that kind, but also because their own ideas about such matters are the same as mine. If they had been planning a Hollywoodish kind of party I would not have accepted, even for my oldest and dearest friends.

As a result, my personal arrangements in connection with the premiere have been altered in one respect but only one. I still plan to be away from Atlanta during the two weeks before the premiere and to leave immediately after the performance, but I will arrive here an hour or two before the evening program in order to attend the party the Press Club is giving.

I realize that this one deviation from my original plan is going to make trouble for me, for it will make it harder for me to decline other invitations. People will want me to add one more hour, and still another hour, to my time in Atlanta that day, in order to attend their parties. That means I will be forced to hold rigidly to my plan to attend only the one party. If I should attempt to make any more changes, I would soon find myself in a hopeless tangle.

So I am sure you understand why I cannot accept the invitation to your party. If I had known about it earlier, I might have made your party the one I would attend, for there is no one whose hospitality I would rather accept than yours. But it is too late to talk about that now. I have already accepted the other invitation, there is no way I can get out of it and, to be very frank, I do not wish to do so. I do not think you will misunderstand that last statement, for I believe you can realize how much the girls' action means to me. I can only wish that things were different.

Now, as to your suggestion that The Macmillan Company and Selznick combine with the ladies of the press in one large party—I hardly know what to say about this because, you see, I am merely the guest of the occasion. I do not believe that I could make such a suggestion to the Club, for it might give the girls the impression that I thought their party not grand enough for my high-toned taste. And that is just the opposite of the truth, for a small, quiet party is exactly what I like best.

I do not even know whether to advise you and Mr. Selznick to approach the Club with your offer. They might accept and again they might resent it as a suggestion that they were not capable of giving the right sort of party and needed the help of outsiders in order to give it properly. The girls think that *their* party is going to be the nicest one of all, even though some of the other premiere parties will be much more pretentious, and they might not wish to combine it with a Selznick and Macmillan party.

This is not entirely because Southerners are touchy about such matters; it is largely because of the peculiar attitude Atlanta people have toward my book. Even though you have been very close to "Gone With the Wind" these past three years, I do not believe that you or anyone outside of

Georgia can realize how strongly Atlanta feels about this whole situation. In your letter, you referred to the premiere as "Selznick's show." I don't believe Atlanta people feel that way about it at all. Mr. Selznick will put on the show, of course, but the premiere will be *Atlanta's* night, not Selznick's. Long ago, I gave up thinking of "Gone With the Wind" as my book; it's Atlanta's, in the view of Atlantians; the movie is Atlanta's film; and the premiere will be an Atlanta event, not merely the showing of a motion picture. From the way things are shaping up, my guess is that it will be one of the biggest events in Atlanta's modern history.

If I have succeeded in giving you even a faint conception of Atlanta's strongly possessive feeling toward the book and everything connected with it, perhaps you now understand why I have some doubts that the ladies of the press would wish to have you and Mr. Selznick as joint hosts at *their* party. I believe they would feel that, on this *Atlanta* occasion, they should be the hostesses and you and Mr. Selznick the guests.

That brings me to the one suggestion I can make confidently and with assurance. Cannot you and the others of the Macmillan folks who come to Atlanta be the guests of the Press Club at their party? The president, Medora Perkerson, of the Journal, knows Lois and Harold very well and, I am sure, will be only too happy to issue an invitation to the Macmillan group. And if you accept, it would certainly please me, for it would be the only way in which I could entertain any of you. I couldn't give you a party myself at that time, much as I should like it, because I would have to hire our new City Auditorium and invite five thousand people. If you were the guests of the Press Club you'd be my guests too, and yet I would be able to say to enraged friends who had not been invited, "It wasn't my party, I was only the guest of honor and had nothing to do with the invitations."

I know this sounds very involved, but life is very complicated these days.

P.S. I forgot to say that the plans for the Press party are a deep secret—no one outside the Club, except Katharine Brown, had been told up until I told Lucien and Norman. I was sworn to secrecy on the matter as were the other members because we knew if the news got around we'd be deluged with demands for invitations. So please keep it confidential for us.

Miss Marcella Rabwin   Atlanta, Georgia
Selznick International Pictures, Inc.   May 12, 1939
Culver City, California

Dear Miss Rabwin:

The stills you mailed me on May 8th have just arrived. Thank you so much for them. Of course I found them very exciting. I did not realize that the picture had progressed up to the point of the jail sequence and the Ku Klux raid.* From this distance it would seem that the picture is going into the home stretch and it does not seem possible that your organization can have done so much in so short a time. I think the background of the picture showing Rhett playing poker with the whiskered Federal officers is especially fine. Of course I can't help hoping that he won all their chips in this game!

I wish you would thank Mr. Selznick for me for his kindness in sending me these stills. My husband and I enjoy them so very much—probably no one in the world could be as interested as we are.

Mr. George Brett, Jr.	*Atlanta, Georgia*
The Macmillan Company	*May 19, 1939*
New York, New York	

Dear George:

Your letter of May 15th, written in answer to my letter about the Press Club's premiere party, has arrived. I thank you for your patience in this complicated matter. Many times I feel very guilty when I inflict upon you long letters, for I know how busy you are. I also know how easy it is for misunderstandings to arise when distances are great between letter writers, and when complicated situations come up I can do nothing else except send you what must appear to be a sequel to "Gone With the Wind."

As soon as I received your letter I went to see Medora Perkerson. Fortunately, I arrived some hours before she received the news that The Macmillan Company would bring out her mystery novel, "Who Killed Aunt Maggie?" on September 15th. There would have been no premiere discussion had I made my visit later! She told me that, of course, the Press Club wanted people from The Macmillan Company to come to the party. She said that she and the entertainment committee had already discussed inviting only those who were connected with "Gone With the Wind"—my family, the newspaper people, the Selznick people and the Macmillan group. She said she would take it up soon with her committee and issue a formal invitation, but I want to beat them to it and issue my informal one right now. She said she knew the whole Club would be very flattered to think that you and some of your people would come to their party.

Of course, I know no more about the date of the premiere than I did when I last wrote you. However, this morning Mr. Jere Moore, whom you

---

* In the film, no reference is made to the Ku Klux Klan. The Shantytown raid in which Scarlett's second husband, Frank Kennedy, is killed was conducted by "a great many of our southern gentlemen," including Ashley and Dr. Meade.

have met, telephoned me to say that he had a letter from some Selznick officials who had just returned to New York from Hollywood.* This official said that the picture would be released around Thanksgiving Day and the premiere would probably be in Atlanta. He also said there would be "sixty more shooting days" before production ended. This innocent official also told Jere that the Selznick company would issue five hundred invitations to the premiere and the rest would be paid admissions. At this last information Jere and I laughed uproariously and exchanged mutual congratulations that neither of us had anything to do with giving out those invitations. Poor Mr. Selznick does not know what he is headed into. Five hundred invitations will hardly cover the Atlanta newspapers, let alone the hundreds of Atlanta people who feel that they should be invited. And then there is all the rest of the state. And my geography told me that Georgia is the largest state east of the Mississippi. . . .

Miss Katharine Brown   *Atlanta, Georgia*
Selznick International Pictures, Inc.   *May 20, 1939*
New York, New York

Dear Katharine:

I have been wanting to write to you ever since I returned home but, as usual after a trip, a million things had accumulated. But you know how that is better than I do. I was so interested in every detail John had to tell. I only wish you and he had had at least twenty-four hours' unlimited time, for there were thousands of other things I wanted to know. John said, regretfully, that your time was so short that you had little opportunity to exchange gossip and had to stick to business.†

When he told me that he had told you about the Rhett and Melanie scandal I had to laugh.‡ I would not blame you if you did not believe that, but it is true. For months this controversy raged and I had letters from all points of the compass about it, showing that the idea was widespread. Even more incredible is the fact that a number of people from out of the

---

* Jere Moore, editor of the Milledgeville *Union-Recorder*, was chairman of the Georgia World's Fair Commission for the 1939 New York World's Fair.

† Marsh had gone to New York in his continuing attempts to clarify Mitchell's contract with Selznick as it related to commercial tie-ups.

‡ Mitchell received numerous inquiries from readers questioning whether Rhett and Melanie had an affair; some even went so far as to suggest Rhett was the father of Melanie's second baby.

state made formal calls upon me to ask me to settle the matter, as the controversy was raging in their home town. One very handsome young man came down from North Carolina and told me that he could not go home until he had seen me because the large bridge club, of which he and his wife were members, had been rent asunder on this subject and different members were not speaking to each other. He, being a "Southern gentleman," was firmly convinced of Melanie's chastity and Rhett's respect for her, but he confessed to me that other members of the club were so common that they had no understanding of such matters. I hotly reassured him about the virtue of Mrs. Wilkes, and he went home triumphantly and sent me an inordinate number of red roses. I know that sounds very amusing but for a while it was a great and delicate problem. I realize now that even a good woman cannot risk her reputation by closing the door upon herself and a man with a bad reputation—even if the man and woman are only characters in a book. I'll know better next time.*

Mr. Selznick has sent me a number of stills from the picture and they are very exciting. The last ones showed the Atlanta backgrounds and they had all the authenticity of the pictures from "Brady's Photographic History."† The town looked solid and real and not like a set. I went down to the Historical Society and looked at the pictures of Atlanta in the old days and the very atmosphere of them was like the stills.

There are several questions I am asked every day. People who read about the cast notice that Scarlett's first two children, Wade and Ella, are not mentioned and neither are Will Benteen, Archie or Grandma Fontaine. They want to know if these characters have been omitted. I tell them that I do not know and then add that the book was so long that naturally some characters must be omitted and some incidents telescoped. Can you tell me if these characters have been omitted?‡ And if you do not wish me to make mention publicly of it I will keep it quiet.

I think you will be glad to know of the great interest people showed in the set of stills which were released some while back. These showed the O'Hara family group, Scarlett at the bazaar et cetera. I know you will be glad to hear that everyone has a good word for Vivien Leigh. What interests people most is that her face is never the same twice.

---

* In the scene in the novel where Melanie comforts Rhett after Bonnie's death (page 997), he closes the door to his room behind her.

† *Brady's Photographic History of the Civil War* was a multivolume collection of Matthew Brady's historical photographs documenting the war.

‡ None of these characters were included in the motion picture.

The articles written by Mrs. Kurtz and Sue Myrick are very well received. Sue's articles, especially, evoke enthusiasm. People like my hairdresser, who does not know I know Sue, rave about them. I wish that they were being syndicated over the country instead of appearing in three Georgia papers. I think other sections would like them, too. There is a freshness of viewpoint about them which pleases people. As my hairdresser remarked, "Miss Myrick doesn't say that Clark Gable has a pale pink bathroom and that Miss Leigh takes two lumps of sugar in her coffee and other uninteresting stuff."

Thank you so much for getting things started on the commercial tie-up matter. My brother Stephens had a letter from Mr. Samuels.* While nothing has been definitely settled, we are very glad that things are moving. We appreciate the work you did on this, for it has been a heavy and embarrassing problem to us during the last three years and we will be happy when the whole affair is straightened out to the satisfaction of all concerned.

I wish I could see you and hear all the news. I wish, too, that you could have the long vacation that you deserve. I was somewhat disturbed by the information John brought home that you were having digestive disturbances. You've certainly been under a long strain and you need a long vacation. I hope when GWTW is in the can that you will get it.

Mr. David O. Selznick   *Atlanta, Georgia*
Selznick International Pictures, Inc.   *May 20, 1939*
Culver City, California

My dear Mr. Selznick:

I am sending you a copy of "Southern Treasury of Life and Literature," selected by Stark Young. I am sending it to you because of the excellent essay, "The English Language in the South," by Cleanth Brooks, Jr., Page 350. I realize that you are probably sick and tired of the pros and cons of the so-called Southern dialect. Certainly, you have had enough trouble with it to make you wish you had never heard of it! Just the same, I hope you will read this article, for it is the best thing on the subject I have ever read. Furthermore, it backs up the statements I made at the time you announced the selection of Miss Leigh as Scarlett. I said that the speech of the Southern people of the War days was closer to the English speech than that of other sections of the country. Mr. Brooks explains why this is true.

---

* Robert E. Samuels was one of Selznick's attorneys in New York.

I have been so grateful to you for the stills you have sent me. Of course they have been seen by no one except my husband, father and brother, and all of us find them so interesting.

Belatedly, I am acknowledging your letter of April 24th about the Paris Metro-Goldwyn-Mayer office and their present plan to use the French title of "Gone With the Wind" for the film when it appears in that country. I have passed the information on to the French publishers and I am sure they are glad to know.* Present indications are that my book is doing fairly well in France. I have not received many reviews as yet and will not have a statement of sales from the publishers for some months, so it is too soon to tell whether "Gone With the Wind" will have as good a sale there as in other countries.

I do not know anything at all about moving pictures in the Orient, but I think you will be interested to know that "Gone With the Wind" has sold 150,000 copies in Japan and is very popular there.† The Japanese translator wrote me that not only the "young maidens" but "intellectual college professors" liked it. He said that numbers of newspaper and magazine articles, of both popular and serious natures, had appeared about it. I gather from this that a good groundwork has been laid for the exhibition of your film there.

Mr. and Mrs. Wilbur G. Kurtz   *Atlanta, Georgia*
Selznick International Pictures, Inc.   *June 1, 1939*
Culver City, California

Dear Annie Laurie and Wilbur:

. . . We enjoyed the snapshots you sent us so much and thought them fine. Wilbur, thank you for the check on Mr. Austell's bank and the casualty list.‡ Just for curiosity, I'd like to know if the casualty list was made up in part from the list of the Ninth Georgia Infantry (I believe it was the Ninth) which came from Augusta and Richmond County. It looked familiar, for there were so many Irish names on it and so many Irish enlisted in Augusta.

---

* *Gone With the Wind* was published in France in February 1939 as *Autant en Emporte le Vent*.

† *Gone With the Wind* was released by several publishers in Japan beginning in 1937—without Mitchell's approval and without paying her royalties—under an obscure, early twentieth-century trade agreement between the United States and Japan.

‡ In addition to advising on historical matters, Kurtz designed props for the film, including the bank draft Scarlett used to pay the taxes on Tara (drawn on "The Atlanta National Bank/A. Austell, President"), the casualty lists used in the scene in which anxious Atlantans await word from Gettysburg, and the letter Rhett wrote to Melanie returning her and Scarlett's wedding rings after the Atlanta Bazaar.

A letter from Susan told me that a schedule she had seen showed that the shooting should be over on the 22nd of June and that there would be a five weeks' interval before retakes began. Will you two stay in Hollywood? Or will you come home for five weeks and return to Hollywood? Or will you return for good after the 22nd? We can hardly wait to see you. . . .

Do keep up your articles, Annie Laurie. We read them with so much interest. Everybody reads them and likes them.

John and I are both well and grateful that the summer lull in my mail and business matters has set in. If I could only believe that this lull was the beginning of a permanent state, I would be very happy. I fear, however, that the permanent state will not begin until the picture is released, and so, no one prays more devoutly for the speedy release than we do.

Later

I've just come from the Carnegie Library where I was stopped by one of the young and pretty brunette librarians. I cannot for the moment recall her name, although I know her very pleasantly. She said that she, another librarian whose name I did not get, and Miss Isabel Erlich, of the Reference Department of the Library, were leaving for a trip to the West Coast soon. They expect to be in Hollywood around the 18th of June. She asked me if there was any way in the world they could manage to get on the Selznick lot and see the sets or watch the shooting. She wanted to know if I thought one of you could manage it for them. She had heard about other Atlantans who had been admitted. I told her that the studio had tightened up on admissions and, furthermore, that the final say-so about visitors did not rest with you two. She declared that their trip would not be complete without at least a peek and said that they would write or telephone you when they arrive. She begged that I write you that they were coming so that you would not think them imposters or people who wanted to get extra parts. I said I would write you, and now I have done it! Perhaps you two know Isabel Erlich. She's the little dark girl in the Reference Department who is a combination of ferret and bloodhound where historical references are concerned.

Colonel Telamon Cuyler   *Atlanta, Georgia*
Wayside, Jones County, Georgia   *June 9, 1939*
Dear Colonel Cuyler:

. . . I understand from California newspapers that the shooting on "Gone With the Wind" will be over sometime this month. I suppose Susan and the Kurtzes will be with us soon. I hope so for there are many things I'd like to hear. By the way, I have just learned that in order to shorten the script the producers eliminated Scarlett's first two children, Archie, Will Benteen and Grandma Fontaine. They have introduced a character named Grandma Tarleton, who seems to be a resident of Atlanta. At any rate, she appears in the Gettysburg scene reading the casualty list. I've never met Grandma Tarleton, so I can't tell you much about her!*

Miss Susan Myrick   *Atlanta, Georgia*
Selznick International Pictures, Inc.   *June 10, 1939*
Culver City, California

Dear Sue:

Forgive this note if it sounds curt. Your letter caught me as I'm packing to go to Smith College, my old alma mater. They are going to give me an honorary Master of Arts degree and I am madly rushing to get off.

Please tell Mr. Selznick and the Publicity Department that under no circumstances will I permit them to quote my remarks about your newspaper articles in their promotion program. I haven't the time to tell you all the difficulties it would cause me but here is one of them. During the past three years whenever I have voiced an honest and enthusiastic opinion about anybody's writing I have been in danger of immediately getting a request to use my statement for advertising, and I have had frequent experiences of this kind about newspaper stories. I'm not exaggerating when I tell you that requests for statements about books, magazine articles and newspaper stories have run into the thousands. I've had to turn them all down, even at the risk of appearing most ungenerous and ungracious, but I did not intend to have my name appearing six times a day in newspapers recommending this or that. I might as well go ahead and endorse Pond's cold cream and get it over with, and I have no intention of doing that sort of thing. To make matters worse, there would be the unavoidable suspicion that Mr. Selznick had paid me for the use of my name. This would give a number of people a chance to say that as long as I got paid for the use of my name I did not care how it was used. Of course our friends in Georgia would understand that I am very sincere in liking your articles, but you understand better than most people that I have got to take into consideration what people in other parts of the

---

* The brief scene with a character named Grandma Tarleton, played by Margaret Seddon, was cut from the final film.

country would think. So, caution them not to use my commendation of your stuff in any way, shape or form, directly or indirectly.

I hate to write you this because I honestly do like your stuff a lot, but I can't break my rule on this matter. It has about reached the point where I'm afraid to open my mouth in any words of praise about anything because, with very few exceptions, I get an immediate request for my words to be used for advertising purposes.

Moreover, your stuff does not need any recommendation from me or anyone else. It is good stuff and it can stand on its own feet.

Mr. Michael Bercutt   *Atlanta, Georgia*
Beverly Hills, California   *June 24, 1939*

Dear Mr. Bercutt:

I thank you so much for thinking of me in connection with your one-reel film which you mentioned in your letter of June 16th, but I must decline your offer to be the commentator for this film. I am not doing any work of this nature.

Of course I could not help wondering what kind of film yours was to be because Atlanta has so few "famous landmarks." The town grew so rapidly that most of the historic landmarks have been destroyed.

The ideas I am now going to express may not have entered your head, but I want to mention them as there has been a widespread misconception about the connection of the characters and houses in "Gone With the Wind" with actual people and places in Atlanta. My characters and houses were altogether fictional, with the exception, of course, of actual names of streets and places. Yet, many people have erroneously believed that this or that place was the actual site of Miss Pittypat's house or Scarlett's mansion. This is not true and it has caused me great embarrassment and also stirred justifiable resentment among the descendants of people who lived on these sites. I thought that perhaps you were contemplating a film which might show some of these supposed locations of the homes of my characters and I wanted to let you know that these homes never had any locations except in my own mind.

Miss Marcella Rabwin   *Atlanta, Georgia*
Selznick International Pictures, Inc.   *June 26, 1939*
Culver City, California

My dear Miss Rabwin:

Your letter of June 2nd to my husband arrived just as I was leaving the house for a trip North and I did not have the opportunity to discuss it with him. I expected to be home within four days and thought I could write to you about it then, but my New York trip lengthened out. Immediately on my return to Atlanta I had to go to South Georgia because of the illness and death of a friend. I have just returned. I am very sorry that my absences from the city have kept me from writing about the trailer and one-reel publicity film which Mr. Selznick wishes to use in advertising "Gone With the Wind."

I do not want to write this letter to you, for I find it an embarrassing one to write. To my sorrow, I have been forced to write a number of similar letters to your organization during the past three years and they have been equally difficult. My embarrassment arises from the fact that Mr. Selznick may think such letters mean that I am not sincerely and cordially interested in the picture and very sympathetic with his problems, which I am. But after reading the suggestions in your letter of June 19th to my husband, I can see no other course except to state again my attitude about personal publicity, just as I have stated it time and again before. When I sold the moving picture rights to "Gone With the Wind," a month after the book had been published, I told Miss Katharine Brown and the other Selznick people who were present that the book was theirs to do with as they wished. My contract specified this. I said that I would sell the book, lock, stock and barrel, but only on the condition that my name was never used for promotion or publicity purposes, except as the author of the book. Miss Brown, Mr. Wharton and others understood this perfectly. I thought that this would be all that was necessary, but throughout the following three years I have been forced to write letters to every department of your organization and wearily re-state this stand.

If you will look into the files of letters and telegrams to Mr. Russell Birdwell, of Publicity, beginning around November 24, 1936, you will find that I told him I did not wish to be used in any way whatsoever in connection with the film, except as the author, and I stated my position at length and in detail. I have written the same thing to Mr. Selznick himself on several occasions, notably on March 13, 1939 and March 24, 1939. I have written Miss Katharine Brown several times on this subject, the last time being on March 13, 1939 when Mr. Whitbeck, of Metro-Goldwyn-Mayer, wished to get pictures of me for the trailer. I wrote then that, for reasons I had set out a great many times previously in letters to the Selznick organization, I did not wish to appear in the trailer or in any publicity in connection with the film. I am the author of the book and not the producer of the film. I have had nothing to do with the picture, but there has been a widespread public belief that I was singlehandedly producing "Gone With the Wind." This is unfair to Mr. Selznick and it has been a burden on me. It has multiplied my problems a hundred times. For Mr. Selznick's sake, as well as my own, I have repeatedly, throughout the past three years, disclaimed any connection with the film. So, any mention of me now in the trailer or your other publicity, except as author, would undo three years' work and make me out a liar. For once and for all, I would be linked up with the picture in the public mind in a relationship very different from the true one.

I have written and said these things so often. I wish it were possible that Selznick International Pictures and I could come to some real and permanent understanding on this matter so that I would not be put to the worry and embarrassment of having to write frequent letters restating these facts.

The thing that is most difficult for me to understand is that, whenever these troubles have arisen in the past, I have gotten letters back from Mr. Selznick, Miss Brown, Mr. Birdwell, saying, in effect: "I understand perfectly now. I am sorry I did not understand before. You can count on us to respect your desire to avoid personal publicity." And then, a few months later, the same old trouble comes up again.

Are we going to keep on this way until some new unpleasantness arises after it is too late for me to write long letters and receive fresh assurances of your willingness to respect my wishes? Am I to fear that some effort to ballyhoo me is going to be made right on the eve of the premiere when I will have no choice but to do my talking in the newspapers, instead of privately in letters, and both of us will be involved in a nasty mess which will give joy to the columnists and embarrassment to Selznick International Pictures and me?

I am beginning to wonder if the trouble is that I have maintained a friendly and courteous attitude toward Selznick International Pictures and its members, in spite of our recurrent unpleasantnesses on this one point of using me for publicity. Maybe my continued friendliness and courtesy causes your people or MGM to think that I don't mean what I say, that I am just being coy, that I really *do* want personal publicity and just want to make you beg for it.

My husband, out of friendliness and courtesy, answered your first letter by sending you some printed matter which we use as a matter of routine in answering requests for information, meanwhile asking what use you planned to make of this material and emphasizing that if you were even thinking of making use of me personally, we expected to be informed about it. Then your reply comes back revealing that your original letter was an indirect approach to the same old Whitbeck idea and suggesting that shots of me be included in the trailer. Everybody in the Selznick organization should know by this time that anything of the sort would be highly distasteful to me. I turned down the Whitbeck proposition quite flatly several months ago, and this revival of it, on top of similar experiences in the past, is making me wonder if my continued friendliness since then was a mistake. Is it impossible for your organization to understand the difference between my willingness to be friendly and helpful in any proper way and my very strong unwillingness to be used for publicity purposes?

The friendly, informal manner of my husband's letter to you is typical of the attitude we have always had toward your organization in the past and which we wish to continue to have. The letter Mr. Selznick wrote me in March had led both of us to think that we had finally reached an understanding with your organization about this matter of personal publicity, and so my husband felt no hesitancy in writing you freely and frankly. On the face of it, his letter is not the cautious, guarded communication a person might write to someone in whom he did not have confidence. As a result, he resents as much as I do the fact that there was apparently a hidden motive in your letter.

Of course, if I am attributing motives to you which you did not have, I am sorry. But if all considerations of that kind are waived, the outstanding fact of your letter continues to be that the Selznick organization has not yet given up the idea of using me personally in its publicity, in spite of all the assurances to the contrary that have been given me. That both depresses me, makes me wonder whether I can put faith in your promises, and forces me to take action.

I don't want to reach the point where I must feel suspicious of every letter I get from the Selznick organization. I don't want to be forced into deciding that I cannot afford to be friendly, that I must sever all relations with your organization, perhaps not even attend the premiere. So I am making this further effort to get a real understanding between us about this matter which means so much to me. It is:

> I don't want personal publicity; I don't want publicity of any kind in connection with the movie except *necessary* mentions of me as author of the book; I *mean* this, I am not being coy, and I am tired of writing letters about it. If you occasionally say "By Margaret Mitchell" in reference to my book and make no other mention of me in your publicity, that is what would please me most.

I am sending copies of this letter to Mr. Selznick and Miss Brown and I would like to hear from them about it. If we can't have a clear-cut, *permanent* understanding about this matter, I want to know about it, so our future relations can be adjusted accordingly.

And now I want to tell you how very sorry I am that you happened to be the one to receive this letter. I suppose that you were acting under orders, so I don't hold you personally responsible. But the letter had to be written.

Getting back to the main subject of your letter (and to the friendly cooperation which I hope we are going to retain), we will be glad to supply you with the sales figures on the book and any other information we can. It is not quite clear, however, as to what answer you intended to give to my husband's question about whether you wanted the sales figures immediately. During the coming month, we expect to receive annual or semi-annual statements from a number of the publishers and we can then give you more up-to-date information. But if you want the information immediately, just let me know and I will send you such figures as we have. I don't believe we would be willing to estimate what the total sales are going to be six months from now.

You asked about "dramatic sidelights on the book" and mentioned a story about a group of mountaineers who had one chapter read to them every day. If this story is true, I have never heard of it. However, there have been a number of unusual incidents and I suggest that you write to my publishers for material of this kind. They are The Macmillan Company, 60 Fifth Avenue, New York City. Address your letter to Mr. George P. Brett, president, or to Miss Rosa E. Hutchinson, head of publicity. They probably have a record of such occurrences and I haven't.

You asked, too, about the exotic, far-off places of the world where "Gone With the Wind" had been read. I don't know any better answer to this than to give you the list of countries in which it has been published. It has had a wide sale in Europe, and Japan and South America as well, and in every foreign country where it was published it made a success comparable to its success in the United States. The countries in which translations have been published to date are: Norway, Sweden, Denmark, Finland, Germany, Hungary, Czechoslovakia, Italy, Latvia, Poland, France, Chile and Japan, in addition to its publication in the English language in the United States, Canada, England and the British colonies.

As to your trailer and promotion film, I cannot believe that I am putting any serious problem on you by asking you to leave me out of it, except a mention as the author, and I believe you will agree with me when you stop to think about it. After all, the trailer is intended to advertise the film, not me. And there are so many interesting things to say about the book itself and about the making of the film, I can't see that the trailer would lose anything in "human interest" if I am omitted. The movie public isn't interested in me; they are interested in *your film*, and impatiently waiting for it. Beyond that, the facts of the writing and publication of "Gone With the Wind" are strangely unglamorous, despite the many rumors to the contrary. The truth would make dull telling. My private life, which is a normal one, would make even duller telling. Moreover, it is my private life and I do not wish it publicized.

My best wishes for the success of your film and for a continuance of our friendly relations.

Mrs. Wilbur G. Kurtz   *Atlanta, Georgia*
Selznick International Pictures, Inc.   *June 28, 1939*
Culver City, California

Dear Annie Laurie:

When I returned from Quitman several days ago I wrote Mabel Search, on Good Housekeeping Magazine. I told her who you and Wilbur are and something about your work in Hollywood. I said that you had been writing newspaper articles and having no trouble in placing them and that you now wish to break into something more ambitious. I told her what I could about your prospective article—menus, recipes, human interest sidelights on meals of other days and perhaps little histories of some of the recipes. I requested her to write to you direct if she were interested. If she were not interested I asked her to let me know immediately so that you could submit your article to another publication. I think you or I should hear soon unless she is on her summer vacation. I do hope we will hear good news soon.

I haven't any news to pass on because I have been so busy since my two trips that I haven't seen anyone. No, I take that back. I did go to the Library yesterday and all the librarians rushed out and informed me, with tongues hanging out, that Isabel Erlich and the other two girls had actually met Clark Gable and had their pictures taken on the Peachtree sets, and it was all due to the kindness of that sweet Mrs. Kurtz. Annie Laurie, you are so nice. I know how much pleasure the girls must have had and how grateful they are to you. The Library can hardly wait for their return and I have been invited to come down next Monday and have an eleven o'clock dope in one of those cubby holes upstairs and hear all the returning travelers have to say. Of course I had hoped the girls would see the sets but I knew how busy you were and how strict Selznick International had become about visitors.

After I left Smith College I spent a day or so in New York and had lunch with Katharine Brown. She gave me as much gossip about the film as she could and spoke of her pleasure in seeing you. She said Mr. Selznick could not get along without you two and that everyone on the lot was crazy about you.

I suppose the actual shooting is over now.* Will you and Wilbur stay for retakes? Do you know when you are coming home? Just as soon as you have seen your family please make arrangements to have supper with John and me so we can hear all before you are tired of talking about it.

We haven't heard from Sue in some time and we wonder when she will be home.

---

* The final day of regular shooting was June 27. A "wrap" party was held to celebrate the "conclusion of the damned thing," and the invitation was signed by the four stars and by Fleming as "Big Sam," the foreman at Tara, and Selznick as "Jonas Wilkerson," the Yankee overseer.

CHAPTER Five

"Faster and Funnier by the Hour"
1939 (July–December)

> Things get worse and worse as the premiere comes closer,
> for everyone in the South seems determined to be there for the
> first night. I cannot understand why, for the picture will be the
> same ten years from now as it is today, and I personally would rather
> see it for the first time on some other date than premiere date.
>
> —*Margaret Mitchell to Annie Laurie Kurtz*
> *September 19, 1939*

Miss Lois Cole   *Atlanta, Georgia*
The Macmillan Company   *July 18, 1939*
New York, New York

Dear Lois:

... I have been hoping to get away for a week to visit the Edwin Granberrys on a Florida key in the Gulf, but I have had a persistent summer cold which settled in one ear and has to be treated every day. While it is going very well now, I don't want to put myself at the back of beyond where I can't get to an ear specialist if I need one.

Lois, the many ramifications of GWTW become increasingly incredible and amusing. Yesterday Jimmy Pope called from the Journal and said that a rumor had hit town that Ole Marse Selznick was not going to let the premiere of his picture take place here. The Junior League had already deter-

mined to give a whopping costume ball that night and other civic organizations have made plans. As far as I have been able to determine, all these plans
were made without any word from Mr. Selznick as to whether the premiere
would actually be held here. At any rate, Jimmy said the ladies of the Junior
League and of other organizations descended on Mayor Hartsfield's office
like a pack of well dressed Eumenides.* His Honor, a passionate Confederate and a stout defender of Atlanta's civic rights and honors, leapt eight feet
into the air when the ladies told him the rumor. Jimmy said the reporter at
City Hall phoned in excitedly that it sounded like a WPA riot and he, for one,
wanted a police reserve called out. Mayor Hartsfield announced to the press
that this was the worst outrage since Sherman burned the town. Of course
Atlanta was going to have the premiere. "Why," said the Mayor, "in a large
way the book belongs to all of us." Various members of City Council were
assembled and, for all I know, the Governor, too, and they all began bom-
barding poor Mr. Selznick, who is now in the last stages of the picture (and
of nervous prostration, no doubt) with telegrams telling him he must quiet
the unrest in Atlanta occasioned by this rumor. Jimmy wearily asked me if
I had had any official confirmation that the premiere would be here and I
said "no." No one else bothered with me at all because, after all, I am only the
author, and upon such occasions a highly alarmed author. This morning Mr.
Selznick came through handsomely and said the premiere *would* be held here
but he reserved the right to have a press premiere in Hollywood first, as there
were hundreds of film columnists who had to see it. This is all to the good
because I had been wondering if any of the local citizens would be able to get
into the premiere here if the out-of-town correspondents swarmed in. The
Junior League and the Mayor are soothed and satisfied now and for some
reason I feel hysterically hilarious because it all seems so very strange. . . .†

Miss Katharine Brown   Atlanta, Georgia
Selznick International Pictures, Inc.   July 18, 1939
New York, New York

Dear Katharine:

I had intended to answer your letter of June 30th before this but I was
out of town for a while and then developed one of those infuriating sum-

---

* The Eumenides, in Greek mythology, were female deities of vengeance, similar to the Ro-
man Furies.

† After Selznick confirmed the premiere would be held in Atlanta, the local papers trumpeted the news on their front pages. The *Atlanta Journal*'s July 18 headline read, "'Gone With
the Wind' Premiere Decisively Won for Atlanta: General Selznick Surrenders to Dixie After
Mayor Hartsfield Draws His Sword."

mer colds which settled in one ear. Between the earache and the treatment I have decided that there is little choice. It is better now.

This morning I sent you clippings covering the latest news on the Atlanta front. The grapevine telegraph brought me the information that this is the way the rumor started that the premiere would *not* be held here. Mr. Jock Whitney was supposed to have been in Atlanta sometime within the last week on his way to the Coast and to have stayed at the Georgian Terrace Hotel for a few hours. It was reported that he had told someone at the hotel that the premiere would be held in Los Angeles. This rumor reached the Junior League and they immediately called upon His Honor the Mayor, asking him to do something about it. The Journal telephoned me and asked if I had yet had an official notification from Mr. Selznick as to where and when the premiere would be held. I thankfully said that I had had no such official notification and that when—and if—I did get one I would notify the papers immediately. The Journal reporter remarked gloomily that the noise in the Mayor's office sounded like a WPA riot instead of His Honor conferring with the Junior League. I said that I did not believe Mr. Whitney had made any such statement and that the girls had just latched on to a rumor and had become excited about it. The story in this morning's paper straightens things out. If there are any follow-ups I'll let you have them.

John was so sorry he did not get to see you and to meet Miss Leigh. He said Mr. Samuels was wonderful and I can well believe that. For your part in hastening the closing of this matter I am so very grateful. You were swell about it.*

I am enclosing a clipping from the Journal. It is very much like dozens of other stories which have appeared in the last few months. Everyone from Atlanta who has been fortunate enough to get on the sets has been charmed by what they saw and has said so in the newspapers. I think it's grand publicity for your picture, for the people really mean what they say and sincere enthusiasm carries a lot of weight.

---

* Marsh and Stephens Mitchell had gone to New York to sign a new contract for commercial tie-ups. Under the July 17 agreement with Selznick and Loew's, Inc., Mitchell was paid $1,000 and was to receive a sliding-scale percentage of the profits made on licensed products promoting the film. (In the first week after the movie opened, sales of items such as Scarlett O'Hara dolls, nail polish, quilts, candy, perfume, handkerchiefs, scarves, sweaters, and girdles, along with Rhett Butler tie clips, cuff links, and bow ties, totaled $636,250, according to *Business Week*.)

Miss Marcella Rabwin   *Atlanta, Georgia*
Selznick International Pictures, Inc.   *July 19, 1939*
Culver City, California

My dear Miss Rabwin:

A number of things occurred to delay my answer to your very nice letter of June 29th. I was called out of the city and I contracted a summer cold which made me feel too dull to do any writing and I was further delayed by waiting on American and foreign sales figures.

I am enclosing a copy of a story on the sales figures of "Gone With the Wind," which the Atlanta newspapers will publish next Sunday. Please feel free to use this information if you think it would be of assistance to you. As I believe my husband wrote you, the full figures from abroad are not in yet from several countries. They should arrive within the next six weeks to two months. Will you please let me know if you want these sales figures sent to you as they come in? Of course, if you wish to close up this end of the matter now, I realize you would not wish these additional figures.

Yesterday I mailed Katharine Brown copies of the stories which recently appeared in Atlanta newspapers about the "Gone With the Wind" premiere. I hope she forwards them to Mr. Selznick and that you will see them. I believe you will find them both interesting and amusing. While the attitude of some of our civic leaders may lead the Selznick organization to wonder bewilderingly just who really is producing and releasing the picture, I hope it gives you pleasure to know of the deep and sincere interest Atlanta has in the film. The interest is so deep that it took only a mild rumor about the premiere not being held here to cause an uproar. Everyone seemed very pleased when Mr. Selznick finally settled the matter. It was fine of him to act so swiftly.

Of course our Atlanta Junior League was very upset by the no-premiere rumor because they were planning to give a large costume ball after the premiere. They hoped that Mr. Selznick and any members of the cast who might come to Atlanta would be present. They are all very happy now that they can proceed with their plans.

I heard rumors that Mayor Hartsfield, of Atlanta, and some of the civic organizations intend to stage festivities upon the occasion of the premiere but I know nothing of the details.

Please tell Mr. Selznick how pleased and flattered I and the members of the Atlanta Women's Press Club were when we learned through Katharine Brown that he had promised to attend the pre-premiere buffet supper the Women's Press Club is giving me. This party will be a private one and a rather small one. The only people invited, besides the ladies of the press, are some of the Macmillan people from New York and Mr. Selznick and the members of his cast and his organization. When your plans for your Atlanta trip are complete, please let me know how many people from your organization we may expect. I hope all of you will come to the party the Press Club is giving because it will be the only party I am attending that day and, of course, I want to meet everyone connected with the picture.

Your last letter to me was so fine and understanding and I appreciate it more than I can tell you. I realize how easy it is for misunderstandings to arise when people are separated by great distances. I realize, too, that it is very difficult for anyone who has not been here in Atlanta during the last three years to understand the reason behind my attitude about personal publicity. Thank you so much for all you wrote.

Mr. George Brett, Jr.   *Atlanta, Georgia*
The Macmillan Company   *July 26, 1939*
New York, New York

My dear George:

I am asking Miss Stone to hold this letter until your return, for it is not important enough to break in upon your vacation. All of us regretted that it was necessary to disturb you with that telegram Steve and John had to send when they were in New York.

Here is what I would like to know if you can tell me. How many people from The Macmillan Company will come to Atlanta for the premiere? The reason I ask is that the town is in a swivit about the premiere. Mr. Selznick has definitely stated that it will take place here, probably sometime in the latter part of November. Various organizations have gone into dithers about parties, His Honor the Mayor is flying about planning civic affairs, and everything is stranger than you can image. The members of the Women's Press Club, who are giving me the buffet supper before the premiere, have decided that they must close the invitation list soon. They must know the exact number of guests to be expected so they can make arrangements for refreshments, identification cards et cetera. They are trying to hold the number down as low as possible. They know that when the news leaks out, as it inevitably will, they will be stormed by people wanting invitations, so they want to close the matter up as soon as possible and they requested me to ask you how many they should expect from New York.

A problem has arisen in connection with the premiere which I cannot solve, nor can it be solved in Atlanta. This problem is how may reserved seats to the premiere be obtained? No one here knows whether admission will be by invitation only or whether seats will be sold to the public and at what prices. Yesterday I talked to the manager of the theatre which will exhibit the picture and told him that I expected some of the Macmillan organization to be here, and how would I arrange tickets for them? He said frankly that he did not know and could not assist me. I understood him to say that he would not be in charge at that time. From this I gather that a manager or publicity man will be sent from California or New York to handle the whole affair. May I suggest this course of action to you when you learn how many of your organization intend to come to the premiere— get in touch with Katharine Brown, of the New York Selznick office, and put the matter up to her. While she has nothing to do with the premiere, she will doubtless know who will be in charge and perhaps she can use her influence to see that you get tickets. I would not draw an easy breath if you or any of my other friends at The Macmillan Company arrived in Atlanta on that occasion without tickets, with thousands of people saying they had been promised passes and the theatre seats numbering only 2,100. I imagine the seats will be allotted some time before the premiere, so that even I, the author, would be unable to wangle any for you short of crippling and disabling a requisite number of people holding tickets.

I hope you had a wonderful vacation. I have thought of you frequently during the last month as I remember your description of the place where you are staying. It certainly sounded beautiful and remote.

Miss Katharine Brown   *Atlanta, Georgia*
Selznick International Pictures, Inc.   *August 7, 1939*
New York, New York

Dear Katharine:

Please forgive my delay in answering your letter. I know you and Mr. Selznick wanted a prompt reply. Unfortunately, my secretary is on her vacation and I am swamped with mail; Bessie has been ill; I have been trying to find a new apartment; and the public, frenzied by news of the approaching premiere, have produced new problems (see enclosed clipping).

About the story for Redbook magazine—I wonder if you would do this for me. If it will be very troublesome or in any way embarrassing, please do not hesitate to tell me so. I would like very much to see the article before it is printed, or at least those parts which make mention of me. I realize that may sound very presumptuous to you and may sound even more presumptuous to Redbook. However, I think I discussed with you some of my reasons for wanting to see the story when I talked to you in New York. It is incredible the number of erroneous statements that have been printed about me and "Gone With the Wind" as a book and a movie. Sometimes I am appalled at the errors some of my best friends make, even after I have told them the truth of things.

I would like the Redbook story to be accurate and if I know anything about editors I think they would like it accurate. For instance, I would not like for them to include that error about my having sold "Gone With the Wind" in galley proofs when in actuality I sold it some time after publication when the sales figures were around 400,000 (I think) and I had every assurance of a half million sale in a couple of months. I would not like to embarrass a reputable magazine like Redbook by asking them for a correction. If you could tell Mr. Vetlugin what my situation is and ask him if I could see the story or the parts of it referring to me, I should be very appreciative. But if this isn't convenient to you, for any reason, let me know and I will write him immediately myself.

This will have to be all for today. I will write you tomorrow about the other matter.

Mr. George Brett, Jr.   *Atlanta, Georgia*
The Macmillan Company   *August 8, 1939*
New York, New York

Dear George:

I was delighted to hear that nine of you were coming down. One of the reasons I have delayed writing you about it is that I had to get hold of Medora Perkerson, president of the Press Club, to discuss the matter with her. As you know, Medora is your newest Atlanta author.* Her book comes out on the fifteenth and every friend she has is giving her a party, so it was hard to catch her. She was equally delighted to hear about the Macmillan group. It seems too good to be true that all of you are coming. The Press Club herewith extends an invitation to all of you. The formal invitations and cards will be sent later. Do please tell everyone to hold on to their cards, because even I, the guest of honor, will not be able to get anybody in to the party without a card.

When I think of nine good friends from the Macmillan Company coming to Atlanta, I regret that my visit with all of you will be so short, and be confined to the party alone. But I don't know anything else to do about it.

---

* Perkerson's murder mystery *Who Killed Aunt Maggie?* was published by Macmillan.

Referring back to Medora's book—everyone who has read it, which includes me, thinks it's grand and we all feel that it will have a good sale.

I am looking forward to the dummy of the cheap edition which you said you were sending to me.* As you can imagine, I am very curious to see it. I do have cold feet (for your sake) when you write that you hope to sell 500,000. However, my feet are not as cold as they would have been three years ago. Then I implored Harold Latham not to make a 10,000 first edition because I did not want my publishers left with 7,000 heavy volumes. I am so accustomed to sales miracles by the Macmillan Company that I am not as alarmed as I should be. I wish you would tell Mr. Blanton that I am sending him all good wishes for the success of the 69¢ copy. I do not know to whom he is going to sell these copies but I believe he will do it.

P.S. Would it be *too* grasping of me to ask for the 2,000,000th copy? Or have you promised it?†

Miss Katharine Brown   *Atlanta, Georgia*
Selznick International Pictures, Inc.   *August 8, 1939*
New York, New York

Dear Katharine:

I can't tell you how good and bad I felt when I read the part of your letter in which Mr. Selznick wrote that he wanted me to see the entire uncut picture. I have wanted to see the uncut version so much and so has John. Naturally, I'd rather see it than all the cut versions in the world and it makes me very happy to know that Mr. Selznick wanted me to see it—and in his company.

I felt bad about it because I knew I couldn't see it without endless difficulties and perhaps a great deal of unpleasantness. To be frank, so many difficulties are piling up about the premiere of the picture that I do not have either strength or courage to contemplate adding one more burden to those which I am carrying. It would not be possible for my presence at

---

* The publisher was preparing a paperback Motion Picture Edition of the novel featuring color stills from the film. The book, to be released in conjunction with the movie, would sell for sixty-nine cents.

† In December 1936, Macmillan presented Mitchell the one-millionth copy of *Gone With the Wind*, adding a special page noting its significance. The book is in the Margaret Mitchell Collection in Special Collections at the Atlanta-Fulton Public Library System. In response to the author's request for the two-millionth copy of her novel, Brett promised to "do as careful figuring as we can" to determine when such a book would come off the press. This copy would have been a Motion Picture Edition, but no volume marked as such is in the library's collection, nor does Mitchell mention the two-millionth book again in her correspondence.

a preview to be kept a secret. It might be a secret for a day or a week but not for a longer period. It would be even worse if the secret leaked out long after the premiere, because then everyone would jump on me for being a liar, or at least acting a lie when I gave the impression that the premiere was the first time I had seen the picture.

Already the papers have been after me asking whether I have seen the uncut version or intend to see it. Dearie, our newspaper boys don't miss a trick. They are always two jumps ahead of me. I told them that I had not seen it and did not intend to see it.

I don't think my presence at a secret preview could be kept a secret. In the first place, whenever I léave, even to drive to Marietta, twenty miles away, all my fellow townsmen know exactly where I have gone and why. Within five minutes after I buy tickets for a train trip, it's all over town. Generally people think I am going to Hollywood and the phone begins going like mad. I know newspaper people all over the United States and I cannot think of any fairly large town you could choose for your preview where I do not know newspaper people. Mr. Selznick's presence in any town in the United States could not be kept a secret. Every member of his party would be identified. And when there was one small member who could not be identified, it would not take the newspaper lads long to figure out who she was. Then I would come home and have to go through the mill of having the entire populace stopping me on the street and asking me which scenes were to be cut and is Mr. Gable too thrilling for words and am I disappointed or not. I just don't think I can go through all that, in the light of what the premiere will be.

There are very few things I really like to do. Seeing the uncut version is one thing I want to do most violently. But when I balance up my desires against the attendant difficulties, I'm afraid I must swallow my desires.

You wrote that "I think this means more to Mr. Selznick than you can possibly know." No, Katharine, I really believe I do know how much this would mean to him. And that is why I am so grateful to him for thinking of me. We've been long distance partners in this enterprise. I worked like a dog to write the book and Heaven knows he has worked like a dog to film it. It's only natural that he should want me to see all of his work and not just a part, because he wants me, as author, to see the whole job he, as producer, has done. And I'd give anything if it were possible, but it isn't. John and I have talked the whole thing over for two days and we just don't see how it could be managed. Please tell Mr. Selznick how sorry I am and please make him realize that I mean it.

Mr. *Voldemar Vetlugan*   *Atlanta, Georgia*
Redbook Magazine   *August 17, 1939*
New York, New York

My dear Mr. Vetlugan:

I have just received from Katharine Brown, of Selznick International Pictures, Inc., the proofs of the story "Tiger By the Tail" (and before I go any further, I congratulate you on this catchy and apt choice of title). I thank you most sincerely for your courtesy in permitting me to see the proofs, and I hope that I can return the courtesy by contributing something to its accuracy. I am sure that you and Mr. Van Ryn wish it to be completely accurate, quite as much as I do.* Following are some suggested changes:

I have been under the impression that Miss Leigh's name is "Vivien," not "Vivian," but I may be wrong about this.

I think you have Miss Brown's first name misspelled. Her letters to me are always signed "Katharine," not "Katherine."

Is the spelling of "Pluncket" correct? I have always understood that his name is Walter Plunkett.

Near the bottom of page 98, you refer to me as "*Mrs.* Mitchell." It should be "*Miss* Mitchell." I am Mrs. Marsh, but I use my maiden name, Margaret Mitchell, for writing purposes.

On the whole, the article is very accurate, so far as my knowledge goes, and there is only one other passage where I would like to see a revision made.

On page 12, you say that I sold the motion picture rights to Mr. Selznick on July 15, 1936. This is an error. The correct date is July 30. Also on page 97, you say, "A fortnight passed—the most memorable fortnight in the life of Margaret Mitchell of Atlanta. By August first etc." The fortnight in question was not especially "memorable" for me. I was at that time in the mountains enjoying a vacation, following much more memorable days, and weeks, and "fortnights" some while before then.

This is the one part of your article which is bad from my personal standpoint. I will explain. Among the many groundless rumors which have gotten into circulation about me, and which have caused me much annoyance and embarrassment, is the one that I sold my motion picture rights "while my book was still in galley proofs and before a single copy of the book had been sold." This makes me out a perfect fool and lays me open to the unwanted sympathy of well meaning people who think I "gave away"

---

* The article, which appeared in the October 1939 issue of *Redbook*, was written by Frederick Van Ryn using information the studio provided.

my movie rights. This is far from true, for my movie rights brought me the highest price ever paid, up to that time, for a first novel.

Your article does not repeat the "galley proof" error but, in effect, it conveys almost the same idea, for it says that it was not until a fortnight *after* the sale of the movie rights that the book "had become a national sensation and a 'must' on everybody's bookshelf." The correct date of the sale, July 30, coincides with the time when you say the book had become "a national sensation, etc.," but even that statement is not completely accurate.

Long before the movie sale, the book had aroused national interest. It had a record-breaking advance sale before publication date, June 30. In the month between that date and the sale of the movie rights, more than 250,000 copies had been sold and predictions were being freely made that it would sell 500,000 copies within a few weeks. The book was high on the best seller lists the first week of publication and it quickly jumped to the top. And if I had not had the sales figures to tell me that my book was making an unusual success, I would have known this from the flood of letters which were sweeping in on me from all parts of the country.

I am rehearsing this bit of ancient history, not to boast about my book, but to clear out of your mind any impression you may have, as a result of the rumors, that I blindly sold the movie rights at a time when I was wholly ignorant of my book's possibilities. I hope you will revise that portion of your article so that it will not tend to perpetuate a rumor that makes me out a fool, and Mr. Selznick a knave, and is very unfair to both of us. I asked for, and got, a very high price, and he took a long chance in paying it, and both of us are satisfied.

In conclusion, may I ask that you do not quote any part of this letter in your article? I am glad to help in getting the article accurate but I prefer to remain off-stage. There are a number of reasons for my request but I will not take up your time explaining them. And I doubt if any explanations are necessary, for I think you probably will agree with me that "Tiger By the Tail" is, and should remain, a *Selznick* story. Bringing me into it at this late date would only throw it out of balance.

My thanks again for your courtesy—

Mr. Harold Latham   *Atlanta, Georgia*
The Macmillan Company   *August 21, 1939*
New York, New York

Dear Harold:

Today is the first time I have had a free moment in which to write and thank you for the lovely corsage. The reason I have had no free moments is

Medora and her "Aunt Maggie." You'd never know Aunt Maggie had been killed; she's been the liveliest person in Atlanta for two weeks. Everyone likes Medora so much and is so interested in her book, everyone in Atlanta loves to give parties and all they need is a mild excuse, so there have been four parties a day since the thirteenth of this month. Medora is going strong and looking radiant. I am practically bushed and my complexion is in a dreadful state from party food and late hours. I hear that "Aunt Maggie" had a second printing almost immediately and I was delighted. I do not know how the book is going over the country but it is doing marvelously here and everyone is crazy about it. . . .

I had a note from Mr. Brett a couple of weeks ago, saying that you would be among those who would come to Atlanta for the premiere. That is marvelous news and we are so pleased. Don't let anything happen to upset this plan for we'd be so disappointed if you did not come. I realize that we won't have the opportunity to see a great deal of our Macmillan friends on this occasion, for it appears that the premiere will be the wildest, maddest day since President Jeff Davis unveiled the Ben Hill monument in Atlanta in the eighties, but even a glimpse of you will be fun.*

Mrs. Wilbur G. Kurtz   *Atlanta, Georgia*
Selznick International Pictures, Inc.   *August 22, 1939*
New York, New York

Dear Annie Laurie:

John and I appreciated your long letter of August 13th. It sounds as if the three of you are having a wonderful time and we love hearing about it.† Knowing how busy you are, we appreciate the time you take in writing to us.

Susan Myrick reaches Macon today and her friends called us to invite us to a "welcome home" party tonight. We could not make it, for we are (and have been for some time past) in one of our desperately busy periods. We hope to get Susan up here in a week or so and have a wonderful time hearing of her experiences. . . .

I was glad to learn that work on the montages was under weigh.‡ I would imagine that the most difficult period of the picture was now at

---

* On May 1, 1886, former Confederate President Jefferson Davis attended the unveiling of a monument to Confederate Senator Benjamin Harvey Hill in downtown Atlanta, and more than one hundred thousand people turned out.

† The Kurtzes' youngest daughter, also named Annie Laurie and a student at Wesleyan College in Macon, was visiting her parents in California.

‡ A montage is an editing technique used to suggest the passage of time, often accompanied by special photographic effects and music. There are several montages in *Gone With the Wind*,

hand—the montages, the cutting, the retakes, the musical scoring. I wish it were all completed. In fact, I wish it were completed and released, so that we would have that hurdle behind us. The premiere cannot come soon enough to suit us. I do not look forward to it with any sensations of pleasure, for it will be an ordeal I do not care to contemplate. But once it is over a great many of our problems will be over too. At least, I hope so. At any rate, I will not be beset by people who want to play Scarlett nor annoyed by frenzied folk who are determined that I can secure them sixty passes for the premiere for their clubs.

. . . The wildest rumors arise, such as the one that tickets to the premiere will cost fifty dollars. I have heard every date on the calendar mentioned authoritatively as the day of the premiere. After three and a half years, I am inured to rumors of all kinds and never even listen to them. I marvel at the credulity of the public.

I had to laugh at your anecdote about me, Governor Rivers and Mayor Hartsfield being on the committee to handle the premiere. Whenever you hear this mentioned I would be very pleased if you would tell the speaker that he is a liar. If you feel that you can bring yourself to it you may state exactly what kind of a liar. I have nothing to do with the premiere, thank God, and do not intend to be dragged into it. I have promised that I will be at the theatre at a certain time and there begins and ends my connection with the matter. . . .

So many people have asked when you two will be home and I tell them that I do not know. I imagine you will stay in the West until the picture is in the can. Am I right?

Mr. and Mrs. Edwin Granberry   *Atlanta, Georgia*
Winter Haven, Florida   *August 22, 1939*

Dear Mabel and Edwin:

Of course you do not know that I have had you on my conscience for several months, but I have. Ever since your invitation to come to see you at Long Boat [Key] we have been intending to write you that we were on our way. I've delayed writing each week until we could set a definite date. Finally, it dawned upon us that the summer was practically over and we would be unable to come at all. I cannot tell you what a disappointment this was to both of us. We both needed a vacation so much and we wanted

---

including the opening of the second half, in which footage of swirling dust, flames, and marching soldiers serves as background to two titles, "And the wind swept through Georgia . . . ," followed by the single word "Sherman!"

to see you two. There are so few people with whom we can talk and so few people whose laughter we love as much as yours. And the quiet of Long Boat seemed like Paradise.

This has been the most overworked summer we have had so far. No sooner had one emergency problem been met and settled than another arose. One of our most exasperating new problems arises from the world premiere of GWTW, which definitely will be held in Atlanta on an indefinite date between now and the New Year. I have nothing to do with the premiere; my only connection is that upon this indefinite date I will put on an evening dress and take a seat in a movie with a heart full of relief that the thing is nearly over. . . . The town is very excited about the prospect of a premiere and many groups and individuals wish to give parties upon the occasion. They want us to attend the parties and "use our influence" to make Mr. Gable attend, too. I can deny connection with the movie until I am blue in the face but it does little good. All of this takes up a great deal of time and leaves only the hours after midnight in which to attend to business matters such as foreign translation contracts. From the foregoing you two can understand that we have been busy. Amid all this turmoil I have been apartment hunting. I have been on such hunts for four years, for we need one more room for an office in which to keep our typewriter and file cases. As we also want a glassed in sun porch, we have had difficulties. But I think we've got what we want now and hope to move on the first of September. . . .

Mr. John Embry Horan   *Atlanta, Georgia*
Dalton, Georgia   *August 26, 1939*

My dear Mr. Horan:

You may recall having written to me several times during the spring of 1937 in regard to permission for the use of names of Negro characters from "Gone With the Wind" in connection with the dolls you wished to sell as a tie-up with my book. On account of uncertainties about the tie-up rights at that time, I was unable to give you a definite answer. I am glad to say that this situation has now been clarified and I have reached a definite understanding with the motion picture people. If you are still interested, the person to whom you should write is—

Mr. Irwin Margulies
Loew's, Inc.
Loew Building
1540 Broadway
New York, New York

He has full authority to deal with you about the licensing of commercial production and similar matters.

You have been on my mind many times in the past year and upon several occasions I considered writing you to tell you that I had not forgotten or overlooked your request. But, as I had nothing definite to report, I decided against writing to you. I realize my long silence must have led you to think that I was not interested in your desire to have the mountain people of your section manufacture these novelties. The reverse was true but there was nothing I could do about the matter at that time.

I have written Mr. Margulies and told him of your request.

Miss Katharine Brown   *Atlanta, Georgia*
Selznick International Pictures, Inc.   *August 26, 1939*
New York, New York

Dear Katharine:

I've been out of town with the Georgia newspaper editors on their annual jaunt, which, oddly enough, covered only three counties this time instead of the usual twelve. And there was only one fish fry and one barbecue instead of two in every county, so my complexion is not as wrecked as it might be.

We have finally chosen an apartment and taken the lease and I have worked off most of the new draperies and slip covers, the parties given to Mrs. Perkerson in honor of her book have settled down to one every other day instead of three a day, and all in all life has returned to its normal tenor. This means only twelve to fourteen working hours a day. I tell you, life is strenuous in the South and we are indeed a virile people to bear up under it as well as we do.

All the above mentioned things have kept me from writing you again about the preview.* We've thought it over and talked it over and we always come back to the same decision. Dearly as we would love to see the picture, it seems the [better] part of discretion not to do so. Of course, if, after the premiere, an opportunity rose for us to see an uncut version, we would love to do so, but not if it were any extra trouble to you or Mr. Selznick or anyone in the organization. I do not know much about such matters. I imagine it would be troublesome to put together an uncut version after the cutting has been done. By the way, I've heard scores of people say that

---

* As an alternative, Brown suggested arranging a private screening of the uncut film at Whitney's "Greentree" estate in Manhasset, Long Island.

they would give anything to see everything Mr. Selznick has shot, even if they had to sit hours and bring their lunches in shoe boxes. As I remarked above, we are a virile race et cetera.

You mentioned having a letter from a Mrs. Carter about the Junior League ball. The Leaguer who talked to me was Mrs. Green Warren and I do not know which Mrs. Carter this is.* I'm not a Junior Leaguer, you know, and so I am not in on their plans. To tell the truth, I am not in on the plans of any civic organization here, except the Women's Press Club. I have very carefully stayed out.

Here is something I wanted to discuss with you for some while but was unable to do so during this last frantic month. I am writing you about it at the request of Mrs. Perkerson, President of the Press Club. I could take it up direct with Mr. Selznick but I know how busy he must be at present. So I'm asking you to get me the information if you can. The matter concerns you, too. It is this: the Press Club, having been assaulted to right and left for invitations to their party, have closed down their list of invitations with a snap like a bear trap. They've done their best to keep this a very small party—just the Press Clubbers and their husbands, true loves and the newspaper executives. The only outside people to be invited are a few from the New York Macmillan office and the Selznick people. The girls are getting out their invitations and the cards which go with the invitations. Without the admission card no one can get in. They would like to know how many of your organization they may expect. Of course they want you and your husband if he can come, and Mr. and Mrs. Selznick, the members of the cast and the director. Here is their problem, and it is a delicate one. The wildest rumors take Atlanta about the premiere, one of them being that a solid train of Californians will be here, with the entire movie industry, press agents, photographers, secretaries, grips and prop boys. The Press Club is small and cannot handle a large crowd. They do not want to give offense by not inviting people who should be invited, yet they cannot invite everyone who might come. For instance, if they invited one out-of-town newspaper person they would have to invite them all, and this they could not do.

The same applies to writers from film magazines and publicity men and photographers. Everyone in the Club has out-of-town newspaper friends and many members have friends on film monthlies. They'd be in bad if they invited strangers and did not invite their friends. They would like to know

---

* Mrs. W. Colquitt Carter was president of the Atlanta Junior League.

how many people will be in Mr. Selznick's *personal* party. This includes, of course, the director and any members of the cast who may come.

Is there any way you can find out this for us? This may sound like a strange request but I know that you, who have been here in Atlanta, will understand. The girls would like to know as soon as possible. By the way, have you any idea yet about the approximate date of the premiere? I hear November 15th, I hear Christmas Eve and I hear sometime in 1940. We usually take our vacation sometime in the early winter and go to Florida and I'd like to make our plans in advance, if possible, but I do not want to conflict with any possible premiere date. . . .

Miss Katharine Brown   *Atlanta, Georgia*
Selznick International Pictures, Inc.   *September 1, 1939*
New York, New York

My dear Katharine:

I am sorry if your Publicity department was embarrassed by the typographical errors I caught in the Redbook article. I thought the errors had been made by the magazine's printers or proofreaders, and I called attention to them for no reason except as an act of cooperation with the magazine. When a publication is kind enough to submit proofs of an article to me, in order that I may protect myself against errors, I feel an obligation to return the favor by telling them of all errors I happen to notice, whether they affect me or not.

Of course, it was too bad that Redbook had gone to press before my letter reached them. I have not yet decided whether I will ask them to print a correction. Such corrections, published a month after the error, rarely do any good. So please do not consider this letter as the one which you said you would rewrite and send to Redbook over Selznick's signature. If I decide to ask for the correction, we can then decide on the method of handling it.

I am glad you wrote me at length about your viewpoint on the date of sale of the motion picture rights. It gave me my first real understanding of why we have been at cross purposes over this ever since 1936. Previously, we did not understand each other because we were looking at the matter from entirely different angles. When we discussed this in New York, I thought you looked a little bewildered, but I supposed this was because a great deal of water has flowed under both our bridges since 1936. I thought you had merely forgotten the details of what is now an item of ancient history, and no doubt you thought the same of me.

My files verify your statement that we agreed on the price on July 7th, and you have already verified my statement that the date when I signed the contract was July 30th. According to your way of looking at things, the sale was made as soon as the price was decided on, and you say that is the customary viewpoint in the movie trade. I am not surprised that the movie industry has that attitude, for I am told that most authors never even read their contracts and that the signing of them is purely a formality (for the authors). And, apparently, I was expected to behave the same way, for when the contract was mailed to me, I was warned that I must take it, or else. I was told that it was the official "standard" movie contract, that nobody ever questioned the goodness of it, and that I must not dare to ask for or try to make any changes in it, except very minor ones, or Mr. Selznick would walk out on me and the whole trade would be off.

As you remember, I not only made numerous changes in the contract, but very important ones, and if Selznick had not agreed to the changes I demanded, the sale would never have been made. The price was only one of a great many details which had to be agreed upon before I was willing to sell, and some of the other details were much more important to me than the money involved.

Even in a situation where the contract is a pure formality, a sale is not legally made until the contract has been signed. But in my case the contract was no mere formality. The contract you originally submitted was one I would never have dreamed of signing, and Selznick would never have gotten the movie rights if the contract had not been revised. The agreement on price did not close the sale. It was an agreement on one detail, with the closing of the sale entirely conditional upon the working out of a contract satisfactory to me, and I could have abandoned the trade at any time I pleased up to the time I put my name on the revised contract. So the correct way of stating the case is that the price agreement on July 7th was one step in the working out of a sale that took place when the contract was finally closed up and signed on July 30th. The sale did not take place until July 30th.

So much for the legal angles. After reading your letter, I now understand how we happened to get tangled up. It was your pride versus my pride, and the pleasant thing is that neither of us needs to surrender her pride in order to get the trouble straightened out.

You take pride in the fact that you were enthusiastic about my book "prior to the time it was publicly acclaimed." Certainly I have no objection to that. I am proud of it myself. I have always been proud that the very smart Katharine Brown had faith in my book before it became a best-seller—and such great faith that she urged her company to pay an unprecedented price for the first novel of an unknown author. I am very grateful to you and, if I have not told you so before, I am glad to do it now. I have no desire to detract the least bit from your pride and pleasure or from any business reputation you may have gained from having taken a chance on me.

My pride involved is that I do not intend to be held up to the public as a country fool who was so dumb that she let a slick New York gang swindle her out of her movie rights before she found out they were worth something. That is the meaning which some of the commentators have given to the story that you bought the movie rights "while the book was in galley proofs." The Redbook article is not quite that bad, but it does definitely imply that the success of my book began in the fortnight *after* the movie rights had gotten out of my hands. Which, of course, is not true, even on the basis of the July 7th date. My book was a success even before publication, on June 30th, and by the time the movie rights were actually sold, a month later, my eyes were wide open to the fact that the book, by some accident, had become a national sensation.

I just don't like the gossip which says that you and Mr. Selznick put one over on me, and that I was so dumb I could not prevent you from putting one over on me.

By all means, hold fast to your position that you had "made your decision" about my book before it was publicly acclaimed. The story of your excitement about the book when you first read it and of your frantic efforts to make Mr. Selznick buy it can, as far as I am concerned, be used as much as you please. Personally, I think it is a good story. I have always liked it, as one of the extraordinary, unbelievable events of those first days of the year of the big Wind. That gives you what you want for your pride, I believe.

And for my pride, please see that the Selznick and MGM organizations understand that if any further statements need to be made about the date when the movie rights were sold, the date should be the *correct* one. July 30th, 1936, is the one and only date on which the sale took place. There isn't any other date, for the sale was not made twice.

If you feel compelled to mention the July 7th date, it should be referred to as the date when Katharine Brown succeeded in getting Mr. Selznick to meet my price. But I would prefer that you do not mention that date at all, simply because the public is easily confused, and *two* dates are somewhat more than it can grasp.

You do not need to mention that date in order to tell your side of the story. Your story is just as good without it. And any time that date is mentioned, or any statement is made that you bought the rights before publication or immediately after publication, it puts me in a very bad light. All I want your folks to do is stick to the truth and say that the movie rights were sold on the date when they actually were sold, which is July 30th, 1936.

We seem to write each other some very long letters. I do not mind if they help retain and maintain the very friendly understanding we have had ever since we first met.

P.S. Can you tell me what happened to cause the Selznick-Macmillan split over the movie edition? I have heard nothing, except that there is to be no movie edition, and I am naturally curious. It must have been something serious, for they were far advanced with their plans.*

Miss Willa Gray Martin   *Atlanta, Georgia*
Greenville, South Carolina   *September 3, 1939*

My dear Miss Martin:

Ever since I read your story in the August 27th issue of The Atlanta Constitution, I've been trying to find time to write to you.† As I have been in the midst of moving into a new apartment, there have been very few minutes in which to write. This morning your special delivery letter arrived and I am taking these early morning hours to answer it.

It will be impossible for me to see you on Tuesday, as you requested. My moving has been delayed already by many business matters which have come up during the last two weeks, so I am making no new engagements. There is a second reason why I cannot give the interview you requested. I hope you will understand this reason. I have not given an interview, except on spot news, in something over two years. I am sure you understand what I mean by spot news. If my book is published in another foreign country, if I win a prize, am awarded a degree, become involved in a lawsuit or in any way experience something that is "news," I know that the newspapers are entitled to the information and I do not mind making some brief comment if they ask for it. Such brief comments on a few occasions have been all that I have said for publication in a long time; there has been nothing in the interview category.

---

* As the release date drew closer, Selznick began having second thoughts about allowing Macmillan to use stills from the movie in its new paperback edition. Wanting to ensure that the characters and scenes appeared fresh to moviegoers, the producer demanded publication be delayed until the spring or summer of 1940. Selznick's feelings also influenced the movie's trailer, which featured oil paintings by Kurtz instead of actual scenes from the film.
† Martin's article was headlined "Southern Accent in New York: Selling Scarlett to the Movies."

The truth of the matter is, the interview and feature story material about me was thoroughly worked out within a few months after the publication of "Gone With the Wind," and whatever has been published about me in these past three years has been a deadly dull rehash of those first stories. I know the public is as heartily sick of the repetition as I am. You see, nothing has happened to me since the publication of my book, except that the book has sold incredibly, and certainly that item has been written out, too. Because of the circumstances outlined, I have had to turn down a number of requests for interviews, and magazine editors and my many newspaper friends have put me under a promise that when, and if, I decide to give an interview, I will give them all an even chance at it. If I gave you the interview, I'd have to call them all in, too. As you can see, this would be a very difficult and troublesome affair. I'm awfully sorry, for I appreciate your interest, but that is my situation.

I had intended writing to you, even before your letter arrived this morning. Unfortunately your article in The Constitution last Sunday contained a number of errors. I suppose you got your information from Miss Annie Laurie Williams, so I do not hold you entirely to blame, but the errors are nevertheless troublesome. So, my first request of you is that you do not publish the article any further without at least correcting the errors.

I am very sorry that you did not query me about the facts before the article was published. I have never failed to cooperate with any newspaper writer who queried me. I am so grateful for their consideration and courtesy that I answer with all possible speed.

One of the errors in last Sunday's article—and as a Southerner you will understand that it is not trivial—was the statement about my grandfather "Captain" Mitchell and his friendship with Miss Williams' grandfather. My grandfather was not a captain; he was a sergeant. This statement has been published scores of times whenever any biographical sketch of me has gotten into print. He was not one of the "five survivors of his regiment." It must have been some other regiment and some other "Captain Mitchell." If my grandfather ever knew Miss Williams' grandfather, I never heard of it, nor have any of my Georgia relatives. Of course, he *might* have known him and he might, as you say, have sent letters to Mr. Berryman but there is no basis whatsoever for your statement that "*both* families cherish letters telling of a friendship that lasted long after the war." Our family has no such letters, nor have we heard of any letters. If Miss Williams possesses any letters from my grandfather, she never mentioned them at our single, brief meeting, nor in the few letters she has written me.

My Mitchell family connections are numerous and they know our family history very well. They know my grandfather was not a captain and that he was not one of the five survivors of his regiment. They have no Berryman letters. They think I am responsible for your story and they naturally wonder why, at this late date, I should promote my grandfather to captaincy. This has been a busy and bothersome week explaining that the fault was not mine. They are a family which takes pride in accuracy about such matters, and even when I explain that I knew nothing about the article until I read it in the papers, they still think that I should have been able to prevent our relative from being dragged in, erroneously, for no reason except that Miss Williams presumably thought this would advertise her. Should you sell this article elsewhere, please eliminate all mention of my grandfather.

I am mystified by your statement that you read a letter of mine—shown to you by Miss Williams—written on blue stationery with a "dainty" letter head. I have no recollection of ever having used blue stationery and my letter head does not seem dainty to me, and I cannot recall ever writing Miss Williams of my "refusal to say what actors and actresses I thought should play the leading roles." I have just gone through my files and can find no such letter. Of course, it is possible that I did write such a letter and the carbon is lost. I can remember only one letter to Miss Williams which mentioned Hollywood at all. Miss Williams, for some reason, seemed very anxious for me to go to Hollywood. I replied briefly, "As I told you in New York, I do not want to go to California. I haven't changed my mind about that."

I feel rather strongly about this matter. So many people have annoyed me by saying that I should go to Hollywood and mind Mr. Selznick's business for him. As my connection with the film of "Gone With the Wind" ended on July 30, 1936 when I sold the motion picture rights, I felt (and still feel) that it would have been the rankest impertinence and presumption for me to mix into an affair that was no concern of mine. The implication in your article is that I felt I had the right to name the cast but was restraining myself nobly. Having nothing to do with the picture, I had no right to say anything about Mr. Selznick's cast without appearing to be an obnoxious busybody, meddling where I had no business to meddle. My relations with the Selznick organization have been cordial throughout and I believe that Mr. Selznick has appreciated my efforts not to add to the heavy load he has been carrying by issuing proclamations about a piece of property I had sold lock, stock and barrel.

I do not especially like to learn that Miss Williams has been discussing my business. While she was not my agent (she was employed by my agents,

The Macmillan Company), I thought that business matters of this type were confidential.

The statement that Miss Williams spent "months" trying to find a buyer for my motion picture rights is entirely wrong. My first employment of an agent, The Macmillan Company, to represent me in this was a matter of weeks, rather than months, before the sale was made. At what date thereafter, The Macmillan Company employed Miss Williams to assist them, I do not know. .

As to the statement that nobody wanted to buy the movie rights, even after the book had sold 250,000 copies, that also is entirely wrong. By that time, the sale had been closed and the contract signed, and three weeks before then Selznick had made a firm offer for the rights.

Now that you have read this far, I suppose you think I am angry at you—and perhaps you are angry at me. I am not angry and I hope most sincerely that you are not. I don't enjoy writing letters like this, and I would not do it if I did not feel compelled to. It is the only means I have of checking the many "legends" that have grown up, or been built up, about me since my book was published. Almost without exception, other writers have welcomed the correct information and I hope you will, too.

I am not asking you to publish a correction. In fact, I would prefer that you do not. Corrections frequently do more harm than good. And I hope you will not use my somewhat frank statements in this letter in some other article. My greatest desire these days is to recapture my former quiet life, and the more articles published about me, the more difficult that is.

I hope you will take this letter in the friendly spirit in which it is written.

Mr. Voldemar Vetluguin   *Atlanta, Georgia*
Redbook Magazine   *September 5, 1939*
New York, New York

My dear Mr. Vetluguin:

It was embarrassing, and amusing, that I misspelled your name in my previous letter in which I told you of errors in other names. I am very sorry. We will have to blame that on Selznick also. They gave me your name incorrectly, and I did not find the correct spelling until it was too late. I won't let it happen again.

Please do not be disturbed about my inability to give you the information for your article in time to get the corrections made. I do not hold you to blame for the errors, and if the proofs did not reach me in time—well, that's just too bad and we will hope for better luck next time.

I do not wish you to publish a correction in your next issue. Such corrections are of doubtful value, in my opinion, and sometimes they do more harm than good. But could I be permitted to check the facts if Redbook happens to publish some future article in which I am involved? That safeguard against additional errors would mean far more to me than publication of a correction now. . . .

Please do not publish any part of this letter. I am sincere in my statement that I prefer not to have a correction published. . . . I am most grateful for the consideration you have shown me.

Miss Katharine Brown   *Atlanta, Georgia*
Selznick International Pictures, Inc.   *September 14, 1939*
New York, New York

Dear Katharine:

Your note of September 13th, enclosing the excerpt from Mr. Lewton, has just arrived. It found me in the midst of the wildest chaos imaginable, with the new apartment overrun with workmen. The preview note was the most cheering information I could have had at such an awful time.* I am returning Mr. Lewton's page just as soon as John has read it. Thanks a million for letting me see it.

Of course I was pleased at the audience reaction but I cannot say I was terribly surprised. I can say that in all honesty where you or other people who have worked on the film could not say it. All of you have been so close to it that I imagine by this time you cannot decide whether it is good or bad. All indications I have received have been that it is a wonderful film. Returning travelers from the Coast brought me tales of marvels; the sober and honest comments of the Kurtzes and Susan Myrick have confirmed these impressions; lastly, the complete about face of gossip columnists, who were so picky and malicious six months ago, showed me that the picture is an excellent one. They want to be on the winning side always and I wouldn't be a bit surprised if the very ones who denounced Vivien Leigh will be the first to shout that they always knew she was the right person.

I am so happy for you—so happy for Mr. Selznick. When you hear more details of course I'd like to know. Here's one detail in which I am

---

* Val Lewton, Selznick's West Coast story editor, reported that the first preview of *Gone With the Wind*, held September 9 in Riverside, California, "went over with a tremendous bang." Audience members jumped to their feet, cheered, and hugged each other when Mitchell's name flashed on the screen and gave the film a five-minute standing ovation at the end. A second preview was held October 18 in Santa Barbara, California, and the reaction was "pandemonium all over again," according to film editor Hal Kern.

especially interested. I do not know how you have ended the picture—exactly as I wrote it or with a happy ending or with some intimation that Scarlett eventually got him back. If you ended it as I wrote it, what was the audience reaction? Did the preview cards ask for a happy ending or were they satisfied?*

Dear me! I wish I were in New York this minute. I would take you out and buy you a champagne cocktail so large you'd have to drink it from a beer-bout stein!

P.S. Of course I'll keep this confidential and should I have an official letter it will appear to be my first news.

George Brett, Jr.	*Atlanta, Georgia*
The Macmillan Company	*September 15, 1939*
New York, New York	

I AM WILLING TO GAMBLE WITH YOU ON MOVIE EDITION IF YOU ALSO ARE WILLING TO GAMBLE WITH ME STOP IF I GET NOTHING IF YOU LOSE I SHOULD GET PART OF THE PROFITS IF YOU WIN STOP YOUR PROPOSITION ASK ME TO JOIN YOU IN TAKING THE RISK BUT OFFERS ME NO REWARD FOR MY RISK BEYOND WHAT I WOULD OTHERWISE BE ENTITLED TO EVEN IF YOU SELL A MILLION COPIES STOP WHAT OFFER WILL YOU MAKE ME ON SALES ABOVE THREE HUNDRED FIFTY THOUSAND COPIES IF I ACCEPT YOUR PROPOSED TERMS UP TO THAT FIGURE.†

Mrs. Wilbur G. Kurtz	*Atlanta, Georgia*
Selznick International Pictures, Inc.	*September 19, 1939*
Culver City, California	

Dear Annie Laurie:

If this letter seems choppy please excuse it. We are still in the midst of trying to get settled in the new apartment. You would think that after nineteen days the Empire State Building could be refurbished, let alone a normal sized apartment. But then, you know how workmen are—they'll

---

* Selznick reported that none of the preview comments asked that Scarlett and Rhett be shown getting back together. At the time, the producer was battling with the censors over Rhett's use of the word "damn" in his exit line, so Gable was shown walking out the door after saying, "Frankly, my dear, I just don't care."

† With the Motion Picture Edition back on track, Brett had proposed that Mitchell forgo all royalties on sales below 250,000 copies and accept a two-and-a-half cent royalty—half of what she was entitled to under her contract—for sales above that figure.

tear your house up and then rush off to tear up some other woman's house and you have to get a court order to make them return. When we get the curtains up and the new fly screens fitted I hope we'll be through. I certainly never want to move again. . . .

Saturday I rushed down to Macon to the wedding of a cousin and spent the night with Sue. I heard a lot about the picture but, as our time was short, I did not hear all I wanted to hear. We hope that in a couple of weeks when the apartment is finished Sue will come up for a week-end and tell us more. She is so glad to be home again and the happiness of her Macon friends at having her back is very apparent.

I had learned from reading newspapers that the movie industry was very upset about the war and that staffs were being cut to right and left.* Naturally, I was glad to learn that Wilbur was being kept on. I may be wrong but I think Mr. Selznick will get his money back on GWTW, even without a world market. It appears that there is a violent public interest in the picture and everyone wishes to see it. It may take several years to get back his investment but I don't think he will lose a cent and he will probably make an awful lot of money.

Things get worse and worse as the premiere comes closer, for everyone in the South seems determined to be there for the first night. I cannot understand why, for the picture will be the same ten years from now as it is today, and I personally would rather see it for the first time on some other date than premiere date. I am happy that I am not handling admissions. I cannot help resenting, however, the burden that has come down on us because of the premiere. I know you and Wilbur must have a burden, too, and it will be far worse when you come home, for all your friends will believe that you have an inside track and can produce passes from your pocket in large numbers. Won't it be wonderful when all of this is over! . . .

Annie Laurie, about the speeches you have made about me—let me tell you my ideas on the subject in some detail so that you will get a better understanding of the matter. I know you would not ever say anything about me that was not true and I know that you are too good a friend to ever say anything that was not nice. But the bad part is that your truthfulness and your praise will do neither you nor me much good where the public is concerned and they may cause both of us some embarrassment. This is the reason—you can stand on your feet and tell the truth about me till you drop in your tracks but the people who hear you will hear only half and

---

* On September 1, Germany invaded Poland. Two days later, England declared war on the Nazi regime.

will interpret for themselves that half they comprehend. When they pass on the story of what you have said they will give it their own twist and back up their errors with the statement that it must be true because a good friend of Margaret Mitchell's said it. The next person who passes it on will be even less accurate and by the time it has passed through five hands you would not recognize it, yet it will be attributed to you. Do not think that I am making this up. I have had it happen far too many times since 1936 and have had embarrassing and protesting friends say, "But, Peggy, I never said that. I said just the opposite. How could it have become twisted?" But the things they say *do* become twisted and then my friends have laid themselves open to the charge that they have deliberately misrepresented me. I know that they have not, and they know, but these explanations become embarrassing when some full fledged lie blossoms forth with some good friend's name attached to it.

I'll give you one example—one that came to your ears and which you told me. About two years ago Willie Ethridge, when making a speech before the Wesleyan Alumnae, wanted to show that I had not changed over night because of the success of GWTW.* To prove this she said that the year before GWTW was published she noted that at a press convention I was wearing a pair of ten cent garters, one blue and one pink. After I had sold a million copies she observed that I was still clinging to the same mismatched garters instead of garters with gold and diamond buckles. You know how the story finally ended up—that I went to Marietta with Wilbur and George Cukor and on the way hung my legs out of the car window so that everyone could see I wore one pink and one blue garter. When I traced the story back people told me that Willie Ethridge had said it.

So, for your protection as well as mine, I'd rather you did not make speeches about me. All my friends here have discovered, to their sorrow, that they cannot do this without most unfortunate consequences. Of course, if someone asks you if I am divorced or have children or if I tried twelve publishers before I landed GWTW or if the book went begging for a purchaser in Hollywood, I do hope you will step on these inaccuracies and I will appreciate it if you do. But if you address gatherings and tell them about me sooner or later I will hear that you have said something perfectly dreadful. It's no using feeling bad about this state of affairs; people have always been like this and always will be, and the only possible protection is to give them as little material to garble as possible. Besides, I can't for the

---

* Willie Snow Ethridge, born in Georgia, was a newspaper reporter, columnist, and author. She was married to Mark Ethridge of the Louisville *Courier-Journal*.

life of me understand why anyone should want to know anything about me except that I wrote a book. I have loved many books and have yet to care whether the author was sixteen or sixty, married or single. . . .

Did you know that Jonesboro had opened a little movie house and had named it the Tara? Steve is all for having the premiere held there. I think it seats nearly a hundred. With a straight face, Steve expresses indignation that the premiere will not be held there. Some people have no more sense than to believe him, which delights all of us.

Sue said so many wonderful things about the work you two (she meant you and Wilbur, of course) had done that I am sure your ears must have burned to a crisp. She said she did not think the picture could have been produced without you.

The Editor   *Atlanta, Georgia*
Variety   *September 28, 1939*
New York, New York

Dear Sir:

I have just seen an item from the August 30th issue of Variety which reads as follows:

"'Wind'" Free to Papers

"David O. Selznick, owner of the newspaper as well as the screen rights to 'Gone With the Wind,' announced that he had declined an offer from King Features of $5,000 cash and percentage. Selznick is sending out the serialization free."

This is not correct. The newspaper serialization rights in my novel are not owned by Mr. Selznick. They are owned jointly by me and my publishers, The Macmillan Company, and they are not "free."

I am confident the error was unintentional but it could nevertheless lead to a great many misunderstandings, as you no doubt realize, so I will be grateful if you will publish a correction.

Mr. John Embry Horan   *Atlanta, Georgia*
Dalton, Georgia   *September 30, 1939*

Dear Mr. Horan:

I have received your letter and the enclosure from Metro-Goldwyn-Mayer. I know this must be a disappointment to you, and no doubt many other Georgians would have been interested in having the dolls produced by a home industry.*

Mr. George Brett, Jr.	*Atlanta, Georgia*
The Macmillan Company	*October 2, 1939*
New York, New York	

Dear George:

I rush the enclosed advertisement from House and Garden to you in all haste, hoping it may catch you before you leave for the Coast. I want to call your attention to the statement that House and Garden for November will publish pictures of the interiors of the "Gone With the Wind" houses in *actual color*.† While I do not know if these will be interiors without figures, I do notice the advertisement says "see . . . Leigh as Scarlett," so perhaps there are people in the stills. I thought you might use this for ammunition in your argument with Mr. Selznick. If he is letting House and Garden use color pictures for a November issue (which will be out in the middle of October), there is no reason in the world why he should not permit you to use stills which will be published at a later date.

I'd like to have this advertisement back when you have finished with it. And please do not say where you got it because it might get my friend on House and Garden in trouble.

In haste, and with all good wishes for the success of the California expedition.

Miss Katharine Brown	*Atlanta, Georgia*
Selznick International Pictures, Inc.	*October 2, 1939*
New York, New York	

Dear Katharine:

I am sorry to have let your letters of September 25th and 27th go un-answered this long when I know you wanted an immediate reply. My father has been very ill again and in the hospital, and it was only yesterday that he took a turn for the better. During the bad part of his illness I scarcely had time to open the mail.

---

* MGM denied Horan's request to produce his dolls, noting the studio already had signed a contract with The Alexander Doll Co. to manufacture *GWTW*-related figures.

† The November 1939 issue of *House & Garden* featured an article titled "Decorating for Scarlett O'Hara," by Joseph B. Platt, that included eight color plates of interior sets from the film as well as a full-page color photograph of the exterior of Tara.

First, I want to say that news has been trickling around about how wonderful the picture was at the Riverside sneak preview. There have been several items in newspapers, of course. . . . But the word-of-mouth advertising, which is the best and which costs nothing, has been excellent. No one wants the picture cut; people shake their horns and paw and snort at the notion, and if I were Mr. Selznick I would not bother if it ran six hours. I am so pleased and happy for all of you.

The date you mentioned—sometime between the 15th and the 20th of December—couldn't be better. I like it fine. It fits in, too, with our usual vacation plans, for we like to go away between Christmas and New Year's when John's work will permit it. Please don't change your mind about this date.

Thank you for telling Mr. Dietz about our setup here.* I know it is a difficult one to explain and I appreciate your taking the trouble to explain it and Mr. Dietz's sympathetic understanding. Do I understand that Mr. Dietz will not accompany you and Mr. Ferguson on your trip around October 9th?† You did not mention him in connection with this trip, so I suppose he will come down just before the premiere.

Well, dearie, I guess we really must be going to have a premiere here, for when I was dashing madly through a department store last week to buy Father some extra pajamas the buyer and the salesgirls from the ladies' ready-to-wear ambushed me and told me I'd better come 'round and let them pick me out a dress for the premiere. They had already sold a dozen to members of the Press Club. So, I really believe it's true now!

Mr. Stuart Rose   *Atlanta, Georgia*
Saturday Evening Post   *October 3, 1939*
Philadelphia, Pennsylvania

Dear Mr. Rose:

For all I know, you and the Post are probably sick to death of anything connected with the film of "Gone With the Wind," but on the chance that you are not and are interested in a story, I want to tell you about Susan Myrick, of Macon, Georgia, who has just returned from Hollywood where she was employed as a technical adviser on dialect in that film.

---

* Howard Dietz was director of advertising and publicity for MGM in New York.
† William R. Ferguson was MGM's director of exploitation. He and Brown came to Atlanta in October to meet with city officials and others, including the author's husband, about the upcoming premiere festivities.

Miss Myrick was brought up on a plantation twelve miles from Milledgeville, Georgia, in the deep country. She's been a reporter on the Macon Telegraph for many years and is one of the best known Southern newspaper women. When George Cukor, the first director of "Gone With the Wind," was in Macon several years ago he met Miss Myrick, was impressed by her and took her to Hollywood.

I was in Macon recently attending a wedding and I talked to Miss Myrick about her work and her experiences. I do not know when I have heard such an interesting and amusing recital. She was employed to superintend Southern dialect but it appears that accents were her least important tasks. She had to give immediate and expert answers on how tables were set and served in the old days, at what age little slave boys put on shoes, whether a butler on a deep-country plantation would wear livery, how deeply an old lady and a young lady would curtsey, and thousands of other small but important matters. In fact, there was scarcely a single scene shot that was not shot in her presence.

If ever I saw a good story walking around on two legs, it was Miss Myrick. I don't know if she would write the story but if she did it should be good, so I am passing the word on to you. If you are interested, will you please let me know? Then I'll write her to get in touch with you. If you aren't—then I'll say nothing to her.*

Miss Martha Brunson
University of South Carolina
Columbia, South Carolina

Atlanta, Georgia
October 18, 1939

My dear Martha:

I am so glad to have your letter, even though it did give me a shock to realize that you are grown-up and in the University of South Carolina.

I am glad to learn through your letter of the fine young man you have met, and I take it as a compliment that it was my book which drew you two together.

I know what I must write will disappoint you and your John, and I am very sorry about it. I can do nothing in the world to aid you in securing tickets to the premiere of "Gone With the Wind." You ask that I "use my influence" to assist you in this matter. Martha, I have no "influence" to use. The truth is this: I have had no connection with the production of this film; I have not worked on it in any way; I have no knowledge of

---

* Myrick wrote an article for *Collier's*, the *Saturday Evening Post*'s main rival. "Pardon My Un-Southern Accent" appeared in the magazine's December 16, 1939, issue.

the details of the Atlanta premiere; I do not even know how my husband and I will obtain tickets ourselves. The theatre in which it will be shown seats approximately nineteen hundred people; I have heard that over fifty thousand have already attempted to make reservations and the number increases daily. No one, not even the theatre manager knows how the tickets are to be distributed or how much they will cost.

From the foregoing you can understand why I cannot help you. I am very sorry.

You wrote that you had heard that I might come to Columbia and you were kind enough to ask me to call you up at the University. That was sweet of you and I appreciate it. However, I am at a loss to understand how the rumor got about that I was coming to Columbia, for I have no plans about such a visit.

Miss Katharine Brown   *Atlanta, Georgia*
Selznick International Pictures, Inc.   *October 24, 1939*
New York, New York

Dear Katharine:

The chrysanthemums are gorgeous, the stems are so long that I need an old fashioned churn really to set them off. The apartment looks sumptuously dressed. Thanks so much for them.

I am enclosing some clippings. The Polly Peachtree one was evidently written by Lib Hunt. My, my, what a charmer you are. There was a picture of you and the Governor but I cannot find it now and will send it later. . . .*

Now, sugarfoot, try and get some rest before the storm breaks in December. You are thinner than you ought to be and it is old Doctor Mitchell's diagnosis that you are running on your nerves. You run very well on these nerves but they do need a rest. I hope you can find time for that rest between now and the premiere.

Tell Mr. S. for us what a good job you've done.

Mr. George Brett, Jr.   *Atlanta, Georgia*
The Macmillan Company   *October 28, 1939*
New York, New York

My dear George:

Perhaps, as you say, this is not the time for a play-by-play account of the battle of Brett vs Selznick, but some day I want to hear it all. I imagine

---

* The photo was taken when Brown was in Atlanta working on plans for the premiere.

it probably is as unbelievable as some of my encounters with the movie folks. Perhaps now you may believe some of the stories I told you about them, whereas at the time you probably had the inner thought, "Yes, this Margaret Mitchell of ours has a wonderful imagination, but just a bit too melodramatic."

Why don't you go ahead and put out your own cheap edition for the movie market, according to your own ideas as to the style of it, the date of publication and when and where and how it will be sold? The root of all your trouble, it seems to me, is not that Selznick controls the movie stills you want, but that they know you want them so badly. The very powerfulness of your desire for them has enabled them to get control temporarily over matters of much greater importance than the movie stills themselves—Macmillan's reputation as a publisher, your relations with the booksellers, George P. Brett's blood pressure and the peace and dignity of your organization as a whole. My guess is that if you decided to go ahead without their stills, they probably would come running to ask you to use them. You are in position to give their movie some very valuable publicity, but that is not something they need at the time of the premiere, so they are being very high and mighty. But in the year ahead they will need it, and if they thought they were not going to get it, they might take a more reasonable attitude.

I probably should not say these things. They are your business, not mine. I mean that, for I have never felt that the author should attempt to run the publisher's business for him. You know the ins and outs of these matters in a way that I never could, so you are the one to make the decisions. Besides, you probably will have the whole situation in hand by the time this letter reaches you. So, please understand that I was not talking as "the author," but as a friend, and not attempting to give advice, but merely airing a view of mine about situations of this kind in general.

As to the proposed $2.00 edition, I cannot give you an answer on this until we can clear up a few points about it.* First, I will have to have a more definite proposal than you have submitted; second, I intend to insist upon your recognition of the equitable principle which I outlined,

---

* When it appeared that Selznick would not allow the Motion Picture Edition to be released in time for the premiere, Brett suggested Macmillan issue a special two-dollar hardback edition as a backup. Under her contract, Mitchell was entitled to a 15 percent royalty, or thirty cents a copy. However, Brett claimed the cost of publishing the two-dollar edition would be unprofitable for Macmillan and again asked the author to accept half of her standard royalty, or fifteen cents a copy.

and you agreed to, with reference to the 69¢ edition, because it also applies to this $2.00 edition.

You say there is nothing in our contract which covers a $2.00 edition. I do not agree with you on that. The contract clearly provides for a 15 per cent royalty on any editions that sell for more than $1.50 (half the price of the original edition). So, your request is that I agree to a 50 per cent cut in the royalty which you previously contracted to pay me.

Perhaps I may agree to take the cut. I agreed to a modification of our contract in connection with the 69¢ edition.* I am not unwilling to trade with you on any proposition that may be to the advantage of both of us. But if you want to deviate from the contract, and if you ask me to make concessions in order to help you in a gamble, then I should not be the only one to make concessions. You should make concessions, too, and you should *offer* to make them. It is not right for you to put me in the embarrassing situation of having to ask for them each time.

I thought that my principle had been made clear when we were discussing the 69¢ edition, and that you had agreed it was equitable, which simply means fair and proper. Now, I am wondering if you understood me at all. I cannot help wondering whether you gave in on the 69¢ edition just because you thought you had to and because you thought I was "holding you up." That embarrasses me tremendously, and I most certainly do not intend to do any trading with you on the $2.00 edition until I am certain that you understand the rightness of the principle I have outlined.

Maybe the following will explain what I mean. We have a contract under which you agreed to pay me certain definite and fixed royalties for the privilege of publishing and selling my book. I do not take the risk; you take it. The risk is not on me because I get my fixed royalty, whether you sell a few books or many. Because *you* took the *risk*, you were entitled to the big profits when the book made its big success. No matter how many million copies were sold, I was not entitled to anything more than my *fixed* royalty per copy. And that was entirely fair and proper and equitable, because I had not taken the risk.

Suppose I had come to you, in December 1936, and said: "Look here, you're making a lot more money out of my book than you ever dreamed

---

* Mitchell agreed to accept a two-and-a-half-cent royalty on the Motion Picture Edition that would take effect only if sales reached 250,000; after that, a sliding-scale royalty called for payment of up to eight cents a copy should sales reach 1.4 million. The Publisher's Preface noted the paperback edition was made possible "through the cooperation of Author and Publisher, Publisher and Producer."

of making. What about giving me a cut? What about paying me a bigger royalty? You're paying yourself and everybody in the Macmillan organization a bonus out of the profits on my book. Where's my bonus?" I did not do it then, and I am not doing it now. It would have been highly improper for me to do it. I made a contract and I stuck to it. I do not mean either that I resented the profit you made. You paid me what you had agreed to pay, and I did not expect or want anything more.

But on these two recent propositions, your attitude has been: "Look here, we want to put out some special editions and we don't know whether we can make money on them or not. So, what about you coming in with us on the gamble? We want you to take a reduction in your royalties. This time, we want *you* to take a part of the *risk*. But if we win, we don't intend to give you any reward for your risk. In fact, it never occurred to us that you were entitled to it. We want to travel on a different basis this time from what our contract provides. We want you to surrender your *fixed* royalty, to the extent of 50 per cent, and share the risk with us. But we don't intend for you to share the profits, too. We promised you a 15 per cent royalty and on a $2.00 edition that would be 30¢ a copy. But we want to amend the contract so you will get only half that amount. That means that you are kicking in 15¢ on every copy as your contribution toward putting this deal over, and we need your help. We are going to be partners in taking the risk. But if we do put it over, if we sell ten million copies, we won't be partners in dividing up the profits. All you'll get is your 15¢ a copy, no more, no less."

That may be rather blunt, but I do not mind its bluntness if it makes the idea clear. If it is clear, and if you care to make me an offer on the basis of some reward to me for joining you in the risk, I will be glad to consider it. I will not attempt to suggest what the "reward" should be, but I imagine it should be some sliding scale of royalty payments. I think it should also state whether the $2.00 edition is to be offered during a limited period of time, or the edition should be otherwise identified, so that this new and special royalty arrangement on a particular edition will not become confused with the other provisions of our contract.

I think you are right in saying that the edition would be made available to all Atlanta dealers (perhaps also to all Georgia dealers), instead of being available to Davison's only. This is on the assumption that you may not have anything else to offer here at the time of the premiere. Of course, if you do have something else available, I would have no objection to some arrangement for a special edition offered exclusively by one store.

Incidentally, I learned this morning that matters had taken a new turn and you were considering a de luxe special Atlanta edition. If you do get it out, I suggest that it be in two volumes. Many people have asked for that, because of the heaviness of the one-volume edition. That, however, is merely a suggestion. As to your remark that Luise Sims and I have reached an understanding about a preface or something of the sort, she mentioned this to me once and also suggested using my picture in an "Atlanta edition." I told her I did not want my picture used and also would not want the preface to be a eulogy. If any preface is used, I would wish to see it in advance, of course.*

I hope we understand each other now. I know that your problem is a difficult one and I want to be helpful if I can. All I am asking is that if the contract is to be revised, it be done on a basis that is fair to both of us.

Mrs. Green Dodd Warren   *Atlanta, Georgia*
Atlanta, Georgia   *November 1, 1939*

Dear Irene:

I was in bed with influenza when your letter arrived, and before I had recovered some out-of-town friends came to Atlanta, so I was forced to delay answering you. The plans of the Junior League for the "Gone With the Wind" premiere week seem very interesting and it was kind of you to include the many details, such as the costumes Selznick will lend, the bazaar sets, et cetera. I did not know about all this and of course was glad to hear. You must be proud of the Atlanta Junior League for undertaking such a huge job. Of course, I hope it will be a great success and that the League will make a lot of money which you can spend for those who need it.

You asked me to speak my mind about the picture the editor of the Junior League Magazine wanted. I will speak out and I thank you for telling me in advance of your understanding of my situation. It will be impossible for me to have the picture taken. The reason is that a picture of you and me discussing plans for the ball, as she requested, would be the most misleading picture imaginable, for it would lead all of your readers to believe that I am actively engaged in organizing and promoting the Junior League ball.

---

* Macmillan published a limited-edition two-volume version of *Gone With the Wind* for Atlanta's Davison-Paxon department store. The one thousand sets in a slipcase were hand numbered and sold for $7.50. The first volume contained a notice that the edition was published "in appreciation of Margaret Mitchell's magnificent work in commemorating the life and times of the Old South," but the book did not include a preface or photograph of the author.

You, of course, understand that this is not the case, but others who do not understand would think that I am taking an active part in promoting an affair which honors my book, and indirectly me.

I am taking no part in any of the plans for the many civic and social festivities which will take place at the time of the premiere. If I should busy myself about such matters, I would lay myself open to the criticism that I was trying to promote myself and my book. I think people would be right in criticizing me should I do this, for it would be in the worst possible taste. So I must go to the premiere as a guest, a very flattered and appreciative guest, and take no credit or blame for the picture itself, the Junior League ball or any of the other affairs which will take place at that time.

It is kind of you and the other members of the League to invite me again to your ball. I know it will be interesting to see and I would enjoy being with you. But, as I told you at the time we first discussed the matter, I could not attend for two reasons—I made my plans for the premiere long before I knew the Junior League would give a party. My commitments are already given. (I have many out-of-town friends who will be in Atlanta at that time to see me and not to attend parties.) The second reason is that it would be humanly impossible for me to attend all the affairs which are being planned for the week of the premiere. If I tried to attend even half of them, I would be exhausted and the premiere would be a dreadful burden and an ordeal, rather than a pleasure. For these reasons I have refused all invitations except one. Even before the Junior League thought of their ball the Women's Press Club, of which I am a member, asked to give me a very small and informal party for about thirty people before the premiere and I accepted. That party and the premiere will be the only events I will attend.

Again, I want to tell you how glad I am that your plans are working out the way you wished. And, even though I am not at the ball in person, you will have my very sincere good wishes for a happy occasion, both that night and afterwards in the good you will be able to do for many people who need your help.

Mr. Howard Dietz   *Atlanta, Georgia*
Metro-Goldwyn-Mayer   *November 6, 1939*
New York, New York

Dear Mr. Dietz:

Thank you so much for your telegram of November 4th which brought me the news of the definite date of the Atlanta premiere of "Gone With the Wind."* It was kind of you to notify me before the story broke in the Atlanta papers and I appreciate your courtesy.

The story made the front pages and the top headlines of the Atlanta papers and I believe you would have been pleased at the interest it occasioned.

Mr. George Brett, Jr.   *Atlanta, Georgia*
The Macmillan Company   *November 7, 1939*
New York, New York

My dear George:

We are in hearty agreement on one point, that it would be fine if we could talk in person about the cheap edition matters. I am confident that we could get together and do it promptly, without the burden and the delays of letter-writing. I am sorry I could not get this letter off to you sooner, but with Father continuing quite feeble and the approaching premiere of the movie bringing me a fresh surge of problems, I could not attend to it sooner.

Regardless of whether a $2.00 edition is issued or not, I think it is important for us to understand each other about this matter. If we do, we can work together on various special propositions that will make money for both of us. If we don't, we won't make the money and our personal relationship may be impaired also.

The thing that makes me question whether you yet understand the principle which I tried to explain in my previous letter is this—first, you ignored my statement that I am willing to compromise with you on the amount of the royalty, and then you seemed to be trying to put on me the responsibility of blocking the edition. As you consider this edition a necessary one to satisfy the booksellers and the public in an emergency created by the movie edition tangle, it is a serious accusation if you say, or even imply, that I am the one who blocked it.

If I had stubbornly and inflexibly insisted upon my full 15 per cent royalty on an edition which could not be published profitably on that basis, I would have been guilty of blocking it, very foolishly and shortsightedly. But I did not do that. I stated definitely that I was willing to consider the reduced royalty and I said further, "I am not unwilling to trade with you on *any* proposition that may be of advantage to both of us." I asked only that some appreciation be shown for my willingness to make the concession you asked for, if the venture made a big success.

---

* Dietz alerted Mitchell that he was announcing to the Atlanta newspapers that the world premiere of *Gone With the Wind* was scheduled for 8:15 p.m. on December 15 at Loew's Grand Theatre.

You answered, inflexibly, that I would have to take the flat 15 cents a copy—or else, no matter whether you sold 10,000 copies or 10,000,000. You said, in effect, that my concession was no concession, and that you would consider no adjustment whatsoever excepting one only, the *downward* adjustment you asked *me* to take.

I have expressed my complete willingness to work out a proposition advantageous to both of us. Your proposition is the take-it-or-leave-it kind. So, the inflexibility in this situation is yours, not mine, and if the edition should be blocked that responsibility is yours, not mine. I am counting on you to make certain that my position is not misunderstood within the Macmillan organization or among the booksellers.

This whole thing is a matter of principle with me, a point of honor, in fact. I have no idea that you are going to sell 10,000,000 copies of a $2.00 edition, or 1,000,000, or 100,000. I have serious doubts that any really big volume could be sold at that price, after the book has been on sale for a long time at $1.49, and much less than that in most places. So, the amount of money involved, either way, is not enough to quarrel about. But the principle is. And it becomes a point of honor when I feel that you would not try to trade with me on the basis you suggested, if you had any respect for me. Briefly and bluntly, your proposition is the sort that a grown person might offer to a child, according to my way of looking at it.

I would not express myself so bluntly if I really thought that was your attitude. If I did, I would not be writing you at all. I merely think that you still do not understand what my position is, and that by failing to understand it you are endangering what has been a pleasant and very profitable relationship. . . .

To carry your proposition on the $2.00 edition to the extreme, here is the way it could work out. If you should happen to make a net profit of $1,000,000 on it, after all expenses of every kind, including my royalties, my "compensation" would be a *net loss* of exactly fifty per cent. Just because you needed my help in the beginning and induced me to accept only half of the contract royalty, my pay for helping you would be a big loss, no matter how big your profits were. I cannot believe you would want me to stand the net loss, while you were raking in net profits in big amounts.

My position seems so simple, it is hard for me to believe that you do not understand the fairness of it, and I am inclined to think that you were simply reluctant to make me an offer, for fear that I would not consider it reasonable. I understand something about "the economics of the business." I know that in publishing any book you do not get "out of the red" until you have sold a certain number of copies, and that your profits are small until after you have sold a large number of additional copies. I also know that at a certain point the bigger profits begin and that thereafter they begin to multiply and you have a real success.

In asking that we work out a trade on the $2.00 edition, I never had the idea of your boosting the 15¢ royalty up to 25¢ a copy after the first 5,000, and up to 50¢ after 10,000, with 10¢ increases every 5,000 copies thereafter until I was receiving $1.00 royalty on each copy.

I have sense enough to know that your getting a fair profit is good for me, as well as for you, because it will make you more interested in promoting the sales. I was, and still am, willing for the 15¢ royalty to continue until the volume of sales warranted some increase, in fairness to both of us. I was simply opposed, as a matter of principle, to the unfairness of an arrangement under which my royalty would keep on chugging along at 15¢, even though the sales and your profits mounted into the millions.

So, if you do care to make me an offer, I will be glad to consider it. And, as always in the past, I am willing to trust your figures as to "the economics of the business," as to the volume of sales that would be necessary in order to warrant an increased scale of royalties above the original 15¢.

Now, I have had my say. If you are unwilling to make me an offer, if you are still "inflexible," I want to say that I will accept the flat 15¢ royalty on a $2.00 edition of not exceeding 50,000 copies. I think it is very unfair and that your attitude is very unreasonable. But my contention is for a principle and if you are not willing to agree to it, well, that's that. Failure to have the $2.00 edition or some other edition on the market in the near future will create an embarrassing situation and, while I would not be to blame for it, I would be involved in it. I am too weary these days to get into any embarrassing situation which I can avoid, so if you insist on the flat 15¢ royalty, I agree to it.

Miss Mary DeV. Butler   *Atlanta, Georgia*
Five Oaks   *November 8, 1939*
Athens, Georgia

My dear Miss Butler:

When I had finished your lovely letter I felt that I had heard from an old friend. This feeling did not come from the fact that you wrote many kind and laudatory things about "Gone With the Wind" (though, of course, that gave me much pleasure). It was the sincerity and friendly informality and charm of your words which made me feel that I had known you and your family a long time.

Because of the tone of your letter I am going to be quite frank with you and hope you will understand. I was so very pleased and touched that your mother had thought enough of "Gone With the Wind" to make me a gift. And I was equally pleased that you wished me to come see you in Athens. Both the gift and the visit would give me great pleasure but I do not know when the trip can be managed. In the first place, my father has been very ill and has only very recently returned from the hospital. He is now at home under the care of two nurses and what spare time I have is naturally spent with him. On top of this, I have a very strange problem and burden. As you may have noticed in last Sunday's paper, the moving picture people who have produced "Gone With the Wind" announced that the premiere would be held on December 15th. I had nothing to do with the production of the picture and probably know less about it than anyone else in the world, but since that announcement a deluge has descended upon me and my whole family. Hundreds of people confidently believe I can secure passes for them and my telephone and door bell ring all day long; the mail is heavy with similar requests. Atlanta wishes to do itself proud on this occasion and there are scores of plans for festivities of civic and social natures. When people are not calling about passes they are calling to know if Clark Gable will *really* come to Atlanta. (And I know nothing about the gentleman's plans!) I do not see how I will be able to leave Atlanta until after the premiere, even for a day.

I have gone into these details so that you would not think me ungracious and unappreciative of your interest and that of your mother and your sister. It is simply that I have a job to do which is not my job, and yet I must do it. And so, I will not be able to come to Athens anytime in the near future. I hope "when this cruel war is over" that I can accept your invitation. It would be such fun!

With best wishes to your mother, your sister Katherine and yourself.

Mr. Howard Dietz   *Atlanta, Georgia*
Metro-Goldwyn-Mayer   *November 13, 1939*
New York, New York

Dear Mr. Dietz:

Probably Katharine Brown has already given you my message with reference to the use of my picture in your special program for the "Gone With the Wind" premiere. You have my permission to use the picture if I understand your wishes, and I am writing you this letter so that we will have a clear-cut understanding.

I appreciate the sympathetic attitude expressed in your letter and I also appreciate the reasons why you think my picture should be used in this particular instance. I can see the appropriateness of including my picture in the program with Mr. Selznick and the others, and I agree with you that the absence of my picture might be unfortunate in that it would subject you to the criticism, most unjustly, that you were deliberately ignoring me. I do not know whether you have any of my photographs, so I am enclosing one. In stating the conditions under which it is to be used I do not mean to imply that you would take advantage of this permission; I am merely doing what several generations of lawyers in my family have taught me should always be done in a matter like this to avoid future misunderstandings.

1. This permission is for the use of the enclosed photograph of me in a souvenir program to be prepared by you and distributed at the Atlanta premiere of "Gone With the Wind." (If you are planning an opening in New York similar to the one in Atlanta and wish to use a souvenir program there also, please let me know and it is probable that I can give you the use of the photograph there. But this present permission is for the Atlanta premiere program only.)

2. This does not give permission for the use of my photograph, in small size or as a "blow-up," in theatres generally. On the contrary, I wish to affirm what Miss Brown has probably already told you, that I do not wish my photograph used that way.

3. The cut lines to be used in connection with my photograph in the Atlanta souvenir program are to be submitted to me and approved by me. Any other biographical article about me or background material relating to the history of my book in the program is also to be submitted to me for approval in advance of publication.

4. My photograph is not to be published on the front page of the program and is not to be used at all unless the photographs of Mr. Selznick and the others you mentioned are also used.* A dummy of the program is to be submitted to me in advance and I reserve the right to change the position of my picture in the dummy and to withdraw this permission entirely if my photograph is given undue prominence. (I did not make the motion picture; Mr. Selznick made it and he is the one who deserves the position of prominence. I am the author and it is proper to include my photograph, but only as the author.)

---

* In the program, Mitchell's photograph is published on the same spread with equal-sized shots of Selznick, Fleming, and Sidney Howard.

If these provisions are acceptable to you please write me to this effect. Perhaps you may be somewhat disturbed by my requirement that the dummy be submitted to me. I know that you are probably rushed in getting your advertising and publicity material ready and I promise to give you a reply as soon as the dummy is received. My husband is an advertising man and both he and I are former newspaper reporters, so we know what it is to work against deadlines. Also, I do not mean that you must submit a finished dummy. It can be a rough dummy, merely indicating in pencil what will appear on the different pages and the location of my photograph in relation to the other material.

While I am writing I would like to say a few things about the general subject of publicity. I would like for you to submit to me for approval in advance any publicity matter about me or the background of my book. I believe this will be to your advantage as well as mine, and again I promise to give you a prompt answer on anything of this sort. My one interest in this is that of accuracy. In spite of many personal conversations and long letters to the Selznick people about such matters, embarrassing errors have continued to occur. I suppose this is almost inevitable when a movie company is scattered all the way from New York to California. But that is no comfort when the same errors are repeated over and over. I suppose you recognize also that additional possibilities of errors were created when the handling of all such matters was taken over by your company, with whom I have had no past dealings. I am confident Katharine Brown has explained things to you and I am equally confident of your desire and willingness to avoid errors but, as a practical man, I am sure you will recognize that errors could occur and that submitting the publicity items to me in advance will be a desirable safeguard for both of us.

An example of what I am talking about is the oft-repeated error about the date when Selznick bought the motion picture rights to my book. Shortly after the contract was signed in 1936 a story got into circulation that Selznick bought the movie rights while the book was still in galley proofs. This error has been published so often that many people consider it as true and it bobs up again and again. There is very little I can do to prevent it from being repeated in unauthorized stories, but there certainly is no excuse for it being repeated in publicity items given out by Selznick or you, when I have explained the situation to Selznick not once but several times. It has become a sore spot with me, far beyond its original importance and you cannot blame me for fearing that someone in your office or in California or in Budapest or in Kamchatka will put it out again as an authentic statement of truth unless we have some arrangement under which publicity material of this kind is not to be used at all until it has been approved by me. . . .

The emphasis I have placed on this may make you believe that I am expecting you to put out a great many publicity items about me, so I want to say again that Mr. Selznick made the movie and I am merely the author of the book. I am not asking for publicity and I will, in fact, be happy if the publicity about me is only that which the circumstances call for. I am only interested in knowing that such items about me and the background of the book as you may use are accurate.

Incidentally, while we are on the subject of errors, I have seen recently, for the first time, the special "Gone With the Wind" letterhead your company has been using. As you may already have noticed, it contains two errors: Melanie's name is spelled "Melanee" and Ashley Wilkes's name is spelled "Wilks." The letter which I saw was written two or three months ago, so it is quite probable that you may have already corrected these errors. If not, I would be grateful if they could be changed.*

I was sorry that you did not come to Atlanta with Katharine and Mr. Ferguson, as I was looking forward to meeting you. Obviously, if we could talk over matters of this kind it would be much more satisfactory than attempting to handle them by letter. I am hoping that I will yet have the opportunity to meet you and to talk with you about some of the things in which we are now mutually interested. I have not yet met Mr. Ferguson but I hope to do so on his next trip to Atlanta.†

Mrs. Vivian Latady   *Atlanta, Georgia*
Birmingham, Alabama   *November 14, 1939*

Dear Vivian:

Forgive the haste of this letter. I just wanted to thank you for your sweet letter and your good wishes. Everything has been topsyturvey and all atwit here in Atlanta since the date of the premiere was announced, and I do not see how John and I will be able to draw a breath until after the affair is over. Every civic and social organization plans to give.a party around that time and our phone rings like mad all day long. No announcement

---

* The original letterhead contained a third error that Mitchell missed: "Carreen" was spelled with a single "r." All three mistakes were corrected by the end of the month.

† On November 2, Dietz noted that his correspondence with Mitchell was "particularly exacting." The author's "precise mind" required "equal precision as a counter-attack," he told Selznick. While Dietz believed he and Mitchell were getting along, "it is a bit wearying," he added.

has been made yet about when the tickets will go on sale and what price will be charged. Everyone believes I know the answers to these questions, so they telephone me and I know no more than anyone else. Many thousand reservations have already been sent in, some of them coming from as far-off places as Canada and Mexico; the theatre seats nineteen hundred; so you can imagine what a scramble is going on. . . . People have been reserving hotel rooms for the last week and, as there are to be several conventions in town at the same time, rooms are fading rapidly. I am glad you are going to stay with Augusta so you'll be sure of a place to sleep.*

If I do not see you at this time please overlook it. With the Macmillan publishing company coming down here in a body and Mr. Selznick and his stars, too, I expect to be tied up. . . .

Howard Dietz   *Atlanta, Georgia*
Metro-Goldwyn-Mayer   *November 15, 1939*
New York, New York

THANK YOU FOR YOUR UNDERSTANDING LETTER STOP YOUR ATTITUDE MAKES ME FEEL CONFIDENT THAT WE CAN WORK OUT A SOLUTION TO OUR PROBLEM SATISFACTORY TO BOTH OF US STOP I HEREBY GIVE MY APPROVAL TO THE USE OF MY PHO-TOGRAPH IN YOUR SOUVENIR PROGRAM IN THE POSITION AND MANNER SHOWN IN THE DUMMY AND WITH THE CAPTION YOU MENTIONED STOP I ALSO AGREE TO YOUR USE OF THIS SAME PROGRAM IN OTHER CITIES AS WELL AS ATLANTA STOP I SEE NO REASON WHY THE PHOTOGRAPH SHOULD BE RETOUCHED AS IT HAS BEEN USED SUCCESSFULLY ALL OVER THE WORLD AND ON THE FEW OCCASIONS WHEN IT WAS RETOUCHED IT WAS CHANGED INTO SOMETHING THAT DOES NOT LOOK LIKE ME AT ALL STOP HOWEVER IF YOUR OBJECTION IS TO THE PARTICULAR PRINT I SENT YOU MACMILLAN CAN SUPPLY YOU WITH OTHER PRINTS OF THIS SAME PHOTOGRAPH STOP IN VIEW OF MANY ERRORS IN PUBLICITY MATTER YOU SENT ME I MUST INSIST ON YOUR SUBMITTING ANY STORY ABOUT ME IN THE PROGRAM FOR MY APPROVAL IN ADVANCE AND ALSO THE SELZNICK AR-TICLE IF IT MENTIONS ME OR BACKGROUND OF NOVEL STOP OFFICIAL NATURE OF THE PROGRAM AND THE LARGE CIRCU-

---

* Augusta Dearborn Edwards was a longtime friend of Mitchell's and a bridesmaid at her first wedding.

LATION OF IT YOU ARE PLANNING MAKE IT IMPERATIVE THAT STORIES BE ACCURATE STOP IF THEY ARE ACCURATE THIS WILL PREVENT MANY FUTURE ERRORS WHEREAS ERRORS IN OFFICIAL PROGRAM WOULD HAVE FALSE APPEARANCE OF AUTHENTICITY WHICH WOULD CAUSE ENDLESS TROUBLE STOP LETTER FOLLOWS ABOUT ERRORS IN PUBLICITY ARTICLES AND OTHER MATTERS YOU MENTIONED.

Mr. Howard Dietz   *Atlanta, Georgia*
Metro-Goldwyn-Mayer   *November 16, 1939*
New York, New York

Dear Mr. Dietz:

Enclosed is a copy of a telegram which I sent you just as soon as I could read your letter of November 14th and the enclosed publicity matter. Supplementing my permission for the use of my photograph in your special souvenir program, I am glad to say that you have my permission to use my photograph in "other similar displays such as a more diminutive house program." This means that, in "general displays of producer, author and director" when the proprieties would call for the use of my photograph, you have my permission to use it, with the exceptions stated in my previous letter, that "blow-ups" of my photograph are not to be used in theatre lobbies or otherwise, and that my picture is never to be used on billboards or similar large displays. Even if you should for some reason wish to use photographs of the producer and director on large posters, my personal feeling is that the use of my photograph in this manner would be contrary to the proprieties. Within these limitations, I am willing to give you carte blanche, as you requested.

Please do not take offense at my reference above to the use of my photograph on billboards. I have no idea that you are even thinking of using my photograph in that way, but I will make statements of that type in this letter and others simply because of my desire that we have *clearcut* understandings with each other. We do not know each other and we cannot read each other's minds, but if we can arrive at clearcut understandings matters will be simplified for both of us and we can work together harmoniously in solving our somewhat perplexing problem.

I am glad that we begin our relationship with me granting a permission which you said you thought I would not be willing to grant. I did not immediately assume that you were going to "sensationalize" me and I believe that my permission, even with the not-too-difficult limitations, gives you all that you want in the use of my photograph. I hope that my attitude and also the promptness of my reply have reduced to some extent your "margin of worry" about the publicity matters in general. I see no reason why those problems cannot be solved. Before getting into that general subject, there are one or two other matters in your letter to clear away. "Cut lines" is a newspaperman's phrase down here, which means the same as your "caption." The caption you submitted is quite satisfactory and I did not have any idea of asking you to submit a proof of the engraver's plate. I thank you for having gotten the corrections made in the special "Gone With the Wind" letterhead. I am enclosing a short biographical sketch, as you requested.

Also, I want you to know that in connection with matters such as we are now discussing and others which may arise in the future, my husband has full authority to act for me. I may be out of town from time to time, and I would especially like to get away from Atlanta sometime in the next few weeks on account of the excitement the premiere is stirring up, and I want you to understand in advance that my husband's approval or disapproval on publicity matters et cetera is the same as mine.

Now, with regard to the publicity problem in general, I think the whole problem is described in your statement that the publicity stories "unfortunately were never written during the production when there was plenty of time to do it." That is unfortunate for both of us, but I do not feel that I am the one who should be made to suffer for it. It puts on you a great pressure of time to get the material ready and I am willing to do anything I can to help you get things handled expeditiously, but I do not feel called upon to waive any right to have the stories accurate. Your company acquired the distribution and other rights, including the handling of publicity, on August 25, 1938 and, if you waited more than a year before consulting with me about these matters, I think you should accept your own share of the responsibility for whatever inconvenience may be involved in straightening things out at this late date. It is a large sized inconvenience to me, as well as to you, to have to take the time for this when the approaching premiere has brought me innumerable other problems, and if I am willing to give my time to it I am sure you will meet me halfway.

However, the difficulties do not seem to me to be insuperable. I recognize your necessity to get the job done on time. I am sure you recognize my necessity of having it accurate. If we agree on those two main points, we have already taken a big step toward getting the problems solved. And if you will agree with me on one additional point, I think you will recognize the importance to both of us of having the material checked by me for accuracy. The additional point is this—

1. You have already mentioned that Mr. Birdwell gave you erroneous information on one point, the date when Selznick acquired the motion picture rights. If he has given you wrong information on one point there is no reason to think he will not do it on others, especially when the particular point was one about which the correct information was given to the Selznick people not once but several times. With concrete examples of that kind before us, can you or I have confidence that the information you have been given is authentic?

2. I mentioned before the great mass of untruths which have gotten into circulation about me. I said also that some of them had been published so often many people consider them the authentic truth. Is there any reason to believe that your men in the field will not make use of untruths, in complete good faith, unless some steps are taken to let them know what is true and what is not?

3. You mention the troubles which might arise from "overzealousness of men in the field." That is something I especially want to guard against. My wishes are simple: I don't want your men to take liberties with the facts and I don't want them to take liberties with me; I don't want them to repeat inaccuracies already in circulation or use their imaginations in creating fresh ones, just to get a punch into some story or give it a fresh slant....

The two publicity articles you sent me provide good examples of what I am talking about. The one prepared for Liberty Magazine is a "Margaret Mitchell" story with the movie brought in as a secondary matter. I object to this story for that reason, quite apart from my objections to the large number of errors it contains. As to the other story, for the New York Times, the general approach of it is all right because it is a story about the motion picture. But I do most seriously object to the lead on it because it is completely erroneous and because it seems to drag me in for no reason at all except to drag me in. If there was even the slightest basis of fact for the statements in the lead on this story, I would perhaps have less justification for objecting. But, since the statements are purely the creation of somebody's imagination, I can but think that the writer made it all up, for no reason at all except to put "Margaret Mitchell" in the front of the story. This is the sort of thing I had in mind when I said I objected to taking liberties with facts and taking liberties with me.

To be more specific, May 20, 1936 may be a crucial date in the history of the film, if that happened to be the date when Katharine Brown wired Mr. Selznick about my book. It also may have happened that I went to see my friends, the Kurtzes, on that same day. If I did, my visit to them had nothing to do with making that date a significant one in the history of your picture. Futhermore, the impression is created that my statement to Mrs. Kurtz was the first time I had ever told anyone that I had sold my novel. The truth is that my novel had been announced in Macmillan's catalogue several months before then and, in fact, it had been scheduled for publication during May. The fact that the Book-of-the-Month Club had selected it, and thereby caused postponement of the publication date, had been given wide publicity. Macmillan salesmen had already taken orders for thousands of copies of the book and it was a subject of wide discussion in all parts of the country, if I may judge from the many letters I was receiving even then from booksellers and other total strangers in far away places. Therefore, the implication that my alleged visit to the Kurtzes had some significance is a distortion of the facts, for no apparent reason except to publicize "Margaret Mitchell" instead of the motion picture. In addition, I object to the statement that I "sidled" and "fidgeted," as it is not my habit to do either.

Enclosed is a detailed statement of the other changes and corrections which should be made in the New York Times article. As you will see, they are not numerous and all of them can be easily made. As a whole, the article (except for the lead) is excellent. It is not only interesting but contains the materials for dozens of other interesting stories. . . .

Now, I must say just one thing more. A long time ago, I told the Selznick people that I was tired of writing letters to them about this matter of publicity, and that if my wishes were again disregarded, I would be forced to take more direct action. From my first meeting with them, in 1936, I told them over and over that I was not to be publicized personally. Finally, I had to tell them that if I was dragged in improperly, I would go to bat about it in the newspapers or over the radio, even if this occurred on the very day of the premiere.

If my wishes had been conveyed to you properly, you would not have prepared the Liberty article at all, certainly not without consulting me. So, I have had to inflict a very long letter on you. I am doing it because I want you to understand some of the basic matters which you have not previously understood. I hope we can work together in friendship, and I see no reason why we should not. I do not intend to burden you with other long letters, but if this one helps us to a better understanding, I will consider this time well spent.

Notes on "Gone With the Wind" publicity article "planned for the New York Times"

(See other comments about the lead as given in my letter.)

Page 1, paragraph 2—"working on her first novel for *seven* years." I began writing my novel in 1926 and completed it in 1936. I did not work on it continuously during that time, but, as you have stated it here, it should be "ten years," not seven. In the proposed Liberty magazine article, you say that the writing required "the better part of *four* years." I do not know the exact number of days and years I put in on it, of course. So, suppose we standardize on the phrase "over a period of ten years."

Page 1, paragraph 2—"Native *magnolia* country." North Georgia, where I live and where the story is laid, is not a "magnolia and moonlight" section, in the meaning this phrase has been given on the stage and screen. I thought I had made it very clear in my book that North Georgia is very different from the older parts of the South. Abuse of the word "magnolia" has given it a distorted meaning that is highly distasteful to many Southerners, and I do not want my section referred to as a "magnolia country."

Page 2, paragraph 1—The statement that the book rights in my novel had "just been acquired" by Macmillan in May, 1936, is not correct. At that time, Macmillan had owned the book rights for nearly a year and had already printed many thousand copies, which would have been placed on the market in that month except for the Book-of-the-Month Club postponement.

Page 2, paragraph 2—"Cynara." This is not the title of the poem. It is, "Non sum qualis eram bonae sub regno Cynarae." The best way to express it in your publicity would be, "well-known poem *about* 'Cynara.'"

Page 2, paragraph 4—"Fifty thousand." The correct statement is that sales of the book *before* publication had surpassed fifty thousand, (not "on the first day of publication").

Page 2, paragraphs 3 and 4—You have corrected the date when Selznick acquired the motion picture rights, so as to make it July 30, 1936, for which I thank you, but you have not eliminated the thing that is most objectionable to me. Your story leaves the impression that Mr. Selznick bought the movie rights at a time when the book was unknown, and that its big success occurred *afterwards*, during the four weeks when he was in Honolulu, or the month of August, 1936. By that time, the book had sold more than a quarter million copies, but the important thing to me is that it was already a runaway success at the time I sold the movie rights on July 30th. The book went on sale on June 30th, and the first "best seller" reports thereafter in the New York Times and Herald-Tribune showed it high on the list the first week and at the top the second week, the position it held for many months afterwards.

The erroneous story of the sale of the movie rights, which has been circulated so widely and which you repeat in this article, is offensive to me because it creates the impression that Mr. Selznick was the slick movie man who put one over on the little country girl when she didn't realize how valuable the rights were. It is not true, and I don't like it on either Mr. Selznick's account or my own, so I do not want it repeated.

It is quite all right with me for Katharine Brown to get the credit for recognizing the possibilities of my book before it had been generally acclaimed and for urging Mr. Selznick to buy the movie rights. It is also correct to say that Mr. Selznick *made an offer* for the rights, or sought to buy them, soon after publication, but my final acceptance of the offer was not given until I signed the contract on July 30, 1936, at which time I was most keenly aware that my book was making an unprecedented success.

Page 3, paragraph 1—"Delighted publishers." The foreign language rights in my book were not handled by my publishers. I own the foreign rights and the sale of them was handled by me and my husband, through my foreign agent, of course.

Page 6, paragraph 1—"Burning of Atlanta." The fire scene in the motion picture is NOT the "burning of Atlanta." The event pictured in the film occurred on September 1, 1864, when the Confederate troops evacuated Atlanta and set fire to certain buildings containing war materials to prevent them from falling into Union hands. For the same reason, they also burned a number of freight cars loaded with ammunition. The city in general was not touched by these fires. The real "burning of Atlanta" occurred nearly three months later, in November, 1864. General Sherman and his troops had occupied the city in the interval, and they burned the city when they left in November at the beginning of the "March to the Sea."

If I may make a friendly suggestion, this is a point which you will do well to watch in your publicity. It is not merely a matter of historical preciseness. When you say that the burning occurred when the Confederates evacuated, you are saying that they burned their own city. (On page 12 of this same article, the error is repeated and you also say that they looted their city.) Southerners are very touchy on this point, because Northern defenders of General Sherman's record are constantly saying that Sherman did no burning, that the Southerners burned up their own homes and cities.

Ignorant people who see the movie will probably think they are seeing the burning of Atlanta, but it would be unwise, in my opinion, for you to make that error in your publicity. The same error appears in the Liberty magazine story. In that one, I don't think you are going to help yourself a bit by referring to Mr. Selznick as "General Sherman."

Page 6, paragraph 4—"Blistering comment from the press." This matter is of no concern to me personally, but I believe you have made the statement stronger than the facts justify. You would be correct in saying that the selection of Miss Leigh was one of the controversies stirred up by the movie, but the press comments in general were not "blistering." Some individuals, organizations and newspapers protested, but a great many others favored her selection. In the South, a majority of the newspaper comments were favorable.

Miss Rosa Hutchinson   *Atlanta, Georgia*
The Macmillan Company   *November 16, 1939*
New York, New York

Dear Miss Hutchinson:

As the Atlanta premiere of "Gone With the Wind" has been announced for December 15th in Atlanta, I have had a number of requests from newspapers about the sales figures of the book in this country and Canada. The last figures I have show the sales up through April 1939. They show:

United States	1,744,078
British and Colonial	197,179
Total in English Language	1,941,257

Do these figures check with yours as to the sales totals in April? My impression is that the "United States" figure above includes the sales in Canada as well. If so, can you give me a separate total for Canada? Also would you be willing to make an estimate bringing these figures up to date? I know that April is your annual inventory month but the newspapers always want the figures as of now, so if you care to estimate the present totals, I would be glad to know what they are.*

Mr. Brett has written me about the $2.00 and 69¢ editions to be published around the date of the motion picture premiere. I can mention these editions in the information I give out, if you wish, along with any figures on the advance sales you care to give me. Of course, if you do not want them mentioned until you make your own announcement at some later date, I will not refer to them. Just let me know what your wishes are.

Please forgive the abruptness of this letter. For some time I have intended to write you a long and newsy letter but since the announcement

---

* Latham sent Mitchell an updated report on November 28 that showed total English-language sales of 1,948,807 copies, with Canadian sales accounting for 48,765 of the total.

of the date of the showing of the film I have been busier than ever before in my life. The town is very excited about the visits of the stars and plans are going forward to make this affair the biggest and most exciting in our history. Unfortunately, no announcement has been made as to when the ticket sale will start and how much the tickets will cost. Our telephone goes night and day with calls from people who mistakenly believe I can get them tickets, so I expect to be very busy until December 15th.

Howard Dietz   *Atlanta, Georgia*
Metro-Goldwyn-Mayer   *November 23, 1939*
New York, New York

YOUR PROGRAM EXCELLENT BUT OFFER FOLLOWING CORRECTIONS QUOTE GEORGIA AFTER SHERIDAN UNQUOTE IN LISTING OF CHARACTERS MUST MEAN QUOTE GEORGIA AFTER SHERMAN UNQUOTE AS GENERAL SHERIDAN NEVER OPERATED IN THIS SECTION STOP IN THE CREDITS SPELL IT SUSAN MYRICK NOT SUZAN STOP IN FACTS STORY FIRST PARAGRAPH PLEASE ELIMINATE FIRST DRAFT AND MAKE IT READ QUOTE MOST OF THE BOOK HAD BEEN COMPLETED BY 1929 STOP IN THE SUCCEEDING YEARS UNTIL ITS PUBLICATION IN 1936 MUCH ADDITIONAL WORK WAS DONE IN FILLING IN MISSING CHAPTERS, REWRITING CERTAIN CHAPTERS AND CHECKING THE THOUSANDS OF HISTORICAL AND OTHER FACTUAL STATEMENTS FOR ACCURACY UNQUOTE ALSO SAME PARAGRAPH PLEASE SAY BOOK NOW TRANSLATED INTO SIXTEEN FOREIGN LANGUAGES STOP I HAVE NOT YET RECEIVED PRINTED COPIES OF TWO, THE BRAZILIAN AND RUMANIAN, BUT CONTRACTS WERE SIGNED SOME TIME AGO AND I HAVE BEEN INCLUDING THEM IN THE TOTAL STOP IN THIRD PARAGRAPH FIRST LINE SUGGEST CHANGE MUNITIONS PLANTS TO QUOTE MILITARY SUPPLIES UNQUOTE ATLANTA MANUFACTURED SOME MUNITIONS BUT ITS CHIEF IMPORTANCE WAS AS A DISTRIBUTION CENTER AND WHAT THEY BURNED WAS CARLOADS OF AMMUNITION AND WAREHOUSES FILLED WITH WAR MATERIALS OF ALL KINDS STOP IN CLARK GABLE STORY SECOND PAGE THIRD PARAGRAPH PREFER THAT YOU ELIMINATE QUOTE BEHIND THE WALLS SHE BUILT AROUND HER HOME UNQUOTE THIS LAST MIGHT BE TAKEN LITERALLY AND THEREFORE BE MISLEADING AS I LIVE IN AN APARTMENT AND HAVE BUILT NO WALLS STOP AM WRITING

SOON ABOUT OTHER POINTS IN YOUR VERY FINE LETTER FOR
WHICH I THANK YOU.*

Mr. Howard Dietz   *Atlanta, Georgia*
Metro-Goldwyn-Mayer   *November 24, 1939*
New York, New York

Dear Mr. Dietz:

I feel we are making real progress. Your letter encourages me to believe
that we can work together, for I do not believe there is any essential difference in our viewpoints. So the problem now is merely that of getting
together on the practical details. I agree with you that some matters are not
entirely within our control, but if you and I and your associates understand
each other thoroughly, I see no reason why we should not together be able
to handle the problems that come from the outside.

Enclosed is a copy of my telegram about the souvenir program. I think
it covers that subject fully but, for your information, I want to explain the
reason for one of my corrections. Your statement that I completed a first
draft of my novel in 1929 and then spent the next two years rewriting it
creates a picture that is very different from my method of writing. Some
people do write just that way, get a first draft neatly typed out from front
to back, and then pitch in on the job of revamping and re-modeling. My
book was never complete from front to back until it was ready for delivery
to the printer, several months after Macmillan bought it. I worked on it by
chapters and every chapter was rewritten many times as I went along. By
1929, substantially all of the *story* had been written but there were many
gaps between chapters. The first chapter was not written until after the
manuscript was in Macmillan's hands, although I had previously made
many unsuccessful attempts at a first chapter. And most of the research
work was done after Macmillan bought the book.

The importance of my correction in the program lies in the fact that
the correct information, as above, has been published many times, and I
thought the wrong statement in your official program might prove embarrassing to both of us.

---

* All of Mitchell's corrections were made to the souvenir program. However, Dietz reworked
the *Liberty* article to focus on Gable, and the first paragraph of the piece, which appeared in
the February 1940 issue of the magazine under the headline, "I Was Afraid of Rhett Butler,"
contains the line Mitchell wanted removed: "I can understand perfectly why she built a wall
around her home. Haven't I wanted to do the same thing during the past year?"

Thank you for giving me the correct information about the Selznick-MGM contract. I am sorry that my previous letter did you an injustice and I thoroughly agree with you in wanting your responsibility clear cut before you took charge. Thank you also for offering to pay for telegrams and other expenses in connection with the publicity matter. I sent my telegram last night collect, but don't bother about the previous one.

As to the "essential fact" story which you wish to prepare as the basis for all of your publicity, I will do anything I can to assist you in getting it accurate. The best plan, I suppose, would be for you to send the story to me and let me correct any errors I find in it. But I hope we are now in agreement that it will not be a "Margaret Mitchell" story and that the background material about the book will be in its proper position as *background*. Give the movie the top spot and leave the book and me in a subordinate place. Apart from any question of my wishes and feelings, that policy will do a lot toward simplifying matters for you and me. I recognize that you could not properly leave the book and me out of your publicity entirely, even if you were inclined to do so, but if you bring us in only when it is necessary as a part of the *movie's* background, then there should be no great difficulty in our getting together on the few essential facts you will need.

Whether Macmillan is a reliable source of information is a point we need not argue. In general, my dealings with them have been satisfactory. But, from your past experience in other matters, you know how statements lifted out of their context often acquire different meanings from the original, and how a writer who gets his information second-hand or third-hand often gets just enough to make a distorted and wrong story. The Liberty Magazine article is a good example of this. Most of the statements in it contain some element of truth, but the composite result is far from true. Just to take a random example, you say that my "family" are cotton planters, lawyers, and Methodist ministers. Presumably you refer to my immediate family; actually that statement refers to my ancestors for some generations back.

The only way to avoid errors of that sort is to check the material direct with me and then we both will know that it is correct. Misunderstandings and misinterpretations are certain to occur if the information passes through three or four hands before it reaches you. But we need not worry about that any further in view of your statement that you will check such material with me in the future. . . .

Of course I am interested in "Gone With the Wind" matters and I will be glad to have you keep me informed of interesting developments in the film's career. Don't let this be a burden on you but if your judgment tells you that some item might be of interest to me send it along. Although I have had no part in making the movie, I naturally have a sympathetic understanding of Mr. Selznick's many problems and a friendly desire to see your company and his make a great success.

Now, I want to tell you what a fine job I think you have done on the souvenir program. Even in the rough dummy it is striking and I know it will be beautiful in colors. The pictures of the stars, the little drawings, the lay-out look wonderful to me and I know these programs will be treasured by all fortunate enough to get copies.* You certainly deserve credit and congratulations. Would it be possible for you to send me a dozen copies of the program? I have asked for tickets to the premiere for only a few of my closest relatives here in Atlanta but I would like to send the program to some relatives and dear friends elsewhere as mementoes of the first showing of "Gone With the Wind."†

I am returning the dummy to you herewith.

Mr. John Paschall   *Atlanta, Georgia*
The Atlanta Journal   *November 25, 1939*
Atlanta, Georgia

Dear Mr. Paschall:

Last night when I listened to your voice on the radio my memory went back several years to that stifling hot night in July 1936 when I was a newly hatched author highly alarmed at the prospect of going on the air.‡ I remembered how kind and reassuring you were then and how very pleased I was at the things you said about "Gone With the Wind." (Although I could not believe all of them!) You were so good and understanding then, and last night I had the same warm feeling of pleasure and gratitude that I felt

---

* The twenty-page program sold for twenty-five cents at theaters showing the film. During *Gone With the Wind*'s original release, moviegoers purchased more than 1,750,000 copies of the booklet.

† Mitchell's guest ticket list included eleven passes—for her father, her brother and sister-in-law, her secretary, and several aunts and uncles in Atlanta. Her father was not well enough to attend opening night, but he saw the film the following day.

‡ On November 24, Paschall's *Editorial Hour* on WSB Radio featured interviews with Hartsfield, Alvin B. Cates, president of the Atlanta Chamber of Commerce, and Faber Bollinger, executive vice president of the Atlanta Convention and Visitors Bureau, among others. Details were provided about the Junior League Ball, tickets to the premiere, and the various planned festivities.

in 1936. I am not thanking you only for the wonderful things you *said* but for the thought and the comprehension of my situation which was behind your words. John has told me about his conversation with you and the wise advice you gave. We are both grateful for this advice and we will follow it. What would I do without friends like you? Your advice and your attitude have lightened a burden that was heavy upon us both and have given me the strength to finish out the last lap of this last mile.

Miss Mary DeV. Butler   *Atlanta, Georgia*
Five Oaks   *November 27, 1939*
Athens, Georgia

My dear Miss Butler:

Forgive my delay in acknowledging the letter and the lovely gift. If you have been reading the Atlanta papers during the last two weeks you will understand that the town has been in an excited frenzy. The question in every mind seems to be "how can I get tickets for the premiere?" Automatically questioners turn and ask me. I cannot tell them anything, for I know nothing more than what appears in the newspapers.

The green taffeta trimming your mother made for me is perfectly beautiful and I marvel at the tiny, regular stitches. Please thank her for me and tell her I hope to thank her personally for the gift and for her thought. I have been so busy recently that I have been unable to buy any clothes for the festivities except the white taffeta dress I will wear to the premiere, and it has blue accessories.* And if I do not get the opportunity to do any shopping between now and the fifteenth of December, I am going to cut off the end of the trim, make a little rosette of it and wire it to my flowers so that I will have a real, authentic War-and-Reconstruction article with me.† You and your sister are very lucky to have so sweet a mother, and I am very lucky to have her gift.

Sometimes I feel embarrassed when I think that I had the temerity to write about the War and Reconstruction. Such a book should have been written by a person like your mother, who went through it all, for she knows. But ladies such as your mother were too busy living that life to have the time to write about it.

---

* Mitchell apparently changed her mind about her premiere-night costume. On December 15, the author wore a pink gown of tulle and crepe with puffed sleeves.

† The author carried Mrs. Butler's green taffeta trimming in her purse at the premiere.

Miss Helen B. Parker   *Atlanta, Georgia*
Rich's, Inc., Book Shop   *November 28, 1939*
Atlanta, Georgia

Dear Helen:

You know John and I want to come to your luncheon on the fifteenth and I hope you realize how disappointed we will be if we do not get there. The truth of the matter is that it is very doubtful that I will be able to attend. I have been ill ever since I had the flu and the constant harassments of the frenzied public during the past three weeks have given me no opportunity to regain my strength. I have the choice of going to parties, wearing myself out and not being able to attend the premiere—or I can stay quietly at home and go to the premiere. I think it will be better for me to see the picture. Of course there is always a chance that a miracle will happen and that between now and the fifteenth I will feel better. For the present, however, you had better not include me in your plans. I will ask John if he can go and will let you know.

If it will not inconvenience you too much I wish you would permit me to delay a while in giving you a definite refusal. Would it throw out your plans too much if you did not know until the fourteenth whether or not I could come? I want you to be very frank with me about this, for I know what a job it is to rearrange place cards et cetera.*

With regret I have had to refuse all invitations I have received, with the exception of the small party of the Women's Press Club which I accepted nearly a year ago. It will take place immediately before the premiere.

Colonel Telamon Cuyler   *Atlanta, Georgia*
Wayside, Jones County, Georgia   *November 29, 1939*

My dear Colonel Cuyler:

Nothing but the second battle of Atlanta would have kept me from answering your letters and thanking you most sincerely for the valuable telegrams from Jefferson Davis and Robert E. Lee, which you sent me. I am, as always, sincerely grateful to you for your generosity.

If you have been reading the Atlanta papers you have learned what a state the town is in. There is a pleasing excitement over everything and everyone is looking forward to a marvelous three days. But the whole affair has John and me working till all hours of the night.

---

* Mitchell attended the luncheon.

I have not felt very well since I had the flu, as there has been no opportunity for me to get any rest and recover the weight I lost. So it is very doubtful that I will be able to attend the Junior League costume ball or any of the other festivities and go to the premiere, too. So I will probably stay home on the 14th and 15th and rest up for the big event on the night of the 15th. But I hope you get to the costume ball and I so sincerely hope you get to the premiere. If there was any way whereby I could beg, borrow or steal you a ticket I would do it, for you should be there, but thus far John and I have not received tickets ourselves!*

This is all a very incredible affair and I still believe I will wake up some day and find out it is not true.

Mr. Harold Latham   *Atlanta, Georgia*
The Macmillan Company   *December 1, 1939*
New York, New York

Dear Harold:

This is just a note to acknowledge the royalty check which arrived today. Thank you so much for sending it and for the sweet note that came with it. Who would have ever thought that I'd be getting royalty checks three and a half years after publication! I am so glad you are coming down to the premiere, even if it will not be the quiet and leisurely visit I would like. At least I will get to see you at the Press Club party, and for a nice long visit I will look to your spring trek southward.

Miss Katharine Brown   *Atlanta, Georgia*
Selznick International Pictures, Inc.   *December 4, 1939*
New York, New York

Dear Katharine:

Here are a few of the items from Sunday's papers, not all for Bessie made away with many before I could get them. The papers were practically given over to GWTW. My statement is included and I am sending you several copies.† If you wish to send some to Mr. Selznick, Miss Leigh and

---

* Myrick arranged for Cuyler to receive two tickets to both the ball and the premiere. "But 2 precious tickets makes me in real danger from ladies and girls and old ladies and everyone," he joked to Mitchell. "What *shall* I do? Who shall I ask to hoopskirt and go with me?" At Cuyler's request, local labor leaders chose Katherine Golucke, a young Atlanta schoolteacher and union member, to be his date.

† On Sunday, December 3, the Atlanta newspapers carried a statement from Mitchell in which she said that her part in the celebration would "not be all that I would like" because of

Mr. Gable to show them that in my feeble way I am trying to see that they have a good time, do so. Things are getting faster and funnier by the hour. Everyone who is important is trying to roll the less important for premiere and ball tickets. Many prominent feet are being held to the fire in an effort to make their owners disgorge tickets.

Mrs. O.D. Bartlett   *Atlanta, Georgia*
Atlanta Better Films Committee   *December 5, 1939*
Atlanta, Georgia

Dear Virginia:

Thank you so much for the invitation to the luncheon on December 15. I am sorry that John and I cannot be with you. December 15th will probably be the busiest day of my entire life. Not only will the moving picture people be here but my publishers will be in town too, as well as scores of out-of-town friends. I have not been well recently and am having to forgo many of the festivities so that I will be in shape for the premiere itself. If I am able to be out on the day of the 15th I will have to be with the Macmillan publishing people. But thank you just the same.

Mr. and Mrs. L.W. Robert   *Atlanta, Georgia*
Georgian Terrace Hotel   *December 5, 1939*
Atlanta, Georgia

My dear Mr. and Mrs. Robert:

John and I thank you so much for your invitation to your "after the Wind" breakfast in the wee hours of Saturday morning. Under ordinary circumstances it would give us the greatest pleasure to accept but, as our circumstances will be most extraordinary that week-end, we must regretfully decline. Practically everyone we have ever known will be in Atlanta at that time and we made our plans and engagements a long time ago. I am sorry that we have an engagement which conflicts with your party. I know your breakfast will be so much fun and I am so sorry we cannot be with you. Thank you so much for thinking about us.

---

illness. She encouraged the city's residents to show their visitors that "the best things of the Old South, its courtesy and warm hospitality, have not gone with the wind." She also noted she was looking forward to "my first meeting with Mr. Selznick" and to the premiere, when she would "see the old streets of the little Atlanta I wrote about, and the old houses which have been gone for 75 years, and the people. It will be a strange and unbelievable experience."

Mr. George Ward   *Atlanta, Georgia*
Ward, Stern & Company   *December 6, 1939*
Birmingham, Alabama

My dear Mr. Ward:

I never had a white orchid before and I never expect to have again as beautiful a flower as the one you sent me. The message that came with it was as lovely as the flower itself. How good of you to think of me "before the tumult and the shouting comes"! I have not been very well recently, as I had a brisk siege of influenza a while ago. I have been eating vitamins and liver extract in an effort to get strong before the premiere of "Gone With the Wind" comes. I wore your orchid to the doctor's office yesterday and he said he thought it had done me more good than all his vitamins. . . .

Have you seen Doctor Douglas Southall Freeman's new book, "The South to Posterity"?* To my delight, I found in it references to your mother's spirited and intelligent testimony and I was so glad to know that her words were being given even wider range than they now enjoy.

Mr. George Brett, Jr.   *Atlanta, Georgia*
The Macmillan Company   *December 12, 1939*
New York, New York

Dear George:

Enclosed I am returning to you one copy of your letter of December 7th. I have signed both copies of it and retained one copy in my files, and this will constitute our agreement as to royalties on the $2.00 edition of "Gone With the Wind."

Of course I am glad to accept the new arrangement and I am happy to know that the new developments indicate that the edition may be more successful than you anticipated.† A copy of the book and of the 69¢ edition arrived and I congratulate you on them. I was surprised to learn that the 69¢ edition would go on sale here in Atlanta on the same day as the motion picture premiere, as I was still under the impression that your agreement with the motion picture people would not permit it to be offered anywhere

---

* *The South to Posterity: An Introduction to the Writings of Confederate History* was published in 1939 by Charles Scribner's Sons. Freeman, the longtime editor of the *Richmond News Leader*, won a Pulitzer Prize for his four-volume biography of Robert E. Lee in 1935.

† When manufacturing costs for the two-dollar edition came in lower than expected, Brett offered Mitchell a sliding scale that would pay her royalties of up to twenty-two cents a book on future sales. However, only a single printing of 13,400 copies of this edition was produced.

until next month. I do not yet understand quite clearly what your intentions are with reference to the two editions. Will the 69¢ edition go on sale in each city simultaneously with the first showing of the motion picture in each city and the $2.00 edition being offered generally so as to make copies of the book available in places where the motion picture edition is not on sale? Or is the plan of placing the 69¢ edition on sale simultaneously with the first showing of the movie in various places effective only to some definite date and thereafter the 69¢ edition will be available everywhere?*

I am asking these questions purely out of curiosity. The best news is that you have apparently made some arrangement with the motion picture people more satisfactory to you than you anticipated when I last heard from you.

I have never seen Atlanta in such a turmoil as it has been in recently, and the worst is yet to come. I hope that you and the other Macmillan folks are going to enjoy your visit and my chief regret is that I will not have the opportunity to see as much of you as I would like. You all understand, I am sure, what my situation is.

Miss Hattie McDaniel	*Atlanta, Georgia*
Los Angeles, California	*December 13, 1939*

Dear "Mammy":

Your very fine letter reached me just when the excitement about the Atlanta premiere of "Gone With the Wind" is at its height.

I am so glad you wrote to me and I thank you for your letter and all the nice things you said about my book. Thank you for wanting to play "Mammy." I take that as a compliment to the character. Of course I have seen many still pictures of you in this part and I am looking forward with the greatest interest to seeing you on the screen. Mrs. Kurtz and Miss Myrick have told me so many interesting things about you and how splendid you are as "Mammy."

Should you be in Atlanta at any time, please telephone me. I would like to see you and talk to you.†

---

* Initially, the Motion Picture Edition was scheduled to be released nationwide on February 15, 1940, but as the premiere drew closer, Selznick relented and allowed Macmillan to ship the book to stores in cities where the film opened. Atlanta received its first shipment—thirty thousand copies—on December 11, and the book became available in bookstores there on December 15.

† Atlanta, like most of the South, was racially segregated in 1939. Loew's Grand Theatre did not have a "colored balcony," so McDaniel could not have sat in the auditorium, nor could she have stayed at the Georgian Terrace Hotel with the other celebrities.

The Premiere
1939 (December 13–15)

This is a very happy and exciting day for me, and at this time, I want
to thank everybody in Atlanta for being so nice to me and my poor
Scarlett.

—Margaret Mitchell outside Loew's Grand Theatre
December 15, 1939

On Wednesday, December 13—the same day Mitchell replied to
Hattie McDaniel's letter—the first cast member from *Gone With the
Wind* arrived in Atlanta for the premiere festivities. Ann Rutherford, who played Scarlett's youngest sister, Carreen, came by train with her
mother. The twenty-two-year-old actress, best known as Polly Benedict in
MGM's popular "Andy Hardy" series, was welcomed by Mayor Hartsfield,
who presented her a large bouquet of red roses. In an impromptu interview with reporters at the Georgian Terrace Hotel, where the Hollywood
contingent would stay, Rutherford said she wanted "to see all the famous
places I've heard so much about. . . . Even when I'm eighty-five, I'll look
back with pride and say I had a part in *Gone With the Wind*."[1] That afternoon, a chartered TWA Skysleeper carrying David Selznick; his wife, Irene;
and his brother, Myron; along with Vivien Leigh and her future husband,
Laurence Olivier, and Olivia de Havilland landed at Atlanta's Candler Field
after having left Los Angeles at 11:00 the night before. Kay Brown, who
had been in the city for several days, joined the mayor to welcome her boss

to Atlanta. Evelyn Keyes, who played Suellen O'Hara, and Ona Munson, who portrayed Belle Watling, arrived on a commercial flight about an hour later, and all the visitors were bundled off to the hotel. The general public would not get its first glimpse of the stars until a parade the following day after Clark Gable arrived.

As the guests were driven through town, they saw a city awash in "the *Wind*." Loew's Grand Theatre, where the film would premiere Friday night, was decorated with a three-story white-columned façade surmounted by a huge oval portrait of Gable and Leigh as Rhett and Scarlett. Confederate flags and red, white, and blue bunting hung from the windowsills. On the office building across the street were four large round paintings of the main characters set in star-shaped frames outlined with lightbulbs.* At the mayor's urging, Selznick and Loew's had shipped dozens of original costumes and hats, set drawings, costume sketches, props, and set miniatures to Atlanta, where they were divided among downtown retailers for promotional displays. Just up the street from the theater, the Davison-Paxon department store devoted a window to the eight-foot-tall oil painting of Scarlett in blue velvet that hung in Rhett's bedroom in the film.† With the painting was the cream-colored wedding gown Scarlett wore at her first marriage to Charles Hamilton. Another window highlighted items from Mitchell's personal collection, including foreign-language translations of her novel, original illustrations from the Danish edition, and Civil War mementoes. Inside the store's French Room, additional costumes were on view, including the green velvet gown Scarlett fashioned from the drapes at Tara, Belle Watling's yellow satin dress trimmed with red roses and black lace, and Rhett's Twelve Oaks barbecue outfit.‡ Crosstown rival Rich's department store dedicated four windows to assorted costumes, including Bonnie Butler's blue velvet riding habit and Scarlett's maroon-and-white gown from the scene of Ashley's Christmas furlough, as well as a working model of Tara and numerous set and costume sketches. In addition, the store's millinery department showcased eight hats from the film designed by John Frederics. More costumes worn

---

* The four "roundel" portraits are on display at the Road to Tara Museum in Jonesboro, Georgia.

† The portrait, by Helen Carleton, was presented to the city's High Museum of Art and later found a home in the cafeteria of the city's Margaret Mitchell Elementary School. The painting currently is in the movie museum at the Margaret Mitchell House.

‡ The green velvet drapery dress and Scarlett's wedding gown are among five original costumes in the Selznick Collection at the Harry Ransom Center at the University of Texas.

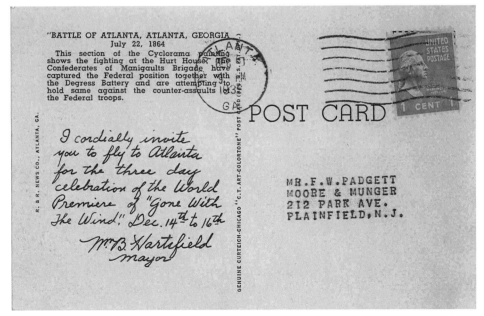

I cordially invite you to fly to Atlanta for the three day celebration of the World Premiere of "Gone With The Wind." Dec. 14th to 16th

Wm. B. Hartsfield
mayor

MR. F. W. PADGETT
MOORE & MUNGER
212 PARK AVE.
PLAINFIELD, N.J.

Atlanta's mayor, William B. Hartsfield, sent postcards of the city's famous Cyclorama to businessmen and government officials across the country, inviting them to "fly to Atlanta" for the premiere festivities. John Wiley, Jr., Collection.

During premiere week, Atlanta's Davison-Paxon department store, which hosted Mitchell's first book signing in 1936, devoted a display window to the author's collection of foreign editions of her novel. Herb Bridges Collection.

The mayor, second from right, greets de Havilland, David and Irene Selznick, and Leigh on their arrival in Atlanta on December 13, 1939. Herb Bridges Collection.

At an informal press reception at their hotel that evening, Leigh, right, told reporters she was "scared to death" and hoped the Atlanta audience would like her. She also called Scarlett "an egotistical little brat who at times needed a good spanking." Herb Bridges Collection.

That night, Selznick, Leigh, and de Havilland met Mitchell for the first time in her Atlanta apartment (shown in the late 1940s). The author's foreign editions of *Gone With the Wind* are on the bookshelf, right. Special Collections and Archives, Georgia State University Library.

Gable's arrival the following afternoon with his wife, actress Carole Lombard, rates a personal welcome from Georgia's governor, Eurith D. Rivers. Herb Bridges Collection.

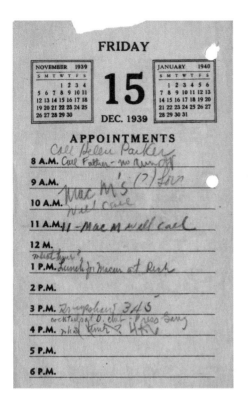

Friday, December 15, was a busy day for Mitchell, including a luncheon at Rich's department store and a cocktail party. She also had to work in a visit with her doctor after she sprained her back. Courtesy of Hargrett Rare Book and Manuscript Library/University of Georgia Libraries.

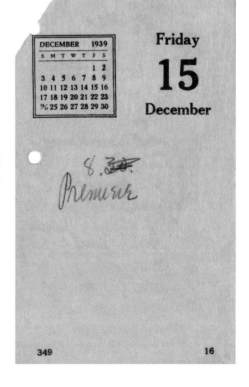

Initially, Mitchell had the premiere listed on her desk calendar for 8:30, but she changed it to 8:00. Courtesy of Hargrett Rare Book and Manuscript Library/University of Georgia Libraries.

At the Friday luncheon at Rich's, Mitchell talks with fellow Pulitzer Prize winner Marjorie Kinnan Rawlings, author of *The Yearling*. Courtesy Special Collections, Atlanta-Fulton Public Library System.

Mitchell and Gable meet for the first time at a cocktail party at the Piedmont Driving Club. Afterward, he tells reporters that she was "the most fascinating woman I've ever met." Special Collections and Archives, Georgia State University Library.

The author poses with the actors and the producer at the country club. Special Collections and Archives, Georgia State University Library.

More than eighty thousand requests were received for the 2,031 tickets available to the premiere, priced at ten dollars each. Eager fans "fought and trampled little children and connived and broke the ties of lifelong friendship" attempting to get passes, Mitchell told a friend. John Wiley, Jr., Collection.

The beams from five searchlights set up outside Loew's Grand Theatre reportedly could be seen fifty miles away. Special Collections and Archives, Georgia State University Library.

Wilbur and Annie Laurie Kurtz arrive at the theater. Herb Bridges Collection.

Mitchell steps away from the microphones outside Loew's Grand after thanking the people of Atlanta "for being so nice to me and my poor Scarlett." Special Collections and Archives, Georgia State University Library.

The author pauses at the entrance to the theater lobby and chats with doorman Ben Cotton while waiting for Selznick, who has her ticket. Herb Bridges Collection.

Four Confederate veterans, each in their nineties and guests of honor at the screening, are greeted by the governor. (Mitchell's friend, Telamon Cuyler, stands behind the "men in gray.") Special Collections and Archives, Georgia State University Library.

There are no known photographs of Selznick inside the theater that night, but he might have sat here, on the aisle in the row in front of Mitchell. Special Collections and Archives, Georgia State University Library.

Just before the film began, the author was thinking that she was "the most fortunate woman in the world." Special Collections and Archives, Georgia State University Library.

While the South's segregation policies kept Hattie McDaniel from attending the premiere, Mitchell cabled the actress early the next morning to congratulate her for her performance as Mammy. Herb Bridges Collection.

As a souvenir of Gable's visit to Atlanta, Mitchell sent him a 1937 Danish edition of her novel, noting that the artist who drew this illustration "had you in mind. . . . As this translation was published long before you were announced for Rhett, you can see that even the Danes wanted you!" John Wiley, Jr., Collection.

Gable and Lombard raised chickens on their ranch in Encino, California. After the premiere, the couple sent Mitchell four dressed hens as a Christmas present. John Wiley, Jr., Collection.

Billed-Bladet

Nr. 5   30. Januar   3. Aargang   1940

WGST

OFELIA SOM SCARLETT O'HARA
1939's Kronborg-Ofelia Vivien Leigh
kommer til Urpremieren i Atlanta paa
"Borte med Blæsten"
Se Reportage inde i Bladet

25 ØRE

The premiere made news across the country and around the world, as evidenced by the cover of this Danish magazine in early 1940. John Wiley, Jr., Collection.

On February 29, 1940, *Gone With the Wind* won a record eight Oscars, including Best Picture and Best Actress. From left, Irene Selznick, Whitney, de Havilland, David Selznick, Leigh, and Olivier. John Wiley, Jr., Collection.

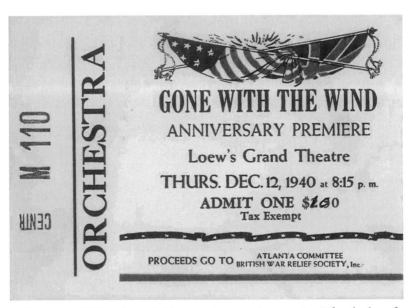

In December 1940, Atlanta held an anniversary "re-premiere" for the benefit of the British War Relief Society. After the announced appearance of Leigh and McDaniel reenacting a scene from the book onstage was canceled, ticket prices were reduced. John Wiley, Jr., Collection.

A giant birthday cake with a single candle decorated the outside of Loew's Grand for the anniversary screening, but bad weather prevented Leigh and Olivier from attending. Herb Bridges Collection.

Mitchell's godson, Turney Allan Taylor Jr., saw the movie for the first time during its 1947 rerelease. Afterward, the nine-year-old told his "Aunt Peggy," "All the time I kept thinking you had written the book, and how you thought of it all." Courtesy of Allan Taylor.

While in Atlanta in 1958 for the premiere of her new film, *The Proud Rebel*, de Havilland paid her respects at the grave of Margaret Mitchell in Oakland Cemetery. Special Collections and Archives, Georgia State University Library.

Selznick sits on the front steps of the postwar Tara. In 1959, when the façade on the back lot was dismantled, the producer told reporters, "Nothing in Hollywood is permanent. Once photographed, life here is ended." Herb Bridges Collection.

by Melanie, Ashley, Carreen, Suellen, Aunt Pittypat, and India were on display at other stores along Peachtree Street.[2]

For those seeking a souvenir of the historic occasion, the city's merchants advertised and displayed a wide selection. In addition to Macmillan's three new editions of the book, numerous *GWTW* novelty items were for sale at department stores and drugstores—dolls, stationery, two boxes of Scarlett chocolates, perfume, dusting powder, nail polish, handkerchiefs, scarves, a paint book, paper dolls, jewelry, and dresses. The city's three newspapers were packed with articles and photographs about the week's events. Specially printed cards from Mayor Hartsfield welcoming guests to Atlanta were slipped under the doors of the city's hotel rooms, and store clerks, waitresses, taxi drivers, and streetcar conductors wore period costumes.

Once at the hotel, where they found flowers from Mitchell in their rooms, Selznick and his party attended an informal press reception where they talked with reporters. De Havilland praised the film and its producer. "I am absolutely convinced that this is by far the greatest picture that ever came out of Hollywood," she said. "If there is any question of giving credit where credit is due, there can be but one answer—David Selznick. It is just an inspiration to have such a man in charge of production. He is a perfectionist from the word 'go' and insists on everything being done right, no matter what the cost."[3] Leigh admitted she was anxious about the city's reaction. "I'm waiting for Friday night with the nervousness of the stage actress awaiting opening night," she said. "I'm scared to death, and I do hope Atlanta will like me. They already have been so charming." As for the character she played, Leigh termed Scarlett "an egotistical little brat who at times needed a good spanking." And when asked if the heroine won her husband back, the actress said no. "Rhett had had enough."[4] Selznick defended the film's length. "As it stands now, with intermission, it runs four hours. There are those who will say, and do say, that this is too long. But it requires this to tell the story, and we have been faithful to the story," he said. "It is Miss Mitchell's story, and we tried to bring it to life in visual form."[5]

After supper, the producer and his two female stars slipped away and were driven to Mitchell's apartment, where they met for the first time the woman whose novel had brought them all together.* According to the *Atlanta Georgian*, the author sat on the floor and kept her audience en-

---

* Irene Selznick and Laurence Olivier accompanied them on their visit with the author. Wilbur and Annie Laurie Kurtz and Sue Myrick reportedly were there as well.

thralled. "In accordance with the true rules of hospitality, she offered her guests, who had flown in from Hollywood late in the afternoon, a drink. But they needed no other stimulus than their hostess' conversation and refused so much as a Southern Comfort," the article claimed.[6] Mitchell also showed the visitors her collection of editions of *Gone With the Wind* from around the world, pointing out to Leigh various artists' conceptions of Scarlett. The Hollywood contingent did not tear themselves away until 1:30 in the morning.[7]

*   *   *

On Thursday, December 14, officials of Loew's, Metro-Goldwyn-Mayer and Macmillan began arriving by plane and train, as did Laura Hope Crews, who portrayed Aunt Pittypat, and Alicia Rhett, who played India Wilkes, as well as actress Claudette Colbert, a friend of Irene Selznick, and the governors of Alabama, Florida, South Carolina, and Tennessee. That morning, the Atlanta chapter of the United Daughters of the Confederacy dedicated a downtown gas lamp as the "Eternal Flame to the Confederacy," and Rutherford charmed six veterans of the conflict, all in their nineties, when she visited the Confederate Soldiers Home of Georgia. At mid-afternoon, the celebrities were driven back to the airport to await the arrival of Gable and his wife, Carole Lombard. Hundreds of people gathered to catch a glimpse of the "King of Hollywood," and female squeals and sighs greeted him as he descended from a plane on which were emblazoned the words "MGM Gone With the Wind: Special Flight to Atlanta Premiere."* After the governor and mayor greeted the couple, they made their way to a waiting car and joined a caravan of convertibles for a triumphal entry into the city. As twilight settled, the cars turned up Peachtree Street. Bands were stationed every few blocks playing "Dixie," and spectators, fifteen and twenty deep on the sidewalks and sitting in upper-office windows, eagerly strained for a glimpse of the stars that had fallen onto Atlanta. First came the supporting cast members and local officials, followed by the cars bearing Georgia Governor Eurith D. Rivers with Selznick and Leigh, and Hartsfield with Gable and Lombard, whose appearance drew the biggest cheers. The parade ended at a side entrance to the Georgian Terrace, and the celebri-

---

* Selznick was perturbed that MGM was claiming the film as its own and cautioned Howard Strickling, the studio's West Coast director of publicity, to avoid "repetitions of this kind . . . in the future."

ties made their way through the lobby and onto a platform constructed at the corner of the hotel's terrace. There, as thousands more jammed the intersection, the ordinary citizens of Atlanta welcomed Scarlett, Rhett, and the others home.

The mayor introduced the cast members and presented each of them with a Wedgwood demitasse set depicting famous people and landmarks of Atlanta history. In turn, the visitors stepped to the microphones to greet the crowd. Keyes paid tribute to the city in which she grew up and where her mother still lived: "You're all wonderful people, and I'm very, very proud of my own hometown." Ever-bubbly Rutherford declared, "I just feel that if I never have another exciting day as long as I live, I shan't mind because I've had this day."

Selznick took the opportunity to express his wish that the city's residents would be happy with the film: "Ladies and gentlemen, we've entered Atlanta with humility and trepidation; we remain in gratitude. And it's our fervent hope that this city, of all cities, will be pleased with our efforts." Vivien Leigh's British accent was quite evident as she told the crowd, "I've spent quite a good deal of my time on Peachtree Street this year, and now that I'm here, it feels, well, just as if I were coming home."

The mayor read a cable of greeting from Leslie Howard, who had returned to England after war broke out with Germany. Hartsfield then announced, "I present to you the man who, by national acclaim, from start to finish, was, is and always Rhett Butler, who now owns Atlanta—Mr. Clark Gable!" The actor waited for the cheers to die down before beginning. "Thank you, ladies and gentlemen. You know, as I started down here this evening, your mayor told me that the population of Atlanta was three hundred thousand. I have seen myself tonight, coming from the airport, three million people!" He then paid tribute to Mitchell and expressed his eagerness to meet the author.[8]

The celebrities went to the hotel's ballroom for a cocktail party hosted by Selznick International and MGM. There, they chatted with dozens of reporters from newspapers and wire services across the country. After a quick supper, the stars dressed for the evening's highlight—the *Gone With the Wind* Ball, sponsored by the Atlanta Junior League, at the city auditorium. While Gable, Leigh, and de Havilland wore evening clothes, the rest of the cast arrived in costumes from the film. As the audience found their seats, a local orchestra played southern melodies, including "My Old Kentucky Home," "Carry Me Back to Old Virginny," "Old Folks at Home," and, of course, a rousing rendition of "Dixie." Onstage, with a large façade of a white-columned southern mansion as a backdrop, a choir from the city's African American Ebenezer Baptist Church performed spirituals such as "I Want to Walk With Jesus" and "Come Along, Children, and Be Baptized."

Master of Ceremonies Clark Howell Jr., publisher of the *Atlanta Constitution* and dressed as Dr. Meade, paid tribute to Mitchell, explaining that she was at home conserving her strength for the following night's premiere. He then introduced the stars and special guests, each of whom stood and waved as spotlights picked them out in their box seats. When Howell announced, "And now, Miss Olivia de Havilland," the light swung to Box G—but the actress was not in her seat. There was scattered, hesitant applause and then a steady buzz of whispers. Suddenly, from the back of the auditorium boomed the voice of Police Captain Jack Malcolm: "Clear the way." A smaller voice shouted, "Here I come!" The audience turned, and the applause grew louder as they realized what was happening. Somehow, in assigning automobiles and escorts for the ball, de Havilland was overlooked. By the time she went down to the lobby, her fellow cast members had left. The hotel's night auditor, a bachelor named Edmund Miller who lived at the Georgian Terrace, summoned a car and driver and escorted her himself. As the police captain cleared a path, he lifted the actress up to Olivier, who gracefully pulled her into the box. De Havilland took several bows for that performance.[9] Howell introduced Leigh by noting that her last name "is pronounced our way" and drew appreciative laughter and cheers when he welcomed Gable "in Junior League fashion" as "Mr. Carole Lombard."[10] As bandleader Kay Kyser and his orchestra took the stage, hundreds of chairs were removed from the main floor. Shortly after 11:00, a grand march began, led by Margaret Palmer, one of Atlanta's debutantes chosen to model the green-sprigged gown Scarlett wore to the Twelve Oaks barbecue. The stars began slipping out and returning to the hotel, but the other guests stayed and danced the night away.

* * *

Premiere day, Friday, December 15, dawned cold. The front pages of the city's newspapers trumpeted, "Rhett Butler at Five Points" and "300,000 Screaming Fans Acclaim Gable in Wildest Welcome in City's History."* Each paper produced a special *Gone With the Wind* souvenir edition, and state and city employees enjoyed a governor-declared holiday. Mitchell,

---

* Five Points is an intersection in downtown Atlanta where several other streets come together at Peachtree Street.

who had stayed quietly in the background the previous two days, had a full schedule on tap.

While Selznick, Gable, Lombard, Leigh, and de Havilland visited the Cyclorama, the city's famed circular painting of the Battle of Atlanta, the other actors attended a "Christmas at Tara" luncheon hosted by the Atlanta Better Films Committee. At the same time, Mitchell was honored at a lunch at Rich's. In attendance were representatives of The Macmillan Company and two other southern Pulitzer Prize–winning novelists, Marjorie Kinnan Rawlings, who wrote *The Yearling*, and Julia Peterkin, author of *Scarlet Sister Mary*. As the meal began, someone pulled Mitchell's chair out for her just as she sat down, and the author tumbled to the floor, injuring her back. Later that afternoon, a doctor taped the sprain so she could continue with the day's events.[11]

After the Cyclorama tour, Selznick and Gable stopped by the governor's mansion, where both men were named honorary colonels. The governor then threw the switch to light up the annual Christmas display of Santa Claus and his reindeer rising from the lawn to the roof of the mansion. Mitchell returned to her apartment and then went across the street to the Piedmont Driving Club, where the Atlanta Women's Press Club was hosting its exclusive cocktail party. There, the author finally met her Rhett Butler. Mitchell and Gable stepped into a private dining room and chatted briefly; the actor later told reporters that she was "the most fascinating woman I've ever met."[12] By 6:00, the guests began returning to their homes or their hotel rooms to prepare for the culmination of the week, when Atlantans, after three and a half years, would see what Hollywood had done with their story.

The Selznicks came to Mitchell's apartment in a limousine to escort the author and her husband to the theater. (Brown originally suggested that she and John Hay Whitney do the honors, but the producer apparently overruled her.)[13] Mitchell wore a full-length white velvet coat decorated with gold and silver threads and carried a corsage of camellias from the producer.* After the short drive downtown, she stepped out of the car, blinking at the harsh glare of spotlights and flashbulbs. Five antiaircraft searchlights cut through the night skies and played across the front of the theater; the beams of light reportedly could be seen fifty miles away. At the urging of Master of Ceremonies Julian Boehm, a prominent Atlanta insurance executive, Mitchell stopped before the microphones to speak to the large crowd of spectators outside and to those listening by radio across

---

* The coat is in the collection of the Atlanta History Center.

the nation: "This is a very happy and exciting day for me, and at this time, I want to thank everybody in Atlanta for being so nice to me and my poor Scarlett. Thank you." Selznick, still hopeful of the South's approval, came next: "Three years of effort have led to this moment. If Atlanta, which is the final judge, approves our efforts, these labors will not have been in vain." The two couples made their way into the theater as Gable and Lombard arrived. The actor paid tribute to the woman he had met just hours before: "Ladies and gentlemen, tonight, I'm here just as a spectator. I want to see *Gone With the Wind* the same as you do. And this is Margaret Mitchell's night, and the people of Atlanta's night. Allow me, please, to see *Gone With the Wind* as a spectator. Thank you."[14]

Most of those lucky enough to have snared tickets had taken their seats by the time the last of the celebrities arrived. As Mitchell and Marsh walked down the aisle, the audience broke into applause. The couple was seated next to Whitney, and to his right were de Havilland and Myron Selznick. When Gable and Lombard entered, they were seated on the other side of Marsh, along with Mayor Hartsfield and his daughter. Leigh, Governor Rivers, Irene Selznick, and Colbert were in front of them, while Olivier was relegated to a seat several rows back.*

The lights dimmed. Composer Max Steiner's overture began, and the curtains parted. From the opening shot of the colonial façade of the Selznick studio, the applause was tremendous. The crowd roared its approval when the frame reading "Margaret Mitchell's Story of the Old South" appeared, followed by the sweeping title, each word filling the screen as the letters seemed to blow across the stage while the lush "Tara's Theme" swelled on the sound track. The mood of the audience was light as Scarlett O'Hara, the belle of the county, flirted and schemed her way through the opening scenes—and met her match in Rhett Butler. At the Atlanta Bazaar, when Dr. Meade announced that General Robert E. Lee had "completely whipped the enemy" and swept the Yankee army from Virginia, the cheers in the theater drowned out those on-screen. As the tide of war turned, quiet gasps and sobs could be heard as Scarlett searched for the doctor among the expanse of wounded Confederate soldiers at the depot. At intermission, Keyes recalled, the crowd was hushed, emotionally drained, and moved as if in slow motion.[15] As the lights went down and Steiner's entr'acte began, the

---

* It is not known where David Selznick sat. No photographs of the producer inside the theater have surfaced, although a couple of photos show two empty aisle seats in the row in front of Mitchell. It has been suggested Selznick watched the film from the projection booth to ensure that everything ran smoothly, viewed it from the back of the auditorium to gauge the audience's reaction, or even paced in the lobby, nervously smoking cigarettes.

audience quietly settled in for the second half. When the word "Sherman!" flashed on the screen, they hissed "like a pit of angered snakes," said Henry McLemore of United Press International. And when Scarlett shot the Yankee deserter on the stairs at Tara, the cheers shook the theater's roof.[16] The story moved quickly, as Scarlett married Frank Kennedy to save Tara and then, after his death, accepted Rhett's marriage proposal, which finally gave her the money and security she longed for. Their beloved daughter Bonnie's tragic fall from her pony, followed by Melanie's moving deathbed scene, brought the film to its dramatic conclusion well after midnight. When Rhett walked out the door with his declaration that he didn't give a damn, Scarlett collapsed on the stairs of their Atlanta mansion, seemingly defeated. But she was roused by the voices of her father, of Ashley and of Rhett, who reminded her of her love for Tara. As the camera moved in on her tear-stained face, she vowed to think about it tomorrow, and the scene dissolved to Scarlett silhouetted against a sunrise at Tara while the music swelled to a crescendo. The audience rose to its feet with a thunderous ovation to pay tribute to the woman who had told their story and to the man who had brought old Atlanta to life on the silver screen.

Boehm called the mayor to the stage. Hartsfield, in turn, invited each of the visiting actors and the producer to join him and take a bow. He then turned to the woman of the hour—Margaret Mitchell.

Hartsfield: And now, I'm going to ask, and I do hope she'll come. I think this is going to be her first public appearance, if she'll do it. How many of you want her to really come down?

[Applause]

Well, you seem to know who I'm talking about. But wait a minute now. I want Rhett Butler—in other words, I want Mr. Clark Gable, and his very beautiful, charming wife, Mrs. Clark Gable—to act as a committee to bring down here Atlanta's own Mrs. John Marsh, Margaret Mitchell.

[Applause]

Yes, she's coming—

[Sustained applause as Mitchell, escorted by Gable and Lombard, makes her way to the stage]

Now—

[Mitchell laughs nervously as the height of the stage microphone is adjusted for her four-foot, eleven-inch frame]

Now, she's really going to speak to you.

[Applause]

Mitchell: *I think everybody who knows me—and I'm sure about three-quarters of the people here do know me—know that I'm not any speaker, and so please excuse me if I stumble through what I'm gonna say.* It's something that's been in my heart since the first month my book was published, and that is: I want to say "thank you," for me and for my poor Scarlett, for all the grand things that everybody here has done—the taxi drivers, the librarians, the bankers, the Junior League, the girls behind the counters, the boys in the filling stations. What could I have done—and my Scarlett—without their kindness and their helpfulness?*

You know, everybody thinks it's just when you're dead broke and you're out of luck that you need friends, but, really, when you have as incredible success as I've had, that's really when you need friends. And, thank Heaven, I've had 'em! And I've appreciated everything the Atlanta people and Atlanta's papers have done for me to be kind to me and to my Scarlett.

And now, I think all of you can understand that this picture was a great emotional experience to me. I know that fan magazines speak of lots of pictures as being that, but to me it is a great experience. I think it was heartbreaking, and I know I'm not the only person that's got a dripping wet handkerchief.

[Laughter]

And I'm not the only person I heard secretly blowing their nose, and mine wasn't so secret!

[Laughter]

I feel like it's been a very great thing for Georgia and the South to see our old Confederacy come back to us. I felt that way all this week, and I was practically giving the Rebel yell tonight.

[Laughter]

It isn't up to me to speak of the grand things these actors have done, 'cause they've spoken so much more eloquently than I could ever do, but I want to

---

* On December 19, Latham wrote to Mitchell, "Your appearance before the microphone was just right. It brought a lump in the throat of this hardened old sinner." However, in a January 5, 1940, letter to a New York agent interested in representing Mitchell on a speaking tour, the editor wrote, "She really is a very shy little person, she hates public appearances, and she does not speak with any assurance. I heard her speak publicly for the first time in Atlanta in connection with the premiere, and I was sorry for her."

speak just a minute about Mr. David Selznick. He's the man that every one of you all cracked that joke about: "Oh, well, we'll wait till Shirley Temple grows up and she'll play Scarlett."

[Laughter]

I want to commend Mr. Selznick's courage and his obstinacy and his determination in just keeping his mouth shut till he got the exact cast he wanted, in spite of everything everybody said. And I think you all will agree with me, he had the absolutely perfect cast. *[17]

---

* In an article in the December 17 *Atlanta Journal*, "Seeing 'GWTW' Picture Was an 'Experience' to Margaret Mitchell," Medora Perkerson quoted the author as "telling friends" that Gable's Rhett "seemed to grow as the story progressed. At the end he was a mature character, not too cynical, no longer impetuous. Clark Gable was the character in my story as I wrote it." She also was quoted as saying, "Vivien Leigh was my Scarlett, and Olivia de Havilland gave me my Melanie as I never hoped for. The whole cast was perfect. I love all my characters and I could ask no more." And of Hattie McDaniel, Mitchell said, "The scene in which Mammy walked up the stairs with Melanie after Bonnie's death was one of the finest I ever saw."

CHAPTER Six

Atlanta's Night, America's Film

1939 (December)–1940

The movie people were all charming and the Atlanta people who
met them fell in love with them. . . . The crowds on the streets were
larger than those which greeted Lindbergh and President Roosevelt,
yet everything was so orderly and well-bred and people did not mob
the stars or try to snatch off their buttons for souvenirs. I was
so proud of the town I nearly burst.

—*Margaret Mitchell to Lillian Harding*
March 26, 1940

Hattie McDaniel	*Atlanta, Georgia*
Los Angeles, California	*December 16, 1939*

THE PREMIERE AUDIENCE LOVED YOU AND SO DID I. THE
MAYOR OF ATLANTA CALLED FOR A HAND FOR OUR HATTIE
MCDANIEL AND I WISH YOU COULD HAVE HEARD THE CHEERS.
CONGRATULATIONS.

The Honorable William B. Hartsfield	*Atlanta, Georgia*
Office of the Mayor, City Hall	*December 16, 1939*
Atlanta, Georgia	

My dear Mayor Hartsfield:

I was glad to have the opportunity last night to congratulate you on
the wonderful way you planned and directed the "Gone With the Wind"
festival, but I want to say it again in this more formal way.

You have done a great thing for Atlanta in handling an event of such magnitude with such smoothness, without a single jarring note in the whole celebration. It was wonderful, and I know it could not have come to pass without your forethought, your planning, your supervision, your leadership. I was glad to see how Atlanta showed to the world that it could do big things, but I was especially happy about the fine spirit that was manifested everywhere. You know how proud of Atlanta I am, but I was never prouder than this week when Atlanta people showed how kindly, friendly, courteous and considerate they are.

Everyone is grateful to you for leading us through the big experience so successfully. I am grateful, too—for that, and for adding the final touch of perfection to my happiness last night by presenting me the beautiful roses on behalf of the City of Atlanta. Your gracious words in presenting them will always remain in my memory.

Chief M.A. Hornsby   *Atlanta, Georgia*
Atlanta Police Department   *December 16, 1939*
Atlanta, Georgia

Dear Chief Hornsby:

It is with great pride in you and Atlanta's police force, that I add my congratulations to those of hundreds of others you must have received. You and your men did a wonderful job during our "Gone With the Wind" festival. Confronted with unprecedented crowds, with traffic tangles, with rerouted automobiles, street cars and buses, your problems must have seemed insurmountable. But everything went off as smoothly as if you and the force handled such affairs every day. The officers were so efficient and so courteous that they contributed much to the success of the whole celebration. It made me feel so proud when I heard Atlanta's famous guests comment so enthusiastically on the manner in which you handled things.

My husband told me of your assurance to him that you and your men would take good care of me. As you know, everything went perfectly, and I am most grateful to you and to the men who escorted me to and from the theatre. I was unable to get their names and I hope you will thank them for me.

Major Clark Howell, Jr.   *Atlanta, Georgia*
The Atlanta Constitution   *December 16, 1939*
Atlanta, Georgia

My dear Major:

Thank you—and the Constitution—for so many things. For the kind support you have given my book ever since it was published, for the wonderful things written about me during Atlanta's "Gone With the Wind" festival. I hope you and the staff of the Constitution realize that when I said briefly, at the premiere, that I thanked the Atlanta papers for their kind friendliness, I was speaking from my heart and speaking inadequately, I am afraid.

I am grateful to you not only for what was written about me but for the fine consideration you showed me in the weeks preceding the premiere when I was ill and fearful that I might not recover my strength in time for last night's big event. But for your understanding—and that of the other Atlanta papers—during that trying time, I doubt that I would have been able to see the picture. I cannot tell you how grateful I am.

On Thursday night I lay in bed and listened to the radio program from the Junior League ball. As I heard your voice giving details with a vividness that brought the whole scene to me, I had a great feeling of personal sorrow that your father was not present. He would have been so proud of you, so proud of Atlanta's splendid festival, so proud of the expert handling of all the week's events. He loved this town so much and did so much to make it what it is. I wish he had been spared to see this town's big party.*

I wanted to tell the Constitution folks individually of my great appreciation of all they have done for me, but it may be some time before I can see them or write them, as I need a rest and must get away on my trip. Won't you please tell them for me? Ralph McGill, Ralph Jones, Mr. Hine, Willard Cope, Lamar Ball, the Society Department, the photographers, and all the others, were so very good to me in what they wrote. I shall never be able to thank them enough.

Mr. John Paschall
The Atlanta Journal
Atlanta, Georgia

Atlanta, Georgia
December 16, 1939

Dear Mr. Paschall:

Before I go away for a little rest I must thank you and the Journal for many things. I am supposed to be good at finding words to put in the mouths of my characters but I find it difficult now to choose the right words for myself. Perhaps it is because I feel so deeply about what you and the Journal have done for me.

I had not intended to speak a piece at the premiere but when I stood there with the cast and Mayor Hartsfield, with the spotlight blinding me, it came over me suddenly that now, if ever, was the opportunity I had longed

---

* Howell's father, the owner and Pulitzer Prize–winning editor of the *Constitution* for nearly forty years, died in 1936.

for, to say "thank you" to everyone. And last, and highest, on my list were the Atlanta newspapers. I'm sure the audience thought I meant thanks for all the wonderful things that had been written about my book. Yes, I meant that, but my most heartfelt thanks were to you personally for your good advice to me recently, and the consideration and forbearance you and the paper showed me during the week or so before the premiere. But for the breathing spell you and the other Atlanta papers gave me, it is doubtful that I would have been able to attend the premiere at all. I was ill and weak, and exhausted by the frenzied demands made on me for tickets, for advice on parties and costumes and displays and hotel reservations. If I had had to go through photographs and interviews by the press, at that time, I would never have had the strength to get to the theatre last night. Thank you for making it possible for me to be at the premiere—to be there happy, excited and grateful.

I have seen today's Journal and, good Heavens, I am really overcome! The affectionate perjury of everyone who wrote about me makes me feel both humble and proud. I hope they know of my gratitude, Medora, Frank, C.B., Robert McKee, Ruth Raine, Susan Jones, Louise Mackay, Pete Craig, Jake Carlton, Ralph Smith, the photographers and all the others on the staff who wrote such wonderful things.

Mr. W.S. Kirkpatrick   *Atlanta, Georgia*
The Atlanta Georgian   *December 16, 1939*
Decatur, Georgia

Dear Mr. Kirkpatrick:

This letter is written in sadness—and in gratitude—to you and to the Georgian. I am sad because I feel as if an old friend had died when the Georgian died.* I am grateful for all the past kindnesses I have received at your and the Georgian's hands. In particular, I want to thank you and the staff for the wonderful things written about me during the "Gone With the Wind" festival. I have certainly been blessed with good friends and I was thinking of such friends as you and the Georgian staff when I spoke my piece at the premiere last night and thanked the Atlanta newspapers.

I am grateful for what the Georgian said about me. I am grateful, too, for the kindness and the understanding you showed me during the two weeks before the premiere. I was ill and harassed by many things and if you and Mr. Paschall and Major Howell and Mr. Caldwell had not been so

---

* On December 12, James M. Cox—former Ohio governor, 1920 Democratic candidate for president, and owner of the *Dayton Daily News* and the *Miami News*—purchased the city's two afternoon newspapers, the *Atlanta Journal* and the *Atlanta Georgian*. Cox announced that he was closing the *Georgian*, and its final edition was printed December 18.

considerate of me at that time I probably would never have gained strength to attend the premiere. I thank you so very much.

John, as a former Georgian reporter, has been very depressed about the breaking up of your fine organization and he joins me in good wishes for each of you. As their names call themselves over in my mind—Dudley, Tarleton, Jimmy Burns, Ed Danforth, Paul Stevenson, Harold Martin, Cliff Fligg, Tom Ripley, Pauline Branyon, the society department, the photographers and all the others—I am impressed again by your ability to assemble a truly remarkable staff. It seems tragic that they will never function together again.

Mr. W.F. Caldwell   *Atlanta, Georgia*
The Associated Press   *December 16, 1939*
Atlanta, Georgia

Dear Mr. Caldwell:

I owe so much of my happiness at the premiere of "Gone With the Wind" to your understanding and considerate attitude. In fact, I probably would not have been at the premiere at all except for you and the Atlanta editors. But for your patience and forbearance in the week before the picture, I might not have had the strength to attend the opening.

As an ex-reporter I understand as well the needs of the A.P. for statements from me, pictures, interviews et cetera. Because I am an ex-reporter, I am doubly grateful for your consideration, for it gave me the opportunity I needed to build up my strength for Friday night.

I could not pick you out of the crowd at the premiere, but I hope you were there and heard my public thanks to the press for their kindness to me. I am sure most of the audience thought I was speaking of the columns about me and my book which have been written recently. Of course, I meant that, for I have felt humbly grateful to the hometown papers and to you for your generosity. But I was speaking especially to you and Mr. Paschall and Major Howell and Mr. Kirkpatrick—thanking you for the consideration which made it possible for me to attend the premiere and to attend it with such tremendous happiness.

Mrs. W. Colquitt Carter   *Atlanta, Georgia*
Atlanta, Georgia   *December 16, 1939*

Dear Mrs. Carter:

Last night, after the premiere, I saw Irene Warren and some of the other members of the Junior League, and I had the pleasure of telling them how proud I was of all of them for the way they handled the ball. Now I want to say the same thing—and more—to you, the president.

I believe I am in a position to judge and evaluate the League's accomplishments better than most people, for I was in the thick of the whole premiere festival and I heard reports and comments and "inside stuff" from hundreds of people, both League members and people not connected with the organization. I know how long the League worked and how hard; I know the plans that went wrong and had to be abandoned for other and better plans; I know the almost unbearable pressure brought to bear on your members for tickets that were not obtainable. Only Junior Leaguers will fully realize what I mean by that last—but I know what all of you went through when it seemed that the whole world wanted to come to your party—and there wasn't room in our Auditorium for the wide, wide world.

You did a great thing for the League and a great thing for Atlanta. Thank you for saying that I helped you. You know I didn't but it was fine of you to say that I did. My small contribution was in putting the League in touch with the right people and the League did the rest.

I'll never have a disappointment so great as I had in missing the League's ball. I lay in bed and listened to it over the radio and thought that few people ever had so hard a choice to make—to go to the ball and miss the premiere, or go to the premiere and miss the ball. Forgive me if I chose the premiere. I had to be there—and I did not have strength for both.

Mr. Harold Martin   *Atlanta, Georgia*
Atlanta, Georgia   *December 16, 1939*

Dear Harold:

Thank you for the fine and flattering things you wrote about me in your premiere story. Thank you, too, for including John's remark. I didn't hear it and he didn't tell me and, but for your story, I'd have missed it.* And I wouldn't have missed it for a pretty. You were so very kind to me and I am grateful.

Mr. O.B. Keeler   *Atlanta, Georgia*
Atlanta, Georgia   *December 16, 1939*

Dear O.B.:

Thanks for what you wrote about me at the premiere. And what thoughts were in my head then? I was thinking that I was the most fortu-

---

* In his article in the *Georgian* on December 16, "Premiere Thrills Gala Throng: Author Paid Emotional Tribute," Martin reported that a radio announcer stopped Marsh outside the theater and asked, "Aren't you proud of your wife?" The author's husband replied, "I was proud of her long before she wrote a book."

nate woman in the world and my mind wasn't on "G.W.T.W." either. I was thinking about the friends who had been so good to me—as you have been.

Love to you and Nelly—

Mr. George Cukor   Atlanta, Georgia
Selznick International Pictures, Inc.   January 9, 1940
Culver City, California

Dear George:

Thanks so much for your Christmas telegram—which we have just received. Immediately after the "Gone With the Wind" premiere, John and I went away on a vacation—which we needed!

The premiere was exciting and fine, of course, but we did miss you. You were almost our first contact with the movies—and a most pleasant one—so we naturally had you and the film linked up together in our minds. It seemed strange not having you here with us at the "birthing."

I know Atlanta lies outside the line of travel for movie people but John and I hope some day you'll get back here and pay us a visit unhampered by frenzied aspirants for the part of Scarlett.

With cordial good wishes from both of us.

Colonel Telamon Cuyler   Atlanta, Georgia
Wayside, Jones County, Georgia   January 9, 1940

My dear Colonel Cuyler:

As you know, John and I went away immediately after the premiere and were away during the holidays. When I returned and opened the Christmas package you sent me I could scarcely believe my eyes. "Battles and Leaders," and for my very own and from you!* The beautiful and poetic page you wrote and pasted in the front of the first volume touched me and made me feel very humble. How kind and generous you are to me and how I wish I had a dozen different ways to say "thank you." I sat up most of the night looking them over, examining first the pages in which you have inserted red paper markers. I have never seen "Battles and Leaders" in this original dress. (I take it that the paper covers *are* the original dress.) The volumes I read as a child and which I consulted in later years were unwieldy and bound in dark cloth—four volumes, I believe. Were they originally brought out in paper and then bound, or were some issued in paper covers and others in stiff backs?

Didn't Atlanta do itself proud at the premiere? I can realize the real magnitude of the affair now that I have a little perspective. While it was

---

* *Battles and Leaders of the Civil War*, edited by Robert Underwood Johnson and Clarence Clough Buel, was published in thirty-two paperback volumes beginning in 1887.

going on, and for three months beforehand, I was so beset by people who thought I could get tickets for them, by influenza and by a thousand harassments that I hardly had time to think about what was actually going on. Now I am so proud of the town! I have one very happy memory of the premiere itself—you standing in the theatre foyer. You looked so distinguished and so appropriately a part of the occasion.

Mr. W.T. Anderson   *Atlanta, Georgia*
Macon Telegraph Publishing Co.   *January 9, 1940*
Macon, Georgia

Dear Mr. W.T.:

John and I wish so much that it were possible for us to be at the Macon premiere of "Gone With the Wind." We feel that it would be a doubly enjoyable occasion—first, because it will do honor to Sue for her wonderful work and, second, because we would have none of the responsibility and very little of the limelight. But we just can't make it. Sue told us it would probably not be held until sometime after the 20th of this month and at that time I will not be able to come to Macon. Sue will tell you why.* We are both more disappointed than you can know and we wish so much that the Macon opening was this week.

I told Sue that the sincerest compliment her work received was that practically no one mentioned the Southern accents of the actors. As you will recall the thousands of columns written in Southern newspapers during the last three years about how impossible it was to make non-Southerners sound like Southerners, this is indeed an incredible state of affairs. When I prodded people for their opinions about the accents they said, "What accents? They talked just like us." Leslie Howard's accent was the only one which came in for any remarks, but no one was very bothered about it. I think the South owes Sue a very great debt for her work in Hollywood.

Mr. Sam Kendrick   *Atlanta, Georgia*
The Associated Press   *January 9, 1940*
Boston, Massachusetts

Dear Mr. Kendrick:

You were the one who sent me the AP wirephotos, weren't you? The note which accompanied them was unsigned but my Hawkshaw instinct

---

* The Macon premiere of *Gone With the Wind* was held January 28 at the city's Grand Theatre, with Myrick as guest of honor. Mitchell, who was recovering from abdominal surgery two weeks earlier, sent a telegram of greeting, as did Selznick, Gable, Leigh, and de Havilland.

tells me it was you. Thank you so very much for them. Thank you especially for putting in three of the photographs of Miss Leigh, Mr. Gable and me. I am going to give the photograph of Mildred Hartsfield in the old fashioned dress to Miss Hartsfield, and I know she will be as pleased as I am.*

When, many months ago, Atlanta began planning for the "Gone With the Wind" premiere, we had no idea that it would turn out to be such a magnificent affair. We knew it would be lots of fun for the home town but we did not dream that it would excite so much interest all over the country and attract to Atlanta so many prominent and celebrated people. What pleased everyone the most (and the moving picture people especially) were the good manners of everyone. The crowds were cordial and enthusiastic but no one tried to snatch buttons and orchids from the stars and, by heroic self-control, people refrained from even asking for autographs, with a few exceptions.

I would have acknowledged your pictures before this, but immediately after the premiere John and I went away on our vacation. I had had influenza shortly before the premiere and was very tired before it was over. We both got a fine rest and have just returned.

Mr. and Mrs. Clark Gable   *Atlanta, Georgia*
Care MGM Pictures   *January 10, 1940*
Hollywood, California

Dear Mr. and Mrs. Gable:

My long delay in acknowledging the chickens you sent us at Christmas time is not due to lack of appreciation. John and I managed to get away on the trip we've been promising ourselves for so long and there wasn't time to write. Thank you so much for the gift—and my father and brother and his wife thank you, too, for I gave them one of the chickens. Father has been ill for several months, was too ill to attend the premiere, and having one of the Clark Gable chickens did him a world of good.†

---

* Mildred Hartsfield, the mayor's daughter, attended the premiere events with her father and sat beside Gable at the ball.

† Gable and Lombard, who lived on a small ranch in the San Fernando Valley, shipped the author four dressed hens on dry ice, along with a note that read, "Some chickens from the farm, to tempt you to come out & visit us." The package arrived on December 22, after Mitchell and her husband had left town, so the author's secretary kept one and gave the others to Mitchell's father, brother, and housekeeper. In an article, "Two Happy People," in the May 1940 issue of *Movie and Radio Guide*, James Street reported that Lombard was "quite proud of her selection of a gift for Margaret Mitchell, who did *Gone With the Wind*—unquestionably her husband's greatest picture. She knew Miss Mitchell (Mrs. John Marsh) is not the kind of person to whom you send an ordinary gift. So when she and her husband returned

Before I go any further I must thank you, Mr. Gable, for something you said (or the newspapers said you said). Perhaps you did not say, as you left Atlanta, that I was "fascinating," but the papers credited it to you and, my, how my stock has gone up! People think it's all very well for me to have written "Gone With the Wind," but, after all, there are lots of books, but to have Clark Gable make such a statement—well, that's a different matter and people look at me with becoming respect. Even my best friends look at me in a speculative way—probably wondering what they overlooked that your sharp eyes saw! I am feminine enough to be quite charmed by such a statement and I thank you.

I know it was a great strain on both of you to come to Atlanta, to face crowds roaring welcome and flashlights every other minute and people who probably said foolish things with the very best of intentions.* It must have been a strain, being whisked here and there with no chance to relax, and I have an idea that probably neither of you looked forward to it with any pleasure. But you did come and you carried off an unprecedented situation with such grace and charm and warm humanness, and I hope you are getting some satisfaction out of the great happiness you gave to many thousands here in Atlanta. For that is what you two did. You didn't know us but everyone felt that they knew you. They'd seen you both on the screen and they welcomed you for your past performances. But especially they knew you, Mr. Gable, as Rhett, whom they had read about and talked about. It wasn't just ordinary neck-craning curiosity that brought thousands onto chilly streets to stand for hours. It was an honest feeling of welcome to someone they knew and knew very well, who, after all, *belonged* to Atlanta. And the town took great pride that you came to see us.

When the picture was over, I couldn't tell you what was in my mind. I had been too moved by it all. I don't know if I could tell you now what I think, for I still have not accustomed myself to the idea of Rhett coming to life and looking at me from the screen. But I do want to say that I've seen practically all of your pictures since "Night Nurse" and I think this is by far the best work you have ever done.† I know I would think that, even if I had not written the book. There was something that I can only describe

---

from Atlanta . . . Mrs. Gable sent four fat chickens to Mrs. Marsh. Of course, sending chickens from California to Georgia is something like sending coal to Newcastle. But anyway, it was an original idea."

* Mitchell was referring to photographers' flashbulbs.

† *Night Nurse*, starring Barbara Stanwyck, was one of Gable's earliest films. He played a brutish chauffeur in the 1931 release by Warner Bros.

as "maturity" in your acting, especially in the last half of the film. Perhaps that word doesn't mean the same thing to you as it means to me, but I can find no other word.

Incidentally, I was surprised at the statements of some of the reviewers that the first half of the film was the best part. I thought the latter part was much better, because of the better rounded character development and because of your fine acting and Miss Leigh's.*

I am sending you as a souvenir of your visit a copy of the Danish translation of "Gone With the Wind." It is illustrated and it is obvious that the artist had you in mind, especially in the bazaar picture. As this translation was published long before you were announced for Rhett, you can see that even the Danes wanted you!

You are both so kind to ask us to come to Hollywood and see your ranch. Neither of us has ever been to California but sometime, when the Big Wind has finally blown itself out, we may come. But we would not be coming to see the famous Carole Lombard and Clark Gable. John and I both liked you as people, two very fine and real people, and it would be a pleasure for us to see you again.

Miss Vivien Leigh   *Atlanta, Georgia*
Selznick International Pictures, Inc.   *January 10, 1940*
Culver City, California

Dear Miss Leigh:

I've been wanting to write to you ever since the Atlanta premiere but John and I went away on our first vacation and have just returned. First, I want to take up the letter you wrote to me on December 14th, after receiving the two-volume edition of "Gone With the Wind." (How I do wish it were on rag paper and set in better type! If ever such a set should appear, be certain I will send it to you.) In your letter you asked if you could send me the set at some later date for an autograph. I realize that when I say I cannot autograph it, I must sound very rude. It seems a small favor to do

---

* Marsh's opinion of Gable changed after seeing the film. As the author's husband wrote to his family in January 1940, he and Mitchell picked up on the actor's tension at the premiere. "He was so anxious for the thing to be a success, and we couldn't keep our minds on the picture for wanting to tell him, 'There, there, Captain Butler!' If that sounds funny, try to imagine yourself sitting next to a man who had staked his career, almost, on that one role, while the film was having its premiere before the audience whose good opinion mattered most of any in the world. It was not a kindly thing to seat him next to us, or us next to him. And when it was over, we were truly happy that we could tell him, honestly, that we liked his work. It is at least ten times better than any other job he has ever done."

for someone whose acting gave me such sheer delight, but autographing is the one thing I do not do.

This is my situation. I have not given an autograph since 1936. At the time the sales of "Gone With the Wind" had rocketed up to the million mark within six months, and the requests for autographs were in proportion. Books were dumped on me through the mail in scores, people came to the door from early dawn till long past midnight. It wasn't that I didn't appreciate the interest people showed in the book. No one will ever know how amazed and how humbly grateful I've been to the public for the reception they gave "Gone With the Wind." But the truth is that for months I had no time to eat uninterruptedly, to sleep, to visit my family, to see my friends. So, three years ago, I swore off autographing. Since then, I have not even inscribed copies belonging to relatives and close friends.* I realized that I couldn't pick and choose and that if I did autograph a copy for one person, I had to do it for all of that person's friends.

I hope you will believe me when I say there is no one for whom I'd rather do this favor than you who brought Scarlett to life in a way that left me shaken and almost speechless. But I just can't do it. I hope you'll understand.

John and I got great satisfaction and happiness from the pleasant visit you paid us that night. It was good of you to come. I knew you must have been weary; certainly you had been under an enormous strain that day, with all the crowds and the flashlights and no time to relax. But you were as sweet and charming as if you'd lived around the corner from us all your life and had just run in for a visit.

I've read the New York papers about the opening there, and with much pleasure. Everyone in Atlanta was pleased, too. Part of our satisfaction, perhaps, came from that natural human feeling of superiority. "We saw her first and we thought she was wonderful." But Atlanta was also happy for your sake, for everyone genuinely liked you, both on the screen and off.

After the premiere, I suddenly felt wonderfully fine and wanted to celebrate, so John and I went to the Driving Club "breakfast," where it seemed that everyone who had attended the premiere had gathered to eat scrambled eggs and sausage. People came up to me with tears in their eyes, to tell me how greatly your Scarlett had moved them. They couldn't tell you, they

---

* Mitchell did make exceptions to her no-autograph rule. She added an inscription to Cole's first edition of *Gone With the Wind* on June 13, 1939, to mark the first birthday of her son: "And more—to my handsome and beloved god-son, Turney Allan Taylor, Jr., from his doting godmother—Peggy." The author also signed numerous foreign-language editions of her novel for Latham, Brett, and others.

said, so they wanted me to know, and I am passing it on to you.* Everyone had his (or her) own opinion as to what was the best thing you did and there were violent arguments that lasted until dawn. Every spot of film in which you appeared had its strong supporters—and still has, for I can't get into an elevator without the operator asking me if I didn't think you were best when you shot the Yankee; taxi drivers insist that you were best in the "birthing" scenes; sales girls behind the counters say you broke their hearts when you came home to Tara; and ladies, young and old, boldly come out in favor of the bedroom scene. Atlanta will be talking for months. You see, we haven't changed much since the days of the Sixties—we are a little town, even if we are a big town, and we do love to talk things over!

When Mr. Olivier was here that night he intimated that you had plans which he could not divulge at the time and I suspected a play in which you would both appear. The New York papers carry a rumor that you will appear in a stage play. I never believe rumors but I do hope this one is true. John and I do not travel much, because we like to stay home, but we get to New York once or twice a year and I know we'd make a special trip to see you two.

My grateful thanks go to you for what you did to—and for—"my poor Scarlett." My good wishes for your success and happiness are sincere and not just a closing formality,

Editor's note: While Mitchell declined to sign Leigh's copy of Gone With the Wind, *the author enclosed a small piece of note paper on which she had written, "To Vivien Leigh,/'Life's pattern pricked with a scarlet thread/where once we work with a gray,/to remind us all how we played our parts/in the shock of an epic day'/Margaret Mitchell." The stanza is from the poem "The Revelation" by Robert W. Service.†*

Miss Alicia Rhett   *Atlanta, Georgia*
Charleston, South Carolina   *January 10, 1940*

Dear Miss Rhett:

I knew that sending an azalea to a Charlestonian was like carrying coals to New Castle but I couldn't find another pretty plant for you. Now that I learn from your letter that you carried it back to Charleston, I'm as proud as can be. In Charleston soil it will probably grow into a tree like the gorgeous azaleas which so delighted us when we went to Charleston to see the gardens.

---

* Leigh and Olivier left Atlanta for New York immediately after the screening.

† On February 8, Leigh replied, "I cannot tell you how much I appreciated your writing, and the verse, which I have placed in the lovely copy of *Gone With the Wind* you gave me." The whereabouts of Leigh's copy of the two-volume edition is not known.

You were kind to ask us to look you up should we come to Charleston again. We would like to do it and we hope we find you there when next we visit your city. It has been a great disappointment to us that we've been too busy to get there in recent years. Perhaps now that the premiere has come and gone, we'll have more time.

When I heard you were to appear in the film, I was delighted. I was so happy that a Southerner was to have a part. Katharine Brown and Susan Myrick and the Wilbur Kurtzes told me such fine things about you as a person and as an actress, and all they said, and more, came true on the screen. You have such genuine dignity, such controlled fire, strange things for one so young as you! I hope I am going to see you on the screen many, many more times.*

Mr. Robert C. Saltmarsh   *Atlanta, Georgia*
New Bedford, Massachusetts   *February 19, 1940*

Dear Mr. Saltmarsh:

There was no need for you to recall yourself and your 1936 letter to me; I remember it with too much pleasure to forget it. I have a good memory for handwriting and when I saw the address on your recent letter and the New Bedford postmark, I said to my husband, "I know this is a letter from Mr. Saltmarsh." (You see, my married name is Marsh and the association of names helped yours to stick in my mind.) And, sure enough, it was from you. Thank you so much for writing me again about the book and the picture, and thank you, too, for the hospitable invitation to visit which you sent us.

As to the invitation—it sounds most enticing but I do not know when we can accept it. I am just out of the hospital following an operation for abdominal adhesions and, while I have done extraordinarily well, my doctor wishes me to take things easily for a very long time—not so much because of the operation but because the last three and a half years have been strenuous ones and he thinks I need rest and quiet at home.

. . . I hope, now that the moving picture of "Gone With the Wind" has been released, my life will quiet down and during the next year I will be able to enjoy the normal things of life, such as traveling about in a leisurely manner.

Atlanta had a three-day celebration of the premiere of "Gone With the Wind." Everyone seemed to enjoy it very much and many people have gone to see the picture three or four times. It is finishing its tenth week here and

---

* *Gone With the Wind* was Rhett's only motion picture. She returned to Charleston and became a well-known portrait artist.

closing in a few days.* I hope to be able to see it again myself. I have read some of the New England papers about the picture and, while I had nothing to do with the production, I could not help feeling pleased that people outside of the South enjoyed it, too. . . .

David O. Selznick	*Atlanta, Georgia*
Selznick International Pictures, Inc.	*March 1, 1940*
Culver City, California	

I WAS SO HAPPY TO READ ABOUT YOUR BIG SWEEP OF THE AWARDS.† PLEASE GIVE MY CONGRATULATIONS TO THE INDIVIDUAL WINNERS AND TO ALL THE MEMBERS OF YOUR ORGANIZATION WHO HELPED TO MAKE GWTW A GREAT PICTURE.

Vivien Leigh	*Atlanta, Georgia*
Selznick International Pictures, Inc.	*March 1, 1940*
Culver City, California	

WE WERE HAPPY BUT NOT SURPRISED TO HEAR THAT YOU HAD WON THE ACADEMY AWARD. CONGRATULATIONS.

Mr. Harold Latham	*Atlanta, Georgia*
The Macmillan Company	*March 1, 1940*
New York, New York	

Dear Harold:

I was so sorry to learn from Lois that you had the flu. Someone had told me that you were in California and Medora and I and your other

---

* *Gone With the Wind*'s reserved-seat engagement ended at Loew's on February 24. An estimated 230,000 tickets were sold—many to repeat viewers, including the author and her husband. After seeing the film on January 12, Marsh told his family that the couple "liked it better than the first time. Seeing it quietly gave us the opportunity to notice many things which we missed entirely at the first showing." On March 1, the movie moved to the city's Rhodes Theatre, where it played an additional three weeks on a continuous-showing basis.

† *Gone With the Wind* was nominated for thirteen Academy Awards. On February 29, the film won eight, including Best Picture, Best Director (Fleming), Best Actress (Leigh), Best Supporting Actress (McDaniel), and Best Adapted Screenplay (Sidney Howard). McDaniel's award marked the first time an African American had been nominated let alone won. The film also received awards for art direction, color cinematography, and editing. Production designer William Cameron Menzies was given an honorary Oscar for his "use of color for the enhancement of dramatic mood" in the motion picture, and Selznick received the Irving G. Thalberg Memorial Award, presented for a body of work that reflects a "consistently high quality of motion picture production." Gable, nominated for Best Actor, lost to Robert Donat in *Goodbye, Mr. Chips*, and Max Steiner lost the award for Best Original Score to Herbert Stothart for *The Wizard of Oz*. An Oscar for costume design was not presented until 1949.

friends here were hoping you would visit us on your way back East. I hope you are taking plenty of time for your recovery. . . .

I've been home from the hospital several weeks now and have climbed down our stairs three times to go to the doctor's office. I've done so very well that I cannot complain if this stage of my convalescence is slow. I can't drive the car and I do not climb stairs easily and I cannot wear high heeled slippers. The doctor warned me that it would be six months before I would be completely strong again, but for once in my life I am not impatient because I feel a hundred per cent better than I did around the time of the premiere. Then it was a footrace between the premiere and the hospital.

After the premiere, when we were at the Driving Club and the crowd was so thick you could not get to our table, you stood up and waved to me and I thought, of all the strange things that had happened since we met in 1935, this was the most incredible. It is unbelievable enough that that untidy manuscript sold so well, but to have it make a famous moving picture that brought you and the other Macmillan folks to Atlanta was just too much for me to take in.

I was so very sorry I did not get to see more of you at that time—sorriest of all that I missed The Macmillan Company's cocktail party.* If I had known that I would be able to go to the Driving Club after the picture, I would have arranged for a party for all of us.

I wish you'd tell your mother how truly sorry John and I were that she could not come. I am so glad she liked the memorial cups. There were to have been a dozen each but, as it turned out, I was fortunate to get the few I did secure. The Historical Society had ordered them from Wedgwood in England and the members had put in their orders. Then the war came along and our orders were cut. I thought I had enough for myself and you three but, to my horror, I discovered two days before the premiere that Mayor Hartsfield had bought fifteen dozen from the Society to give to the movie people for souvenirs from the city. This left the members short, and there was squalling and outcrying from this member. I didn't know till I actually had my hands on them whether I could get any. If we manage to get others when the war is over I want to fill out the dozen for your mother. Please let me know what color they were. . . .

Harold, I hear many fascinating rumors about my activities at present. Word comes to me that, on the one hand, I have completed a sequel to "Gone With the Wind" and, on the other hand, that I am writing a murder mystery. (Probably I am being mixed with Medora.) I just wanted to tell

---

* Macmillan held an open house the afternoon of December 14 in George Brett's suite at the Georgian Terrace Hotel.

you, in case you heard these rumors, that there is no truth in them. While the actual showing of the picture has let off a lot of steam and diverted interest from me, the sale of the movie edition is rolling up a heavy mail and keeping alive a number of the problems which have kept me busy for three years, so there has not been an opportunity to think of writing.

I never thanked you for the box of books you sent while I was in the hospital, but I did appreciate them so much and they kept me busy and entertained. "How Green Was My Valley" is a beautiful book and I wondered if it was one of your discoveries.*

David O. Selznick   *Atlanta, Georgia*
Selznick International Pictures, Inc.   *March 2, 1940*
Culver City, California

YOU ARE AMAZINGLY GENEROUS IN OFFERING TO SEND ME THE TROPHY BUT I WOULD NOT THINK OF ACCEPTING IT. THE AWARD WAS NOT FOR NOVEL-WRITING BUT FOR MOVIE MAKING SO THE TROPHY'S PROPER PLACE IS WITH YOU.† NOBODY KNOWS BETTER THAN I DO HOW MANY DIFFICULTIES YOU HAD TO OVERCOME IN MAKING THE MOVIE AND I AM TRULY HAPPY AND PROUD TO SEE YOUR GREAT ACHIEVEMENT ACCLAIMED BY THE ACADEMY AND THE PUBLIC.

Mr. David O. Selznick   *Atlanta, Georgia*
Selznick International Pictures, Inc.   *March 6, 1940*
Culver City, California

Dear Mr. Selznick:

Thank you for letting me know of the rumor the Journal wired you about.‡ That was the first time I had heard of it. I have become somewhat

---

* *How Green Was My Valley*, by Richard Llewellyn, was published in the United States by Macmillan in 1940. The film version, directed by John Ford and starring Walter Pidgeon and Maureen O'Hara, was released in 1941 by Twentieth Century-Fox and won the Academy Award for Best Picture.

† On March 2, Selznick wired Mitchell that he was going to send her the Academy Award he won for Best Picture of 1939 because "without your great book there would have been no award." Nearly sixty years later, on December 15, 1999, the producer's Oscar statuette sold for $1.54 million at an auction at Sotheby's in New York; the buyer was entertainer Michael Jackson.

‡ When newspapers reported Selznick's offer to send Mitchell his Oscar, a rumor surfaced that the producer also planned to send her an additional $50,000 because of the film's great success.

toughened to strange rumors these past four years but, of course, they can be rather startling if they are sprung on a person unexpectedly. So, I am grateful to you for forewarning me about this new one.

I have waited twenty-four hours before answering your wire, so that I might perhaps, learn more of this rumor and pass it on to you. But no newspaper or news service has queried me and no friend or stranger has phoned or wired me about it. Frankly, I doubt that such a rumor is in wide circulation, for I believe I would have heard of it if it were. I hope you are not letting it worry you.

Now I want to thank you personally for the beautiful red roses you sent me while I was in the hospital. It was nice of you to think of me. I'm making a fine and leisurely recovery and will take things quietly for some months to come.

Please give our kindest regards to Mrs. Selznick.

David O. Selznick   *Atlanta, Georgia*
Selznick International Pictures, Inc.   *March 7, 1940*
Culver City, California

SUPPOSE YOU HAVE SEEN TIME MAGAZINE STORY THIS WEEK ABOUT ACADEMY AWARDS WHICH CREDITS YOU WITH SAYING YOU PLAN TO SEND CHECK TO ME. ATLANTA CONSTITUTION IS USING THIS FRIDAY AS A BASIS OF STORY WHICH IN THEIR NIGHT EDITION TONIGHT CARRIED FOLLOWING HEADLINE QUOTE PROFITS OF MOVIE TO BE SHARED BY MISS MITCHELL. SELZNICK SAYS HE WILL SEND EXTRA CHECK TO AUTHORESS UNQUOTE WHEN WE SAW THIS JOHN PHONED THEM AND THEY PROMISED TO TREAT IT AS RUMOR AND NOT POSITIVE FACT IN LATER EDITIONS HE ALSO TOLD THEM THIS WAS OUR FIRST KNOWLEDGE OF THE WHOLE MATTER AND WE PREFERRED NOT TO DISCUSS IT AT THIS STAGE. I AM SORRY YOU ARE BEING CAUSED THIS EMBARRASSMENT.

Mr. Walter Winchell   *Atlanta, Georgia*
New York Mirror   *March 15, 1940*
New York, New York

Dear Mr. Winchell:

Recently I have been caused considerable embarrassment by widespread circulation of rumors that Mr. Selznick was going to send me, or had already sent me, a "bonus" check because of the great success of the motion picture "Gone With the Wind," and also that he was sending me the Academy Award which he received. The rumor was published in various forms in newspapers and magazines but your column a few days ago made the flat and unqualified statement that the trophy and the money *had* been sent to me by Mr. Selznick. The enclosed story from this morning's Atlanta Constitution gives the facts, and I am writing to ask you to publish a correction. As you will note from the enclosed story, the award was offered me by Mr. Selznick but I declined it because I thought it properly belonged to him. No bonus check was sent or offered.

My difficulty during the period while the rumors were in circulation was that I was put into a false position. I knew that the rumors should be denied, but I felt that Mr. Selznick was the one to do this. As to the award, I regarded his offer of it to me as confidential unless he chose to make it public. As to the bonus, there was nothing I could say except that I had not received it, had not been notified that I would receive it, and had no intimation from Mr. Selznick that he was even thinking about sending it. This I stated to the newspapers in answer to their inquiries, but the public, nevertheless, continued to believe that I had received the bonus and was attempting to conceal it. Many people quoted you as their authority because of the unqualified statement you published that it had been sent to me. The result was about the same as if I had won the Irish Sweepstakes and I have received many offers of assistance in spending money which I had never received. Now that Mr. Selznick has stated that there is no basis for the bonus rumor, you will be doing me a great service if you will publish the correction. I feel that you owe this to me, as the public belief that I had actually received the bonus was based very largely on your unqualified statement that it *had* been sent to me.

Couldn't I get you to query me in the future about statements relating to me before you publish them? I spent several years as a newspaperwoman and I have an understanding of newspaper matters. Other columnists and writers will tell you that I make a practice of giving prompt answers to reasonable questions, and I believe that both of us would be better off if you *could* query me in the future before publishing rumors about me. A great many of them have gotten into circulation, for some reason or other, since "Gone With the Wind" was first published, and most of them are wrong.

Miss Nell Battle Lewis   *Atlanta, Georgia*
Raleigh News and Observer   *March 15, 1940*
Raleigh, North Carolina

Dear Miss Lewis:

At this late date I want to tell you how much I enjoyed your column which appeared last month after you had witnessed the film, "Gone With the Wind." The column was headed "Scarlett Materializes." Mrs. John Huske Anderson, of Raleigh, sent it to me and I enjoyed it so very much. I would have written you sooner to tell you what a fine column I thought it was, but at the time it arrived I was recovering from a trip to the hospital.

I was especially interested in your paragraph about the lack of applause when the Confederate battle flag was shown fluttering over the acres of wounded Confederate soldiers at the car shed. Here in Atlanta at the premiere there was a great deal of applause early in the picture, and later on where Scarlett shot the Yankee deserter on the stair the tense audience practically yelled. But during the scene you mentioned there was a deathly stillness, just as you noted in the Raleigh theatre. Afterwards a number of us were talking it over, each giving reasons why the audience had been so still. One man summed it up this way—"Have you ever felt like applauding in a Confederate cemetery on Memorial Day? No, you haven't; you feel something too deep for applause." I think he was on the right track. Had the Confederate flag been shown for the same length of time over a crowd of charging soldiers or even going down a dusty road in retreat, I think audiences would have yelled themselves hoarse. During that scene they probably felt as they do in a Confederate cemetery.

I'm so glad you mentioned the work Miss Susan Myrick, of Macon, did on Southern speech. The best compliment I heard about the so-called "Southern dialect" was that no one was aware of it! And all of us would have been dreadfully aware had the actors spoken as if they had their mouths full of hot okra.

I'd like to pass on to you a compliment from my husband. He liked especially your summation of Scarlett in the second paragraph and at the end of the column, and he said, "I always like Miss Lewis's stuff. She writes with so much understanding, and with force, and common sense, too." I hope you don't mind the "common sense." From a man, that's a high compliment!

Mrs. Hugh Harding   *Atlanta, Georgia*
Pasadena, California   *March 26, 1940*

Dear Lillian:

I know you will understand my long delay in answering your letter of February 11th when I tell you that I was in the hospital at the time it arrived. I am just now getting back to the office and picking up the threads. . . .

I had delayed the operation from month to month, waiting to get the premiere of "Gone With the Wind" behind me, and the movie producers kept moving the date up and up. Finally, the date was set for mid-December, but unfortunately I had a case of flu, so by the time Atlanta was in a furore over our three-day celebration I was not up to much. I wasn't able to go to the Junior League costume ball at the Auditorium or to the newspaper reception for the stars. Both of these affairs were held the day before the picture was shown. But I did get to attend the rather small party the Women's Press Club gave for me and the movie people in the late afternoon of the premiere day and, of course, to the picture that night. The movie people were all charming and the Atlanta people who met them fell in love with them. I wish you, as an old Atlantan, could have been here, for we will never see the town so excited again. The crowds on the streets were larger than those which greeted Lindbergh and President Roosevelt, yet everything was so orderly and well-bred and people did not mob the stars or try to snatch off their buttons for souvenirs. I was so proud of the town I nearly burst.

I wish I had some news of old friends to send to you but I haven't. With the influenza and the premiere and my hospital trip, I've been out of circulation since December and I am just now seeing a few people. I haven't even the smallest juicy tidbit to send you. . . .

Mr. George Brett, Jr.   *Atlanta, Georgia*
The Macmillan Company   *April 8, 1940*
New York, New York

Dear George:

Steve handed over to us your letter and the enclosed letter from Paul Jeral about my mythical case of leukemia. John is out of the hospital now and I am feeling fine, though still wabbly in the knees, and so we considered the matter and I wrote the enclosed letter to Mr. Jeral. I hope it may draw from him the source of his information and then I can land on the source like a duck on a June bug and stop this rumor before it spreads too far. Sometimes, I've had luck in nipping these affairs in the bud, so thank you for sending the letter on to Steve.

Please have no hesitancy about communicating matters of this type to me should any ever arise in the future. I want to know about them so that I can take steps to prevent such rumors spreading. I have had a great many rumors to contend with in the last four years and I sometimes wonder whether all authors are so plagued and embarrassed. I have had, according to legend, a broken back from which I would never recover, incurable blindness, blindness which was cured by the same surgeon who operated on the King of Siam, a wooden leg, three children, a divorce from John, and a pregnancy—twins at that. This last was most embarrassing. It was Caroline Miller, Georgia author of "Lamb in His Bosom," who was pregnant but I got the credit for it up until the time her child was actually born. So far, the leukemia is a brand new story and I hope it doesn't get very popular. I am at a loss to understand why the public appears to want me to be in a doomed condition.

Far from being doomed at present, I am twenty pounds heavier than I have ever been in my life and most embarrassingly fat. As I can take no exercise until the end of June, I suppose I will have to trundle my avoirdupois about for a while longer—and doubtless take to wearing Mother Hubbards, as I can find nothing which will fit me. . . .

Needless to say, the news about the 69¢ edition and its phenomenal sale just about bowled me over.* By the way, I was interested in The Macmillan Company's announcement in Publishers' Weekly some time ago about the rebinding of the movie edition.† You must have worked fast and well to have stopped it so effectively. It's amazing how many people there are in the world who are anxious to cash in on other people's work.

As I have been getting about for the first time in the last two weeks, I have been catching up on back gossip from friends. Everyone who had the pleasure of attending the Macmillan tea at the Georgian Terrace during the premiere celebration was loud in their remarks about what a good party it was. Personally, I'll never get over missing it, but in the light of hindsight I think I did the wise thing to have only one day out of three. Otherwise, I don't believe I would have managed to get to the premiere.

Mr. and Mrs. Edwin Granberry   *Atlanta, Georgia*
Winter Park, Florida   *April 11, 1940*
Dear Mabel and Edwin:

For many months I've been wanting to write to you but our lives have been "first one thing and then another"—as I will relate hereafter. . . .

Last summer we fully expected to get down your way and we kept saving things to tell you but it seemed that the tempo of things speeded up in-

---

* A second printing of 350,000 copies of the Motion Picture Edition was ordered for January and a third printing of the same size for February. The cover of the later editions carried the tagline "Complete and Unabridged."

† As the movie began opening across the country, several entities purchased Macmillan's paperback in bulk, rebound the volumes in hard covers (usually with the still of Gable and Leigh pasted on the front), and resold them at a higher price. On February 24, Macmillan ran a full-page "Notice to the Trade" in *Publishers Weekly* warning that such books were a violation of its rights and that the company intended to halt "this tampering."

stead of lessening. We did not get our fall vacation either because I had flu and, on top of it, there arrived the excitement about the Atlanta premiere of the film. This incredible frenzy which took the town began three months beforehand and words are inadequate to picture what happened. Our theatre holds only two thousand and all the population of Atlanta, Georgia and the late Confederacy were firmly convinced that they should get inside. As the time drew nearer and the news of the excitement spread, people from all parts of the United States decided they wanted to come, too. There was a widespread belief that I had a million tickets to the premiere in my pocketbook and for a "pretty, please" I would gladly yield up fifty or sixty to anyone who wanted them. People fought and trampled little children and connived and broke the ties of lifelong friendship and bribed and brought political influence to get tickets. And we had two tickets for ourselves, and we only possessed them five hours before the premiere! I don't believe our phone quit ringing for three months. . . .

For myself, there has been no writing. For four years there has not been a minute when I did not have eight pressing things to do. We hoped that when the picture was finally shown and the interest in it on the wane things would quiet down—and, thank God, they have, but we are still far from having any leisure. Perhaps the next six months will see us out of the woods. I hear many interesting stories about my alleged new book. Even good friends who should know me better stop me on the street and tell me about it and upbraid me for not confiding in them. It seems that it is a sequel to "Gone With the Wind," and by common consent the title is "Back With the Breeze." It is evidently a highly moral tract in which everyone, including Belle Watling, undergoes a change of heart and character and reeks with sanctimonious dullness. I am happy to announce that I have written no such book and still happier that such a book lies outside my feeble capabilities.

Speaking of rumors, we have just picked up a new one which is a trifle disturbing. As it came out of Florida, I am wondering if you two have heard it? A New York man who had been in Florida wrote The Macmillan Company that he had heard I was suffering from the incurable blood disease, leukemia, but he knew a refugee Austrian physician who had perfected a cure for it. While he did not go into details, I understand that the cure involves eating the entrails of freshly slaughtered animals. It all sounded like a first cousin of the cure of old age so vividly presented by Aldous Huxley in his recent book, "After Many a Summer."* I wrote

---

* Huxley's *After Many a Summer* tells the story of a Hollywood millionaire who tracks down a European nobleman who found the gift of eternal life but not of eternal youth. Published in

asking the man where he picked up this error, but have heard nothing. As I am now so fat I practically waddle and am in excellent shape, it is hard to know how this lie got started. . . .

Miss Mary DeV. Butler   *Atlanta, Georgia*
"Five Oaks"   *April 17, 1940*
Athens, Georgia

My dear Miss Butler:

When I saw the letter in your handwriting, accompanied by the rolled-up Edgefield Advertiser, I felt distressed, for something told me that they bore the news of your mother's death. I hardly wanted to open your letter, for I felt a pang of grief for your grief and that of your sisters. While I never met your mother, I felt as if I knew her—perhaps because it had been my privilege to know a few other great ladies of the old South. I am grateful to you for writing me about her passing and for sending me the copy of the Advertiser, and I am even more grateful for your reiterated statement that she had enjoyed "Gone With the Wind." . . .

I hope your mother realized how much I prized the green Confederate trimming. It was dear of her to make it for me and it has been admired by many people who have seen it.*

With deepest sympathy for your loss,

The Honorable William B. Hartsfield   *Atlanta, Georgia*
Office of the Mayor, City Hall   *April 29, 1940*
Atlanta, Georgia

My dear Mayor Hartsfield:

Foreign clippings about the release of "Gone With the Wind" are beginning to trickle in. It is a matter of great pride to me that European newspapers have given pages of pictures and columns of type to the *Atlanta* premiere. I feel very proud of my home town. I am enclosing a page from a Dutch magazine (or newspaper) which has your picture in it.

1939 in London by Chatto and Windus, the book was released in the United States as *After Many a Summer Dies the Swan*.

* The day after the premiere, Mitchell's secretary sent Mrs. Butler a piece of the green silk trimming the author had carried in her purse at the theater, along with a camellia from Mitchell's corsage. In a thank-you note, the elderly woman wrote, "Among all the soul-satisfying things that were done to gladden my ninetieth Xmas your sending the camellia & that scrap of 'Gone With the Wind' trimming that had *really accompanied you to the Premiere* was the crowning point of the occasion."

Miss Katharine Brown   *Atlanta, Georgia*
Selznick International Pictures, Inc.   *May 1, 1940*
New York, New York

Dear Katharine:

Forgive me for having delayed so long in answering your inquiry to John about autographing a copy of the movie edition for Mr. Selznick. To tell the truth, I thought John had answered the inquiry himself and I was distressed to find that, due to this misunderstanding, such a long time has elapsed. We are just beginning to clear up business and mail dating back to November, and in the course of this clearance I discovered that the request had gone unanswered.

I am terribly sorry that I cannot autograph Mr. Selznick's movie edition, but I have not autographed a book, album, picture, handkerchief, bed quilt, pencil stub or any object whatsoever in several years. Around the time "Gone With the Wind" hit the million mark, I had to stop autographing in self-defense, because the books were coming in in hundreds. I discovered that it was not a matter of just autographing one or two books, for every time I obliged one person everyone who knew that person sent me their book. I was in a position where I could not pick and choose without offending everyone I refused, and so I had to call a halt. Since that time I have not even autographed for relatives or close friends. Please tell Mr. Selznick how very sorry I am that I cannot oblige him. I know it seems like a very small favor, and in itself it is, but if I did it it would open the floodgates again. . . .

As for me, I am positively obese. I put on about twenty pounds while in the hospital and while convalescing. This delighted John and my doctors but I scarcely share their delight, as there seems to be no garment, except smocks or Indian blankets, which will cover me. I cannot swim or take any other exercise for a month or so, so I suppose I must bear my weight as philosophically as possible.

I have been getting around and seeing people for the last month and they are still talking about the picture and the premiere. Everybody had such a wonderful time and it will go down in Atlanta history side by side with that great day in the eighties when Jefferson Davis, then an old man, paid a visit to Atlanta.

If you know when Vivien Leigh and Laurence Olivier will open in New York I wish you'd let me know, for I'd like to wire them or send them some flowers.

Vivien Leigh   *Atlanta, Georgia*
51st Street Theatre   *May 9, 1940*
New York, New York

WE SEND ALL GOOD WISHES FOR A WONDERFUL NEW YORK SUC-
CESS TO YOU, MR OLIVIER AND THE REST OF THE CAST.*

Mr. Sam A. Cousley   *Atlanta, Georgia*
Rockford Register-Republic   *May 9, 1940*
Rockford, Illinois

Dear Mr. Cousley:

I appreciated your letter sending me the copy of your editorial from
the Rockford Register-Republic of April 1st, and I am sorry I have been
delayed in thanking you for it.† Only recently have I returned to my office
after a surgical operation and there was an unavoidable accumulation of
unanswered mail while I was away.

Ever since my novel was published, in 1936, I have been receiving letters
requesting me to write a sequel. To all of them I have given the same answer—
that I did not contemplate writing a sequel because, to me, the story of the
lives of Scarlett and Rhett ended on the last page of "Gone With the Wind."
As to what happened to them and their friends and enemies thereafter—well,
anybody's guess is as good as mine, for I do not know.

I suppose it was to be expected that the showing of the motion picture
would increase the public discussion of a possible sequel. These rumors
have gotten into print and statements have been published to the effect
that the motion picture people might produce a sequel whether I wrote
one or not. So far as I can learn, there is no foundation of any kind for
these rumors. Recently Mr. David Selznick, the producer of the motion
picture, was quoted in one of the New York papers to the effect that the
rumors were unfounded.

I enjoyed your editorial because of its thoughtful and intelligent attitude toward the subject of a sequel to "Gone With the Wind" and sequels
in general. I agree with you that "nothing can spoil a good book so quickly
as a bad sequel." My observation has been the same as yours, that a sequel
is often an anti-climax.

Thank you again for giving me the pleasure of reading your editorial.

---

* Leigh and Olivier opened in *Romeo and Juliet* on Broadway on May 9.

† Cousley's editorial, "Back with the Breeze?," advised Mitchell to "permit Scarlett and Rhett
to stay right where 'the wind' took them." Bringing them back to life in a sequel "might be a
good financial bet but it likely would be a great literary mistake," he wrote.

Miss Katharine Brown   *Atlanta, Georgia*
Selznick International Pictures, Inc.   *June 14, 1940*
New York, New York

My dear Katharine:

It was a great pleasure hearing from you again, especially the good news that you are at last taking that vacation. I read in the newspapers that Mr. and Mrs. Selznick are spending the summer in the East, and I hope this means that they also are enjoying some relaxation from the high pressure of the past few years.

Things are better with us. John is thriving, with the help of his leave of absence and his first opportunity in four years to catch up on lost sleep. I still have unpleasant reminders of my operation and at times am very discouraged by my slow progress, but the operation must have done me good for I now weigh more than 120 pounds. That is more than I have weighed in many years. I am still forbidden any strenuous exercise, and I am looking forward to the time when I can begin bending and twisting the excess poundage off my middle. Our best news is that life is finally beginning to quiet down for us. Our dream for many years was that this would happen after the movie had been shown, and recently it has seemed that we were right, for the mail has dropped off sharply. Of course, the war may be a factor in that. With everyone so worried by events in Europe, it is difficult to imagine anyone writing fan letters. But, whatever the cause may be, I hope the trend continues, for I am indescribably weary of the unnatural life I have been leading for nearly five years, and I yearn to get back to my own work again.

About the sequel rights, your inquiry was not unexpected, as there have been so many stories in the newspapers about proposed or possible sequels to the movie. I appreciate the frankness with which you discussed the situation and I will answer in the same manner, as follows:

1. I have no plans at this time for writing a sequel to "Gone With the Wind"; 2. I would not consider selling the right to create a sequel, to Mr. Selznick or anybody else.

As to your third question, about the approach you took in asking for my views before making a money offer, that was the correct one. And my answers are what I really think. They are not designed to lead you into making a higher offer than you originally intended. I am not horse trading.

Please give Mr. Selznick my thanks for his offer and tell him that if I have stated my answers to his questions briefly and to the point, there was no intention to be curt. There are some exceedingly strong reasons behind my refusal, and I am quite willing for him to know what they are.

Disregarding all other angles of the situation, there would be no point to Mr. Selznick's making me an offer, because I could not write a sequel now if my life depended on it. Writing anything would be impossible now, because I have no leisure at all, I haven't the physical strength, and the impulse to write under present circumstances is completely lacking.

I said earlier that things were beginning to quiet down for John and me, and *beginning* was just what I meant. There has been some lessening of the merciless pressure that has been on us for nearly five years, but that is all. My life is still far from quiet and my work is still heavy. Before I will be able to even think about further writing, there will need to be a period of calm and rest in my life, and that still seems to be far away. You can't write books in the middle of a tornado or when one has just passed over you.

You, Katharine, have been closer to me than anyone else in the Selznick organization, but even you could have no more than the faintest conception of what my life has been since 1936 and how seriously important it is that nothing shall interfere with the quieting down process now under way.

From the time I sold the movie rights to Mr. Selznick until just a few weeks ago, I have had the movie-mad population of the continent on my neck, asking foolish questions and making foolish suggestions. I had hundreds of would-be Scarletts on my doorstep, and scores who wanted to write scripts or design costumes or sell you genuine Confederate uniforms or just to get on the set to watch the shooting. I have had the organizations who wanted me to make Mr. Selznick do this or do that, and the newspapers pursuing me for information that I did not have or could not give, and a thousand and one other annoyances and bothers. It has cost me money, affected my health, stretched my working time to twenty hours a day, and almost quenched my desire to write.

You and Mr. Selznick know what I'm talking about, for you have had similar problems, but your situation was different from mine. Making movies and wrasslin' with the movie public is your business. It isn't mine, I had no training for that kind of thing and no experience in it, and I did not hire out to do that kind of job for you when I sold you the movie rights. But I did do it, at a sacrifice of my own real work—writing. At a sacrifice of my health, too, and my privacy and my peace of mind and many other things that are the most important things in the world to me.

Mr. Selznick's sequel offer is an invitation to me to plunge back into that frenzy when I am only just beginning to escape out of it. And my answer is that I would not do it for all the money in California, and New York too. Even if I had a sequel already written (and I definitely have *not*), I would not sell it to you now, for I do not believe I could yet force myself to undergo another siege such as the one that is just ending. I am determined to get my health back, and I want the opportunity to try to do some more writing, but neither would be possible if I had to go through another year like 1939, or 1938, or 1937. So, I have two very strong reasons for opposing a movie sequel:

First—Because of the stresses and strains of the past four years, for which your movie was largely responsible; and because I am completely out of practice in writing, as a result of having had all of my time taken up by other duties, including unpaid work for the benefit of the Selznick company, it would be completely impossible for me to write a sequel at this time, even if my life depended on it;

Second—Even if, by some miracle, the sequel were already written, the making of a movie from it would probably cause disturbances in my life similar to those which I have suffered for four years as a result of your making of the original movie. I am fearful that this might have a serious effect on my health by preventing me from leading my normal life for an additional long period of time.

Most of my statements so far have been based on conditions existing now or in the immediate future, so I suppose I should also give you my ideas in general with reference to a sequel.

Whether I will ever attempt to write a sequel, I honestly do not know. I have said many times that I believe the story comes to its natural and proper ending at the point where it ends, but I also know that there is a public demand for a sequel, for I have been receiving letters since 1936 asking for one. Because of the many other demands on my time and attention since 1936, I have never attempted to decide whether I might write a sequel some day. In fact, I have scarcely given the matter a serious thought, for all matters relating to creative writing have been crowded out of my mind by the pressure of other duties, and in this period of turmoil I have intentionally avoided making decisions about the future.

In all of this uncertainty, there is one thing I can say definitely and certainly. I have not commercialized my book's success and I do not intend to do it. I am not going to turn out stuff to "catch the market," just because I know a market exists. I have turned down offers amounting to a sizeable fortune from folks willing to buy anything I might write, good or bad, and I intend to continue turning them down. When, and if, I ever write anything else, it will be as good as I know how to make it, and not something cheaply and hastily written to cash in on "Gone With the Wind's" success. Which means that it will have to be written as I choose to write it and as slowly as I please to write it, not something written to order and according to somebody else's ideas.

As to the suggestion of my selling Mr. Selznick or anybody else the right to create a sequel to my novel, that is out of the question. It would make me guilty of commercializing my success in the rankest possible manner, and I would never be able to look myself in the face again if I did such a thing. It would be a violation of all of my own standards of honor, and it would also make me contemptible in the eyes of a great many people. You have found out how strongly Southern people, and many others, feel about my book, and many of them would never forgive me if I sold you Scarlett and Rhett to do with as you pleased. On top of that, I would be held responsible for whatever sequel you wrote. No matter how often it was announced that I had nothing to do with your sequel, people who did not like it would put the blame on me. Seriously, I cannot think of a better way by which I could make my life miserable for the next twenty years than to permit you to produce a sequel which I had not written.

Finally, a sequel might cause serious damage to two things which are very valuable to me—my literary reputation and the financial asset which I have in "Gone With the Wind." When I wrote the book, I never suspected that it would be a success, but it turned out to be something that is liked by people all over the world. Its success, commercially and from a literary standpoint, is apparently because of the "lifelikeness" of Scarlett and the other characters which I created. As the book now stands (without a sequel), it has a large commercial value; it is a source of profit to me and may continue to be for years to come. But I might destroy that value if I became over-anxious to make money and threw together a sequel, hastily and without the care and thought I gave to the original book. Unless the sequel measured up to its predecessor, it could easily make the public disgusted with the characters and with me, and thereby damage my literary reputation and the popularity of "Gone With the Wind."

Sequels to successful novels have been failures more often than successes, so the matter of a sequel to my novel is not something to be considered lightly. Certainly, it is not something to be attempted when I am weary and sub-normal in health and pressed by many other duties. And most certainly, it is not a job to be entrusted to a stranger. No one could know and understand my characters as well as I do, and if a stranger wrote a sequel, he would be certain to change and distort my characters. The commercial and literary asset which I have in "Gone With the Wind" depends very largely on the characters and the high standing they have won in the public mind. I don't want them to lose that standing and I don't want their personalities changed. Both things would be very damaging to me.

My literary reputation for the future would be in your hands from the moment I sold you the right to create a sequel. If your sequel was a cheaply commercial job, or if it was a conscientious job which nevertheless failed to please the public, my future reputation might be tarnished to such an extent that the public would refuse to buy some book I might write in the future. My name and my book's name and the names of my characters are linked together in the public mind, and a bad sequel to my book, even though not written by me, would have a very bad effect on the public standing of "Margaret Mitchell" as an author.

As you see, I have quite a collection of reasons for not being interested in Mr. Selznick's offer for the sequel rights, but please tell him that I am still his enthusiastic admirer and, if I should happen to write another book some day, I certainly hope that he will be the producer of the movie—assuming that he wishes to do so, of course. The remarkably fine job he did with "Gone With the Wind" has given him my good will in a large way and, if I ever become entangled with Hollywood again, I shall be disappointed if my affairs are not in his capable hands.

My very best regards to him and Mrs. Selznick and to you.

Mr. Harold Latham	*Atlanta, Georgia*
The Macmillan Company	*July 3, 1940*
New York, New York	

Dear Harold:

Of course I will be glad to cooperate with you in your plans for disposing of the overstock of the motion picture edition of "Gone With the Wind." I was sorry to learn from your letter of July 2nd that Macmillan had suffered a loss on the final printing of the 69¢ edition.

Whether the surplus stock should be remaindered at some later date or be disposed of now to the Pocket Books Company or Grosset & Dunlap is a business matter about which your judgment is far better than mine. I am willing to abide by your judgment and, in order that you may proceed with your arrangements, I am glad to give my approval to the proposal outlined in your letter of July 2nd. That is, I agree to accept a royalty of one cent a copy if you are able to effect a bulk sale of the surplus stock of this edition on the basis you have outlined or some substantially similar basis.*

---

* As the movie's showings wound down in the late spring of 1940, sales of the Motion Picture Edition plummeted, and most of the third printing was returned to the publisher.

Katharine Brown   Atlanta, Georgia
Selznick International Pictures, Inc.   July 15, 1940
New York, New York

MACMILLAN PROPOSAL OUTLINED IN YOUR LETTER WAS NOT
INITIATED BY ME BUT I HAVE APPROVED IT AND AGREED TO
ACCEPT GREATLY REDUCED ROYALTY SIMPLY BECAUSE THE
PROPOSED PLAN APPEARS TO BE BEST AND MOST PRACTICAL
WAY OF DEALING WITH SURPLUS BOOKS. ALSO I THOUGHT THIS
ORDERLY DISPOSAL OF BOOKS WAS PREFERABLE TO UNDIGNI-
FIED DUMPING OF THEM ON REMAINDER SHELVES. HOWEVER
IF YOU HAVE GOOD REASONS FOR OBJECTING, PLEASE DON'T BE
SWAYED BY MY OPINIONS.

Dr. Wallace McClure   Atlanta, Georgia
U.S. Department of State   August 8, 1940
Washington, D.C.

Dear Doctor McClure:

I would be very glad to have the pirated Chinese edition of "Gone With
the Wind" which you so kindly offered to me. Thank you so very much.
It will round out my collection of foreign editions and it is all I will ever
get out of China, I suppose. No, I have never seen this Chinese edition. My
only information about it came from letters and from brief references in
the newspapers some time ago. . . .

I have thought of you so often since the war situation became grave
and one country after another became involved. I know how hard you have
worked to solve the international copyright problems of American authors
and what a disappointment it must be for you that the war came before the
United States had joined the international convention. My sincere wishes
that your efforts may bring results at some future date. . . .*

I heard that there was a threatened radio dramatization in Argentina.
As Selznick International Pictures own the radio rights, this was the

---

Macmillan sold the overstock to Grosset & Dunlap, which rebound the books in hard-
cover, added a dust jacket, and sold them for fifty cents when the film was rereleased in
December 1940.

* The United States was not a member of the Berne Convention for the Protection of Literary
and Artistic Works, an international agreement governing copyright. This caused American
authors, especially Mitchell, a great deal of trouble around the world. The United States
eventually joined the Universal Copyright Convention of Geneva in 1955.

problem of Selznick and MGM, not mine, thank goodness. I have heard, but am not certain, that this radio piracy was stopped.

Selznick and Metro-Goldwyn-Mayer had reports from Japan that a pirated movie of "Gone With the Wind" was being produced there. Later information, which came to me through several people, shows that MGM probably has the situation in hand. While I wish MGM all the luck in the world in this matter—still, I would like to see a Japanese movie of my novel. If they placed it back in the sixties, the Japanese Confederates would doubtless be marching forth to defend Atlanta in Samurai armor and Scarlett would be dashing about in a 'ricksha instead of a buggy.

Mr. Julian V. Boehm   *Atlanta, Georgia*
Atlanta, Georgia   *August 16, 1940*

Dear Julian:

In many newspapers on the European continent you appear in pictures labeled as David O. Selznick, de producer van de film or M. David Selznick, le producteur du film. I thought you might be interested in seeing yourself under this alias, and so I am sending you this clipping from a Dutch newspaper. While neither John nor I pretend to read Dutch, we have puzzled out enough of this story to know that it tells the history of "Gone With the Wind" and goes into many details about our Atlanta premiere.

While I am talking about the premiere, I want to thank you, belatedly, for the firm, kind hand that was under my arm when I stepped from Mr. Selznick's car on that exciting night and for the fine things you said about me.

Miss Katharine Brown   *Atlanta, Georgia*
David O. Selznick Productions, Inc.   *September 1, 1940*
New York, New York

Dear Katharine:

A month has gone by since your letter and I feel very guilty about my delay in acknowledging it. Thank you so much for it and for Mr. Selznick's remarks about the sequel.

My secretary is on her vacation, Bessie, the cook, is airing herself in Miami, I've been hunting for a new office, I've been making bandages at the Red Cross five hours every day, I've been taking my father, who is a little better, out riding as frequently as he can go. All these are reasons for my procrastination. Speaking of the bandage making, my health has improved enormously, else I couldn't be working at this job. I usually fold operating sheets which appear to me to be eight yards long and ten wide. They must be folded about thirty six times to make an eight inch square package. You know how short I am. I have to do all the swoops and bends and leaps of an adagio dancer to manage the sheets. The long legged girls who should be doing this work sit demurely on tall stools, winding bandages about their fingers. Incidentally this work has taken two inches from my waist line besides giving me a very comfortable feeling that I am helping in a good cause. . . .

Of course, I've kept up with the dissolution of SIP and the birthing of DOS Productions.* It sounded very interesting and we have wondered how it will affect you. You won't have to go to California, I hope.

Speaking of going to California, Medora Field Perkerson sold her "Who Killed Aunt Maggie?" to Republic and she is going West, soon. I'll enclose a clipping about it if I can find it. I thought you might be in California and might run into her and think you were having nightmares about being back at the Press Club Tea at the Premiere.

Something has come up recently that I want to ask you about. If you know the answers I wish you would tell me. And if you don't know the answers, please tell me who can set me right.

A couple of weeks ago, the Atlanta papers got me out of bed and asked me how come I hadn't told them that I was going to N.Y. to go on the air with the radio version of "GWTW." When I replied bewildered, that I didn't even know the rights had been sold, they read me an article by McManus, the radio columnist on PM, which stated flatfootedly that "Margaret Mitchell herself will take the air during the prologue period, to give a proper Tara flavor."†

Naturally I was seething because this was my first intimation that any radio sale was cooking and I had had no invitation to go on the air and been given no chance to refuse to go on—which I would have done. I denied the whole thing and the Atlanta papers carried the story. I wired PM and got a correction but, of course, the damage was already done. People who

---

* In May 1940, Selznick International Pictures began a multiyear liquidation process, and on August 7, a new entity, David O. Selznick Productions, was incorporated.

† The PM article, "'Gone With the Wind' Joins the Radio Serials," by John T. McManus, claimed the program would run for a year as a Sunday night serial to promote the film's upcoming "popular price" release. The article featured several photographs of various actors at rehearsal, including Helen Claire as Scarlett, Don McLaughlin as Rhett, Georgette Harvey as Mammy, and Agnes Moorehead as Aunt Pittypat. These actors, McManus claimed, would perform a two-month prologue about Scarlett's early life. The final cast would be chosen after nationwide auditions, he said, and Selznick stood to make $500,000 on the project.

had asked me to go on the air commercially wanted to know why I had accepted Vicks' offer and refused theirs; everybody who wanted to get into the radio show demanded that I get them an audition, out of town papers wanted to know the details and I had to spend endless hours on street corners telling my fellow townsmen that it was all a lie. In other words, in a minor way, things got as gummy as when the search for Scarlett was afoot.

Naturally, I was mad and am still mad for my name was misused, without my permission and it got me into a lot of trouble and worry just when I had hoped life was settling down. I couldn't figure out who started the whole thing and I still can't figure it out. But I want to know who it was for I intend to land on them with tommyhawk and scalping knife. Do you know who could have been responsible for this erroneous statement. McManus of PM? The publicity department of Vicks? The Pub man at CBS? The MGM publicity department? Hal Kemp of Stack-Goble advertising agency? Or who? If you can set me right on this I'd certainly be grateful because I want to put the guilty party on notice that I will not have my name used to ballyhoo their radio serial.*

Yesterday, I saw a brief item in the papers that the Vicks-CBS-Selznick-MGM radio deal had been called off or had fallen through.† Naturally, we are curious about what really happened—whether the news story was a premature break or whether Mr. S. decided that the radio serial would cut in on the profits of the reissue of GWTW next spring or what. As I was very definitely affected by the news story of the sale and the PM item I can't help wondering.

Did I write you that the news perculated about, some time ago, that Mr. Selznick had made "GWTW" at least two hours longer and had been forced to cut out two hours? Everyone stopped me on the street and asked that I get *every foot* he had shot and have it run here in Atlanta. When I'd say feebly that such a show would doubtless run for six hours, every one

---

* On August 31, Mitchell wrote a strongly worded, seven-page, single-space letter to Selznick expressing her anger over the radio situation and demanding that a clause be added to her contracts with Selznick and Loew's that would invoke a monetary penalty in the future if her name were misused for publicity again. However, she did not send the letter, possibly because she learned the deal had collapsed.

† The premature announcement about *Gone With the Wind* on radio seemed to be a case of advertising and publicity representatives jumping the gun, resulting in what *Variety* termed a "debacle." The agreement between Vick's Chemical Company (which had signed on to sponsor the program), the Stack-Goble Advertising Agency, and CBS Radio collapsed when Selznick International and MGM declared that such a serial would be too competitive with the film's upcoming rerelease.

said they wouldn't mind at all, they'd bring fried chicken in shoe boxes and stuffed eggs in Kleenex and have a wonderful time. People said they saw no reason why the rest of the United States should have such a treat but that there was no reason why Atlanta, etc. etc.

I think you'll probably do well with the film in South America if publishing figures mean anything. I've had a Spanish edition out in Chile and other Spanish speaking countries for nearly two years and recently the publishers have brought out a two volume edition, a better translation. While it's hard to get definite figures, I understand the book has done well—this includes Mexico, too. The Portuguese edition, in Brazil, is going like wildfire, to judge by Atlanta newspaper people who are just back from there. Biggest sale of any book in many years. The Brazilians feel a kinship with the happenings of the book because they, too, have a "North" and a "South," an agricultural half and an industrial one. And the slaves, which made the agricultural part so rich, were freed in the Eighties.

John sends his best and so do I and we hope your rest has done you worlds of good.

Mr. Harold Latham   *Atlanta, Georgia*
The Macmillan Company   *October 6, 1940*
New York, New York

Dear Harold:

I had lunch with Norman yesterday and he told me of his plan for The Macmillan Company to entertain for Medora the day before "Aunt Maggie's" premiere. He was not sure whether it would be an afternoon or an evening party, as the Atlanta Historical Society also wishes to give Medora a party and they are waiting to hear from her as to whether an afternoon or evening party would be more satisfactory. As soon as Medora lets the Historical Society know, then Norman can make his plans for afternoon or evening festivities. Regardless of whether the Macmillan party is held at midnight or at high noon, it wouldn't be complete without your presence. You will be the real host of the occasion, whether you are there in person or in spirit, but it would be so much fun to have you in person. Won't it be possible for you to arrange your autumn trip so that you can be here on the 23rd or 24th of October. . . .

I did not mean to bring in business on this personal letter, but I might forget to mention this later on. I have just bought an 89¢ copy of "Gone With the Wind." It is the movie edition minus the photographs, and very nicely bound in red cloth with a fanciful pictorial map on the front. I notice that the Macmillan imprint is missing from the spine of the book and I wonder who brought it out. There are two misspelled words on this little map. The name of General Stephen D. Lee is spelled "Lea" and Rough and Ready appears as "Rough and Ready's." Of course I get the blame for these inaccuracies. Is it too late to have these errors changed? Have all the printings of this edition appeared which will appear? If the Grosset and Dunlap edition which we discussed some months ago has a jacket design with any legends on it, could I check it before it is printed? General Robert E. Lee's name might appear as "Lea" and then I would have to go somewhere where no extradition papers could reach me.*

Mrs. James D. Robinson   *Atlanta, Georgia*
British War Relief Society   *December 2, 1940*
Atlanta, Georgia

Dear Mrs. Robinson:

Thank you so much for your letter of November 26th, about the anniversary showing of "Gone With the Wind."† It was good of you to write me about it. As my secretary wrote you, I have been out of town and that is why my answer has been delayed.

My sincere thanks for your invitation to be present at the showing of the picture. It was sweet of you to say that "without you I feel sure it would not be nearly so great a success." Of course, I am happy to have you say something so nice, but I know the performance will be a great success, whether I am present or not. The British War Relief is a cause which touches all hearts and the ladies of Atlanta associated with you have a long history of making a success of anything they undertake.

Of course, all my good wishes go to you and the other members of the British War Relief Society. At this time I can think of no more worthy cause than yours. It is a cause that I have been working for in several ways for

---

* The book Mitchell purchased with a map labeled "The Flight to Tara" on the cover was one of five thousand copies of the movie edition Macy's department store rebound on its own to sell at a special price. Latham reported that when Macmillan found out, the publisher insisted the store remove the stills from the volume because Macmillan's agreement with Selznick did not authorize a hardback Motion Picture Edition.

† To kick off the release of *Gone With the Wind* at "popular prices"—twenty-five, forty, and fifty-five cents—Loew's announced that a "second premiere" of the film would be held in Atlanta on December 12.

nearly a year—by donations to several different organizations, by collecting clothes for the Friends of Children, Inc., and by making surgical dressings for the Red Cross.

It was good of you to invite me to call at your headquarters and talk things over with you and Mrs. Dickey. I hope I can do this, although I cannot say just now when I will have the opportunity because of other engagements.

In fact, it is very doubtful that I will be able to attend the performance on December 12th, because my husband and I have planned to be out of town on a vacation trip during most of December. It will be a great disappointment if I am unable to be with you, but it appears impossible for me to rearrange my plans which were made long before I ever heard about the anniversary showing of the picture.

I know the foregoing calls for an explanation and I will tell you about it frankly, although it is not a matter I enjoy discussing.

In your letter you said, "Of course you are familiar with all the arrangements which are being made in regard to the anniversary premiere of 'Gone With the Wind.'" Instead of knowing all about the arrangements, I really know very little about them. Until yesterday, I knew almost nothing at all, except what I had read in the papers. On yesterday, Miss Katharine Brown, of the Selznick organization, gave me an outline of proposed plans, but that was almost my first definite and official information from the motion picture people. The only previous information I received from them was a brief telephone call to my husband from Mr. Coleman last week, just before we left on our trip to Kentucky.* And as you know, I have had no information of the plans of the British War Relief Society or any communication from you until your letter of November 26th, which was awaiting me on my return.

All of this puts me in a false position, through no fault of my own, and I find it highly embarrassing. It makes me appear to be absenting myself from Atlanta at that time through indifference or lack of interest, and that is not the case. Months ago my husband and I made plans for a vacation trip this December visiting friends we have not been able to see during the past four years because of the pressure of business matters arising from "Gone With the Wind." Not only were our plans made before the movie showing was announced but friends we expect to visit had made their arrangements also. At this late date and upon such short notice, it is extremely doubtful that we could give up our trip and cause our friends

---

* Elmer Bradley Coleman was MGM's southeastern exploitation manager.

inconvenience and disappointment. So it is practically certain that we will have to be away from Atlanta on December 12th.

I cannot help feeling a trifle indignant that I was not informed early, by the movie people, of their plans. Whether or not I could have changed my plans then, I do not know, but the advance notice might have made it possible. When the movie people decided on the December 12th date, they had made no effort to find out if I would be in Atlanta at that time. Their representatives were here for two or three weeks before their newspaper announcements on Thanksgiving Day, but they neither telephoned nor wrote me. Nor did the British War Relief Society give me any official information of plans until your letter arrived.

In view of the above, of course it is unnecessary for me to say that none of the plans for the anniversary showing were of my making. I had no part in them and I did not know the motion picture people were even thinking of a "second premiere" until I read the stories in the newspapers. I am sorry that matters have fallen out this way but I can only be frank and trust that you will understand it. Again let me wish you great success in your undertaking and a very happy and exciting occasion for all concerned.

Miss Lois Cole   *Atlanta, Georgia*
The Macmillan Company   *December 10, 1940*
New York, New York

Dear Lois:

. . . Right now we are undergoing ordeal by "second premiere." The anniversary showing is on the 12th. Miss Leigh and Mr. Olivier will appear to speak for the British Relief and the proceeds will go to the Relief. I will not undertake to give you all the horrors of this situation, but for two weeks we have had a terrible time with the Metro-Goldwyn-Mayer people. They had never even told me the date of the "premiere" or consulted me in any manner, and then, without warning, they announced that Vivien Leigh and Hattie McDaniel would appear on the stage and do the corset lacing scene.* It so happens that I own the dramatic rights and they should know it, and the whole affair constituted a barefaced attempt at infringement if I ever met one. And, dearie, I have met every form of infringement that the broad Empire of Rome can bring, and have not yet lowered my arm. Of course I could have sued the hell out of them, and I would have done it

---

* While the city's segregation policy prevented McDaniel from sitting in Loew's Grand Theatre, she could have performed on the stage.

except for the unfortunate and innocent ladies of the Atlanta British Relief unit. I gave, without charge, this portion of my dramatic rights for the benefit of the British, and asked only that Metro-Goldwyn-Mayer and Selznick guarantee me copyright and copyright protection. They were perfectly horsey about it for days, saying that I should not only donate but take the risk. Finally, just as the contract was about to be signed, with me giving the rights to the skit and the movie people guaranteeing protection, the whole thing blew up. The reason for this was that Hattie McDaniel could not get away from a picture she was in. A wire sent to Hattie three weeks before would have revealed this but it had not occurred to any of these screwballs to send such a wire. So our Kentucky trip was cut short for nothing and this last wild ten days was useless. These movie people are crazy as bedbugs.

I will, however, except Katharine Brown, who seems to understand how normal people tick. When the trouble got hot Selznick sent her down here and she managed to inject a little common sense and courtesy into the whole affair. You can perhaps imagine the anguish of the prominent Atlanta matrons of the British Relief. They are having to refund money on their tickets because, without the skit, they did not feel that they could charge five dollars. If we can just live till after the 12th we will try to get away to Florida and we hope that a visit to Marjorie Rawlings in the swamps near Ocala will sooth our nerves. . . .

Mr. and Mrs. Laurence Olivier   *Atlanta, Georgia*
Georgian Terrace Hotel   *December 11, 1940*
Atlanta, Georgia

My dear Mr. and Mrs. Olivier:

Like everyone else in Atlanta, John and I are happy to have you in our city again. Our only regret is that your stay will be so brief. Of course I will see you at the breakfast-luncheon of the British Relief unit and very probably we will ride to the theatre in your car that night.

We had hoped to have a brief private visit with you and hoped it might be managed on Wednesday night. Now we learn that your plans have been changed and you will arrive on Thursday. Of course it would give us great pleasure if you could come to our house by yourselves just to see us—by ourselves—no reporters, no photographers, no publicity men. There are so many things we'd like to say quietly to both of you. But if your time is too short and the demands of the press and other engagements will make your stay a rushed one, then do not give a thought to a visit with us. We will understand and hope that on some other occasion it may be possible.

I have discussed this matter with Susan Myrick and should you discover that you do have the opportunity she can doubtless arrange the matter in her own efficient way.

I will arrive half an hour early at the breakfast and be on hand to see you.*

Mr. David O. Selznick, President   *Atlanta, Georgia*
Selznick International Pictures, Inc.   *December 11, 1940*
New York, New York
Mr. Nicholas M. Schenck, President
Loew's, Incorporated
New York, New York

Gentlemen:

As you may know, it was originally planned that the featured attraction of the so-called "second premiere" of "Gone With the Wind" in Atlanta on December 12th would be a staged dramatization of a scene from my novel, with Vivien Leigh and Hattie McDaniel as the actors. Later the idea was abandoned because Hattie McDaniel was not available. But before that denouement, your representatives had entangled me in a difficult and highly embarrassing situation which cost me a great deal of work, worry, trouble, annoyance and expense. In addition, the false position in which I was placed was one which gravely endangered my standing before the public.

The situation involved me because the dramatic rights in my novel belong to me. Your proposed dramatization could not be presented without my consent and permission. But, without having even asked for my permission, your Mr. Ferguson announced in the newspapers that the dramatization would be presented. In fact, I was not consulted in any way before the public announcement was made.

Out of that bad beginning grew complications which were not cleared up until after two weeks of hard work. During that period, my time was taken up, my other affairs were interfered with and delayed, I was forced to break off a vacation trip and return to Atlanta to clear up the problem, and my attorney and my business manager gave many days and nights of hard work to the job. In addition to paying them for their services, my other

---

* Bad weather on the day of the screening diverted the plane carrying Leigh, Olivier, and British film director Alfred Hitchcock to Augusta, Georgia. The celebrities missed the British War Relief brunch and the film that night; they were driven to Atlanta the next day for a brief visit before heading back to the West Coast.

direct expenses were large. To top matters off, later developments showed that you had caused me all of this trouble and expense for no good reason, that it was all useless and needless.

In view of all the circumstances, the expense which you caused me should properly be borne by you, not me. You also owe me some compensation for the trouble you put on me and for my loss of time. *I am, therefore asking for a payment of five thousand dollars.*

This is the first time I have ever asked compensation of this nature from you, but it is not the first time you have caused me trouble and expense by careless or reckless trespasses on my rights. In the past I have never dealt with you on a coldly business basis. I have given you services which you could not have hired me to do. I have stood in front of you and fought your battles for you. I have spent large amounts of my own money and my time in protecting and safeguarding your rights. In all of my dealings with you, I have worked on a basis that was helpful, friendly and considerate, rather than cold-bloodedly businesslike. From the time I first sold you my movie rights, I have had no financial interest in anything that happened to you, but I have nevertheless done many things to help you, and I have never asked anything from you except CONSIDERATION.

Now, finally, you have forced me to the conclusion that I made a mistake in trying to deal with you on the past basis. The recent incident is the last straw. On several previous occasions, you have tried my patience to the breaking point, but when you apologized and promised emphatically that such things would never happen again, I accepted the apologies and promises. Because I thought you *meant* them. Now you have forced me to believe either that you have no real intention to treat me fairly or that your companies are so large and loose-jointed you have no control over your subordinates. Perhaps your own personal and official attitude toward me is fair and friendly, but that is no protection for me if your subordinates trespass on my rights, abuse the friendship I have shown you and misuse my time and strength. You are responsible for the actions of your subordinates and, beginning now, I expect to hold you to strict accountability.

If the bill I am now submitting is paid, we will consider the recent incident closed. As to the future, I can only say that I can no longer afford to have my time and money wasted and my friendship imposed upon by the careless and thoughtless acts of your subordinates. You have demonstrated that my past methods of dealing with you were wrong. If further troubles occur, I will be forced to take whatever steps are necessary for my protection.

In order that you may have the facts before you, I will give you a history of the recent incident as briefly as possible. When Mr. Ferguson made the newspaper announcement of the proposed dramatization without asking my permission, I regarded it as a flagrant and inexcusable trespass on my rights and I instructed my attorney to enjoin the performance and file suit against you for breach of contract. Before he had completed drawing up the papers, a telegram arrived from your Miss Katharine Brown asking for the necessary permission. I also learned that Mr. Ferguson had induced the Atlanta ladies of the British War Relief unit to sponsor the "premiere" by promising them the stage performance and assuring them that it would make the event a success.

Partly because I did not wish to disappoint the Atlanta ladies, who had been imposed upon by Mr. Ferguson, just as I had, and partly because of my friendship for Miss Brown, I reverted to my attitude of the previous four years, and I decided to grant the favor you had asked.

I had nothing to gain from what you wished to do. On the contrary, I have always been opposed to dramatizations of my novel piecemeal. Also I was fearful that your four-minute dramatization might in some way damage or endanger my dramatic rights in the book as a whole. But, over the years, I had gotten into the habit of helping you out of your many difficulties and, after Miss Brown's telegram arrived, I pitched into the situation with the same friendly attitude I had had since 1936.

The contract I authorized my attorney to negotiate with you donated the performance rights for the sketch, without charge to you and for the benefit of the British Relief, for a single performance on December 12th. I asked nothing from you except that you protect me from any copyright difficulties that might result from my generosity in giving you, without any charge, the use of part of my dramatic rights.

The situation had developed at the very time when my husband and I planned to leave on a vacation, his first visit to his Kentucky birthplace in twenty years. The problem you had dumped into my lap forced us to delay our departure for two days but, when we left, we thought the difficulty was over. Having made what I considered a very generous offer, I supposed that you would be glad to accept it. And if it had been accepted promptly, I would not be writing you this letter. Instead, your lawyers haggled over it for ten days.

They balked on my one requirement about copyright protection. They wanted me not only to be generous to you but also to stand all the risks and penalties that might result from my generosity. They wanted to take all the benefits and give me all of the burdens. They were seeking a favor—a favor from which I would not benefit in any way, one which I had refused to many other people, one which I would never have granted to you except for reasons of generosity—yet they wanted to dictate the basis on which I granted the favor, a basis which relieved you of any and all responsibilities. I was showing you the highest degree of consideration and was being met with the very opposite of consideration.

It disrupted our vacation, for we were constantly pursued by telephone calls and telegrams. Before the trip was half over, we were forced to hurry back to Atlanta. At that time, it seemed that the whole "premiere" might collapse because no agreement had been reached about the dramatic rights. I was in danger of being dragged into a public scandal if your representatives tried to save their own faces by laying the blame on me before the public.

We came home and after three more days and nights of wrangling, your attorneys agreed that you should accept your proper responsibility. Mr. Decker telephoned my attorney that the amended contract we had worked out was acceptable, except for two minor changes in language to which I agreed.* Mr. Decker said that the contract would be signed and sent to me by airmail that night. Then two hours later he wired us that the whole thing had blown up.

I then learned about your inability to obtain the services of Hattie Mc-Daniel for the Atlanta performance. So, the outcome of it all was that you had put me to great trouble and expense in order to obtain the use of my dramatic rights, when you had not put yourself into position to make use of them. I need not have been entangled in the situation at all, but I was entangled in it, through no fault of my own. Expense and trouble were put on me, uselessly and needlessly, all because of the careless disregard of my rights by your representatives and the generally inconsiderate manner in which I was treated. It was expense and trouble which your subordinates created and I am entitled to compensation for it.

A considerable part of the five thousand dollars I am asking for is actual and direct expenses. It includes the services of my attorney and my business manager, day and night for the greater part of two weeks, several consultations with my New York attorney about copyright matters affecting dramatizations, a large volume of long distance telephone calls and telegrams, overtime work by my secretary, taxicabs and transportation, losses from delays and interference with my other work, losses because you forced me to break off my vacation trip after I had spent considerable money in preparation for it.

What value should be placed on my own loss of time, inconvenience, annoyance and disruption of plans, I will not attempt to say. If I charged

---

* David O. Decker was an attorney with MGM in New York.

you a proper amount, the total would be larger than I am asking. In setting the total at five thousand dollars, I have included a reasonable amount for my time, but I have not included anything as damages on account of the worry and harassment to which I was subjected.

I would like to have an immediate payment of this bill as my books close on December 31st.*

Mrs. Albert E. Thornton   *Atlanta, Georgia*
British War Relief Society   *December 14, 1940*
Atlanta, Georgia

Dear Mrs. Thornton:

I am enclosing a check for $100 for the British War Relief. I had intended to bid at least $100 on the articles which were to have been offered at the auction. Since there was no auction, I am sending the money to you direct.

I think you and all the hard-working people in the Atlanta branch did a wonderful job, and I hope it gives you all the sense of satisfaction you deserve. I never saw so many obstacles put in the way of a worthy cause, but the way you handled them was fine to see.

John and I saw Mr. and Mrs. Olivier very briefly while they were here and to say that they were upset and disappointed at missing the luncheon is putting it very mildly. I told them as much about the luncheon as there was time to tell and they were sincerely touched by all that had been planned for them and the British Relief.

The orchids I wore at the luncheon were so beautiful. I am so grateful to all of you for them. I think you were so sweet to remember me in the midst of all your problems.

Please let's have lunch sometime and swap experiences. I personally feel as if I had been through the Battle of the Beaches of Dunkirk, and I know your sensations must be similar.†

---

* Mitchell received a check for $5,000 on February 7, 1941.

† In September 1941, Mitchell donated a Danish edition of *Gone With the Wind*—like the one she gave Gable—to a British War Relief auction in New York. The author included a calling card on which she had written, "Dear Mrs. Thornton: This is the Danish edition of 'Gone With the Wind.' I think the illustrations are charming," and signed it: "Margaret Mitchell Marsh."

CHAPTER **Seven**

In the Wake of the Storm
1941–1949

So, on the night of the premiere, I knew before the film began
to roll that it would be a great picture and before many minutes
had passed, I knew it was even greater that I could have expected.
Yes, I have always thought myself fortunate that Selznick
International produced "Gone With the Wind."

—*Margaret Mitchell to John Hay Whitney and David O. Selznick*
August 31, 1942

Mr. George Brett, Jr.   *Atlanta, Georgia*
The Macmillan Company   *April 15, 1941*
New York, New York

Dear George:

John and I have just returned from our trip and I am writing you right
away about your letter of April 7th. I have talked with Steve and John about
the offer from Press Alliance, Inc. for the right to make a newspaper pictorial strip of "Gone With the Wind" and here are our ideas.

Our understanding of what this offer refers to is the same as yours,
that "pictorial strip" means "funnies," or rather one of the type of "funnies"
which have become popular in recent years and which are, for all practical
purposes, a newspaper serial story in pictures not necessarily funny.

As to the question of who owns the right to authorize such a pictorial strip, I believe that right belongs to me. Under my contract with you,

Macmillan is given a share of any money I might receive from a newspaper serialization of my novel, but my understanding has always been that this refers only to serial publication of the actual novel, as it appears in book form. I don't understand that it refers to a serialization in pictures, as in a newspaper strip. The latter would be a presentation of my story in an entirely different medium or form of art. The book publishing rights which Macmillan acquired from me did not give you any right to dramatize my story in a series of pictorialized incidents, which is what a newspaper strip would be. You have the right to publish my story as a novel, and I still retain the right to publish it in pictorialized form, if I choose to do so.

However, there is no need for us to argue about this, as I am strongly opposed to any pictorial strip based on my novel. Before giving my reasons for that, let me answer your question as to whether the movie people would have to be consulted about this offer.

In the commercial tie-up contract which I worked out with Selznick and Loew's in 1939, we included a provision stating that the movie people would *not* have the right to put my book into a newspaper comic strip or to authorize anybody else to do it. I think we've made it clear enough that the movie people have no right to do this, but, if I were to authorize a newspaper strip, the movie people might be brought into the situation in the following way. Whoever bought the rights to produce the strip might wish to capitalize on the popularity of the movie by making the people in the strip look like the people in the movie. It would be natural for them to wish to make Rhett look like Clark Gable and to make Scarlett look like Miss Leigh et cetera, and they might otherwise wish to follow the same arrangement of incidents as was in the motion picture. That is something I would have to prevent, or try to prevent. If I didn't, if the newspaper strip was to a greater or a smaller degree a serialization of the movie rather than an original creation based on my story, it seems to me that it would be trespassing on the rights of the movie companies and I would have to obtain their permission and perhaps give them a part of the money received from the strip.

Those complications are one of the big reasons why I am opposed to selling the newspaper strip rights. In any contract I might make with Press Alliance, Inc. or any other newspaper syndicate, I would specify very strongly that their strip must be a picturization of my novel and not of the movie. But I think we would have a lot of trouble making them comply with the contract. And I see trouble of several other kinds in any such arrangement.

As you know, I have not given anybody the right to publish a sequel to my novel or to sequelize it in any other way, and I have fought down several attempts to do this without my permission. Press Alliance, Inc. wants to acquire the right to sequelize my story, in addition to serializing it. Their letter which you sent me states that ". . . our idea is to work out further episodes in cooperation with Miss Mitchell, after the material included in the book has been utilized." I do not intend to sell them or any other syndicate the right to produce a sequel to my novel in a newspaper strip, and that would be specified in any contract I might make with them, but again I am afraid we might have difficulties in holding them to the contract.

In addition, you know how opposed I have always been to condensations or adaptations of my story. I imagine that any newspaper strip would condense it and make adaptations. On top of these other things, I have doubts that any newspaper strip would be properly dignified. If it wasn't it would damage both The Macmillan Company and me. Both the book's reputation and my own literary reputation would suffer. . . .

Of course if a very large sum of money was involved I might be forced to give the matter further consideration but I doubt that the newspaper strip rights would bring any substantial sum, so I will appreciate if you will notify Press Alliance, Inc. that I am not interested in their offer.

Mrs. Hattie McDaniel-Crawford   *Atlanta, Georgia*
Los Angeles, California   *May 12, 1941*

My dear "Mammy":

It was good of you to send us your wedding announcement and my husband and I send you and your husband our very best wishes for your happiness.*

I would have acknowledged your enclosed letter sooner but because of the serious illness of my father I have been unable to get to my office. To tell the truth, I have felt that I owed you a letter for a long time because every time I see "Gone With the Wind" (and I have seen it five times) my appreciation of your genius in the part of Mammy has grown. I have felt ungenerous that I have not written you fully about how wonderful I think you were. I do not weep easily but now I have wept five times at seeing you and Miss de Havilland go up the long stairs.† In fact, it's become a joke among my friends—but they cry, too!

My clipping service brings me news of the picture from the far parts of the world. As you know, it has had a wonderful success wherever it has

---

* McDaniel married her third husband, James Lloyd Crawford, on March 21, 1941.

† Mitchell refers to the scene in which Mammy tells Melanie of Rhett's grief over the death of his daughter in a riding accident.

played. Sometimes foreign reviewers have not liked this or that incident in the film and have criticized the acting of this or that player, but one and all they have been unanimous in praising your performance.

When our Hollywood visitors were here for the world premiere the Mayor of Atlanta presented them with sets of Wedgwood after-dinner coffee cups. These cups were made for and sold by our Atlanta Historical Society. On them are scenes of old Atlanta. I had intended giving these cups myself, but our Mayor was an energetic man and he beat me to them. Now, I am sending you and your husband, as a wedding gift, some of these cups, and it will give me great pleasure to know that they are in your possession.

I am looking forward to seeing you in many fine portrayals. "The Great Lie" has been here in Atlanta but I missed it, as I was spending my time with my father. I hope to catch it soon at a second-run house.*

With sincere good wishes for your happiness and your success.

Miss Katharine Brown   *Atlanta, Georgia*
David O. Selznick Productions, Inc.   *May 22, 1941*
New York, New York

My dear Katharine:

We were so sorry to learn that you had been ill. The best I can hope for you is that your stay in the hospital will be as beneficial to you as mine was to me.

Now, as to your wish to come down here on June 15th and talk about a musical production of "Gone With the Wind"—yes, do come down. You know John and I always like to see you, whether it be for business or pleasure, and we will enjoy a visit with you. However, I should say frankly that my willingness to discuss Mr. Selznick's proposition in regard to the musical production does not mean that I am making any trade with you or will make any trade with you. I'm just open to discussion; that's all. After having had the first comparatively peaceful months since the summer of 1936, I am loath to surrender this peace and plunge myself back into the devil's cauldron.

If you decide to come, I beg of you not to tell anyone why you are coming. I don't want any rumors to get about erroneously stating that I am negotiating with Mr. Selznick on this matter. I don't want any items in New York gossip columns stating that "Katharine Brown has flown to Atlanta to discuss Mr. Selznick's forty million dollar musical production of 'Gone

---

* *The Great Lie*, a 1941 Warner Bros. film, starred Bette Davis, George Brent and Mary Astor and featured McDaniel in a supporting role.

With the Wind' with the author, Margaret Mitchell." If anything like this got out I just wouldn't feel like discussing the matter at all.

Here is another angle on your visit. My father has been desperately ill for three weeks and we never expected him to live, until four days ago. He is better now, although quite sick. I have been spending most of my time with him. If he took a turn for the worse, I would, of course, have to wire you that I could not see you. I'm sorry I can't be more definite, but that is the situation. I do not want you to delay your trip here because of father's illness. Frankly, I do not think he will ever be much better than he is now and should you wait six months to come he might be worse. Even if I were tied up at the hospital during part of your visit, John could discuss the matter with you.

We are looking forward to seeing you.

Paramount Pictures, Inc.   *Atlanta, Georgia*
Hollywood, California   *September 4, 1941*

Gentlemen:

On August 29, 1941, I sent a telegram giving my consent to the use of a reference to and an excerpt from "Gone With the Wind" and to a use of my name in the motion picture version of "Louisiana Purchase," now being made by you, stating that a letter giving details would follow.*

I grant to Paramount Pictures, Inc. the license and permission to use the scene submitted on August 5th, 1941, to David O. Selznick Productions, Inc., which was forwarded by Selznick to me for my approval and consent. This license and permission extends only to the current film version of "Louisiana Purchase," and this scene may not be used in any other dramatization or picturization.

The scene must be played verbatim as submitted to me, with the exception pointed out in my telegram—that is, the excerpt from "Gone With the Wind" must be quoted verbatim. I do not consent to the change in language of my book for which you requested permission.

No other rights collateral to or flowing from this scene or from this permission and license are to be acquired by Paramount Pictures, Inc. by reason of this permission and license.

---

* In the 1941 film *Louisiana Purchase*, Bob Hope, as Pelican State politician Jim Taylor, begins a filibuster by announcing he is going to read "a brief statement on the glories of the South—*Gone With the Wind*, by Margaret Mitchell." He picks up a copy of the book and turns to the first page. The scene then dissolves to a hoarse, disheveled Taylor reading the last lines of the novel.

Mr. Wesley W. Stout
Saturday Evening Post
Philadelphia, Pennsylvania

Dear Mr. Stout:

I had never heard the remark you attributed to Percy Hammond about his hobby being "not writing," but I can't tell you how much I enjoyed it.

Thank you for giving me the dates of your vacation. I will try to arrange my next trip North so as not to come at a time when you are away from Philadelphia. The reason for my trip will be a visit to Wilmington, Delaware, to see my husband's family, and the time will depend largely on when John can leave his work here.

In the past I have been grateful to you on several occasions for querying me about various matters involving me, and now, after reading your item about Katharine Hepburn's biography, I am more grateful than I can tell you that you asked me about this before printing it. When I read that sentence in your letter, it actually made me weak because of the sudden picture it flashed into my mind of those years when practically everybody in the United States was trying to trap me into stating my preference for Scarlett—and also in the knowledge, from bitter experience, of the enormous amount of trouble it would have caused if the item had been published by the Post.

Let me say now, flatfootedly, I never endorsed Katharine Hepburn for the part of Scarlett. From first to last, I never endorsed anybody or expressed the vaguest preference for anybody. And, to answer your question more directly, Katharine Hepburn was *not* my choice for Scarlett. Nobody was my choice; that is the literal truth, even though nobody apparently believed me then and perhaps nobody believes me now.

It is hard for me to understand why Miss Hepburn should make such a statement. The only basis she could have for it is that she knows my inner thoughts better than I do, and that my inner thoughts are just the opposite of my public denials. For I did make a public denial that she was my choice and I do not know how she could have failed to see it, for it was published in all the New York papers, in Life magazine (November 7, 1938), and in newspapers generally over the country.

The "Hepburn incident" in the fall of 1938 was the climax of those unbelievable events between the publication of my novel and the announcement in December 1938 that Vivien Leigh had been given the role of Scarlett. You have probably forgotten the details but you may remember that commentators remarked that the controversy, over who should play

Scarlett, was equalled by nothing except a Presidential election. It was a strange phenomenon, especially to me, and I wanted no part of it, but never was a person so pulled and hauled about as I was. And never did a person have to fight harder to prevent her name from being misused to promote the candidacy of one actress or another.

When I sold the screen rights to David Selznick, it was with the understanding that I would have nothing to do with the picture in any way and must never be called upon to express an opinion or do any work on it. I knew nothing about the production of motion pictures, whereas Mr. Selznick has made name and fame in that field. Even if I had had strong preferences for the cast, which I did not, I would have kept silent. I would no more have presumed to tell him how to make his movie than I would permit him to tell me how to write a book. So, I had thought when I unloaded the movie rights that my problems were over, but they had just begun, and the years thereafter until the film was released were a nightmare.

It is not possible for me to give you any understanding of the many and varied and incredible kinds of pressure that were brought to bear on me to make me come out in favor of one or another actress. People went to any lengths to try to entrap me into some statement they could twist in favor of their candidate. But, so help me, I never opened my mouth. I tried to be polite under this bombardment and to remain courteous in the face of frenzied people. As you can imagine, this was somewhat difficult.

And then something happened that is really incredible. Mrs. Ogden Reid, of the New York Herald Tribune, announced that Katharine Hepburn was my choice for Scarlett! On October 11, 1938, Mrs. Reid telephoned me from New York to urge me to attend some sort of women's forum dinner in New York. I thanked her and declined. Thereafter Mrs. Reid spoke at length of Miss Hepburn, who was to make a talk at the dinner. Over and over she spoke words of praise for Miss Hepburn's acting, each time asking if I did not agree with her. My notes on this telephone conversation show that I, too, spoke words of praise for Miss Hepburn, saying that I enjoyed her work in "Little Women" so much—and, I may add, my remarks were sincere. At this, Miss Reid moved in on me with horse, foot and tanks, asking if I did not think Miss Hepburn the perfect type for Scarlett. I thought, "Oh, good God, here we go again," and told her that I had a strict rule of never discussing who should play Scarlett, that I never made any statements about it, one way or the other, that it was a matter for Mr. Selznick to decide, not me, and that I truly did not care who got the role. I also said, with considerable restraint, that here in the South we had quick ears for voices and that Miss Hepburn's perfect New England accent would scarcely be acceptable to people of this section.

The next thing I knew the news services and the press were on my neck, saying that the New York newspapers were stating that Mrs. Reid had "disclosed that she had visited Margaret Mitchell, author of 'Gone With the Wind,' at her home at Atlanta, Georgia, and that Miss Mitchell had expressed a strong preference for Miss Hepburn for the screen role of the heroine of her famous novel." Of course they wanted a statement from me.

As you can imagine, I was on the spot—a spot I had occupied, wearily and far too often, during those years. It would have pleased the papers very much had I said flatly that Mrs. Reid had lied, and you can imagine what fine reverberations that would have had in gossip columns all over the country. At the risk of having you think me stuffy and old fashioned, I want to say that I think "brawling and feuding" in the public press is in very poor taste and, short of direct attacks upon my moral character or my private life, I do not make controversial statements. I told the press the whole situation and implored them to state my position without writing anything which might embarrass the innocent Miss Hepburn or the not-so-innocent Mrs. Reid. The papers were very kind about it. Life for November 7, 1938, for instance, said, "In introducing her, Mrs. Ogden Reid, vice-president of the Tribune, nominated Miss Hepburn for Scarlett O'Hara in the movie 'Gone With the Wind,' intimated the suggestion was Author Margaret Mitchell's choice. Politely, Miss Mitchell denied this, said she had no preferences." I am enclosing a copy of a story the Atlanta Journal printed. When these stories came out Mrs. Reid wired, saying she was "terribly sorry if I have caused you any annoyance," and then wrote. Her letter said, "I feel that I owe you an apology for not having asked if you minded me saying what I did." (What she had said was that Miss Hepburn was my choice "first, last and always," according to a copy of her remarks which she enclosed.) She could give little explanation for her conduct except that she thought I was merely being coy and "over-retiring" and that any movie producer ought to welcome my opinion.

Well, the "Who will play Scarlett?" controversy was ended a few months later when Miss Leigh's selection was announced and that phase of my life was over. Or is it over? If you should publish Miss Hepburn's statement that she was my secret choice, I am afraid the controversy would break out again, not as widespread and excited as before, but enough to put on me the burden of writing many letters and issuing fresh denials—and the time when I can do some more writing will be still further postponed, for the

Scarlett controversy is one of the principal things that have used up my time and prevented me from attempting any writing since 1936.

Possibly, Miss Hepburn is quite innocent in her statement. It may be that Mrs. Reid led her to believe that I did secretly favor her. But it is not true and I hope you will not publish the falsehood.

I have been very frank with you in this letter, franker than I generally am, and perhaps far more frank than is wise. But I know enough of you by now to believe that you will keep this confidential.

I wish more editors of my acquaintance had been like you in the past and had asked me questions before hurrying into print. My life would certainly have been far less eventful.*

With many thanks,

Miss Helen L. Cornforth   *Atlanta, Georgia*
Rocky Hill, Connecticut   *October 1, 1941*

Dear Miss Cornforth:

When I came to the end of your letter and read your statement that you were fourteen years old, I was truly surprised because I had received the impression that you were a much older person. I thank you for your letter. It was a thoughtful one and it showed great perception. You are right—most readers took it for granted Scarlett was the heroine of my book, but, to me, the author, Melanie was the true heroine. There have been some readers like you who were more impressed by her than by Scarlett, but such readers are few and far between. The flamboyance of Scarlett evidently overshadows the more solid virtues of Melanie and I suppose it is only natural that most people are more interested in the victories of the flesh than in those of the spirit.

It was good of you to tell me that my Melanie had done something nice for you. I wish you could have seen Miss DeHavilland as she looked when she came to call on me the night before the Atlanta premiere of the motion picture. She was much smaller than I thought she would be and looked no older than a high school girl. She wore no makeup and her hair was plainly done. She looked as lovely off the screen as she does on it. Miss Leigh came with her and she was a surprise, too, for she is quite tiny and she, too, had a charming, innocent, little-girl look.

---

* The article, "The Hepburn Story," by Lupton A. Wilkinson and J. Bryan III, appeared in the January 3, 1942, issue of *Saturday Evening Post*. The only reference to *Gone With the Wind* was in the opening sentence, which said Hepburn lost the role of Scarlett O'Hara "through her studio's timidity."

Because of your interest, I am sending you a pamphlet printed by my publishers.* It deals with the background of "Gone With the Wind" and I hope you will like it.

Miss Katharine Brown   *Atlanta, Georgia*
David O. Selznick Productions, Inc.   *October 4, 1941*
New York, New York

Dear Kay:†

You are a grand person to take so much trouble about the GWTW chandeliers. I am truly grateful to you and I know the doctors will be equally grateful when I tell them. The doctor at the head of the building committee (the one who talked to me the day you were here) has really been having a fit with a fringe on it ever since he got the notion that their new Academy of Medicine had a chance of getting Mr. Selznick's and Rhett's chandelier. He confided to me the other day that he wasn't sleeping at all well and got up and walked the floor at three a.m. when he thought how posterity would come to view his building and the chandelier. All over again, I had that strange feeling I always get at the way this section takes the book and the picture. As I told you, they no longer belong to me or Mr. Selznick.

I have not told the doctor of your connection with Mr. Selznick. I merely said that a friend of mine who was connected with the movie business knew Joe Platt and would make inquiries. I believe I can get all medical treatment free from this doctor. Unfortunately, he is a skin specialist and my skin does pretty well for the most part. But if they do get the chandelier and I do get the seven years' itch, I am sure I will be well taken care of. The doctor is out of town now but will return Monday and I will relay the contents of your letter of October 2nd to him. Thanks so much. It really means a great deal to the medical men here. Do not bother about writing Mr. Klune about checking the commercial house. Mr. Platt's information is all they will need. . . .‡

It was grand seeing you and we wish you'd come oftener.

---

* The twenty-two-page booklet, *Margaret Mitchell and Her Novel* Gone With the Wind, was put out by Macmillan in October 1936 to answer some of the many questions the company received from readers.

† This appears to be the only time Mitchell called Brown "Kay" in a letter; she usually called her "Katharine."

‡ Platt reported that all of the chandeliers used in *Gone With the Wind* were reproductions rented from prop companies. Ray Klune was the film's production manager.

Miss Katharine Brown   *Atlanta, Georgia*
David O. Selznick Productions, Inc.   *October 24, 1941*
New York, New York

Dear Katharine:

... I have been out of town junketing about South Georgia on drafty day coaches and catching the world's worst cold. Otherwise, I would have written you to thank you for your further efforts on the chandelier. I came home ill and have been harassed beyond endurance by one of the doctors who has developed an obsession about having the chandelier. I told him I had done all I could possibly do and the rest was up to him. What I am now going to write is, of course, confidential, but if a certain circumstance should arise I want you to quote me. I am very much afraid that behind my back and without my knowledge this doctor will use my name in an attempt to pry the chandelier out of the owner or get a cheaper price. For all I know, he may even approach Mr. Selznick on the matter. I want you and Mr. Selznick and everybody concerned to know that I am asking no favors whatever on this subject, really have no connection with it except a willingness to do the doctors a favor by finding out where it was, and do not intend to be connected with the matter in any way. Of course I'd like for them to have the chandelier if they want it, but that is their little red wagon and not mine, and I have no intention of harassing anyone about it or trying to bring pressure on anyone.

I came home through Macon and spent the night with Sue. I told her that I was writing you and she asked me to send you her love. She's up to her neck in the Little Theatre, for they are putting on "The Man Who Came to Dinner."

Miss Katharine Brown   *Atlanta, Georgia*
David O. Selznick Productions, Inc.   *November 3, 1941*
New York, New York

Dear Katharine:

You will recall that when we were waiting for your airplane we were discussing vehicles for Ingrid Bergman.* You said that if ever I had a notion to pass it on to you. I have a notion and it is one I mentioned to you two or

---

* In 1938, Brown went to Sweden and persuaded Bergman to sign a contract with Selznick. The actress made her American film debut, opposite Leslie Howard, in 1939's *Intermezzo*, which Selznick produced concurrently with *Gone With the Wind*.

three years ago. It is Mary Johnston's "To Have and to Hold." I believe you told me at that time that someone else owned the rights to this book. . . .

About the confounded chandelier—I have just heard the West Coast people who owned it wanted $4,000 for it and the doctors couldn't reach that price, so they dropped the matter.* I do not know whether they will buy the reproduction which is in New York. Having been harassed by the obsessed dermatologist until I was broken out in an allergic rash, I really do not care at this point. Anyway, I am very grateful to you for all the trouble you took!

Miss Katharine Brown   *Atlanta, Georgia*
David O. Selznick Productions, Inc.   *November 14, 1941*
New York, New York

Dear Katharine:

Thank you for writing me about the Metro trailer in which the words "Gone With the Wind" are used. I have no objection at all to the use of the title in this fashion, and I will appreciate it if you will pass this information on to the proper persons.† By the way, if you should ever meet the author of "The Vanishing Virginian," Rebecca Yancey Williams, of Richmond, I am sure you will like her a lot. She and her husband are very fine people.

David O. Selznick   *Atlanta, Georgia*
Selznick International Pictures, Inc.   *December 24, 1941*
Culver City, California

THE CHRISTMAS SEASON WILL ALWAYS BRING BACK MEMORIES OF THE EXCITING EVENTS WE SHARED WITH YOU IN DECEMBER 1939. OUR SINCERE GOOD WISHES TO YOU AND MRS SELZNICK FOR CHRISTMAS AND THE NEW YEAR.

---

* On October 31, Dr. Howard Hailey, president of the Fulton County Medical Society, wrote to Mitchell, "We were unable to get the price of $4,000 reduced so, therefore, the idea had to be abandoned." However, the website for the former Academy of Medicine building, now part of the Georgia Institute of Technology and used as a venue for wedding receptions, meetings, and dinners, touts its "rotunda accented by the famous Czechoslovakian chandelier seen in the movie *Gone With the Wind*."

† The trailer for MGM's forthcoming motion picture *The Vanishing Virginian* opened with a large map of the southeastern United States. The camera moved to a close-up of Georgia as the narrator noted, "Out of Georgia came *Gone With the Wind*." The camera then moved to Florida: "Out of Florida came *The Yearling*." Finally, it swung to Virginia: "From Virginia came another great story, *The Vanishing Virginian*."

Mrs. Sidney Howard   *Atlanta, Georgia*
Stockbridge, Massachusetts   *December 31, 1941*

Dear Mrs. Howard:

Please forgive my delay in answering your letter of December 10th. As my secretary wrote you, I have been on the jump since the war broke out.*

I am so very sorry to write you that I cannot find any letters from Mr. Howard to me.† I had several letters from him, probably written in 1936 or early 1937, telling of some of his Hollywood problems and mentioning that he hoped to bring you with him to visit in Atlanta. That was during the most nightmarish period of my life and what became of his letters I do not know. I did not have a regular full time secretary then and I believe I destroyed most letters which did not deal with business matters. I still have not completely crawled from under the debris that the "wind" left. When I get the opportunity to go through the piles of stuff that have accumulated in six years, it may be that I will find a letter from Mr. Howard somewhere in the clippings and boxes and souvenirs. If I should, of course I will let you know immediately. I am sorrier than I can say that I cannot help you.

My husband and I have thought of you and Mr. Howard so often, for we were so regretful that your visit to Atlanta never took place and never can take place. We had had the greatest admiration for his work long before he did "Gone With the Wind" and it was a constant source of pride and relief that he was the one who did the work. We hoped some day to talk over with him the strange and idiotic experiences he had in Hollywood.

I remember with extraordinary vividness meeting you at the Press Club tea at the Piedmont Driving Club during the "Gone With the Wind" premiere. I've often hoped that you would come back to Atlanta, perhaps on your way to Florida, and that you would let us know you were here. Please do phone us should you ever be in town. It would give us great pleasure to have you for dinner.

---

* On December 7, 1941, the Japanese bombed the U.S. Pacific Fleet at Pearl Harbor, Hawaii. Congress declared war the next day.

† Howard was killed on August 23, 1939, when a tractor he was trying to start at his Tyringham, Massachusetts, farm lurched forward, pinning him against a wall. When his screenplay for *Gone With the Wind* was recognized with an Academy Award, Howard became the first posthumous Oscar winner.

Mr. and Mrs. David O. Selznick   *Atlanta, Georgia*
David O. Selznick Productions, Inc.   *December 31, 1941*
Culver City, California

Dear Mr. and Mrs. Selznick:

I was not at home for Christmas but was, of all places, in the Brooklyn Navy Yard. The new cruiser "Atlanta," which I christened last fall, was commissioned by the Navy on Christmas Eve and I made a hurried trip North to be present at the ceremonies. I had little sense of Christmas time until I returned home and opened the large and exciting package you sent. Then I experienced all the pleasures I had missed and many others, too, and I cannot thank you enough, both for the gift and for my pleasure. The three silver platters are so very lovely and the box in which they are displayed is a thing of beauty and fine workmanship in itself. John and I have examined and re-examined the platters and each time our pleasure has been greater. It may interest you to know that their initial use will be at a small party for Sue Myrick, who is to be our guest on New Year's Day. As we had no Christmas fun, we are inviting a few of the newspaper people you met on your visit here, and we will have the silver on the table bearing baked ham and fruit cake and other New Year's nicknacks. I know all of our guests will admire this Irish silver even as we do. Thank you again for sending the very thing which would please me most.

I hope you haven't become wearied of hearing about the film of "Gone With the Wind," for there are some things I want to tell you even at this late date. Time and again in the last few years, I've wished so much to have one unhurried day with you, Mr. Selznick, so that I could tell you some of the many fine things I've heard about your picture. I know you are enough of an artist to appreciate the honest statements of humble people as much as those of great critics and prominent personages. John and I have seen the picture five times—the last three times being in small neighborhood houses. The audiences were interestingly compounded of self-important people seeing the picture for the seventh or eighth time and others who were having their first experience because the earlier price had been prohibitive for them. I have wished that you could sit in one of these small movies, unknown to anyone, and see the genuinely moving effect the film has even on those who can almost quote the whole scenario. I know it would make you feel amply repaid for the nerve-racking years you spent in producing it. And always, when the film has finished, numbers of people, mostly strangers, stop me in the lobby and talk and talk as though under a spell.

You know how an old movie is almost as dated as an old newspaper, but that isn't the case with "Gone With the Wind." People still discuss it and almost the first question I am asked when visiting in strange towns is, "And what did you really think of Clark Gable or Vivien Leigh or Olivia de Havilland?" When I was visiting at the Brooklyn Navy Yard and was the guest of an admiral at a thoroughly Navy party, at a time when the news from Manila was bad, I expected that all conversation would be about the Pacific Fleet. But no, I was interested and grateful that the Naval people fell to talking about the film with avidity, arguing different points with genuine interest. I thanked Heaven for this subject of conversation which kept us all from dwelling too much on the Eastern situation.

I am sure that the war is causing many problems in your industry and that many headaches are being experienced as moving picture producers try to anticipate what will interest a wartime public six months from now. I know you do not have to bother about this. You are going to give solid and sincere entertainment, and the public appreciates this, be it peace or war. So, John and I are wishing you a prosperous New Year, and that wish is not a conventional formality.

With many thanks for the beautiful silver,

Mr. Clark Gable   *Atlanta, Georgia*
MGM   *January 19, 1942*
Hollywood, California

Dear Mr. Gable:

Your wife brought so much beauty and gaiety and uplift of spirits to millions of people that all of us who ever saw her feel a sick, stunned sense of loss.* We can only faintly estimate what her going means to you who knew her best, and our sincere sympathies are with you. My husband and I are grateful for the privilege of having met her briefly at the time of the "Gone With the Wind" premiere. We will never forget her.

---

* Lombard was killed on January 16, 1942, in a plane crash outside Las Vegas while returning from a war bond rally in her home state of Indiana. Mitchell recalled the actress for the Atlanta newspapers: "She was so interested in raising chickens and that's mainly what we talked about. She asked me if her husband could talk with me privately for a few minutes and I thought how nice she was, just like any other good wife, to be arranging things for him. She and her husband sent me a chicken packed in ice for Christmas that year. It was good. I remember that when we went to the premiere of the picture I saw her slip Clark her handkerchief during a sad scene when Bonnie died. I'm sure I heard him when he tooted his nose."

Miss Katharine Brown   *Atlanta, Georgia*
David O. Selznick Productions, Inc.   *February 16, 1942*
New York, New York

Dear Katharine:

I was in New York recently for a hurried week-end and telephoned your office but got no answer, for it was Saturday. The weather was bad and I acquired my usual New York sore throat and earache and had to return home speedily. I hope you are having better weather in California than the kind New York was enduring when I was there.

Katharine, we do not mind discussing the musicalization at all and you must know by now that we like to hear from you, whether it is on business or personal matters. I have no objection to selling the rights for a musicalization of "Gone With the Wind" if we can get together on a satisfactory proposition, both as to amount of money and talent search. I know we have talked about this matter a number of times and a few letters have passed between us but—just to discuss the money angle of it—Mr. Selznick has not yet come out with a definite dollars and cents price. I do not see how we can begin to work out the details of this sale until a definite sales price has been made by him and accepted or rejected by me. As I told you when you were here in Atlanta last, I'd like an offer made me of a flat sum in cash plus a percentage of the royalties. I do not think any amount of money in the world would make it worth while to me to undergo again the horrors of a talent search and the indignities inflicted by movie publicity men. But you have said that these matters could be adjusted, too. So, if they can be adjusted and if the price Mr. Selznick is willing to give me is sufficient, I'll be glad to do business with him. But tell him he'll have to make me a price of a flat sum plus a percentage before we can begin to trade. . . .

Miss Katharine Brown   *Atlanta, Georgia*
David O. Selznick Productions, Inc.   *March 16, 1942*
New York, New York

Dear Katharine:

It's all right with me if you and Mr. Selznick wish to wait until the middle of the year for further discussion about the musicalization. John and I are up to our necks in civilian defense at present and Steve is on one of the draft boards, so we wouldn't have much time for business matters anyhow. When Mr. Selznick has the opportunity to formulate definite notions, we'll be glad to hear from you.

In your reference to an option, I understand that you refer to one after we may have come to some agreement, and not to an option now. I mention this so we won't have any misunderstandings. I have no objections to your waiting until next summer to submit your offer but I am not bound to you in the meantime. If something attractive should develop from some other source, I am free to act on it.

Laura Hope Crews was in town with "Arsenic and Old Lace."* Mrs. Kurtz took me to the matinee and I took Miss Crews and the Kurtzes and Sue Myrick out for cocktails. Our time was brief but it was lots of fun and it was good to rehash the Second Battle of Atlanta with veterans.

Miss Katharine Brown   *Atlanta, Georgia*
David O. Selznick Productions, Inc.   *July 17, 1942*
New York, New York

Dear Katharine:

Of course I was prepared for the news but it was with a sense of sadness that I learned that you and the Selznick outfit were going separate ways. It is difficult for John and me to think of you and Selznick Productions as separate entities. Heaven knows you were an aid and comfort in our relations and I'm glad we had you with us at that time. Wherever you go, you'll be a valuable person and someone is going to be lucky if he gets you.

You know by now how limited my knowledge is of moving pictures and producers. I've heard of H.S. but at this moment I cannot place him or what he has done.† When and if you make this connection, and have the time, I wish you'd write and tell us about him. The things you wrote about his personality make it appear that he'd be a fine person to work for.

Sue Myrick was in town the other night and was pleased to know that I had seen you. She said to send you her best when I wrote.

Of course John and I will call you up when next we come to New York, though Heaven knows when that will be. I'm afraid our traveling is over for some time to come.

Our best to you and Jim.

P.S. Does this mean that Mr. Selznick is going in the army?

---

* *Arsenic and Old Lace*, a comedy by Joseph Kesselring, tells the story of two spinster sisters who poison lonely old men with a glass of their homemade elderberry wine. The play opened on Broadway in 1941 and played 1,444 performances.

† Hunt Stromberg was an independent film producer. While at MGM, he made such movies as the *Thin Man* series with William Powell and Myrna Loy, *Marie Antoinette*, and *The Women*, Cukor's first motion picture after being fired from *Gone With the Wind*.

Mr. Virginius Dabney   *Atlanta, Georgia*
Richmond, Virginia   *July 23, 1942*

Dear Mr. Dabney:

I know I should wait until I have finished your book, "Below the Potomac," before writing to you, but war work and my father's serious illness leave me little time for reading these days and I do not know when I will have the pleasure of completing your book.* So, after reading only one chapter, "The South That Never Was," I am writing to thank you for the fine things you said about Susan Myrick and me, and for the accuracy of your observations about my reactions to the film, "Gone With the Wind."

I was so very pleased at the credit you gave Susan for the Southern accent (or rather, for the lack of Southern accent) in the film. I've always felt that she did not get enough credit outside of her own section for the truly miraculous job she did. For nearly three years the South rared and pitched and muttered threats about seceding from the Union again if "you all" was used when addressing one person or if any actor spoke as if he had a mouth full of hot buttered okra. Unfortunately for me, who had nothing to do with the film, a great deal of this raring and pitching took place on our doorstep, in our parlor and over our telephone, as embittered Southerners demanded that I "do something" to keep travesties of our accent from the film. Susan was the one who "did something"—and far better than I could have done. I thought the finest praise she received was this—after the premiere here in Atlanta, I went to a large party and encountered some of our dowagers who had been most belligerent about the Southern accent. I questioned, "And what did you think about the accent in the picture?" They looked at me and said, rather blankly, "What accent?"

I am glad you made the statement about the prologue of the motion picture and its reference to cavaliers in the South. Some people gave me the credit for writing it and thought it was "just beautiful"; others, who knew the section about which I wrote, belabored me for dislocating one of the central ideas of the book. It was useless for me to protest that I had nothing to do with the matter. I certainly had no intention of writing about cavaliers. Practically all my characters, except the Virginia Wilkeses, were of sturdy yeoman stock.†

---

* *Below the Potomac: A Book about the New South*, was published in 1942 by D. Appleton-Century Company.

† Dabney noted that the accents in the film were "a miraculous exception" to the usual synthetic southern speech in most Hollywood movies and gave Myrick the credit. He also charged that the film's opening prologue—which begins, "There was a Land of Cavaliers and Cotton Fields called the old South"—"distorts" the milieu of Mitchell's novel.

Thank you for your statement about the profusion of white columns on the Georgia plantation homes. Many of us were hard put not to burst into laughter at the sight of "Twelve Oaks." We agreed afterwards that the only comparisons we could bring to mind was with the State Capitol at Montgomery, Alabama. In the pages of unwritten history, no fiercer fight was ever fought than the one centering around columns on the motion picture "Tara." The Georgians present at the making of the film, Susan Myrick and Mr. and Mrs. Wilbur Kurtz, of Atlanta, weren't able to keep columns off of "Tara" entirely, but they managed a compromise by having the pillars square, as were those of our Upcountry houses in that day, if they had columns at all.

I think this chapter, "The South That Never Was," is fine and thoughtful writing. However, I believe that we Southerners could write the truth about the ante-bellum South, its few slaveholders, its yeoman farmers, its rambling, comfortable houses just fifty years away from log cabins, until Gabriel blows his trump—and everyone would go on believing in the Hollywood version. The sad part is that many Southerners believe this myth even more ardently than Northerners. A number of years ago some of us organized a club, The Association of Southerners Whose Grandpappies Did Not Live in Houses With White Columns. May I extend you an invitation to join? Its membership would be enormous if all of the eligibles came in.

Since my novel was published, I have been embarrassed on many occasions by finding myself included among writers who pictured the South as a land of white-columned mansions whose wealthy owners had thousands of slaves and drank thousands of juleps. I have been surprised, too, for North Georgia certainly was no such country—if it ever existed anywhere—and I took great pains to describe North Georgia as it was. But people believe what they like to believe and the mythical Old South has too strong a hold on their imaginations to be altered by the mere reading of a 1,037-page book. So I have made no effort to defend myself against the accusation but it was a great satisfaction to me that a man of your perceptiveness knew that my South was not "The South That Never Was." I thank you for your understanding and for what you wrote.

My husband and I remember with pleasure meeting you several years ago at the Biltmore in the company of Julian Harris, Mark Ethridge, et cetera.* We will be happy to renew this acquaintance should you ever be in Atlanta again.

---

* Julian Harris, a son of author Joel Chandler Harris, was a former editor of the *Atlanta Constitution* and the *Chattanooga Times* and the southern correspondent for the *New York Times*.

With renewed thanks for the understanding of my attitude which you expressed in your book,

Mr. John Hay Whitney   *Atlanta, Georgia*
Mr. David O. Selznick   *August 31, 1942*
Selznick International Pictures, Inc.
New York, New York

Dear Mr. Whitney and Mr. Selznick:

I came home from a long day at the Red Cross, too tired to take my shoes off, and started going through the day's mail. At the bottom of a stack of very dull correspondence, I found your letter. Tired as I was, I had to read it twice before it made sense, and thereafter weariness of foot and head left me immediately. It was not only the very generous check clipped to the letter but the letter itself which raised my spirits and, at the same time, almost made me cry.*

It is true that you two and I and hundreds of others have been associated in the most phenomenally successful event in motion picture or theatrical history. All of us, even to the humblest needleworker in the wardrobe department, have had a part in a great undertaking which has given pleasure to millions of people and, if I am any judge, will continue to give pleasure for many years to come. And all of us have a right to feel a sense of pride, and wonderment too. Yes, there were periods of strain and weariness and years of disruption of life and routine. Such things, I daresay, are unavoidable in any great undertaking, be it a great motion picture or the prosecution of a war. No, I will "never have cause to regret" that your company made the film version of my book. I have seen the picture five-and-a-half times now and have examined it from many angles—musical score, costumes, bit players et cetera, and I like it better each time. And each time the film reaches out and takes my hand to lead me down paths that seem ever new, for I forget in watching that I was the author of the book and am able to view the film with fresh eyes.

At the Grand Theatre here in Atlanta, they play the theme music from "Gone With the Wind" in the interludes between pictures and when the last performances of the night are over. Frequently John and I and many other Atlantans remain in our seats to listen to it, not only because it is beautiful but because we want to recapture the sensations of the first time

---

* On the final dissolution of Selznick International Pictures, Inc., Selznick and Whitney sent Mitchell a check for $50,000 for "your part in making the outcome of the company's activities so successful."

we heard it at the premiere. I never hear this music without feeling again the strange mixture of emotions that I experienced on that night nearly three years ago when I sat in this same theatre and saw the film for the first time. I doubt if I could describe those emotions but they did not include fear that it would not be a great picture.

Years before, I had seen your "David Copperfield" and loved it. When I saw it I realized that here was a producer of both genius and integrity who was breaking all Hollywood rules by producing the book the author wrote, by translating onto the screen what was in the author's mind and the author's heart, adding to it his own color, firing it with his own imagination, heightening effects with his own genius. So, on the night of the premiere, I knew before the film began to roll that it would be a great picture and before many minutes had passed, I knew it was even greater than I could have expected. Yes, I have always thought myself fortunate that Selznick International produced "Gone With the Wind."

As for the check, I can only say "thank you." Its unexpectedness heightened my pleasure in receiving it and, coming at this particular period in our history, it is more welcome than it could be at any other time. I hope it will make you gentlemen happy to know that a large part of it will go for defense bonds and for the assistance of those organizations which need so much money these days—the Red Cross, the USO et cetera.

I will, of course, be glad to join with you in keeping this whole matter confidential. It is fine of you to wish to have it handled that way and you can count on my cooperation.

The war and your work keep you busy these days but perhaps the war and your work will bring you to Atlanta some time. Should that happen, it would give John and me great pleasure to see you, even if briefly between planes. As we are veterans of the same "war," it would be fun to refight this war together.

My good wishes to you both and, again, my very sincere thanks for your letter and the check.

Miss Beatrice Prall, Librarian   *October 23, 1942*
Public Library   *Atlanta, Georgia*
Saginaw, Michigan

Dear Miss Prall:

The reason the Library patron could not find the words which open the moving picture of "Gone With the Wind" in the book was that these words do not appear in the book. I am not the author of this prologue. I am sorry that I cannot tell you who wrote these opening words, as I had nothing to do with the production of the film and did not write a line of the scenario or the additional dialogue. However, I will hazard the guess that the late Sidney Howard was the author of these words. Mr. Howard wrote the script of "Gone With the Wind."

In the concocting of moving pictures many hands stir the broth and many brains go into the preparations. It is possible that some other writer was the author of these poetic words. I advise you to write to the producer himself, Mr. David O. Selznick, David O. Selznick Productions, Inc., Culver City, California, and ask him for definite information.*

At the time of the premiere of "Gone With the Wind" in Atlanta, Mr. Selznick presented me with a bound copy of the "shooting script" of "Gone With the Wind" and I am copying for you the prologue as it appears in this script:†

> "There was a land of Cavaliers and
> Cotton Fields called the old South . . .
> Here in this patrician world the
> Age of Chivalry took its last bow . . .
> Here was the last ever to be seen
> of Knights and their Ladies Fair,
> of Master and of Slave . . .
> Look for it only in books, for it
> is no more than a dream remembered,
> a Civilization gone with the wind . . ."‡

Thank you for telling me that the Library was again having a run on "Gone With the Wind." Even after all this time, I have never become accustomed to what has happened to my book and each nice thing I hear about it makes me feel just as queer as the first nice thing.

---

* Ben Hecht wrote the prologue and other titles in the film.
† In December 1939, Selznick presented more than fifty bound and inscribed copies of the *Gone With the Wind* screenplay to various cast and crew members, original investors in Selznick International, and others associated with the film. Interestingly, the copy he gave to the author, which is in the Margaret Mitchell Collection in Special Collections at the Atlanta-Fulton Public Library System, is the only known copy, other than his personal one, that is not signed.
‡ The on-screen prologue varies slightly from the script. In the film, the second line reads, "Here in this pretty world Gallantry took its last bow . . ."

Dr. Herman L. Turner   *Atlanta, Georgia*
Covenant Presbyterian Church   *November 5, 1942*
Atlanta, Georgia

Dear Doctor Turner:

It was very kind of you to relay to me the letter from your English friend about the long run of "Gone With the Wind" in London.* It is incredible, isn't it? And the most incredible thing of all is that I was told that during the worst of the bombings, when much of London lay in ruins, people were going to the theatre to see little Atlanta destroyed. When I first heard of this I wondered why people who had suffered such disasters did not go to see something light and amusing to take their minds off their troubles. After thinking it over, I've come to the conclusion that perhaps the knowledge that other people suffered similar disaster and yet rose again, with little to help them except their own courage, was a heartening experience. Only recently the film was released in the English "provinces" and yesterday I heard from the mother of an Atlanta boy stationed in England. She said her son and other Atlanta soldiers had been to see the picture several times. If it brings back memories of home—even a home the boys never saw—it makes me very happy.

Mr. David O. Selznick   *Atlanta, Georgia*
David O. Selznick Productions, Inc.   *December 19, 1942*
Culver City, California

Dear Mr. Selznick:

I have just returned home and found your letter of December 3rd waiting for me. With the hot breath of Christmas on my neck and my work for the Red Cross on my back, I'll not try to answer it now but I will do so immediately after the holidays.

Mid-December will always bring memories of you and Mrs. Selznick, the other famous people from Hollywood and the Atlanta premiere. I

---

* *Gone With the Wind* had a triple premiere in London on April 18, 1940, at the Empire, Palace, and Ritz theaters. Among those at the gala screenings were Leslie Howard, fellow British actor Robert Donat, and First Lord of the Admiralty—and future prime minister—Winston Churchill. The film initially played five weeks at the Ritz, eight weeks at the Palace, and twelve weeks at the Empire. It reopened at the Ritz on Leicester Square on August 2, 1940, and ran for 201 weeks through the worst of the London Blitz. "Once our cash box was damaged and the front doors blown off," the manager recalled, "but we never missed a performance." The film closed on June 8, 1944, two days after the Allies' D-Day invasion of Europe.

am not the only one who remembers this anniversary. Yesterday at the canteen, a number of women smiled and said, "About this time three years ago we were just getting over the premiere and our orchids had just about given up the ghost!"

I do not know what your plans are for this coming year or for any of our wartime years, but I wish you great success in them. I know whatever you do will be fine.

John and I send our sincere good wishes to you and Mrs. Selznick and your family for a happy and peaceful Christmas season.

Mr. David O. Selznick   *Atlanta, Georgia*
David O. Selznick Productions, Inc.   *January 4, 1943*
Culver City, California

Dear Mr. Selznick:

My long silence concerning your kind letter of December 3rd and your beautiful Christmas gift must make me seem remiss and unappreciative. This is not the case, for I was so pleased and grateful to you for both. I was out of the city when your letter arrived and I had scarcely stepped off the train when I was called on a Red Cross job which has just finished. The traveling Army War Show of several thousand men and their equipment was parked in the park across the street from our apartment and a Red Cross canteen was opened for them in the neighborhood. I can sew and so I drew the mending detail. I spent the holiday season sewing on buttons and altering overcoats and patching holes in trousers. Between this job and the time I must spend with my father in the hospital, I have not drawn a free breath since early December.

I cannot tell you what a joy your Christmas basket was. All my meals were snatched at the canteen, they generally consisted of a doughnut and a saltine cracker from the hands of some hungry soldier. Late at night, I would get a can opener and explore the contents of your basket, with the result that I had doughnuts by day and pate de fois gras, green turtle soup, Gorgonzola cheese and rum cakes by night. I recommend highly this diet for all canteen workers and thank you so much for this exotic fare in the midst of an underfed and overworked month. We haven't had the plum pudding yet, as we are saving it for some special occasion such as the furloughs of old friends now in the army.

It is good of you to still be interested in having me write something for you for the films. Unfortunately, as the war deepens my time for writing lessens. As I have had no time at all for writing since 1936, it is difficult to see how I would have less time now, but that is true. My war work is heavy and the increasing feebleness of my sick father occupies what time I can take from war work. There just isn't a minute left over for writing. I sincerely hope my life will not always be as crowded and that the time will come when I can again think about work, but that time is not now.

Of course I read everything I see about you and the newspapers carry many interesting hints and rumors about your activities. I have long since learned not to believe what I read in gossip columns but, just the same, I can't help being interested and curious, and I'll be happy when I sit in a theatre and see once more David O. Selznick's name upon the screen.

My very best to you and Mrs. Selznick.

1st Lieutenant Clark Gable   *Atlanta, Georgia*
U.S. Air Force   *January 8, 1943*
Tyndall Field, Florida

Dear Mr. Gable:

Yesterday's paper brought the news that you had won your wings as an air gunner and John and I send you our congratulations and sincere good wishes. I do not know where you will be sent and I do not suppose you know either at this time but, if, by any chance, you should be stationed anywhere near Atlanta, we hope you will come to see us. Needless to say, if you did come, we would do what we could to keep your visit a private one and not a newspaper holiday, although I know that would be difficult. I remember with interest and pleasure our brief meeting at the time of the premiere of "Gone With the Wind," when, for a brief period, you were not the world's best known screen star, not the glamorous and sought after Gable, but an honest person who wanted to talk about honest things like raising chickens.

Because pictures of you and me were broadcast everywhere at the time of the premiere, I have had some very amusing experiences, as we seem linked in the public mind and the public refuses to believe I am not the final authority on you and your military career. A couple of months ago, I went to visit old friends in Moultrie, Georgia, just to spend a quiet week-end and see their children whom I had never met. There is a flying field and air camp at Moultrie, and I found that both camp and town were in an understandable state of excitement.* Newspapers had carried stories that you had gone on leave and when I arrived in Moultrie I

---

* The U.S. Army Air Force's Spence Air Base opened at Moultrie in 1941.

found myself in the flattering but embarrassing position of having come to Moultrie to meet you. I was not told this at first but I could not help noticing the air of expectant excitement. I finally learned the truth and, I am afraid, caused great disappointment (and suffered loss of prestige) when I said I had no idea where you were and certainly did not expect you at Moultrie. I'd like to add that the feeling of these nice people in South Georgia was not the somewhat hysterical and hero-worshipping feeling which has doubtless caused you trouble in the past. One and all thought you were "regular" and they had a feeling of pride in your enlistment and the fine record you had made.

Again, congratulations. I hope you are sent where you want to go.

Mr. Paul D. O'Brien   *Atlanta, Georgia*
O'Brien, Driscoll & Raftery   *January 27, 1943*
New York, New York

Dear Mr. O'Brien:

I hope you will pardon my delay in answering your letter of January 12th. I intended to acknowledge it, but almost simultaneous with its arrival came the news of the loss of the cruiser "Atlanta."* I was sponsor of this ship at her christening and the news was a shock to me, as it was to the rest of the city. Since then, a hot campaign to raise thirty-five million dollars to replace the cruiser has been going on and I have hardly been in my office.

We thank you very much for the figures you sent us on the cost of large New York theatrical productions. We found them interesting and informative. However, we find ourselves back at our original starting point and faced with the same situation. That is, we think Mr. Selznick should make us an offer. Then we can talk business.

In trying to get back of business matters and understand human motives behind business conduct, I'd like to ask you a personal and confidential question. Does Mr. Selznick hesitate to make me an offer because he thinks I have such exaggerated ideas of the value of my property that I would be indignant unless he offered a billion dollars? Do you think that is why he has not talked dollars and cents to me and has dodged away from making me an offer? If so, he is quite wrong. I know the dramatic rights are valuable and, being a normal human being, I want to realize

---

* The USS *Atlanta* was sunk on November 13, 1942, during the Battle of Guadalcanal.

something from them, but I do not put any exaggerated value on them. I hope and believe I am willing to accept a price which would be fair to everyone concerned.

I was frank with you when you were here in Atlanta, when I told you of my ignorance of theatrical matters and costs et cetera. I was not being coy nor was I hoss-trading when I told you that I wanted an offer made me—on the basis of a flat sum and a percentage. The only way I know how to do business is: I have something which someone wants to buy, they make me an offer, I either accept or reject it. If I reject it, then the would-be purchaser and I get together to try to iron out our differences and frequently, by compromise and adjustment on both sides, a happy conclusion is reached.

When you were in Atlanta, I outlined some of the provisions I would want included in any contract and I discussed, as frankly as I was able, the general basis on which I might be willing to trade. I cannot go any further than that, and the next step is up to Mr. Selznick. If I had in my mind some specific figure which I wanted him to meet, I would not hesitate to tell you. But I have not thought of even an approximate amount, and I would not know how to go about setting a price. The figures you sent me are interesting and they may be helpful at some later stage of the discussions, but right now there is nothing to discuss because no offer has been made.

In conclusion, if you and Mr. Selznick are waiting for me to make you an offer, you may as well forget about the whole matter. Mr. Selznick is the one to make the offer, not me, partly because he is the one who initiated this discussion but chiefly because he knows, and I do not, what kind of offer he is in position to make. All of this seems so obvious to me that, frankly, his conduct in the whole situation seems very strange.

Corporal Johnny Wood
Armed Forces Induction Center
Cincinnati, Ohio

Atlanta, Georgia
June 28, 1943

My dear Corporal Wood:

While I appreciate the interest you and your friends have shown in "Gone With the Wind" as book and film, I cannot tell you the price paid me for the moving picture rights. I have never made public announcement of the amount and do not intend to do so. Please tell your friends with whom you were discussing the matter that it's a "military secret." At the time I sold the film rights I was told that I received the highest amount ever paid for a first novel. I do not know if this record still stands.

Mr. Paul D. O'Brien   *July 26, 1943*
O'Brien, Driscoll & Raftery   *Atlanta, Georgia*
New York, New York

My dear Mr. O'Brien:

Again I owe you and Mr. Selznick an explanation and an apology for my delay in answering your last letters. After I wrote you in March, I entered Johns Hopkins Hospital in Baltimore for a spinal operation. I had had an old back injury which had plagued me for some years and I have been too busy since "Gone With the Wind" to have it attended to. I thought my stay in the hospital would be brief and my recovery swift. Unfortunately, the opposite has been true, and only this last week have I been able to turn my attention to business matters. I am very sorry, for I know you must think me very dilatory.

As the discussions about the sale of the musicalization rights of "Gone With the Wind" have dragged on so long, I know it would be well to settle it one way or the other. The best way, I believe, to expedite matters is for you to draw up and send to me a contract for the purchase of these rights. This does not mean that I will sign it immediately and send it back to you; it does mean that I am now well enough to talk business with you. With a formal contract before me, I can deal more quickly with the matter than in the past when our negotiations have been of a somewhat vague character.

As I told you when you were here in Atlanta, the financial arrangements of the sale are one thing, but more important to me than the money is the quiet and peace of my life, which I feel will be seriously disturbed by the musicalization. It may be a year before I have completely recovered from my operation. At least, I have been told that I must take things quietly for that length of time. You can perhaps understand that I do not wish to have my health jeopardized by a repetition of the harassments to which I was subjected during the filming of "Gone With the Wind." So, in drawing the contract, do not fail to include protection for me against bedevilment by Mr. Selznick's promotional men seeking to entangle me personally in their promotion of the show.

July 27, 1943

P.S. I have just finished talking to you over the phone. As I told you, I did not think there was any rush about closing up the matter, as I understood Mr. Selznick did not wish to go into production until after the war. In view of your statements about the theatrical boom and the success of "Oklahoma,"

I can understand the change in his attitude.* I believe the best way to handle the matter would be for you to submit a written contract. This would give us something definite to discuss and perhaps we can come to an agreement.

I hope you will keep confidential my statement about my health. There is no secret about the fact I went to the hospital and had the operation, but please keep confidential my statement that it may be a year before I am completely well. . . .

Miss Katharine Brown   *Atlanta, Georgia*
Samuel Goldwyn Productions   *February 22, 1944*
New York, New York

Dear Katharine:

It was sweet of you to send me the clipping and to be worried about possible trouble it might cause me.† As John and I have just returned from the editors' convention at the University of Georgia, we haven't been home to hear any such rumor. If it does arise we'll handle it as best we can, for it is a legend which pops up about once every six months. I'm sure no one would believe the truth—that we like you and look on you as a friend and veteran of the same campaign in which we fought. All that bothers me is that scores of people whom I did not telephone and who I fondly hoped would not learn of my presence in New York will now know and doubtless write me, not-mad-but-very-very-hurt. But we've handled that situation before, too, so don't worry about it. Seeing you makes it all worth while.

I wish so much we had had a longer time together, for we've remembered so many things we intended to say and did not. We've spoken so often of your venture into the legitimate drama and felt distressed about the result. You were such a good sport about it that your very attitude made us feel sorrier. Better luck next time, for we hope there will be a next time and a successful one.

As usual, Sue Myrick was at the newspaper convention but we scarcely got to speak to her. We had a number of foreign correspondents, home from various fronts, who gave lectures and then fell so in love with the editors that, instead of going home immediately, they stayed for the whole affair. This was in the main due to the charms of Miss Myrick,

---

* *Oklahoma*, the first musical by the team of Richard Rodgers and Oscar Hammerstein, opened on Broadway on March 31, 1943; it ran for 2,243 performances.

† A brief mention in Radie Harris's "New York Runaround" column in the February 16 issue of *Variety* noted Mitchell and Brown had had lunch in New York, "which gives rise to the suspicion that the 'Gone With the Wind' lady from Atlanta has another novel in preparation."

and, as she was generally three deep in correspondents, we scarcely had the opportunity to say hello.

Love from us both,

Dr. Charles E. Mayos   *Atlanta, Georgia*
Davenport, Iowa   *February 23, 1944*

Dear Dr. Mayos:

When I returned from the North, my secretary showed me the letter you sent her and her reply. You are indeed a thoughtful friend and I appreciate your letter and your encouraging remarks about my condition.

I had been sponsor of the other cruiser "Atlanta" which was sunk off Guadalcanal, and when I was appointed sponsor of the new cruiser "Atlanta" I was determined to christen it if I had to do it from a stretcher held up by a squad of bluejackets. But that wasn't necessary, and I got through the affair very well and very happily and I do not think anyone except my husband and my naval aide, an old friend, knew how tired I was or that I had to be "histed" up and down the steep stairs which led to the launching platform.* I have always thought the best analgesic for chronic pain is interesting activity, and in this case my theory worked out as successfully as usual. . . .

A friend of mine in the diplomatic service in Sweden has just sent me a large souvenir program of "Gone With the Wind" done in color.† It contains pictures of the actors, scenes from the film and a picture of me. It seems so strange to see words beneath my picture and not be able to read them. It seems stranger still to know that the story of an almost forgotten American war should be shown in Sweden in the midst of the world's worst war. I should think that the Swedes who are walking the tightrope of neutrality would want to see something gay, such as the doings of Miss Ginger Rogers, rather than a grim story of death and destruction. . . .

Mr. Thomas Coleman   *Atlanta, Georgia*
Columbia, South Carolina   *March 29, 1944*

Dear Mr. Coleman:

Thank you so much for your kind letter about "Gone With the Wind." You say you have seen the film of it seven times. I did not think anyone

---

* The second USS *Atlanta* was launched on Feb. 6, 1944.

† *Gone With the Wind* opened in Sweden in October 1941, and, according to news reports, most of the Swedish royal family attended the Stockholm premiere.

had beaten my record, which is five-and-a-half times.* The last time, I had the rare good fortune of seeing it in comfortable surroundings, sitting on a low sofa buttressed with cushions, at a private showing for Ambassador Grew who had just returned from internment in Tokyo.† I must say that a comfortable seat improved "Gone With the Wind"!

I am so glad you liked my book, and gladder still you wrote and told me so.

Mrs. Sidney Howard   *Atlanta, Georgia*
Stockbridge, Massachusetts   *June 9, 1944*

Dear Mrs. Howard:

Some time ago you wrote asking if I had any of Mr. Howard's letters. I told you that I thought I had destroyed them but that they might be hidden in the piles of "Gone With the Wind" clippings and correspondence. Recently I have been trying to clear out the accumulation of the last six years, and I am happy to say that I have found Mr. Howard's letters and I am enclosing them. Do not bother about making copies of them and returning them, as you suggested in your letter. Please keep them. I know you and his children will have much more pleasure and delight in them than I—and that is saying a great deal!

I know it is asking a lot of you to make this request, but I will make it just the same. Would it be possible to arrange that these letters to me would not be published in any collection of Mr. Howard's letters? The reason for this peculiar request is that when I sold the movie rights of "Gone With the Wind" I refused to have anything to do with the making of the film. I refused to go to Hollywood, to write additional dialogue, to advise on the script or production. I obstinately stood by this decision, in the face of considerable pressure from Hollywood. The position I had taken prevented me from discussing the movie script with Mr. Howard, or even reading it, and the only

---

* Mitchell's "half" viewing reportedly was on the night of the December 12, 1940, anniversary showing in Atlanta, when the author spent part of the evening at the airport waiting in vain for the plane carrying Leigh and Olivier to land.

† Joseph Grew was the U.S. ambassador to Japan at the time of the attack on Pearl Harbor. He was interned by the Japanese for nine months and returned to the United States in August 1942. When Grew visited Atlanta the following year, he mentioned that he had never seen *Gone With the Wind*. A private screening of the film was arranged for March 2, 1943, in the Green Room at the Fox Theatre. He sat beside Mitchell and later recalled her reaction to the film—"laughing and crying, taking as fresh and detached delight in it as if it were her first time, and she had nothing to do with it but enjoy it."

help I ever gave him was by obtaining the historical information regarding two or three questions he asked me. Because of his honest desire to have the Southern background correct, and also because of my high respect for him, I would have been glad to do more, but circumstances made me take a hands-off attitude on everything relating to the movie.

If the opposite impression were given by the publication of Mr. How-ard's letters, it would be highly embarrassing to me. And I am afraid that is just what would happen. So many people are careless readers and it would be easy for them to jump to wrong conclusions, simply because the script writer and the author wrote letters to each other occasionally. It would simplify things for me if the letters were not published at all.

Private David A. Timmons   *Atlanta, Georgia*
324th Medics, HQ   *August 31, 1944*
Camp Maxey, Texas

Dear Mr. Timmons:

I can understand your interest in tracing your family history and per-haps I can give you a lead. One of my father's sisters, Aline Mitchell, married Mr. Willis Menifee Timmons. Their address is 1315 Wieuca Road, N.E., At-lanta. Perhaps he can give you some information about the Timmons family.

I know what I am now going to write will seem rude and impatient to you, but I do not mean it that way. It is only that the Betty Timmons you mentioned in your letter has caused me so much trouble and embarrass-ment since 1936 that my heart sinks when I read in your letter that you believe I dedicated "Gone With the Wind" to her. "Gone With the Wind" is dedicated to my husband and his initials appear on the dedication page of the book.‡ I had never seen or heard of Miss Betty Timmons until some time in 1936 when she gave an interview to a New York newspaper, in which she said I was her aunt, had modeled the character Scarlett O'Hara on her, and had promised to permit her to play the part of Scarlett in the motion picture. As I had not even known of this young lady's existence until I read this as-tounding assertion in the New York paper, you can perhaps understand how disconcerted I was. Thereafter, during the four years when the picture was in production, I was beset by hundreds of people who said that if I could get my "niece" into the movies I could do a similar service for them. I cannot begin to tell you the embarrassment and trouble this caused me. Miss Timmons wrote one letter saying that she had made no such assertion, but I cannot

---

‡ The dedication in *Gone With the Wind* reads, "To J.R.M."

believe a newspaper reporter could make up such a story out of whole cloth. I have no idea where Miss Timmons is but heard that she was married and living in New York. I would be grateful to you if you would tell any of your relatives who might be interested the truth about this matter.

I hope Mr. Willis Timmons can tell you something about the Timmons family history which will be of value to you.

Mrs. Edith Ford   *Atlanta, Georgia*
Time, Inc.   *October 4, 1944*
Atlanta, Georgia

Dear Mrs. Ford:

Thank you for the Time news sheet about the liberated French wanting to know "when is 'Gone With the Wind' coming?" This item made me realize how long this war has been going on, when hardly any European country has seen this film. I heard in a round-about way that the Germans captured a copy of the film when they took Paris. It was in the vaults of Metro-Goldwyn-Mayer. Neither French nor Germans were permitted to view it, but rumors were current that Hitler saw it and permitted a half-dozen of his high-ranking advisers to see it.*

Mrs. William L. Plummer   *Atlanta, Georgia*
Atlanta, Georgia   *December 11, 1944*

Dear Honey:

You are more than generous to let me have the original invitation for the Paris premiere of "Gone With the Wind."† Of course I love having it and will cherish it, but if you or your husband ever regret giving it to me I will part with it. The story in the paper, which you sent, was most interesting. I wonder how I would have felt seeing that picture so far away from Georgia and under such circumstances. I think the scenes of 1864 Atlanta would have made me so homesick I would have wept.

---

* A United Press report from Berlin on January 18, 1941, noted that "a small group of German actors and producers saw *Gone With the Wind* at a private showing today. The audience was selected by Propaganda Minister Goebbels."

† Plummer's husband, a U.S. Army Air Force colonel stationed near Paris, attended the private screening of *Gone With the Wind* on November 24, 1944, at the Cine Press on the Champs-Élysées. The showing, which was hosted by American Ambassador Jefferson Caffery, began at 6:30 p.m., and a buffet supper was served at intermission. "It was like seeing it for the first time and I got a real thrill out of it," Plummer wrote his wife. "It made me homesick, but proud to be a Georgian."

I was interested to know that the film was shown privately and will not be released to the general public for some time. I hope the French people will like it.

Please write and tell your husband how much I enjoyed his remarks about the picture and how nice he is to let me have the invitation on the paper of the Embassy. Please tell him, too, the following which may interest him. My book was banned in Germany and occupied countries some time before Pearl Harbor. Of course the moving picture would have been banned, too, but the producers had refused to have it exhibited in any Fascist country. There was one copy of the film in the vaults of MGM in Paris and this film was captured when the Germans took the city. Rumors came out through the Underground that the film, closely guarded, was sent to Berlin where it had a private showing before a group of five—Hitler and his four closest boy friends. I've wondered since what they thought of it. They did not think a story or a movie which had to do with a conquered people who became free again would be a good thing to show in Germany or occupied countries.

Mr. David O. Selznick   *Atlanta, Georgia*
David O. Selznick Productions, Inc.   *January 2, 1945*
Culver City, California

Dear Mr. Selznick:

John and I have just returned from our vacation at Sea Island. It is nice to take vacations at that time because when we come home we have Christmas all over again. There was your package, so beautifully wrapped. The antique Lowestoft cup and saucer have a bronze-gold design of pheasants and butterflies—a strange shade which is rare indeed. We have a bronze-pink Persian rug. It is almost the same shade. I am going to plant a small bushy house plant in this cup and keep it in my bedroom where it will pick up the colors of the rug. The candy in the cup was so good. It tasted like pre-war candy and reminded me how many things we took for granted are hard to get now and are luxuries. I thank you so much for this beautiful present and for your thought of me at Christmas time.

I noticed in the morning paper that the road show of "A Doll's House" is to play here in a week or so and that among the others in the cast is Jane Darwell.* I do not know Miss Darwell but have a great admiration for her and I hope I have the opportunity to take her to tea during her stay here.

---

* Jane Darwell played Dolly Merriwether in *Gone With the Wind*. *A Doll's House*, by Henrik Ibsen, was first staged in Denmark in 1879.

I know Mrs. Wilbur Kurtz will enjoy seeing her again if she (Mrs. Kurtz) is able to go out. Mrs. Kurtz has been ill off and on for a year and her worry over her two sons overseas and the recent death of her son-in-law in action have not improved her condition.

I hope you will remember us both to Mrs. Selznick, whom we liked so much when we met her here. With good wishes for the coming year,

Mr. Paul D. O'Brien   *Atlanta, Georgia*
O'Brien, Driscoll & Raftery   *January 10, 1945*
New York, New York

Dear Mr. O'Brien:

As Miss Baugh wrote you, we've been away on our vacation. As soon as we returned I took up your letter about Mr. Selznick's offer for the dramatic rights to "Gone With the Wind." I have studied your letter and the proposed contract carefully.

Please tell Mr. Selznick that, while I thank him for his continued interest in a dramatization musicalization of "Gone With the Wind," I must refuse his offer. As near as I can figure it out, he is offering me $2,500 for all the dramatic rights—musicalization, operatic, dramatic, dramatico-musical et cetera—plus motion picture rights. (This $2,500 is against four per cent of the gross weekly box office receipts, but there is no assurance that there would ever be any box office receipts.) The way it looks to me is that Mr. Selznick might produce a stage version for two or three nights only. Then my percentage would stop, but he would be in position to make a movie musical, from which I would get no percentage or any other compensation. In other words, $2,500 might be all I would ever get for the dramatic rights in toto. I would certainly be a dope to accept this offer because I have been offered $2,500 for the straight dramatic rights alone.

This offer does not measure up to even the minimum requirements of the Dramatists' Guild basic agreement.

To tell the truth, I am not especially anxious to sell. I had thought that by this time my life would have settled down considerably and many of my business burdens would be things of the past. It has not worked out this way, and I am still confronted with many business details which keep me busy. My foreign business is in a tangle because of the war and it will take me until two years after peace to straighten it out. I do not feel that this is the time for me to consider deliberately bringing trouble on myself when I am already wrestling with unavoidable troubles. I am less enthusiastic than ever about the sale of the musical and dramatic rights, in the light of Mr.

Selznick's offer which wants me to give away a valuable property with no assurance of any return beyond the original $2,500. . . .

Mr. Paul D. O'Brien   Atlanta, Georgia
O'Brien, Driscoll & Raftery   March 1, 1945
New York, New York

Dear Mr. O'Brien:

Again I regret my delay in answering your letter. It seems I am always late in acknowledging messages from you and Mr. Selznick. Heavy pressure of war work and the reopening of my business affairs in some foreign countries have kept me on the jump.

I thank you and Mr. Selznick for your interest in keeping me from being pestered by publicity resulting from published rumors. I do not know how such stories as the one in Variety and in Louella Parsons's column get into circulation.* Certainly they do not originate down here, as my husband and I have long since learned never to mention anything in any way connected with "Gone With the Wind"—publishing, moving picture, theatrical, musical or tie-ups—to anyone. It will be a happy day when no one gives a hoot and "Gone With the Wind" does not rate even a line in a paper. Then perhaps I can do my Red Cross work without having to answer questions from everyone I meet. Please tell Mr. Selznick I appreciate his trouble in writing.

Lieutenant (j.g.) Richard Harwell   Atlanta, Georgia
USS YMS 89   March 23, 1945
FPO San Francisco, California

Dear Mr. Harwell:

How much I enjoyed your letter of February 21st about your experiences in New Zealand. It is always difficult for me to imagine our Atlanta boys half way across the world, and I find it even more difficult to imagine an Atlanta boy being asked questions about me in New Zealand. So "Gone With the Wind" was playing at the theaters in Auckland at Christmas time! I hear it is still running in London and in its fifth year. I wouldn't be surprised if its popularity is due to the attendance by homesick Southerners anxious to see a bit of the South, even if it is synthetic. . . .

---

* In late January, Variety reported that Selznick was going to tackle a "tuned" version of Gone With the Wind called "Scarlett O'Hara" in the next year or two. In a small story in the Atlanta Constitution, the producer denied the story and said he was "distressed" over the trouble such reports caused Mitchell.

Those of us at home have happier hearts these days, as the war news seems better. I'm glad to say there is none of the false optimism current now as there was six months ago. People do not feel that the war in the Pacific will be over immediately. They are just supremely grateful to the people fighting the war that it *is* being shortened by their efforts. Atlanta is in the midst of its annual Red Cross money-raising campaign, and this time it's nearly a million dollars to be raised. This town has never yet fallen down on a big job and I don't think it will fall down on this one, as nearly $200,000 were collected in three days. People who work down-town have the excitement of getting large sums of money. As I ring door bells here in a residential section, the pickings are small and a ten dollar bill enormous. It never fails to rain whenever I go out for any patriotic purpose, and after this war I believe I will rent myself out to the Farm Bureau for use in dust bowls.

I hope you are well and as happy as one can be far away from home. I hope it won't be too long before we meet again and talk leisurely about Confederate medicine instead of the medicine of this war.*

Mr. David O. Selznick   *Atlanta, Georgia*
David O. Selznick Productions, Inc.   *July 18, 1945*
Culver City, California

Dear Mr. Selznick:

Thank you for your letter of June 26th. I appreciate your frank and friendly attitude and your straightforward manner of dealing with the much discussed subject of an operetta version of "Gone With the Wind." You ask that I make no deal with anyone else for the sale of these rights without giving you the opportunity to make a proposal. I am not in any way binding myself to a deal with you and I am not giving you an option on the musico-dramatic rights, but I will not dispose of them without at least giving you the opportunity to submit an offer.

However, I must make the reservation that your offer must be submit-ted within a reasonable time after I notify you that I am considering a sale of the rights. When and if I so notify you, I couldn't be bound to delay a sale to somebody else for an indefinite time while waiting for you to get ready to make an offer. So the understanding is that I will give you the *opportunity* to

---

* In 1950, Harwell's first of many books on Civil War–related topics, *Confederate Music*, was published by the University of North Carolina Press. Mitchell read his manuscript, and he dedicated the volume "To Margaret Mitchell Marsh."

submit your offer, but I would not be blocked from trading with somebody else if you failed to submit your offer within a reasonable time.

It would be useless for me to deny that I have had offers for the musicalization and dramatic rights to "Gone With the Wind." I have been receiving them from time to time since the publication of my book. I always find it difficult to make prospective buyers understand that my main interest in such a sale is that I shall be protected from the disruption of my life and the invasion of my privacy which seem attendant on motion picture and stage productions. During the five or six years of my father's illness, life would have been unbearable if at the time when his condition was claiming my attention I was having to fight the press agents of theatrical companies. Since my father's death, I have had a little taste of quiet life and I have no desire to surrender it.* I want to do my Red Cross work, see my friends and live like a normal human being. For these reasons I am not anxious to enter into an agreement with you or anyone else to produce an operetta. But when—and if—I change my mind, rest assured I will notify you. We have been associated with each other long enough for you to believe me when I make that statement.

So many people ask me when "Gone With the Wind" will play a return engagement. A number of children who were not old enough to see the picture when it was last here have requested that I ask you when it will come back. So I am asking for them, and because I'd like to see it myself.†

John and I hope you will remember us to Mrs. Selznick.

Captain Thomas Horan	*Atlanta, Georgia*
Oakland ASF RSH	*July 21, 1945*
Oakland, California	

Dear Tom:

. . . I wish I had some news of an elevating or an interesting nature to write you, but I haven't. After some four years of making surgical dressings at the Red Cross and selling bonds, I cannot make them sound interesting in a letter, and those two things are my usual outside activities. I can't make my business affairs at home any more interesting than my war activities,

---

* Eugene Mitchell died on June 17, 1944.

† Selznick replied on July 20, promising not to bother Mitchell again about the musical stage rights. He also explained that he had sold his financial interest in *Gone With the Wind* after the dissolution of Selznick International but said he would contact MGM, which now owned a majority share of the film, about rereleasing the movie or arranging a private screening for her and her friends in Atlanta.

for it's just business matters and auditors and lawyers. One by one I am beginning to hear from my foreign publishers, some of them battered and storm-tossed. My French publisher is bringing out a "semi-luxe" edition and two days ago the Atlanta papers carried a story that the film of "Gone With the Wind" had opened in Paris at the Opera House—the first film ever to be shown there. Tickets were $100 and it was for the benefit of repatriated citizens.* I kept wondering if Lon Chaney, the Phantom of the Opera, was lurking about. Lon Chaney! I am an old, old woman.†

Thanks for your letter, Tom. It was good to hear from you.

Mr. J. Robert Rubin   *Atlanta, Georgia*
Metro-Goldwyn-Mayer, Inc.   *August 8, 1945*
New York, New York

My dear Mr. Rubin:

I am sorry that I have delayed this long answering your letter of July 30th which contained your kind offer to have "Gone With the Wind" screened in Atlanta for me and my friends. My husband has been ill and I have not been able to answer until now.

I appreciate your offer very much and think it generous of you. I have just talked with Mr. Zoellner in the Atlanta office and expressed my appreciation to him. But I want to tell you, as I told him, that there has been a mistake in meaning, as frequently happens when things pass through two or three hands. It wasn't that I wanted a private or "semi-private" screening of "Gone With the Wind"; it was that I wanted to know when it would be released again and play in our Atlanta theatres. I wrote Mr. Selznick and asked him if he knew when it would be released again. He misunderstood my meaning.

This is the reason I asked this question. Of course I'd like to see the picture again myself, but the main reason I asked was that so many people have asked me to find out when the picture would return here. I finally got tired of saying I did not know and promised all who asked me that I would "write to Mr. Selznick." It may interest you to know the two major types of people who wish to see the picture.

---

* A special benefit showing of *Gone With the Wind* was held on July 10 at the Paris Opera House. Newspapers reported that the event featured "distinguished Parisians dressed to kill" and seventy-two Republican Guards in red, white, and gold uniforms lining the marble staircase.
† Lon Chaney starred in the 1925 silent film *Phantom of the Opera*.

The first is adults who have had long arguments with friends about whether something appears in my book alone or in the picture too. I am called upon a wearying number of times to state that while I gave Scarlett three children Mr. Selznick permitted her only one. People wish to see the picture again to clarify such matters.

The second large group is comprised of children who are twelve or thirteen years old. When the picture last played here they were considered too young to see it. Now they have grown up (in their own estimation) and have read the novel and wish to see the picture, for they have heard their parents discuss it. Many children have been promised a visit to the film of "Gone With the Wind" for a birthday or Christmas present. So they phone me or back me in corners on the streets and ask me when it will return, for they firmly believe I own the film and doubtless keep it in my top bureau drawer.

I thank you for offering to let me see the picture and take a few friends with me, but I must refuse. After all, I have to live in Atlanta and I doubt if I could live here if I took a few people and did not take several hundred who thought they should go. But you were nice to make the offer.

Mrs. Marcus A. Goodrich [Olivia de Havilland]   *Atlanta, Georgia*
c/o David O. Selznick   *October 9, 1946*
Culver City, California

My dear Miss Melly:

On the day when you and your husband came to Atlanta, I had gone early to the hospital to be with my husband and I was there most of the day. So I did not know that you were here. If my old cook, who was with me at the time of the "Gone With the Wind" premiere, had answered the phone when you called, she would have known who you were, taken the bus to the hospital and told me the news. As it was, when I did get the afternoon paper and phone the Georgian Terrace, you and Mr. Goodrich had gone. The next morning there was the beautiful plant with your card. I took it to the hospital, where it was greatly admired by my husband and all who saw it; and when John came home several days ago, your plant came home carefully carried in my lap. It is still blooming on the sill of John's bedroom window and, as he can walk a few steps now, he waters it and calls it his private garden.

How very sorry I am that I missed you. How kind and considerate of you both to express concern about John and "not wish to bother me." I wish I had had some advance notice that you were coming. It would have given me such pleasure to do some small thing for you and Mr. Goodrich.

Please come back again. I know moving picture actors and actresses seldom realize how close to them their admirers feel, how well strangers feel they know them. My husband and I, even as thousands of other people in Atlanta, feel such warm friendship for you and claim you as an old Atlantan on the basis of you having once been Mrs. Ashley Wilkes before you became Mrs. Marcus A. Goodrich.

My husband is recovering from a severe heart attack and I hope he will be able to get out again in a few months.* He asks me to send you and your husband his own very sincere wishes for your happiness and to tell you that he looks forward to seeing the revival of "Gone With the Wind" when it appears here sometime next spring. You see, you did the difficult and rare thing of making a virtuous woman attractive. In real life that is not too difficult but on stage or screen a good woman generally comes off second to a bad one.

David O. Selznick   *Atlanta, Georgia*
David O. Selznick Productions, Inc.   *December 24, 1946*
Culver City, California

JOHN AND I HOPE 1947 WILL BE THE VERY BEST YEAR YOU HAVE EVER HAD WITH GREAT STARS, FINE PICTURES AND MUCH PERSONAL HAPPINESS. ALL GOOD WISHES TO YOU.

Mr. David O. Selznick   *Atlanta, Georgia*
David O. Selznick Productions, Inc.   *January 13, 1947*
Culver City, California

Dear Mr. Selznick:

The container for the luscious candies you sent me at Christmas time was a beautiful china bowl covered with delicate flowers. I put lily bulbs in the bowl immediately and when I see how tall they are grown I realize how remiss I have been in not expressing my appreciation long before now. I do not know whether you know that my husband has been ill for a year—since Christmas Eve of 1945, to be exact—and has been in bed most of the time. He is better now and is able to walk about the apartment, but from before this past Christmas until after New Year's he was not doing well at all, and so I have been unable to write and thank you for your thought of us. I think I appreciated your gift all the more this year than I

---

* Marsh suffered a massive heart attack on Christmas Eve 1945, shortly after he and Mitchell arrived at Sea Island, Georgia.

would normally have done, for it was a somewhat anxious Christmas, and upon such occasions the thoughts of friends far away are doubly valued. I doled the candy out to John, and it was delicious. And the bowl with the growing lilies excites comments from all who see it. We both thank you so much for thinking of us.

While John's heart is recovering, he is still facing a considerable period in the house, as you will recall our apartment is up several flights of steep stairs. I have hardly been out of the house myself in a year except to buy groceries, and John and I both feel that we are very out of touch with the world. Last week I consulted with the movie editor of the Atlanta Journal about buying a film projector and renting films. I am the least mechanical person in the world, and if you read an Associated Press despatch in the near future stating that an unexplained accident has put both Mr. and Mrs. Marsh in the hospital you will understand that I became entangled with the projector and the films. I am hoping that by getting the projector and tacking up a sheet on our dining room wall, I can bring a little bit of the outside world into our apartment. I mentioned my plans to some of the children in our apartment and they immediately wanted to know if I was going to show "Gone With the Wind," because they want to come see it.

John and I have read all newspaper stories we could lay our hands on about the bewildering (to us) situation of you and United Artists. We find it difficult from this distance to understand what it is all about but, knowing you, we are betting on you.*

I am looking forward to seeing "Duel in the Sun."† It will be the first picture I have seen in over a year, and I do not intend to miss it.

With all good wishes,

The Honorable William B. Hartsfield
Office of the Mayor, City Hall
Atlanta, Georgia

Atlanta, Georgia
March 25, 1947

---

* In 1941, Selznick became a partner in United Artists. Five years later, a long-simmering disagreement over how the company handled the distribution of Selznick's films led partners Mary Pickford and Charlie Chaplin to rescind their contract with the producer. Selznick sued, and in February 1947, the parties reached an agreement under which United Artists canceled $1.5 million in production loans and paid the producer $2 million for his share of the company.

† *Duel in the Sun*, an epic western produced by Selznick and released in 1946, featured an all-star cast, including Jennifer Jones, Gregory Peck, Joseph Cotton, Lionel Barrymore, and Lillian Gish, with Butterfly McQueen in a minor role. The film grossed more than $11 million but was savaged by critics, one of whom dubbed it "Lust in the Dust."

Dear Bill:

I have been laid up with flu or else I would have thanked you sooner for that most interesting broadside on the picketing of "Song of the South."* It seems odd to me that there has been considerable publicity about the Communist picketing of this film and very little about the same happening to "Gone With the Wind." If I was not always laboring under loads heavier than I can carry and always having someone very ill on my hands, I'd try to write something that would be at least one lick in this fight. All of us, and especially Southerners, are in a fight with such people, and I find it alarming that not one person in a thousand realizes it. Anything else you get on this subject will be read with great interest by John and me. . . .

Mr. Boyd Fry   *Atlanta, Georgia*
Loew's Grand Theatre   *June 27, 1947*
Atlanta, Georgia

Dear Mr. Fry:

Thank you so much for the passes to "Gone With the Wind" and the cordial note which accompanied them. I hope I will have the opportunity to use them and I know they will give me and my family great pleasure. Unfortunately, my husband has been ill for eighteen months and of course he will be unable to attend. Most of my time is occupied with him, and that is why I do not know when I can go to see the picture.

When I saw the photograph of the crowds in front of your theatre, my reaction was very different from yours, I am sure. My heart sank at the thought of having to stand in line for so long a time when I could spare so little time from duties at home. Then came your passes, and that problem was settled. I am very appreciative. I hope the picture has a long run, and I believe it will, for during the past few years the day never passed that people did not telephone and inquire when the film would be reissued.†

---

* *Song of the South*, Walt Disney's 1946 live action/animated musical version of Joel Chandler Harris's tales of Uncle Remus, was the target of protestors who said the film perpetuated the myth of "happy slaves."

† One of the film's first-time viewers that year was Mitchell's godson, Turney Allan Taylor Jr. On October 12, the nine-year-old wrote to "Aunt Peggy," "Last Saterday [*sic*] mother and father took me to see the motion picture Gone with the Wind. I liked it a lot. It is the best movie I ever saw, better even than Henry V. All the time I kept thinking you had written the book, and how you thought of it all. I thought it was sad when Bonnie was killed and it was awful when people were waiting to hear their boys were killed. I thought Vivien Lee [*sic*] played her part very well."

Mr. E. Verbeke   *Atlanta, Georgia*
Editions Brugeoises   *July 2, 1947*
Bruges, Belgium

Dear Mr. Verbeke:

My thanks for your letter of June 4th, giving me the information I had requested in my letter of May 27th. I received the payment in dollars representing the 158,400 francs but I was under the impression that this was 100% of the royalties due and I paid over to Mrs. Bradley 10% of the amount I received, just before your letter arrived.* Mrs. Bradley and I can adjust this between ourselves, of course, but I will be grateful if you can send me a statement in connection with any future royalty payment, so we can avoid misunderstandings of this kind.

I have been informed by Metro-Goldwyn-Mayer that the motion picture of "Gone With the Wind" would be released in Belgium during June. In other countries the showing of the motion picture has stimulated sales of the book and I hope it will have the same effect in Belgium, for your sake and mine. Here in the United States the film is being reissued and it is now on display in Atlanta at the same theatre where the picture was given its premiere showing in December 1939. Apparently it still has a strong hold upon the public, for the theatre has been crowded each day, with people standing on the outside waiting to get in. Today it was announced that the picture was being held over for an additional week.

My best regards and thanks again for your letter.

Mrs. William A. Post   *Atlanta, Georgia*
Birmingham, Alabama   *August 29, 1947*

Dear Vivian:

I did not dream there were again such beautiful things in the world as the handkerchief you sent me. I had seen embroidery like this before the war but not since then, and had come to believe such exquisite work was a thing of the past. If you tell me that you embroidered it yourself, I'll fall down daid with admiration. Really, I wouldn't put it beyond you because you are so smart in so many ways I wouldn't be surprised if you could embroider too. It was so nicely scented that John kept it over his nose for about five minutes breathing in the smell. I just hope "Gone With the Wind" comes back to your theatre every week if it produces things like this!

---

* E. Verbeke was Mitchell's publisher in Belgium. Jenny Bradley was the author's agent in France.

I got to see it too when it reached our neighborhood theatre. I had thought I wouldn't care very much about it this time, as I have seen it six or seven times, but after the bad beginning the picture had, it began to take hold and I enjoyed it all over again, especially the music, which I appreciate more each time I hear it. . . .

Mr. Harold Latham   *Atlanta, Georgia*
The Macmillan Company, Inc.   *September 12, 1947*
Atlanta, Georgia

Dear Harold:

If you will just tell the lady "no," I'll be very grateful and it will save me from having to write another letter—or probably six or seven letters, if I may judge by my experience with movie people.* Of course it wouldn't be polite for me to tell any of them that their bright idea about obligingly writing a sequel for me is not their bright idea alone. It always hurts people's feelings to think they aren't being original, so each time this matter comes up I have to act surprised as though I'd never heard of it before. It's been coming up for about eleven years now and is one of the five or six problems I have which keep me so busy that I never have time to write any books. By the time I have written five or six letters to one agent or editor or ghost writer or movie producer or story editor, and managed to keep them from coming to Atlanta to see me, there is another one with the same bright idea and I have to write five or six letters to him. By the time I've been around the circle of all the movie agents and all the story editors, the number one person is all gingered up and ready to give me another go. In addition to this, these people always bring in people like you or other friends or acquaintances of mine and try to put pressure on me through them, and that takes even more letter writing. I have never understood why these people use my friends to try to pressure me, for, after all, I can read and write and I can cipher, too, after a fashion. I am not mentally deficient, so I am able to understand what they write to me and I do not need to have it explained to me. So if you'd just tell her "no," it would simplify matters for me. The weather has been too hot recently and I have been too tired for me to be polite and, if I am not quick and polite, before I know it people from Hollywood will be bouncing off every plane and expecting to be entertained, and then the gossip columns will be full of the news that

---

* Carol Brandt, international story editor of MGM, had written to Latham about the possibility of Mitchell selling the studio sequel rights to *Gone With the Wind* and asked him to contact the author.

the great director, Mr. So-and-So, is conferring in Atlanta with the shy little author and the sequel to "Gone With the Wind" will be produced in 96 reels by day-after-tomorrow. Then I will have to land on all the gossip columnists, the Associated Press, the INS and the UP.* I've been through it again and again, so just tell her no. . . .

Dr. James C. Bonner   *Atlanta, Georgia*
Georgia State College for Women   *November 6, 1947*
Milledgeville, Georgia

Dear Dr. Bonner:

I am sure there is no one in the United States who would appreciate your article on "Plantation Architecture" more than I. I will admit, however that two other people might possibly be runners-up in interest, and for the same reason. Those two people are Miss Susan Myrick, of Macon, and Mr. Wilbur Kurtz, of Atlanta, both of whom did time in Hollywood as technical advisers on the film of "Gone With the Wind." Their herculean efforts to keep Corinthian columns from the smokehouses and other more humble outhouses of Mr. Selznick's Clayton County have never been properly appreciated by Southerners—and if their efforts were properly known, I am quite sure most Southerners would heartily resent all these two honest people did to keep down the size and number of white columns which appeared in "Gone With the Wind." It has been my experience that most Southerners are firmly convinced, because of the many moving pictures they have seen, that everyone in the South lived in houses of the size and general architecture of the State Capitol at Montgomery, Alabama.

I enjoyed your article so very much and read it aloud to my husband. In spots we both laughed till tears came to our eyes, remembering the moving picture people's startled horror when told of the somewhat crude and frontier-like dwellings which mainly graced our up-country red hills. I had gone to a lot of trouble in my research about the architecture of the 1850s and 1860s and had made sure that there were indeed a few white columned country homes in the county. But I very definitely described "Tara" as an ugly and sprawling habitation built with no architectural plan and growing as need for growth arose. I didn't have anything to do with the filming of "Gone With the Wind" and so am not responsible for the architecture. I did, however, hear echoes from the West Coast of the brisk fight that went on to keep "Tara" from looking like a Natchez house complete with Corinthian columns, Spanish moss and lacy iron grill work.

----

* INS was International News Service. UP was United Press.

So I am sure you can understand what pleasure your article brought me. Could I have another copy, please? Someone is sure to steal this copy I have and I would not like to be without one. I am glad that I am now receiving the Journal of Southern History, for I am looking forward with pleasure to other historical papers from you.

Mr. Wright Bryan	*Atlanta, Georgia*
The Atlanta Journal	*November 6, 1947*
Atlanta, Georgia	

Dear Wright:

I will be very grateful if the Journal will print the enclosed letter to cinch what you said in your column. Mr. Shearer's story is already causing me a great deal of trouble and I would like to go on record about his mis-statement that I wasn't at the premiere.* For the price of a 3¢ stamp, Mr. Shearer could have learned the truth from me about such matters but he didn't take the trouble.

Possibly the New York Times article will be put in the Journal's GWTW morgue file. If so, please make a notation on it that "Gone With the Wind" sold a million copies during the first six months of its life, instead of a half-million as Mr. Shearer stated. That was the all-time record up to that time.

For what it's worth, I have just seen copies of cables from Brussels where the first post-war showing of "Gone With the Wind" was held in mid-October. The film has never had a real Continental run. It showed briefly in Stockholm in 1940, perhaps just one showing for charity. And there was that showing in France at the Paris Opera House, also for charity, immediately after the liberation (Bill Plummer was there and has told me interesting things about it). So this opening in Brussels is the real Continental premiere. One of the New York officials of MGM sent me these cables:

Brussels, October 22 —

"GWTW PURSUES ITS TRIUMPHAL RUN AT METROPOLE WORKING AT FULL CAPACITY SINCE OPENING DATE *** THEATRE SOLD OUT ONE WEEK IN ADVANCE STOP PICTURE ENJOYS TREMENDOUS POPULARITY AND APPEAL WORD OF

---

* In an article, "GWTW: Supercolossal Saga of an Epic" in the October 26, 1947, issue of the *New York Times Magazine*, Lloyd Shearer claimed that "everyone who was anyone took part in the celebration, except the publicity-shy Margaret Mitchell. With her husband, John R. Marsh, she stayed at home that night, taking care of an ill father."

MOUTH PUBLICITY TERRIFIC STOP ALL MOST IMPORTANT PAPERS PUBLISHED UNUSUALLY LONG RICHLY ILLUSTRATED ARTICLES PRAISING EXCEPTIONAL VALUE GWTW"

Brussels, October 23 —

"FOLLOWING PRESS COMMENTS GWTW STOP LE SOIR QUOTE SAW GWTW FOR THE THIRD TIME AND ENJOYED IT IMMENSELY UNQUOTE LE MATIN QUOTE WE WOULD NEED AN ENTIRE PAGE TO TELL ABOUT THE FINE QUALI-TIES OF THE PICTURE WHICH ABSOLUTELY DESERVES ITS REPUTATION PERIOD THE TECHNICOLOR HAS NEVER BEEN EQUALED UNQUOTE LA FLANDRE LIBERALE QUOTE GWTW IS THE BEST LITERARY ADAPTATION EVER MADE UNQUOTE LE PHARE QUOTE CLARK GABLE WHO LIVES THE PART OF RHETT BUTLER DOES A MAGNIFICENT PIECE OF ACTING UN-QUOTE VRAI QUOTE VIVIEN LEIGH IS SUPERB AS SCARLETT UNQUOTE LA LANTERNE QUOTE YOU CANT AFFORD TO MISS GWTW UNQUOTE HEBDO QUOTE FLEMINGS DIREC-TION BRINGS TO THE SCREEN SCENES UNSURPASSED FOR THEIR DRAMATIC INTENSITY UNQUOTE LE LBIRE BELGIQUE QUOTE GWTW MAKES SCREEN HISTORY UNQUOTE POUR-QUOI PAS QUOTE THE INTERPRETATION OF THE ACTORS IS VERY BEST UNQUOTE"

Editor   *Atlanta, Georgia*
The Atlanta Journal   *November 9, 1947*
Atlanta, Georgia

Editor, The Journal:

I want to thank The Journal and Wright Bryan for the two columns Mr. Bryan wrote recently commenting on a story about "Gone With the Wind" by Lloyd Shearer in the New York Times Magazine on Oct. 26. It is not only appreciation of the nice things said about me and my book which prompts this letter. I am also grateful to Mr. Bryan for correcting a startling misstate-ment about me in the article—that I did not attend the premiere of "Gone With the Wind" in Atlanta in 1939. Many people have asked me or written me about this error. Of course I attended the premiere and would not have missed it, so I thank The Journal for clearing up the misinformation.*

---

* Allan Taylor, Lois Cole's husband, corrected Shearer's misstatement in a letter to the edi-tor of the *New York Times*, printed November 9: "The 'publicity-shy' Miss Mitchell, it is true,

Mr. Bryan's amusingly written conjecture that Frank Daniel, of The Journal, had established the letters "GWTW" as a symbol for "Gone With the Wind" is quite true. Mr. Daniel was the first person to use them in this fashion. I can remember when the New York papers began to pick them up, and then papers all over this country and Europe followed suit.

Mr. F. van Veen   Atlanta, Georgia
Antwerp, Belgium   January 16, 1948

Dear Mr. van Veen:

Thank you so much for your letter about the film of "Gone With the Wind." It interested me more than you can know. I wanted to learn the opinion of people in other countries about the film, and I was glad to have yours.

Let me tell you immediately that I took no offense at your frank statement of your disappointment in the film. I had nothing to do with the production of the film. I did not write the scenario, advise with the producer or go to Hollywood. I have heard too often that the protests of authors avail nothing with the producers of motion pictures.

Yes, I understand what you mean when you say that you were disappointed that the love story was emphasized and the war pushed into the background. I, more than anyone else, had a sudden sense of shock when, on viewing the film for the first time, I saw that the siege and fall of Atlanta, which was around September of 1864, came so close upon the heels of the news of the Battle of Gettysburg, July 1863, for an uninformed person might believe they were part of the same battle. I understand that Mr. Selznick, the producer, had originally photographed many war scenes, but when it was discovered that the film lasted six hours he was forced to eliminate two hours of the film and felt that most of his audiences would prefer that he eliminate war instead of love.*

I thank you so much for the kind things you wrote me about my book. Coming as they did from someone who had just lived through a dreadful war and occupation, I appreciate them all the more.

---

remained somewhat in the background during the preliminary celebrations. . . . But she and her husband were definitely on hand in Atlanta's Grand Theatre for the opening. . . . To have stayed away would not have been in keeping either with Miss Mitchell's sense of duty or her understandable interest in seeing the picture."

* While earlier drafts of the screenplay contained some war scenes, most of these were not filmed. In addition, Selznick's edits after the first preview consisted mostly of eliminating a few small scenes and trimming others as well as characters' entrances and exits.

Mr. Walter Plunkett   *Atlanta, Georgia*
David O. Selznick Productions, Inc.   *January 19, 1948*
Culver City, California

Dear Walter:

I've just received your letter about your friend, Howard Greer's ex-pected visit to Atlanta. I'm getting this reply off to you as soon as I can, so please excuse the brevity. I'd love to gossip with you about a million things in this letter but will not, and hope some day you will be here in person.

It's very doubtful that I can see Mr. Greer and I want you to know why so that if he should phone here and I am not even able to answer the phone you both will know I am not being upstage. It's been going on three years since I "met" anybody. John has been seriously ill—and almost fatally—for over two years, after a heart attack. He is recovering very well now and is even able to take short automobile rides. I just stopped seeing people dur-ing his illness and have never started again. You can't nurse a sick man and handle a full-time foreign and domestic business and have the opportunity to go places and see people. Under ordinary circumstances it would give me much pleasure to meet any friend of yours, but these days I don't have the time or the strength.

I must tell you that we have a 16mm projector and we rent films. How happy we are to see your name so very often.

Mr. Elliott Springs   *Atlanta, Georgia*
Lancaster, South Carolina   *January 27, 1948*

Dear Elliott:

I had had you on my mind for two weeks, as I wanted to thank you for the two beautiful decks of cards you sent at Christmas time. Now you beat me to the draw with your nice letter about seeing "Gone With the Wind" for the sixth time. Thank you for all of them—the cards, the letter and for being so interested in the picture.

Yes, John is considerably better—so much better that he was able to sit through a return engagement of "Gone With the Wind" here in Atlanta, al-though he was completely bushed in the process. He is now well enough to go across the street to the Driving Club for short intervals in the afternoon and to see people and, in general, to have more fun. It was out of the question for him to think of going back to the Power Company, even in the far distant future, and it made me very happy to know he wasn't going to try. . . .*

---

* Marsh resigned from Georgia Power in September 1947.

Mr. David O. Selznick   *Atlanta, Georgia*
David O. Selznick Productions, Inc.   *March 11, 1948*
Culver City, California

Dear Mr. Selznick:

This is a much delayed letter thanking you for the fine present you sent us at Christmas. The old-fashioned glasses in Steuben crystal are really handsome and we are proud to have them. I hope you can excuse our tardiness in writing.*

Peggy has been struggling for a month with the current bronchial virus infection which I understand swept Los Angeles some weeks ago. Every night she has said, "I haven't yet thanked Mr. Selznick for those beautiful glasses. How unappreciative he must think we are!" So I told her I would write to you for her.

As you may know, I have been a semi-invalid since a bad heart attack two years ago. Before then, I had been handling Peggy's many and complicated business affairs. When I fell sick she picked up that load on top of what she was already carrying, plus the care of a sick husband. The two years have been strenuous for her, and she has often had to be negligent in writing letters to old friends. But she has succeeded in doing the heavy job which has descended upon her.

We have not yet seen your "Duel in the Sun," for I was not well enough to go to the theatre when it showed here in Atlanta. But we have been seeing some of your earlier pictures. The movies have always been one of my favorite diversions. After I had been shut up here in the house for many months and neither of us had seen a movie of any kind, Peggy discovered that we could rent a 16mm projector and also films. Since then, we have been having movies here at home two or three nights a week, usually for just the two of us.

Naturally, the choice of films is very limited. Westerns and Grade B stuff make up the bulk of the catalogue. But some of the very fine pictures that were being produced ten or fifteen years ago—better than most of the recent ones—have been available and it has been a real treat to see them again.

Among them were your "Star is Born," "Made for Each Other" and "The Young in Heart."† Looking at them in the quiet of our living room,

---

* This letter was written by Marsh on Mitchell's behalf.

† *A Star Is Born* (1937), the original version of the much-filmed story, starred Fredric March and Janet Gaynor. *Made for Each Other* (1939) featured Jimmy Stewart and Carole Lombard, and *The Young in Heart* (1938) starred Gaynor, Douglas Fairbanks Jr. and Paulette Goddard.

these many years after their first presentation, confirms our original impression that you gave them something the ordinary picture does not have. We tried to get your "David Copperfield" but we hear that it has never been put on 16mm.

Of course, GWTW is the best of all. I don't have to tell you of the crowds it attracted when it was shown here in 1947. I wasn't strong enough to sit through the whole performance, but I saw it in segments by going on three different days. I would not have missed it!

We read in the newspapers about your activities from time to time and we hope that all is going well with you. Our best wishes to you, as always.

Miss Hedda Hopper   *Atlanta, Georgia*
Hollywood, California   *March 23, 1948*

Dear Miss Hopper:

I am grateful to you for your letter of March 5th, and its enclosures—the letter from Mr. Morris Mink of Portland, Oregon, and the photograph of Mr. Mink, his friends and the fake Margaret Mitchell—interested my husband and me very much. I would have thanked you long before this but Atlanta has been through the same virus epidemic Los Angeles had a couple of months ago, and I have been laid up with a mild case of it.

The snapshot of the fake Margaret Mitchell shows her to be the same woman who was photographed and interviewed as me in Mexico City last summer and whose picture and interview also appeared in a San Antonio, Texas, paper around the same date. She seems to have had a very good time in Mexico City and was entertained as me. One nice newspaperwoman columnist in Mexico City wrote me about the number of Martinis the woman could down, and the astonishment of the Mexican guests who had not thought "Southern ladies able to hold so much." She also talked a great deal about her "new book," which was a sequel to "Gone With the Wind" and would soon be on the screen with Clark Gable in it. From newspapers all over the Southwest I have been able to reconstruct the woman's portrait very well, but by the time I learn she has been in some town and posed as me she has disappeared into thin air and reappears somewhere else while I am trying to nab her in the former place.

For some years I have been plagued by the rumor that I am writing a sequel and that the entire cast of "Gone With the Wind" would appear in it. It has taken me so much time denying this sequel business that I have had very little time to do anything else. Most of these rumors came out of Hollywood and for some time I was completely bewildered as to how they started. Now I am perfectly certain this woman is at the bottom of them. She goes to earth for a certain number of weeks or months and then apparently she cannot stand it any longer and she bursts forth as me, giving interviews about the book she is writing, the prominent moving picture personalities she knows and intimate gossip about motion picture stars. Eventually her statements find their way into gossip columns, and then I begin to get telegrams and letters about the whole affair.

The woman has been quiet for several months, but I think she must be loose again in Hollywood, for this morning I received a letter from a schoolgirl in California expressing pleasure that the sequel to "Gone With the Wind" would soon appear on the screen, with Clark Gable in it but not Vivien Leigh "because Vivien Leigh refuses to act opposite Gable any more." The young lady had read this in a Los Angeles paper. The last chummy little item about Miss Leigh sounds very much like the fake Margaret Mitchell's statement.

Some day perhaps I'll manage to catch the woman while she is giving interviews or autographing copies of "Gone With the Wind," and it will certainly be a relief to me.

You have been so kind about this whole troublesome affair. I did see the piece you ran in your column and I was so grateful to you for it. It did a lot of good in this section and I know it did more good in the West, as is evidenced by Mr. Mink's letter. I am returning the snapshot to Mr. Mink and writing to him, in the hope I can get a lead on "Margaret Mitchell" and perhaps find out where she holes up between the times of posing as the author of "Gone With the Wind."

David O. Selznick   ·   *Atlanta, Georgia*
David O. Selznick Productions, Inc.   *December 24, 1948*
Culver City, California

JOHN AND I ARE THINKING OF YOU AND WISHING YOU THE BEST CHRISTMAS OF ALL AND THE MOST SUCCESSFUL NEW YEAR.

Mr. David O. Selznick   *Atlanta, Georgia*
David O. Selznick Productions, Inc.   *January 3, 1949*
Culver City, California

Dear Mr. Selznick:

The silver serving pieces you sent for Christmas are so beautiful and "different" in design, and we admire them so much. The sturdiness combined with the graceful simplicity of line are marks of a truly fine designer. We are enjoying them now and will continue to do so in the future. You are kind indeed to think of us at Christmas time and I want to tell you that you were part of the very nicest Christmas we ever had.

Our social activities this year may seem unexciting to other people but they were wonderful to us, because John had recovered enough to go out to dinner with my brother and sister-in-law at Christmas time and to attend briefly "open houses" two friends were giving. We sat up late Christmas Eve and after midnight opened Christmas parcels. After John's long illness, it has been very exciting to have him well enough to enjoy life and his friends. And of course it has been a happy time for me, for there were many times when I did not know whether he would ever be able to get out of bed again.

Now that he is better, I am trying to crawl out from under the enormous stack of business matters which have accumulated in the years of his illness. A great part of these business matters are in connection with the foreign editions of "Gone With the Wind." During John's illness I had to handle just the most pressing matters. Now I am trying to be more businesslike and to clean up more than three years' accumulation of work. John was beginning to get sick just at the end of the war when my foreign publication affairs were in chaos for the most part. Some of my publishers were dead, others had disappeared, some who survived the occupation were penniless and without food or paper or printing machinery, others had lost all their records, some had to be dealt with through our military missions et cetera. Now as I turn to straighten out my affairs once more, I find them in almost as chaotic condition as before, due to political changes in Europe during the last three years. With some of my publishers I do not think of sales reports or the payment of money; it's mainly—if I send them food and clothing will they ever receive them? I sometimes wonder if there is any use in straightening out my foreign affairs when a number of my publishers have had their businesses "nationalized."

I never believe anything I see in the papers, especially in moving picture gossip columns, but I was certainly interested in an item (true or false) that you might produce "Uncle Tom's Cabin." I am one of the few of my age and generation who read "Uncle Tom's Cabin," as it was a forbidden book like "Three Weeks" when I was a child. My mother was a very smart woman and she said every Southerner should read "Uncle Tom's Cabin" and should be required to read it because it showed how mean Yankees were to Negroes any time they had a chance!*

My husband sends you his good wishes for a successful new year and wants me to tell you that we have had many of your older films for our 16mm projector and how much we enjoy them. When we see your trade mark coming up, we know we are in for a wonderful evening.

---

* The antislavery novel *Uncle Tom's Cabin; or, Life Among the Lowly*, by Harriet Beecher Stowe, was published in 1852. *Three Weeks*, by Elinor Glyn, was an erotic romance novel published in 1907.

Mr. Harold E. George   *Atlanta, Georgia*
10th Street Theatre   *May 6, 1949*
Atlanta, Georgia

Dear Mr. George:

My husband and I thank you so much for the passes you sent us for the return engagement of "Gone With the Wind" at your theatre. We used them last night and enjoyed the picture so much. We would have told you so personally before leaving the theatre but it was so late that we decided not to bother you. I was interested to see that the theatre was packed and even the very front rows in use. A great many people seemed to be repeaters, for they knew beforehand what was going to happen and started laughing or crying before the cause for laughter or tears appeared on the screen.

We appreciate your courtesy very much and we thank you for it.

Miss Katharine Brown   *Atlanta, Georgia*
MCA Management, Ltd.   *August 1, 1949*
New York, New York

Dear Katharine:

I am enclosing a clipping from The Journal, which I would like to have back when you have read it. I call your attention particularly to the item about Howard H[ughes]. I could not recall that he attended the premiere. If he did, I did not meet him.* Sue Myrick says she does not remember him being here. I can't find anyone who does recall meeting him. Just for curiosity and to keep the records straight, I would like to know if he was here. He is such a big shot I know somebody would have met him.

Thanks for what you did about the matter John took up with you.†

We hope to be in New York when it is a little cooler and look forward to seeing you then.

---

* A column by Hugh Park titled "Around Town" recounted several humorous incidents associated with the *Gone With the Wind* premiere as told by an Atlanta woman who worked with Elmer Bradley Coleman of MGM in December 1939. One of her anecdotes claimed that when she went to Howard Hughes's hotel room to deliver him $400 he had asked for, she found him talking on the phone while wearing only a towel.

† On July 26, John Marsh authorized Brown, now an agent with MCA Management, Inc., to explore possible interest in the television rights to *Gone With the Wind*. In Mitchell's 1936 contract with Selznick, the author had retained the rights for live dramatic versions of her story on television.

Epilogue: Tomorrow Is Another Day

K ay Brown replied to Mitchell on August 8. She noted that the column about the premiere "brought all kinds of memories back" and agreed that Howard Hughes had not been in Atlanta in December 1939. "I am sure I would have known it." She also denied the columnist's claim that John Hay Whitney's bed at the hotel collapsed in the middle of the night. As for the story that "one of the genteel old Southern ladies in the picture got plastered," needed help getting dressed, and was "still as oiled as a hoot owl" at the premiere,[1] the actual account was "much funnier," Brown recalled. "My secretary was the one elected to do the dressing job and I was the one that took her to the theatre."* Brown closed, "With love to you both."[2] It was the last letter the two women would exchange.

In Atlanta that week, Mitchell was occupied with the usual day-to-day business that had been part of her life in recent years. She prepared several overseas care packages for her publishers and other acquaintances, some of whom were now behind the Iron Curtain. Since the end of World War II, she had regularly shipped them boxes of food, vitamins, and clothing and usually included a few toys as well because "I remember my disappointment as a child when a parcel would be opened, and there would be nothing in it for me."[3] While Selznick had not raised the issue of a sequel recently, readers of the novel continued their quest to learn more about the saga of Scarlett and Rhett. An eager fan from Illinois wrote to Macmillan

---

* Neither the columnist nor Brown named the "oiled" woman, but the car assignment list for the evening of December 15 shows that Brown and her husband rode to the theater with Laura Hope Crews.

421

about a story titled "Whispering Winds," a continuation of Gone With the Wind, "which I think could be arranged into a very interesting book."[4] And a visitor just back from Italy told the author of an amusing incident at a screening of the movie in Milan. In a scene in which Frank Kennedy calls Scarlett "sugar," the Italian subtitles translated his endearment as "something like coffee," which brought gales of laughter from the audience.[5]

On Thursday, August 11, the Constitution carried a small article about the death of eighty-three-year-old Harry Davenport, who portrayed Dr. Meade in Gone With the Wind.[6] Later that day, Mitchell called her former managing editor at the Journal, John Paschall, who was in the hospital after suffering a heart attack.[7] The author herself had not been feeling well for several days. After supper, she suggested to Marsh that they go see a movie; an air-conditioned theater would provide a comfortable break from the evening heat and oppressive humidity.[8] A Canterbury Tale, a British wartime mystery involving an American GI, a British soldier and a young woman from London, was showing at the nearby Peachtree Art Theater; the 1944 film had been released in the United States earlier that year. Since her husband's heart attack, Mitchell always drove when they went out. She found a parking space on the west side of Peachtree Street, across from the theater. Arm in arm, the couple looked both ways and began crossing the thoroughfare that her novel had made famous across the globe. It was about 8:20 p.m. When they were about halfway, the pair spotted an automobile speeding toward them out of a broad curve to the south. There was no time to speak. As Marsh recalled, "In one of those split-second decisions I decided that the safe course was to go forward. Peggy apparently decided the safe course was to run back to the curbing we had just left."[9]

Behind the wheel was twenty-nine-year-old Hugh Dorsey Gravitt, an off-duty cab driver with twenty-four previous police citations; most were for speeding, but he also had been charged with disorderly conduct, running red lights and stop signs, and reckless driving.[10] He later admitted having drunk several beers. Farther down Peachtree, as he sped north, two young boys crossing the street had been forced to jump out of his way.[11] When Gravitt spotted Mitchell and Marsh, he blew the horn, slammed on the brakes, and swerved to the left, trying to swing around the couple. Instead, he skidded straight into the fleeing author's path. It was a scene, Marsh said, "I'm afraid I'll see the rest of my life."[12] Gravitt's car struck Mitchell and dragged her about fifteen feet.

Someone at the theater called an ambulance, which rushed her to Grady Hospital downtown. As word of the accident spread, telephone calls, telegrams, cards, and letters began pouring in from around the world;

Mitchell's friends took turns at the hospital switchboard tracking the hundreds of calls of concern. Selznick, who was in Europe on his honeymoon with actress Jennifer Jones, sent seven orchids to the hospital. George Brett wired Marsh, expressing the concern of everyone at Macmillan. Lois Cole was with her family at a remote cabin and unable to make a flight to Atlanta; Harold Latham had just begun a vacation in Maine and Canada. Like friends and fans everywhere, they kept abreast of the situation through newspaper and radio reports. An official of the Book-of-the-Month Club said she could recall "no other comparable situation when a whole country was waiting to hear what happened to an author, except when Rudyard Kipling almost died of pneumonia during a visit to New York in 1900."[13] Throughout the weekend, the media carried regular updates on Mitchell's condition, and she appeared to be rallying: "Margaret Mitchell 'Definitely Better' in Fight Against Death" and "Peggy is Getting Mad—Beginning to Fight," the *Atlanta Journal* reported. Her doctor said that the author occasionally murmured such things as "It hurts" and "I'll take care of that in the morning" but that she was never fully conscious.[14] Late in the morning on Tuesday, August 16, Mitchell took a sudden turn for the worse. Doctors rushed to prepare to operate to relieve pressure on her brain, but at 11:59 a.m. the author died.[15] She was forty-eight years old. As Marsh wrote his family later, "The marvel was that she stayed alive as long as she did, for the brain damage was very severe. The doctor says that the chances are that she could never have recovered fully. I could not wish that she had survived if it was only for years of invalidism."[16]

The tributes poured in. President Harry Truman called Mitchell "an artist who gave the world an eternal book" and "a great soul who exemplified in her all too brief span of years the highest ideals of American womanhood."[17] Governor Herman Talmadge extended his sympathy, noting, "The people of Georgia, the people of the nation and millions in foreign lands who have read and been inspired by her great and famous book will be saddened."[18] Clark Gable told the Associated Press that Mitchell's death was "a very deep personal loss. She was a woman with a great literary gift, and I shall ever be obligated to her for the finest role I ever played." He predicted that *Gone With the Wind* "will endure as a classic to stand as a monument to her memory."[19] In England, Vivien Leigh, who was preparing to play Blanche DuBois in the London stage premiere of *A Streetcar Named Desire*, recalled the author "of whom I shall ever have the most enchanting memories, never ending gratitude, admiration and affectionate homage. That the strength of her pen could emanate from that delightful and diminutive person will ever be a source of bewilderment and joy to all who were happy enough to know her."[20] That evening, Atlanta's WCON Radio aired a special program that recounted Mitchell's life story while Max Steiner's music from the film played in the background.

The funeral was held at 10:00 on the morning of August 18, one week after the accident. Three hundred admittance cards had been hand delivered the previous afternoon. Mayor Hartsfield ordered flags lowered to half-staff at City Hall and at the Atlanta Cyclorama and arranged for the service to be broadcast over loudspeakers to a large crowd outside the funeral home. The governor asked state employees to pause for three minutes as a silent tribute. Olivia de Havilland sent a spray of red roses. After a short service, the funeral procession crossed Peachtree Street and made its way to the city's historic Oakland Cemetery, where Mitchell was buried next to her parents and infant brother in the "red Georgia earth she loved and glorified for generations yet unborn."[21]

That Sunday, the Rev. Charles L. Allen, pastor of Grace Methodist Church in Atlanta, delivered a sermon about bearing sorrow titled "When a City's Heart is Broken by the Death of One It Loves."[22] Later that month, *Life* magazine devoted three pages to Mitchell's life and funeral and included a photo of Gravitt outside his jail cell.* Bookstores in Atlanta sold out of the novel, and back orders for copies climbed into the hundreds. Theaters across the South clamored to show the film, but only a limited number of prints were still in circulation from its rerelease in 1947. When the city's Piedmont Drive-In screened *Gone With the Wind* for two days later that month—the booking had been made before the accident—eager theatergoers backed up traffic for three miles. Two neighborhood theaters ran the film as well, and the Piedmont and a sister drive-in brought the film back the following week.[23]

* * *

While Mitchell's story of feisty Scarlett O'Hara and her fight for survival brought hope to millions of readers around the globe during World War II, many did not get a chance to see Hollywood's version until years later. The film opened in 1940 to record business in England and other nations in the British Empire as well as in several Central and South American countries, but the war slammed the door shut in many of the largest and most lucra-

---

* On November 17, Gravitt was found guilty of involuntary manslaughter and sentenced to twelve to eighteen months in prison. He was paroled in October 1950 after serving almost eleven months. Gravitt died on April 15, 1994, at the age of seventy-four.

tive foreign markets, including France, Germany, and Italy. Even after the Allies' victory in 1945, monetary policies restricting the amount of funds that could be transferred to the United States from recovering economies further delayed the movie's release. But as the new decade dawned, many in Europe and Asia got their first look at the cinematic Scarlett and Rhett. In May 1950, Parisians flocked to see *Autant en Emporte le Vent* on the big screen. When *Gone With the Wind* opened in Japan in September 1952, shortly after the Allied occupation ended, the picture broke all box office records.* And after the film finally made it to West Germany in 1953, war-weary citizens in Berlin—along with numerous moviegoers who reportedly slipped across the border from communist-controlled East Germany—jammed theaters showing *Vom Winde Verweht*.

In the United States, the film continued to rack up unprecedented grosses. A wide-screen version of *Gone With the Wind* was released in 1954 and drew a new generation of fans, as well as many repeat viewers, to the nation's theaters. The movie opened May 20 at Loew's Grand Theatre in Atlanta at a screening sponsored by the Atlanta Smith College Club, with proceeds used to establish a Margaret Mitchell Memorial Scholarship. Two of the film's cast members were special guests—Ann Rutherford and Cammie King, who played Bonnie Blue Butler and was then a sophomore at the University of Southern California—and Rich's department store mounted an exhibit of material associated with Mitchell and the motion picture. *Gone With the Wind* took in $7.5 million at the box office, making it one of the highest-grossing films of the year. In 1961, as the country began a four-year commemoration of the centennial of the Civil War, the film returned to the theater circuit, opening in Atlanta on March 10, preceded by a costume ball. Selznick, Leigh, and de Havilland made a return trip to the city and helped unveil two portraits, one of Mitchell and the other of Gable, who had died the previous November. The movie added another $6.7 million to MGM's coffers.

At about the same time, the author's brother, who had inherited *Gone With the Wind*'s literary rights on Marsh's death, hired Kay Brown as an agent for his sister's estate. With the novel's copyright due for renewal in 1964, Stephens Mitchell renegotiated with Metro-Goldwyn-Mayer for

---

* The Japanese have a special affinity for Mitchell's story. The motion picture has been rereleased in the country several times. *Gone With the Wind* made its dramatic stage debut in Japan in 1966; a musical version with music and lyrics by Harold Rome, opened four years later. In addition, the movie made its worldwide television debut in Japan in 1975, a year before Americans got their first glimpse of Selznick's masterpiece on the small screen.

a 10 percent share of the film's future earnings. Over the next several decades, millions of dollars for the author's heirs were generated from additional releases of the film in 1967 and 1974; the movie's premiere on U.S. television in 1976—for which NBC-TV paid $5 million—and a later $35 million deal for additional showings on CBS-TV; its 1983 debut on home video; and a resurgence in marketing *Gone With the Wind* dolls, plates, music boxes, and puzzles.

*   *   *

Three-quarters of a century after its world premiere in Atlanta, *Gone With the Wind* remains the most popular motion picture ever made, with nearly 226 million paid admissions in the United States and another 38 million in Great Britain.[24] While spiraling ticket costs long ago bumped the movie from its top spot on the list of all-time box office champions, the 1939 classic is still the leading grosser when figures are adjusted for inflation. By one estimate, the movie has earned the equivalent of $3.3 billion.[25] And Selznick's magnum opus regularly appears on moviegoers' lists of all-time favorites; in 2011, it ranked number one in an ABC-TV/*People* magazine survey. Even the story's dialogue has become a part of our everyday language. A poll by the American Film Institute proclaimed Rhett Butler's exit line—"Frankly, my dear, I don't give a damn"—the most famous movie quote of all time.

For decades, film critics, movie historians, and social commentators have analyzed the movie, those who made it and the fans who love it, in an effort to understand and explain *Gone With the Wind*'s continuing appeal. Noted film professor and commentator Andrew Sarris may have come closest to the answer in an essay aptly titled "This Moviest of All Movies":

> I can never hope to explain to my more serious film students why the gnarled trees and stately mansions of [production designer] William Cameron Menzies, the morosely melodic score of Max Steiner, and the ineffable beauty and cruelty of Vivien Leigh could cast such a hypnotic spell even on moviegoers who should have known better. . . . There is something in most of us that will always treasure Selznick's flair for old-fashioned, full-bodied narrative even as we pay lip service to the most anemic forms of celebration in the modern cinemah. And, ultimately, there is Vivien Leigh's smile on the screen like a sliver of sunlight piercing the heart.[26]

Both Mitchell and Selznick understood the power of an "old-fashioned, full-bodied narrative." From her earliest days of reading and writing, the author knew that a good plot was key. When her imagination, her love of history, and her genius for words came together in *Gone With the Wind*, Mitchell gave birth to a story of unforgettable characters torn by passion and war—a tale that renowned historian Henry Steele Commager deemed "a dramatic recreation of life itself."[27] And in taking the novel from page to screen, Selznick, according to the grateful author herself, carefully translated what was in her mind and in her heart, "adding to it his own color, firing it with his own imagination, heightening effects with his own genius."[28] When her literary prowess and his cinematic flair melded in *Gone With the Wind*, the result was an enduring legend in the pantheon of cinema and in the hearts of moviegoers everywhere.

Cast of Characters

The following are brief biographical sketches of key people with whom Margaret Mitchell corresponded about the motion picture *Gone With the Wind*:

Russell Birdwell (1903–1977): The director of advertising and publicity at Selznick International Pictures in the 1930s, Birdwell and Mitchell rarely saw eye to eye. The legendary PR man, who coined the phrase "Wherever ego, I go," could never seem to grasp the author's reluctance to exploit her fame or allow him to do so. His publicity stunts are legendary. To promote the 1937 film *The Prisoner of Zenda*, he had a dozen residents of the small town of Zenda, Ontario, Canada, flown to New York for the movie's premiere. The following year, he arranged for actress Carole Lombard, starring in *Made for Each Other*, to be named honorary mayor of Culver City for a day; she promptly declared a city holiday, and all of the studio's employees took the day off. Birdwell was the brains behind the nationwide "Search for Scarlett," but shortly after filming began on *Gone With the Wind* in early 1939, he left Selznick International to form his own publicity firm. In the mid-1940s, he worked with Howard Hughes to promote Jane Russell's film debut in *The Outlaw*. Focusing on the actress's legendary cleavage, Birdwell ads asked, "How would you like to tussle with Russell?" and "What are the two reasons for Jane Russell's rise to stardom?"

George Brett Jr. (1893–1984): Like his father and grandfather before him, Brett served as head of the U.S. branch of The Macmillan Company. He began working for the publisher as a stock clerk in 1914 and was elected president of Macmillan in September 1931, when his father became chairman of the board; he remained president until his retirement in 1958. The publisher and the author of *Gone With the Wind* battled over several issues, including agent Annie Laurie Williams representing Mitchell on the sale of the movie rights and his request for the author to accept reduced royalties on two editions of her novel released at the time of the film's premiere. The publisher's collection of foreign editions of Gone With the Wind, several inscribed by Mitchell, as well as the original typescript of the final four chapters of her book are in Special Collections at the Pequot Library in Southport, Connecticut.

Katharine "Kay" Brown (1902–1995): Producer David O. Selznick's East Coast story editor, Brown first brought Gone With the Wind to his attention in May 1936 and kept up the pressure until he agreed to buy the movie rights in early July. A graduate of Wellesley College, Brown joined Selznick International in 1935. She and Mitchell first met during final negotiations on the movie contract, and Brown, later promoted to Selznick's East Coast representative, became the producer's main liaison with the author. After Mitchell's death, Brown continued to unofficially advise Mitchell's husband and then her brother, who hired her as an agent for the estate in the early 1960s. In 1975, she brokered a deal with Richard Brown and Darryl F. Zanuck to produce a movie sequel to Gone With the Wind. While the project eventually fell through, it opened the door to two authorized book sequels—Scarlett, by Alexandra Ripley, in 1991, and Rhett Butler's People, by Donald McCaig, in 2007. Brown was interviewed in the 1988 documentary The Making of a Legend: Gone With the Wind, produced by Selznick's sons.

Lois Cole (1902–1979): Cole, a longtime friend of Mitchell and the first person outside the author's family to read the full manuscript of Gone With the Wind, was born in New York City. She graduated from Smith College in 1924 and began her publishing career with Harcourt, Brace & Co. In 1928, she joined Macmillan's branch in Atlanta, where she first met the author. In 1932, Cole and her husband, Allan Taylor, moved to New York, and she became an assistant editor at Macmillan. It was at Cole's urging that Harold Latham asked Mitchell about the manuscript of Gone With the Wind in the spring of 1935. Mitchell was godmother to Cole's son, Turney Allan Taylor Jr., born in 1938. Cole left Macmillan in 1945 and later worked for Thomas Y. Crowell Co. and then William Morrow & Co., where she edited Margaret Mitchell of Atlanta, by Finis Farr, published in 1965.

George Cukor (1899–1983): The original director of Gone With the Wind, Cukor was a special favorite of Mitchell after visiting the author in Atlanta in the spring of 1937. Even though he was fired just three weeks after filming began in early 1939, several scenes he directed remain in the final film, including the evening prayers at Tara, Mammy lacing Scarlett for the barbecue, the Paris Hat sequence, and most of the scenes around the birth of Melanie's baby. After he and Selznick parted company, Cukor went on to direct *The Women* (1939), *The Philadelphia Story* (1940), *Gaslight* (1944), *Born Yesterday* (1950), *A Star Is Born* (1954), and *My Fair Lady* (1964), for which he won the Academy Award for Best Director.

Telamon Cuyler (1873–1951): Cuyler was a Georgia lawyer, writer, and collector of Confederate memorabilia. Born Telamon Cuyler Smith, in 1905 he successfully petitioned a Georgia court to change his surname to Cuyler, a family name on his mother's side. Several years later, after his wife, Grace Barton, left him and filed for divorce, he sued his mother-in-law for $500,000 in damages, claiming that she had alienated his wife's affections. Cuyler first wrote to Mitchell shortly after *Gone With the Wind* was published and continued the correspondence until her death. To thank him for his help with historical research on the film, Susan Myrick arranged for him to receive two tickets to both the Junior League Ball and the premiere.

Olivia de Havilland (1916–): The winner of two Academy Awards for Best Actress—in *To Each His Own* (1946) and *The Heiress* (1949)—de Havilland's first Oscar nomination, in the Best Supporting Actress category, came for her role as Melanie Hamilton in *Gone With the Wind*. In 1944, de Havilland won a landmark court ruling that limited an actor's contract to calendar years; previously, studios maintained that such pacts could be extended to make up for nonproductive work periods, such as suspensions. Since the early 1950s, the actress has lived in Paris. She returned to Atlanta in 1961 to celebrate the Civil War Centennial rerelease of *Gone With the Wind* and again in 1967 to launch its 70mm wide-screen release; by that time, she was the last survivor among the film's four stars. In 2008, President George W. Bush presented her the National Medal of Arts "for her persuasive and compelling skill as an actress in roles from Shakespeare's Hermia to Margaret Mitchell's Melanie." He also cited her "independence, integrity, and grace [that] won creative freedom for herself and her fellow film actors."

Hobart "Hobe" Erwin (1897–1950): An interior decorator in New York, Erwin spent more than a year doing preliminary work on *Gone With the Wind*. He accompanied Cukor to Atlanta in the spring of 1937 and was the subject of an article in the *Atlanta Journal* headlined "How Will Tara Look in the Movies?" After his trip South, Erwin corresponded regularly with Mitchell, who answered many of his questions about architecture and even the wallpaper at Tara, Twelve Oaks, and the Butler mansion. When production on the film continued to be delayed, Erwin resigned to focus on his design firm, Erwin & Jones. He was one of two art directors on Selznick's 1933 *Dinner at Eight* at MGM; that same year, he served as set decorator on RKO's *Little Women*, directed by Cukor and featuring costumes by Walter Plunkett.

Clark Gable (1901–1960): The "King of Hollywood" was reluctant to take the role of Rhett Butler, fearful that he could never please the millions of people who had read the book and formed in their minds their own image of Rhett. Of course, his role in *Gone With the Wind* became the one for which he is still remembered; he was nominated for an Academy Award as Best Actor but lost to Robert Donat in *Goodbye, Mr. Chips*. Gable was one of the biggest stars in the Golden Age of Hollywood. He won an Oscar for the 1934 comedy *It Happened One Night*, with Claudette Colbert. After the death of his third wife, Carole Lombard, Gable married twice more. He died of a heart attack on November 16, 1960, and is entombed next to Lombard at Forest Lawn Cemetery. Gable's son, John Clark, was born to his fifth wife, Kay Spreckels Gable, in March 1961.

William B. Hartsfield (1890–1971): Atlanta's mayor at the time *Gone With the Wind* premiered, Hartsfield worked tirelessly to snare the opening for the city. He first wrote to Selznick in March 1937 about launching the film in the author's hometown and continued to push for the event over the next two years. Once Selznick confirmed that Atlanta would host the world premiere, Hartsfield led the city's businessmen in ensuring that the festivities were a great success; he mailed postcards to thousands of people across the country, inviting them to visit Atlanta in December 1939. First elected in 1937, Hartsfield served six terms. Atlanta's airport, the world's busiest, was named for him after his death.

Leslie Howard (1893–1943): One of England's best-known stage and screen actors, Howard was an early choice for the role of Ashley Wilkes in *Gone With the Wind*. However, like Gable, he was not eager to play the role. His reluctance stemmed from the fact that he was about twenty years older than the character, and Howard's performance is considered by many to be one of the weakest in the film. At the same time he was working on *Gone With the Wind*, he also was starring in *Intermezzo*, Ingrid Bergman's American film debut, at Selznick International—sometimes shooting scenes for one picture in the morning and scenes for the other that afternoon. Howard returned to England in the fall of 1939 after his country declared war on Nazi Germany. He was killed on June 1, 1943, when the plane in which he was flying to London from Portugal was shot down by the Luftwaffe over the Bay of Biscay.

Sidney Howard (1891–1939): One of the nation's leading dramatists, Howard was Selznick's first choice to craft a screenplay from Mitchell's novel. He won a Pulitzer Prize in 1925 for his play *They Knew What They Wanted*. Howard began work on the *Gone With the Wind* script in late 1936, and, although more than a dozen other writers took a stab at the screenplay over the next two years, he received sole screen credit. Howard was killed in August 1939 when a tractor he was trying to start at his Tyringham, Massachusetts, farm lurched forward, pinning him against a wall. On February 29, 1940, he won an Academy Award for Best Adapted Screenplay for *Gone With the Wind*—the first posthumous winner in Oscar history.

Annie Laurie Fuller Kurtz (1884-1946): The wife of artist and historian Wilbur G. Kurtz, Annie Laurie Kurtz was her husband's assistant during the filming of *Gone With the Wind*. Born in Clayton County, Georgia, she was a daughter of William Allen Fuller, a railroad conductor who foiled an attempt in April 1862 by a small band of Union soldiers to commandeer a Confederate train and take it across Union lines into Tennessee. The incident became known as "the Great Locomotive Chase." Annie Laurie Kurtz wrote numerous lengthy letters to Mitchell from Hollywood in which she shared the latest gossip from behind the scenes at the studio.

Wilbur G. Kurtz (1882-1967): Although born in Illinois and reared in Indiana, Kurtz became one of the premier historians of Georgia and the Civil War after he moved to Atlanta in 1912. Years later, in the fall of 1935, Mitchell asked him to review the section of her manuscript that covered Sherman's march on Atlanta from Chattanooga. He also was an artist renowned for his historical subjects. At Mitchell's suggestion, Kurtz was hired as a historian by Selznick International. He went to the studio for preliminary work for several weeks in early 1938 and returned in November, remaining for more than a year. Kurtz later served as a technical adviser for two Disney films—*Song of the South* in 1946 and *The Great Locomotive Chase* in 1956.

Harold Latham (1887-1969): Editor in chief at Macmillan, Latham has gone down in history as "the man who discovered *Gone With the Wind*." Born in New Jersey, he joined Macmillan's advertising department shortly after graduation from Columbia University in 1909. In the early 1920s, he wrote several novels for young boys. He later moved to editorial and became vice president in 1931. Four years later, Latham, then editor in chief, visited Atlanta on a book-scouting tour and wrangled a tatterdemalion manuscript from Mitchell, a former newspaper reporter. Shortly after leaving Atlanta, he sent the manuscript on to New York, where Lois Cole, with her husband's help, read and organized the pages. In 1965, he released his autobiography, *My Life in Publishing*. His collection of foreign editions of *Gone With the Wind*, some inscribed by Mitchell, are in the collection of the Kearny Public Library in Kearny, New Jersey.

Vivien Leigh (1913-1967): After two and a half years of searching for the perfect Scarlett O'Hara, Selznick settled on little-known British actress

Leigh. Born in India, she got her start on the London stage and made several films in England before nabbing the role of the century in *Gone With the Wind*, for which she won the Academy Award for Best Actress. Leigh and actor Laurence Olivier married in 1940. She won a second Oscar for playing another famous southern belle, Blanche DuBois, in 1951's *A Streetcar Named Desire*. Leigh suffered several nervous breakdowns, and her manic-depressive behavior strained her marriage to Olivier. The couple divorced in 1960. Leigh attended the Civil War Centennial premiere of *Gone With the Wind* in Atlanta and won a Tony Award for the musical *Tovarich* in 1963. She died on July 8, 1967, at the age of fifty-three.

Carole Lombard (1908–1942): The beautiful blonde actress known for her screwball comedies—and at one time the highest paid woman in Hollywood—accompanied her new husband, Clark Gable, to Atlanta for the world premiere of *Gone With the Wind*. (The two were married in March 1939 during a break in the filming of the picture.) After the Japanese attack on Pearl Harbor in December 1941, Lombard threw herself into the war effort. A little more than a month later, on January 16, 1942, while returning from a war bond rally in Indiana, she was killed when her plane crashed outside Las Vegas. President Franklin Roosevelt noted, "She loved her country. She is and always will be a star, one we shall never forget, nor cease to be grateful to." In June 1942, Gable and actress Irene Dunne christened the USS *Carole Lombard*.

Hattie McDaniel (1895–1952): For McDaniel, the groundbreaking Academy Award she received for *Gone With the Wind*—the first time an African American had been nominated, much less won—was a mixed blessing. The youngest of thirteen children, she got her start as a singer and then made her way to Hollywood. Her role of Mammy brought her to the pinnacle of success in her chosen profession but made her a target for attacks by many of her race who felt that her role as a slave was demeaning. McDaniel had a famous retort—"I'd rather make seven hundred dollars a week playing a maid than seven dollars a week being one"—but the controversy took its toll on her career and her health. Unable to participate in the Atlanta festivities because of the city's segregated facilities, McDaniel was the first person to whom Mitchell wrote after the premiere. The actress left her Academy Award to Howard University, but the plaque has been lost.

Susan "Sue" Myrick (1893–1978): Myrick, who served as a technical adviser on southern manners and customs on *Gone With the Wind*, first met Mitchell at the inaugural Georgia Press Institute convention in 1928, and the two newspaperwomen became lifelong friends. During the filming of the motion picture, she kept a diary, wrote numerous letters to the author with behind-the-scenes gossip and produced a series of "Straight from Hollywood" columns for newspapers in Macon, Georgia, and Atlanta. After Myrick returned home, Selznick hired her to give talks about her experiences as a way to promote the film in the South in late 1939 and early 1940. Most of her columns were published in 1982 as *White Columns in Hollywood: Reports from the* GWTW *Sets*, edited by Richard Harwell. Myrick's letters, diary entries, and later articles about Mitchell and the film are featured in two books by her niece, Susan Lindsley—*Susan Myrick of* Gone With the Wind: *An Autobiographical Biography* (2011) and *Margaret Mitchell: A Scarlett or a Melanie?* (2012).

David O. Selznick (1902–1965): The man known as the "Producer Prince" was the youngest son of an Eastern European émigré who would become an early pioneer in silent movies. When his father lost his company and his fortune, Selznick felt honor-bound to redeem the family name. After working at several of the major Hollywood studios, he established his independent Selznick International Pictures in Culver City in 1935. He remains the only producer who has won back-to-back Academy Awards for Best Picture—for *Gone With the Wind* (1939) and *Rebecca* (1940). Hoping to duplicate the success of "the *Wind*," Selznick tried in vain for years to persuade Mitchell to write a sequel to Scarlett's story; he also talked of mounting a stage version of the novel. He died of a heart attack on June 22, 1965, and his obituary in the *New York Times* read as he had predicted: "Producer of '*Gone With the Wind*' Dies."

John Hay "Jock" Whitney (1904–1982): Whitney, one of the richest men in the United States, became involved with the motion picture industry in 1933 when he and producer Merian C. Cooper cofounded Pioneer Pictures; he also invested in Technicolor. Two years later, he became chairman of the board of Selznick International Pictures. His position won him a seat next to Mitchell at the Atlanta premiere. After the December 19, 1939, New York opening, he hosted a party at his family's Fifth Avenue mansion; following the Hollywood premiere on December 28, he held a similar gathering at Ciro's on Sunset Boulevard. For Christmas that year, Whitney gave Selznick a gold watch with an inscription in his own handwriting: "David—Xmas 1939. Praise de Lawd. Jock." President Dwight Eisenhower appointed Whitney U.S. ambassador to England in 1957. He also purchased the *New York Herald Tribune* and served as its publisher until it closed in 1966.

Annie Laurie Williams (1894–1977): Although Mitchell never accepted Williams as her agent, the former actress and newspaper reporter was on the front lines in handling the sale of the movie rights to *Gone With* *the Wind*. Born in Texas, Williams dreamed of becoming an actress. She worked in vaudeville for a while but eventually became a features writer for the *New York Morning Telegraph*. In 1929, she established her own literary agency in New York, and her first major sale was *Magnificent Obsession*, by Lloyd C. Douglas. Macmillan hired Williams on its own to handle the sale of Mitchell's novel but misled the author into believing that the publisher was representing her. Williams later made deals for *Of Mice and Men* and *The Grapes of Wrath*, both by John Steinbeck; *Forever Amber*, by Kathleen Winsor; and *Auntie Mame*, by Patrick Dennis.

Acknowledgments

T his book would not exist, of course, without Margaret Mitchell. She wrote it; I simply served as editor. Well, "simply" may not be the most accurate term. Mitchell was a prolific letter writer. From the time she sold her novel to Macmillan until her death fourteen years later, she wrote thousands upon thousands of letters, and I read a great many of them, tagging those in which she discussed the motion picture version of her novel. I then narrowed this still-vast selection to a few hundred that tell the story of the making of the movie *Gone With the Wind* and its reception around the world. Reading all those letters was never boring; as you have seen, Mitchell had a wonderful way of expressing herself. I wrote a prologue to set the stage for those unfamiliar with the author's story. I added informational footnotes within the text of the letters to provide context and identify people and events that readers might not recognize and created a summary of the film's Atlanta premiere. And I wrote an epilogue to wrap up the tale. But, in the end, this remains Margaret Mitchell's book.

However, on the journey from individual letters to a finished volume, I owe a great deal of thanks to many others as well. First and foremost is Paul Anderson Jr., who, with his father and Thomas Hal Clarke, for many years oversaw the literary rights of *Gone With the Wind*. I also thank Deacon Steve Swope, president of GWTW Partners LLC, which was established in 2012 after the death of Joseph Mitchell, the author's nephew and last immediate survivor. Margaret Mitchell's letters are copyrighted by GWTW Partners LLC and reprinted with its permission.

Mitchell often compared writing to digging ditches. Fellow writers (and family members and friends of writers) can relate: a project such as this is grueling work and tends to take over your life. With my apologies for being distracted and grouchy at times over the past several years,

I offer special thanks to my parents, John and Harriett Wiley; my sister and brother-in-law, Linda and Glenn Collins; and my niece and her husband, Kristin and Cory Bentley. Through it all, their love, support, encouragement, and patience never wavered. Thanks, too, to members of my Dominion family, who did not complain when I took an inordinate amount of vacation time while working on this book. And I'm lucky to have a third family as well—fellow *Gone With the Wind* fans around the world. While I appreciate all of them for their enthusiasm for this project, I must single out one individual: Herb Bridges, the world's foremost authority on *Gone With the Wind*. Herb passed away suddenly in September 2013, and his death leaves a void in the *Gone With the Wind* world—and in my life. I knew Herb for nearly forty years, and over that time, our relationship grew from that of an eager student absorbing knowledge from an experienced teacher to a close personal friendship. His encyclopedic knowledge, wise counsel, and honest opinions were as invaluable to this book as they were to my first, *Margaret Mitchell's* Gone With the Wind: *A Bestseller's Odyssey from Atlanta to Hollywood*. And speaking of that first book, I owe a special shout-out to my *Odyssey* coauthor, Ellen F. Brown. An excellent writer and a researcher extraordinaire, Ellen taught me many things during our writing partnership. Perhaps the most valuable lesson was how to step back from a subject I love so much and take a fresh and objective look. I hope I have done that with this book, too.

Copies of all but a handful of the letters reprinted here are at the Hargrett Rare Book and Manuscript Library at the University of Georgia in Athens. There, more than one hundred thousand letters and carbons of letters, telegrams, notes, contracts, court documents, photographs, and newspaper and magazine articles document Mitchell's life and the enduring entertainment phenomenon she created. I have been a regular visitor to the library over the past decade (I think I'm just a few points shy of honorary Bulldog status!), and the staff members in Special Collections have become friends. Everyone there goes out of their way to be helpful, but three deserve special recognition: Mary Ellen Brooks, Hargrett's director emeritus who knows the Mitchell collection better than anyone; Melissa Bush, who can point me in the right direction no matter what questions I ask; and Mary Palmer Linnemann, who responded quickly to my panicked e-mails when I forgot some small tidbit in the files that I needed. I also would be remiss not to mention those in the library vault who pulled so many file boxes for me and the student workers who copied so many letters and documents. At the Harry Ransom Center at the University of Texas, which holds the even more massive David O. Selznick Collection,

Steve Wilson, film director, and Emilio Banda were extremely helpful when I spent time in Austin going through the files there. Steve also graciously tracked down information for me after I got home. And at the Atlanta-Fulton Public Library, Kelly Cornwell, manager of special collections, likewise checked Atlanta city directories and newspapers on microfilm to help answer many questions.

Several relatives of Mitchell's friends and family members went out of their way to help me—sharing memories and photographs and giving me permission to quote from family letters: Susan Lindsley, niece of Susan Myrick; Wilbur G. Kurtz III, grandson of Wilbur and Annie Laurie Kurtz; Kate Barrett, daughter of Kay Brown; Craig Zane, nephew of John Marsh; and Allan Taylor, son of Lois Cole. Allan also has my eternal gratitude for the wonderful foreword he wrote for this book; as "Aunt Peggy's" godson, Allan is in a unique position to pay tribute to Mitchell. His parents and his sister, Linda, who died in 2011, would be as proud of what he wrote as I am.

Thank you to those who read all or parts of the manuscript and caught typos, asked questions, and offered constructive criticism: Ellen F. Brown, Alan Carter, Linda Collins, Linda Harp, Mickey Kuhn, and Diana McInerney. And for their help in a variety of ways, I thank Beth Bailey and Danielle Conroy, Road to Tara Museum, Jonesboro, Georgia; Lucinda Barrett, daughter of Kay Brown; Otis Brumby III, *Marietta Daily Journal*; Doug Buerlein; Elizabeth Chase and E. Kathleen Shoemaker, Manuscript, Archives, and Rare Book Library, Emory University; Simon Elliott, Special Collections, Charles E. Young Research Library, University of California, Los Angeles; Molly Haskell; Kim Hatcher, Georgia Department of Natural Resources; Tom Heyes; Ellen Johnston, Special Collections, Georgia State University Library; Jenny Lee, Rare Book and Manuscript Library, Butler Library, Columbia University; Andrea Pereira, United Press; Pam Roberts, Georgia Public Broadcasting; Mark Roesler, CMG Worldwide; Robbie Salmons and Matt Sked, Richmond Printing; Landon Simpson; Susan E. Snyder, The Bancroft Library, University of California, Berkeley; Vicki Starnes, Crawford Long Museum, Jefferson, Georgia; Adriana Trigliani; Thomas Venning, Christie's London; Sue VerHoef, Atlanta History Center; Marianne Walker; and Bo Williams and Dorothy Wright, Total Printing.

Finally, where would a writer be without his agent and publisher? Thank you, Jeanne Fredericks, for the faith you had in two new authors in 2009 and for working so hard to sell this book in an even more unsettled publishing world. I'm also thrilled to work again with Taylor Trade Publishing, including old friends Rick Rinehart, Kalen Landow, and Alden Perkins, as well as new friends Karie Simpson, Sam Caggiula, Bruce R. Owens, Beth Easter, and David Luljak. In this case, familiarity breeds only comfort and confidence.

In closing, I circle back to where I began—Margaret Mitchell. After her book took the nation by storm and she became one of the most famous women in the world, the author fought hard to maintain her privacy. She often asked recipients not to quote from her letters and instructed her husband to destroy her personal papers should she die first. When this happened, he began carrying out her wishes within days of the funeral. Luckily for us, John Marsh—encouraged by Mitchell's longtime secretary, Margaret Baugh—soon realized the importance of preserving her letters, both for business reasons and as a record of the remarkable history of *Gone With the Wind*, and he stopped the destruction. The author's files, along with additional material that has been added to the collections over the years, comprise a treasure trove for researchers, historians, and scholars. Knowing how Mitchell felt about her privacy, I admit that I sometimes was uneasy reading her letters, wondering what she would think. But after many years of studying her life, I feel confident in saying that if there were one thing she prized more dearly than privacy, it was accuracy. Kay Brown once called the author "the most genuinely accurate person I know." With this book, I gave Margaret Mitchell the chance to tell the story of the making of the motion picture *Gone With the Wind*—and its effect on her life—in her own words. That is something she would have appreciated—and for which she just *might* forgive me.

Notes

Key to Endnotes: Document Repositories

AHC   James G. Kenan Research Center, Atlanta History Center, Atlanta (Margaret Mitchell Collection)

Columbia   Rare Book and Manuscript Library, Butler Library, Columbia University, New York (Annie Laurie Williams Collection)

HRC   Harry Ransom Humanities Research Center, University of Texas, Austin (David O. Selznick Collection)

NYPL   Manuscripts and Archives Division, New York Public Library, New York (Macmillan Company Records)

UGA   Hargrett Rare Book and Manuscript Library, Richard B. Russell Special Collections Libraries, University of Georgia, Athens (Margaret Mitchell Family Papers, Mitchell-Marsh Family Papers, Stephens Mitchell Family Papers, Gone With the Wind Papers, Gone With the Wind Literary Estate Papers)

Introduction

1. Margaret Mitchell to Katharine Brown, August 8, 1939, UGA.
2. Katharine Brown to Margaret Mitchell, August 10, 1939, UGA.
3. "Notes by M. E. Baugh—for Farr: 'Margaret Mitchell of Atlanta,'" February 1965, UGA.
4. Margaret Mitchell to O. B. Keeler, December 16, 1939, UGA.
5. Margaret Mitchell to Sidney Howard, January 4, 1937, UGA.
6. Margaret Mitchell to Mr. and Mrs. Edwin Granberry, April 11, 1940, AHC.
7. Prologue, *A Star Is Born*, Selznick International Pictures, Inc., 1937.
8. Lois Cole, "The Story Begins at a Luncheon Bridge in Atlanta," *New York Times Book Review*, June 25, 1961.
9. Ibid.

Prologue

1. Stephens Mitchell, "Memoir of Margaret Mitchell," 1962, 22, UGA.
2. Ibid., 24.
3. Ibid., 22.
4. Franklin M. Garrett, *Atlanta and Environs*, vol. 2 (Atlanta: Lewis Historical Publishing Co., 1954; facsimile reprint, Athens: University of Georgia Press, 1969), 464.
5. Mitchell, "Memoir of Margaret Mitchell," 12.
6. Virginia Morris, untitled article written for *Photoplay*, 1939, UGA.
7. John Marsh to Mary Marsh, July 25, 1937, as quoted in Marianne Walker, *Margaret Mitchell & John Marsh: The Love Story behind* Gone With the Wind (Atlanta: Peachtree Publishers, 1993), 364.
8. Richard Harwell, ed., *GWTW: The Screenplay* (New York: Macmillan, 1980), 7.
9. Mitchell, "Memoir of Margaret Mitchell," 17.
10. Ibid.
11. Patrick Allen, ed., *Margaret Mitchell: Reporter* (Athens, GA: Hill Street Press, 2000), xv.
12. Mitchell, "Memoir of Margaret Mitchell," 17.
13. Finis Farr, *Margaret Mitchell of Atlanta* (New York: William Morrow, 1965), 76.
14. Ibid., 77.
15. Margaret Mitchell to Julia Collier Harris, April 28, 1936, UGA.
16. Margaret Mitchell to Julian Harris, April 21, 1936, UGA.
17. Margaret Mitchell, interview by Medora Field Perkerson, WSB Radio, July 3, 1936.
18. Farr, *Margaret Mitchell of Atlanta*, 86.
19. Lois Cole, memorandum [on Margaret Mitchell manuscript], n.d. [April–May 1935], private collection of Allan Taylor.
20. Charles W. Everett, report [on Margaret Mitchell manuscript], n.d., quoted in Farr, *Margaret Mitchell of Atlanta*, 101.
21. Harold Latham to Margaret Mitchell, July 17, 1935, UGA.
22. "Agreement between Mrs. Margaret Mitchell Marsh and The Macmillan Company," August 6, 1935, NYPL.
23. J. Donald Adams, "A Fine Novel of the Civil War," *New York Times Book Review*, July 5, 1936.
24. Julia Peterkin, "The Old South Lives Again," *Washington Post*, July 12, 1936.
25. Stephen Vincent Benet, "Georgia Marches Through," *Saturday Review of Literature*, July 4, 1936.
26. Charles Hanson Towne, "A Fine Civil War Novel," *New York American*, June 30, 1936; Charles A. Wagner, "Books," *Daily Mirror*, July 3, 1936.

27. William W. Hawkins Jr. to Everett Hale, February 12, 1936, NYPL.

28. Everett Hale to William W. Hawkins Jr., February 17, 1936, NYPL.

29. Lois Cole to Margaret Mitchell, March 9, 1936, NYPL.

30. Annie Laurie Williams to Margaret Mitchell, March 5, 1936, Columbia.

31. Lois Cole to Margaret Mitchell, March 9, 1936, NYPL.

32. Margaret Mitchell to Annie Laurie Williams, March 20, 1936, Columbia.

33. Lois Cole to Margaret Mitchell, April 9, 1936, NYPL.

34. Ibid.

35. Margaret Mitchell to Harold Latham, May 25, 1936, NYPL.

36. Katharine Brown to David O. Selznick, teletype, May 20, 1936, HRC.

37. Katharine Brown to David O. Selznick, teletype, May 21, 1936, HRC.

38. David O. Selznick to Katharine Brown, teletype, May 25, 1936, HRC.

39. Annie Laurie Williams to Bosley Crowther, June 5, 1956, Columbia.

40. Harold Latham to George Brett Jr., May 20, 1936, NYPL.

41. Harold Latham to Margaret Mitchell, May 21, 1936, UGA.

42. Harold Latham to Annie Laurie Williams, May 26, 1936, NYPL.

43. Harold Latham to Margaret Mitchell, May 27, 1936, UGA.

44. Harold Latham to Margaret Mitchell, June 15, 1936, UGA.

45. Margaret Mitchell to Lois Cole, June 15, 1936, NYPL.

46. Katharine Brown to Silvia Schulman, teletype, July 7, 1936, HRC.

47. Lois Cole to Margaret Mitchell, July 8, 1936, NYPL.

48. David Thomson, *Showman: The Life of David O. Selznick* (New York: Alfred A. Knopf, 1992), 27.

49. Ibid., 11.

50. Margaret Mitchell to John Hay Whitney and David O. Selznick, August 31, 1942, UGA.

51. Rudy Behlmer, ed., "Selznick on the Writing of Memos," in *Memo from David O. Selznick* (New York: Viking Press, 1972), xxii–xxiii.

52. Alva Johnston, "The Great Dictater," *Saturday Evening Post*, May 16, 1942.

53. Margaret Mitchell to Harold Latham, August 13, 1936, UGA.

54. John R. Marsh to The Macmillan Company, July 27, 1936, UGA.

55. Margaret Mitchell to Herschell Brickell, July 26, 1936, UGA.

56. Margaret Mitchell to Stark Young, November 30, 1936, UGA.

57. Stark Young to Margaret Mitchell, n.d. [December 1936], UGA.

58. Ibid.

59. Stephens Mitchell to Katharine Brown, December 19, 1967, UGA.

60. Margaret Mitchell to M. D. Mermin, September 30, 1938, UGA.

61. Mitchell, "Memoir of Margaret Mitchell," 112.

62. "Agreement between Margaret Mitchell Marsh and Selznick International Pictures, Inc.," July 30, 1936, UGA.

63. John R. Marsh to Macmillan, July 27, 1936.

The Premiere

1. "Atlanta's Hospitality Delights Charming Ann Rutherford As Young Actress Is Engulfed by Southern Atmosphere," *Atlanta Constitution*, December 14, 1939.
2. "Atlanta Windows Vibrant with Color, Rich in History for 'Gone With the Wind' Opening" and "Glamour of 'Old South' Ablaze in Atlanta Windows for 'Gone With the Wind' Premiere," *Women's Wear Daily*, December 15, 1939.
3. Cary Wilmer, "Olivia Relished Her Part in Film," *Atlanta Constitution*, December 14, 1939.
4. Lee Rogers, "Miss Leigh Thinks 'Scarlett' a Brat, at Times Needed a Good Spanking," *Atlanta Constitution*, December 14, 1939.
5. Willard Cope, "'Gone With Wind' Not to Be Cut at Least for Year, Selznick Says," *Atlanta Constitution*, December 14, 1939.
6. Inez Robb, "Margaret Meets Her Brain-Child: Retiring Author and Stars in Three-Hour Chat," *Atlanta Georgian*, December 14, 1939.
7. Ibid.
8. "Dixie Hails 'Gone With the Wind,'" *News of the Day* newsreel, December 1939.
9. Jack Spalding, "Olivia de Havilland Steals Show at Ball—and She's Late," *Atlanta Constitution*, December 15, 1939.
10. "Notables See Gala 60's Revived at Sparkling Ball," *Atlanta Constitution*, December 15, 1939.
11. Yolande Gwin, "Gable, Miss Mitchell Talk Alone after He Begs a Chat," *Atlanta Constitution*, December 16, 1939.
12. Ibid.
13. Katharine Brown to Margaret Mitchell, December 8, 1939, UGA.
14. Recording of *Gone With the Wind* premiere, December 15–16, 1939, UGA.
15. *The Making of a Legend*: Gone With the Wind, Turner Entertainment Company/Selznick Properties, Ltd., 1988.
16. Henry McLemore, "South Won't Secede from Hollywood, McLemore Believes," *Atlanta Journal*, December 16, 1939.
17. Recording of *Gone With the Wind* premiere.

Epilogue

1. Hugh Park, "Around Town," *Atlanta Journal*, June 24, 1949.
2. Katharine Brown to Margaret Mitchell, August 8, 1949, UGA.
3. Farr, *Margaret Mitchell of Atlanta*, 219.

4. [Unidentified reader] to The Macmillan Company, August 11, 1949, NYPL.

5. "Fatal Trip to Show Was Snap Decision," *Atlanta Journal*, August 17, 1949.

6. "Harry Davenport, Vet Actor, Dies," *Atlanta Constitution*, August 11, 1949.

7. Margaret Mitchell's desk calendar, 1949, UGA.

8. "Fatal Trip to Show Was Snap Decision."

9. John R. Marsh to Mother and Family, August 26, 1939, UGA.

10. "Cab Driver in Accident Booked 24 Times Before," *Atlanta Journal*, August 12, 1949.

11. Margaret Shannon, "40-Mile Speed Claimed for Mitchell Death Car," *Atlanta Journal*, November 15, 1949.

12. Ibid.

13. Lois Cole to Margaret Baugh, October 26, 1949, UGA.

14. Margaret Shannon, "'Unavoidable,' Gravitt's Plea," *Atlanta Journal*, November 16, 1949.

15. William Key, "Margaret Mitchell Dies at 11:59 after Five-Day Battle for Life," *Atlanta Journal*, August 16, 1949.

16. Ibid.

17. Harry S. Truman to John R. Marsh, August 17, 1949, UGA.

18. Herman E. Talmadge to John R. Marsh, August 16, 1949, UGA.

19. "Miss Mitchell, 'Gone' Author, Dies of Hurts," *Roanoke Times*, August 17, 1949.

20. Ibid.

21. Celestine Sibley, "Mitchell Burial Today in Oakland; Rites at 10," *Atlanta Constitution*, August 18, 1949.

22. "Author's Death Sermon Theme," *Atlanta Journal*, August 17, 1949.

23. Paul Jones, " 'GWTW' Book, Film at Peak of Demand," *Atlanta Journal*, August 26, 1949.

24. "All-Time Top 232 Movies by U.S. Theatre Attendance," http://mrob. com/pub/film-video/topadj.html; "Movies Which Sold the Most Tickets in Great Britain in the 20th Century," http://www.imdb.com/list/ Ee5pLbhMWdw.

25. "Highest-Grossing Films Adjusted for Inflation," http://en.wikipedia. org/wiki/List_of_highest-grossing_films.

26. Andrew Sarris, "This Moviest of All Movies," *Atlantic Monthly*, March 1973.

27. Henry Steele Commager, "The Civil War in Georgia's Red Clay Hills," *New York Herald Tribune*, July 5, 1936.

28. Margaret Mitchell to Whitney and Selznick, August 31, 1942.

Bibliography

Books

Allen, Patrick, ed. *Margaret Mitchell: Reporter*. Athens, GA: Hill Street Press, 2000.

Balio, Tino. *United Artists: The Company Built by the Stars*. Madison: University of Wisconsin Press, 1976.

Behlmer, Rudy, ed. *Memo from David O. Selznick*. New York: Viking Press, 1972.

Borkowski, Mark. *The Fame Formula: How Hollywood's Fixers, Fakers and Star Makers Created the Celebrity Industry*. London: Sidgwick & Jackson, 2008.

Bridges, Herb. Gone With the Wind: *The Three-Day Premiere in Atlanta*. Macon, GA: Mercer University Press, 1999.

Bridges, Herb, and Terryl C. Boodman. Gone With the Wind: *The Definitive Illustrated History of the Book, the Movie, and the Legend*. New York: Simon & Schuster, 1989.

Brown, Ellen F., and John Wiley, Jr. *Margaret Mitchell's* Gone With the Wind: *A Bestseller's Odyssey from Atlanta to Hollywood*. Boulder, CO: Taylor Trade Publishing, 2011.

Cameron, Judy, and Paul J. Christman. *The Art of* Gone With the Wind. New York: Prentice Hall, 1989.

Davis, Anita Price. *The Margaret Mitchell Encyclopedia*. Jefferson, NC: McFarland, 2013.

Eskridge, Jane, ed. *Before Scarlett: Girlhood Writings of Margaret Mitchell*. Athens, GA: Hill Street Press, 2000.

Farr, Finis. *Margaret Mitchell of Atlanta*. New York: William Morrow, 1965.

Flamini, Roland. *Scarlett, Rhett, and a Cast of Thousands: The Filming of "Gone With the Wind."* New York: Macmillan, 1975.

Garrett, Franklin M. *Atlanta and Environs*. Vol. 2, Atlanta: Lewis Historical Publishing, 1954. Facsimile reprint, Athens: University of Georgia Press, 1969.

Gewirtz, Arthur. *Sidney Howard and Clare Eames: American Theater's Perfect Couple of the 1920s*. Jefferson, NC: McFarland, 2004.

Granberry, Julian, ed. *Letters from Margaret*. Miami: 1st Book Publishing, 2001.

Hamann, G. D. Gone With the Wind *in the 30s and 40s*. Hollywood, CA: Filming Today Press, 2008.

Harwell, Richard, ed. *GWTW: The Screenplay*. New York: Macmillan, 1980.

——, ed. *Margaret Mitchell's* Gone With the Wind *Letters, 1936–1949*. New York: Macmillan, 1976.

Haver, Ronald. *David O. Selznick's* Gone With the Wind. New York: Bonanza Books, 1986.

——. *David O. Selznick's Hollywood*. New York: Alfred A. Knopf, 1980.

Lindsley, Susan. *Margaret Mitchell: A Scarlett or a Melanie?* Atlanta: ThomasMax Publishing, 2012.

——. *Susan Myrick of* Gone With the Wind: *An Autobiographical Biography*. Atlanta: ThomasMax Publishing, 2011.

Mitchell, Margaret. *Gone With the Wind*. New York: Macmillan, 1936.

Molt, Cynthia Marylee. Gone With the Wind *on Film: A Complete Reference*. Jefferson, NC: McFarland, 1990.

Ott, Frederick W. *The Films of Carole Lombard*. Secaucus, NJ: The Citadel Press, 1972.

Pratt, William. *Scarlett Fever: The Ultimate Pictorial Treasury of* Gone With the Wind. New York: Macmillan, 1977.

Pyron, Darden Asbury. *Southern Daughter: The Life of Margaret Mitchell*. New York: Oxford University Press, 1991.

Taylor, Helen. *Scarlett's Women:* Gone With the Wind *and Its Female Fans*. London: Virago Press, 1989.

Thomson, David. *Showman: The Life of David O. Selznick*. New York: Alfred A. Knopf, 1992.

Walker, Marianne. *Margaret Mitchell & John Marsh: The Love Story behind* Gone With the Wind. Atlanta: Peachtree Publishers, 1993.

Wiley, John, Jr. Gone With the Wind: *Atlanta's Film, Atlanta's Night*. Dublin, GA: "Gone With the Wind Collectors Newsletter," 1990.

Articles

"2 Atlanta Girls among 4 in Finals for Lead Role in 'Gone With Wind.'" *Atlanta Constitution*, February 6, 1937.

Adams, J. Donald. "A Fine Novel of the Civil War." *New York Times Book Review*, July 5, 1936.

"Atlanta Officer Attends G.W.T.W. Premiere in Paris." *Atlanta Constitution*, December 7, 1944.

"Atlanta's Hospitality Delights Charming Ann Rutherford as Young Actress Is Engulfed by Southern Atmosphere." *Atlanta Constitution*, December 14, 1939.

"Atlanta Windows Vibrant with Color, Rich in History for 'Gone With the Wind' Opening." *Women's Wear Daily*, December 15, 1939.

"Author's Death Sermon Theme." *Atlanta Journal*, August 17, 1949.

Beamish, Joe. "Matches and Joe." *Post-Standard* [Syracuse, NY], April 18, 1937.

"Beautiful Women Scarce, Movie Talent Scout Says." *The State* [Columbia, SC], n.d.

Benet, Stephen Vincent. "Georgia Marches Through." *Saturday Review of Literature*, July 4, 1936.

Bernstein, Matthew. "Selznick's March: The Atlanta Premiere of *Gone With the Wind*." *Atlanta History: A Journal of Georgia and the South*. Atlanta: Atlanta Historical Society, Inc., Summer 1999.

Brumby, Otis A. "Jambalaya," *Cobb County Times*, October 22, 1936.

Bryan, Wright. "Grew Deeply Moved by 'Gone With The Wind.'" *Atlanta Journal*, March 3, 1943.

——. "GWTW Begins Fifth Year of Run in London." *Atlanta Journal*, April 16, 1944.

——. "GWTW Keeps on Setting Worldwide Records." *Atlanta Journal*, October 30, 1947.

"Cab Driver in Accident Booked 24 Times Before." *Atlanta Journal*, August 12, 1949.

"Capitol Hill's Windy Enough." *New York Telegraph*, February 28, 1939.

"Cashing in on 'Gone With the Wind." *Business Week*, December 30, 1939.

Cerf, Bennett. "Trade Winds." *Saturday Review of Literature*, June 16, 1945.

"Clark Gable Wins His Wings as Air Gunner." *Atlanta Constitution*, January 7, 1937.

Cole, Lois. "The Story Begins at a Luncheon Bridge in Atlanta." *New York Times Book Review*, June 25, 1961.

Commager, Henry Steele. "The Civil War in Georgia's Red Clay Hills." *New York Herald Tribune*, July 5, 1936.

Cope, Willard. "'Gone With Wind' Not to Be Cut at Least for Year, Selznick Says." *Atlanta Constitution*, December 14, 1939.

Cousley, Sam A. "Back with the Breeze?" *Rockford Register-Republic*, n.d.

Daniel, Frank. "Champion Father for Scarlett." *Atlanta Journal*, July 4, 1937.

——. "First 'Secession' Comes over Vivien Leigh as Scarlett of the Screen." *Atlanta Journal*, January 20, 1939.

——. "'Gone With the Wind' Costuming Puzzles Expert, Here to Plan It." *Atlanta Journal*, January 20, 1937.

——. "Hollywood Scouts Arrive to Find Atlanta Film-Mad." *Atlanta Journal*, December 2, 1936.

"Demands $500,000 for Love He Lost: Telamon Cuyler Sues His Rich Mother-in-Law, Following His Wife's Divorce." *New York Times*, November 23, 1913.

Everett, Thankful. "She Found Idea for Thriving Business in 'Gone With Wind.'" *Chattanooga News*, June 7, 1937.

"Fatal Trip to Show Was Snap Decision." *Atlanta Journal*, August 17, 1949.

"Fleming to Replace Cukor for Filming." *Atlanta Constitution*, February 15, 1939.

Forth, Sally. "'Gone With the Wind' Movie Rights Sold by Margaret Mitchell." *Atlanta Constitution*, July 18, 1936.

"Glamour of 'Old South' Ablaze in Atlanta Windows for 'Gone With the Wind' Premiere." *Women's Wear Daily*, December 15, 1939.

"'Gone With The Wind' Awarded Pulitzer Prize." *Atlanta Georgian*, May 4, 1937.

"'Gone With Wind' to Be Filmusical." *Variety*, January 31, 1945.

Gwin, Yolande. "Gable, Miss Mitchell Talk Alone after He Begs a Chat." *Atlanta Constitution*, December 16, 1939.

——. "Mrs. Roosevelt's Maid Visits Here, but White House Talk Is Taboo." *Atlanta Constitution*, July 30, 1937.

——. "'Postage-Due' Letter Wins Movie Role for Georgia Girl: Thelma Wunder Went to Hollywood, Director Saw, She Conquered." *Atlanta Constitution*, October 1, 1937.

——. "Socialite, with O'Hara Dash, Races Madly to See Cukor." *Atlanta Constitution*, April 7, 1937.

Harris, Radie. "New York Runaround." *Variety*, February 16, 1944.

"Hartsfield Asks World Premiere of 'Gone With the Wind' in Atlanta." *Atlanta Constitution*, March 20, 1937.

Harwell, Richard, ed. "Technical Adviser: The Making of 'Gone With the Wind,' The Hollywood Journals of Wilbur G. Kurtz," *Atlanta Historical Journal*, Atlanta: Atlanta Historical Society, Inc., Summer 1978.

Hefferman, Harold. "Gable and Shearer 'Cinch Nominations' to Play Leads in 'Gone With the Wind.'" *Atlanta Constitution*, June 24, 1938.

"Hollywood Orders Red Georgia Mud: 'Gone With the Wind' Characters Will Be Spattered with the Right Hue." *Atlanta Constitution*, January 16, 1939.

Johnston, Alva. "The Great Dictater." *Saturday Evening Post*, May 16, 1942.

Jones, Paul. "'GWTW' Book, Film at Peak of Demand." *Atlanta Journal*, August 26, 1949.

"Journal Readers Pick Cast for 'Gone With the Wind.'" *Atlanta Journal*, April 13, 1937.

Key, William. "Margaret Mitchell Dies at 11:59 after Five-Day Battle for Life." *Atlanta Journal*, December 16, 1949.

Lewis, Nell Battle. "An English Scarlett." *Raleigh News & Observer*, January 22, 1939.

———. "Scarlett Materializes." *Raleigh News & Observer*, February 18, 1940.

Manning, A. D. "Norma Spurns Scarlett Role in 'Gone With the Wind,' and It's All Very Annoying to Margaret Mitchell." *Atlanta Constitution*, August 1, 1938.

"Margaret Mitchell Is Selected among Nation's 10 Women of Year." *Atlanta Journal*, January 8, 1937.

"Margaret Mitchell May Aid on S-I 'Gone.'" *Variety*, February 24, 1937.

"Margaret Mitchell Puts 'Okay' on First Screen 'Stills' of Novel." *Atlanta Constitution*, February 14, 1939.

"Margaret Mitchell's Gown to Reflect the 'Old South.'" *Atlanta Constitution*, December 10, 1939.

Martin, Harold. "Premiere Thrills Gala Throng: Author Paid Emotional Tribute." *Atlanta Georgian*, December 16, 1939.

Martin, Willa Gray. "Southern Accent in New York: Selling Scarlett to the Movies." *Atlanta Constitution*, August 27, 1939.

McGill, Ralph. "Gone With the Wind." *Red Barrel*, September 1936.

McLemore, Henry. "South Won't Secede from Hollywood, McLemore Believes." *Atlanta Journal*, December 16, 1939.

McManus, John T. "'Gone With the Wind' Joins the Radio Serials." *PM*, August 19, 1940.

"Miss Leigh Gets O.K. as 'Scarlett' by U.D.C. Head." *Atlanta Constitution*, January 23, 1939.

"Miss Lombard Liked Atlanta on 1939 Visit; Margaret Mitchell Recalls Chat with Star about Chickens." *Atlanta Constitution*, January 18, 1942.

"Miss Mitchell, 'Gone' Author, Dies of Hurts." *Roanoke Times*, August 17, 1949.

Munday, Pfc. David E. "No Air Raid Can Stop 'Gone With Wind.'" *Atlanta Journal*, August 26, 1943.

News from Selznick International Pictures, Inc.: "David O. Selznick Outbids All Producers for 'Gone With the Wind,'" July 23, 1936.

———. "George Cukor Assigned to Direct 'Gone With The Wind' for David O. Selznick." September 11, 1936.

———. "Sidney Howard Gets Assignment to Adapt 'Gone With The Wind' for David O. Selznick." October 29, 1936.

"Notables See Gala 60's Revived at Sparkling Ball." *Atlanta Constitution*, December 15, 1939.

Othman, Frederick C. "Cukor Quits 'Gone With Wind' in Row over Filming of Scenes." *Atlanta Journal*, February 14, 1939.

Park, Hugh. "Around Town." *Atlanta Journal*, June 24, 1949.

Parsons, Louella. "$65,000 Rumored as Price for 'Gone With the Wind.'" *Atlanta Georgian*, July 18, 1936.

——. [Untitled]. *Los Angeles Examiner*, June 24, 1938.

Paul, Elliot. "Hemingway and the Critics." *Saturday Review of Literature*, November 6, 1937.

"Peggy Denies 'Absence' from GWTW Premiere." *Atlanta Constitution*, November 9, 1947.

Perkerson, Medora. "Seeing 'GWTW' Picture Was an 'Experience' to Margaret Mitchell." *Atlanta Journal*, December 17, 1939.

Peterkin, Julia. "The Old South Lives Again." *Washington Post*, July 12, 1936.

"Premiere Seats $100 Up as Paris Sees 'Scarlett.'" *Atlanta Journal*, July 19, 1945.

Robb, Inez. "Margaret Meets Her Brain-Child: Retiring Author and Stars in Three-Hour Chat." *Atlanta Georgian*, December 14, 1939.

Rogers, Lee. "Miss Leigh Thinks 'Scarlett' a Brat, at Times Needed a Good Spanking." *Atlanta Constitution*, December 14, 1939.

Sarris, Andrew. "This Moviest of All Movies." *Atlantic Monthly*, March 1973.

"Selznick 'Distressed' by Report That He Will Film GWTW Musical." *Atlanta Constitution*, February 18, 1945.

Shannon, Margaret. "40-Mile Speed Claimed for Mitchell Death Car." *Atlanta Journal*, November 15, 1949.

——. "'Unavoidable,' Gravitt's Plea." *Atlanta Journal*, November 16, 1949.

"Shearer Gives Up Role of Scarlett." *New York Times*, August 1, 1938.

Shearer, Lloyd. "GWTW: Supercolossal Saga of an Epic." *New York Times Magazine*, October 26, 1947.

Shipp, Nelson M. "Remarks at Cusseta Bring Statement on 'Gone With the Wind.'" *Columbus Enquirer*, June 11, 1938.

Sibley, Celestine. "Mitchell Burial Today in Oakland; Rites at 10." *Atlanta Constitution*, August 18, 1949.

Sobol, Louis. "The Voice of Broadway." *New York Journal*, September 24, 1936.

——. "The Voice of Broadway." *New York Journal*, October 6, 1936.

Spalding, Jack. "Olivia de Havilland Steals Show at Ball—and She's Late." *Atlanta Constitution*, December 15, 1939.

Street, James. "Two Happy People." *Movie and Radio Guide*, May 1940.

"Suit Seeks to Stop Film of 'Gone With the Wind.'" *Atlanta Journal*, February 4, 1940.

"Tara Replica Urged as Monument to Margaret Mitchell." *Atlanta Journal*, June 28, 1938.

"'Then and Now.'" *Variety*, September 23, 1936.

Towne, Charles Hanson. "A Fine Civil War Novel." *New York American*, June 30, 1936.

United Press. "Margaret Mitchell Reported Paid $52,000." *Atlanta Journal*, July 17, 1936.

——. "Nazis See Banned Film." *New York World-Telegram*, January 18, 1941.

Van Ryn, Frederick. "Tiger by the Tail." *Redbook*, October 1939.

Wagner, Charles A. "Books." *Daily Mirror* [New York], July 3, 1936.

Wilkinson, Lupton A., and J. Bryan III. "The Hepburn Story." *Saturday Evening Post*, January 3, 1942.

Williams, Gladstone. "'Gone With Wind' Premiere Is Set for September Here." *Atlanta Constitution*, December 26, 1938.

Wilmer, Cary. "Olivia Relished Her Part in Film." *Atlanta Constitution*, December 14, 1939.

Winchell, Walter. "On Broadway." *Atlanta Journal*, March 12, 1940.

Miscellaneous

"Agreement between Margaret Mitchell Marsh and Selznick International Pictures, Inc." July 30, 1936, UGA.

"Agreement between Mrs. Margaret Mitchell Marsh and The Macmillan Company." August 6, 1935, NYPL.

"All-Time Top 232 Movies by U.S. Theatre Attendance." http://mrob.com/pub/film-video/topadj.html.

Baugh, Margaret. "Notes by M.E. Baugh—for Farr: 'Margaret Mitchell of Atlanta.'" February 1965, UGA.

Cole, Lois. Memorandum [on Margaret Mitchell manuscript]. N.d. [April–May 1935], private collection of Allan Taylor.

"Dixie Hails 'Gone With the Wind.'" *News of the Day* newsreel, December 1939.

Gone With the Wind pressbook. London: National Screen Service, Ltd, 1967.

"Highest-Grossing Films Adjusted for Inflation." http://en.wikipedia.org/wiki/List_of_highest-grossing_films.

The Making of a Legend: Gone With the Wind. Atlanta: Turner Entertainment Company/Selznick Properties, Ltd, 1988.

Marsh, John Robert. "Codicil to the Will of John Robert Marsh concerning the Manuscript of 'Gone With the Wind.'" July 26, 1951, UGA.

Mitchell, Stephens. "Memoir of Margaret Mitchell." 1962, UGA.

Morris, Virginia. Untitled article written for *Photoplay*. 1939, UGA.

"Movies Which Sold the Most Tickets in Great Britain in the 20th Century." http://www.imdb.com/list/Ee5pLbhMWdw.

Myrick, Susan. Untitled article about Sherwood Anderson's visits to Macon. N.d., private collection of Susan Lindsley.

Recording of *Gone With the Wind* premiere. December 15-16, 1939, UGA.

Index

Note: Where appropriate, significant individuals have a second index entry for letters written to them by Margaret Mitchell, e.g., "Selznick, David O., letters to." Fictional characters from the novel or film are alphabetized according to first name, e.g., "Scarlett O'Hara."